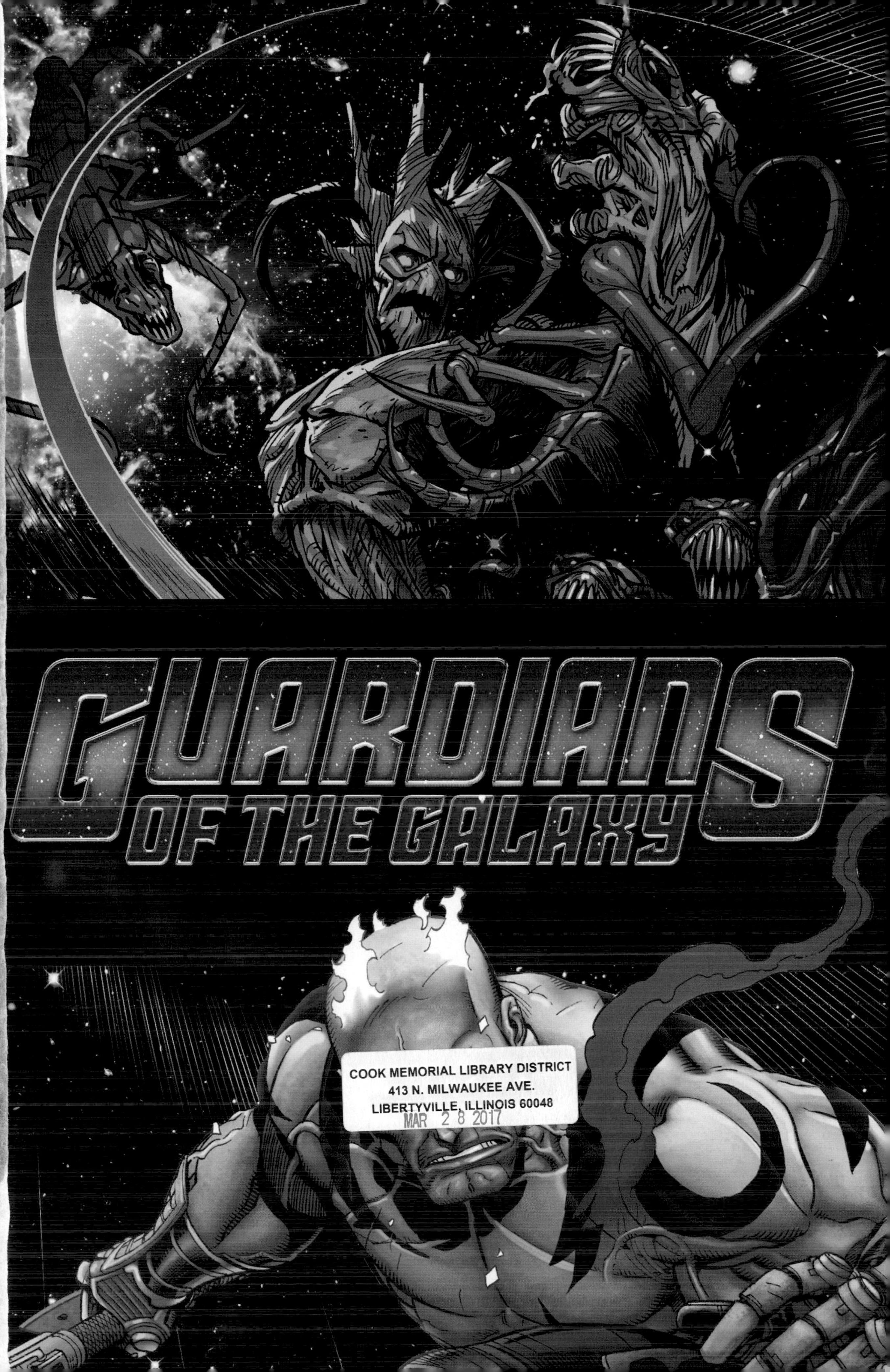
GUARDIANS
OF THE GALAXY

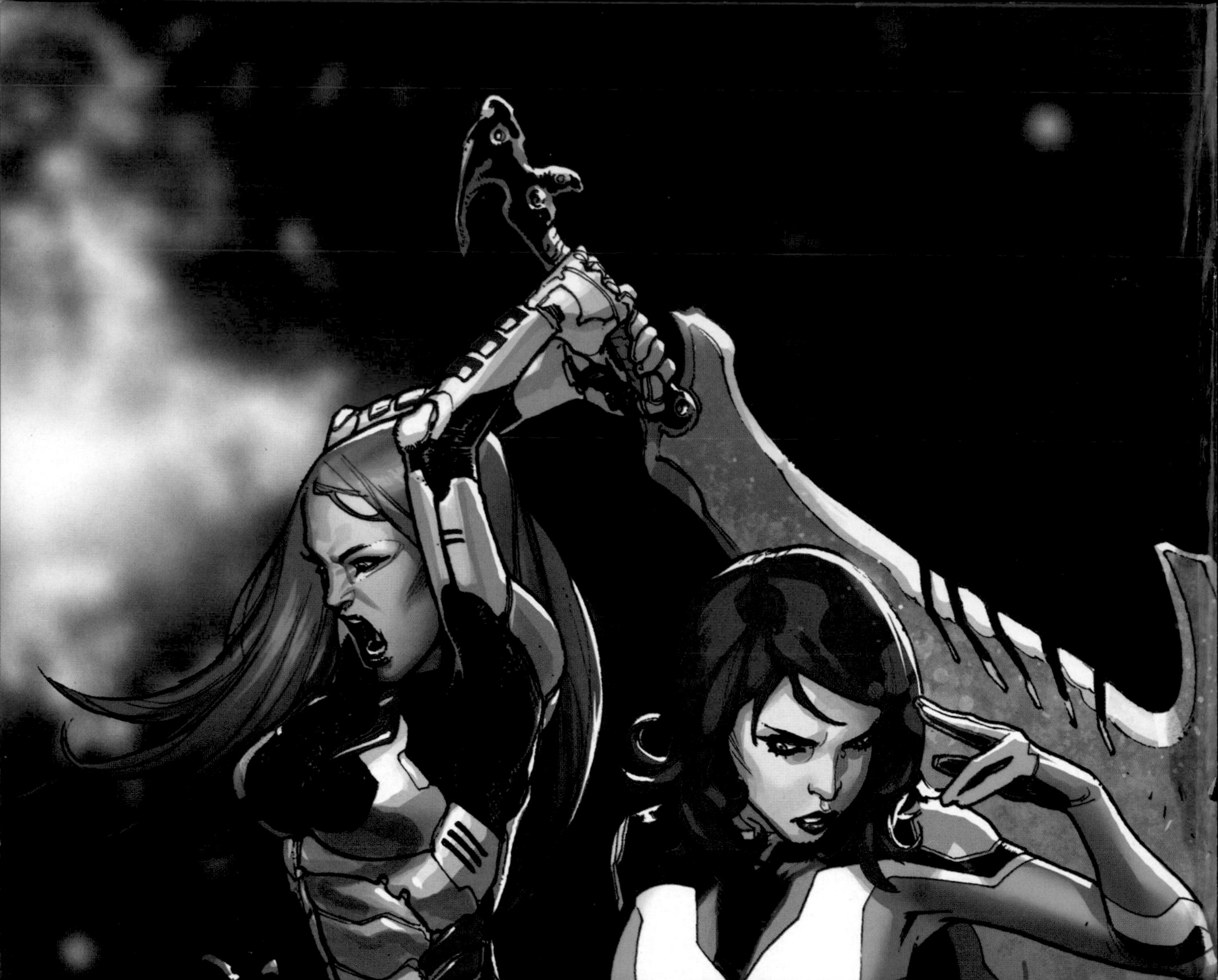

COLLECTION EDITOR: JENNIFER GRÜNWALD ASSISTANT EDITOR: SARAH BRUNSTAD
ASSOCIATE MANAGING EDITOR: ALEX STARBUCK EDITOR, SPECIAL PROJECTS: MARK D. BEAZLEY
SENIOR EDITOR, SPECIAL PROJECTS: JEFF YOUNGQUIST SVP PRINT, SALES & MARKETING: DAVID GABRIEL
BOOK DESIGNER: ADAM DEL RE

EDITOR IN CHIEF: AXEL ALONSO CHIEF CREATIVE OFFICER: JOE QUESADA
PUBLISHER: DAN BUCKLEY EXECUTIVE PRODUCER: ALAN FINE

GUARDIANS OF THE GALAXY VOL. 2. Contains material originally published in magazine form as GUARDIANS OF THE GALAXY #11-17, ALL-NEW X-MEN #22-24 and FREE COMIC BOOK DAY 2014 (GUARDIANS OF THE GALAXY) #1. First printing 2016. ISBN# 978-0-7851-9824-6. Published by MARVEL WORLDWIDE, INC., a subsidiary of MARVEL ENTERTAINMENT, LLC. OFFICE OF PUBLICATION: 135 West 50th Street, New York, NY 10020. **Printed in China.** ALAN FINE, President, Marvel Entertainment; DAN BUCKLEY, President, TV, Publishing and Brand Management; JOE QUESADA, Chief Creative Officer; TOM BREVOORT, SVP of Publishing; DAVID BOGART, SVP of Operations & Procurement, Publishing; C.B. CEBULSKI, VP of International Development & Brand Management; DAVID GABRIEL, SVP Print, Sales & Marketing; JIM O'KEEFE, VP of Operations & Logistics; DAN CARR, Executive Director of Publishing Technology; SUSAN CRESPI, Editorial Operations Manager; ALEX MORALES, Publishing Operations Manager; STAN LEE, Chairman Emeritus. For information regarding advertising in Marvel Comics or on Marvel.com, please contact Jonathan Rheingold, VP of Custom Solutions & Ad Sales, at jrheingold@marvel.com. For Marvel subscription inquiries, please call 800-217-9158. **Manufactured between 9/18/2015 and 11/16/2015 by R.R. DONNELLEY ASIA PRINTING SOLUTIONS, 0, 0, CHINA.**

10 9 8 7 6 5 4 3 2 1

STAR-LORD   GAMORA   ROCKET RACCOON   GROOT   DRAX   ANGELA

GUARDIANS OF THE GALAXY

GUARDIANS OF THE GALAXY #11-13
ARTIST: **SARA PICHELLI WITH STUART IMMONEN** (#12) &
   DAVID MARQUEZ (#13)
ADDITIONAL INKS, #12: **WADE VON GRAWBADGER**
COLORIST: **JUSTIN PONSOR**
COVER ART: **SARA PICHELLI** & **JUSTIN PONSOR**

GUARDIANS OF THE GALAXY #14
PENCILERS: **NICK BRADSHAW WITH JASON MASTERS** &
   TODD NAUCK
INKERS: **NICK BRADSHAW, WALDEN WONG,**
   JASON MASTERS & **TODD NAUCK**
COLORISTS: **JUSTIN PONSOR** WITH **JASON KEITH**
COVER ART: **NICK BRADSHAW** & **JUSTIN PONSOR**

"GROOT'S TALE"	"FIGHT FOR THE FUTURE"
WRITER: **ANDY LANNING**	WRITER: **DAN ABNETT**
PENCILER: **PHIL JIMENEZ**	ARTIST: **GERARDO SANDOVAL**
INKER: **LIVESAY**	COLORIST: **RACHELLE ROSENBERG**
COLORIST: **ANTONIO FABELA**	

GUARDIANS OF THE GALAXY #16
ARTISTS: **NICK BRADSHAW, DAVID MARQUEZ** &
   JASON MASTERS
COLORISTS: **JUSTIN PONSOR, EDGAR DELGADO** &
   JOSE VILLARRUBIA
COVER ART: **NICK BRADSHAW** & **JUSTIN PONSOR**

ALL-NEW X-MEN #22-24
PENCILER: **STUART IMMONEN**
INKER: **WADE VON GRAWBADGER**
COLORIST: **MARTE GRACIA**
COVER ART: **STUART IMMONEN,**
   WADE VON GRAWBADGER
   & **MARTE GRACIA**

FREE COMIC BOOK DAY 2014 (GUARDIANS OF THE GALAXY) #1
PENCILER: **NICK BRADSHAW**
INKER: **SCOTT HANNA**
COLORIST: **MORRY HOLLOWELL**
COVER ART: **SARA PICHELLI** & **JUSTIN PONSOR**

GUARDIANS OF THE GALAXY #15
PENCILERS: **NICK BRADSHAW** & **CAMERON STEWART**
INKERS: **NICK BRADSHAW, CAMERON STEWART** &
   WALDEN WONG
COLORIST: **JUSTIN PONSOR**
COVER ART: **NICK BRADSHAW** & **JUSTIN PONSOR**

GUARDIANS OF THE GALAXY #17
PENCILER: **NICK BRADSHAW** & **MICHAEL OEMING**
INKERS: **NICK BRADSHAW, MICHAEL OEMING** &
   WALDEN WONG
COLORIST: **JUSTIN PONSOR**
COVER ART: **ED MCGUINNESS, MARK FARMER** &
   JUSTIN PONSOR

LETTERER: **VC'S CORY PETIT**
ASSISTANT EDITOR: **XANDER JAROWEY**
ASSOCIATE EDITOR: **JORDAN D. WHITE**
EDITORS: **ELLIE PYLE, MIKE MARTS** & **NICK LOWE**

CYCLOPS MARVEL GIRL ICEMAN BEAST ANGEL KITTY PRYDE X-23

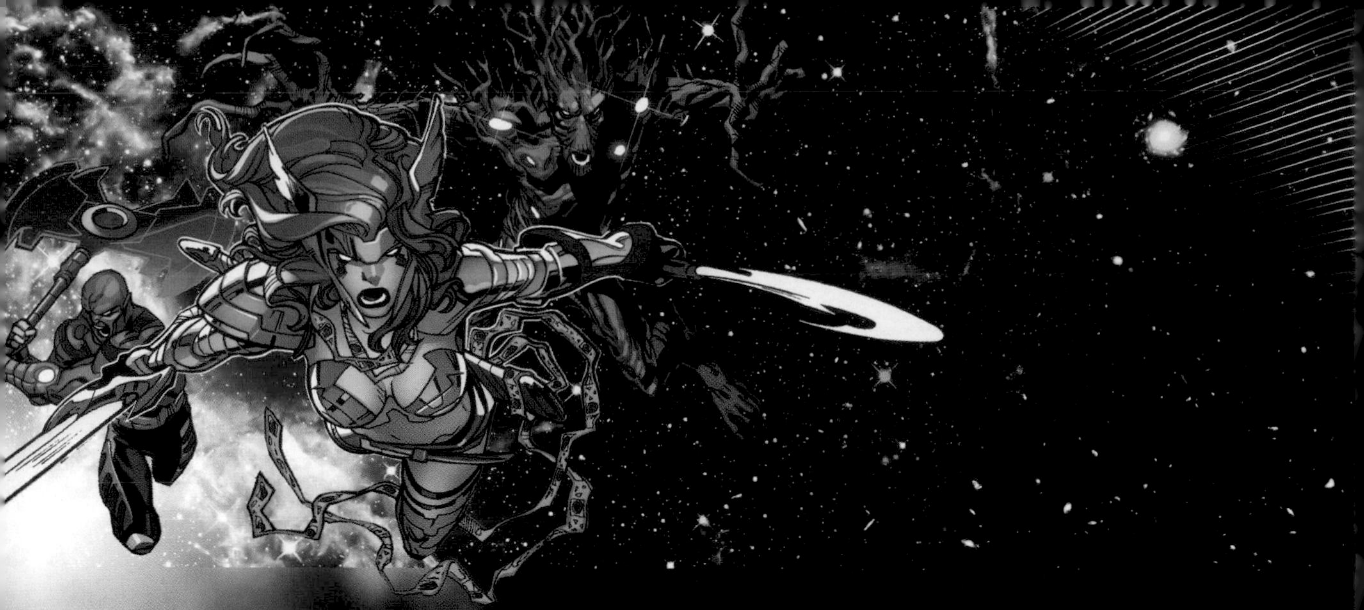

PREVIOUSLY IN *GUARDIANS OF THE GALAXY*...

PETER QUILL'S ESTRANGED FATHER, THE KING OF SPARTAX, TRIED TO CAPTURE THE GUARDIANS FOR DISOBEYING HIS NEW RULE THAT NO ALIEN HAND MAY TOUCH THE PLANET EARTH. IN RETURN, PETER SHAMED HIM WITH SOME COLORFUL PUBLIC DEFIANCE.

THE HUNTER/WARRIOR ANGELA HAS COME TO THIS GALAXY BECAUSE OF A TIME-SPACE CONTINUUM ACCIDENT. SHE IS TRYING TO FIGURE OUT HER PLACE IN THE GALAXY.

THANOS' ARMY CAME VERY CLOSE TO TAKING THE PLANET EARTH, BUT THE GUARDIANS HELPED SAVE THE PLANET. THE MAD TITAN HAS DISAPPEARED.

PREVIOUSLY IN *ALL-NEW X-MEN*...

THE ORIGINAL X-MEN WERE BROUGHT TO THE PRESENT TO HELP SHOW THE PRESENT-DAY X-MEN HOW FAR THEY HAVE STRAYED FROM XAVIER'S DREAM. AFTER LEARNING OF THEIR FUTURE, THE ORIGINAL X-MEN FOUND THEMSELVES IN CONFLICT WITH ONE ANOTHER AS THEY TRIED TO COME TO GRIPS WITH WHAT THEIR DESTINY WILL BRING. THIS ESPECIALLY AFFECTED JEAN GREY AND SCOTT SUMMERS AS THEY LEARNED OF THEIR FUTURE TOGETHER AND JEAN'S SUBSEQUENT DEATHS.

ALTHOUGH THEY HAVE ATTEMPTED TO RETURN TO THEIR OWN TIME, THEY DISCOVERED THAT THEY ARE, IN FACT, STUCK IN THE PRESENT. RECENTLY MOVING FROM WOLVERINE'S JEAN GREY SCHOOL TO PRESENT-DAY CYCLOPS' NEW XAVIER SCHOOL, THEY HAVE BEEN JOINED BY THE NEWLY RESCUED X-23. YET THIS NEW HOME MAY NOT BE AS SAFE AND SECURE AS THEY HAVE BEEN LED TO BELIEVE.

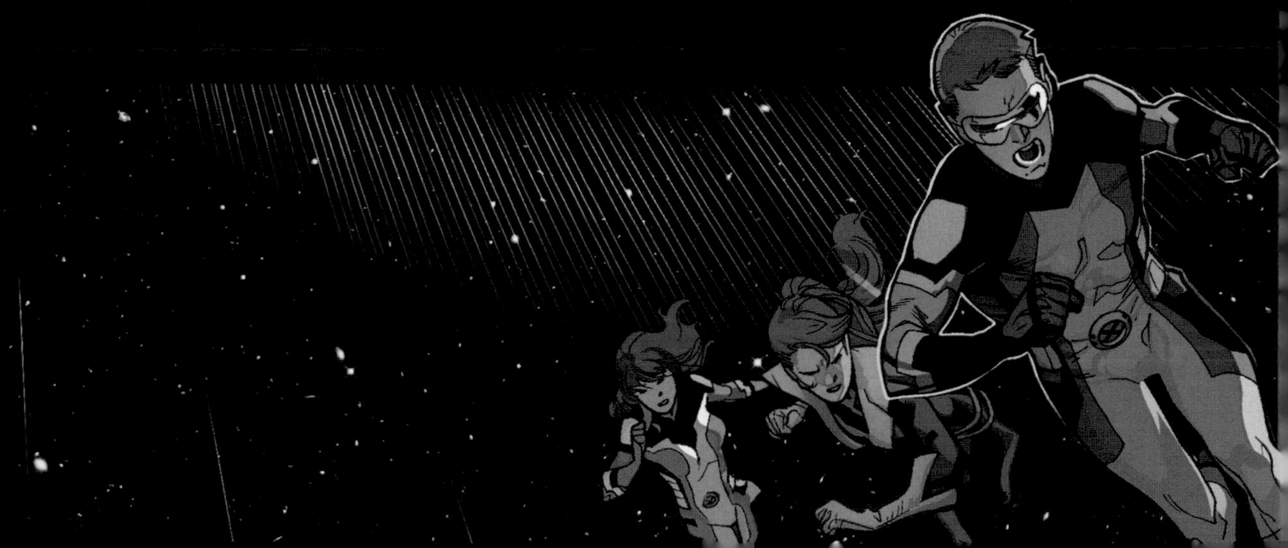

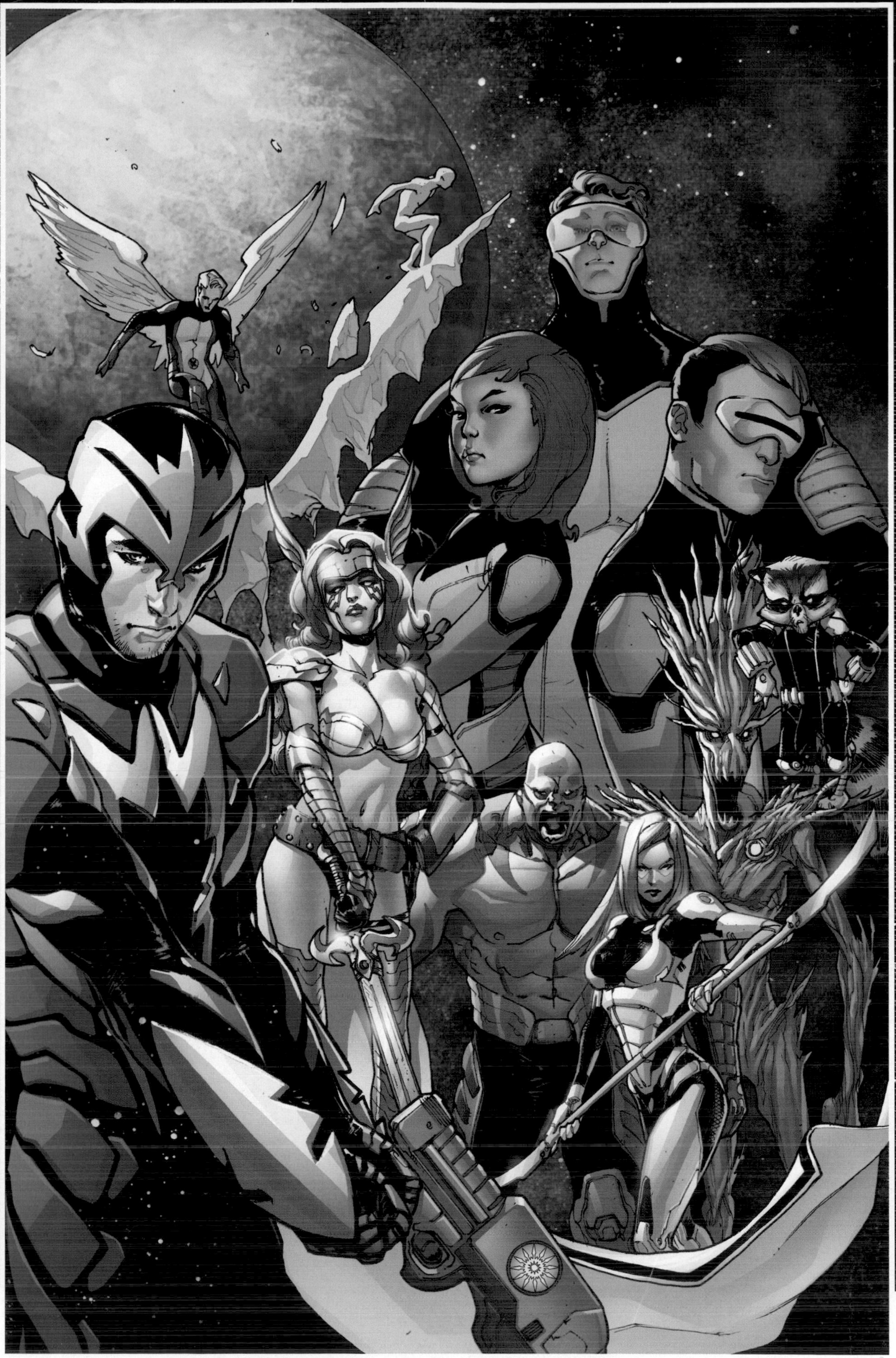

GUARDIANS OF THE GALAXY 11

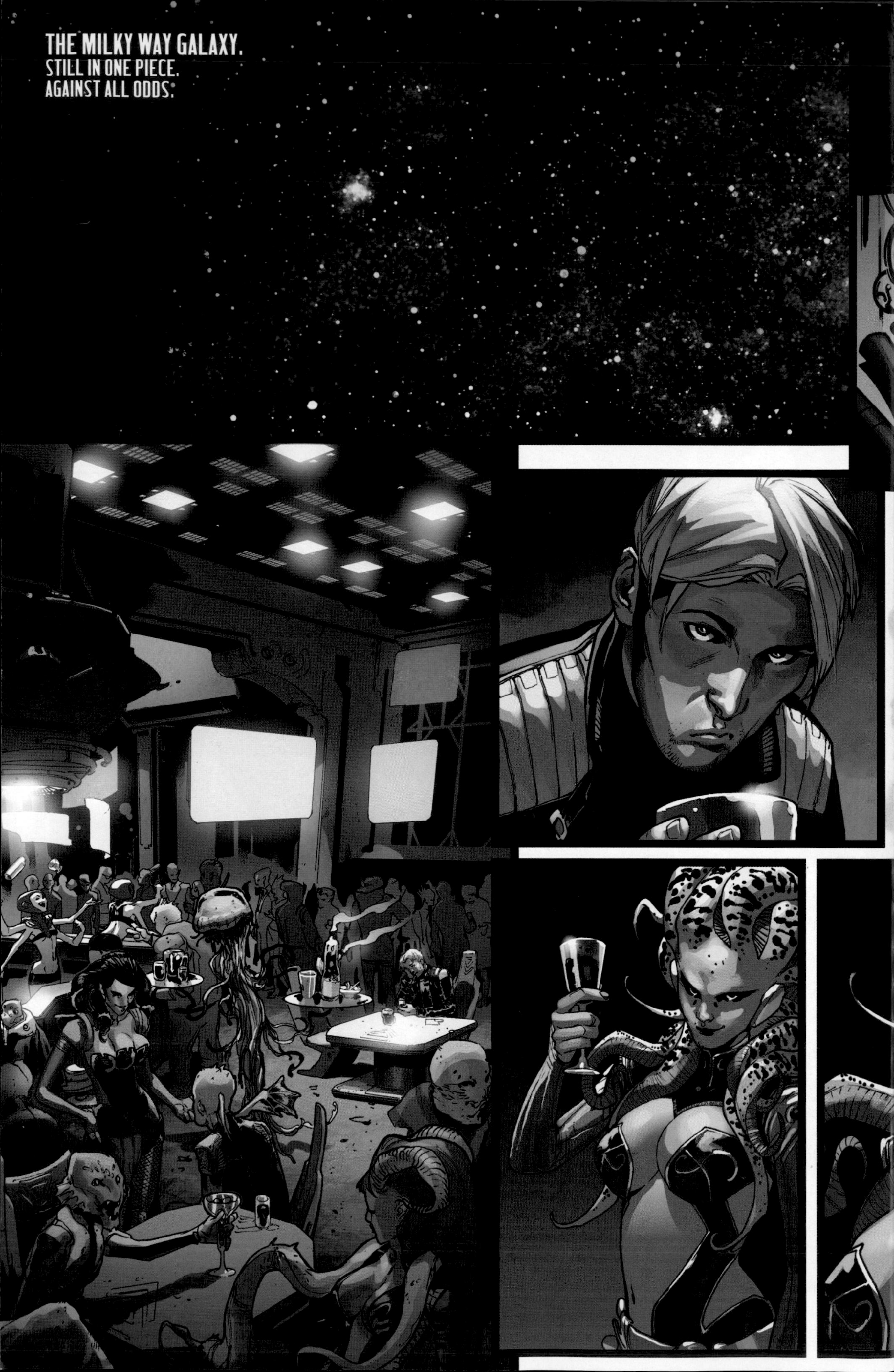
THE MILKY WAY GALAXY.
STILL IN ONE PIECE.
AGAINST ALL ODDS.

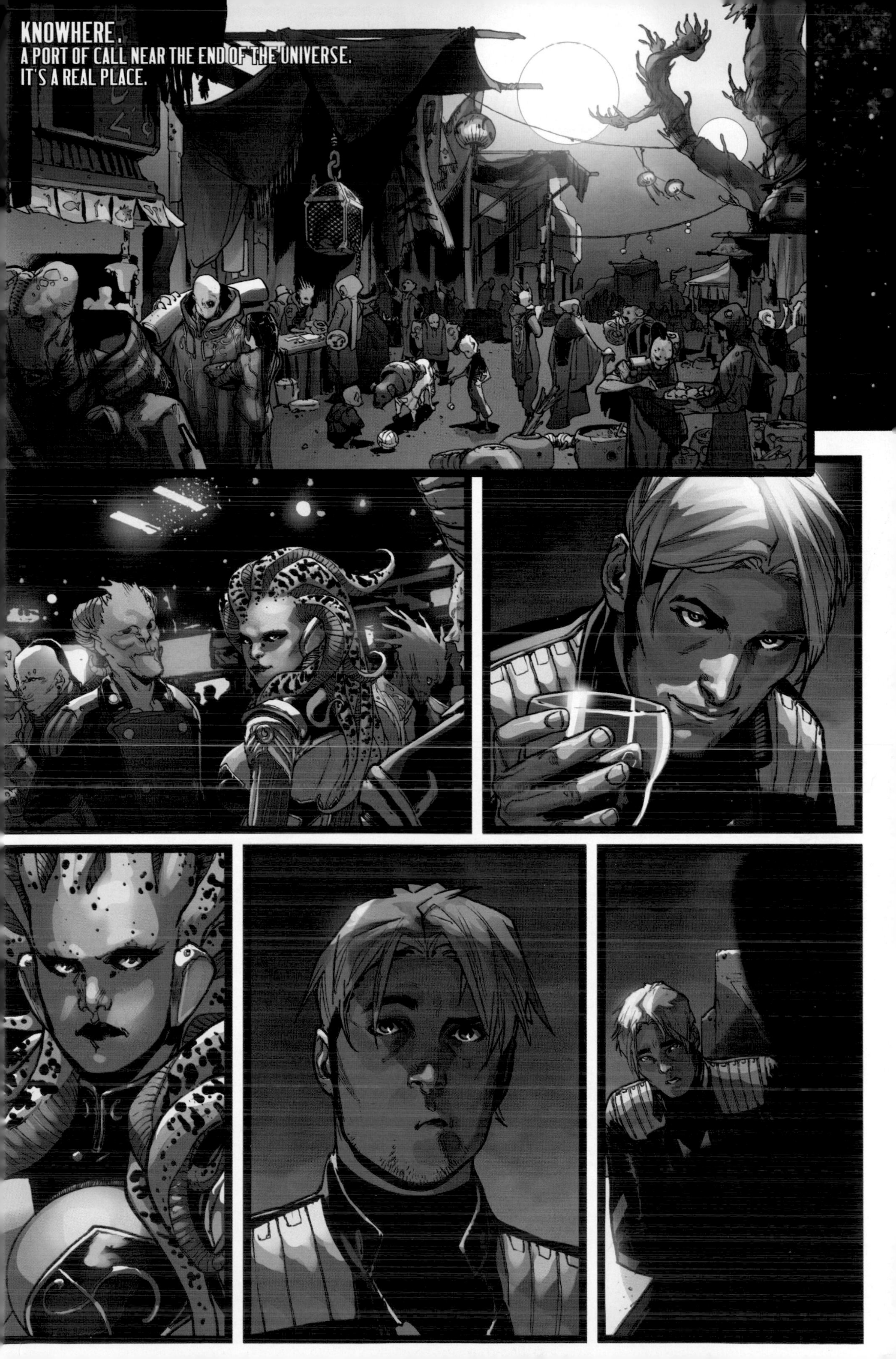
KNOWHERE.
A PORT OF CALL NEAR THE END OF THE UNIVERSE.
IT'S A REAL PLACE.

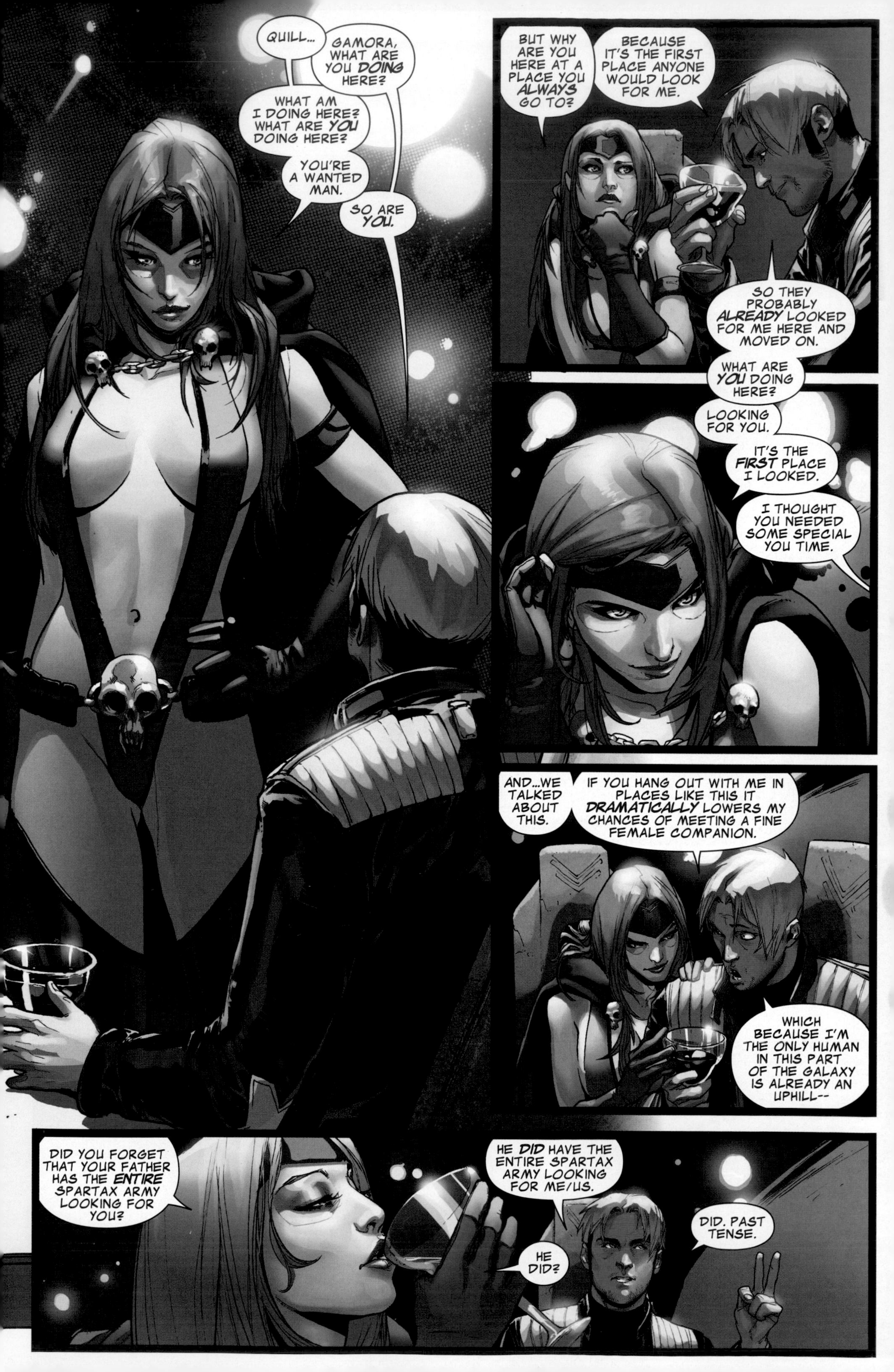
QUILL...
GAMORA, WHAT ARE YOU DOING HERE?
WHAT AM I DOING HERE? WHAT ARE YOU DOING HERE?
YOU'RE A WANTED MAN.
SO ARE YOU.
BUT WHY ARE YOU HERE AT A PLACE YOU ALWAYS GO TO?
BECAUSE IT'S THE FIRST PLACE ANYONE WOULD LOOK FOR ME.
SO THEY PROBABLY ALREADY LOOKED FOR ME HERE AND MOVED ON.
WHAT ARE YOU DOING HERE?
LOOKING FOR YOU.
IT'S THE FIRST PLACE I LOOKED.
I THOUGHT YOU NEEDED SOME SPECIAL YOU TIME.
AND...WE TALKED ABOUT THIS.
IF YOU HANG OUT WITH ME IN PLACES LIKE THIS IT DRAMATICALLY LOWERS MY CHANCES OF MEETING A FINE FEMALE COMPANION.
WHICH BECAUSE I'M THE ONLY HUMAN IN THIS PART OF THE GALAXY IS ALREADY AN UPHILL--
DID YOU FORGET THAT YOUR FATHER HAS THE ENTIRE SPARTAX ARMY LOOKING FOR YOU?
HE DID HAVE THE ENTIRE SPARTAX ARMY LOOKING FOR ME/US.
HE DID?
DID. PAST TENSE.

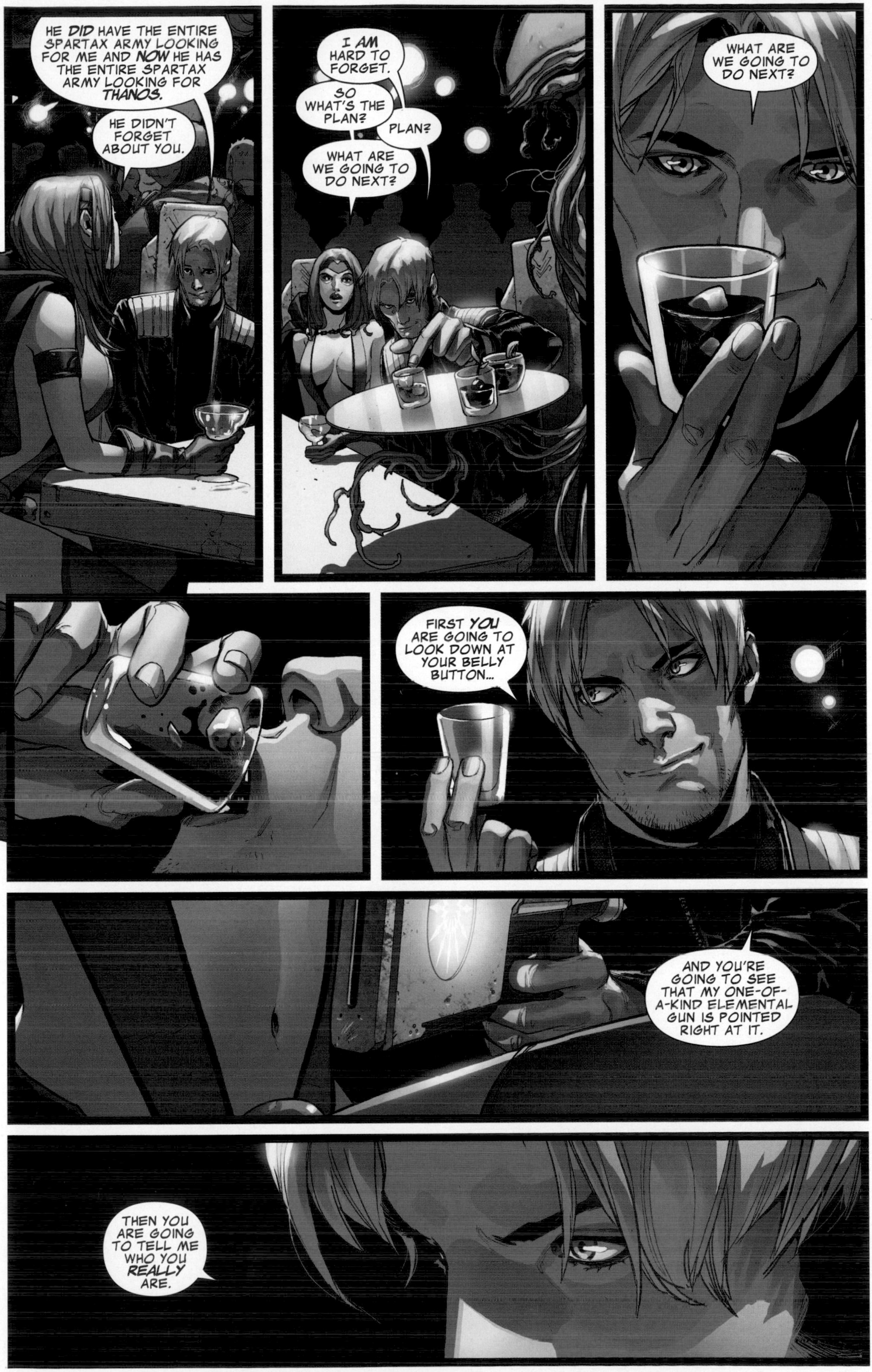

HE DID HAVE THE ENTIRE SPARTAX ARMY LOOKING FOR ME AND NOW HE HAS THE ENTIRE SPARTAX ARMY LOOKING FOR THANOS.
HE DIDN'T FORGET ABOUT YOU.
I AM HARD TO FORGET.
SO WHAT'S THE PLAN?
PLAN?
WHAT ARE WE GOING TO DO NEXT?
WHAT ARE WE GOING TO DO NEXT?
FIRST YOU ARE GOING TO LOOK DOWN AT YOUR BELLY BUTTON...
AND YOU'RE GOING TO SEE THAT MY ONE-OF-A-KIND ELEMENTAL GUN IS POINTED RIGHT AT IT.
THEN YOU ARE GOING TO TELL ME WHO YOU REALLY ARE.

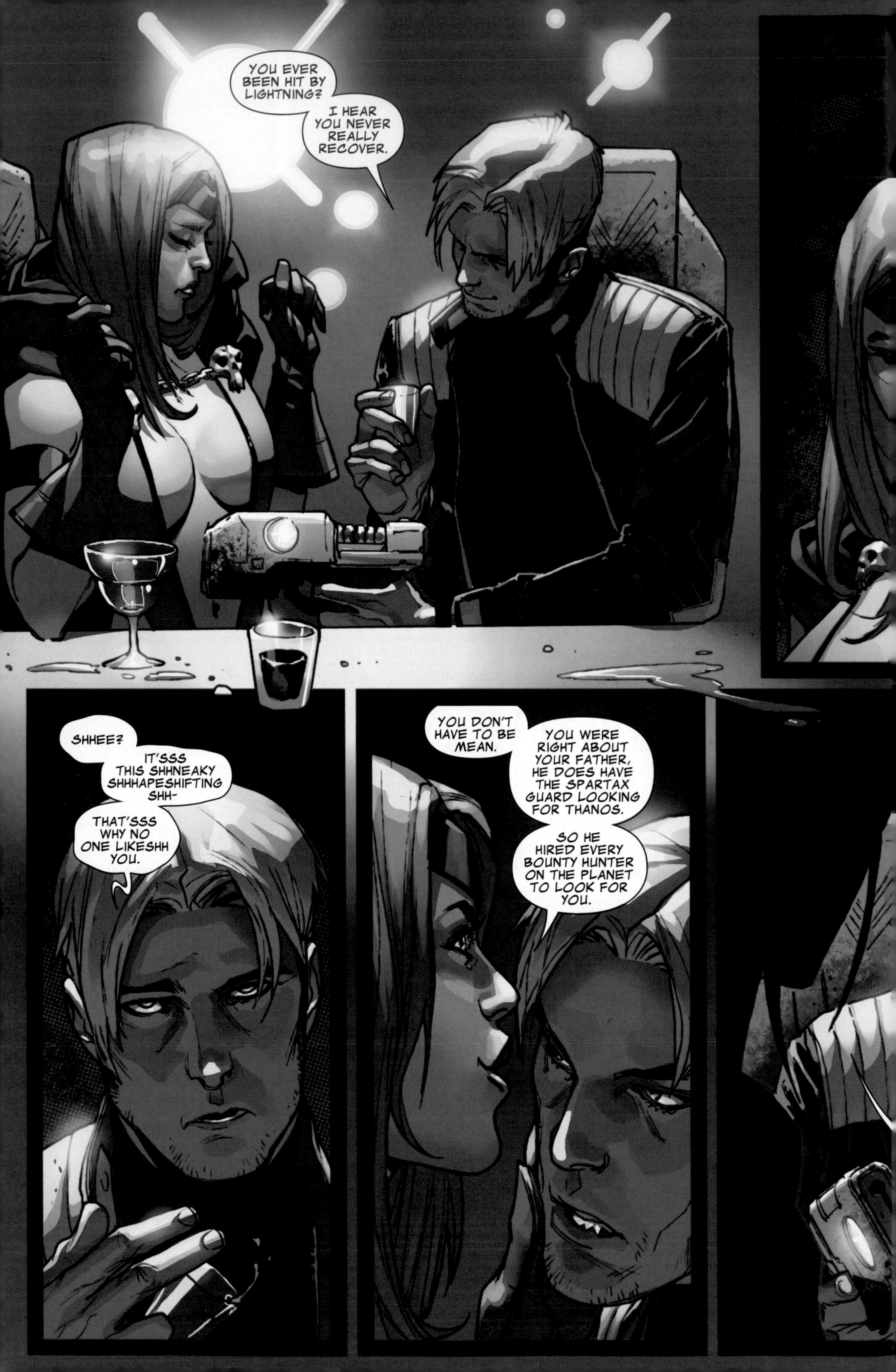
YOU EVER BEEN HIT BY LIGHTNING?
I HEAR YOU NEVER REALLY RECOVER.
SHHEE?
IT'SSS THIS SHHNEAKY SHHHAPESHIFTING SHH-
THAT'SSS WHY NO ONE LIKESHH YOU.
YOU DON'T HAVE TO BE MEAN.
YOU WERE RIGHT ABOUT YOUR FATHER, HE DOES HAVE THE SPARTAX GUARD LOOKING FOR THANOS.
SO HE HIRED EVERY BOUNTY HUNTER ON THE PLANET TO LOOK FOR YOU.

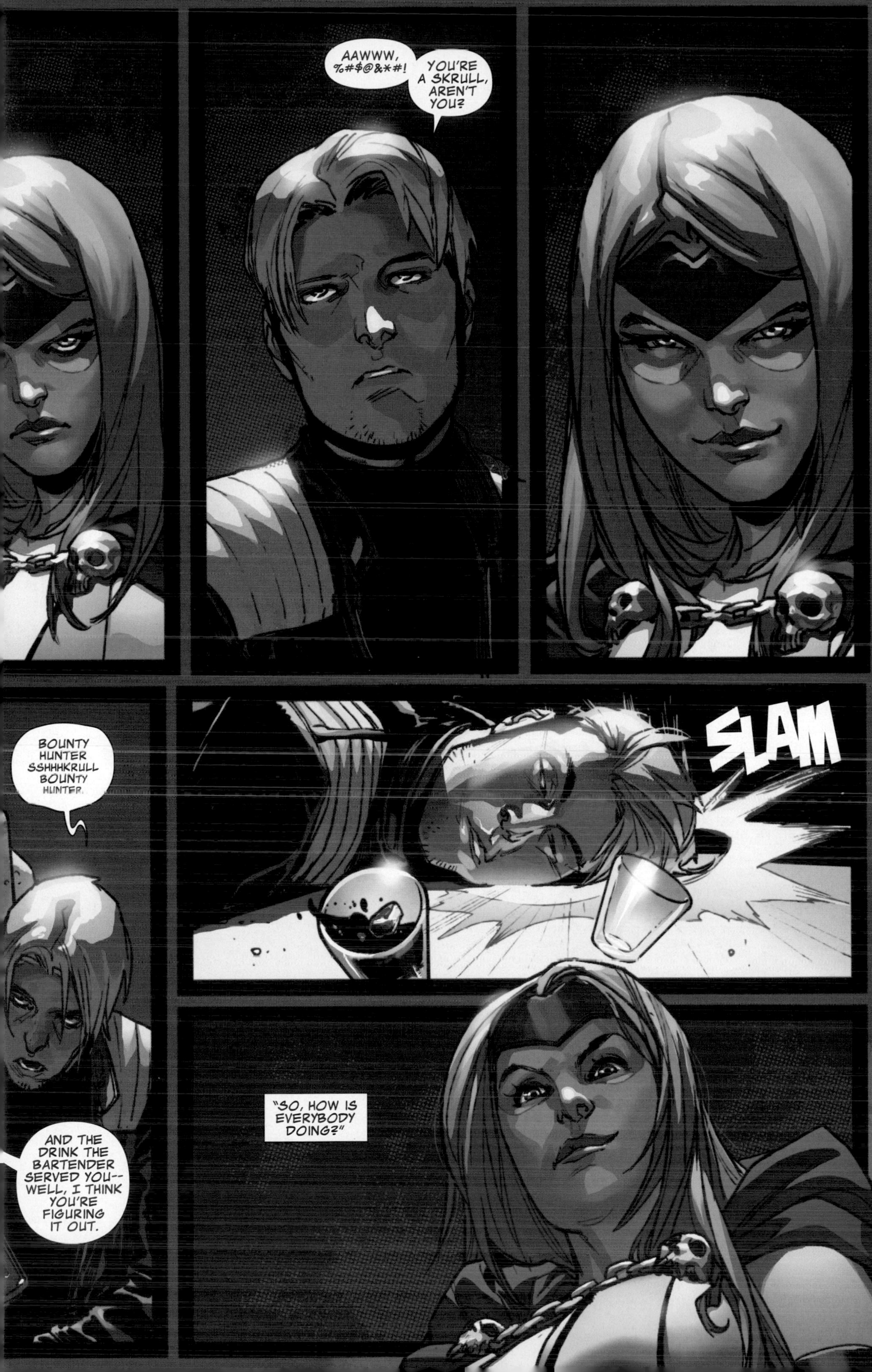
AAWWW, %#$@&*#!
YOU'RE A SKRULL, AREN'T YOU?
BOUNTY HUNTER SSHHHKRULL BOUNTY HUNTER.
SLAM
"SO, HOW IS EVERYBODY DOING?"
AND THE DRINK THE BARTENDER SERVED YOU-- WELL, I THINK YOU'RE FIGURING IT OUT.

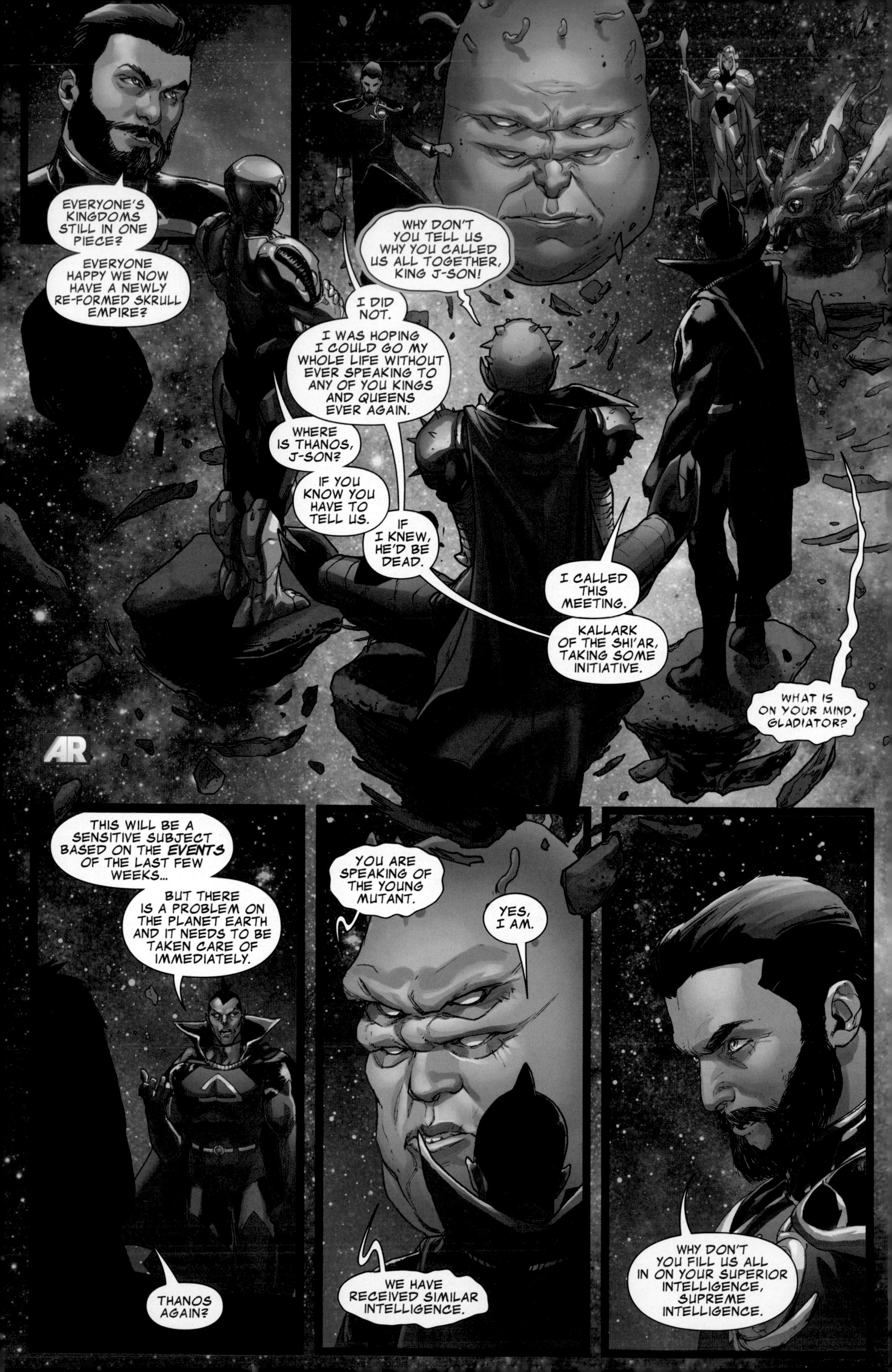
EVERYONE'S KINGDOMS STILL IN ONE PIECE?
EVERYONE HAPPY WE NOW HAVE A NEWLY RE-FORMED SKRULL EMPIRE?
WHY DON'T YOU TELL US WHY YOU CALLED US ALL TOGETHER, KING J-SON!
I DID NOT.
I WAS HOPING I COULD GO MY WHOLE LIFE WITHOUT EVER SPEAKING TO ANY OF YOU KINGS AND QUEENS EVER AGAIN.
WHERE IS THANOS, J-SON?
IF YOU KNOW YOU HAVE TO TELL US.
IF I KNEW, HE'D BE DEAD.
I CALLED THIS MEETING.
KALLARK OF THE SHI'AR, TAKING SOME INITIATIVE.
WHAT IS ON YOUR MIND, GLADIATOR?
THIS WILL BE A SENSITIVE SUBJECT BASED ON THE EVENTS OF THE LAST FEW WEEKS...
BUT THERE IS A PROBLEM ON THE PLANET EARTH AND IT NEEDS TO BE TAKEN CARE OF IMMEDIATELY.
THANOS AGAIN?
YOU ARE SPEAKING OF THE YOUNG MUTANT.
YES, I AM.
WE HAVE RECEIVED SIMILAR INTELLIGENCE.
WHY DON'T YOU FILL US ALL IN ON YOUR SUPERIOR INTELLIGENCE, SUPREME INTELLIGENCE.

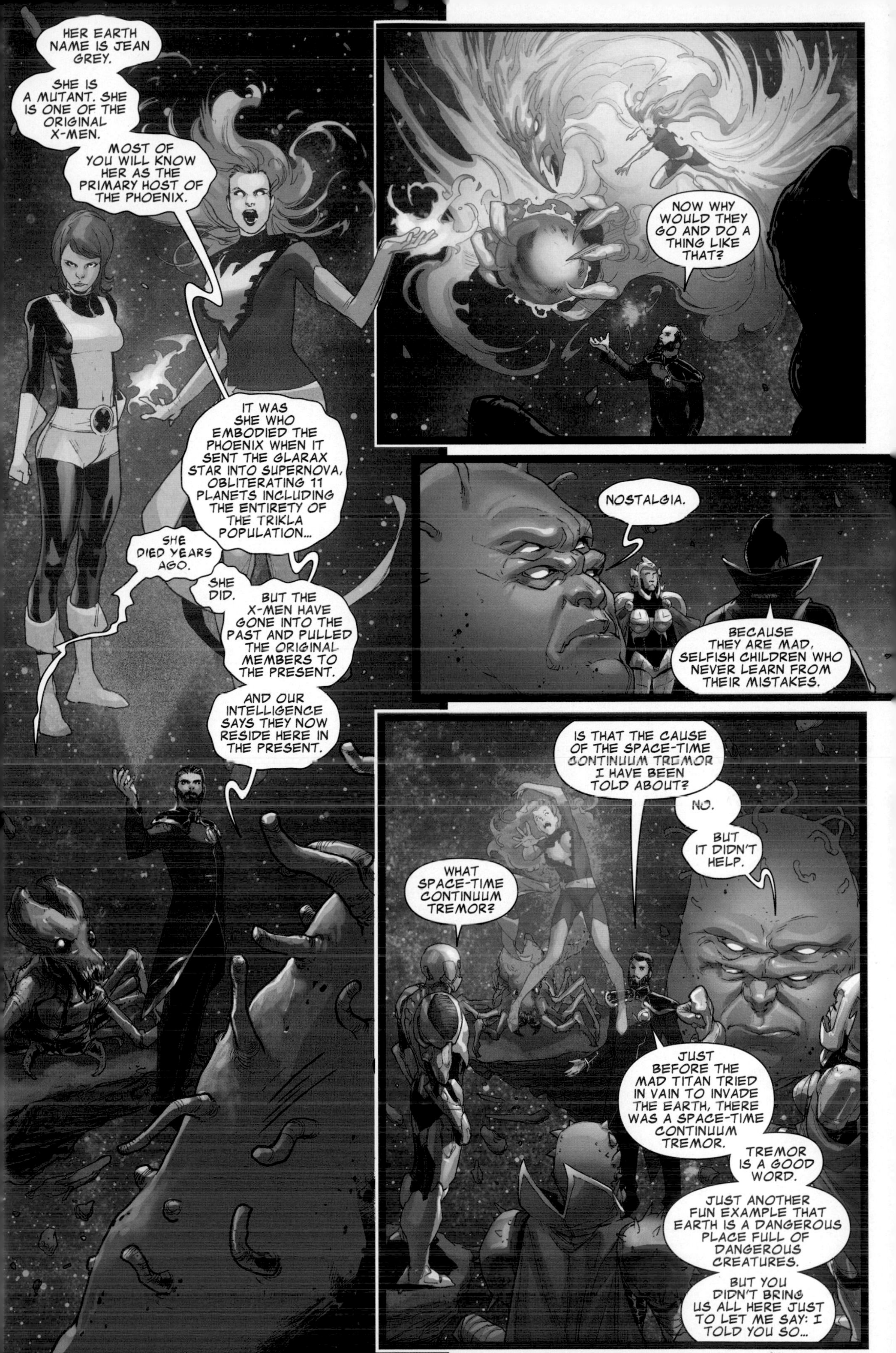
HER EARTH NAME IS JEAN GREY.
SHE IS A MUTANT. SHE IS ONE OF THE ORIGINAL X-MEN.
MOST OF YOU WILL KNOW HER AS THE PRIMARY HOST OF THE PHOENIX.
IT WAS SHE WHO EMBODIED THE PHOENIX WHEN IT SENT THE GLARAX STAR INTO SUPERNOVA, OBLITERATING 11 PLANETS INCLUDING THE ENTIRETY OF THE TRIKLA POPULATION...
SHE DIED YEARS AGO.
SHE DID.
BUT THE X-MEN HAVE GONE INTO THE PAST AND PULLED THE ORIGINAL MEMBERS TO THE PRESENT.
AND OUR INTELLIGENCE SAYS THEY NOW RESIDE HERE IN THE PRESENT.
NOW WHY WOULD THEY GO AND DO A THING LIKE THAT?
NOSTALGIA.
BECAUSE THEY ARE MAD, SELFISH CHILDREN WHO NEVER LEARN FROM THEIR MISTAKES.
IS THAT THE CAUSE OF THE SPACE-TIME CONTINUUM TREMOR I HAVE BEEN TOLD ABOUT?
NO.
BUT IT DIDN'T HELP.
WHAT SPACE-TIME CONTINUUM TREMOR?
JUST BEFORE THE MAD TITAN TRIED IN VAIN TO INVADE THE EARTH, THERE WAS A SPACE-TIME CONTINUUM TREMOR.
TREMOR IS A GOOD WORD.
JUST ANOTHER FUN EXAMPLE THAT EARTH IS A DANGEROUS PLACE FULL OF DANGEROUS CREATURES.
BUT YOU DIDN'T BRING US ALL HERE JUST TO LET ME SAY: I TOLD YOU SO...

PICHELLI AFTER BYRNE.

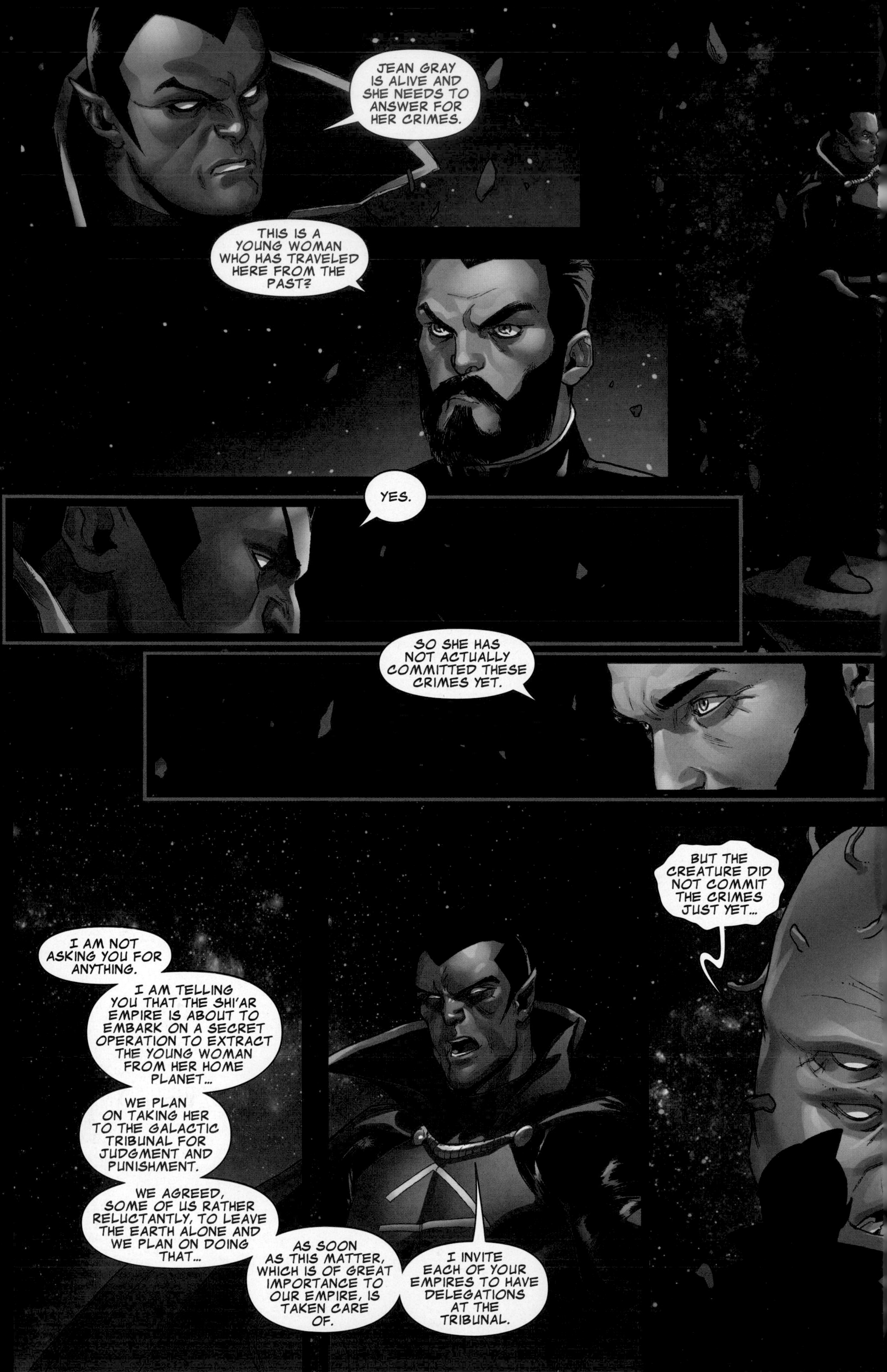
JEAN GRAY IS ALIVE AND SHE NEEDS TO ANSWER FOR HER CRIMES.
THIS IS A YOUNG WOMAN WHO HAS TRAVELED HERE FROM THE PAST?
YES.
SO SHE HAS NOT ACTUALLY COMMITTED THESE CRIMES YET.
BUT THE CREATURE DID NOT COMMIT THE CRIMES JUST YET...
I AM NOT ASKING YOU FOR ANYTHING.
I AM TELLING YOU THAT THE SHI'AR EMPIRE IS ABOUT TO EMBARK ON A SECRET OPERATION TO EXTRACT THE YOUNG WOMAN FROM HER HOME PLANET...
WE PLAN ON TAKING HER TO THE GALACTIC TRIBUNAL FOR JUDGMENT AND PUNISHMENT.
WE AGREED, SOME OF US RATHER RELUCTANTLY, TO LEAVE THE EARTH ALONE AND WE PLAN ON DOING THAT...
AS SOON AS THIS MATTER, WHICH IS OF GREAT IMPORTANCE TO OUR EMPIRE, IS TAKEN CARE OF.
I INVITE EACH OF YOUR EMPIRES TO HAVE DELEGATIONS AT THE TRIBUNAL.

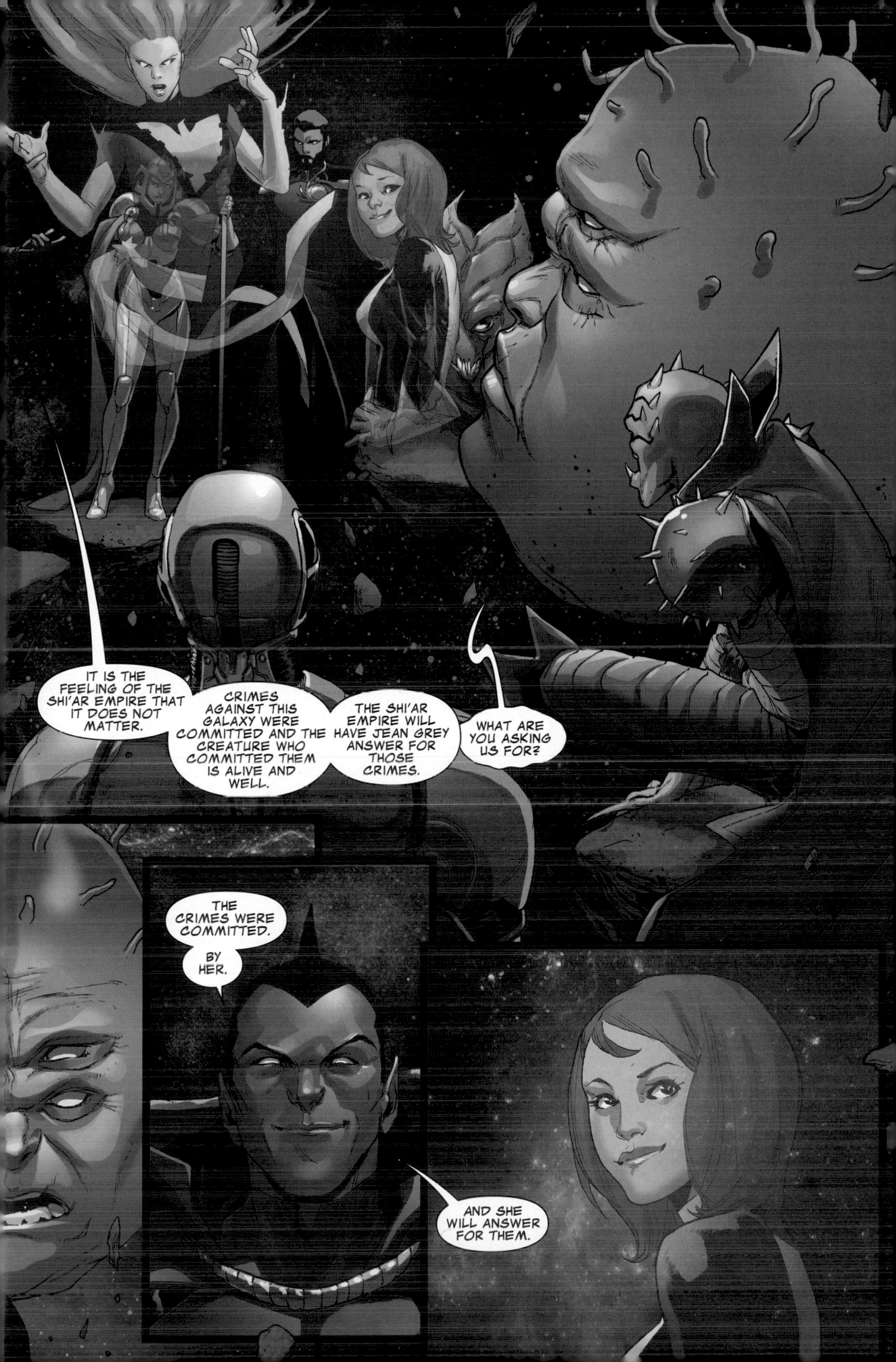
IT IS THE FEELING OF THE SHI'AR EMPIRE THAT IT DOES NOT MATTER.
CRIMES AGAINST THIS GALAXY WERE COMMITTED AND THE CREATURE WHO COMMITTED THEM IS ALIVE AND WELL.
THE SHI'AR EMPIRE WILL HAVE JEAN GREY ANSWER FOR THOSE CRIMES.
WHAT ARE YOU ASKING US FOR?
THE CRIMES WERE COMMITTED.
BY HER.
AND SHE WILL ANSWER FOR THEM.

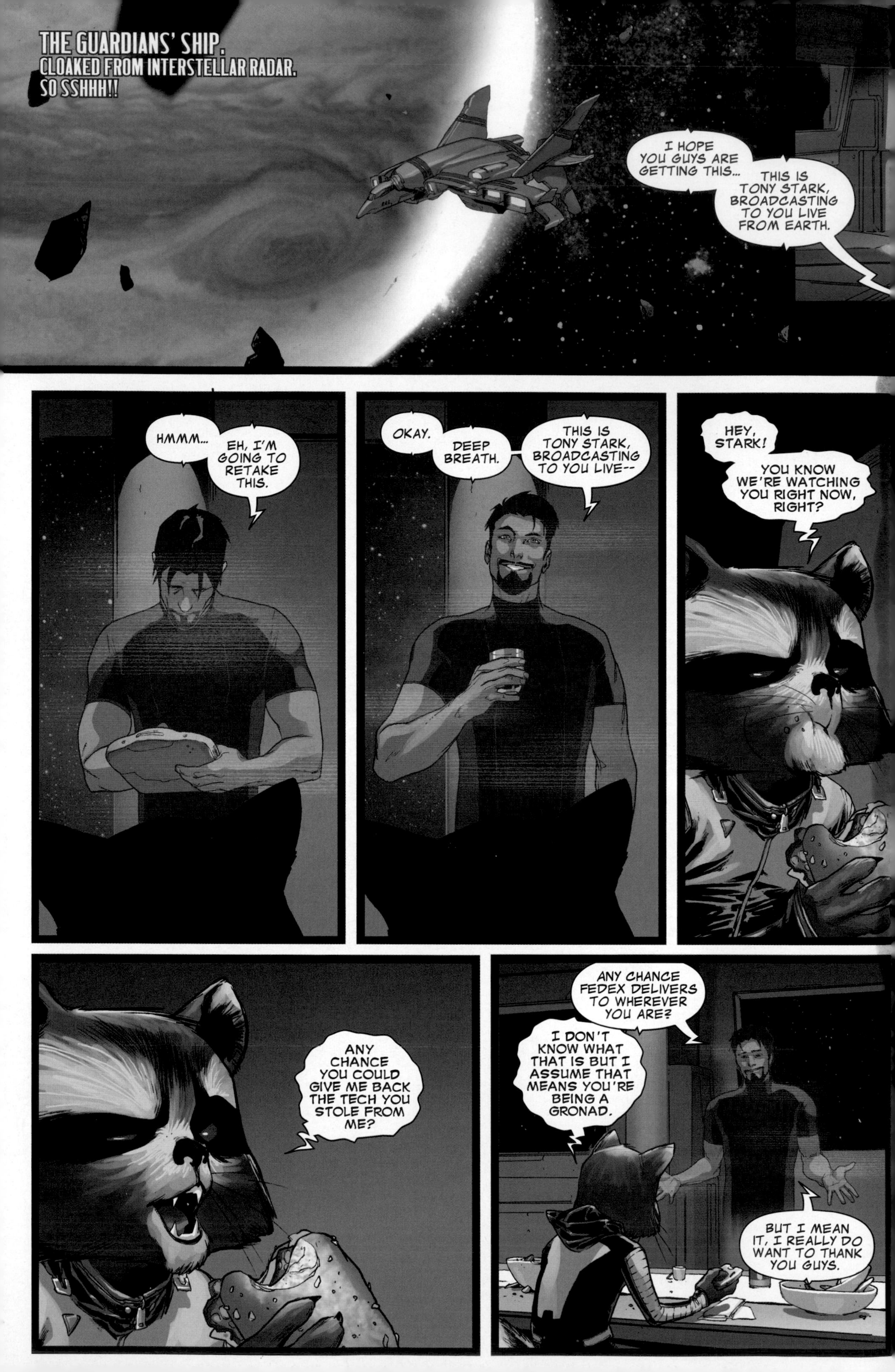
THE GUARDIANS' SHIP. CLOAKED FROM INTERSTELLAR RADAR. SO SSHHH!!
I HOPE YOU GUYS ARE GETTING THIS...
THIS IS TONY STARK, BROADCASTING TO YOU LIVE FROM EARTH.
HMMM...
EH, I'M GOING TO RETAKE THIS.
OKAY.
DEEP BREATH.
THIS IS TONY STARK, BROADCASTING TO YOU LIVE--
HEY, STARK!
YOU KNOW WE'RE WATCHING YOU RIGHT NOW, RIGHT?
ANY CHANCE YOU COULD GIVE ME BACK THE TECH YOU STOLE FROM ME?
ANY CHANCE FEDEX DELIVERS TO WHEREVER YOU ARE?
I DON'T KNOW WHAT THAT IS BUT I ASSUME THAT MEANS YOU'RE BEING A GRONAD.
BUT I MEAN IT, I REALLY DO WANT TO THANK YOU GUYS.

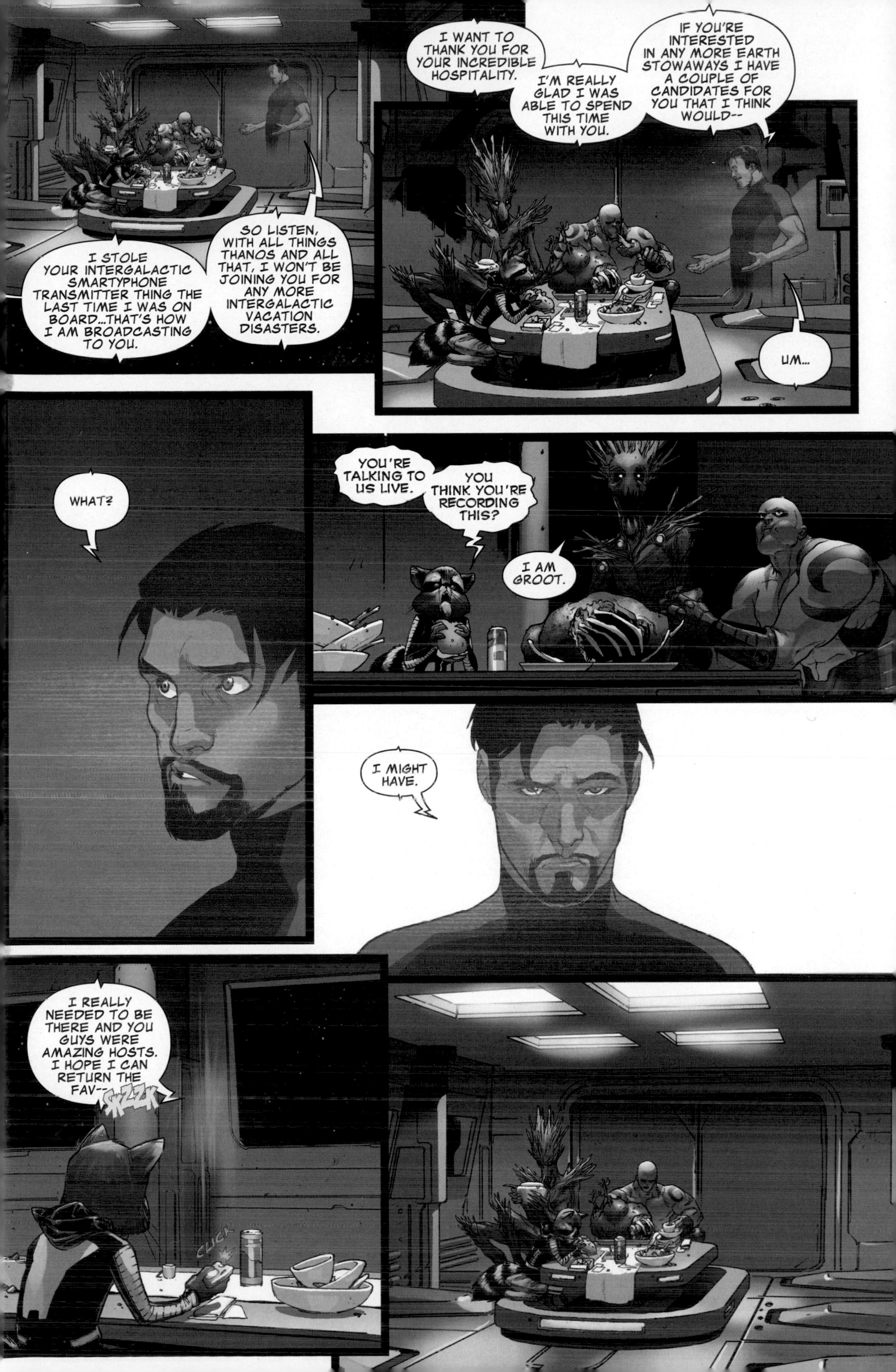
I STOLE YOUR INTERGALACTIC SMARTYPHONE TRANSMITTER THING THE LAST TIME I WAS ON BOARD...THAT'S HOW I AM BROADCASTING TO YOU.
SO LISTEN, WITH ALL THINGS THANOS AND ALL THAT, I WON'T BE JOINING YOU FOR ANY MORE INTERGALACTIC VACATION DISASTERS.
I WANT TO THANK YOU FOR YOUR INCREDIBLE HOSPITALITY.
I'M REALLY GLAD I WAS ABLE TO SPEND THIS TIME WITH YOU.
IF YOU'RE INTERESTED IN ANY MORE EARTH STOWAWAYS I HAVE A COUPLE OF CANDIDATES FOR YOU THAT I THINK WOULD--
UM...
WHAT?
YOU'RE TALKING TO US LIVE.
YOU THINK YOU'RE RECORDING THIS?
I AM GROOT.
I MIGHT HAVE.
I REALLY NEEDED TO BE THERE AND YOU GUYS WERE AMAZING HOSTS. I HOPE I CAN RETURN THE FAV--
SKZZK
CLICK

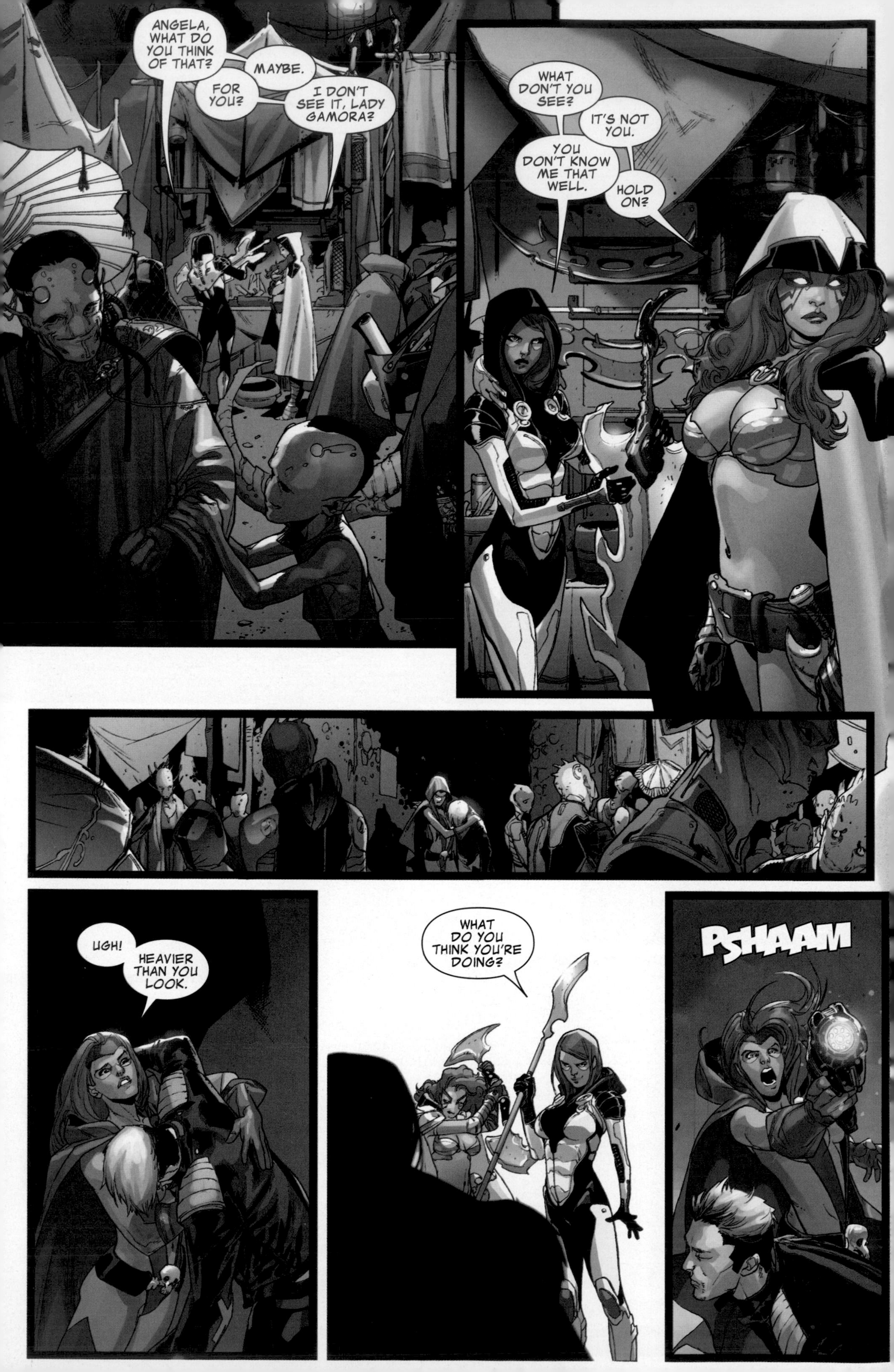
ANGELA, WHAT DO YOU THINK OF THAT?
MAYBE.
FOR YOU?
I DON'T SEE IT, LADY GAMORA?
WHAT DON'T YOU SEE?
IT'S NOT YOU.
YOU DON'T KNOW ME THAT WELL.
HOLD ON?
UGH!
HEAVIER THAN YOU LOOK.
WHAT DO YOU THINK YOU'RE DOING?
PSHAAM

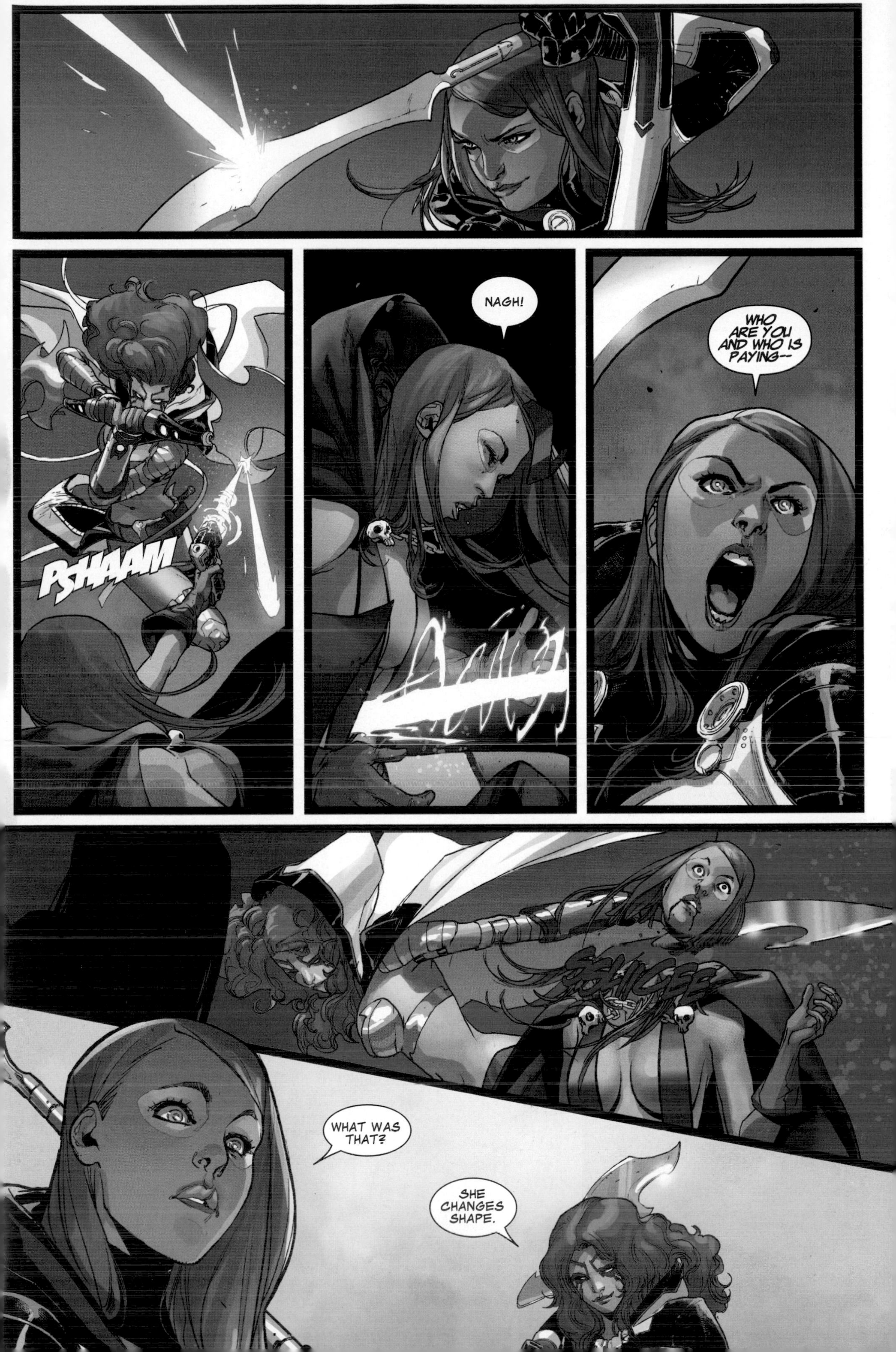
PSHAAM
NAGH!
WHO ARE YOU AND WHO IS PAYING--
SSHICK
WHAT WAS THAT?
SHE CHANGES SHAPE.

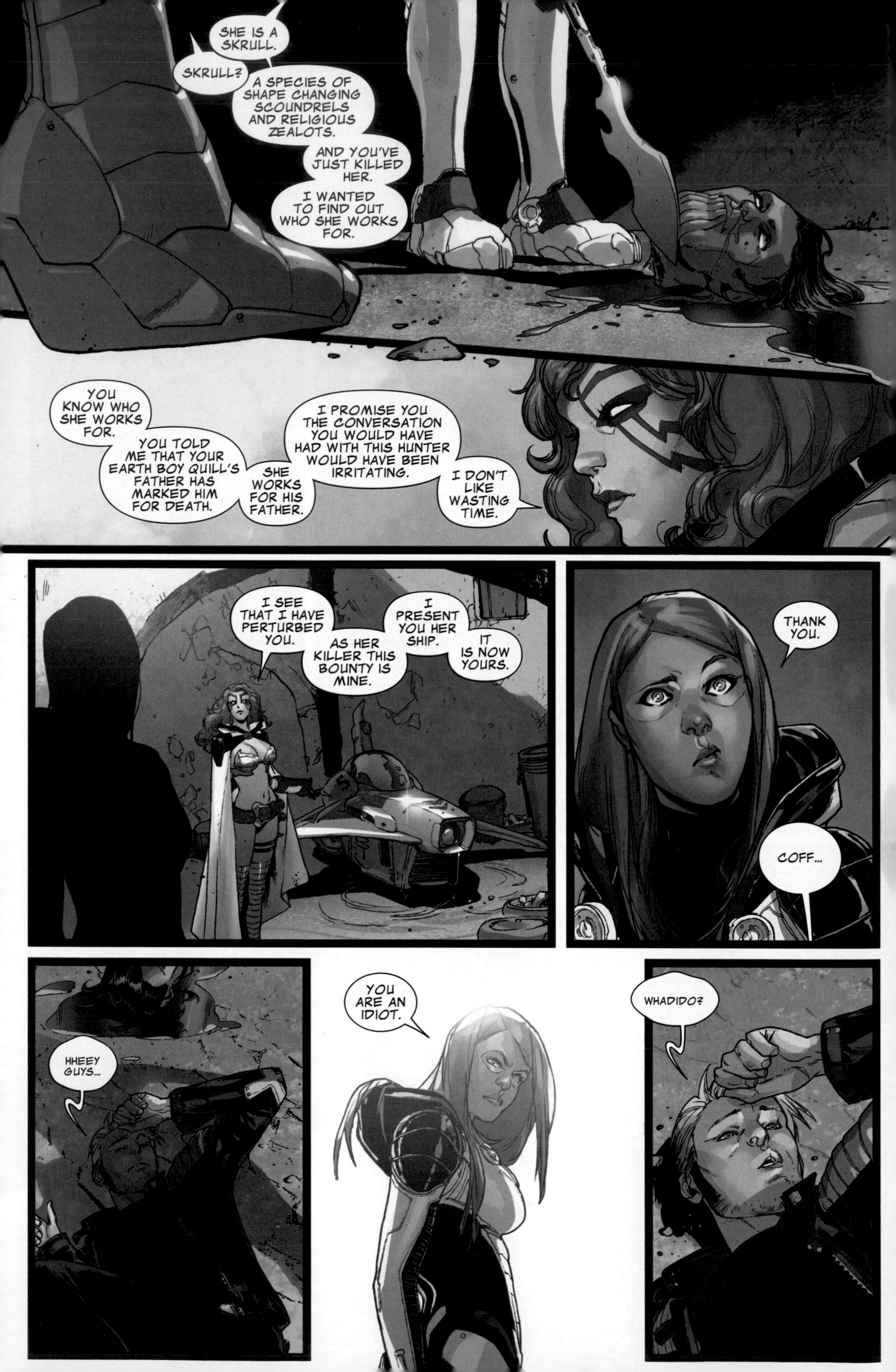
SHE IS A SKRULL.
SKRULL?
A SPECIES OF SHAPE CHANGING SCOUNDRELS AND RELIGIOUS ZEALOTS.
AND YOU'VE JUST KILLED HER.
I WANTED TO FIND OUT WHO SHE WORKS FOR.
YOU KNOW WHO SHE WORKS FOR.
YOU TOLD ME THAT YOUR EARTH BOY QUILL'S FATHER HAS MARKED HIM FOR DEATH.
SHE WORKS FOR HIS FATHER.
I PROMISE YOU THE CONVERSATION YOU WOULD HAVE HAD WITH THIS HUNTER WOULD HAVE BEEN IRRITATING.
I DON'T LIKE WASTING TIME.
I SEE THAT I HAVE PERTURBED YOU.
AS HER KILLER THIS BOUNTY IS MINE.
I PRESENT YOU HER SHIP.
IT IS NOW YOURS.
THANK YOU.
COFF...
HHEEY GUYS...
YOU ARE AN IDIOT.
WHADIDO?

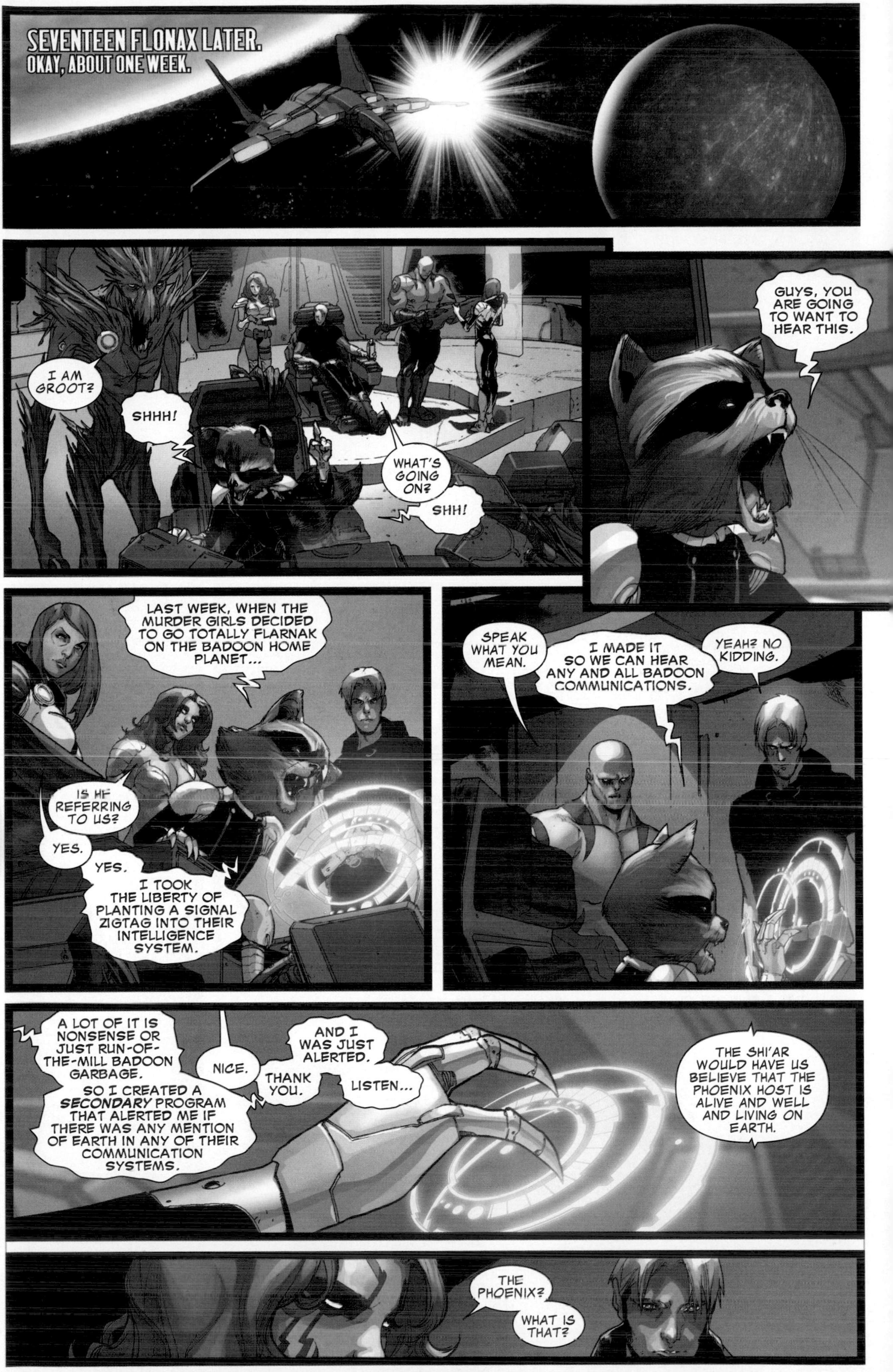
SEVENTEEN FLONAX LATER.
OKAY, ABOUT ONE WEEK.
I AM GROOT?
SHHH!
WHAT'S GOING ON?
SHH!
GUYS, YOU ARE GOING TO WANT TO HEAR THIS.
LAST WEEK, WHEN THE MURDER GIRLS DECIDED TO GO TOTALLY FLARNAK ON THE BADOON HOME PLANET...
IS HE REFERRING TO US?
YES.
YES.
I TOOK THE LIBERTY OF PLANTING A SIGNAL ZIGTAG INTO THEIR INTELLIGENCE SYSTEM.
SPEAK WHAT YOU MEAN.
I MADE IT SO WE CAN HEAR ANY AND ALL BADOON COMMUNICATIONS.
YEAH? NO KIDDING.
A LOT OF IT IS NONSENSE OR JUST RUN-OF-THE-MILL BADOON GARBAGE.
SO I CREATED A SECONDARY PROGRAM THAT ALERTED ME IF THERE WAS ANY MENTION OF EARTH IN ANY OF THEIR COMMUNICATION SYSTEMS.
NICE.
THANK YOU.
AND I WAS JUST ALERTED.
LISTEN...
THE SHI'AR WOULD HAVE US BELIEVE THAT THE PHOENIX HOST IS ALIVE AND WELL AND LIVING ON EARTH.
THE PHOENIX?
WHAT IS THAT?

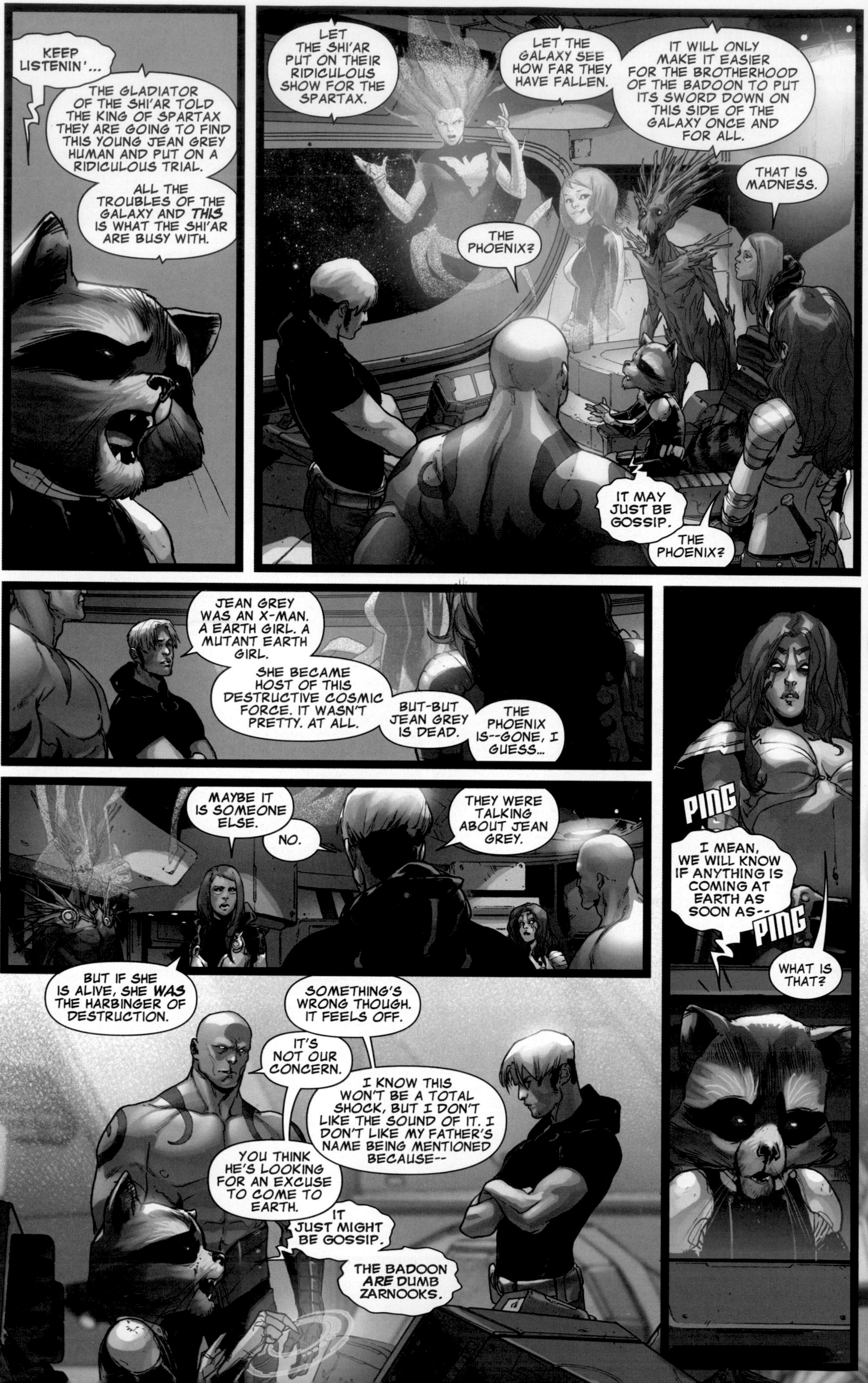
KEEP LISTENIN'...
THE GLADIATOR OF THE SHI'AR TOLD THE KING OF SPARTAX THEY ARE GOING TO FIND THIS YOUNG JEAN GREY HUMAN AND PUT ON A RIDICULOUS TRIAL.
ALL THE TROUBLES OF THE GALAXY AND THIS IS WHAT THE SHI'AR ARE BUSY WITH.
LET THE SHI'AR PUT ON THEIR RIDICULOUS SHOW FOR THE SPARTAX.
LET THE GALAXY SEE HOW FAR THEY HAVE FALLEN.
IT WILL ONLY MAKE IT EASIER FOR THE BROTHERHOOD OF THE BADOON TO PUT ITS SWORD DOWN ON THIS SIDE OF THE GALAXY ONCE AND FOR ALL.
THAT IS MADNESS.
THE PHOENIX?
IT MAY JUST BE GOSSIP.
THE PHOENIX?
JEAN GREY WAS AN X-MAN. A EARTH GIRL. A MUTANT EARTH GIRL.
SHE BECAME HOST OF THIS DESTRUCTIVE COSMIC FORCE. IT WASN'T PRETTY. AT ALL.
BUT-BUT JEAN GREY IS DEAD.
THE PHOENIX IS--GONE, I GUESS...
MAYBE IT IS SOMEONE ELSE.
NO.
THEY WERE TALKING ABOUT JEAN GREY.
PING
I MEAN, WE WILL KNOW IF ANYTHING IS COMING AT EARTH AS SOON AS--
PING
WHAT IS THAT?
BUT IF SHE IS ALIVE, SHE WAS THE HARBINGER OF DESTRUCTION.
SOMETHING'S WRONG THOUGH. IT FEELS OFF.
IT'S NOT OUR CONCERN.
I KNOW THIS WON'T BE A TOTAL SHOCK, BUT I DON'T LIKE THE SOUND OF IT. I DON'T LIKE MY FATHER'S NAME BEING MENTIONED BECAUSE--
YOU THINK HE'S LOOKING FOR AN EXCUSE TO COME TO EARTH.
IT JUST MIGHT BE GOSSIP.
THE BADOON ARE DUMB ZARNOOKS.

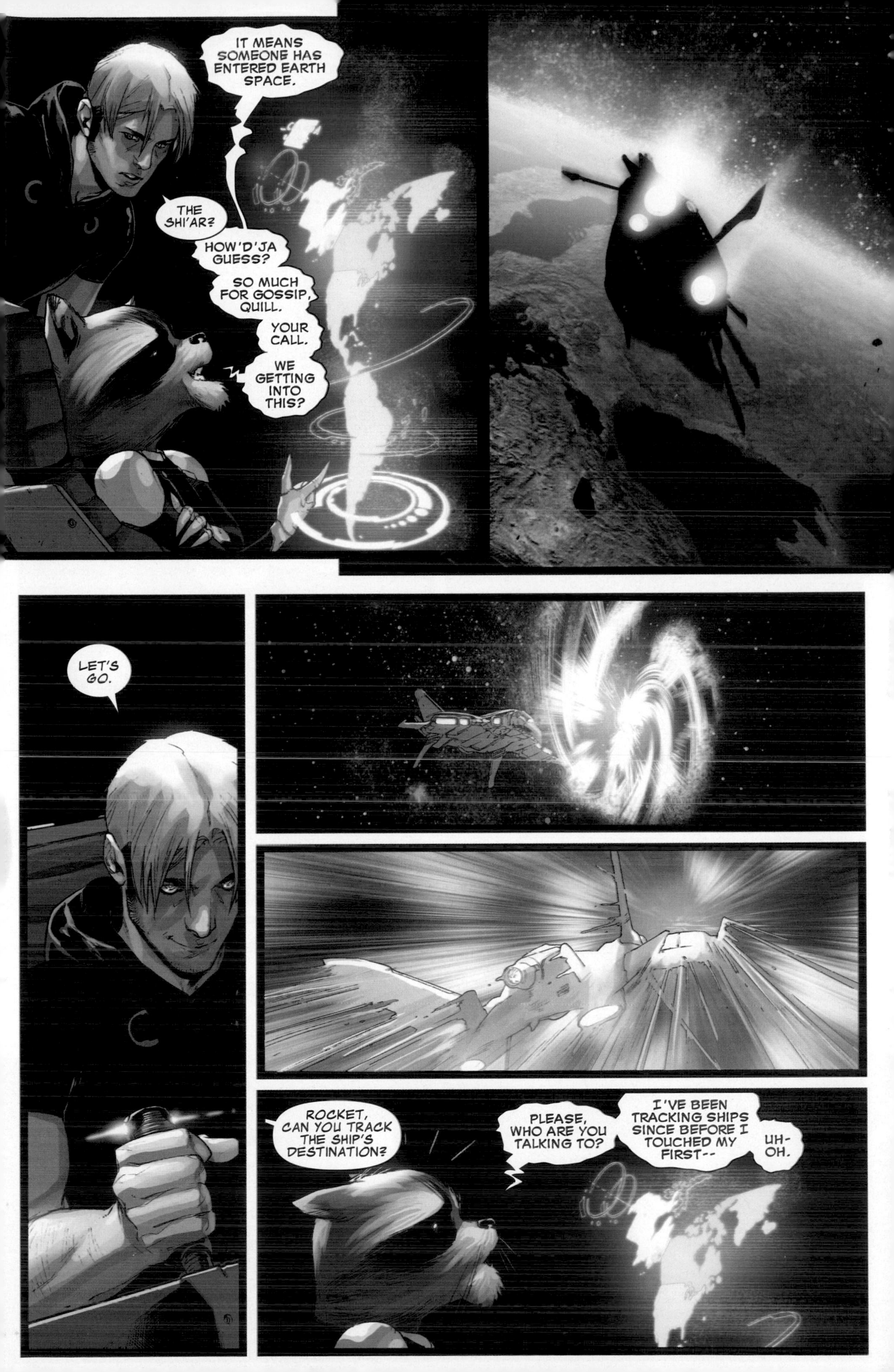
IT MEANS SOMEONE HAS ENTERED EARTH SPACE.
THE SHI'AR?
HOW'D'JA GUESS?
SO MUCH FOR GOSSIP, QUILL.
YOUR CALL.
WE GETTING INTO THIS?
LET'S GO.
ROCKET, CAN YOU TRACK THE SHIP'S DESTINATION?
PLEASE, WHO ARE YOU TALKING TO?
I'VE BEEN TRACKING SHIPS SINCE BEFORE I TOUCHED MY FIRST--
UH-OH.

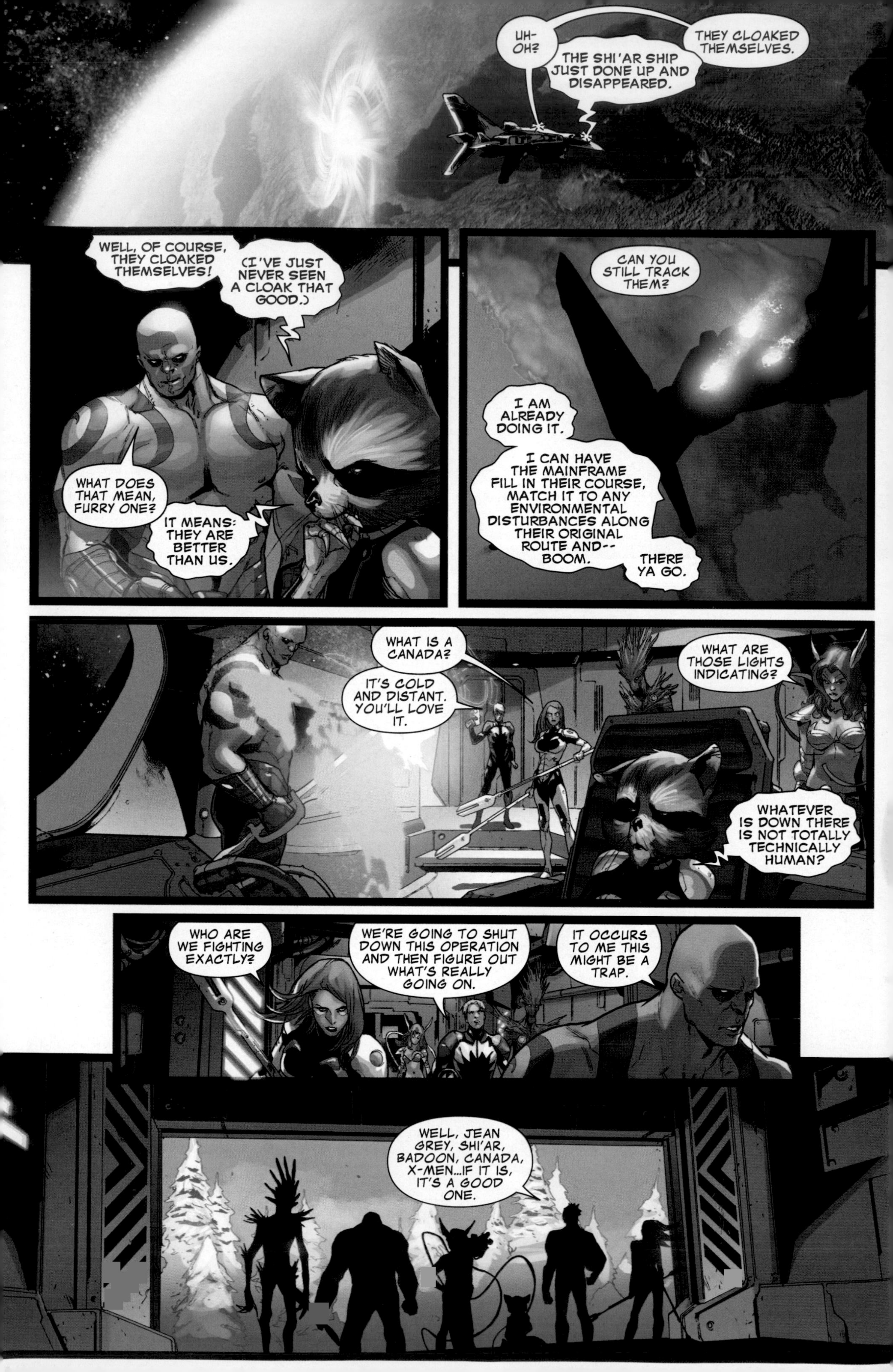

UH-OH?
THEY CLOAKED THEMSELVES.
THE SHI'AR SHIP JUST DONE UP AND DISAPPEARED.
WELL, OF COURSE, THEY CLOAKED THEMSELVES!
(I'VE JUST NEVER SEEN A CLOAK THAT GOOD.)
WHAT DOES THAT MEAN, FURRY ONE?
IT MEANS: THEY ARE BETTER THAN US.
CAN YOU STILL TRACK THEM?
I AM ALREADY DOING IT.
I CAN HAVE THE MAINFRAME FILL IN THEIR COURSE, MATCH IT TO ANY ENVIRONMENTAL DISTURBANCES ALONG THEIR ORIGINAL ROUTE AND-- BOOM.
THERE YA GO.
WHAT IS A CANADA?
IT'S COLD AND DISTANT. YOU'LL LOVE IT.
WHAT ARE THOSE LIGHTS INDICATING?
WHATEVER IS DOWN THERE IS NOT TOTALLY TECHNICALLY HUMAN?
WHO ARE WE FIGHTING EXACTLY?
WE'RE GOING TO SHUT DOWN THIS OPERATION AND THEN FIGURE OUT WHAT'S REALLY GOING ON.
IT OCCURS TO ME THIS MIGHT BE A TRAP.
WELL, JEAN GREY, SHI'AR, BADOON, CANADA, X-MEN...IF IT IS, IT'S A GOOD ONE.

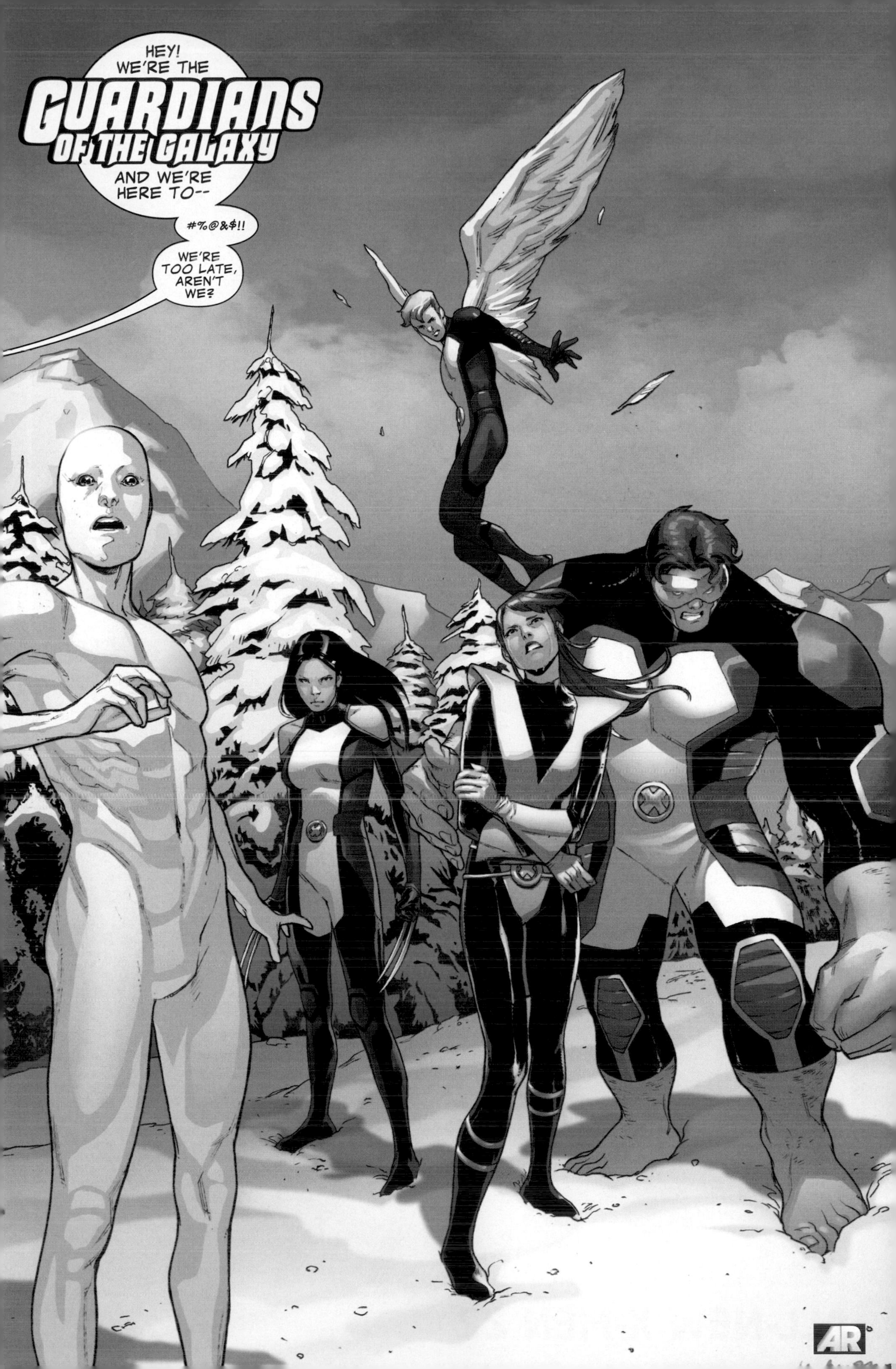
HEY! WE'RE THE GUARDIANS OF THE GALAXY AND WE'RE HERE TO--
#%@&$!!
WE'RE TOO LATE, AREN'T WE?
AR

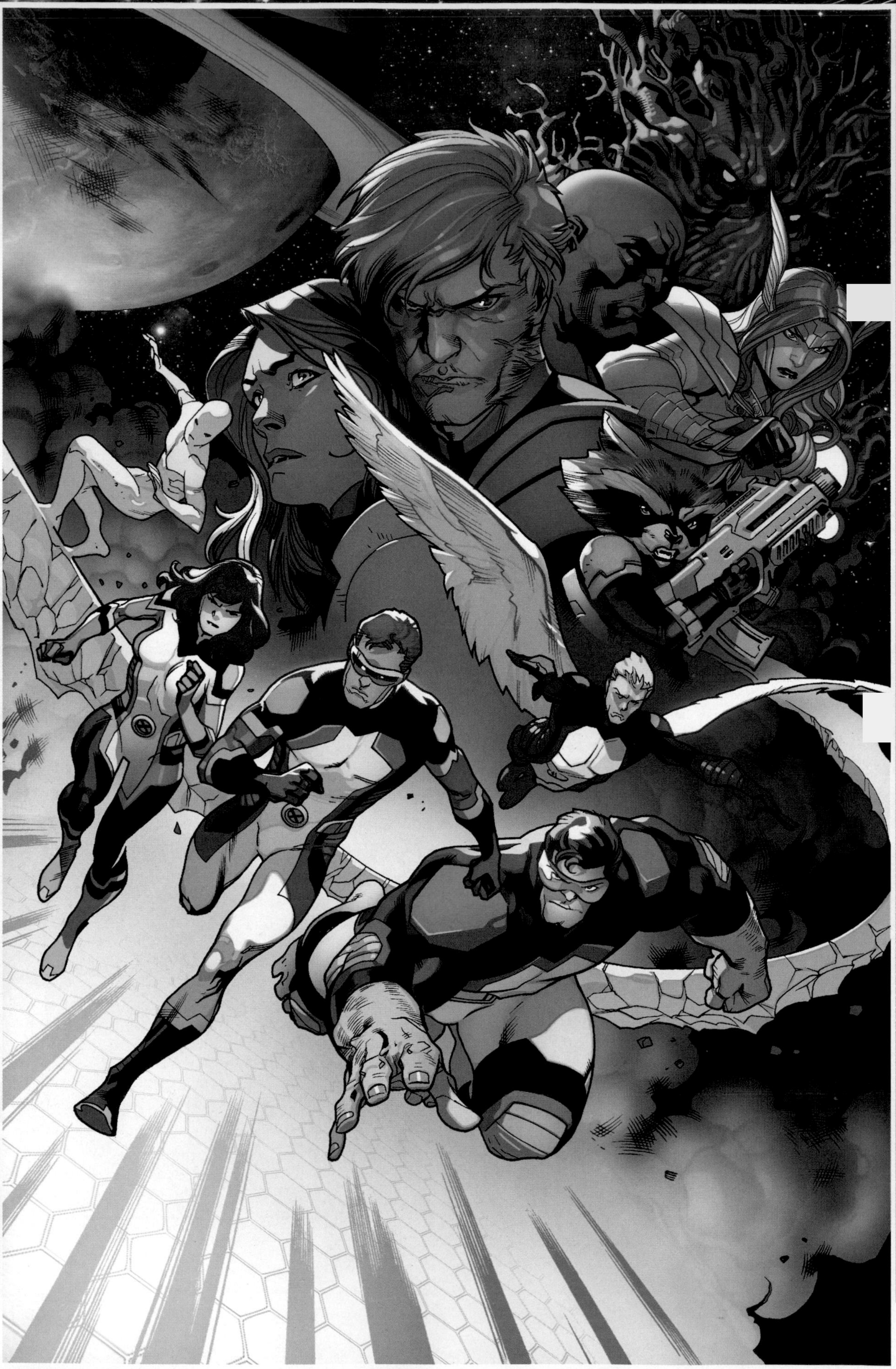

ALL-NEW X-MEN 22

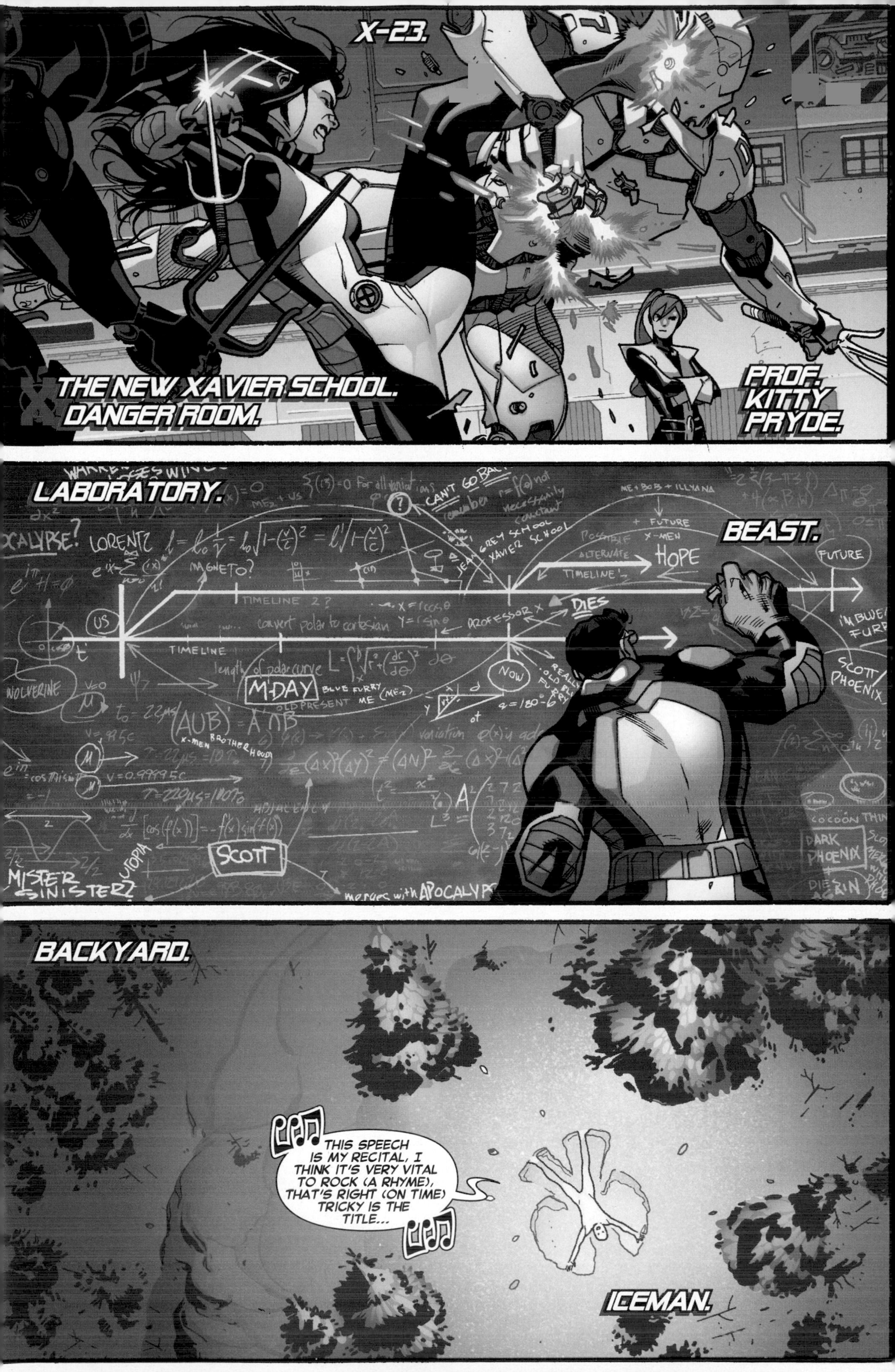
X-23.
THE NEW XAVIER SCHOOL. DANGER ROOM.
PROF. KITTY PRYDE.
LABORATORY.
BEAST.
BACKYARD.
THIS SPEECH IS MY RECITAL, I THINK IT'S VERY VITAL TO ROCK (A RHYME), THAT'S RIGHT (ON TIME) TRICKY IS THE TITLE...
ICEMAN.

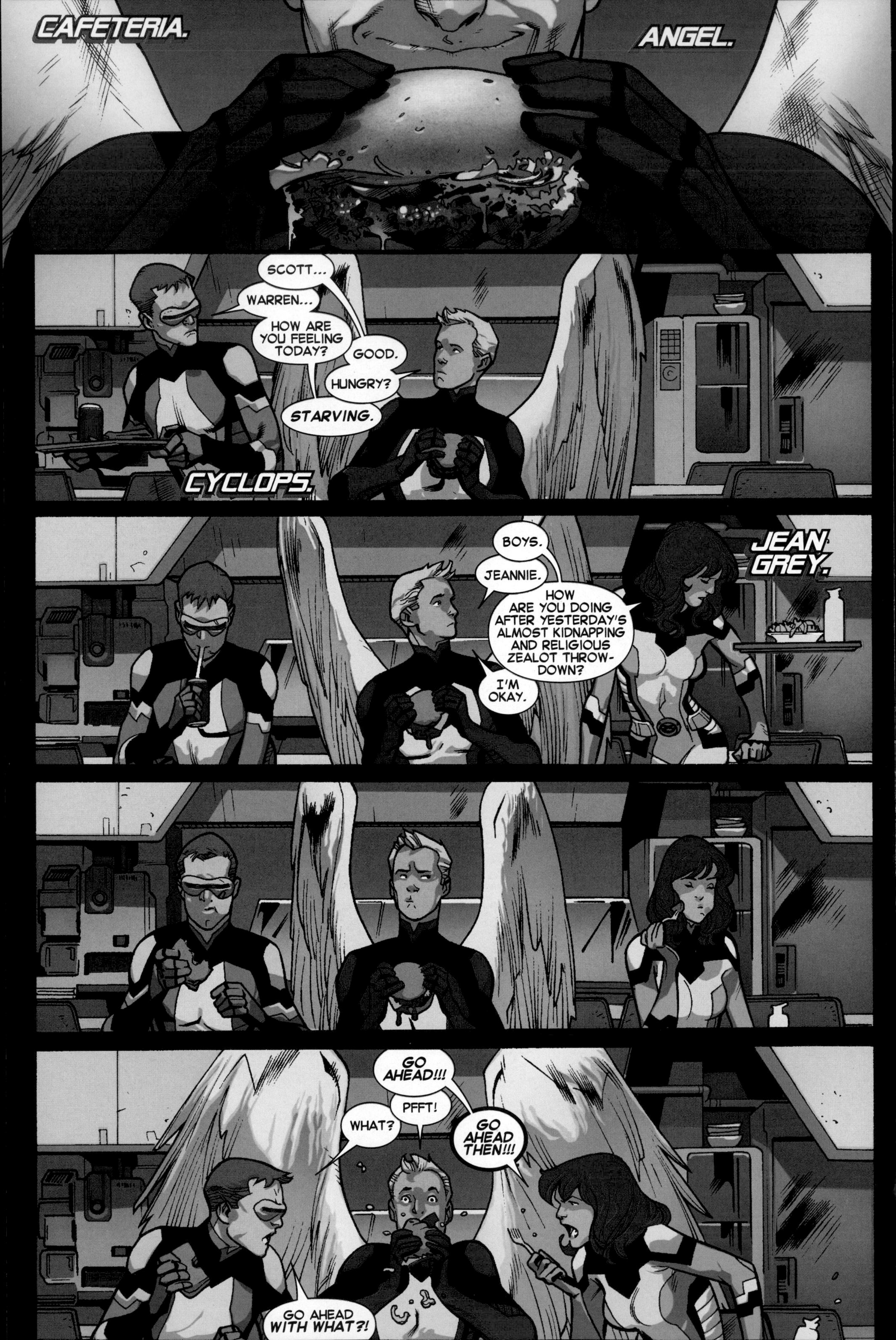
CAFETERIA.
ANGEL.
SCOTT...
WARREN...
HOW ARE YOU FEELING TODAY?
GOOD.
HUNGRY?
STARVING.
CYCLOPS.
BOYS.
JEANNIE.
JEAN GREY.
HOW ARE YOU DOING AFTER YESTERDAY'S ALMOST KIDNAPPING AND RELIGIOUS ZEALOT THROW-DOWN?
I'M OKAY.
GO AHEAD!!!
PFFT!
WHAT?
GO AHEAD THEN!!!
GO AHEAD WITH WHAT?!

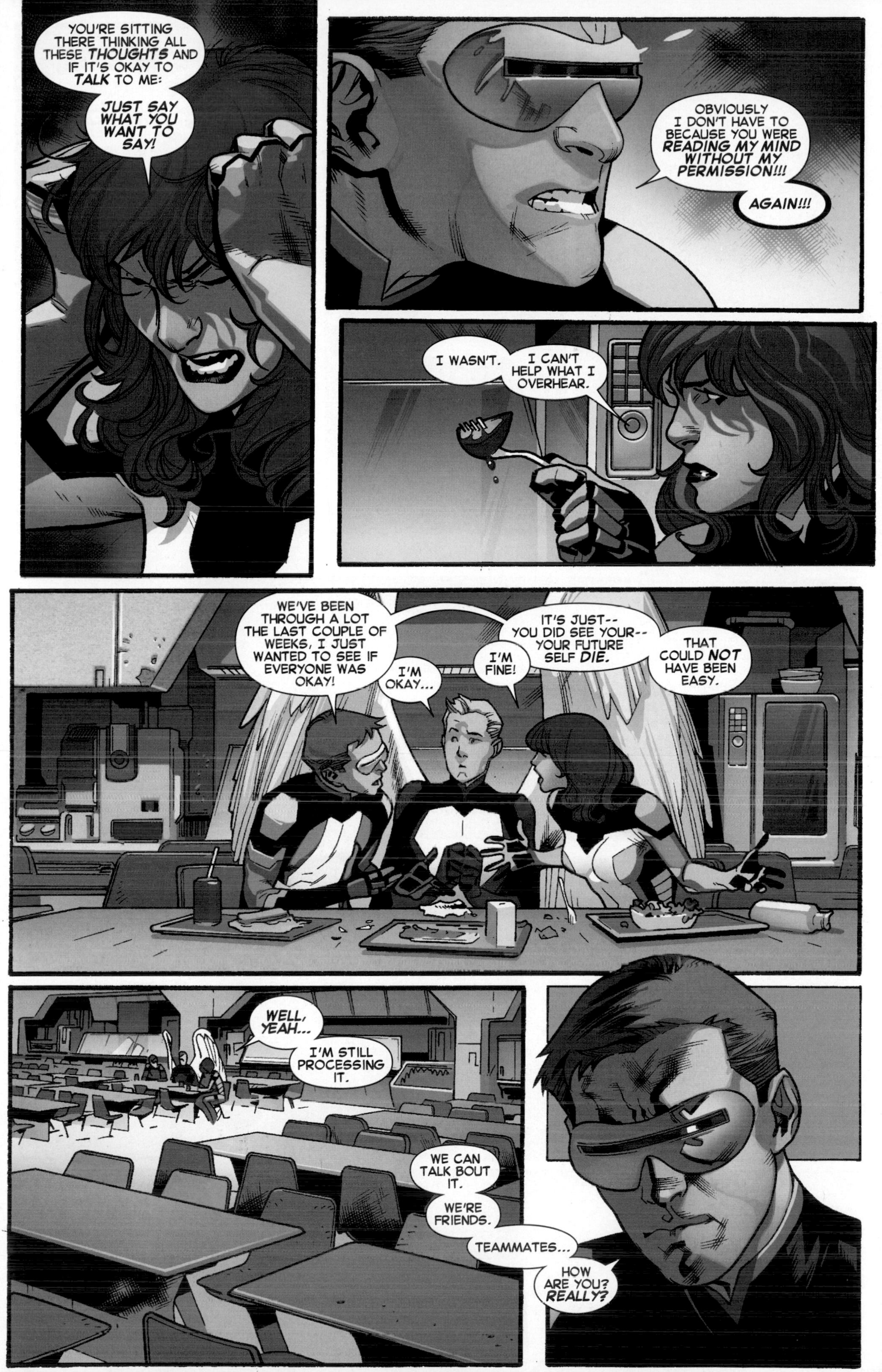
YOU'RE SITTING THERE THINKING ALL THESE THOUGHTS AND IF IT'S OKAY TO TALK TO ME:
JUST SAY WHAT YOU WANT TO SAY!
OBVIOUSLY I DON'T HAVE TO BECAUSE YOU WERE READING MY MIND WITHOUT MY PERMISSION!!!
AGAIN!!!
I WASN'T.
I CAN'T HELP WHAT I OVERHEAR.
WE'VE BEEN THROUGH A LOT THE LAST COUPLE OF WEEKS, I JUST WANTED TO SEE IF EVERYONE WAS OKAY!
I'M OKAY...
I'M FINE!
IT'S JUST-- YOU DID SEE YOUR-- YOUR FUTURE SELF DIE.
THAT COULD NOT HAVE BEEN EASY.
WELL, YEAH...
I'M STILL PROCESSING IT.
WE CAN TALK BOUT IT.
WE'RE FRIENDS.
TEAMMATES...
HOW ARE YOU? REALLY?

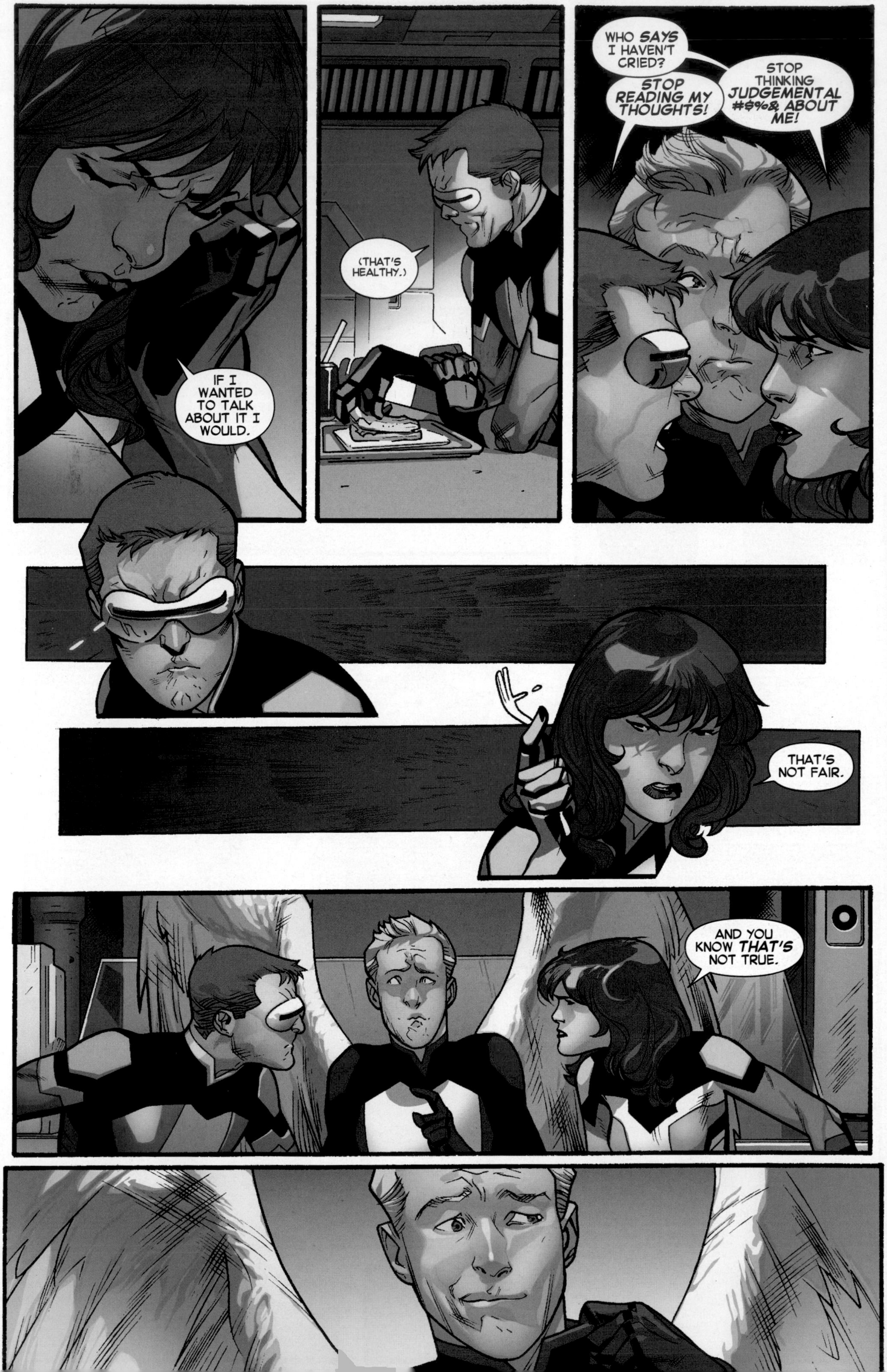
IF I WANTED TO TALK ABOUT IT I WOULD.
(THAT'S HEALTHY.)
WHO SAYS I HAVEN'T CRIED?
STOP READING MY THOUGHTS!
STOP THINKING JUDGEMENTAL #$%& ABOUT ME!
THAT'S NOT FAIR.
AND YOU KNOW THAT'S NOT TRUE.

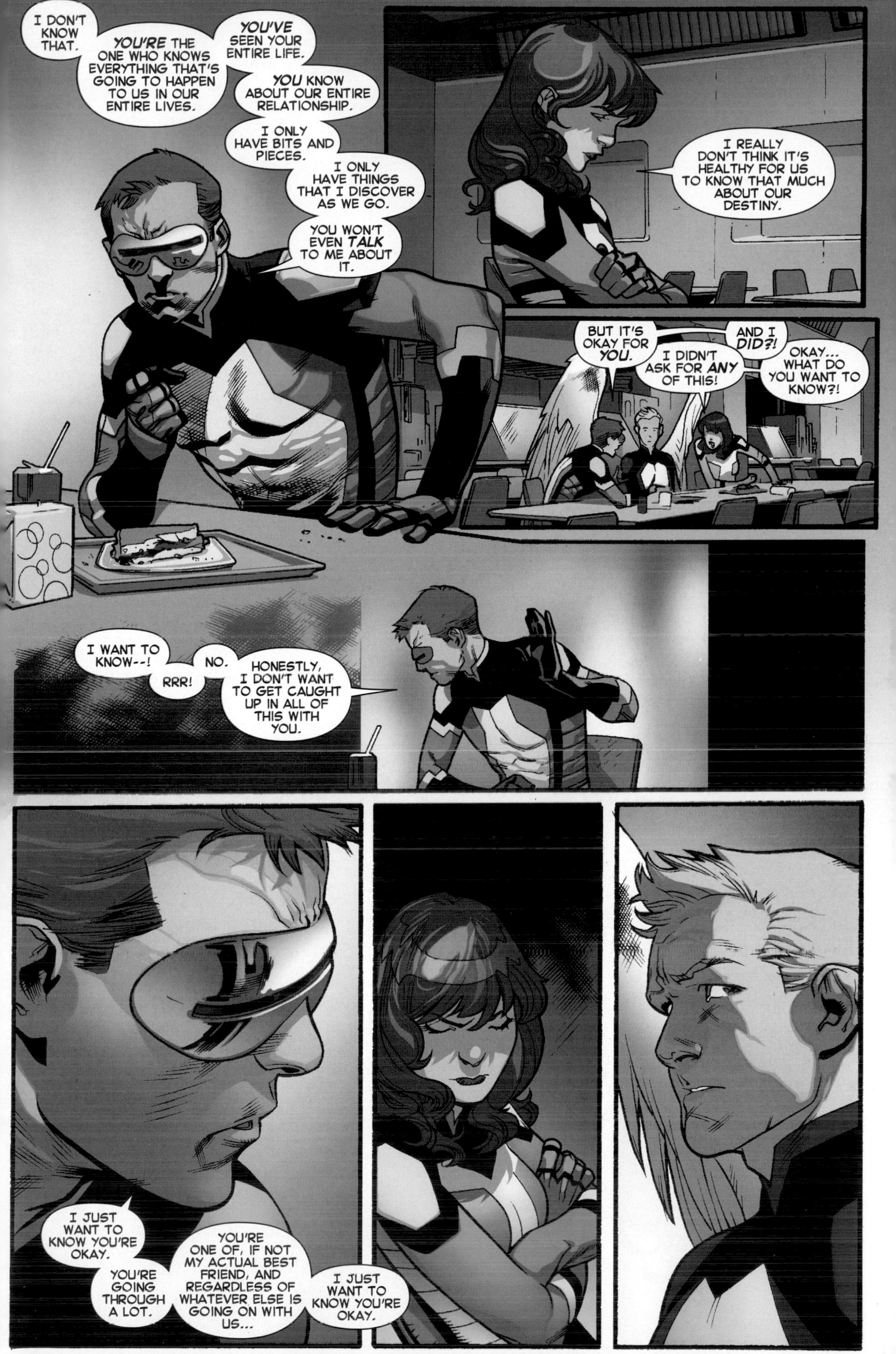
I DON'T KNOW THAT.
YOU'RE THE ONE WHO KNOWS EVERYTHING THAT'S GOING TO HAPPEN TO US IN OUR ENTIRE LIVES.
YOU'VE SEEN YOUR ENTIRE LIFE.
YOU KNOW ABOUT OUR ENTIRE RELATIONSHIP.
I ONLY HAVE BITS AND PIECES.
I ONLY HAVE THINGS THAT I DISCOVER AS WE GO.
YOU WON'T EVEN TALK TO ME ABOUT IT.
I REALLY DON'T THINK IT'S HEALTHY FOR US TO KNOW THAT MUCH ABOUT OUR DESTINY.
BUT IT'S OKAY FOR YOU.
AND I DID?!
I DIDN'T ASK FOR ANY OF THIS!
OKAY... WHAT DO YOU WANT TO KNOW?!
I WANT TO KNOW--!
NO.
RRR!
HONESTLY, I DON'T WANT TO GET CAUGHT UP IN ALL OF THIS WITH YOU.
I JUST WANT TO KNOW YOU'RE OKAY.
YOU'RE GOING THROUGH A LOT.
YOU'RE ONE OF, IF NOT MY ACTUAL BEST FRIEND, AND REGARDLESS OF WHATEVER ELSE IS GOING ON WITH US...
I JUST WANT TO KNOW YOU'RE OKAY.

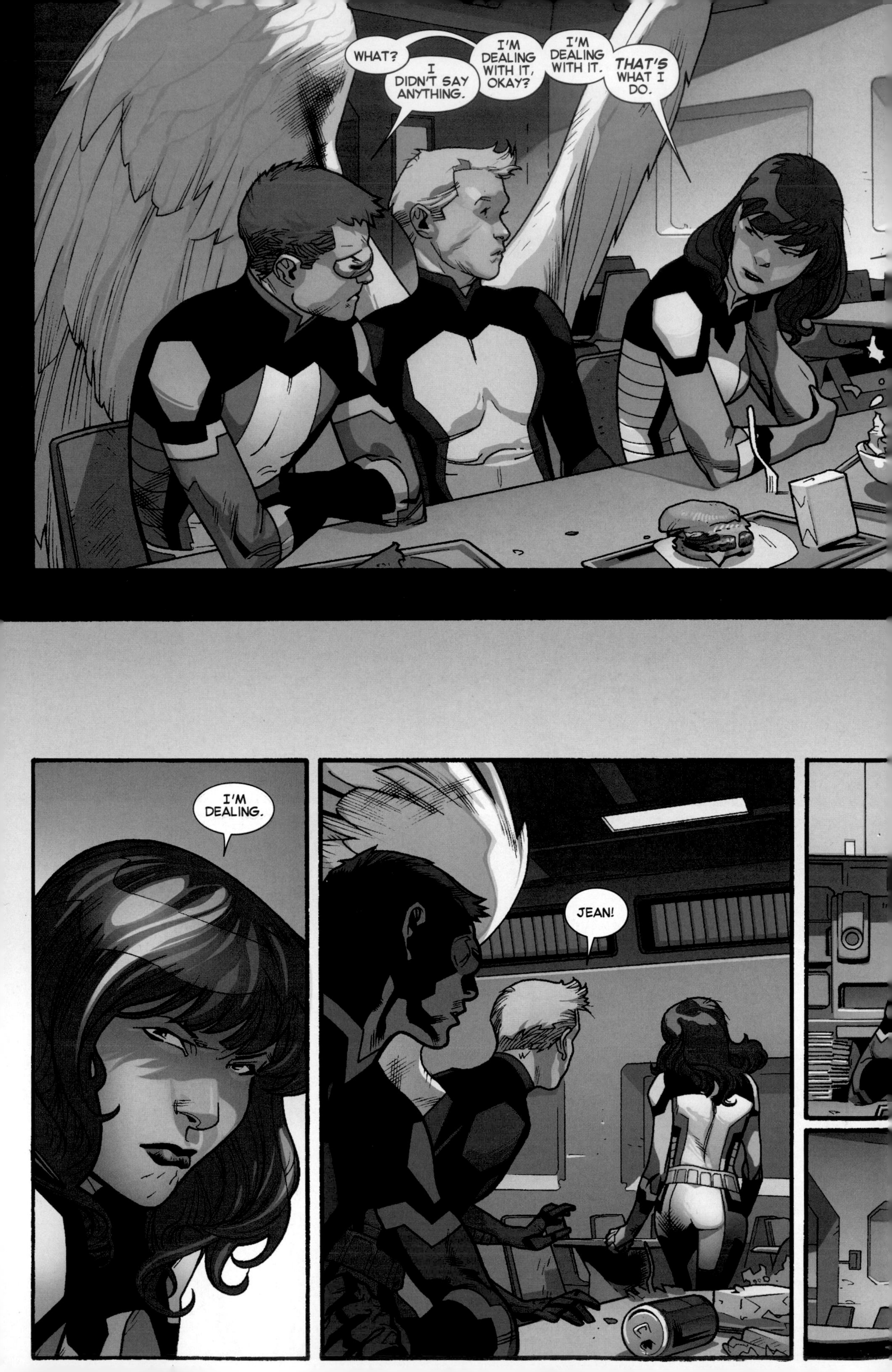
WHAT?
I DIDN'T SAY ANYTHING.
I'M DEALING WITH IT, OKAY?
I'M DEALING WITH IT.
THAT'S WHAT I DO.
I'M DEALING.
JEAN!

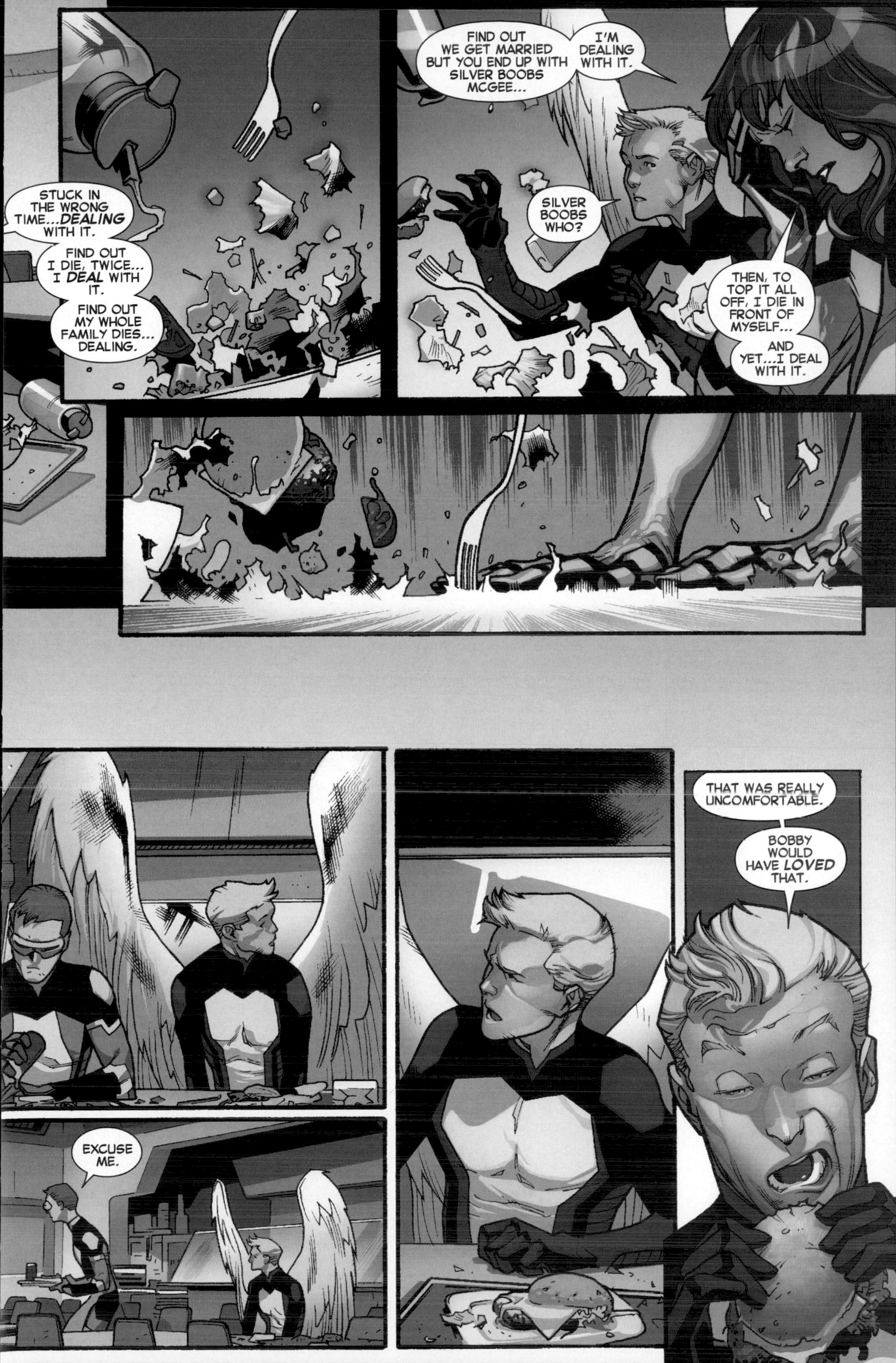
STUCK IN THE WRONG TIME...DEALING WITH IT.
FIND OUT I DIE, TWICE... I DEAL WITH IT.
FIND OUT MY WHOLE FAMILY DIES... DEALING.
FIND OUT WE GET MARRIED BUT YOU END UP WITH SILVER BOOBS MCGEE...
I'M DEALING WITH IT.
SILVER BOOBS WHO?
THEN, TO TOP IT ALL OFF, I DIE IN FRONT OF MYSELF...
AND YET...I DEAL WITH IT.
EXCUSE ME.
THAT WAS REALLY UNCOMFORTABLE.
BOBBY WOULD HAVE LOVED THAT.

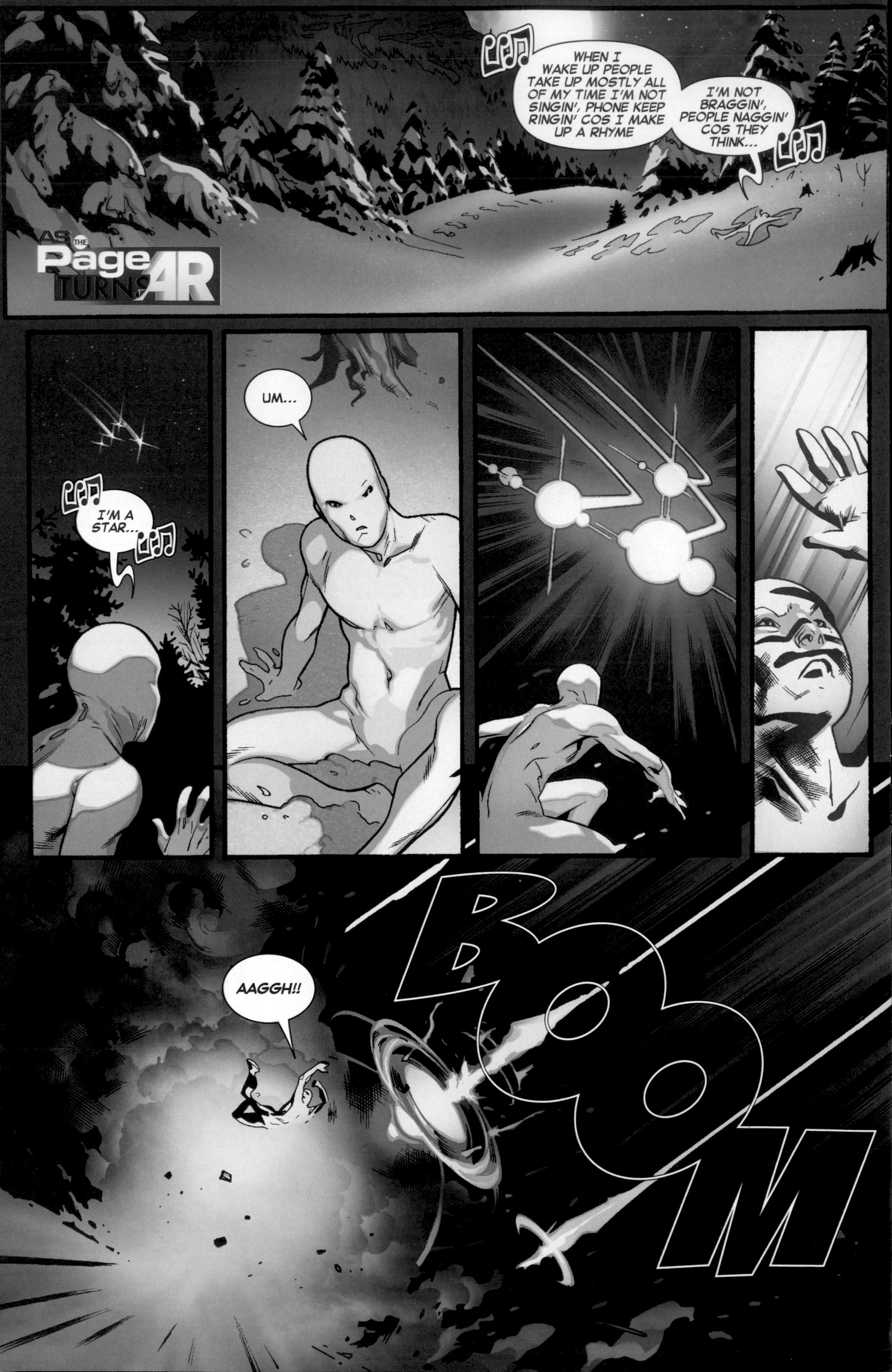
WHEN I WAKE UP PEOPLE TAKE UP MOSTLY ALL OF MY TIME I'M NOT SINGIN', PHONE KEEP RINGIN' COS I MAKE UP A RHYME
I'M NOT BRAGGIN', PEOPLE NAGGIN' COS THEY THINK...
AS THE Page TURNS AR
I'M A STAR...
UM...
AAGGH!!
BOOM

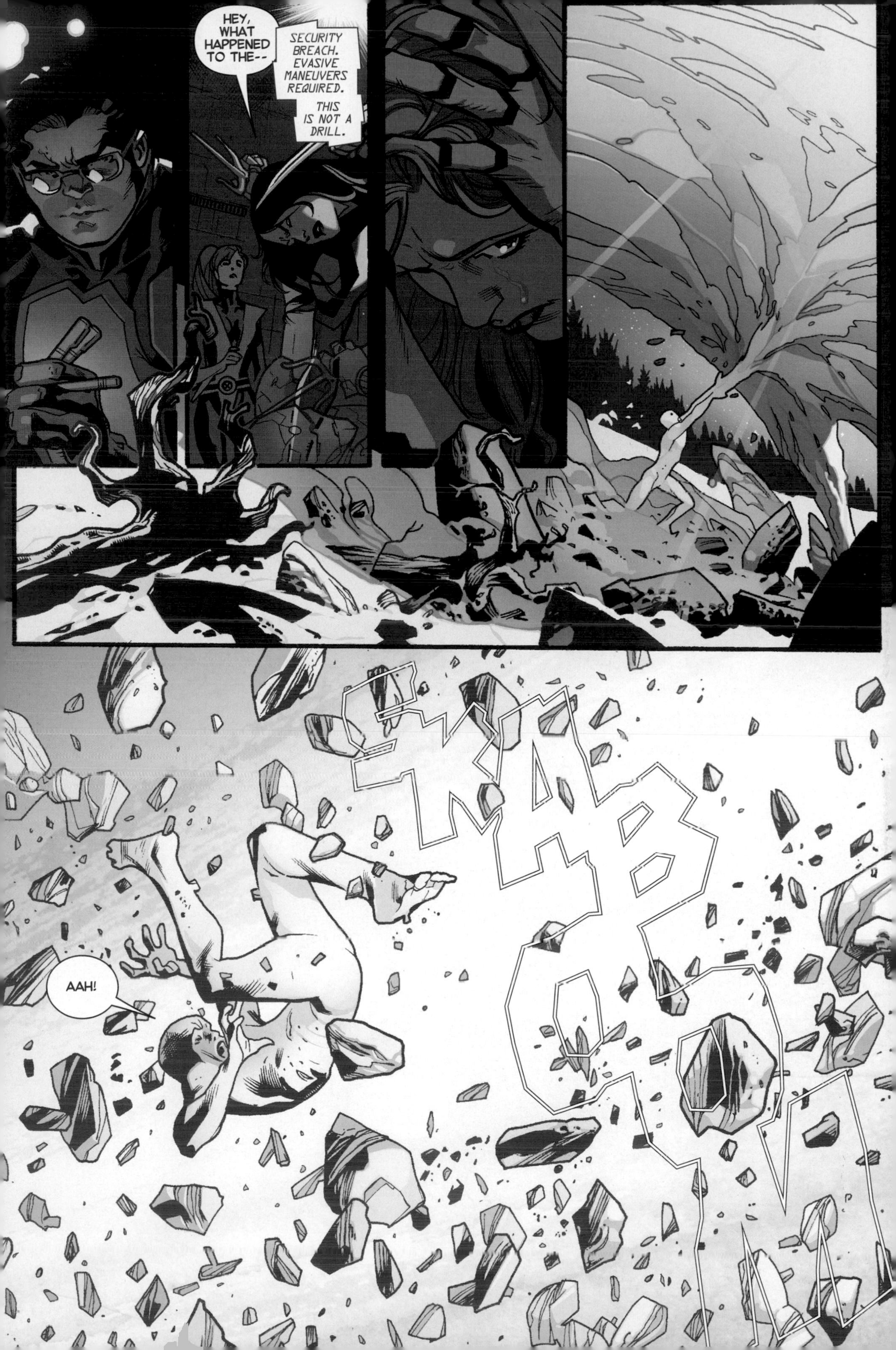
HEY, WHAT HAPPENED TO THE--
SECURITY BREACH. EVASIVE MANEUVERS REQUIRED.
THIS IS NOT A DRILL.
AAH!

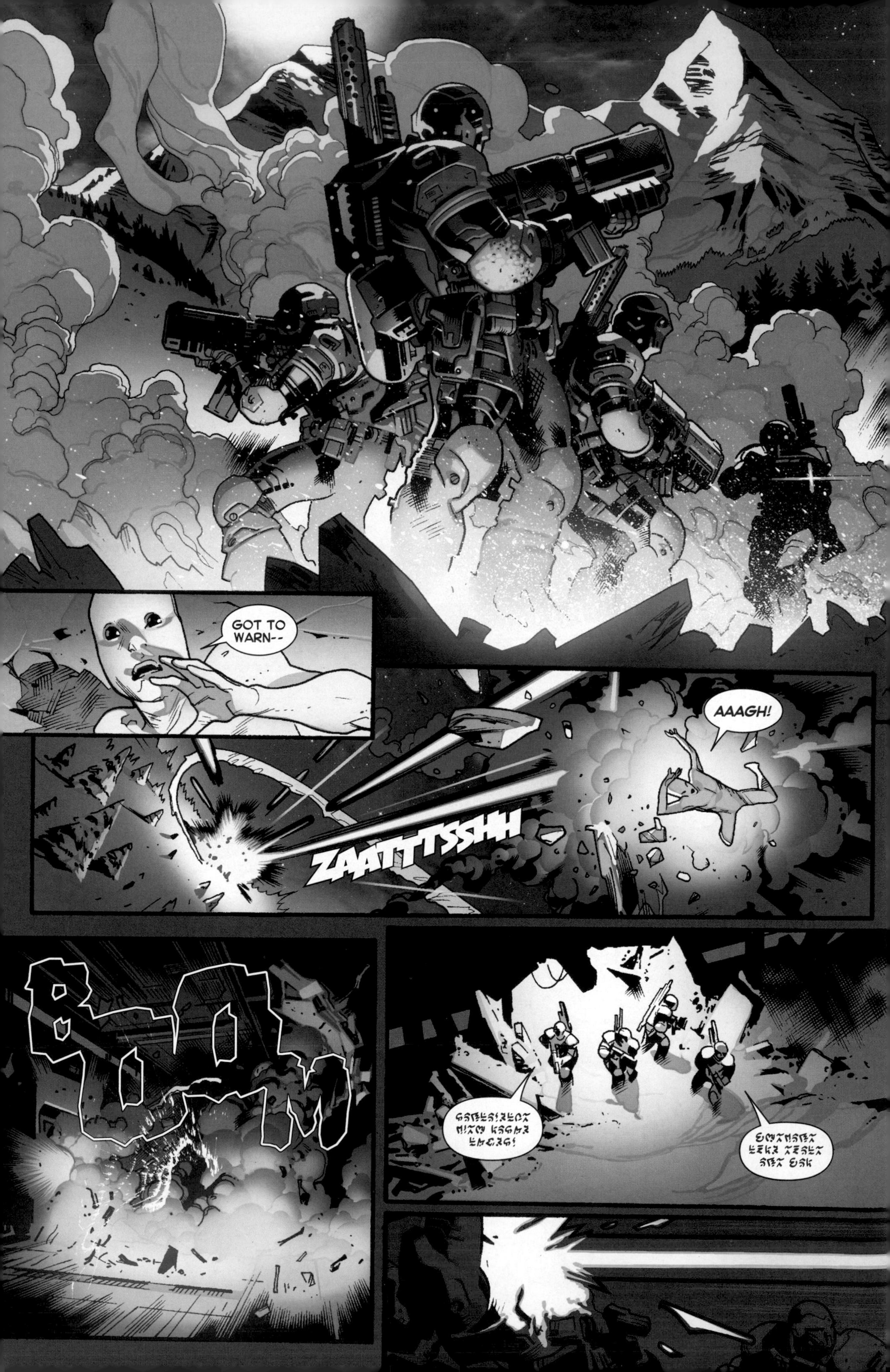
GOT TO WARN--
AAAGH!
ZAATTTSSHH
BOOM

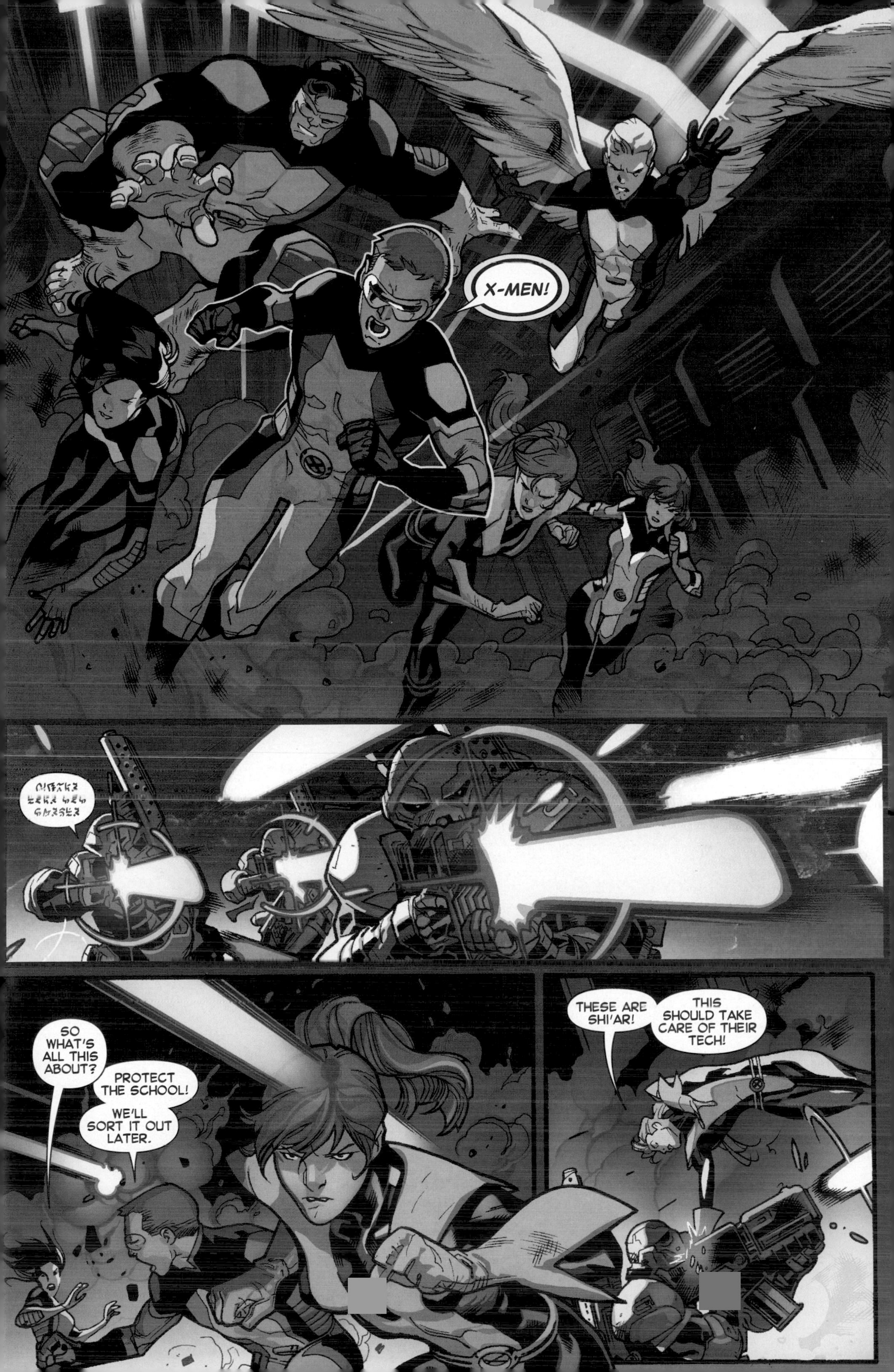
X-MEN!
SO WHAT'S ALL THIS ABOUT?
PROTECT THE SCHOOL!
WE'LL SORT IT OUT LATER.
THESE ARE SHI'AR!
THIS SHOULD TAKE CARE OF THEIR TECH!

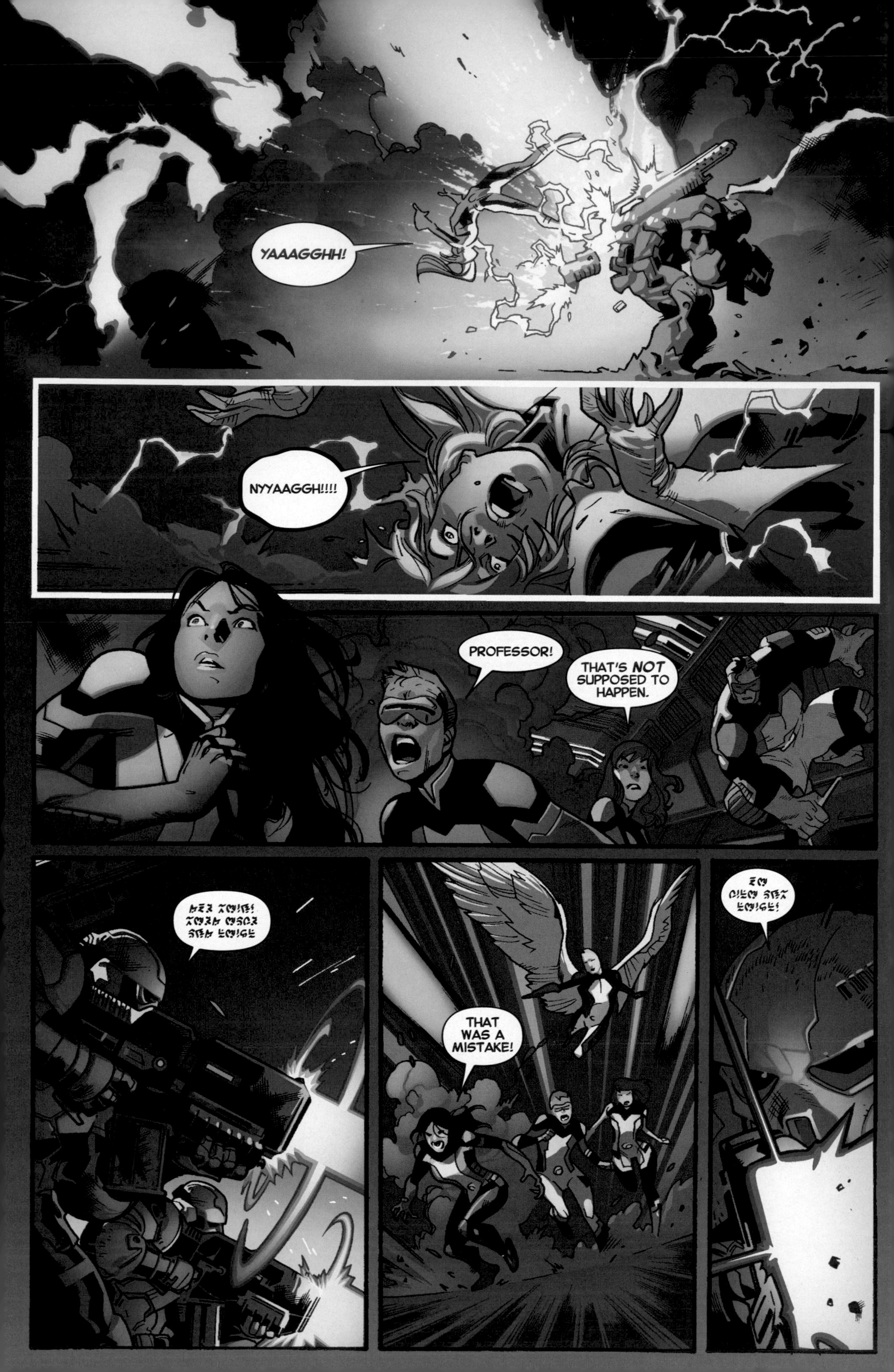
YAAAGGHH!
NYYAAGGH!!!!
PROFESSOR!
THAT'S NOT SUPPOSED TO HAPPEN.
THAT WAS A MISTAKE!

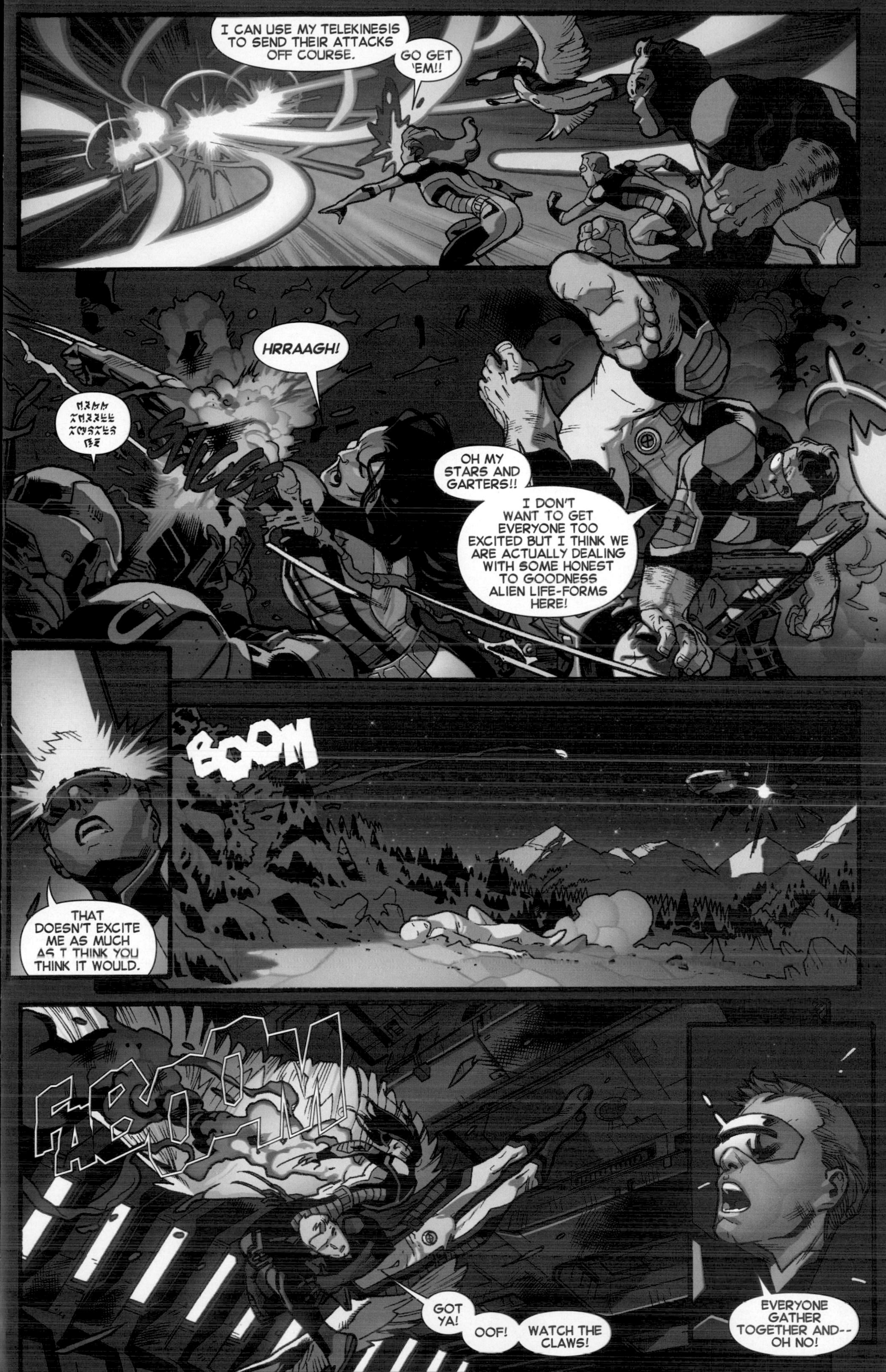
I CAN USE MY TELEKINESIS TO SEND THEIR ATTACKS OFF COURSE.
GO GET 'EM!!
HRRAAGH!
OH MY STARS AND GARTERS!!
I DON'T WANT TO GET EVERYONE TOO EXCITED BUT I THINK WE ARE ACTUALLY DEALING WITH SOME HONEST TO GOODNESS ALIEN LIFE-FORMS HERE!
BOOM
THAT DOESN'T EXCITE ME AS MUCH AS I THINK YOU THINK IT WOULD.
GOT YA!
OOF!
WATCH THE CLAWS!
EVERYONE GATHER TOGETHER AND-- OH NO!

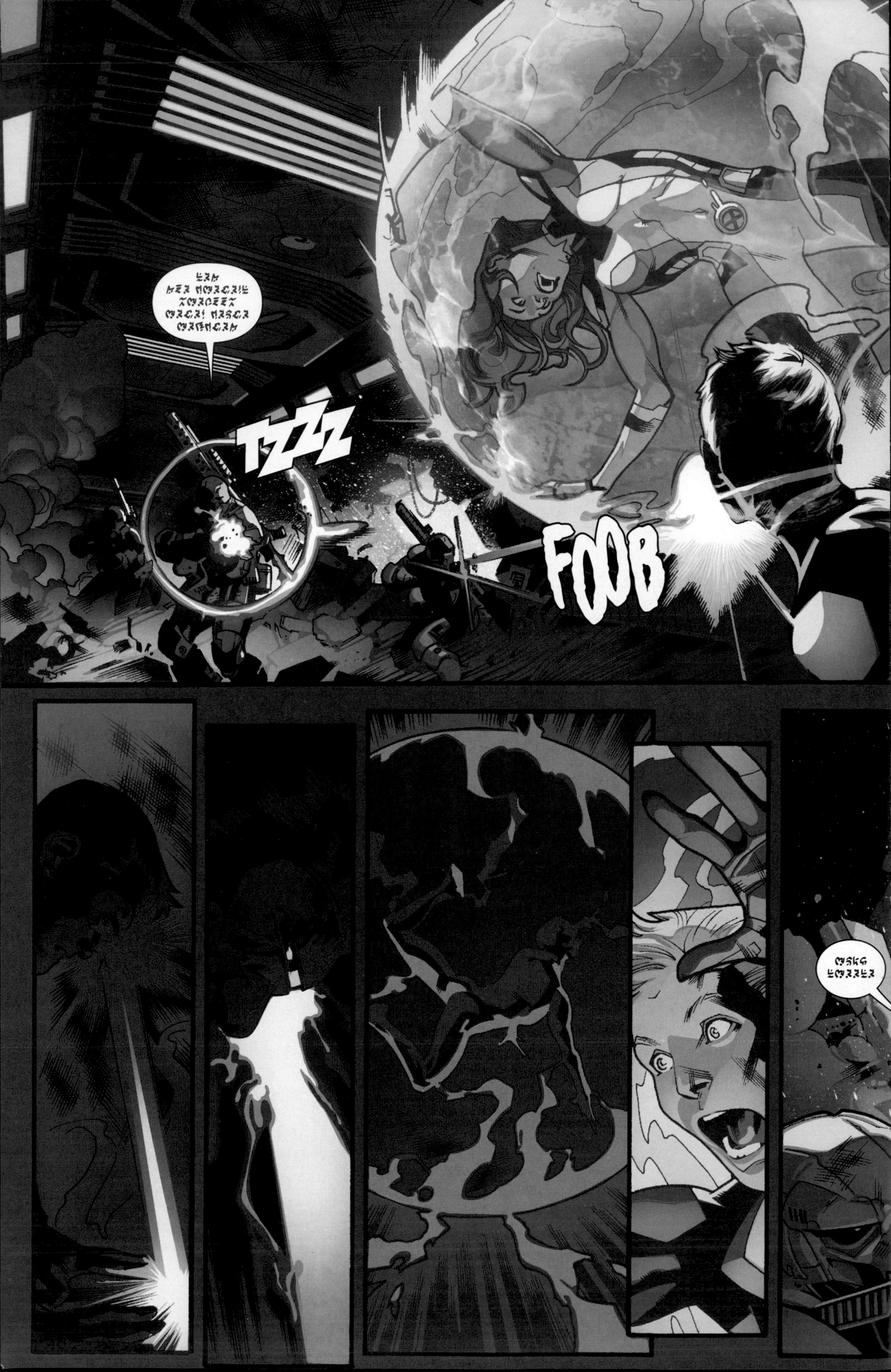
TZZZ
FOOB

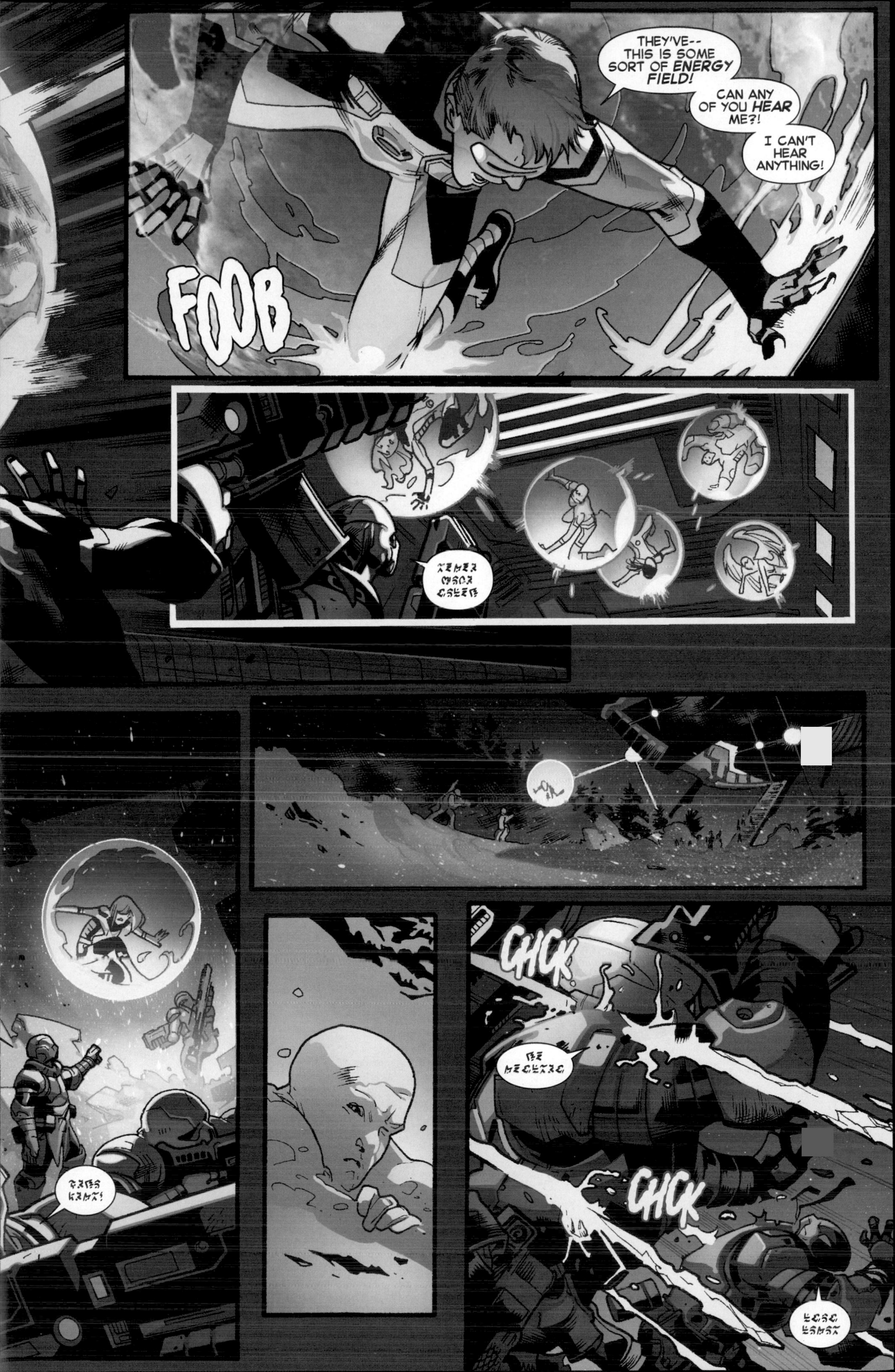
THEY'VE-- THIS IS SOME SORT OF ENERGY FIELD!
CAN ANY OF YOU HEAR ME?!
I CAN'T HEAR ANYTHING!
FOOB
CHCK
CHCK

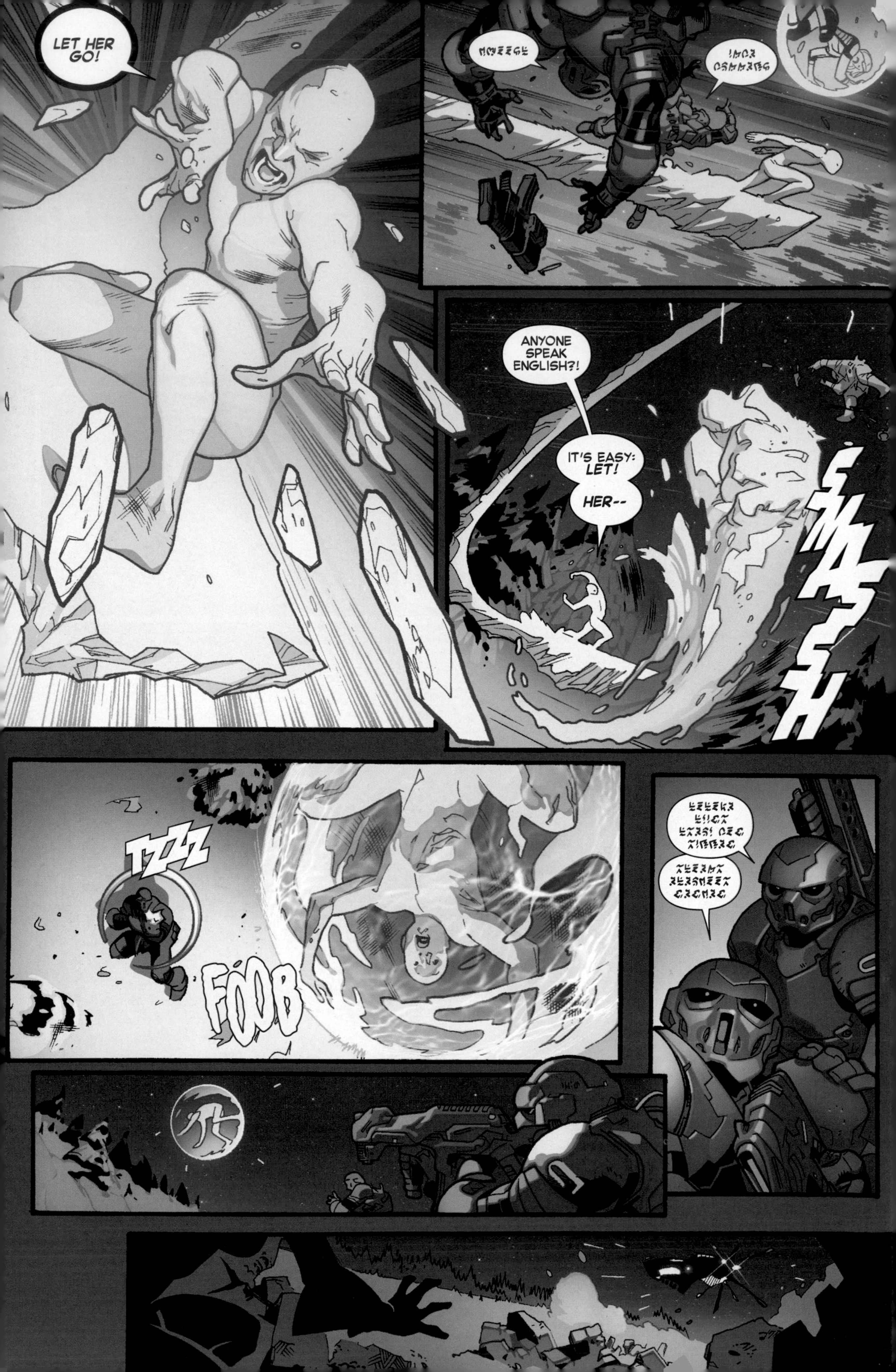
LET HER GO!
ANYONE SPEAK ENGLISH?!
IT'S EASY: LET!
HER--
SMASH
TZZZ
FOOB

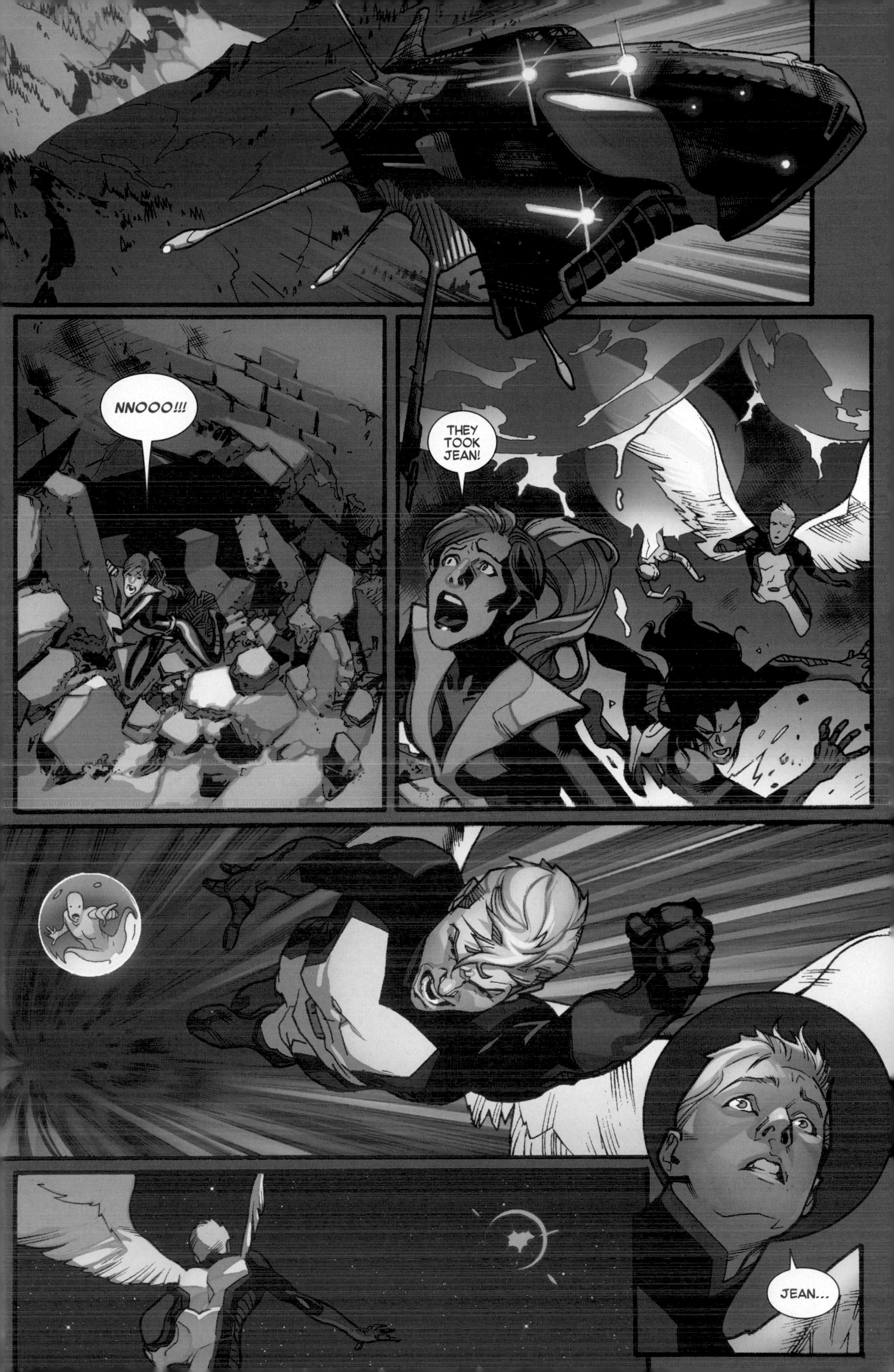
NNOOO!!!
THEY TOOK JEAN!
JEAN...

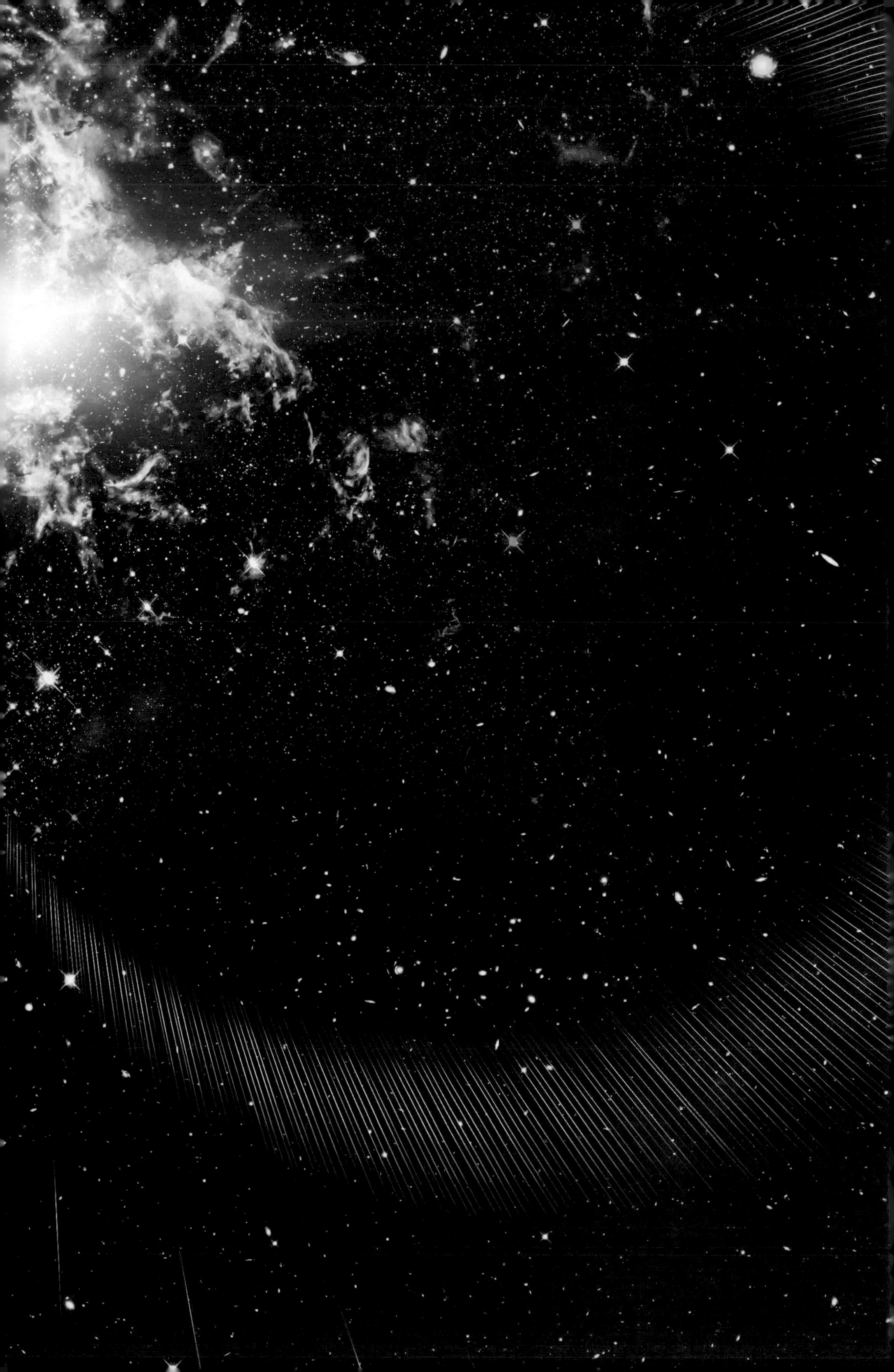

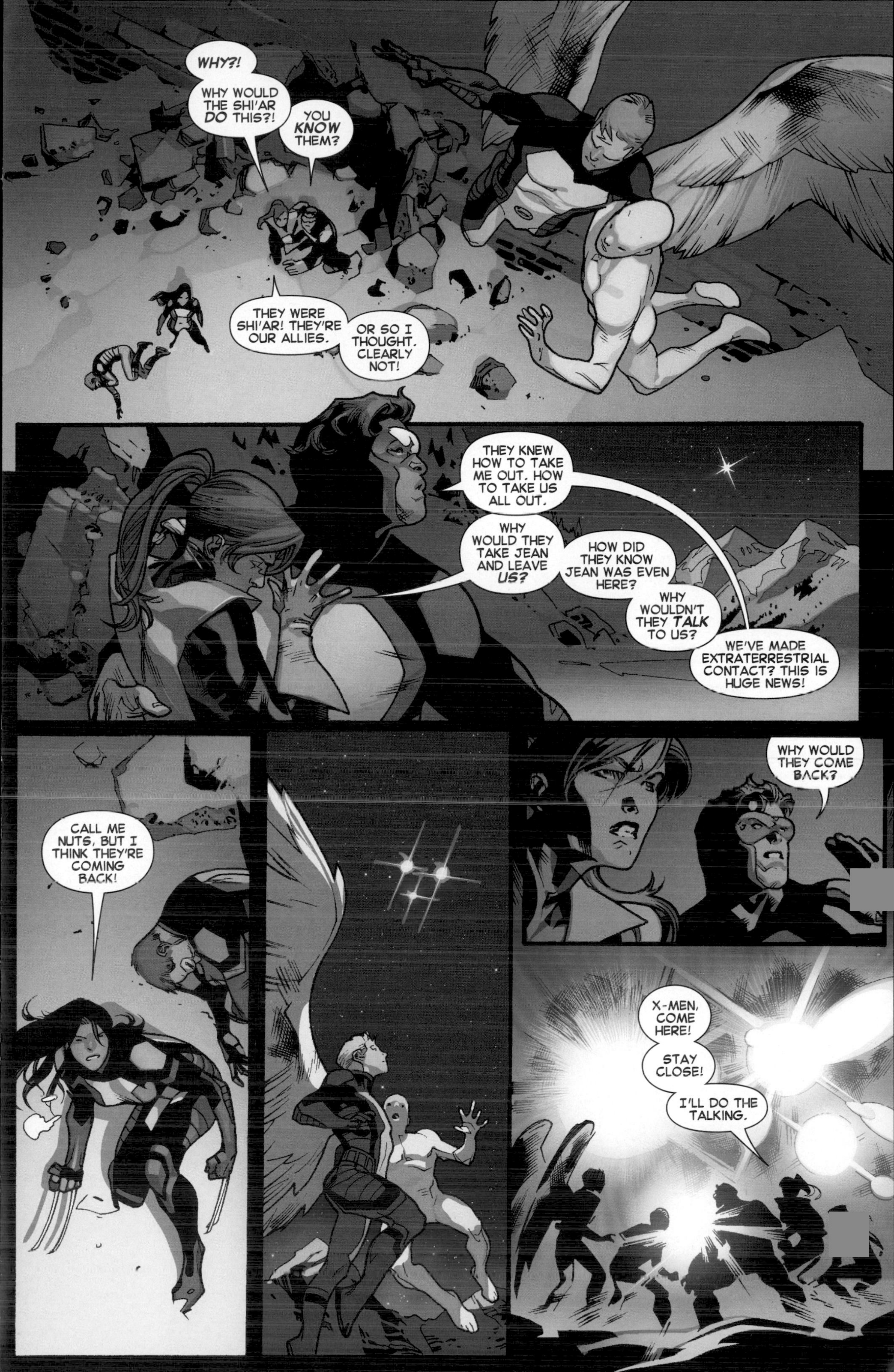
WHY?!
WHY WOULD THE SHI'AR DO THIS?!
YOU KNOW THEM?
THEY WERE SHI'AR! THEY'RE OUR ALLIES.
OR SO I THOUGHT. CLEARLY NOT!
THEY KNEW HOW TO TAKE ME OUT. HOW TO TAKE US ALL OUT.
WHY WOULD THEY TAKE JEAN AND LEAVE US?
HOW DID THEY KNOW JEAN WAS EVEN HERE?
WHY WOULDN'T THEY TALK TO US?
WE'VE MADE EXTRATERRESTRIAL CONTACT? THIS IS HUGE NEWS!
CALL ME NUTS, BUT I THINK THEY'RE COMING BACK!
WHY WOULD THEY COME BACK?
X-MEN, COME HERE!
STAY CLOSE!
I'LL DO THE TALKING.

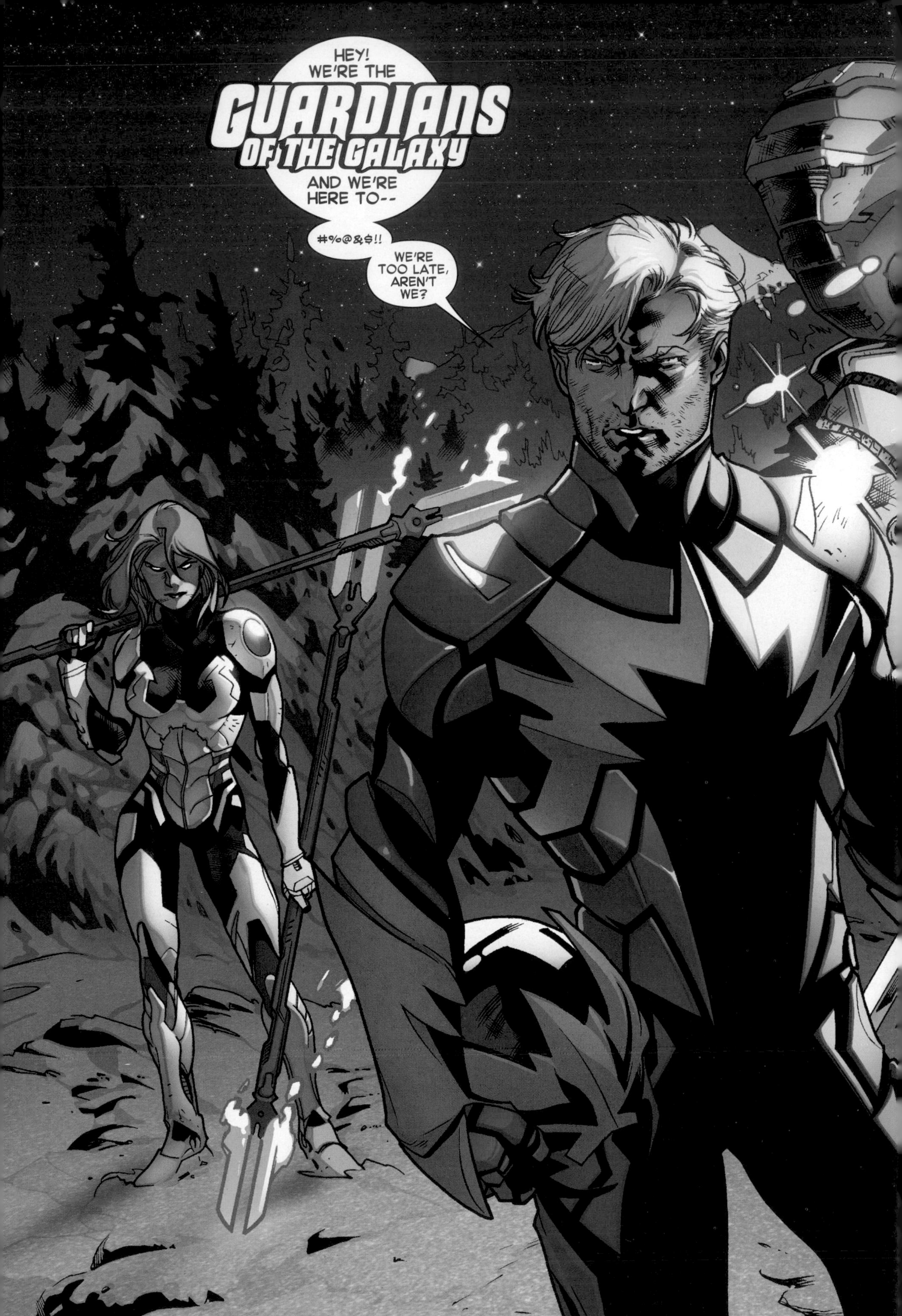
HEY! WE'RE THE GUARDIANS OF THE GALAXY AND WE'RE HERE TO--
#%@&$!!
WE'RE TOO LATE, AREN'T WE?
AR

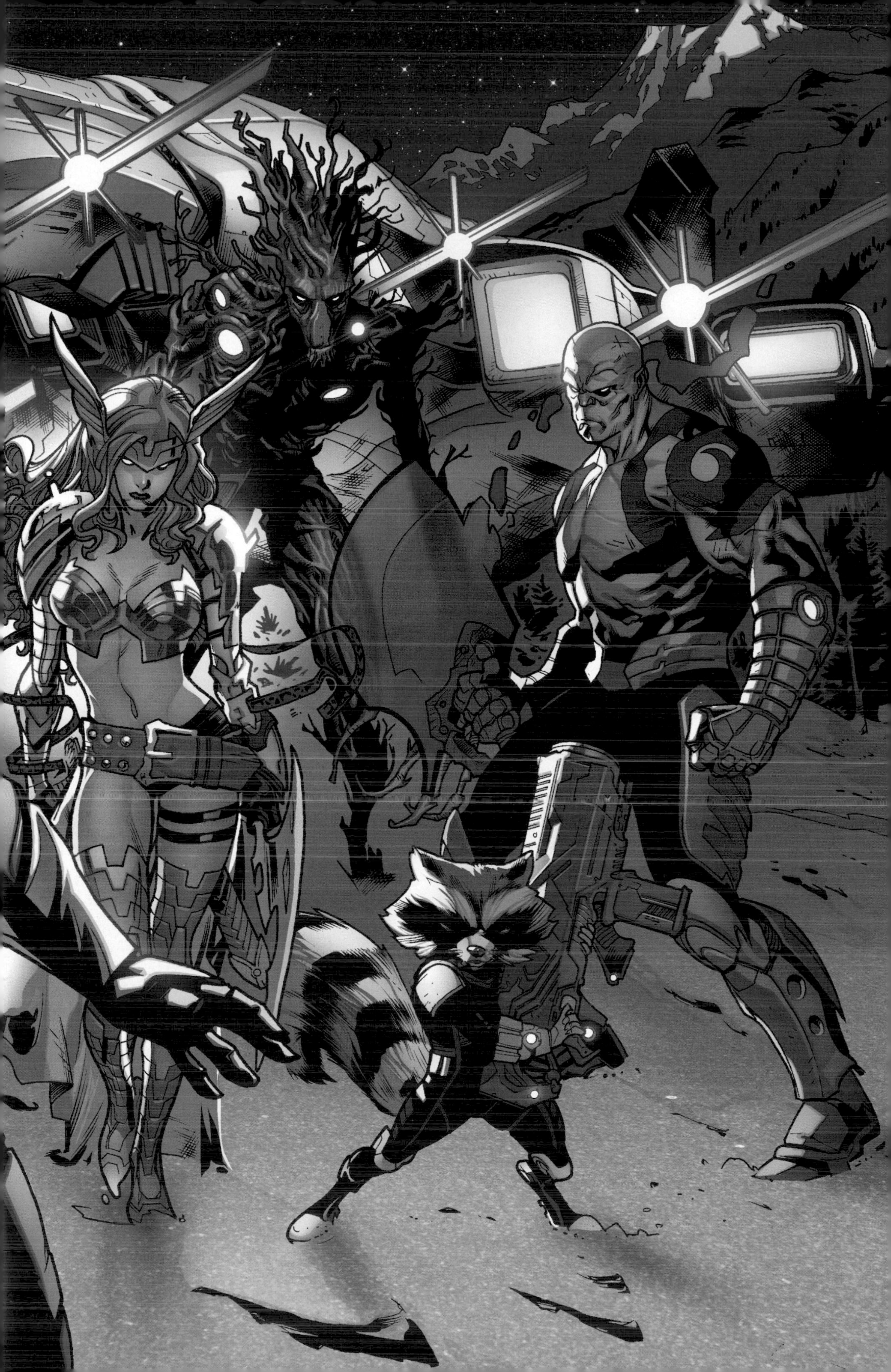

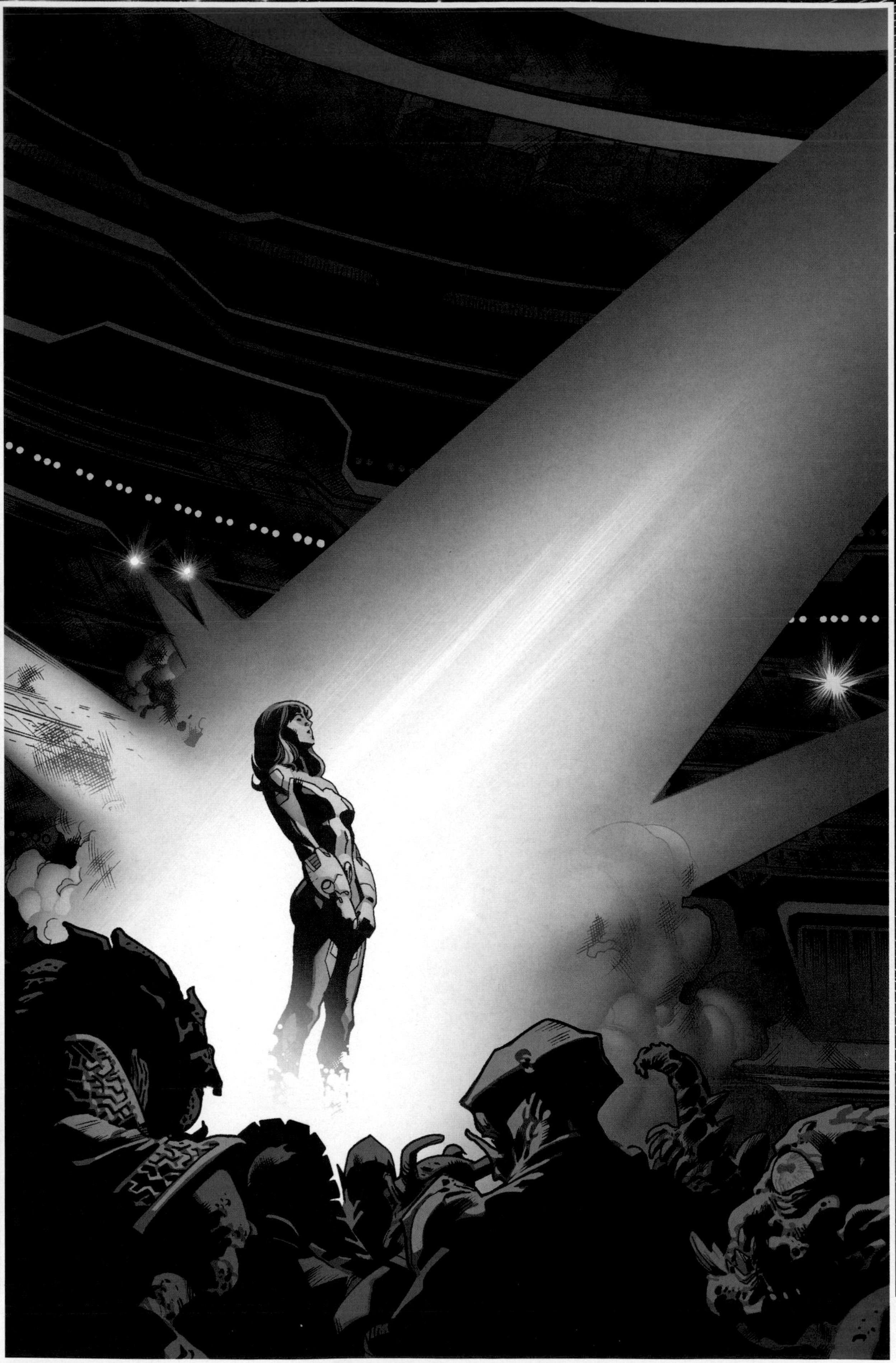

ALL-NEW X-MEN 23

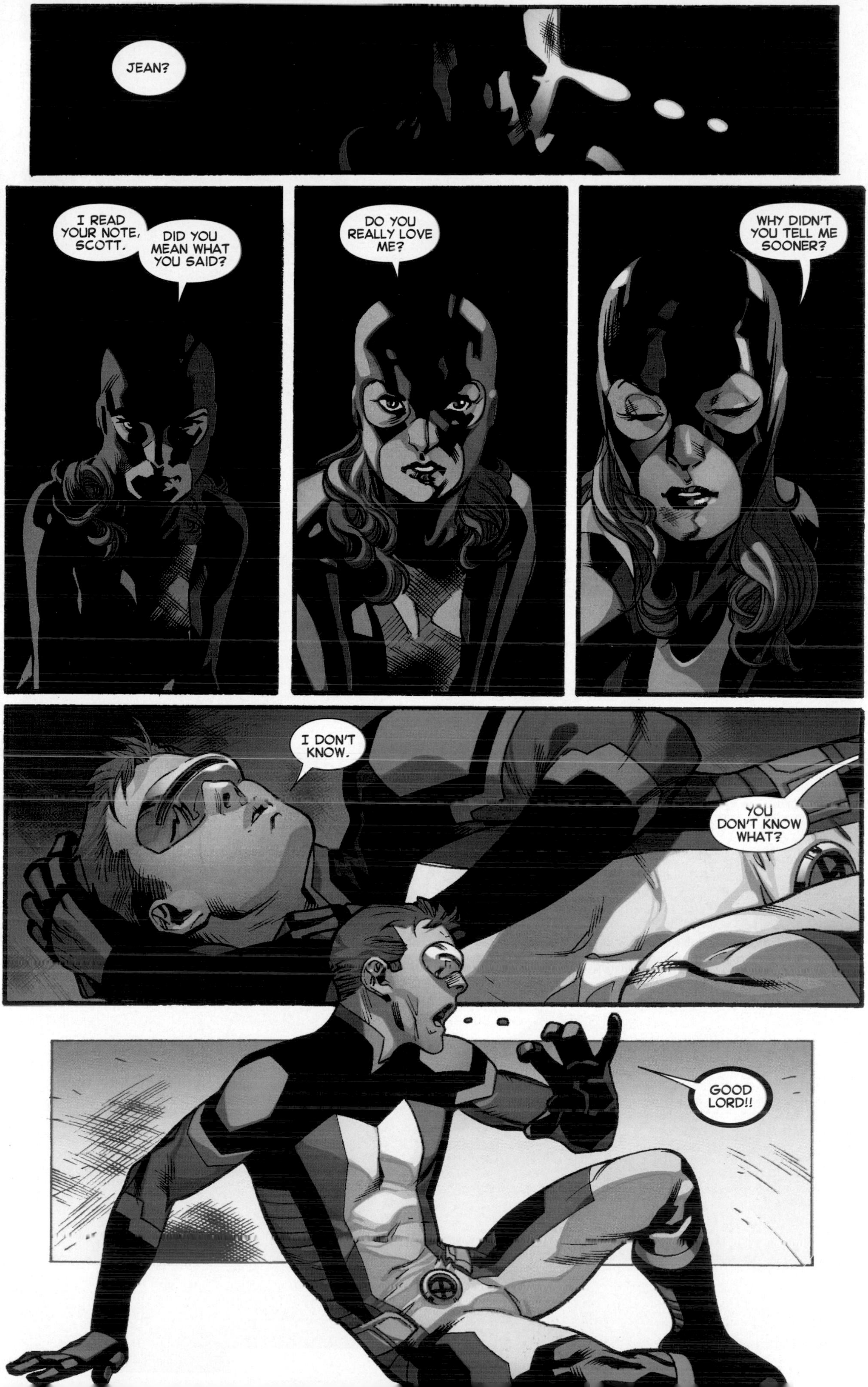
JEAN?
I READ YOUR NOTE, SCOTT.
DID YOU MEAN WHAT YOU SAID?
DO YOU REALLY LOVE ME?
WHY DIDN'T YOU TELL ME SOONER?
I DON'T KNOW.
YOU DON'T KNOW WHAT?
...
GOOD LORD!!

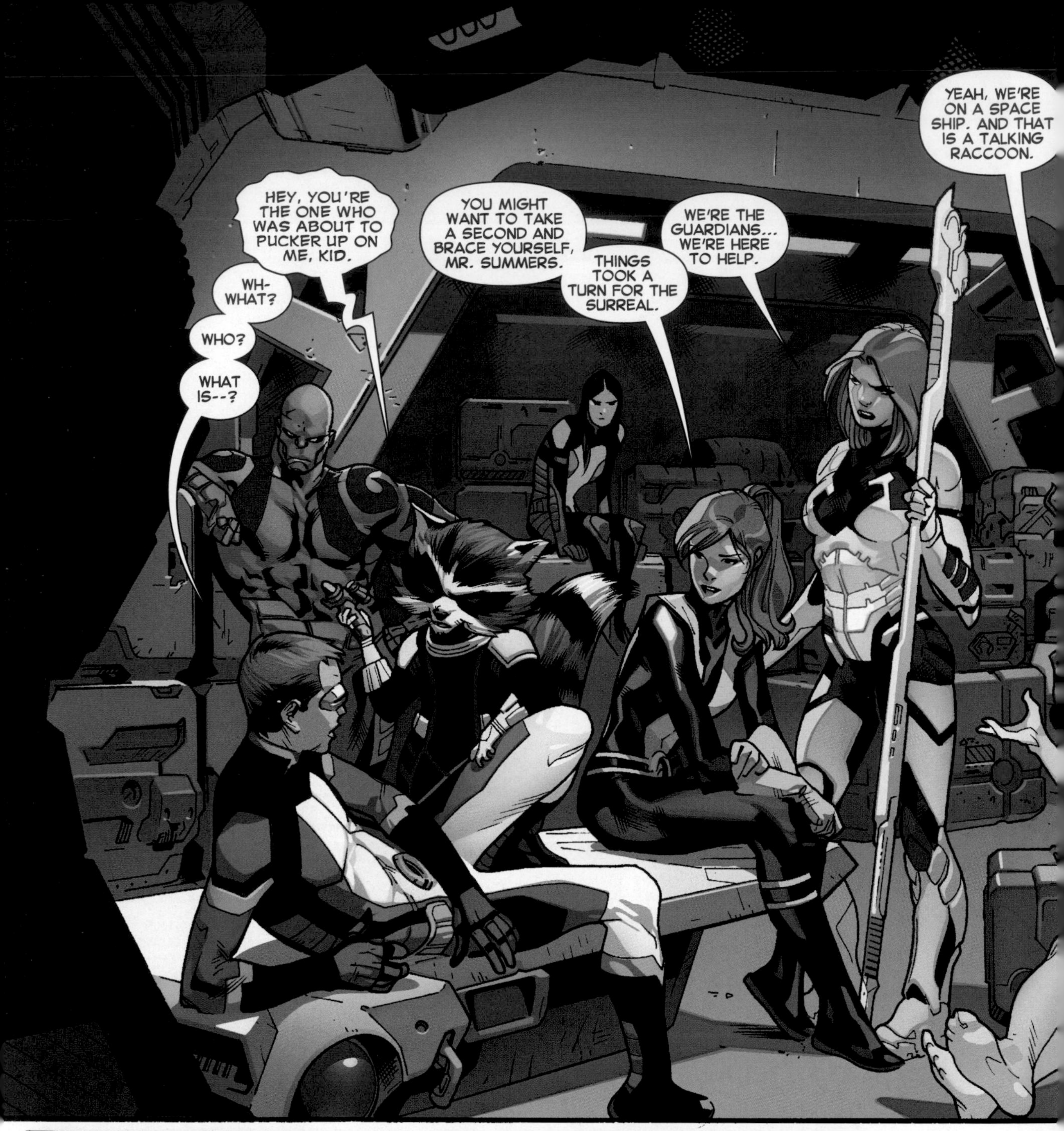
HEY, YOU'RE THE ONE WHO WAS ABOUT TO PUCKER UP ON ME, KID.
WH- WHAT?
WHO?
WHAT IS--?
YOU MIGHT WANT TO TAKE A SECOND AND BRACE YOURSELF, MR. SUMMERS.
THINGS TOOK A TURN FOR THE SURREAL.
WE'RE THE GUARDIANS... WE'RE HERE TO HELP.
YEAH, WE'RE ON A SPACE SHIP. AND THAT IS A TALKING RACCOON.

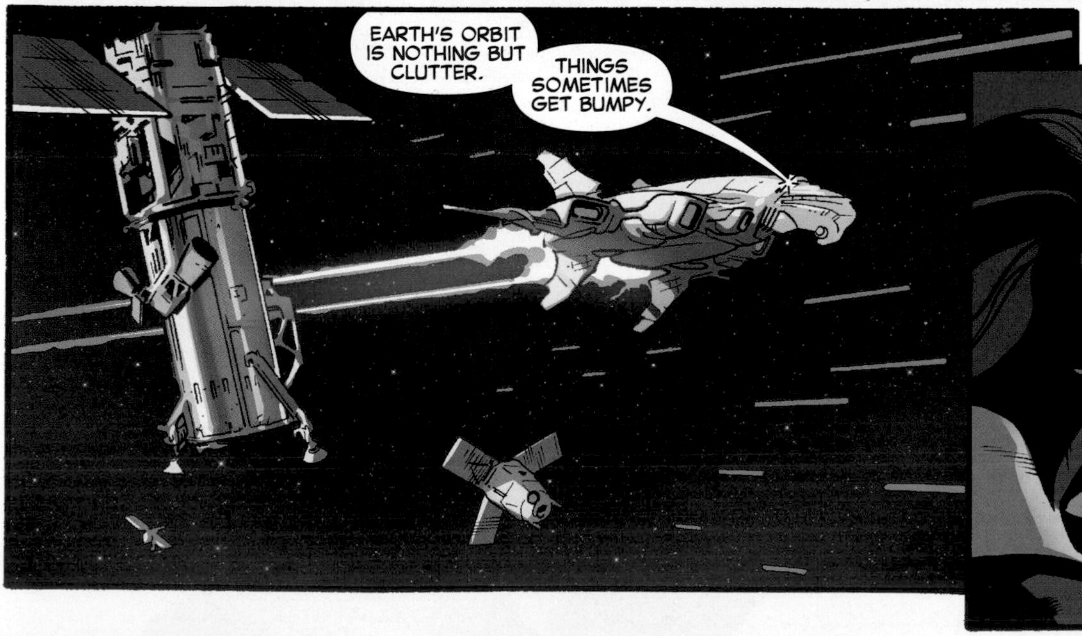
EARTH'S ORBIT IS NOTHING BUT CLUTTER.
THINGS SOMETIMES GET BUMPY.

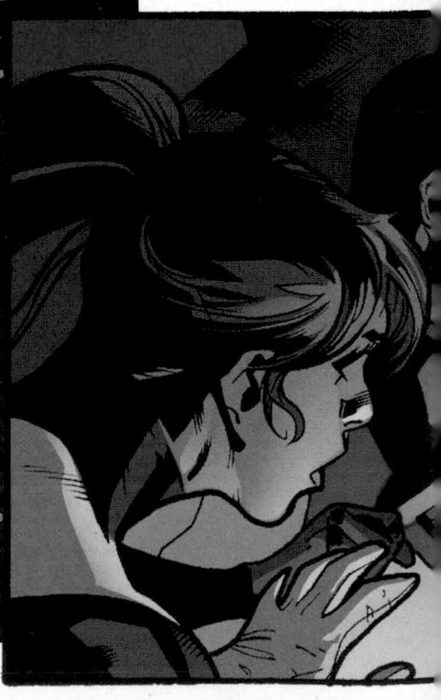

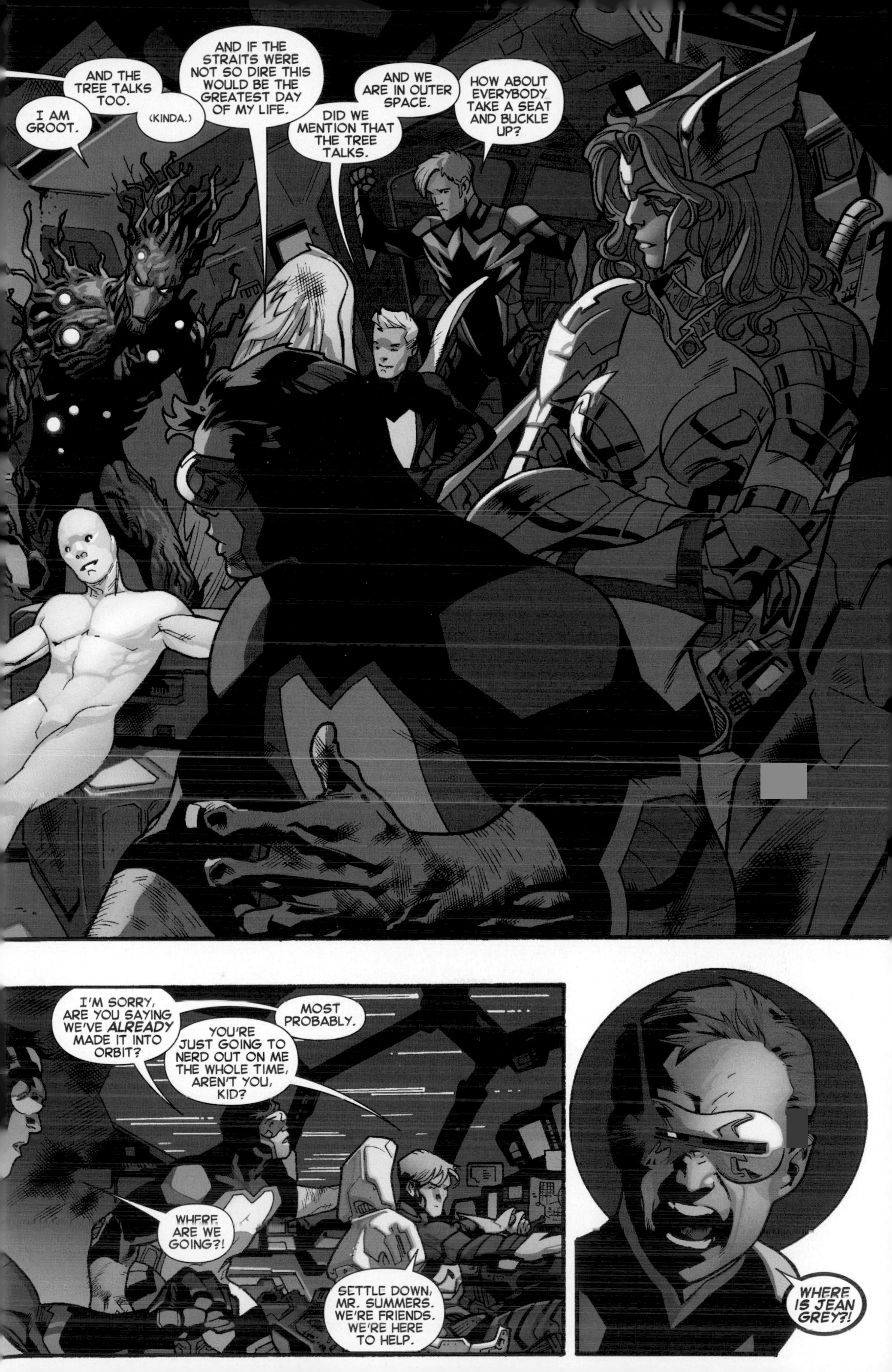
AND THE TREE TALKS TOO.
I AM GROOT.
(KINDA.)
AND IF THE STRAITS WERE NOT SO DIRE THIS WOULD BE THE GREATEST DAY OF MY LIFE.
AND WE ARE IN OUTER SPACE.
DID WE MENTION THAT THE TREE TALKS.
HOW ABOUT EVERYBODY TAKE A SEAT AND BUCKLE UP?
I'M SORRY, ARE YOU SAYING WE'VE *ALREADY* MADE IT INTO ORBIT?
MOST PROBABLY.
YOU'RE JUST GOING TO NERD OUT ON ME THE WHOLE TIME, AREN'T YOU, KID?
WHERE ARE WE GOING?!
SETTLE DOWN, MR. SUMMERS. WE'RE FRIENDS. WE'RE HERE TO HELP.
WHERE IS JEAN GREY?!

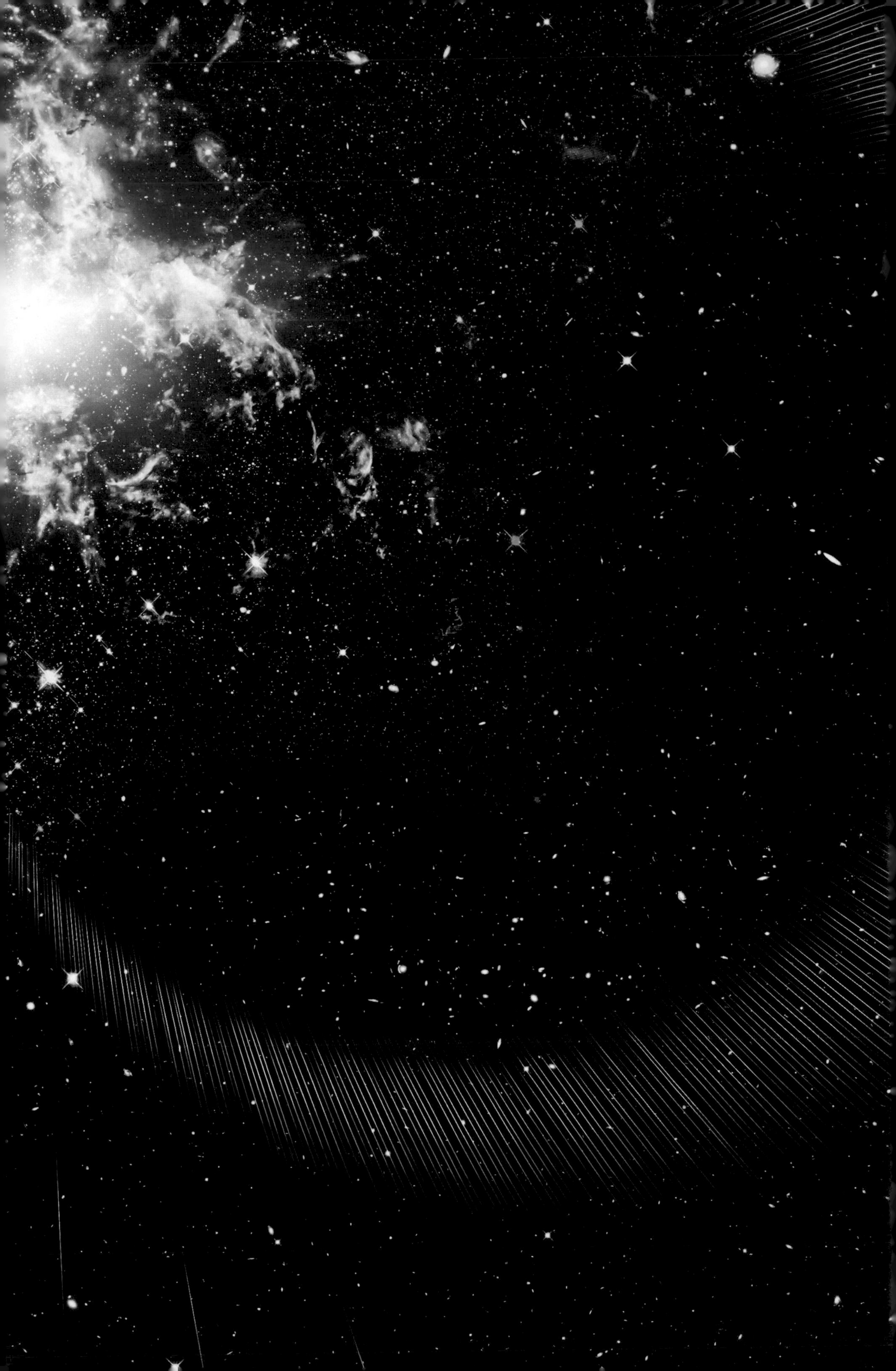

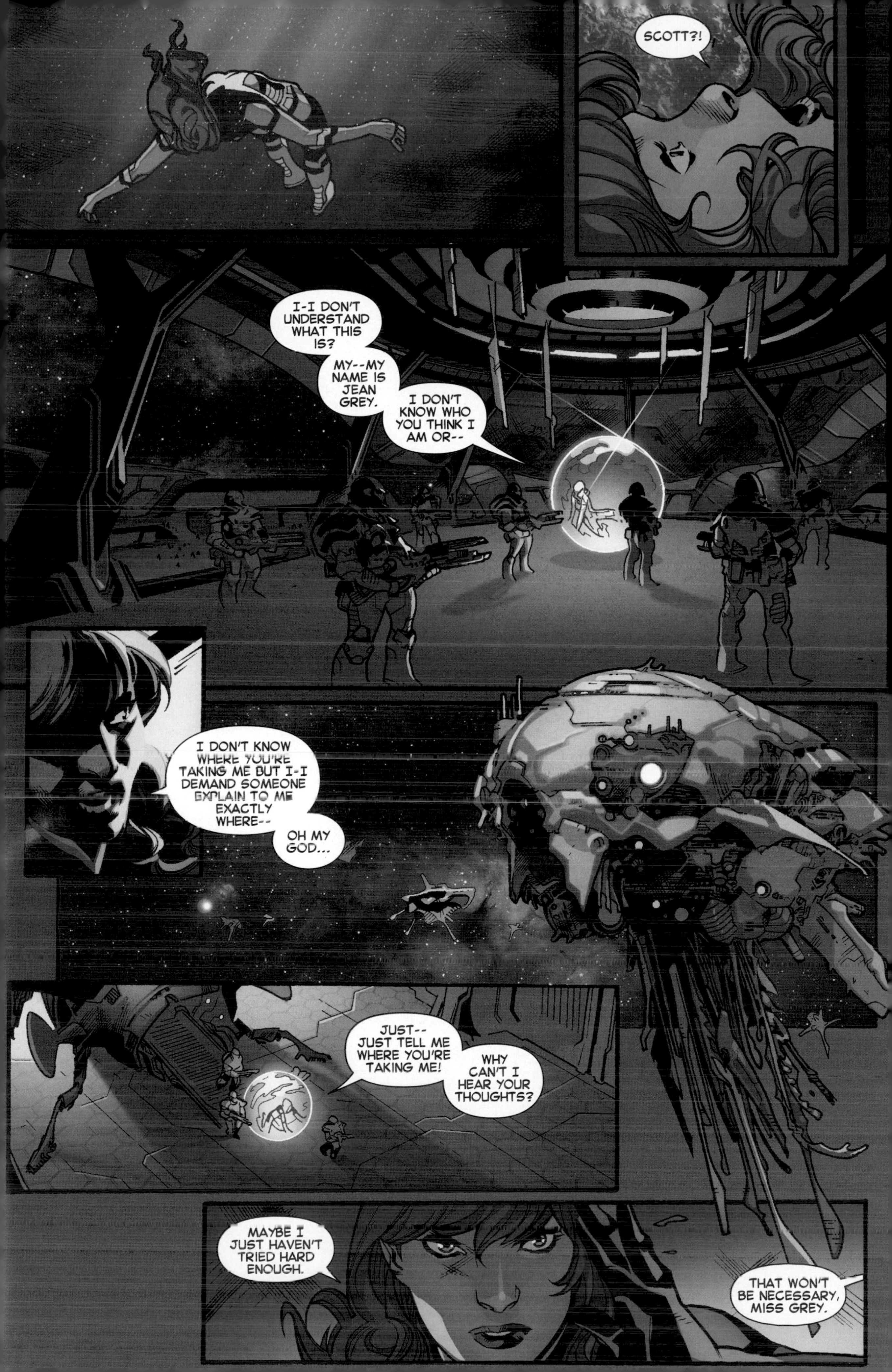

SCOTT?!
I-I DON'T UNDERSTAND WHAT THIS IS?
MY--MY NAME IS JEAN GREY.
I DON'T KNOW WHO YOU THINK I AM OR--
I DON'T KNOW WHERE YOU'RE TAKING ME BUT I-I DEMAND SOMEONE EXPLAIN TO ME EXACTLY WHERE--
OH MY GOD...
JUST-- JUST TELL ME WHERE YOU'RE TAKING ME!
WHY CAN'T I HEAR YOUR THOUGHTS?
MAYBE I JUST HAVEN'T TRIED HARD ENOUGH.
THAT WON'T BE NECESSARY, MISS GREY.

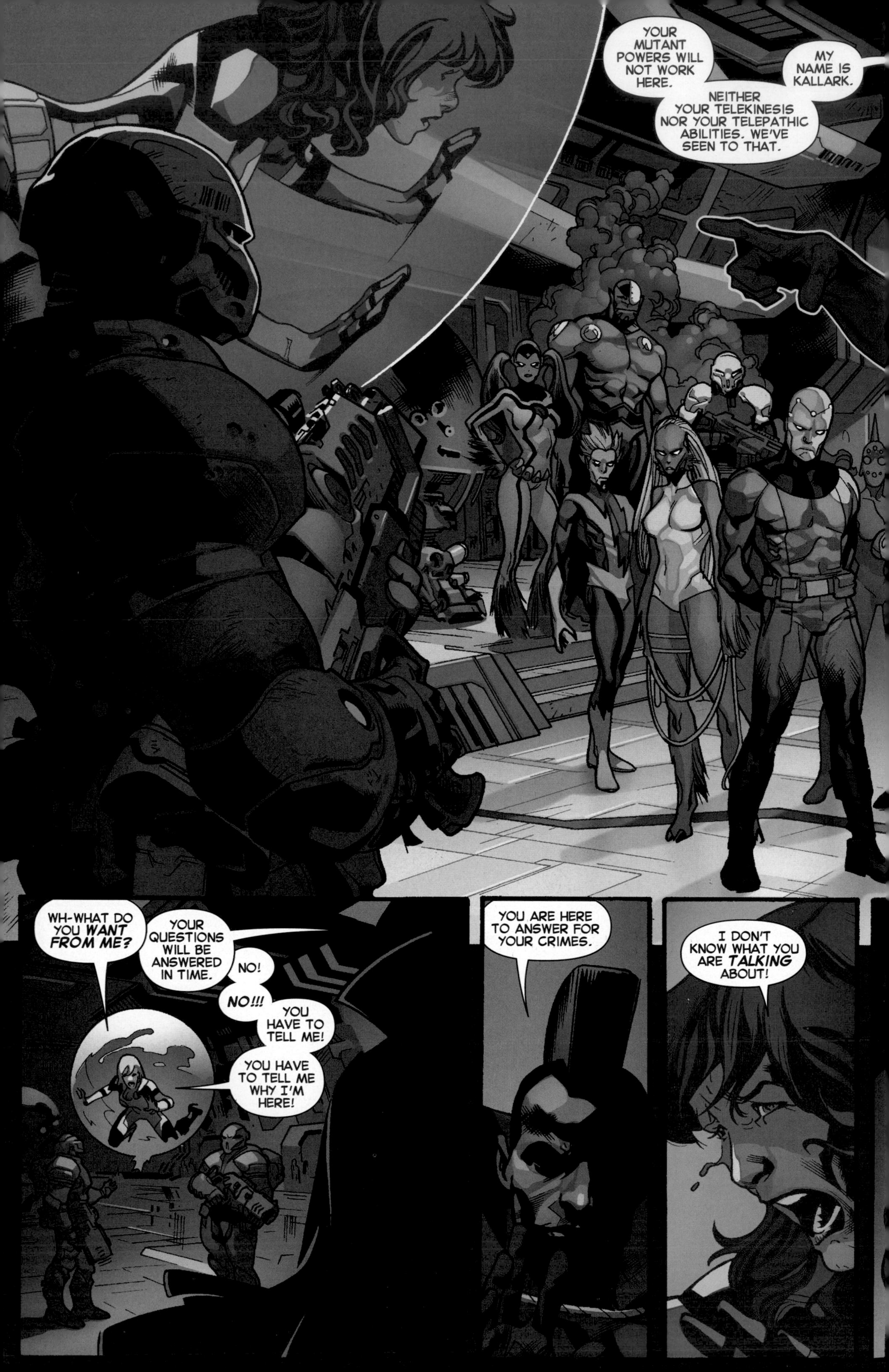
YOUR MUTANT POWERS WILL NOT WORK HERE.
MY NAME IS KALLARK.
NEITHER YOUR TELEKINESIS NOR YOUR TELEPATHIC ABILITIES. WE'VE SEEN TO THAT.
WH-WHAT DO YOU *WANT FROM ME?*
YOUR QUESTIONS WILL BE ANSWERED IN TIME.
NO!
NO!!!
YOU HAVE TO TELL ME!
YOU HAVE TO TELL ME WHY I'M HERE!
YOU ARE HERE TO ANSWER FOR YOUR CRIMES.
I DON'T KNOW WHAT YOU ARE *TALKING* ABOUT!

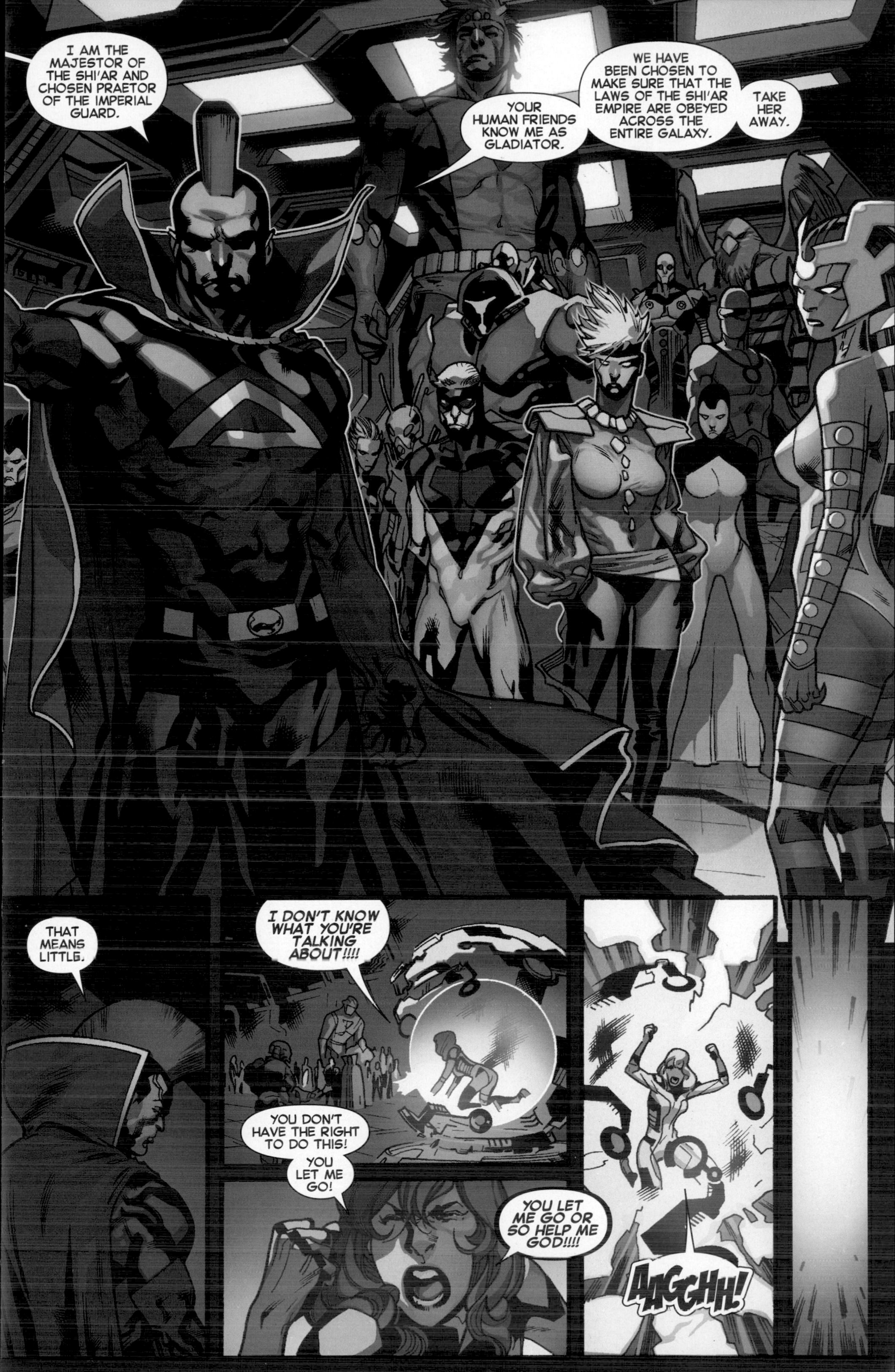
I AM THE MAJESTOR OF THE SHI'AR AND CHOSEN PRAETOR OF THE IMPERIAL GUARD.
YOUR HUMAN FRIENDS KNOW ME AS GLADIATOR.
WE HAVE BEEN CHOSEN TO MAKE SURE THAT THE LAWS OF THE SHI'AR EMPIRE ARE OBEYED ACROSS THE ENTIRE GALAXY.
TAKE HER AWAY.
THAT MEANS LITTLE.
I DON'T KNOW WHAT YOU'RE TALKING ABOUT!!!!
YOU DON'T HAVE THE RIGHT TO DO THIS!
YOU LET ME GO!
YOU LET ME GO OR SO HELP ME GOD!!!!
AAGGHH!

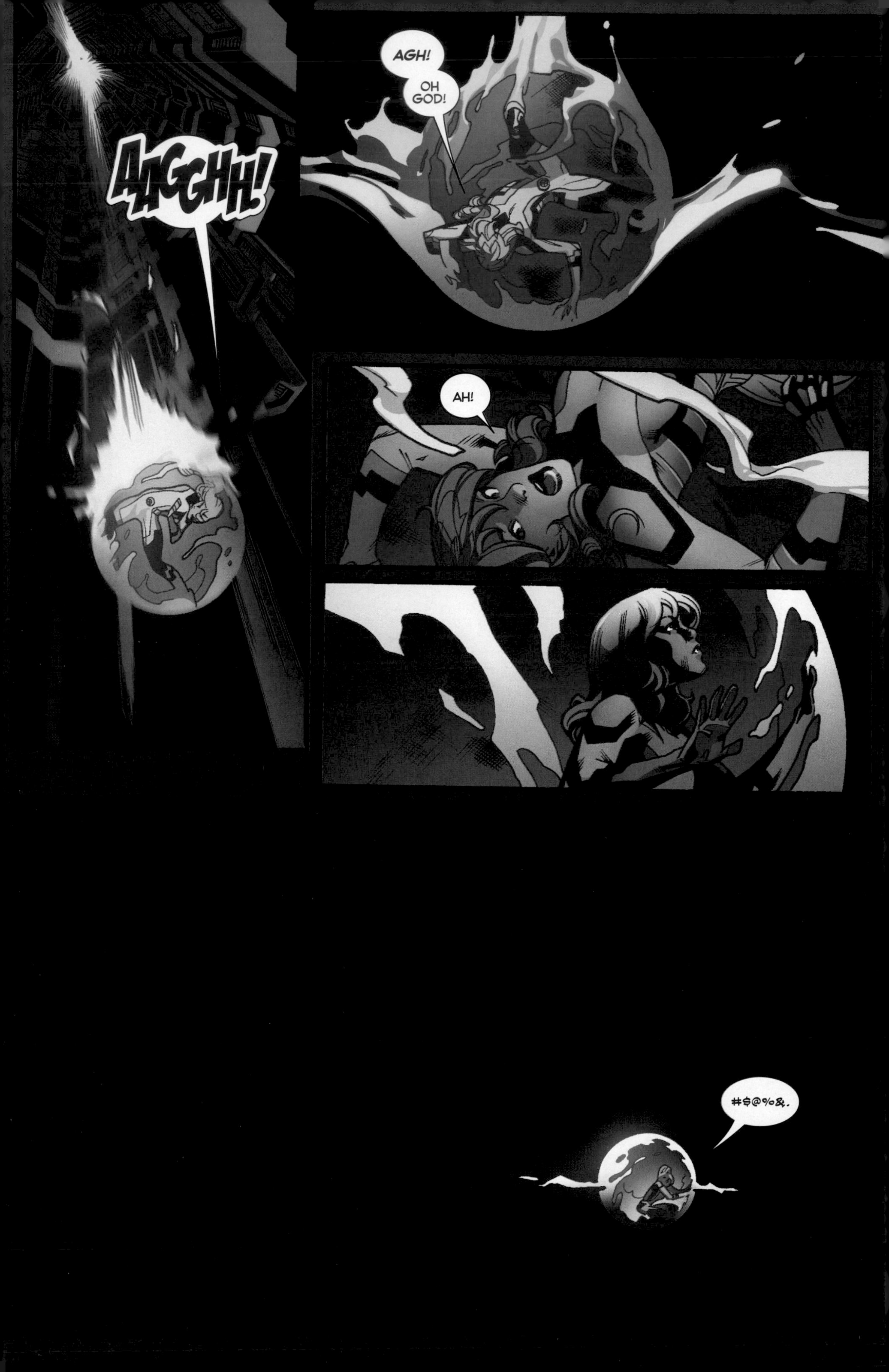
AAGGHH!
AGH!
OH GOD!
AH!
#$@%&.

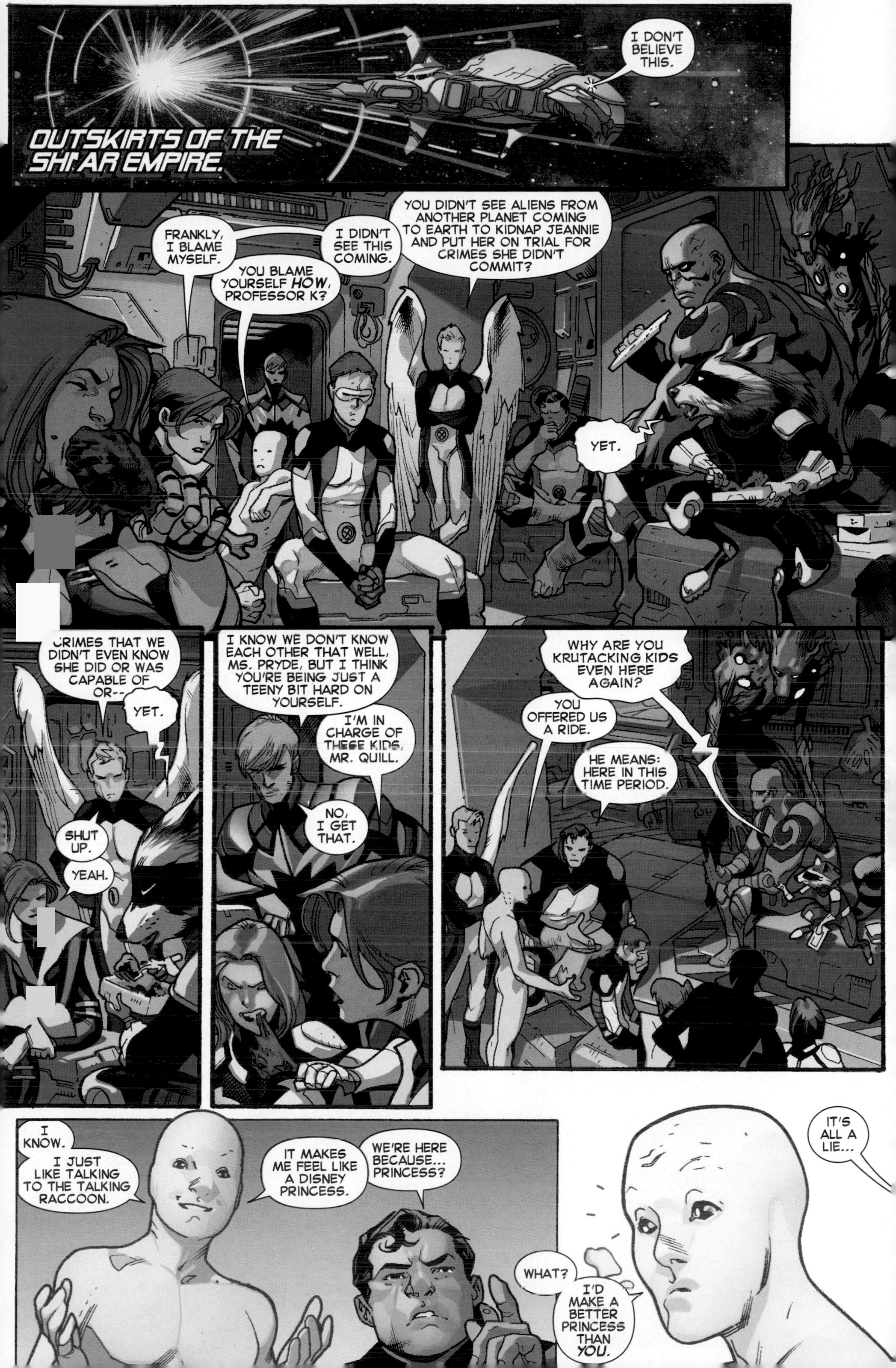
I DON'T BELIEVE THIS.
OUTSKIRTS OF THE SHI'AR EMPIRE.
FRANKLY, I BLAME MYSELF.
I DIDN'T SEE THIS COMING.
YOU DIDN'T SEE ALIENS FROM ANOTHER PLANET COMING TO EARTH TO KIDNAP JEANNIE AND PUT HER ON TRIAL FOR CRIMES SHE DIDN'T COMMIT?
YOU BLAME YOURSELF HOW, PROFESSOR K?
YET.
CRIMES THAT WE DIDN'T EVEN KNOW SHE DID OR WAS CAPABLE OF OR--
YET.
SHUT UP.
YEAH.
I KNOW WE DON'T KNOW EACH OTHER THAT WELL, MS. PRYDE, BUT I THINK YOU'RE BEING JUST A TEENY BIT HARD ON YOURSELF.
I'M IN CHARGE OF THESE KIDS, MR. QUILL.
NO, I GET THAT.
WHY ARE YOU KRUTACKING KIDS EVEN HERE AGAIN?
YOU OFFERED US A RIDE.
HE MEANS: HERE IN THIS TIME PERIOD.
I KNOW.
I JUST LIKE TALKING TO THE TALKING RACCOON.
IT MAKES ME FEEL LIKE A DISNEY PRINCESS.
WE'RE HERE BECAUSE... PRINCESS?
IT'S ALL A LIE...
WHAT?
I'D MAKE A BETTER PRINCESS THAN YOU.

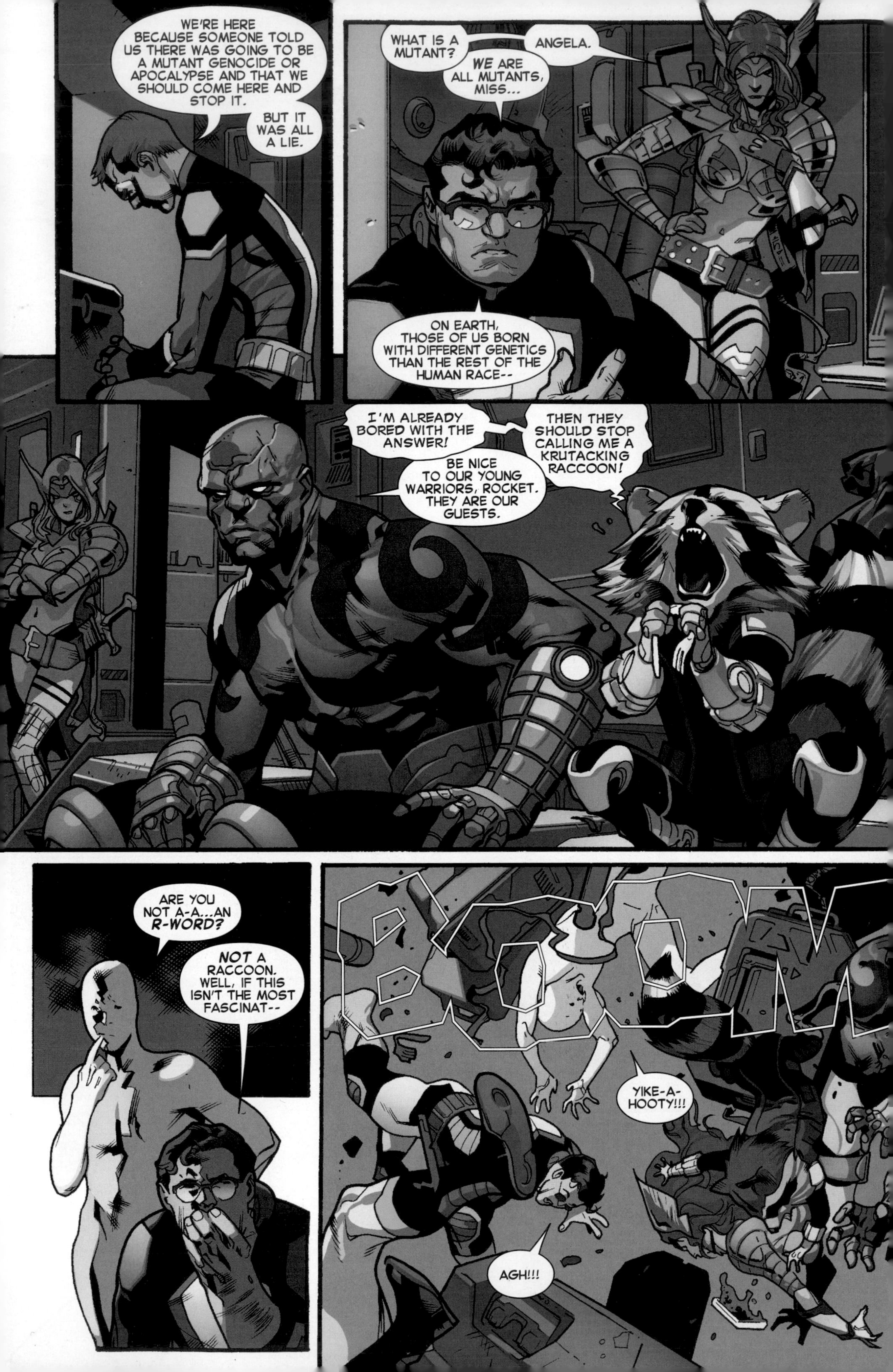
WE'RE HERE BECAUSE SOMEONE TOLD US THERE WAS GOING TO BE A MUTANT GENOCIDE OR APOCALYPSE AND THAT WE SHOULD COME HERE AND STOP IT.
BUT IT WAS ALL A LIE.
WHAT IS A MUTANT?
ANGELA.
WE ARE ALL MUTANTS, MISS...
ON EARTH, THOSE OF US BORN WITH DIFFERENT GENETICS THAN THE REST OF THE HUMAN RACE--
I'M ALREADY BORED WITH THE ANSWER!
BE NICE TO OUR YOUNG WARRIORS, ROCKET. THEY ARE OUR GUESTS.
THEN THEY SHOULD STOP CALLING ME A KRUTACKING RACCOON!
ARE YOU NOT A-A...AN R-WORD?
NOT A RACCOON. WELL, IF THIS ISN'T THE MOST FASCINAT--
BOOM
YIKE-A-HOOTY!!!
AGH!!!

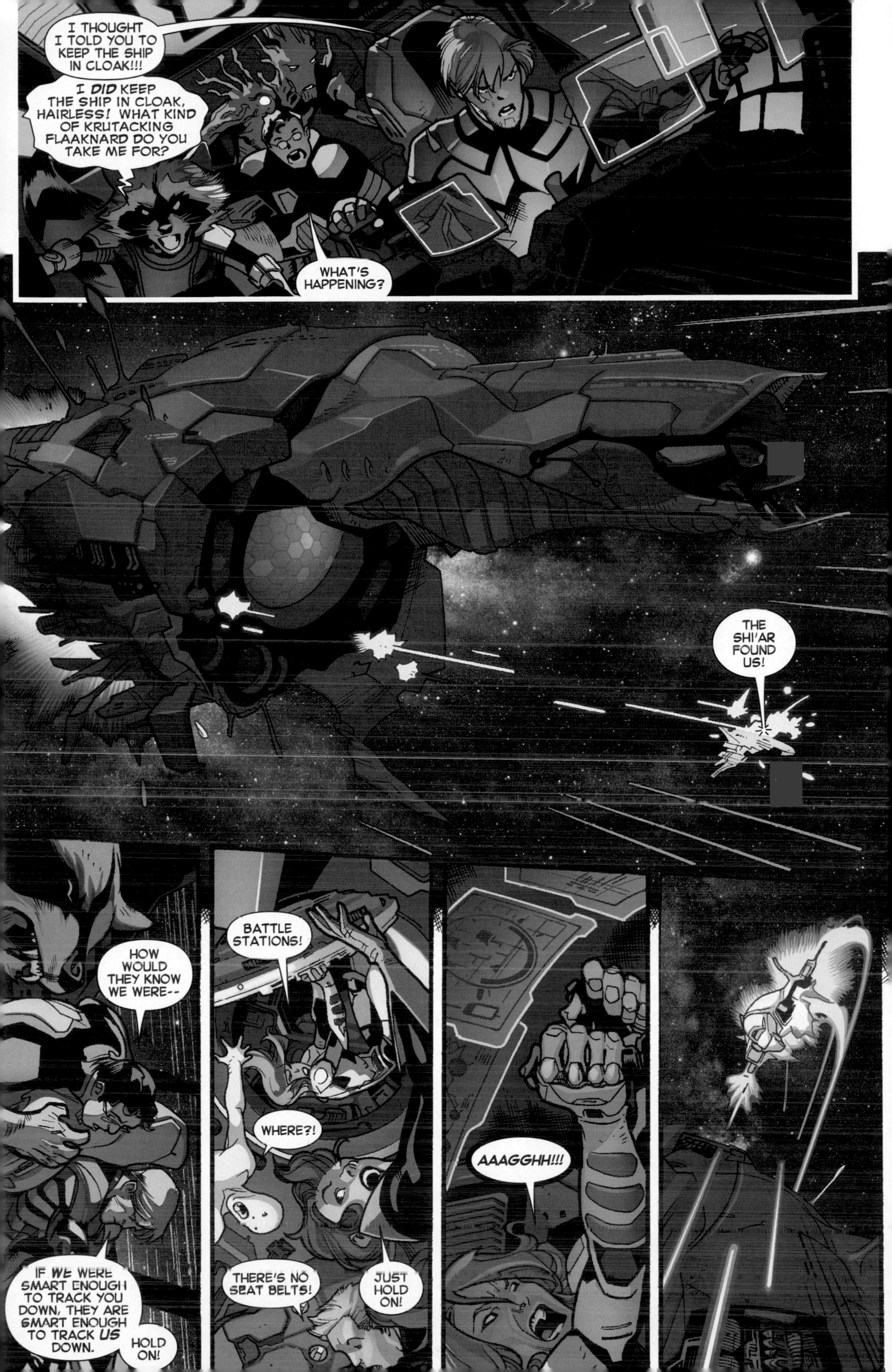
I THOUGHT I TOLD YOU TO KEEP THE SHIP IN CLOAK!!!
I DID KEEP THE SHIP IN CLOAK, HAIRLESS! WHAT KIND OF KRUTACKING FLAAKNARD DO YOU TAKE ME FOR?
WHAT'S HAPPENING?
THE SHI'AR FOUND US!
HOW WOULD THEY KNOW WE WERE--
IF WE WERE SMART ENOUGH TO TRACK YOU DOWN, THEY ARE SMART ENOUGH TO TRACK US DOWN.
HOLD ON!
BATTLE STATIONS!
WHERE?!
THERE'S NO SEAT BELTS!
JUST HOLD ON!
AAAGGHH!!!

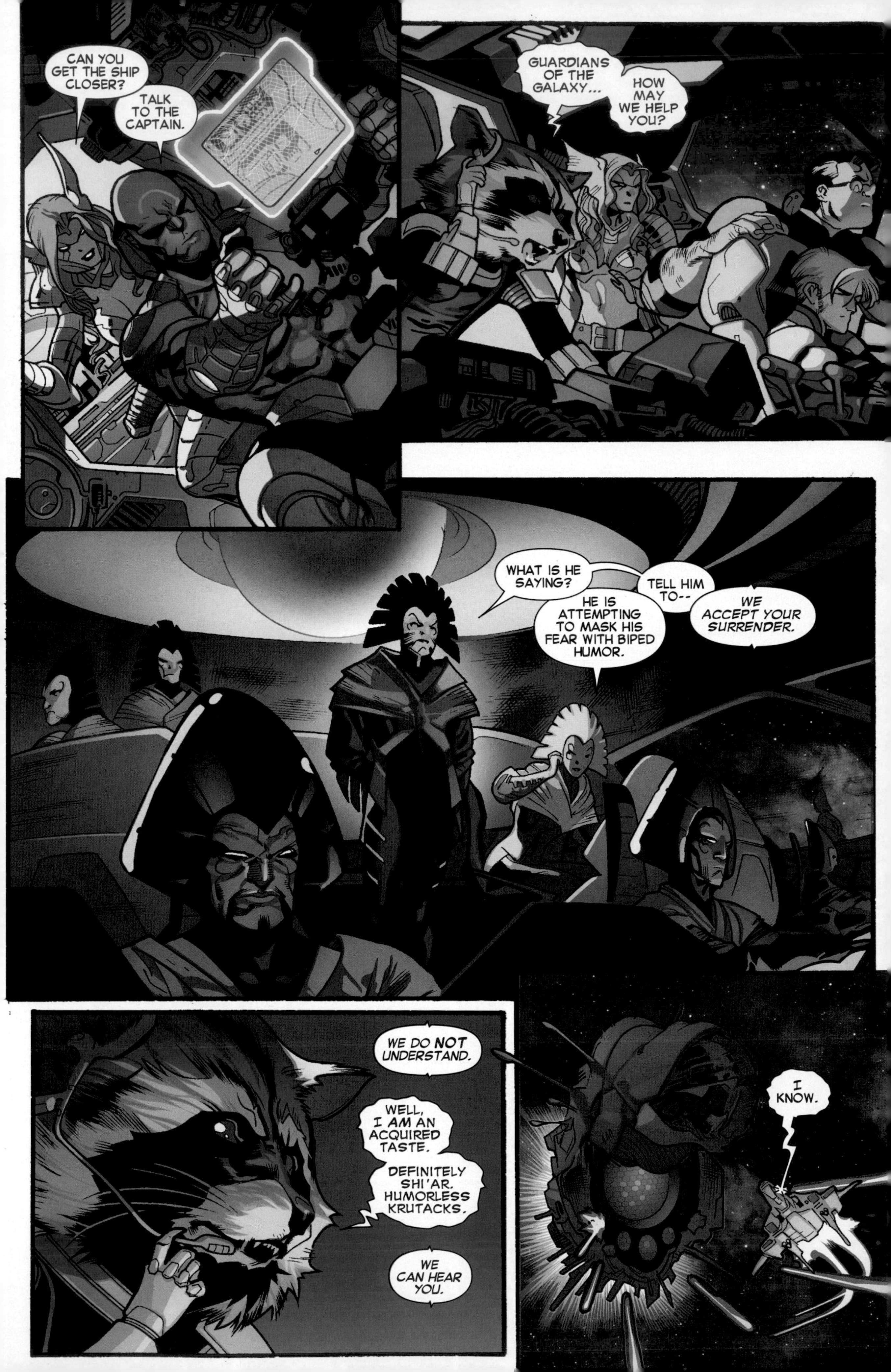
CAN YOU GET THE SHIP CLOSER?
TALK TO THE CAPTAIN.
GUARDIANS OF THE GALAXY...
HOW MAY WE HELP YOU?
WHAT IS HE SAYING?
HE IS ATTEMPTING TO MASK HIS FEAR WITH BIPED HUMOR.
TELL HIM TO--
WE ACCEPT YOUR SURRENDER.
WE DO NOT UNDERSTAND.
WELL, I AM AN ACQUIRED TASTE.
DEFINITELY SHI'AR. HUMORLESS KRUTACKS.
WE CAN HEAR YOU.
I KNOW.

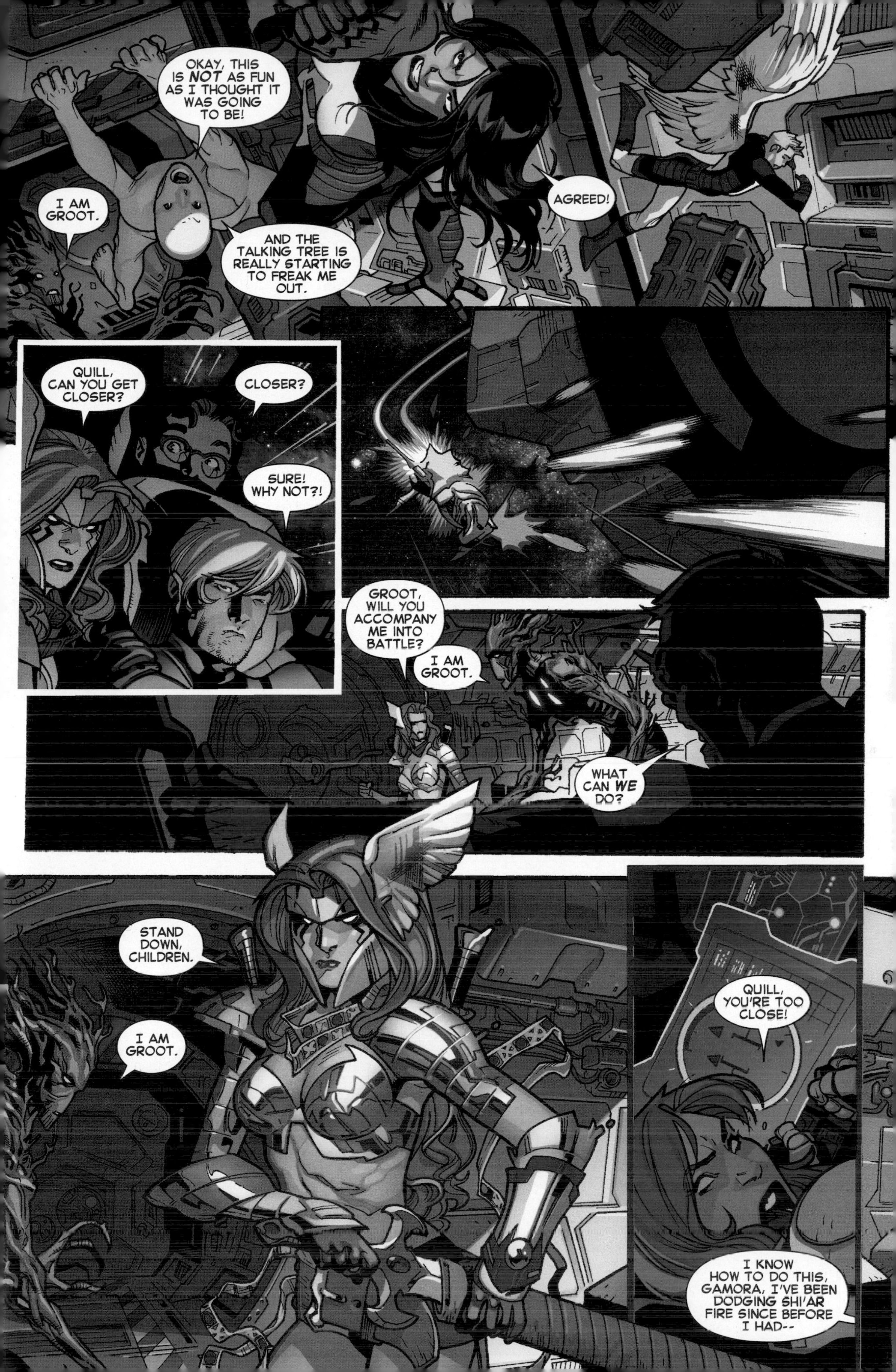
OKAY, THIS IS NOT AS FUN AS I THOUGHT IT WAS GOING TO BE!
I AM GROOT.
AND THE TALKING TREE IS REALLY STARTING TO FREAK ME OUT.
AGREED!
QUILL, CAN YOU GET CLOSER?
CLOSER?
SURE! WHY NOT?!
GROOT, WILL YOU ACCOMPANY ME INTO BATTLE?
I AM GROOT.
WHAT CAN WE DO?
STAND DOWN, CHILDREN.
I AM GROOT.
QUILL, YOU'RE TOO CLOSE!
I KNOW HOW TO DO THIS, GAMORA, I'VE BEEN DODGING SHI'AR FIRE SINCE BEFORE I HAD--

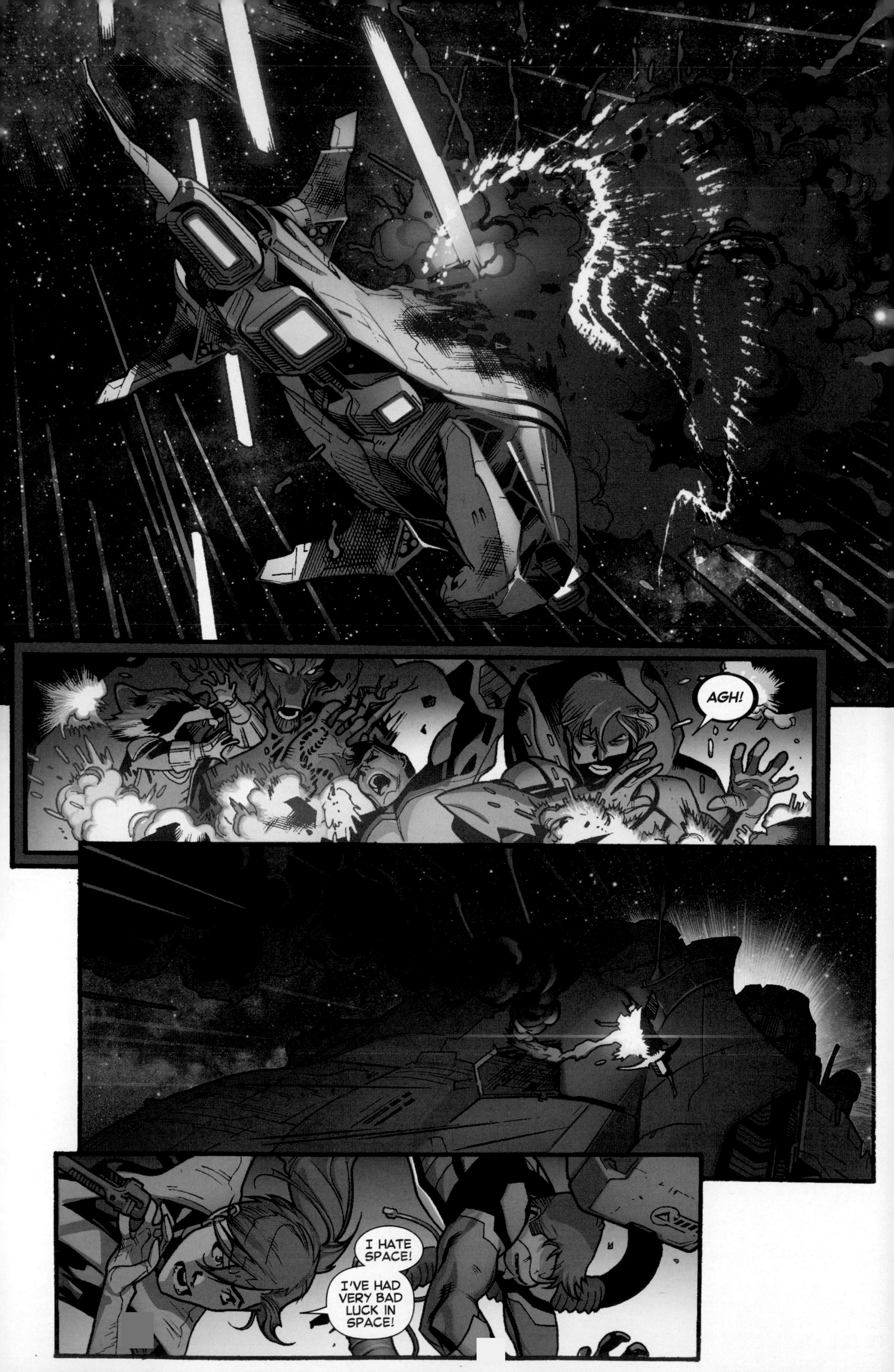
AGH!
I HATE SPACE!
I'VE HAD VERY BAD LUCK IN SPACE!

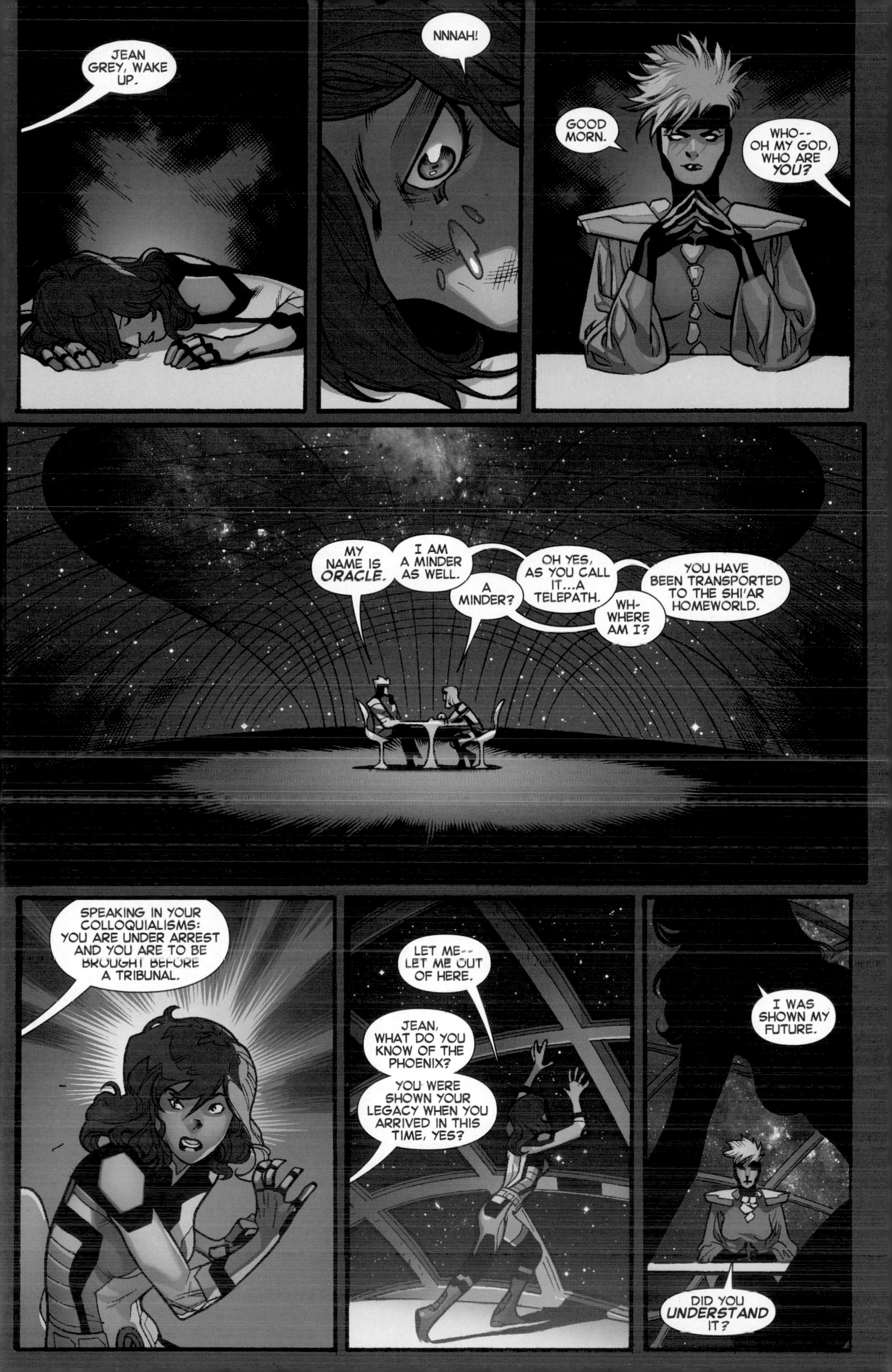
JEAN GREY, WAKE UP.
NNNAH!
GOOD MORN.
WHO-- OH MY GOD, WHO ARE YOU?
MY NAME IS ORACLE.
I AM A MINDER AS WELL.
A MINDER?
OH YES, AS YOU CALL IT...A TELEPATH.
WH-WHERE AM I?
YOU HAVE BEEN TRANSPORTED TO THE SHI'AR HOMEWORLD.
SPEAKING IN YOUR COLLOQUIALISMS: YOU ARE UNDER ARREST AND YOU ARE TO BE BROUGHT BEFORE A TRIBUNAL.
LET ME-- LET ME OUT OF HERE.
JEAN, WHAT DO YOU KNOW OF THE PHOENIX?
YOU WERE SHOWN YOUR LEGACY WHEN YOU ARRIVED IN THIS TIME, YES?
I WAS SHOWN MY FUTURE.
DID YOU UNDERSTAND IT?

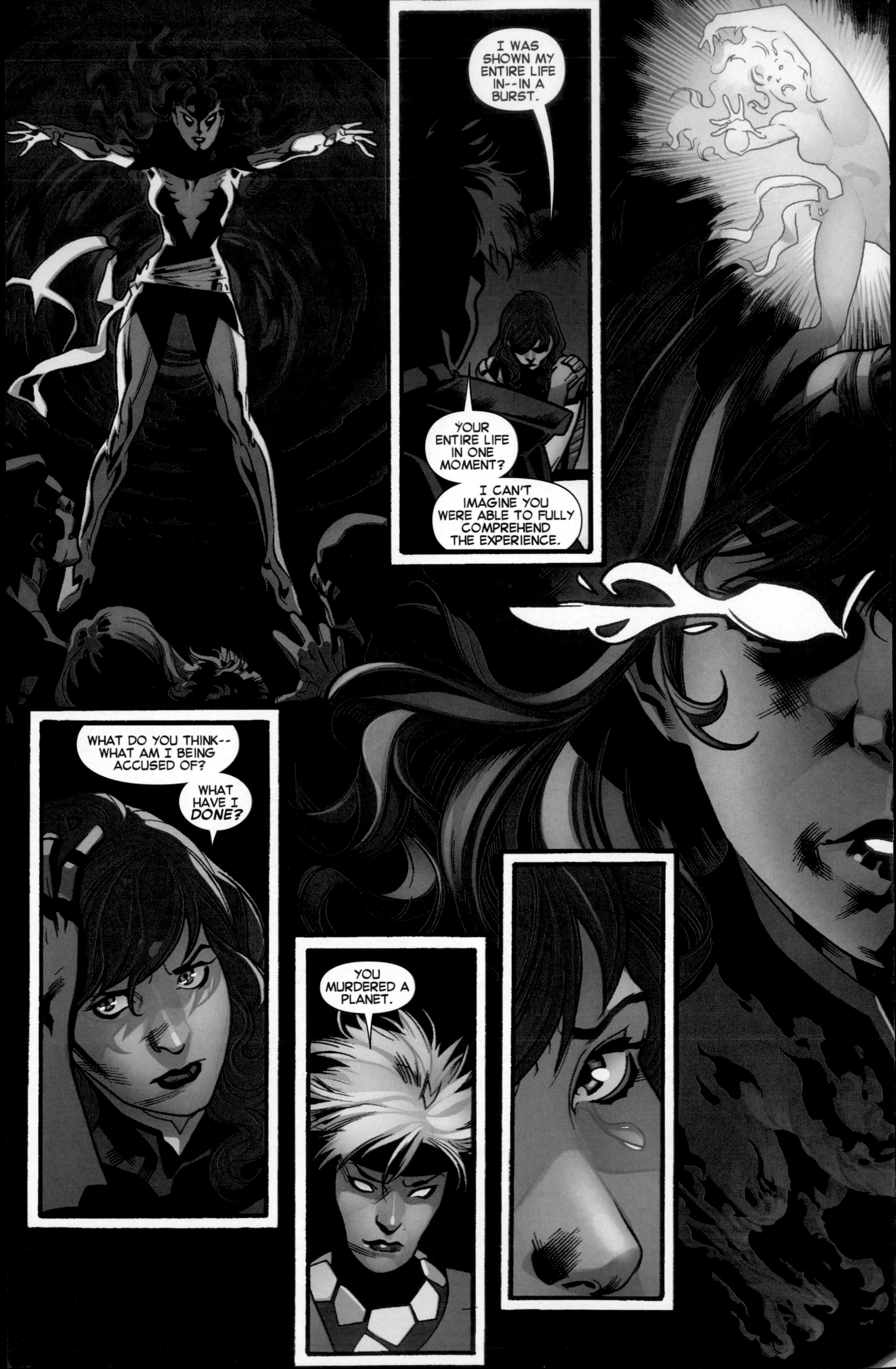
I WAS SHOWN MY ENTIRE LIFE IN--IN A BURST.
YOUR ENTIRE LIFE IN ONE MOMENT?
I CAN'T IMAGINE YOU WERE ABLE TO FULLY COMPREHEND THE EXPERIENCE.
WHAT DO YOU THINK--WHAT AM I BEING ACCUSED OF?
WHAT HAVE I *DONE?*
YOU MURDERED A PLANET.

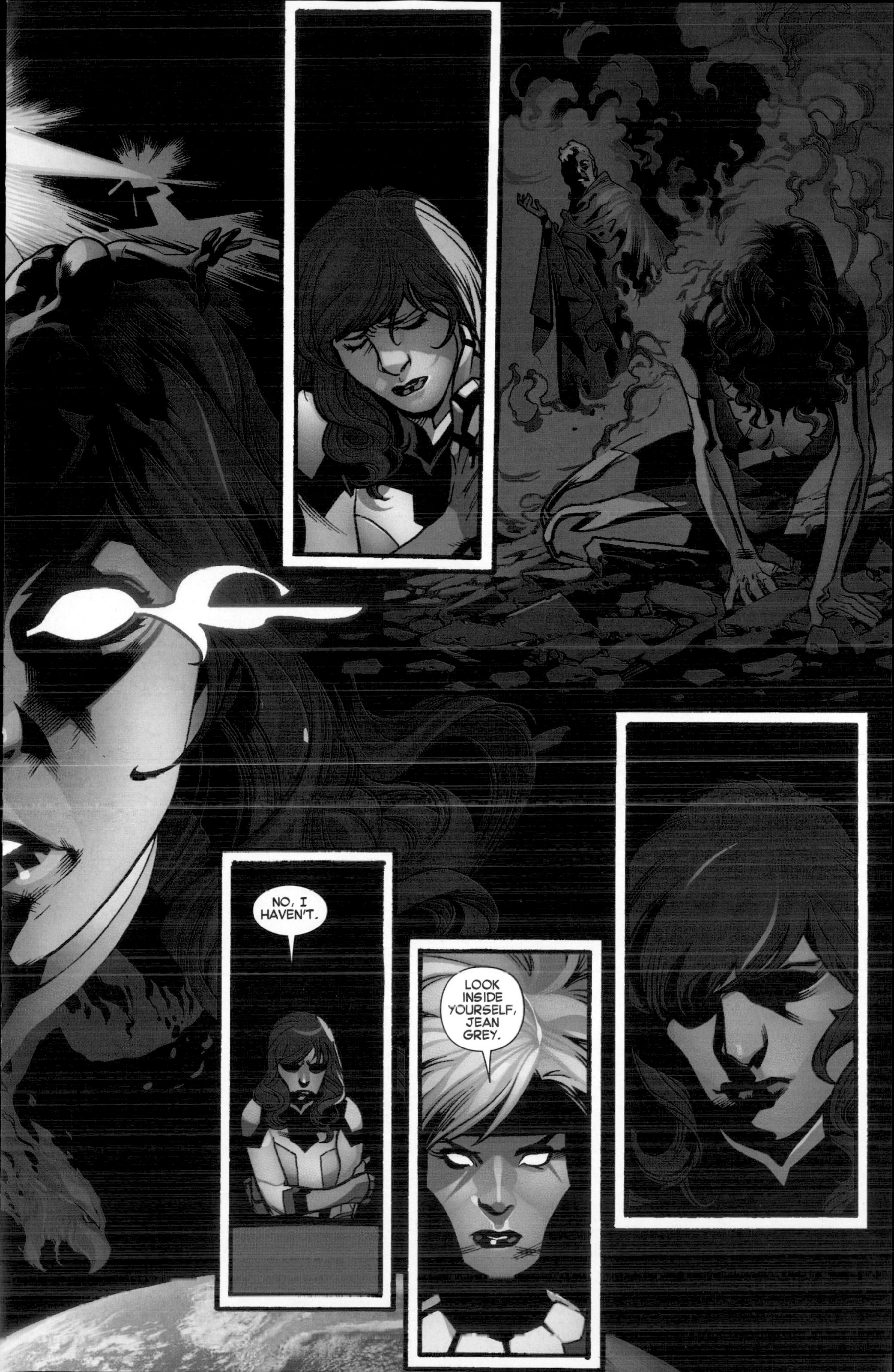
NO, I HAVEN'T.
LOOK INSIDE YOURSELF, JEAN GREY.

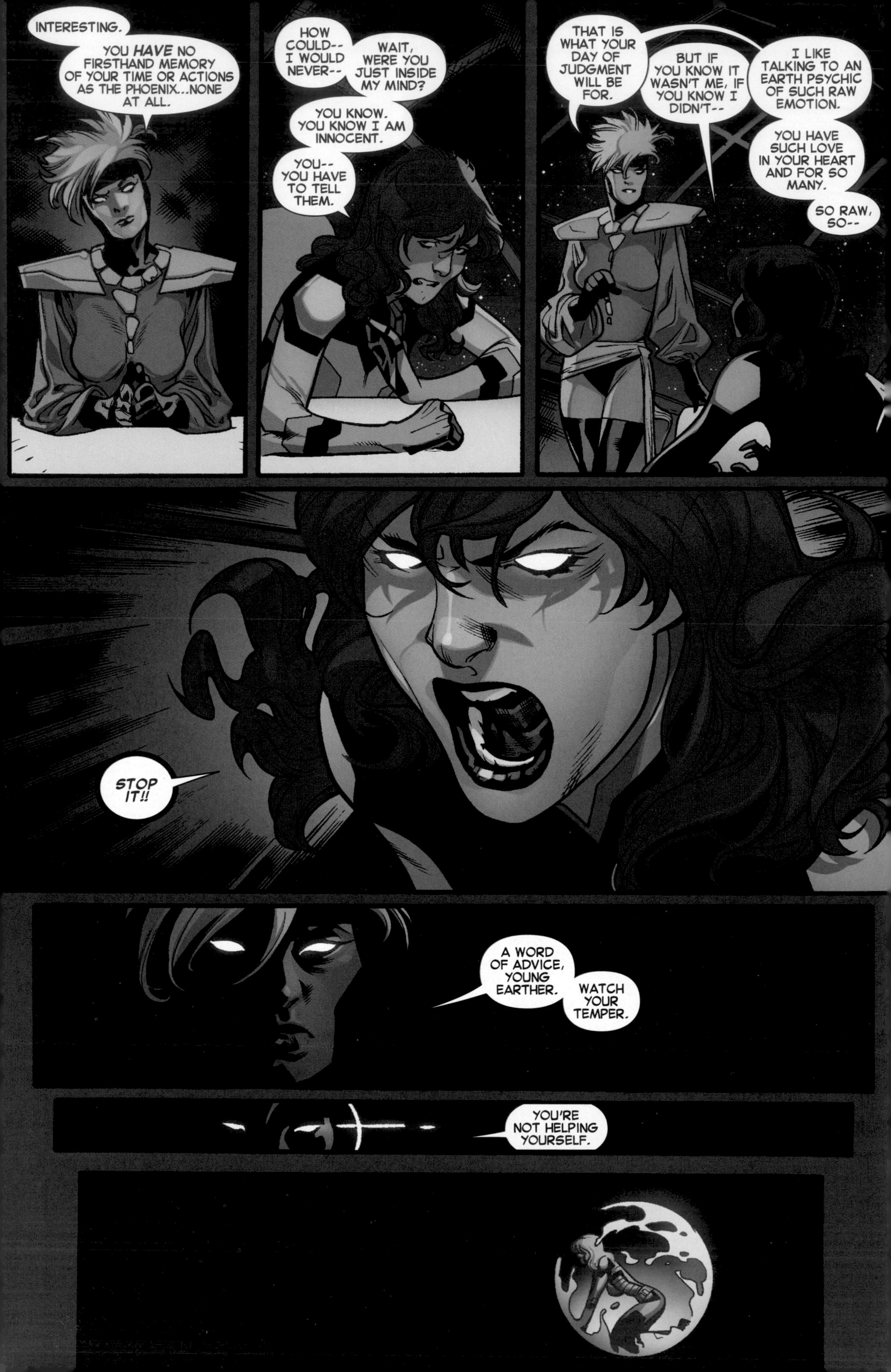
INTERESTING.
YOU HAVE NO FIRSTHAND MEMORY OF YOUR TIME OR ACTIONS AS THE PHOENIX...NONE AT ALL.
HOW COULD-- I WOULD NEVER--
WAIT, WERE YOU JUST INSIDE MY MIND?
YOU KNOW. YOU KNOW I AM INNOCENT.
YOU-- YOU HAVE TO TELL THEM.
THAT IS WHAT YOUR DAY OF JUDGMENT WILL BE FOR.
BUT IF YOU KNOW IT WASN'T ME, IF YOU KNOW I DIDN'T--
I LIKE TALKING TO AN EARTH PSYCHIC OF SUCH RAW EMOTION.
YOU HAVE SUCH LOVE IN YOUR HEART AND FOR SO MANY.
SO RAW, SO--
STOP IT!!
A WORD OF ADVICE, YOUNG EARTHER.
WATCH YOUR TEMPER.
YOU'RE NOT HELPING YOURSELF.

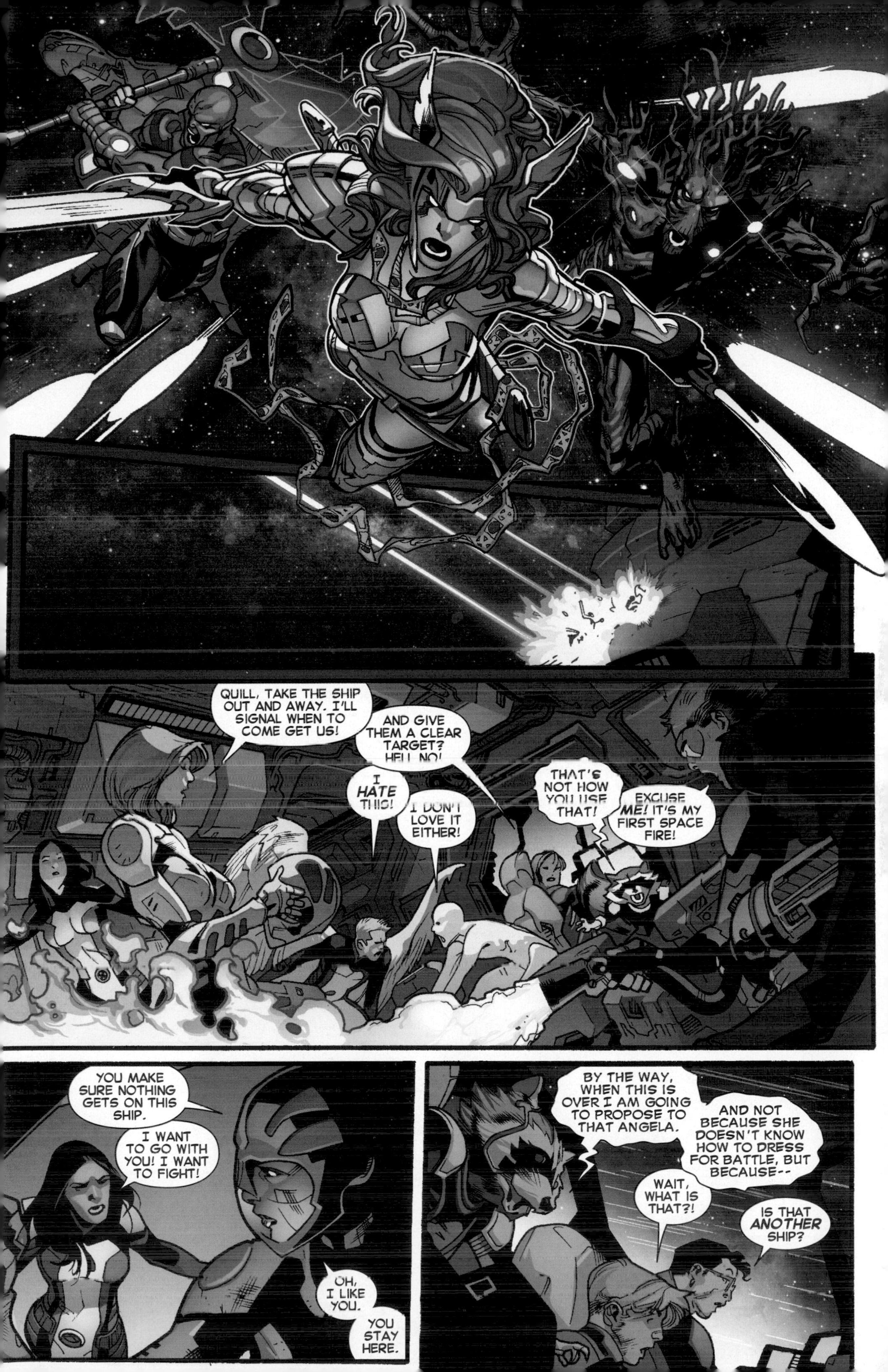
QUILL, TAKE THE SHIP OUT AND AWAY. I'LL SIGNAL WHEN TO COME GET US!
AND GIVE THEM A CLEAR TARGET? HELL NO!
I HATE THIS!
I DON'T LOVE IT EITHER!
THAT'S NOT HOW YOU USE THAT!
EXCUSE ME! IT'S MY FIRST SPACE FIRE!
YOU MAKE SURE NOTHING GETS ON THIS SHIP.
I WANT TO GO WITH YOU! I WANT TO FIGHT!
OH, I LIKE YOU.
YOU STAY HERE.
BY THE WAY, WHEN THIS IS OVER I AM GOING TO PROPOSE TO THAT ANGELA.
AND NOT BECAUSE SHE DOESN'T KNOW HOW TO DRESS FOR BATTLE, BUT BECAUSE--
WAIT, WHAT IS THAT?!
IS THAT ANOTHER SHIP?

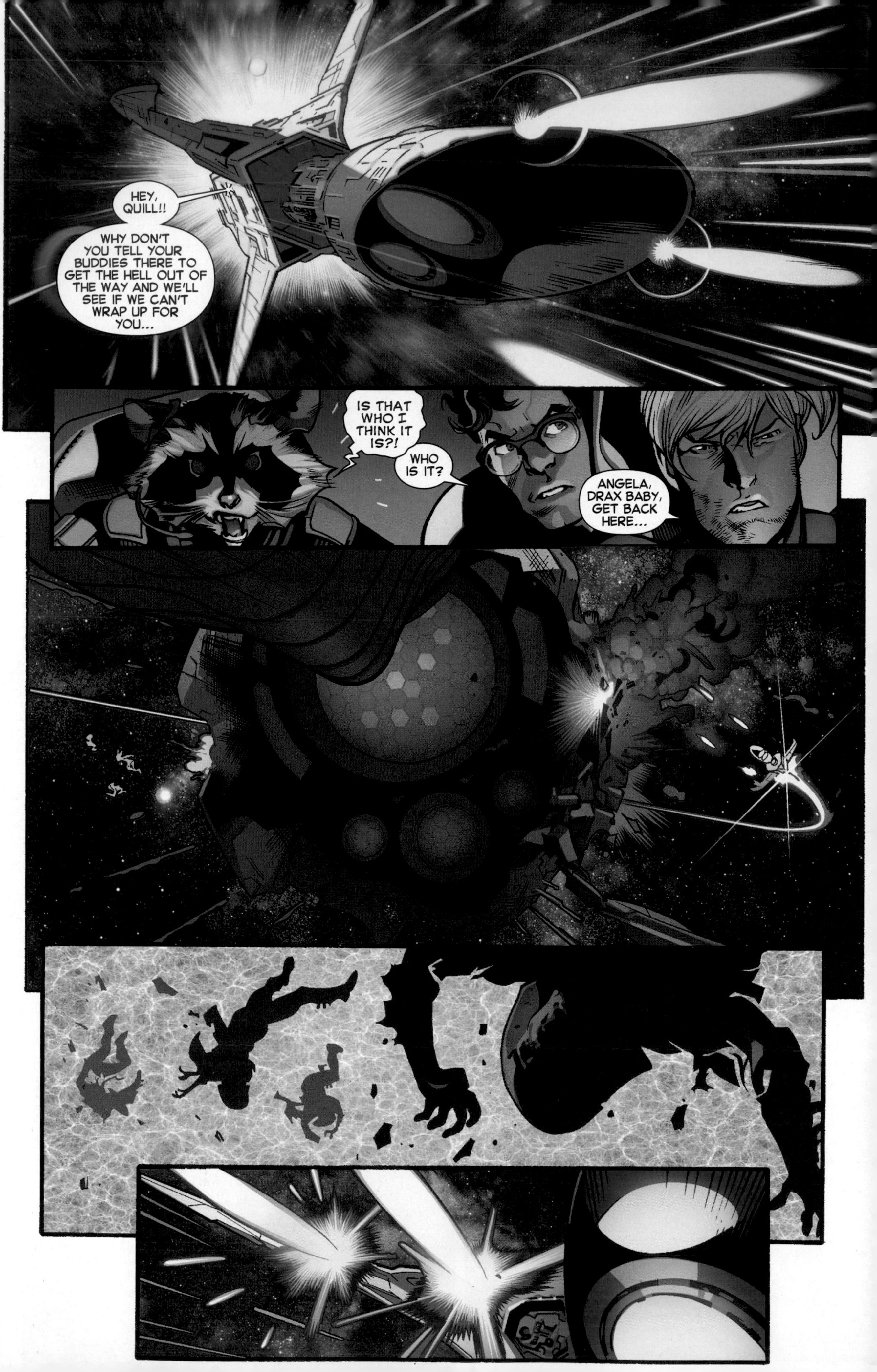
HEY, QUILL!!
WHY DON'T YOU TELL YOUR BUDDIES THERE TO GET THE HELL OUT OF THE WAY AND WE'LL SEE IF WE CAN'T WRAP UP FOR YOU...
IS THAT WHO I THINK IT IS?!
WHO IS IT?
ANGELA, DRAX BABY, GET BACK HERE...

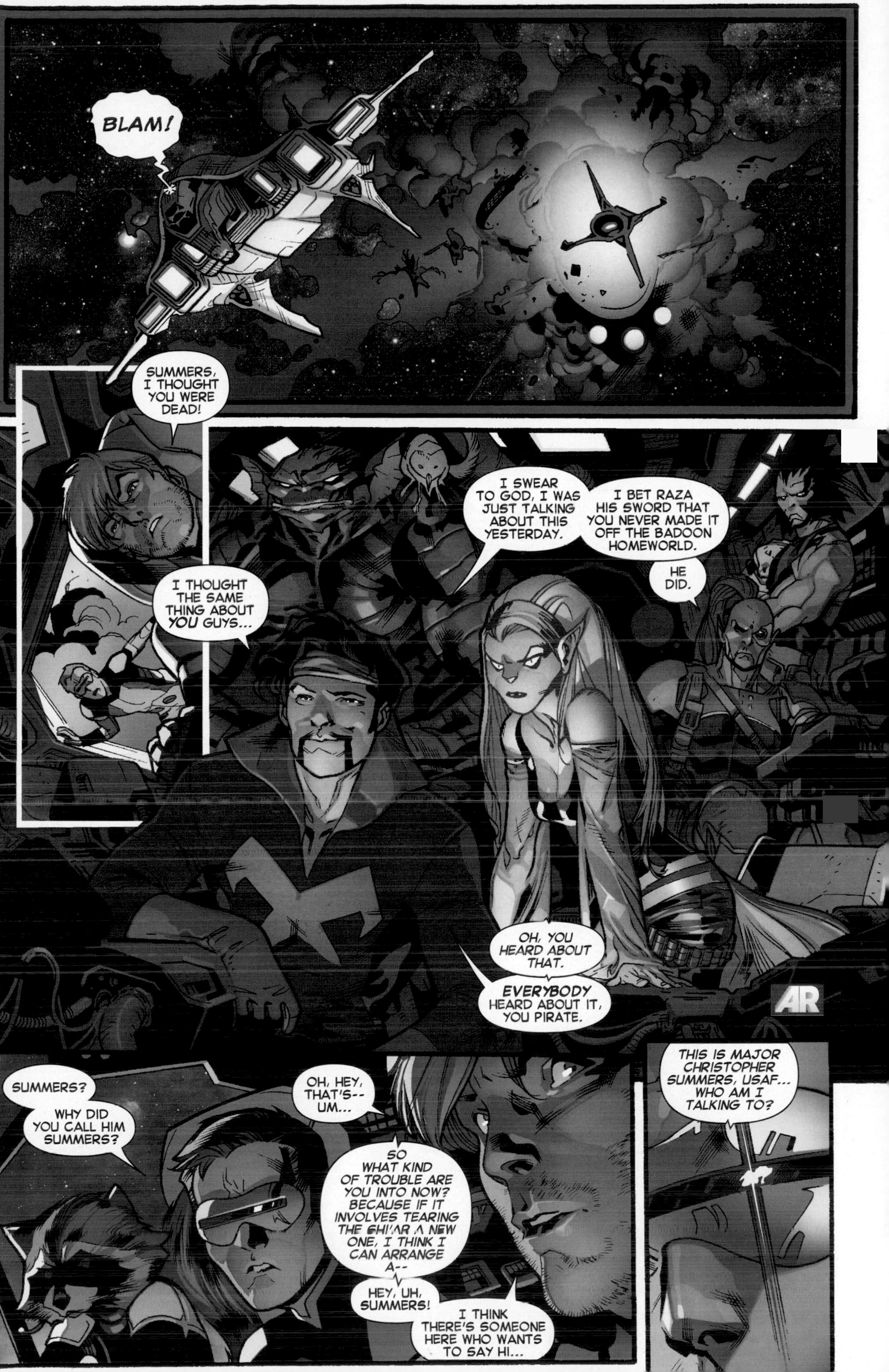

BLAM!
SUMMERS, I THOUGHT YOU WERE DEAD!
I THOUGHT THE SAME THING ABOUT YOU GUYS...
I SWEAR TO GOD, I WAS JUST TALKING ABOUT THIS YESTERDAY.
I BET RAZA HIS SWORD THAT YOU NEVER MADE IT OFF THE BADOON HOMEWORLD.
HE DID.
OH, YOU HEARD ABOUT THAT.
EVERYBODY HEARD ABOUT IT, YOU PIRATE.
SUMMERS?
WHY DID YOU CALL HIM SUMMERS?
OH, HEY, THAT'S-- UM...
SO WHAT KIND OF TROUBLE ARE YOU INTO NOW? BECAUSE IF IT INVOLVES TEARING THE SHI'AR A NEW ONE, I THINK I CAN ARRANGE A--
HEY, UH, SUMMERS!
I THINK THERE'S SOMEONE HERE WHO WANTS TO SAY HI...
THIS IS MAJOR CHRISTOPHER SUMMERS, USAF... WHO AM I TALKING TO?

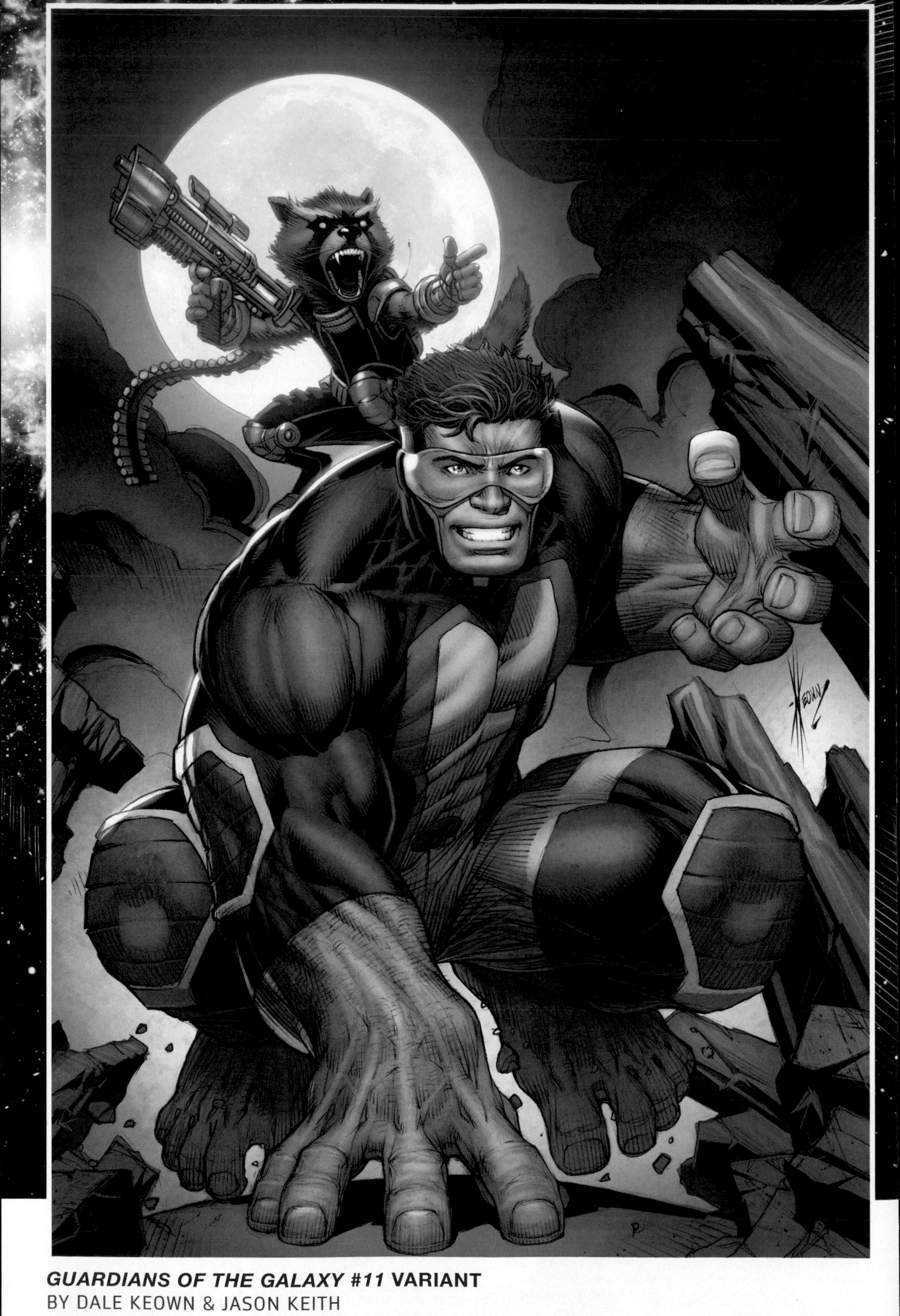

***GUARDIANS OF THE GALAXY #11* VARIANT**
BY DALE KEOWN & JASON KEITH

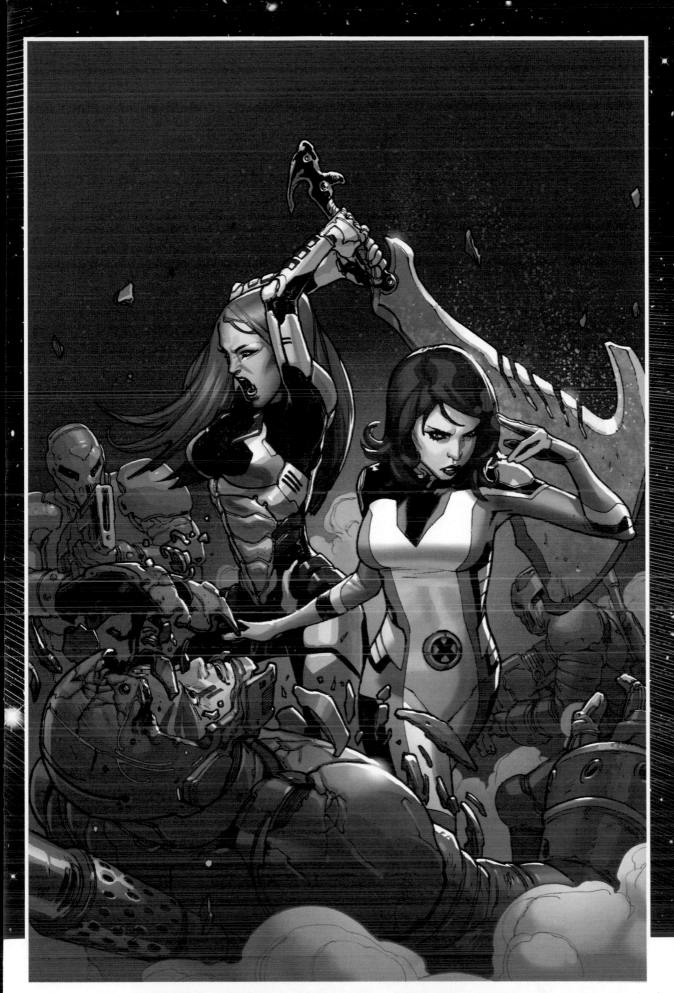

GUARDIANS OF THE GALAXY 12

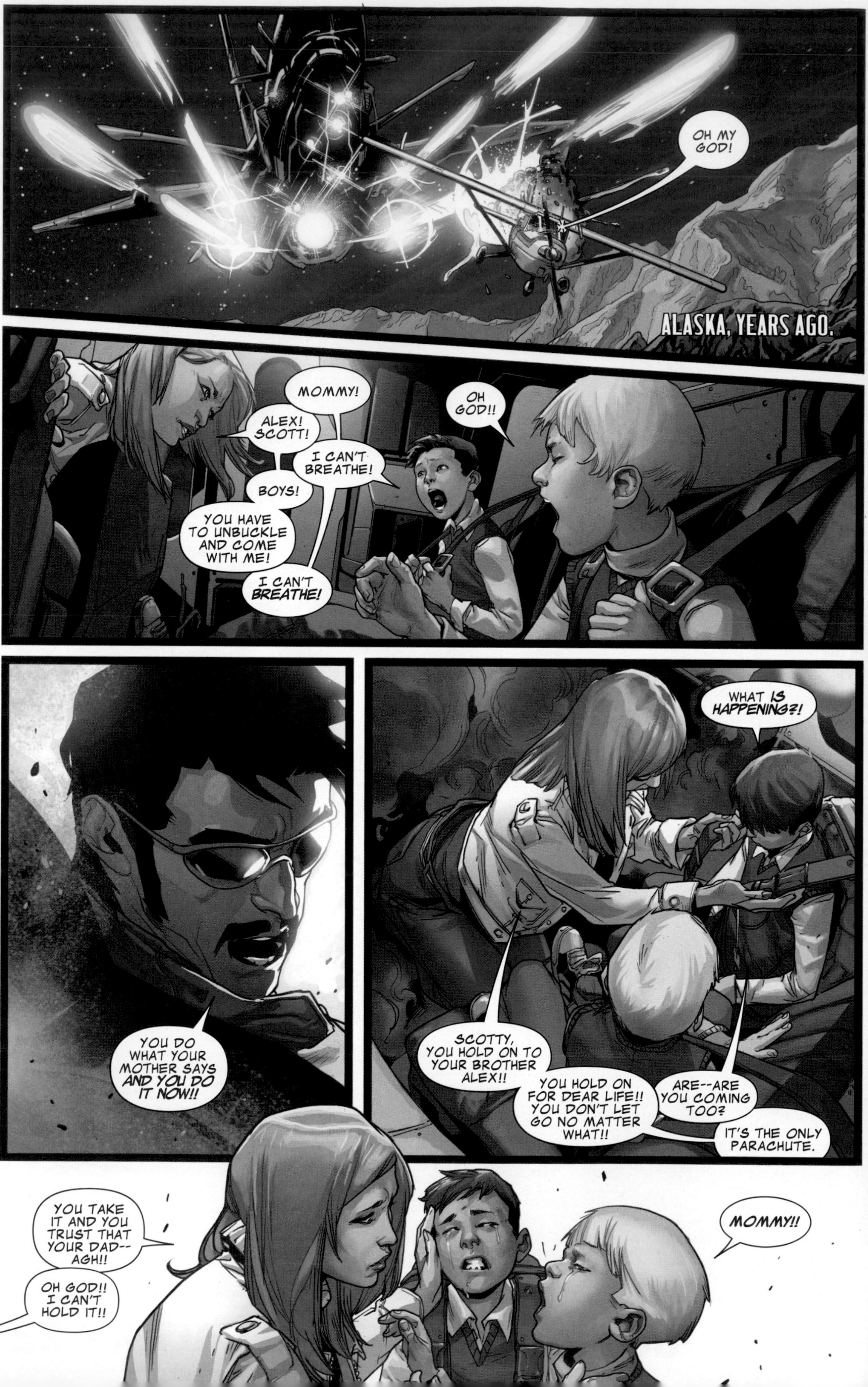
OH MY GOD!
ALASKA, YEARS AGO.
ALEX! SCOTT!
MOMMY!
I CAN'T BREATHE!
OH GOD!!
BOYS!
YOU HAVE TO UNBUCKLE AND COME WITH ME!
I CAN'T BREATHE!
YOU DO WHAT YOUR MOTHER SAYS AND YOU DO IT NOW!!
WHAT IS HAPPENING?!
SCOTTY, YOU HOLD ON TO YOUR BROTHER ALEX!!
YOU HOLD ON FOR DEAR LIFE!! YOU DON'T LET GO NO MATTER WHAT!!
ARE--ARE YOU COMING TOO?
IT'S THE ONLY PARACHUTE.
YOU TAKE IT AND YOU TRUST THAT YOUR DAD-- AGH!!
OH GOD!! I CAN'T HOLD IT!!
MOMMY!!

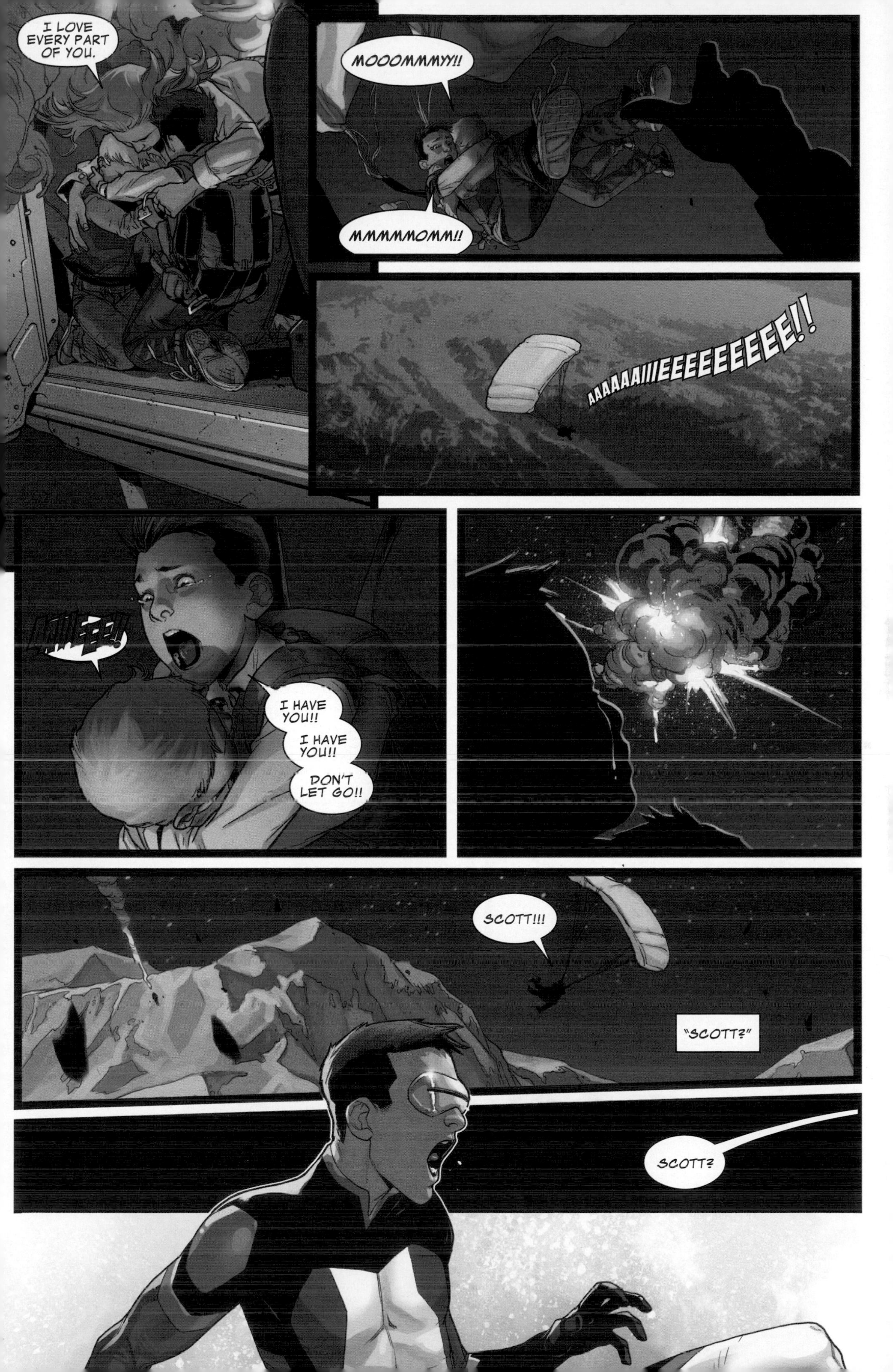
I LOVE EVERY PART OF YOU.
MOOOMMMYY!!
MMMMMOMM!!
AAAAAAIIIIEEEEEEEEE!!
I HAVE YOU!!
I HAVE YOU!!
DON'T LET GO!!
SCOTT!!!
"SCOTT?"
SCOTT?

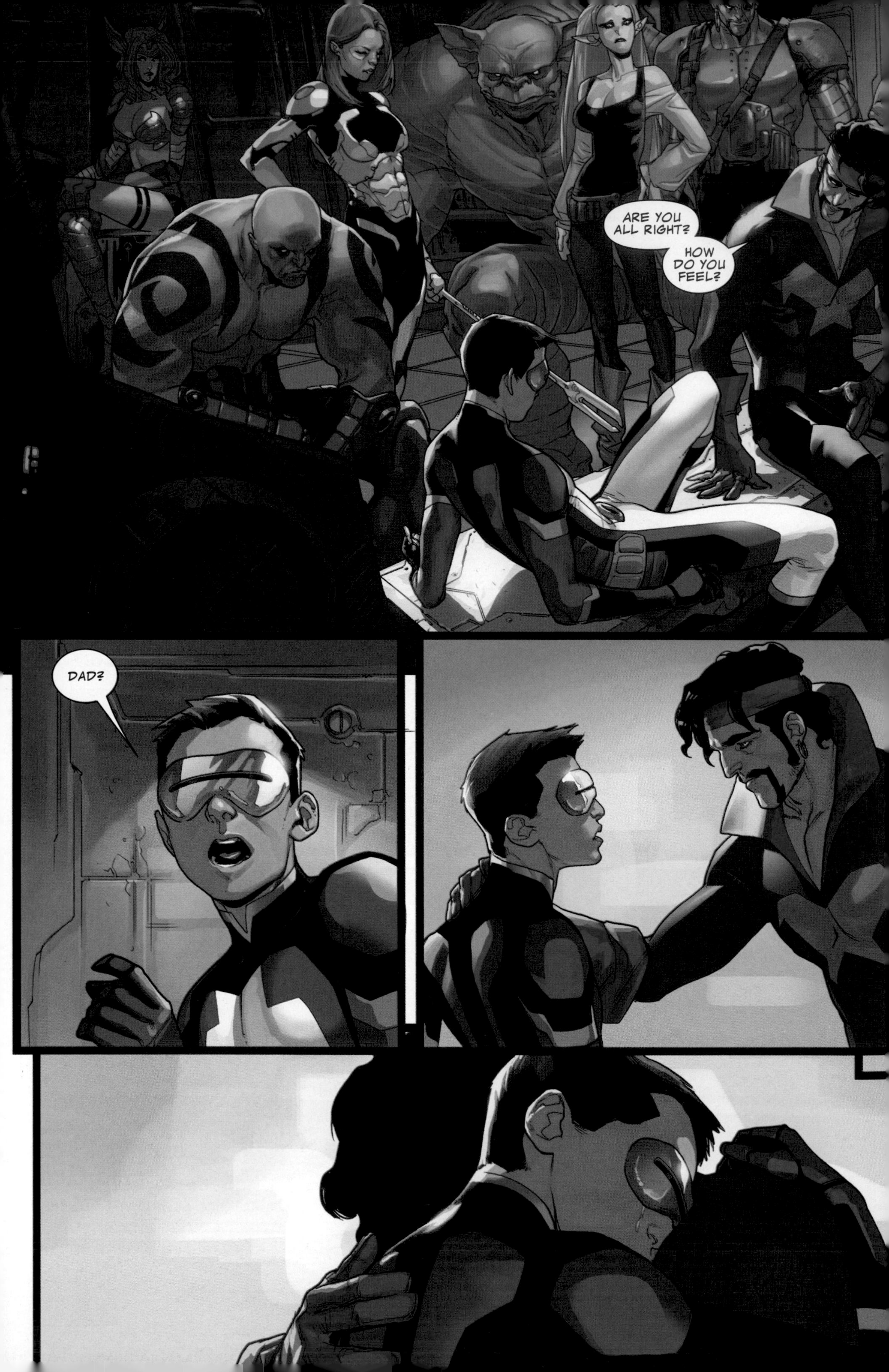
ARE YOU ALL RIGHT?
HOW DO YOU FEEL?
DAD?

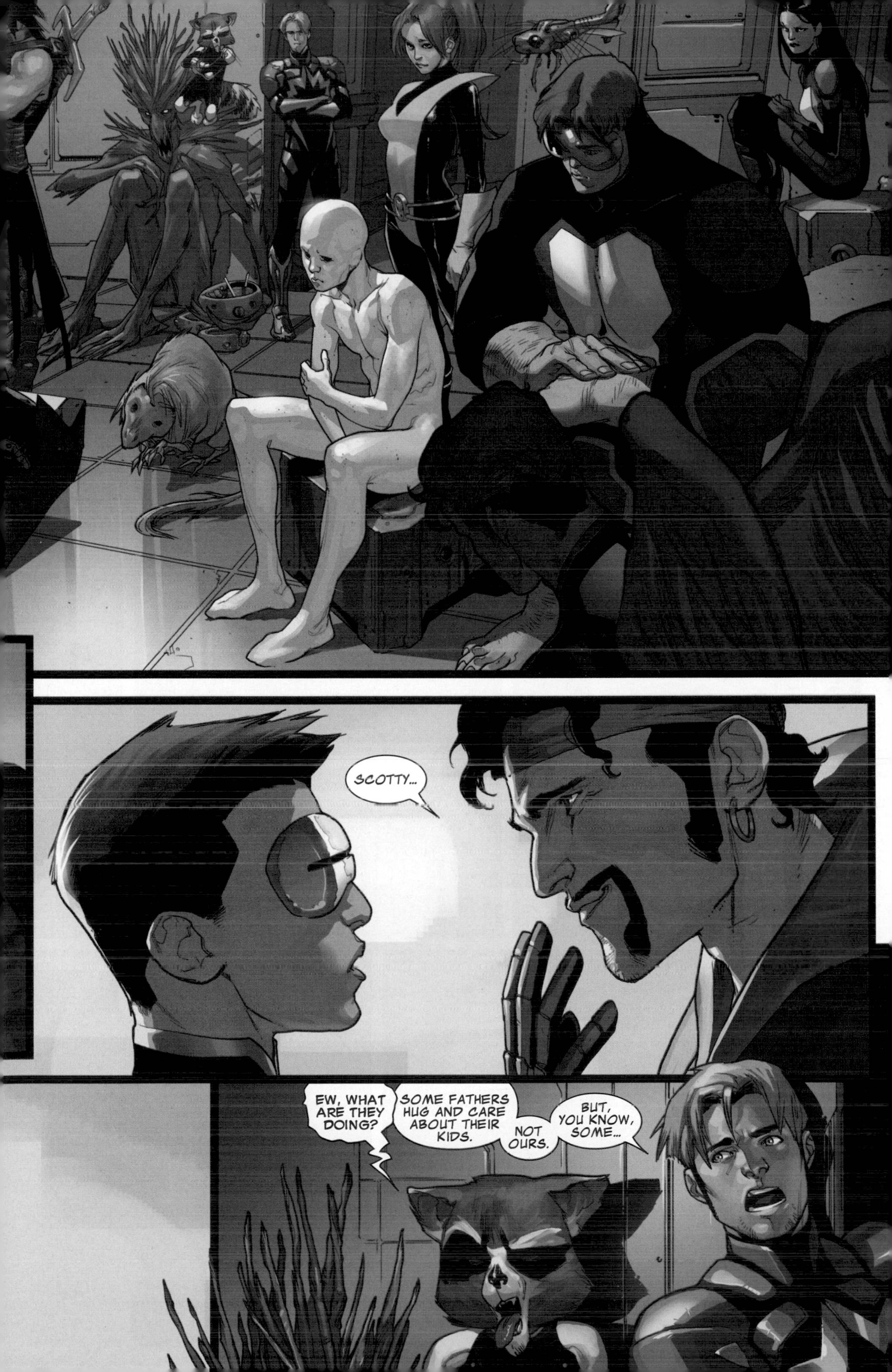
SCOTTY...
EW, WHAT ARE THEY DOING?
SOME FATHERS HUG AND CARE ABOUT THEIR KIDS.
NOT OURS.
BUT, YOU KNOW, SOME...

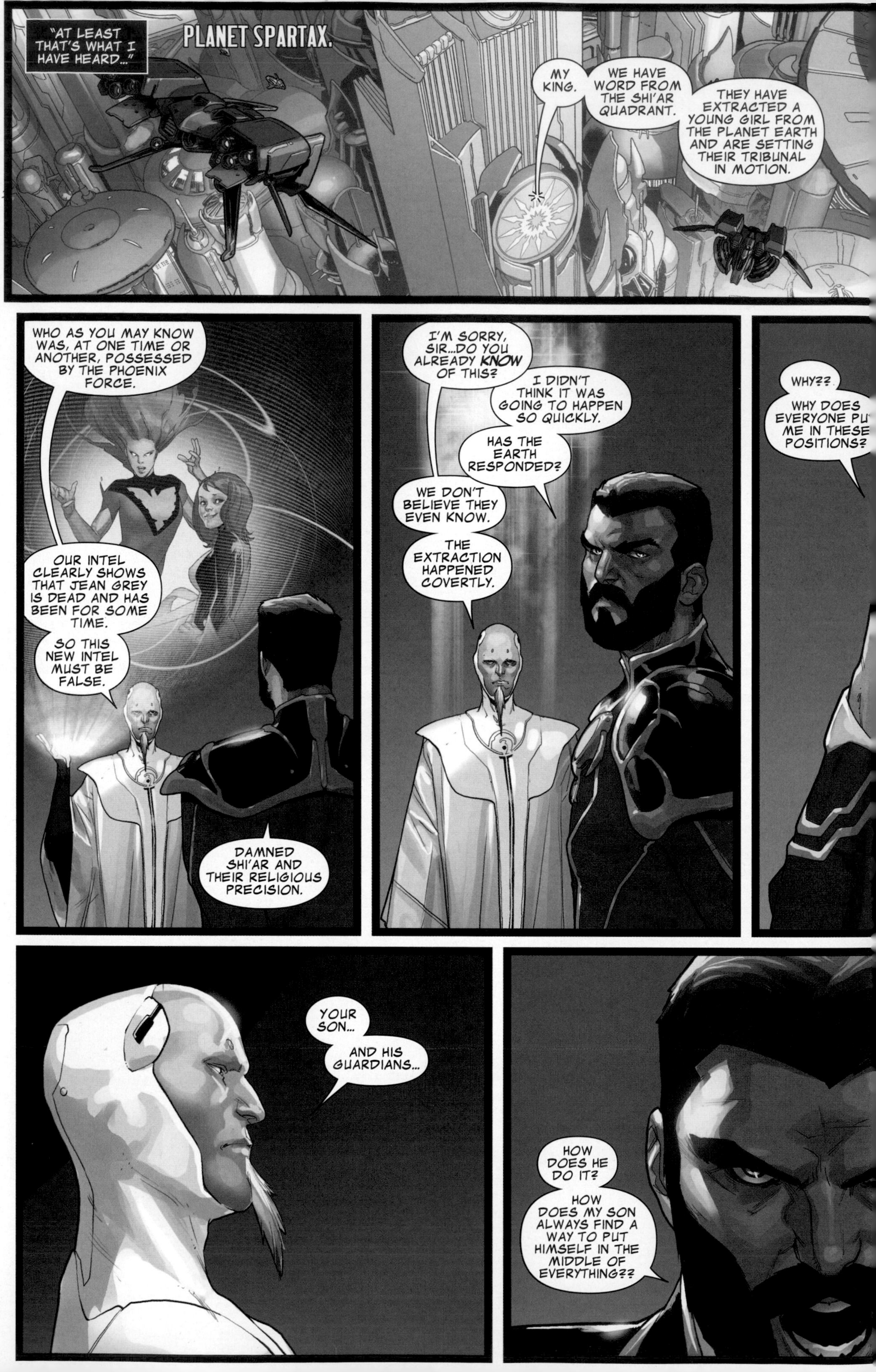
"AT LEAST THAT'S WHAT I HAVE HEARD..."
PLANET SPARTAX.
MY KING.
WE HAVE WORD FROM THE SHI'AR QUADRANT.
THEY HAVE EXTRACTED A YOUNG GIRL FROM THE PLANET EARTH AND ARE SETTING THEIR TRIBUNAL IN MOTION.
WHO AS YOU MAY KNOW WAS, AT ONE TIME OR ANOTHER, POSSESSED BY THE PHOENIX FORCE.
OUR INTEL CLEARLY SHOWS THAT JEAN GREY IS DEAD AND HAS BEEN FOR SOME TIME.
SO THIS NEW INTEL MUST BE FALSE.
DAMNED SHI'AR AND THEIR RELIGIOUS PRECISION.
I'M SORRY, SIR...DO YOU ALREADY *KNOW* OF THIS?
I DIDN'T THINK IT WAS GOING TO HAPPEN SO QUICKLY.
HAS THE EARTH RESPONDED?
WE DON'T BELIEVE THEY EVEN KNOW.
THE EXTRACTION HAPPENED COVERTLY.
WHY??
WHY DOES EVERYONE PU ME IN THESE POSITIONS?
YOUR SON...
AND HIS GUARDIANS...
HOW DOES HE DO IT?
HOW DOES MY SON ALWAYS FIND A WAY TO PUT HIMSELF IN THE MIDDLE OF EVERYTHING??

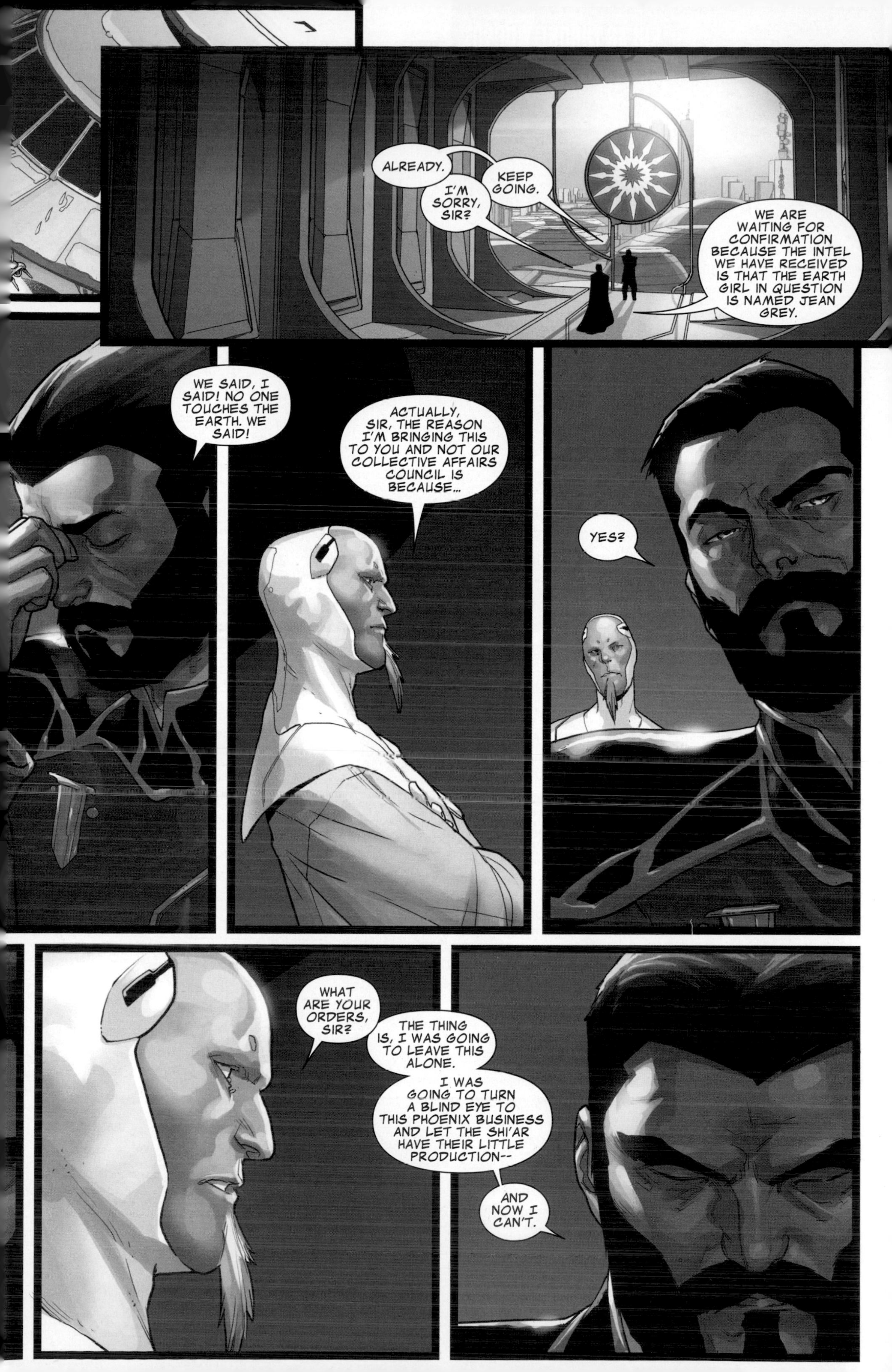

ALREADY.
KEEP GOING.
I'M SORRY, SIR?
WE ARE WAITING FOR CONFIRMATION BECAUSE THE INTEL WE HAVE RECEIVED IS THAT THE EARTH GIRL IN QUESTION IS NAMED JEAN GREY.
WE SAID, I SAID! NO ONE TOUCHES THE EARTH. WE SAID!
ACTUALLY, SIR, THE REASON I'M BRINGING THIS TO YOU AND NOT OUR COLLECTIVE AFFAIRS COUNCIL IS BECAUSE...
YES?
WHAT ARE YOUR ORDERS, SIR?
THE THING IS, I WAS GOING TO LEAVE THIS ALONE.
I WAS GOING TO TURN A BLIND EYE TO THIS PHOENIX BUSINESS AND LET THE SHI'AR HAVE THEIR LITTLE PRODUCTION--
AND NOW I CAN'T.

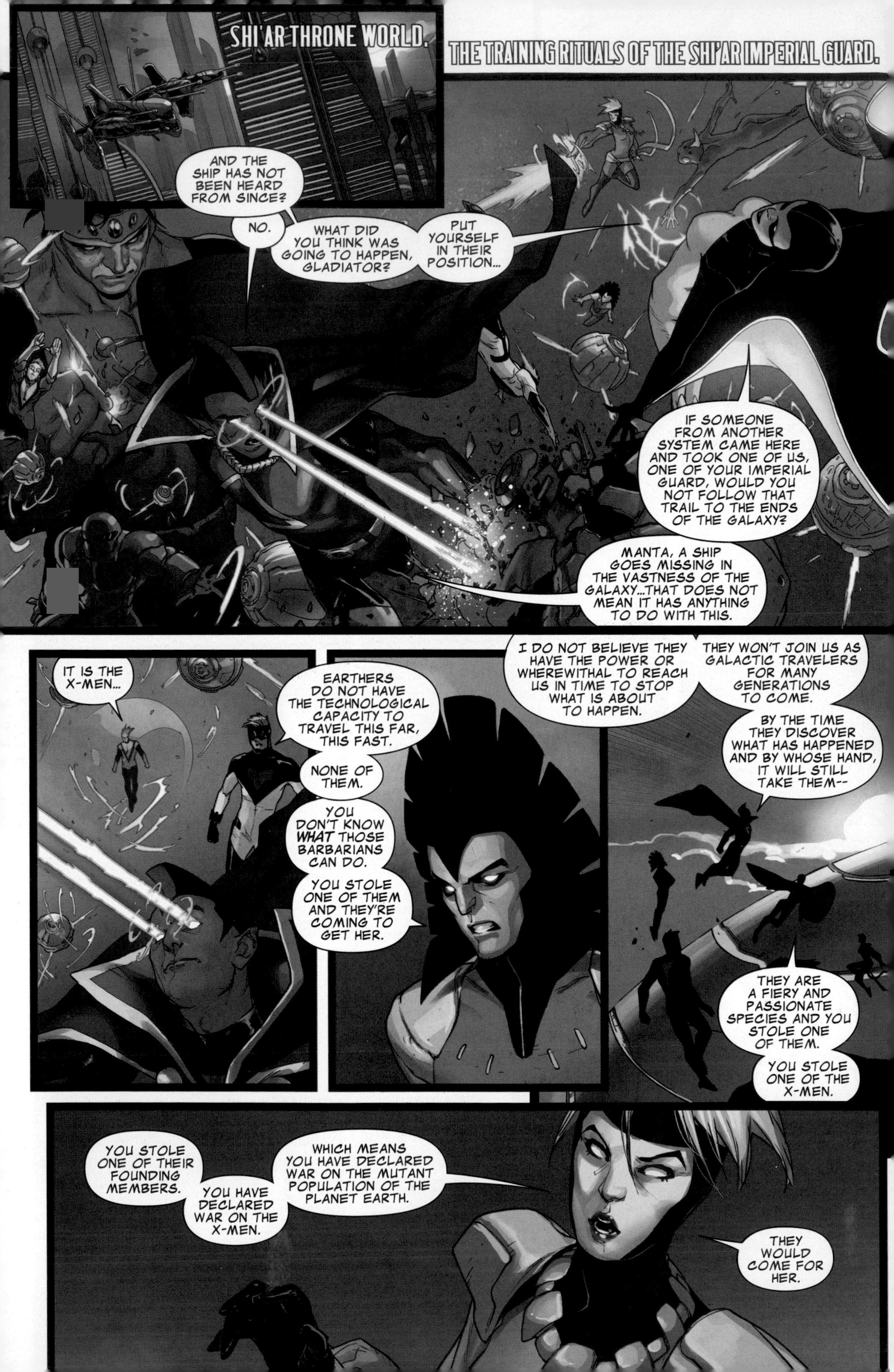
SHI'AR THRONE WORLD.
THE TRAINING RITUALS OF THE SHI'AR IMPERIAL GUARD.
AND THE SHIP HAS NOT BEEN HEARD FROM SINCE?
NO.
WHAT DID YOU THINK WAS GOING TO HAPPEN, GLADIATOR?
PUT YOURSELF IN THEIR POSITION...
IF SOMEONE FROM ANOTHER SYSTEM CAME HERE AND TOOK ONE OF US, ONE OF YOUR IMPERIAL GUARD, WOULD YOU NOT FOLLOW THAT TRAIL TO THE ENDS OF THE GALAXY?
MANTA, A SHIP GOES MISSING IN THE VASTNESS OF THE GALAXY...THAT DOES NOT MEAN IT HAS ANYTHING TO DO WITH THIS.
IT IS THE X-MEN...
EARTHERS DO NOT HAVE THE TECHNOLOGICAL CAPACITY TO TRAVEL THIS FAR, THIS FAST.
NONE OF THEM.
YOU DON'T KNOW WHAT THOSE BARBARIANS CAN DO.
YOU STOLE ONE OF THEM AND THEY'RE COMING TO GET HER.
I DO NOT BELIEVE THEY HAVE THE POWER OR WHEREWITHAL TO REACH US IN TIME TO STOP WHAT IS ABOUT TO HAPPEN.
THEY WON'T JOIN US AS GALACTIC TRAVELERS FOR MANY GENERATIONS TO COME.
BY THE TIME THEY DISCOVER WHAT HAS HAPPENED AND BY WHOSE HAND, IT WILL STILL TAKE THEM--
THEY ARE A FIERY AND PASSIONATE SPECIES AND YOU STOLE ONE OF THEM.
YOU STOLE ONE OF THE X-MEN.
YOU STOLE ONE OF THEIR FOUNDING MEMBERS.
YOU HAVE DECLARED WAR ON THE X-MEN.
WHICH MEANS YOU HAVE DECLARED WAR ON THE MUTANT POPULATION OF THE PLANET EARTH.
THEY WOULD COME FOR HER.

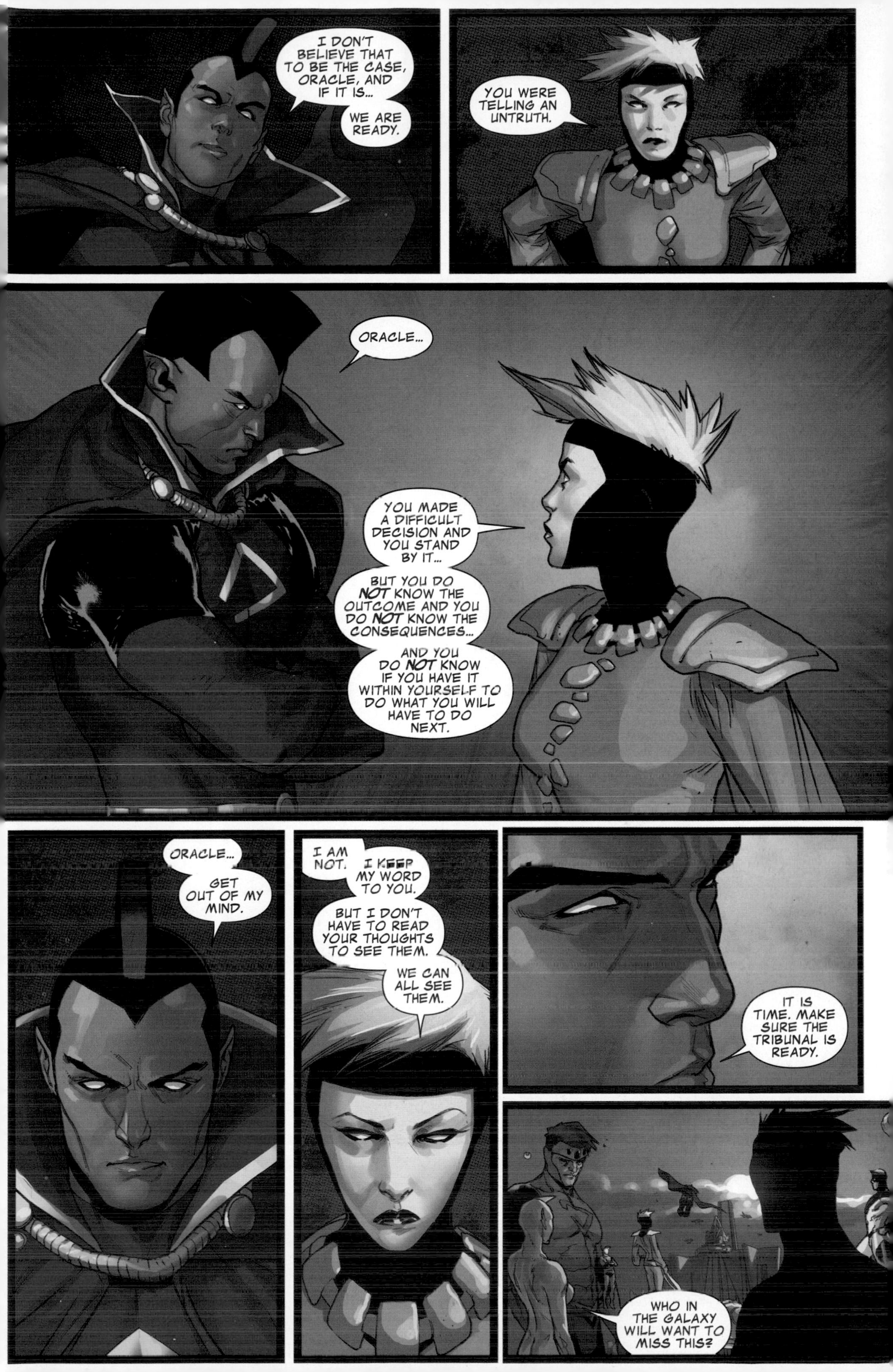
I DON'T BELIEVE THAT TO BE THE CASE, ORACLE, AND IF IT IS...
WE ARE READY.
YOU WERE TELLING AN UNTRUTH.
ORACLE...
YOU MADE A DIFFICULT DECISION AND YOU STAND BY IT...
BUT YOU DO NOT KNOW THE OUTCOME AND YOU DO NOT KNOW THE CONSEQUENCES...
AND YOU DO NOT KNOW IF YOU HAVE IT WITHIN YOURSELF TO DO WHAT YOU WILL HAVE TO DO NEXT.
ORACLE...
GET OUT OF MY MIND.
I AM NOT.
I KEEP MY WORD TO YOU.
BUT I DON'T HAVE TO READ YOUR THOUGHTS TO SEE THEM.
WE CAN ALL SEE THEM.
IT IS TIME. MAKE SURE THE TRIBUNAL IS READY.
WHO IN THE GALAXY WILL WANT TO MISS THIS?

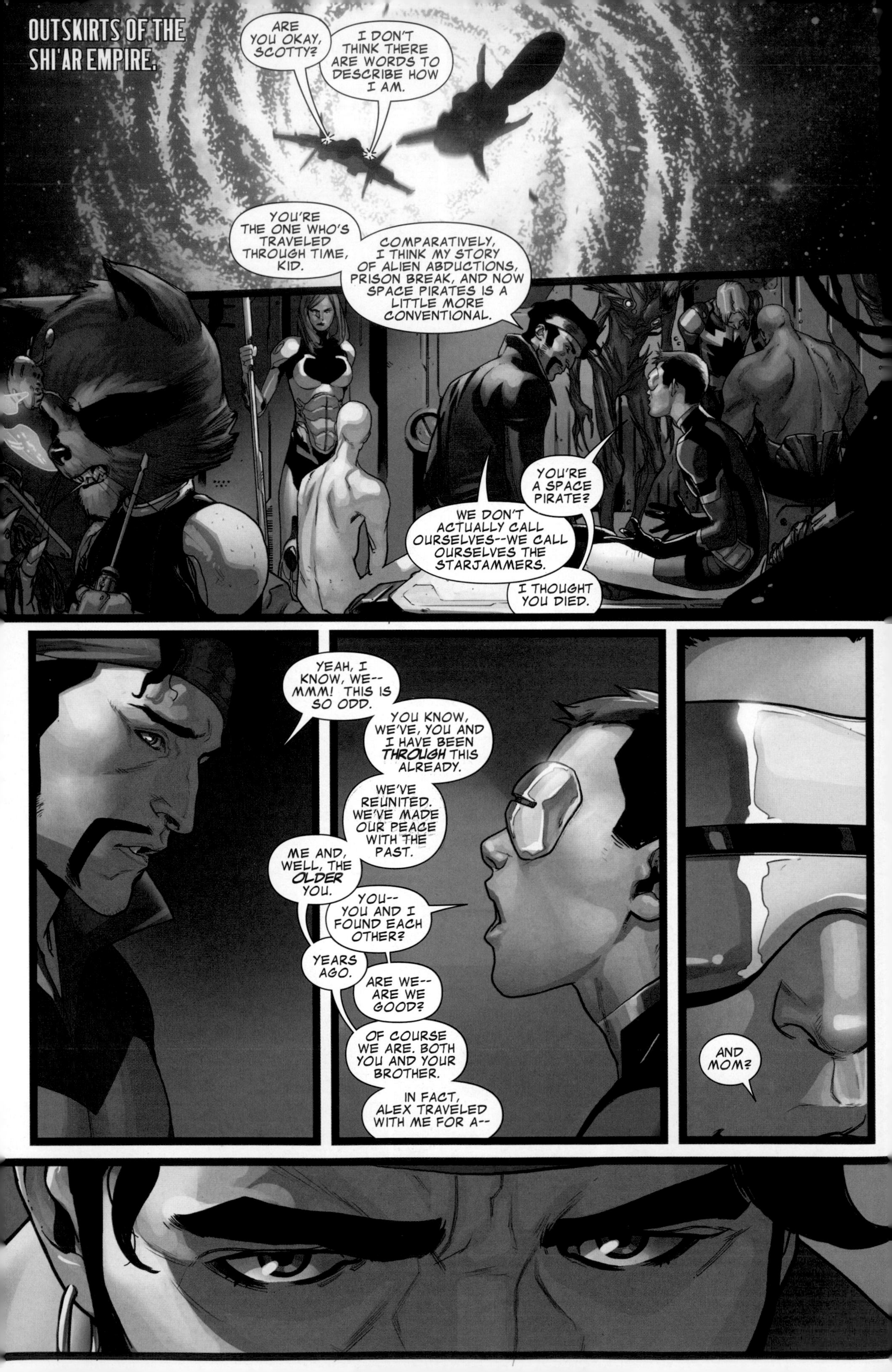
OUTSKIRTS OF THE SHI'AR EMPIRE.
ARE YOU OKAY, SCOTTY?
I DON'T THINK THERE ARE WORDS TO DESCRIBE HOW I AM.
YOU'RE THE ONE WHO'S TRAVELED THROUGH TIME, KID.
COMPARATIVELY, I THINK MY STORY OF ALIEN ABDUCTIONS, PRISON BREAK, AND NOW SPACE PIRATES IS A LITTLE MORE CONVENTIONAL.
YOU'RE A SPACE PIRATE?
WE DON'T ACTUALLY CALL OURSELVES--WE CALL OURSELVES THE STARJAMMERS.
I THOUGHT YOU DIED.
YEAH, I KNOW, WE-- MMM! THIS IS SO ODD.
YOU KNOW, WE'VE, YOU AND I HAVE BEEN THROUGH THIS ALREADY.
WE'VE REUNITED. WE'VE MADE OUR PEACE WITH THE PAST.
ME AND, WELL, THE OLDER YOU.
YOU-- YOU AND I FOUND EACH OTHER?
YEARS AGO.
ARE WE-- ARE WE GOOD?
OF COURSE WE ARE. BOTH YOU AND YOUR BROTHER.
IN FACT, ALEX TRAVELED WITH ME FOR A--
AND MOM?

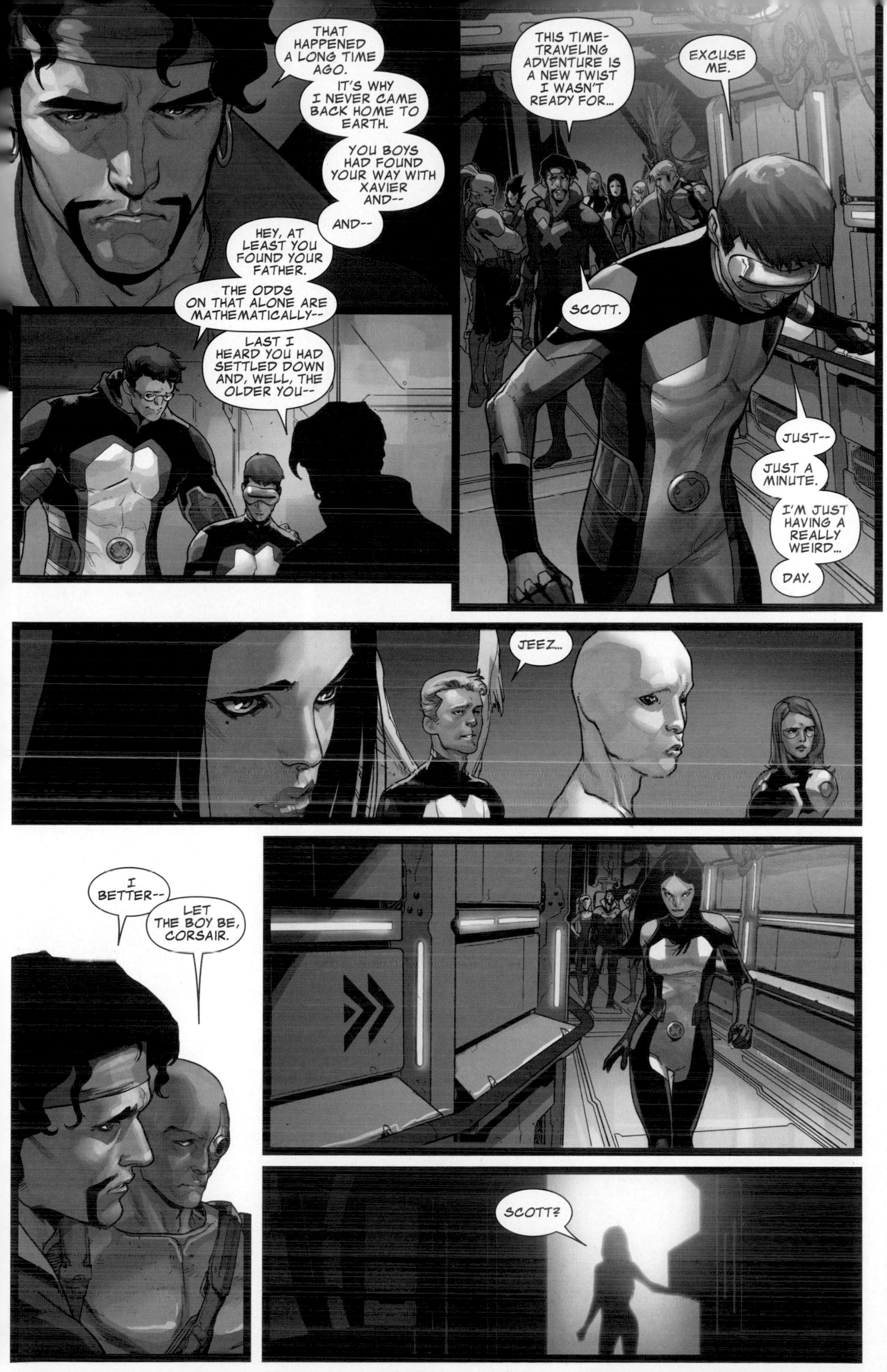
THAT HAPPENED A LONG TIME AGO.
IT'S WHY I NEVER CAME BACK HOME TO EARTH.
YOU BOYS HAD FOUND YOUR WAY WITH XAVIER AND--
AND--
HEY, AT LEAST YOU FOUND YOUR FATHER.
THE ODDS ON THAT ALONE ARE MATHEMATICALLY--
LAST I HEARD YOU HAD SETTLED DOWN AND, WELL, THE OLDER YOU--
THIS TIME-TRAVELING ADVENTURE IS A NEW TWIST I WASN'T READY FOR...
EXCUSE ME.
SCOTT.
JUST--
JUST A MINUTE.
I'M JUST HAVING A REALLY WEIRD...
DAY.
JEEZ...
I BETTER--
LET THE BOY BE, CORSAIR.
SCOTT?

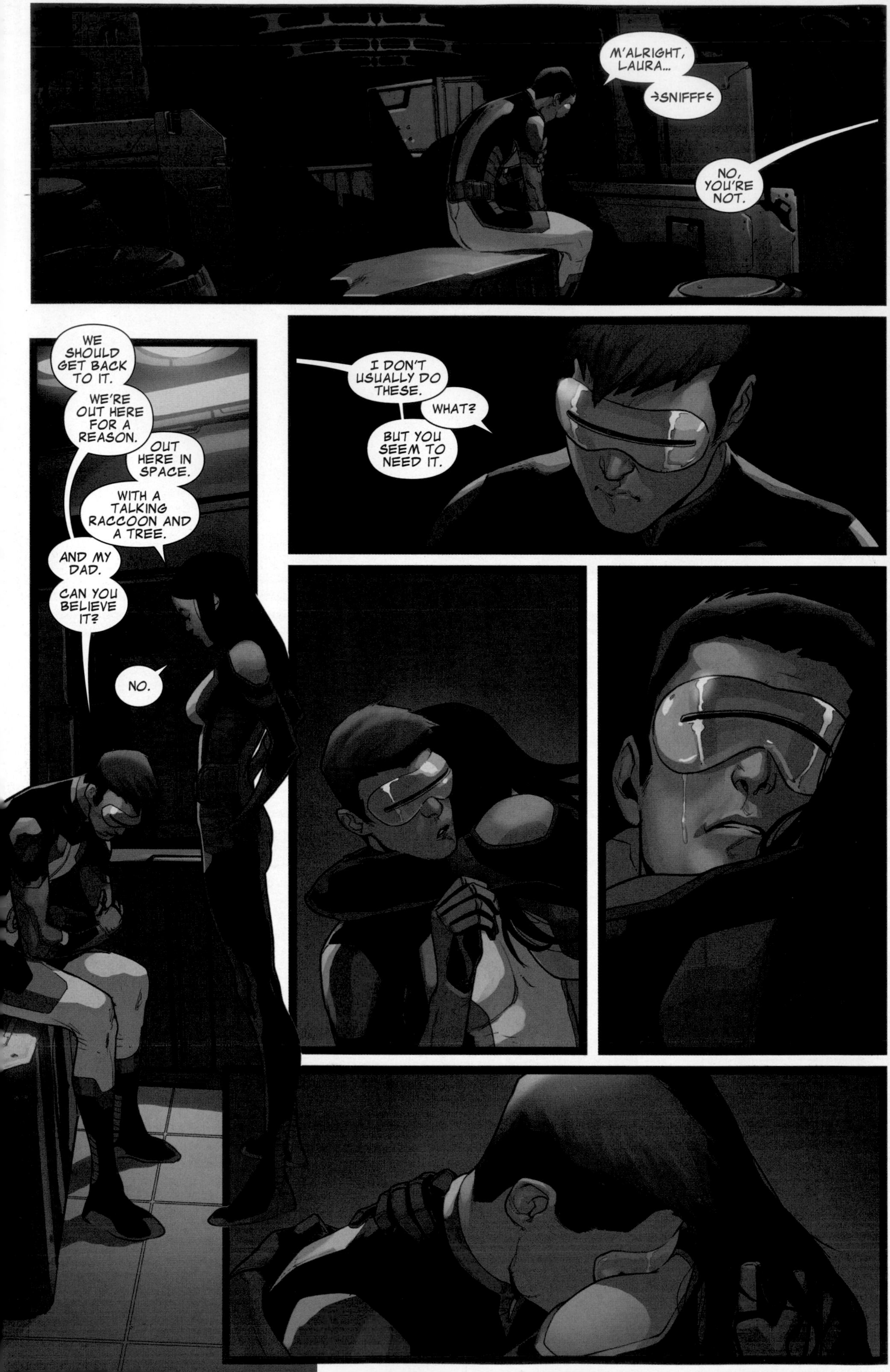
M'ALRIGHT, LAURA...
≯SNIFFF≮
NO, YOU'RE NOT.
WE SHOULD GET BACK TO IT.
WE'RE OUT HERE FOR A REASON.
OUT HERE IN SPACE.
WITH A TALKING RACCOON AND A TREE.
AND MY DAD.
CAN YOU BELIEVE IT?
NO.
I DON'T USUALLY DO THESE.
WHAT?
BUT YOU SEEM TO NEED IT.

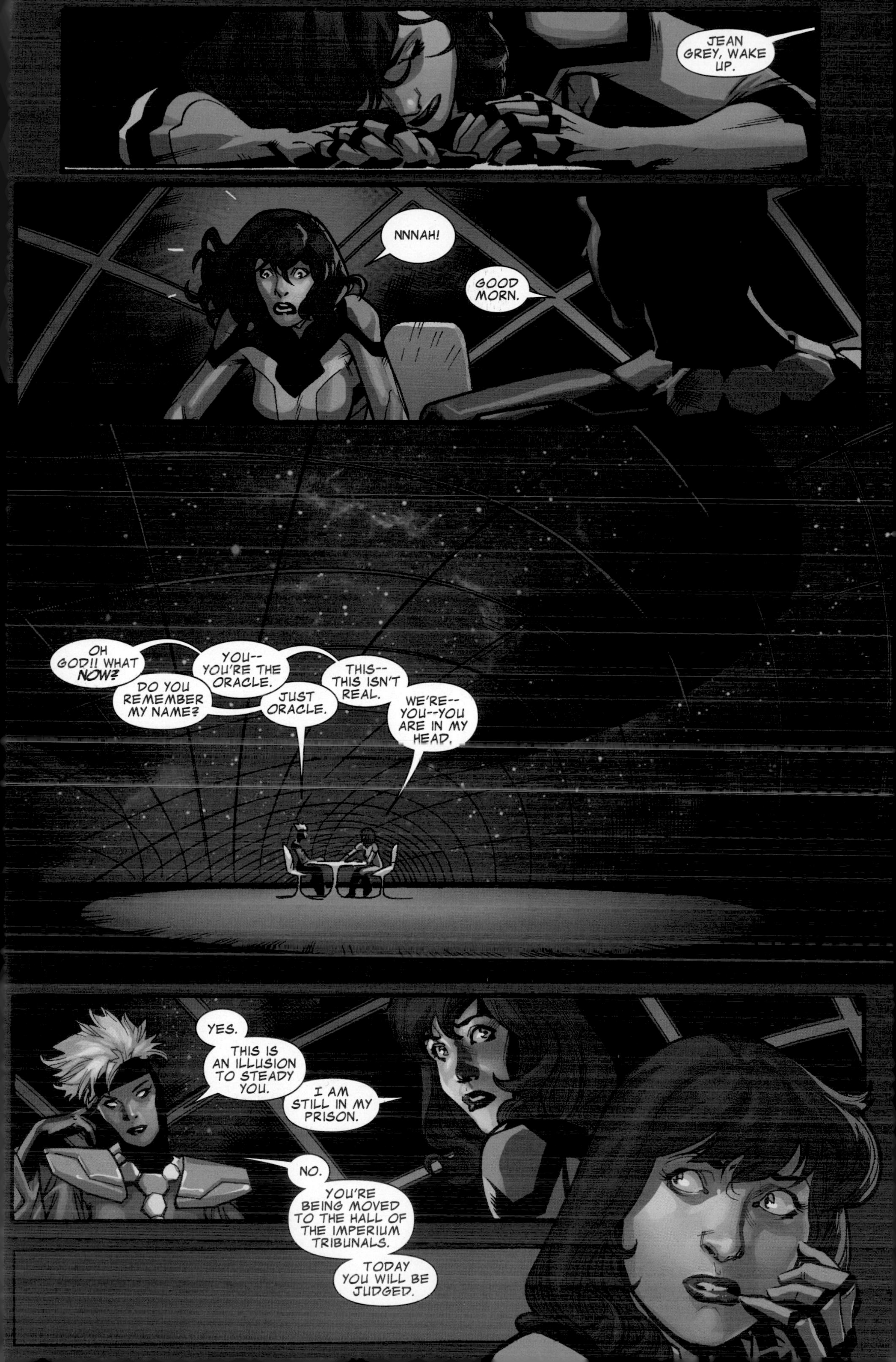
JEAN GREY, WAKE UP.
NNNAH!
GOOD MORN.
OH GOD!! WHAT NOW?
DO YOU REMEMBER MY NAME?
YOU-- YOU'RE THE ORACLE.
JUST ORACLE.
THIS-- THIS ISN'T REAL.
WE'RE-- YOU--YOU ARE IN MY HEAD.
YES.
THIS IS AN ILLUSION TO STEADY YOU.
I AM STILL IN MY PRISON.
NO.
YOU'RE BEING MOVED TO THE HALL OF THE IMPERIUM TRIBUNALS.
TODAY YOU WILL BE JUDGED.

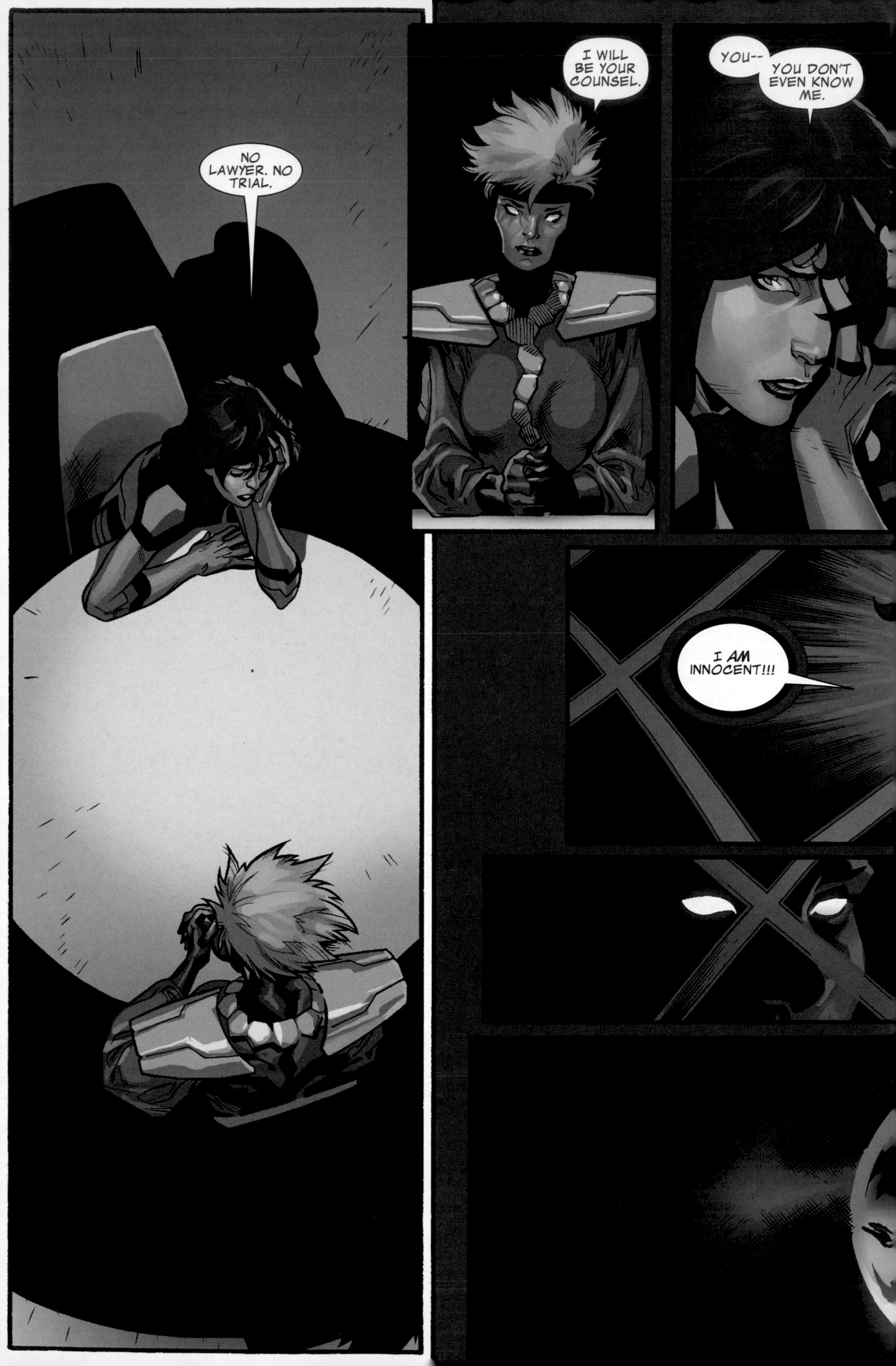
NO LAWYER. NO TRIAL.
I WILL BE YOUR COUNSEL.
YOU--
YOU DON'T EVEN KNOW ME.
I AM INNOCENT!!!

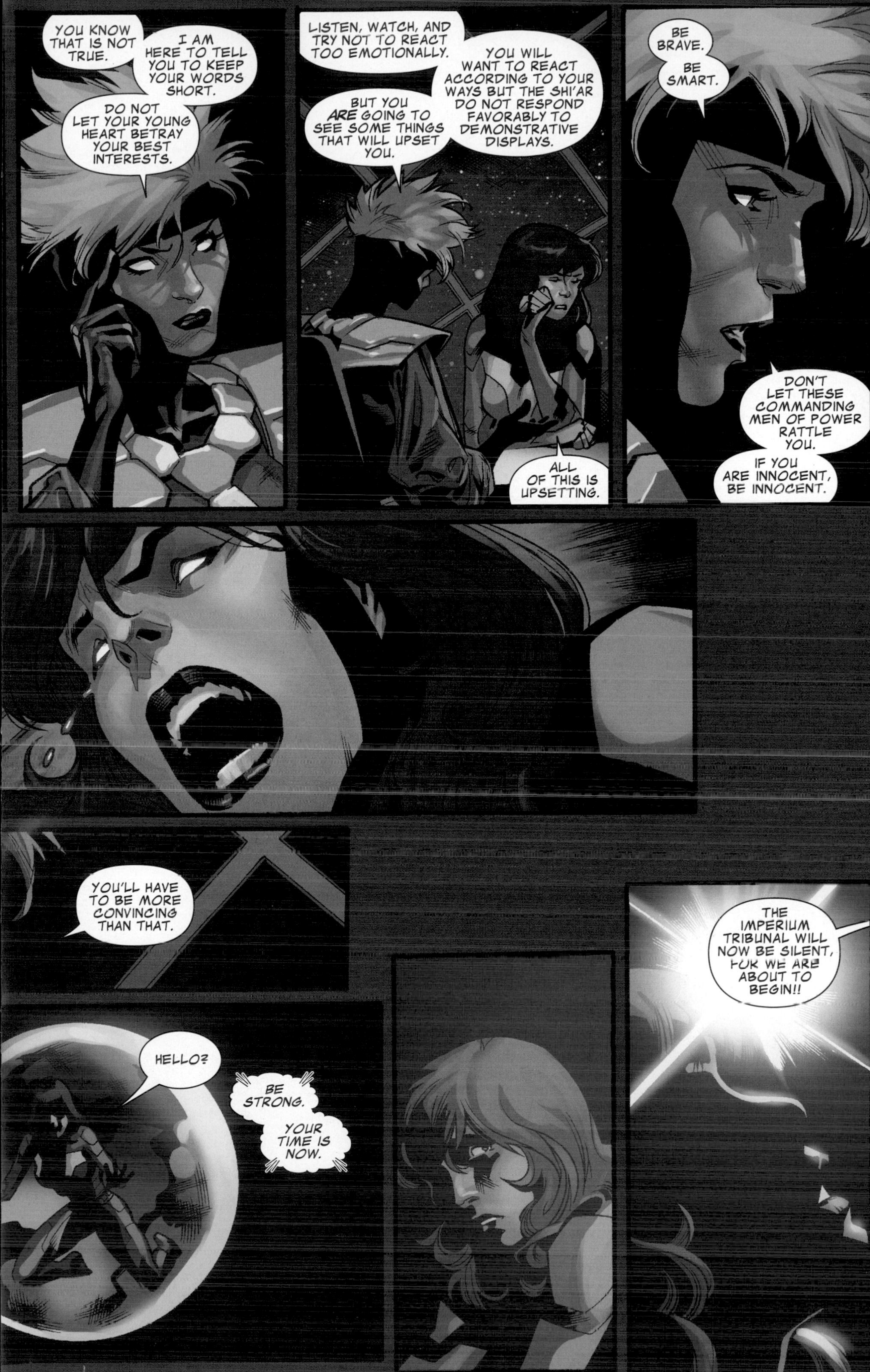
YOU KNOW THAT IS NOT TRUE.
I AM HERE TO TELL YOU TO KEEP YOUR WORDS SHORT.
DO NOT LET YOUR YOUNG HEART BETRAY YOUR BEST INTERESTS.
LISTEN, WATCH, AND TRY NOT TO REACT TOO EMOTIONALLY.
BUT YOU *ARE* GOING TO SEE SOME THINGS THAT WILL UPSET YOU.
YOU WILL WANT TO REACT ACCORDING TO YOUR WAYS BUT THE SHI'AR DO NOT RESPOND FAVORABLY TO DEMONSTRATIVE DISPLAYS.
ALL OF THIS IS UPSETTING.
BE BRAVE.
BE SMART.
DON'T LET THESE COMMANDING MEN OF POWER RATTLE YOU.
IF YOU ARE INNOCENT, BE INNOCENT.
YOU'LL HAVE TO BE MORE CONVINCING THAN THAT.
HELLO?
BE STRONG.
YOUR TIME IS NOW.
THE IMPERIUM TRIBUNAL WILL NOW BE SILENT, FOR WE ARE ABOUT TO BEGIN!!

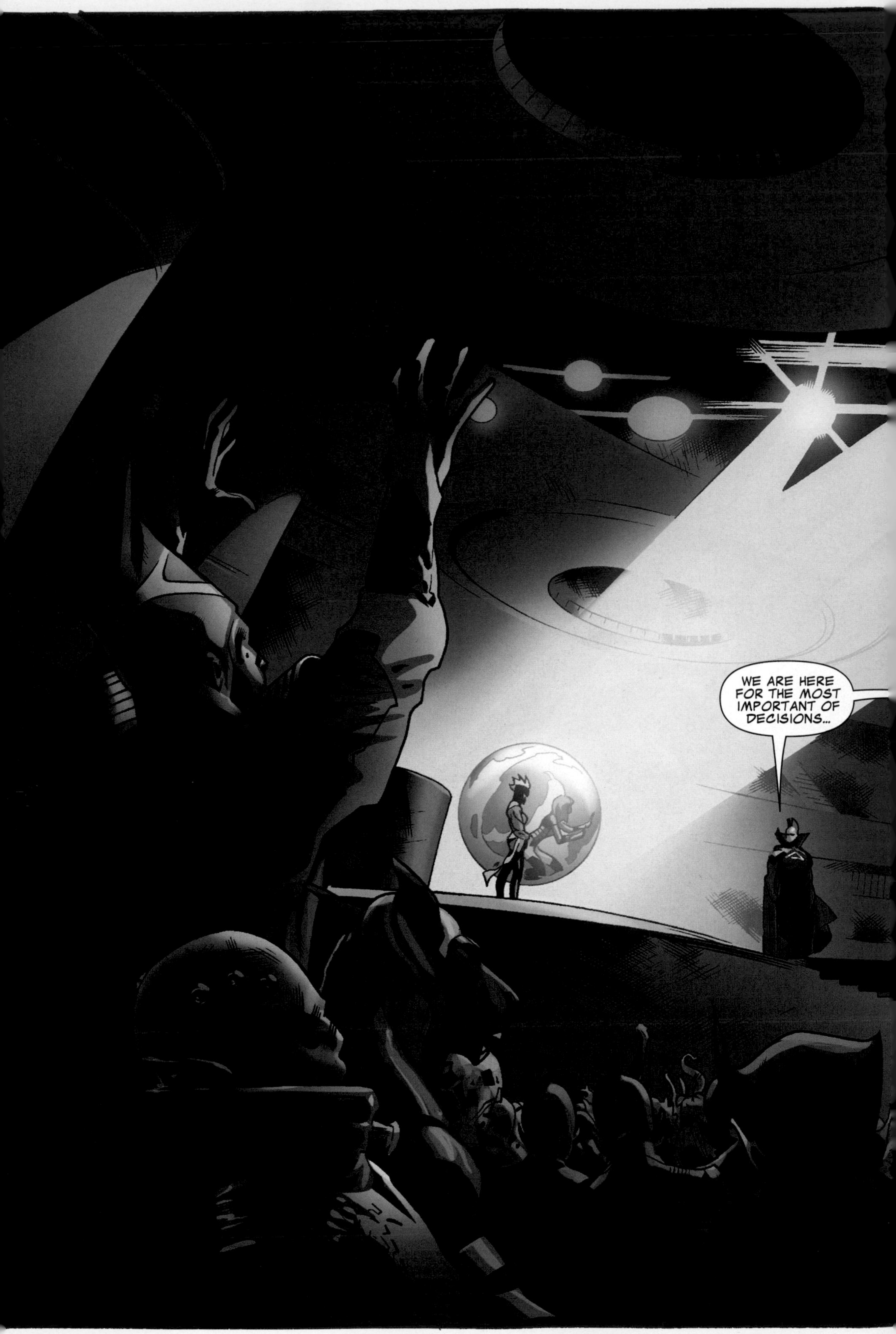
WE ARE HERE FOR THE MOST IMPORTANT OF DECISIONS...

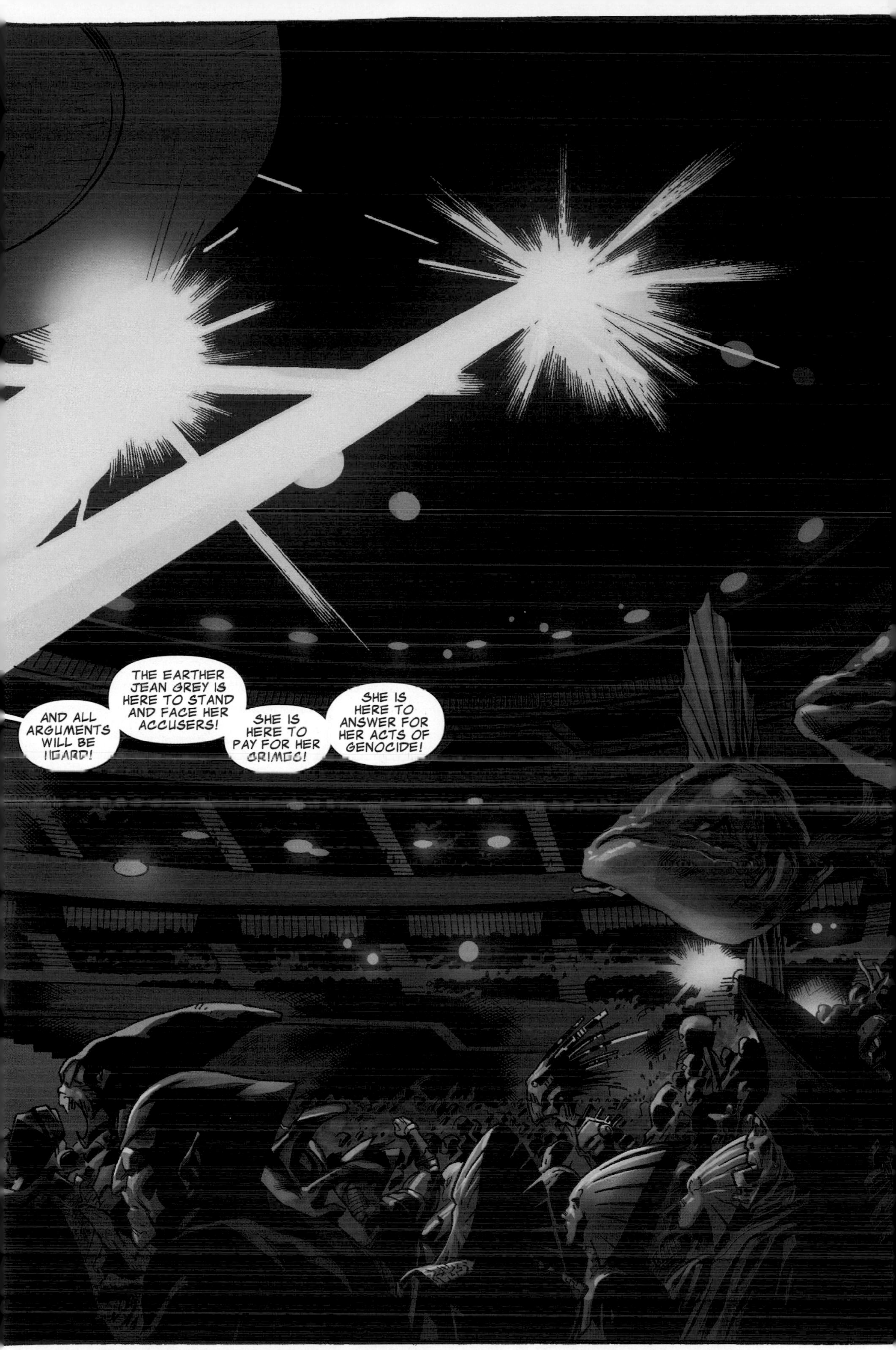
THE EARTHER JEAN GREY IS HERE TO STAND AND FACE HER ACCUSERS!
AND ALL ARGUMENTS WILL BE HEARD!
SHE IS HERE TO PAY FOR HER CRIMES!
SHE IS HERE TO ANSWER FOR HER ACTS OF GENOCIDE!

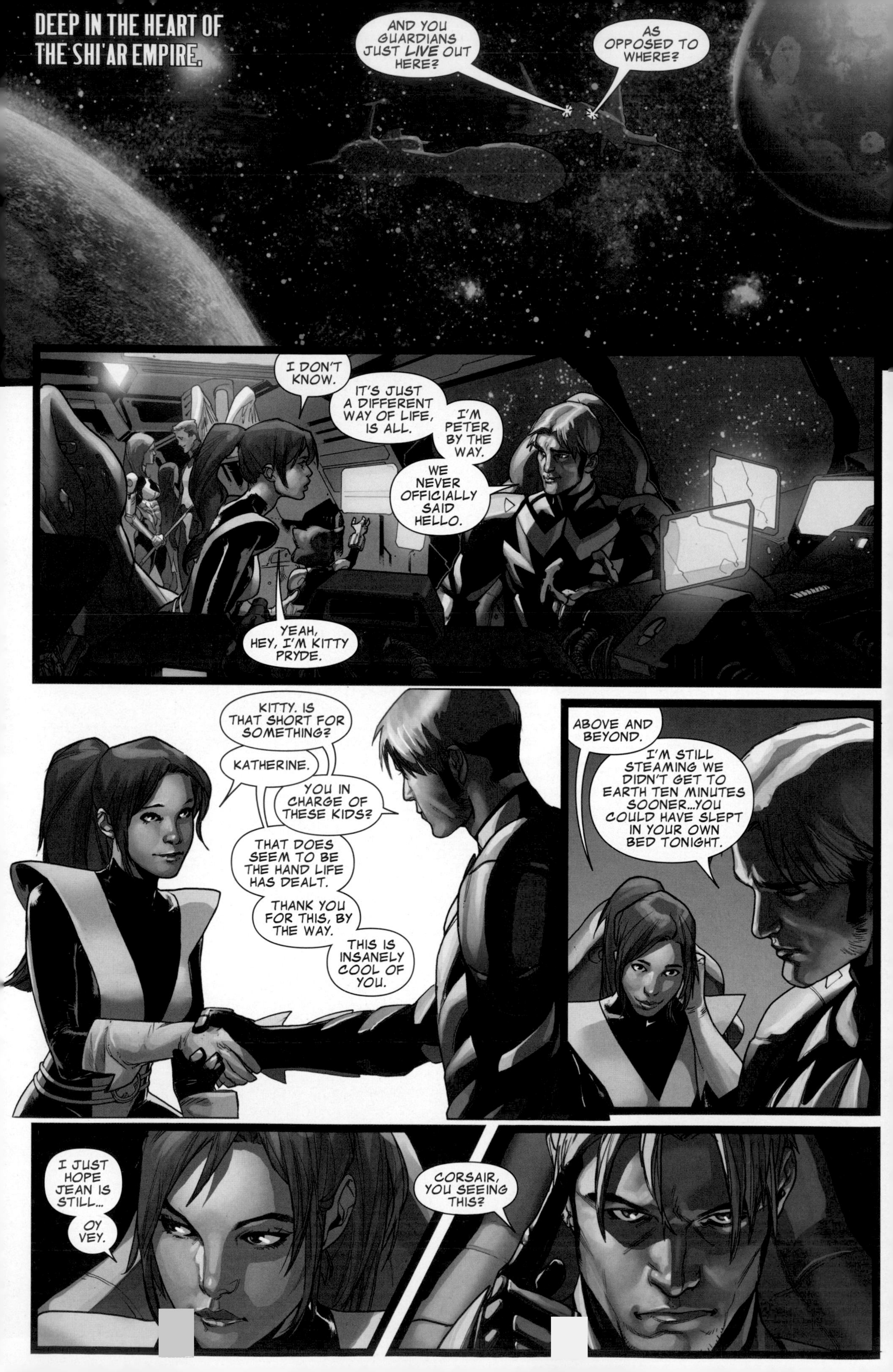
DEEP IN THE HEART OF THE SHI'AR EMPIRE.
AND YOU GUARDIANS JUST LIVE OUT HERE?
AS OPPOSED TO WHERE?
I DON'T KNOW.
IT'S JUST A DIFFERENT WAY OF LIFE, IS ALL.
I'M PETER, BY THE WAY.
WE NEVER OFFICIALLY SAID HELLO.
YEAH, HEY, I'M KITTY PRYDE.
KITTY. IS THAT SHORT FOR SOMETHING?
KATHERINE.
YOU IN CHARGE OF THESE KIDS?
THAT DOES SEEM TO BE THE HAND LIFE HAS DEALT.
THANK YOU FOR THIS, BY THE WAY.
THIS IS INSANELY COOL OF YOU.
ABOVE AND BEYOND.
I'M STILL STEAMING WE DIDN'T GET TO EARTH TEN MINUTES SOONER...YOU COULD HAVE SLEPT IN YOUR OWN BED TONIGHT.
I JUST HOPE JEAN IS STILL...
OY VEY.
CORSAIR, YOU SEEING THIS?

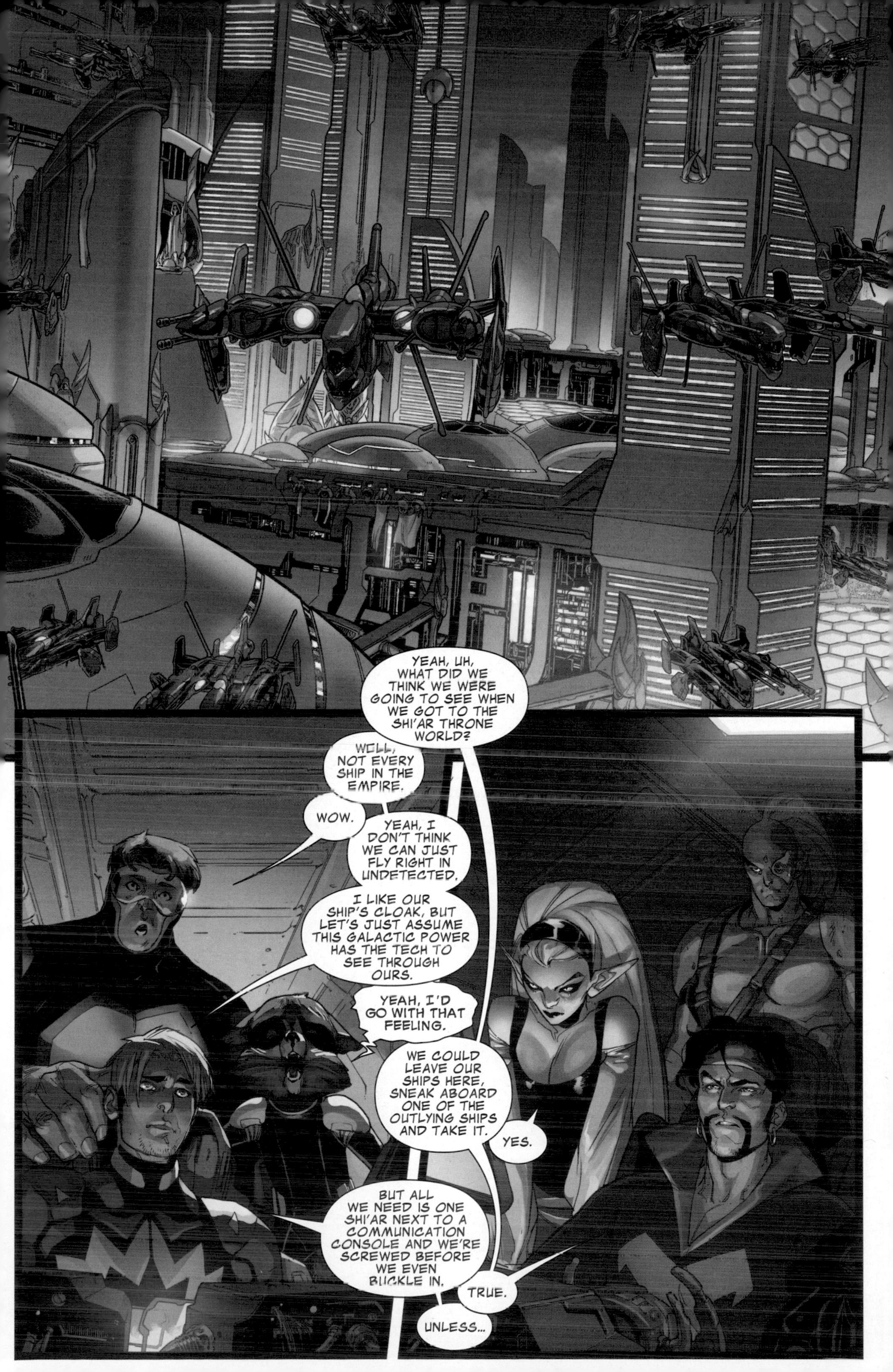

YEAH, UH, WHAT DID WE THINK WE WERE GOING TO SEE WHEN WE GOT TO THE SHI'AR THRONE WORLD?
WELL, NOT EVERY SHIP IN THE EMPIRE.
WOW.
YEAH, I DON'T THINK WE CAN JUST FLY RIGHT IN UNDETECTED.
I LIKE OUR SHIP'S CLOAK, BUT LET'S JUST ASSUME THIS GALACTIC POWER HAS THE TECH TO SEE THROUGH OURS.
YEAH, I'D GO WITH THAT FEELING.
WE COULD LEAVE OUR SHIPS HERE, SNEAK ABOARD ONE OF THE OUTLYING SHIPS AND TAKE IT.
YES.
BUT ALL WE NEED IS ONE SHI'AR NEXT TO A COMMUNICATION CONSOLE AND WE'RE SCREWED BEFORE WE EVEN BUCKLE IN.
TRUE.
UNLESS...

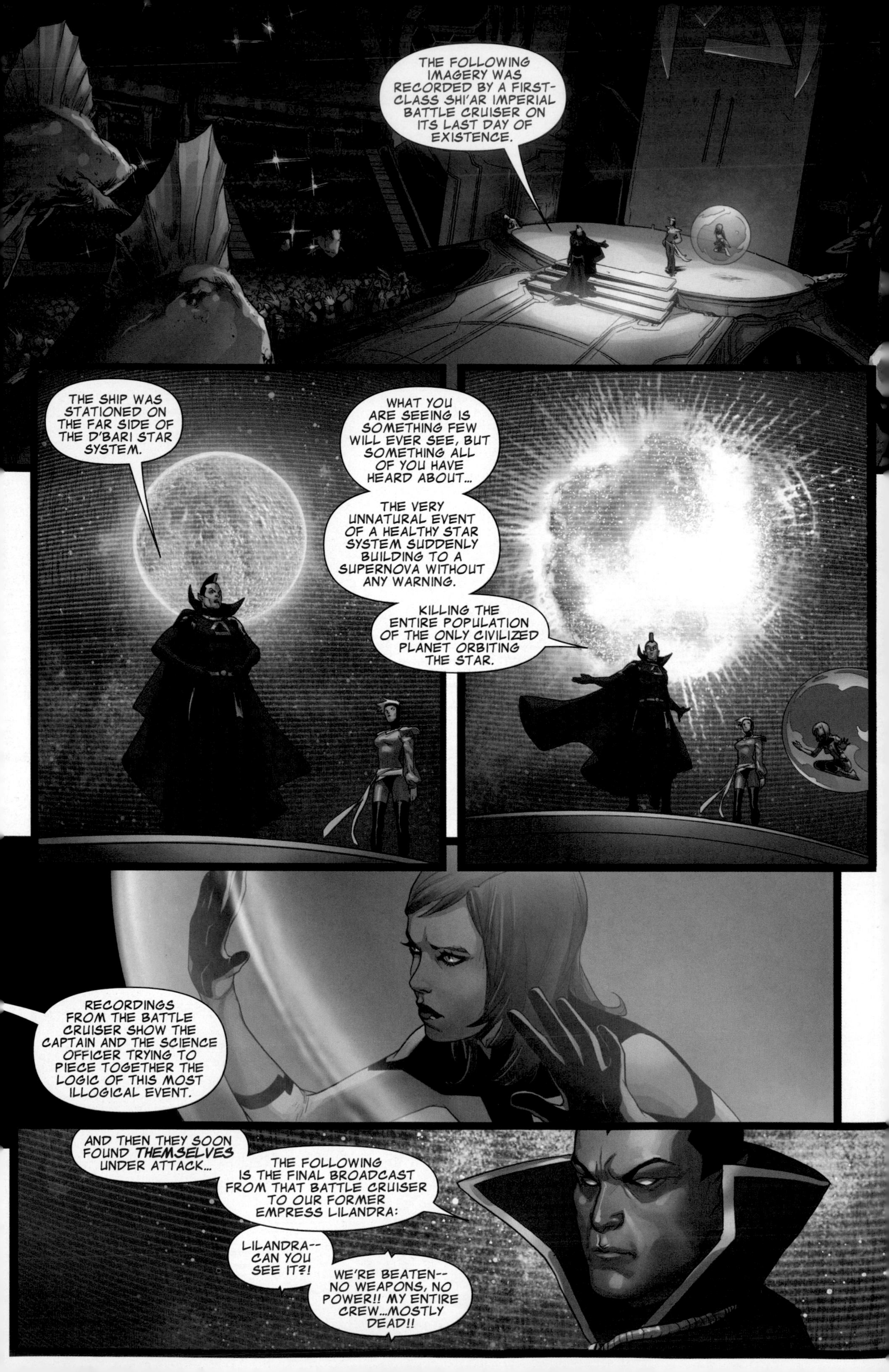
THE FOLLOWING IMAGERY WAS RECORDED BY A FIRST-CLASS SHI'AR IMPERIAL BATTLE CRUISER ON ITS LAST DAY OF EXISTENCE.
THE SHIP WAS STATIONED ON THE FAR SIDE OF THE D'BARI STAR SYSTEM.
WHAT YOU ARE SEEING IS SOMETHING FEW WILL EVER SEE, BUT SOMETHING ALL OF YOU HAVE HEARD ABOUT...
THE VERY UNNATURAL EVENT OF A HEALTHY STAR SYSTEM SUDDENLY BUILDING TO A SUPERNOVA WITHOUT ANY WARNING.
KILLING THE ENTIRE POPULATION OF THE ONLY CIVILIZED PLANET ORBITING THE STAR.
RECORDINGS FROM THE BATTLE CRUISER SHOW THE CAPTAIN AND THE SCIENCE OFFICER TRYING TO PIECE TOGETHER THE LOGIC OF THIS MOST ILLOGICAL EVENT.
AND THEN THEY SOON FOUND THEMSELVES UNDER ATTACK...
THE FOLLOWING IS THE FINAL BROADCAST FROM THAT BATTLE CRUISER TO OUR FORMER EMPRESS LILANDRA:
LILANDRA-- CAN YOU SEE IT?!
WE'RE BEATEN-- NO WEAPONS, NO POWER!! MY ENTIRE CREW...MOSTLY DEAD!!

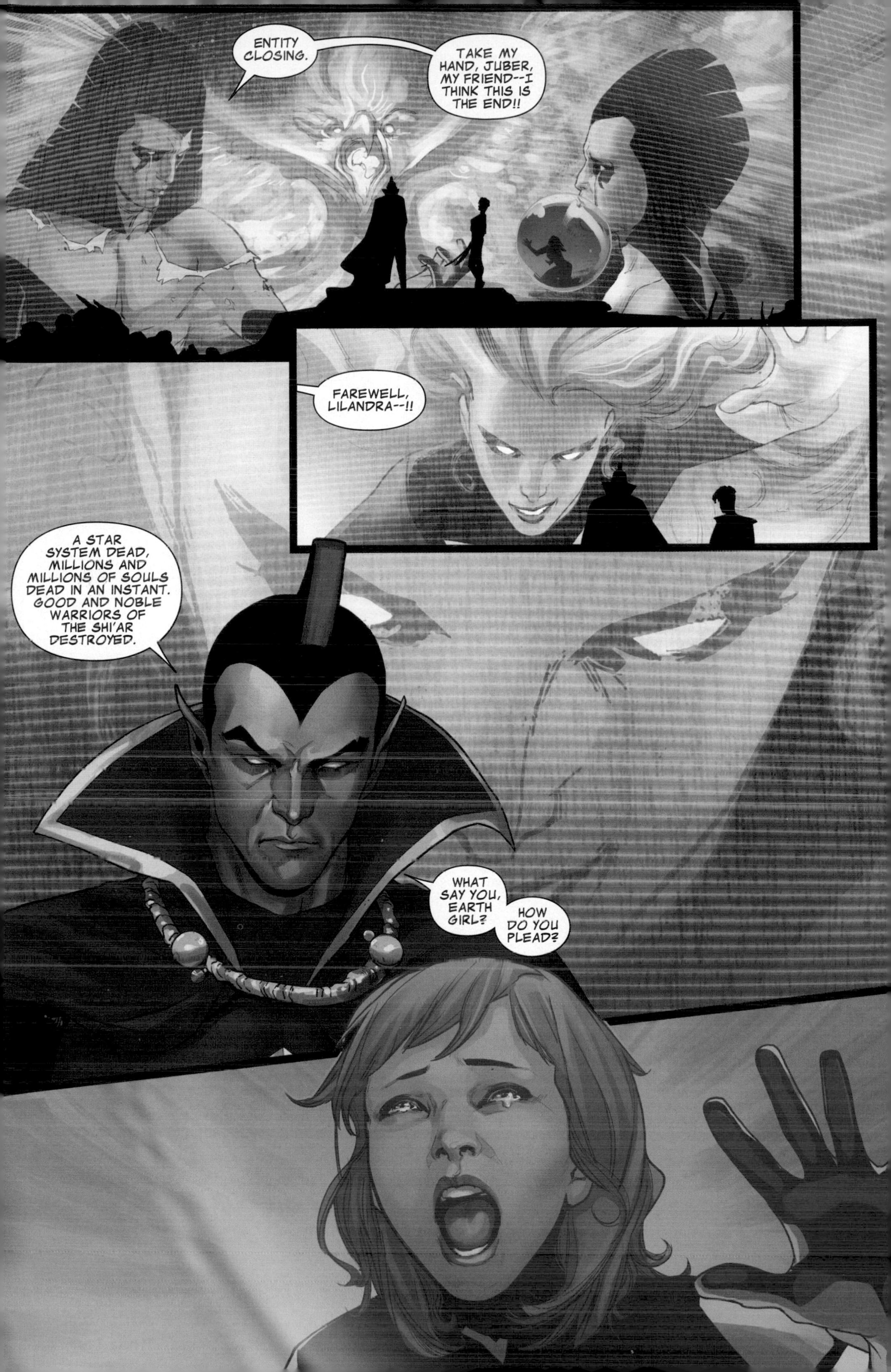
ENTITY CLOSING.
TAKE MY HAND, JUBER, MY FRIEND--I THINK THIS IS THE END!!
FAREWELL, LILANDRA--!!
A STAR SYSTEM DEAD, MILLIONS AND MILLIONS OF SOULS DEAD IN AN INSTANT. GOOD AND NOBLE WARRIORS OF THE SHI'AR DESTROYED.
WHAT SAY YOU, EARTH GIRL?
HOW DO YOU PLEAD?

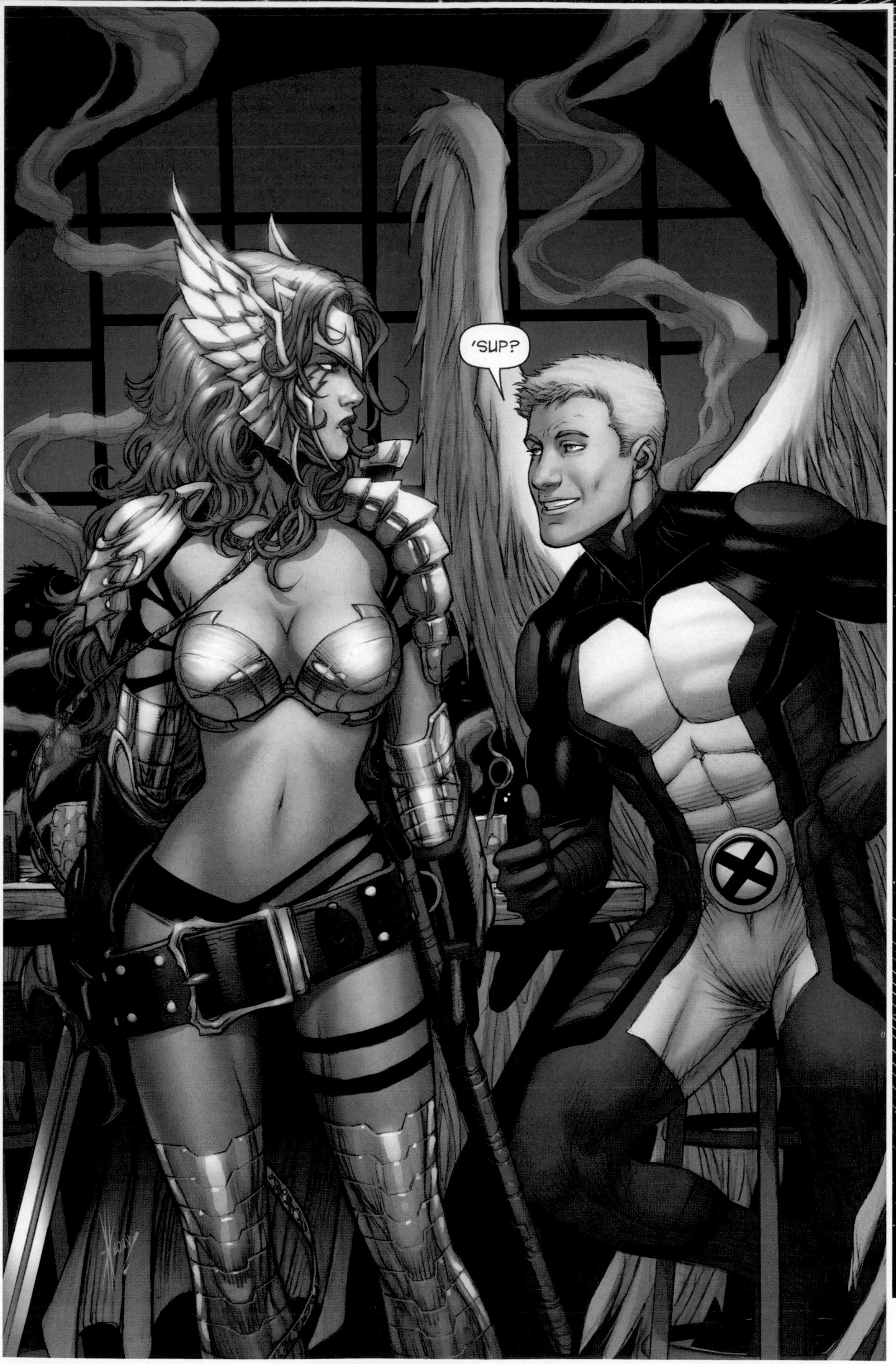
'SUP?

***GUARDIANS OF THE GALAXY* #12 VARIANT**
BY DALE KEOWN & JASON KEITH

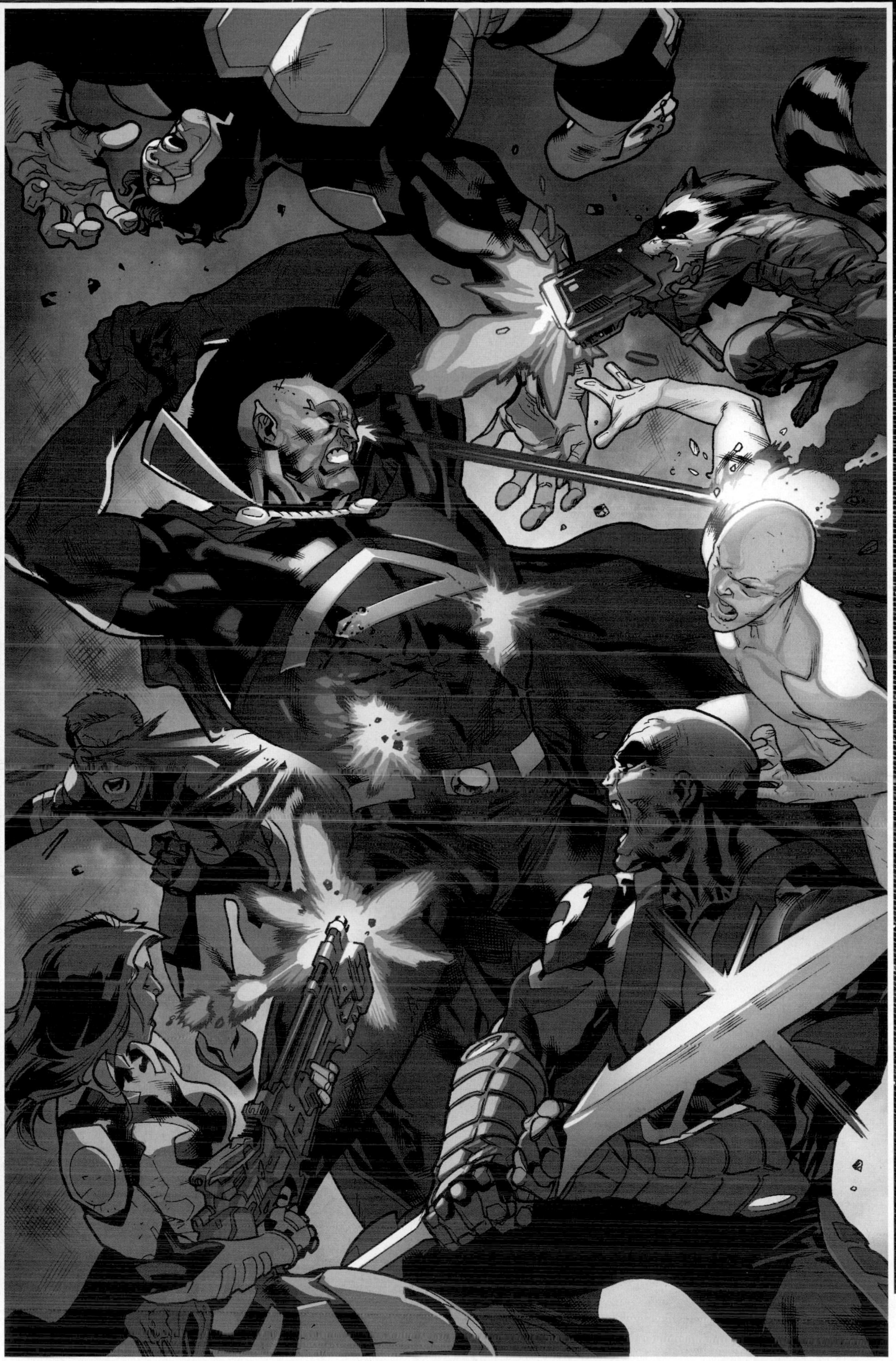

ALL-NEW X-MEN 24

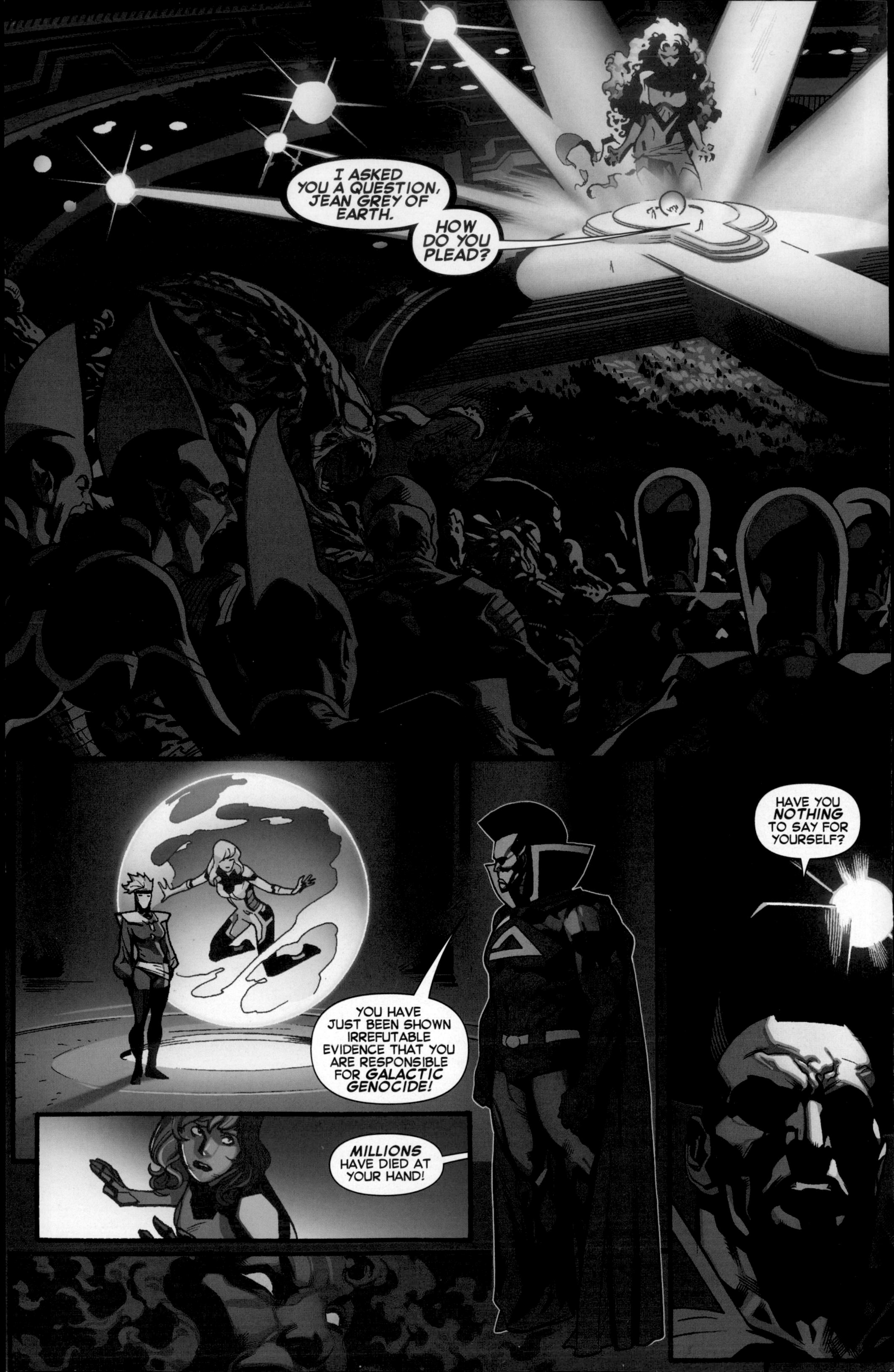
I ASKED YOU A QUESTION, JEAN GREY OF EARTH.
HOW DO YOU PLEAD?
YOU HAVE JUST BEEN SHOWN IRREFUTABLE EVIDENCE THAT YOU ARE RESPONSIBLE FOR GALACTIC GENOCIDE!
MILLIONS HAVE DIED AT YOUR HAND!
HAVE YOU NOTHING TO SAY FOR YOURSELF?

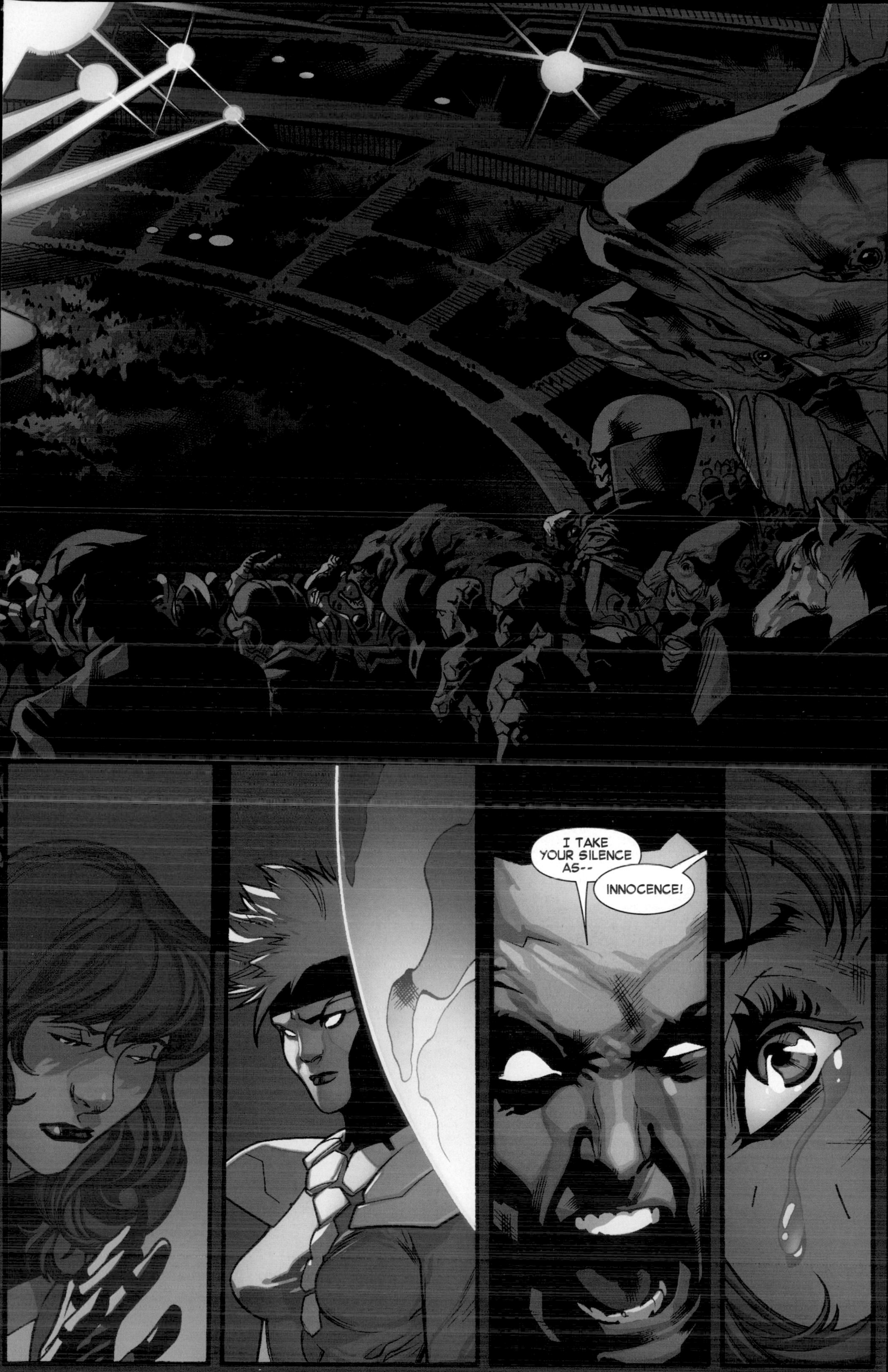
I TAKE YOUR SILENCE AS--
INNOCENCE!

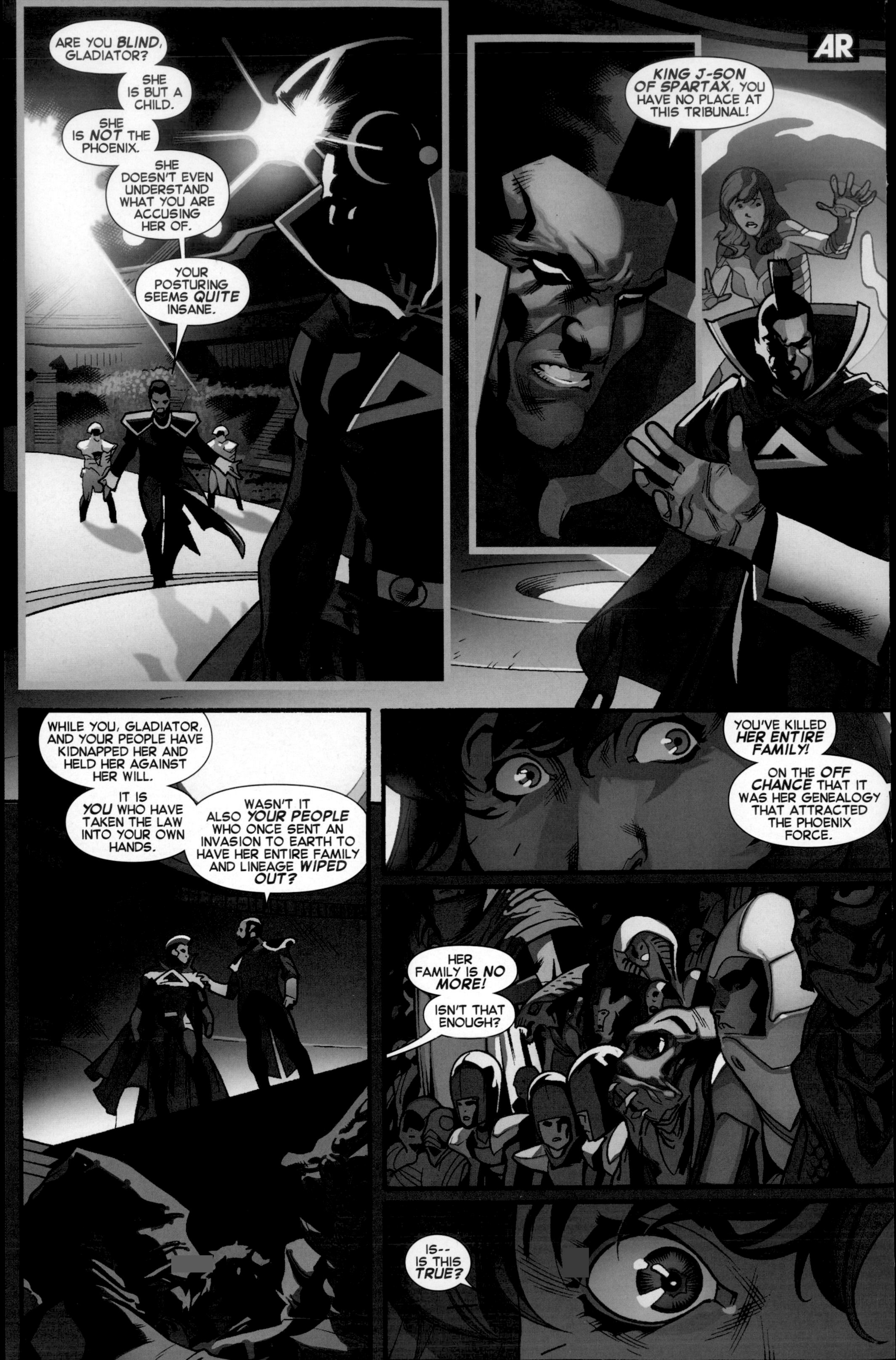
ARE YOU BLIND, GLADIATOR?
SHE IS BUT A CHILD.
SHE IS NOT THE PHOENIX.
SHE DOESN'T EVEN UNDERSTAND WHAT YOU ARE ACCUSING HER OF.
YOUR POSTURING SEEMS QUITE INSANE.
KING J-SON OF SPARTAX, YOU HAVE NO PLACE AT THIS TRIBUNAL!
WHILE YOU, GLADIATOR, AND YOUR PEOPLE HAVE KIDNAPPED HER AND HELD HER AGAINST HER WILL.
IT IS YOU WHO HAVE TAKEN THE LAW INTO YOUR OWN HANDS.
WASN'T IT ALSO YOUR PEOPLE WHO ONCE SENT AN INVASION TO EARTH TO HAVE HER ENTIRE FAMILY AND LINEAGE WIPED OUT?
YOU'VE KILLED HER ENTIRE FAMILY!
ON THE OFF CHANCE THAT IT WAS HER GENEALOGY THAT ATTRACTED THE PHOENIX FORCE.
HER FAMILY IS NO MORE!
ISN'T THAT ENOUGH?
IS-- IS THIS TRUE?

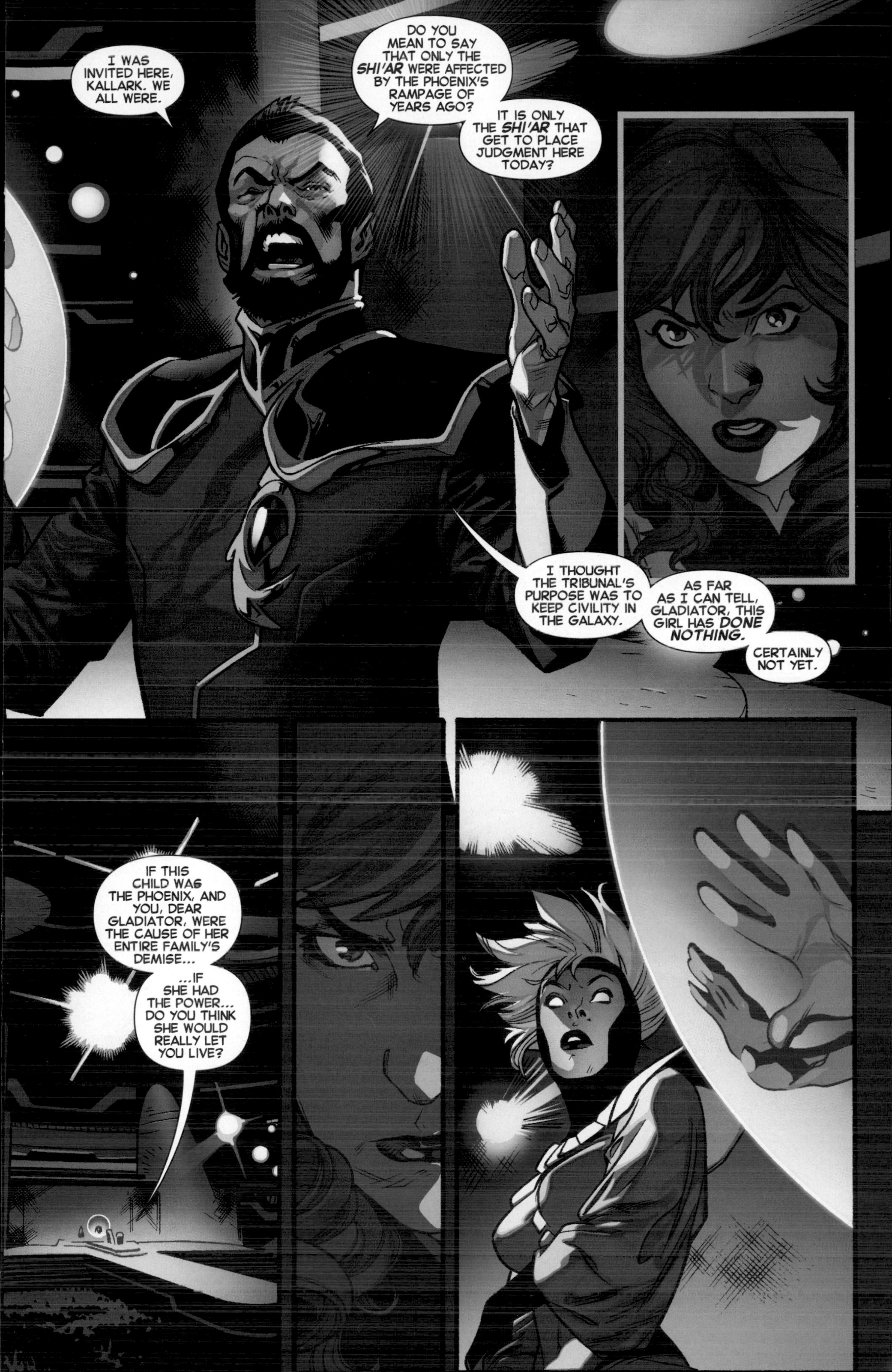

I WAS INVITED HERE, KALLARK. WE ALL WERE.
DO YOU MEAN TO SAY THAT ONLY THE SHI'AR WERE AFFECTED BY THE PHOENIX'S RAMPAGE OF YEARS AGO?
IT IS ONLY THE SHI'AR THAT GET TO PLACE JUDGMENT HERE TODAY?
I THOUGHT THE TRIBUNAL'S PURPOSE WAS TO KEEP CIVILITY IN THE GALAXY.
AS FAR AS I CAN TELL, GLADIATOR, THIS GIRL HAS DONE NOTHING.
CERTAINLY NOT YET.
IF THIS CHILD WAS THE PHOENIX, AND YOU, DEAR GLADIATOR, WERE THE CAUSE OF HER ENTIRE FAMILY'S DEMISE...
...IF SHE HAD THE POWER... DO YOU THINK SHE WOULD REALLY LET YOU LIVE?

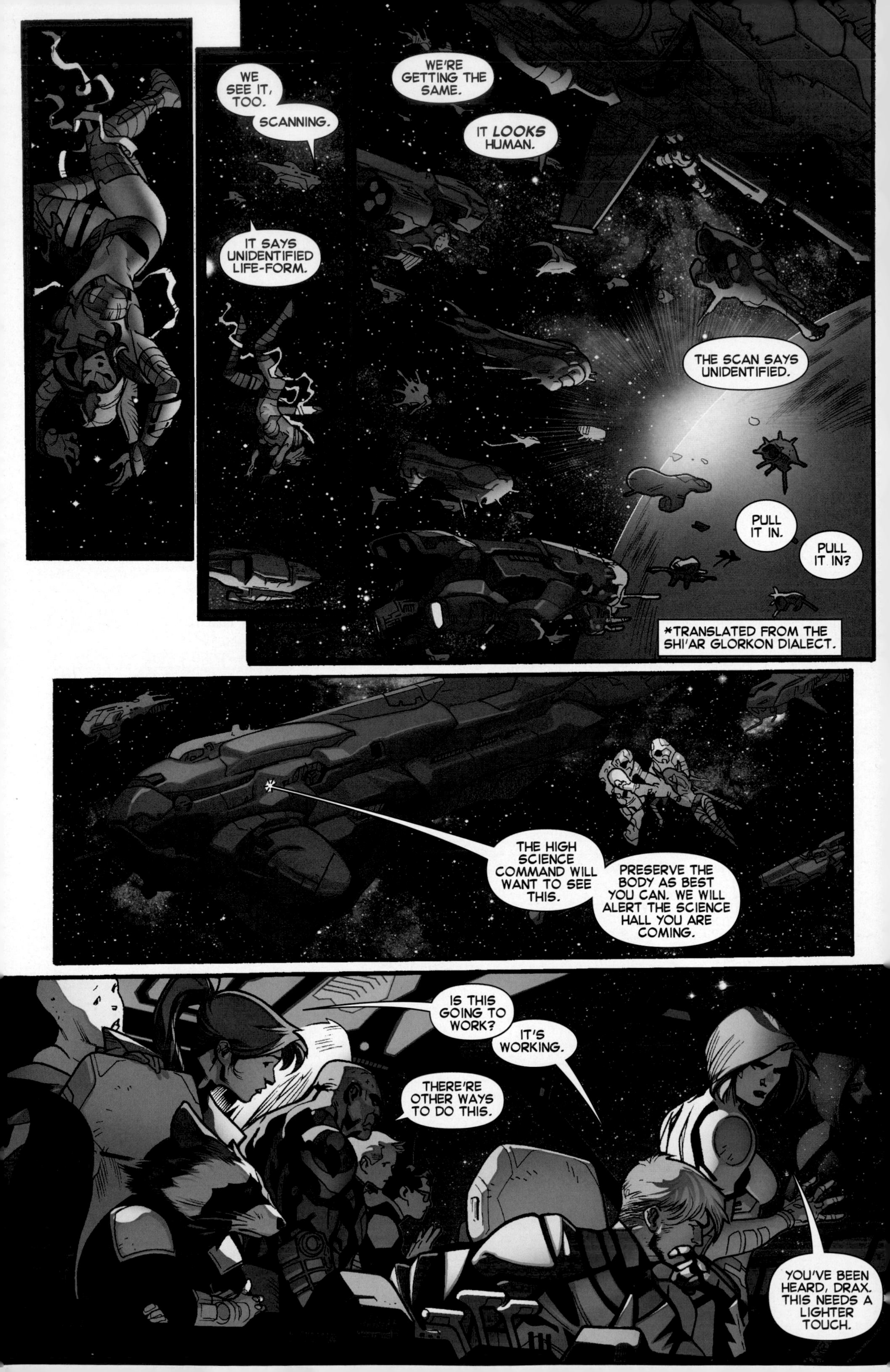
WE SEE IT, TOO.
SCANNING.
WE'RE GETTING THE SAME.
IT LOOKS HUMAN.
IT SAYS UNIDENTIFIED LIFE-FORM.
THE SCAN SAYS UNIDENTIFIED.
PULL IT IN.
PULL IT IN?
*TRANSLATED FROM THE SHI'AR GLORKON DIALECT.
THE HIGH SCIENCE COMMAND WILL WANT TO SEE THIS.
PRESERVE THE BODY AS BEST YOU CAN. WE WILL ALERT THE SCIENCE HALL YOU ARE COMING.
IS THIS GOING TO WORK?
IT'S WORKING.
THERE'RE OTHER WAYS TO DO THIS.
YOU'VE BEEN HEARD, DRAX. THIS NEEDS A LIGHTER TOUCH.

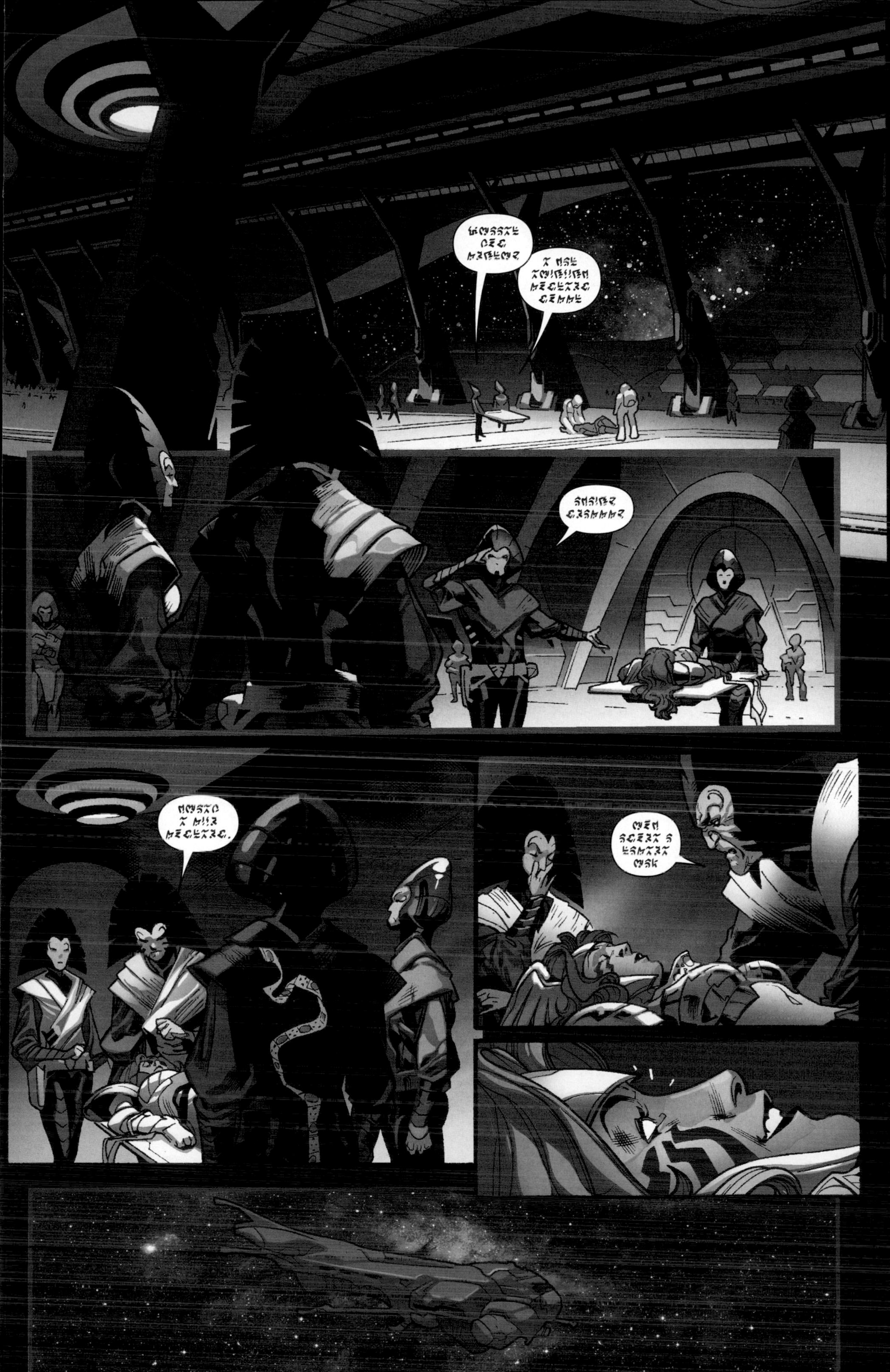

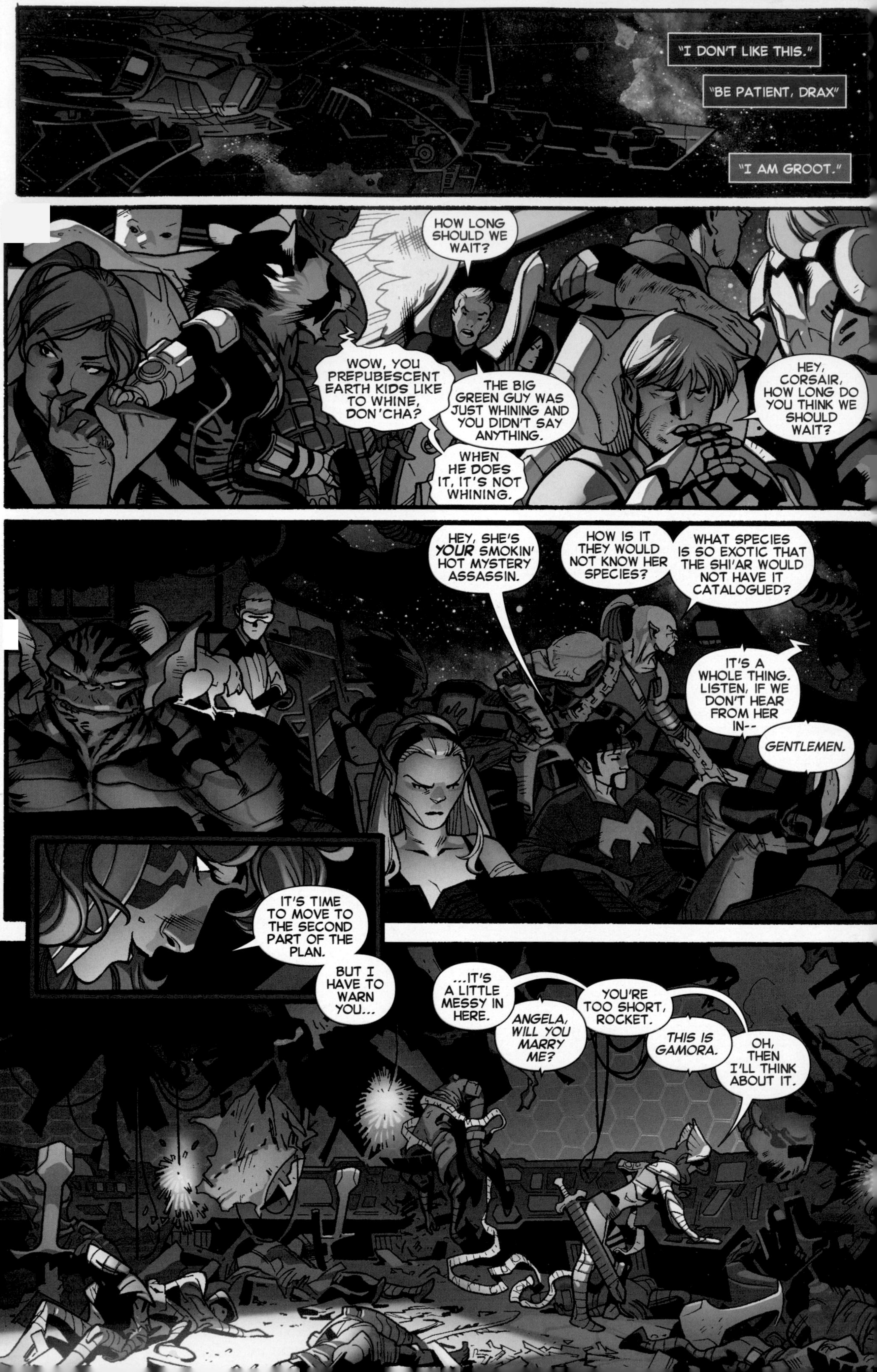
"I DON'T LIKE THIS."
"BE PATIENT, DRAX"
"I AM GROOT."
HOW LONG SHOULD WE WAIT?
WOW, YOU PREPUBESCENT EARTH KIDS LIKE TO WHINE, DON'CHA?
THE BIG GREEN GUY WAS JUST WHINING AND YOU DIDN'T SAY ANYTHING.
WHEN HE DOES IT, IT'S NOT WHINING.
HEY, CORSAIR, HOW LONG DO YOU THINK WE SHOULD WAIT?
HEY, SHE'S YOUR SMOKIN' HOT MYSTERY ASSASSIN.
HOW IS IT THEY WOULD NOT KNOW HER SPECIES?
WHAT SPECIES IS SO EXOTIC THAT THE SHI'AR WOULD NOT HAVE IT CATALOGUED?
IT'S A WHOLE THING. LISTEN, IF WE DON'T HEAR FROM HER IN--
GENTLEMEN.
IT'S TIME TO MOVE TO THE SECOND PART OF THE PLAN.
BUT I HAVE TO WARN YOU...
...IT'S A LITTLE MESSY IN HERE.
ANGELA, WILL YOU MARRY ME?
YOU'RE TOO SHORT, ROCKET.
THIS IS GAMORA.
OH, THEN I'LL THINK ABOUT IT.

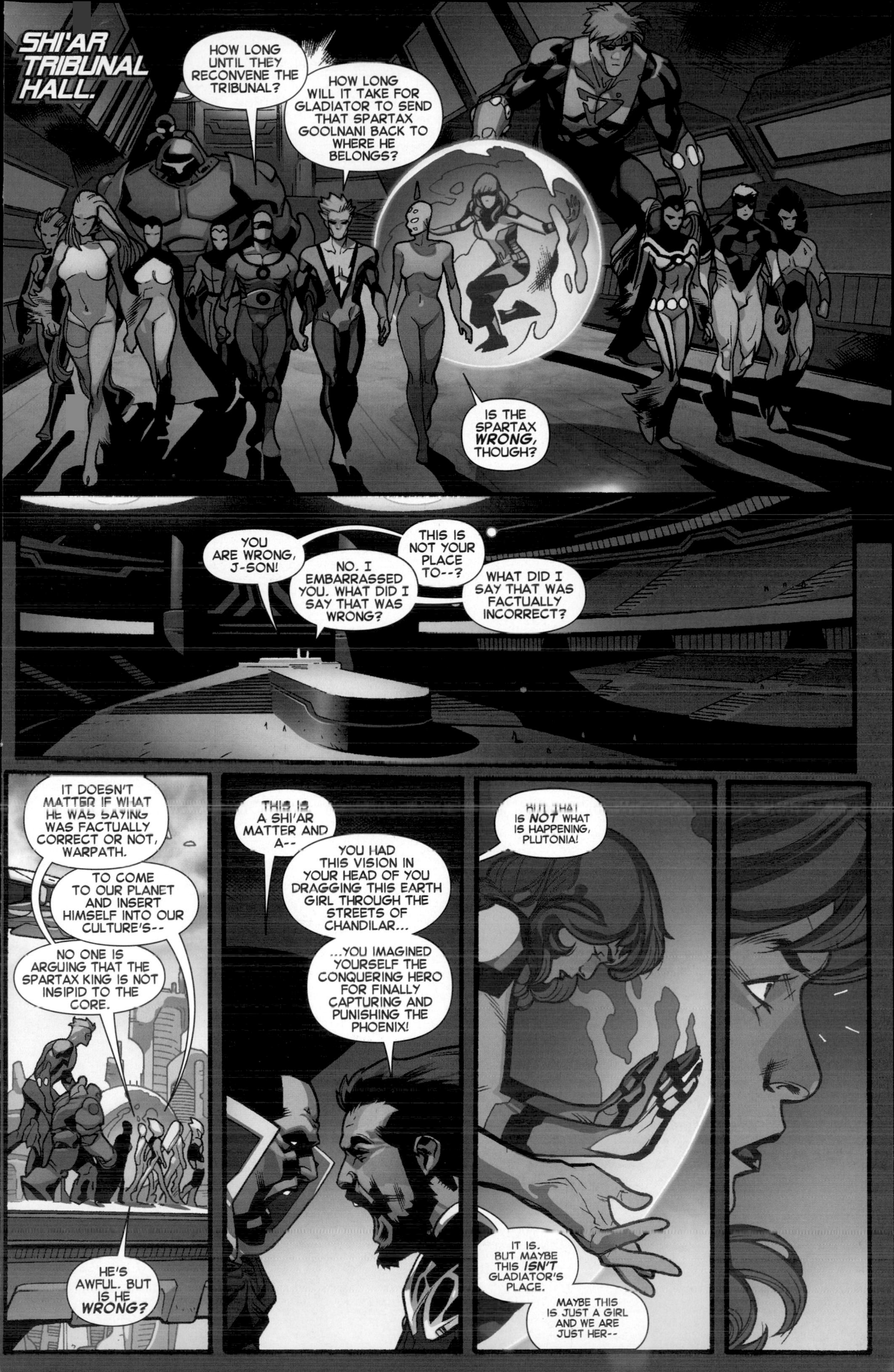
SHI'AR TRIBUNAL HALL.
HOW LONG UNTIL THEY RECONVENE THE TRIBUNAL?
HOW LONG WILL IT TAKE FOR GLADIATOR TO SEND THAT SPARTAX GOOLNANI BACK TO WHERE HE BELONGS?
IS THE SPARTAX *WRONG,* THOUGH?
YOU ARE WRONG, J-SON!
THIS IS NOT YOUR PLACE TO--?
NO. I EMBARRASSED YOU. WHAT DID I SAY THAT WAS WRONG?
WHAT DID I SAY THAT WAS FACTUALLY INCORRECT?
IT DOESN'T MATTER IF WHAT HE WAS SAYING WAS FACTUALLY CORRECT OR NOT, WARPATH.
TO COME TO OUR PLANET AND INSERT HIMSELF INTO OUR CULTURE'S--
NO ONE IS ARGUING THAT THE SPARTAX KING IS NOT INSIPID TO THE CORE.
HE'S AWFUL. BUT IS HE *WRONG?*
THIS IS A SHI'AR MATTER AND A--
YOU HAD THIS VISION IN YOUR HEAD OF YOU DRAGGING THIS EARTH GIRL THROUGH THE STREETS OF CHANDILAR...
...YOU IMAGINED YOURSELF THE CONQUERING HERO FOR FINALLY CAPTURING AND PUNISHING THE PHOENIX!
BUT THAT IS *NOT* WHAT IS HAPPENING, PLUTONIA!
IT IS. BUT MAYBE THIS *ISN'T* GLADIATOR'S PLACE.
MAYBE THIS IS JUST A GIRL AND WE ARE JUST HER--

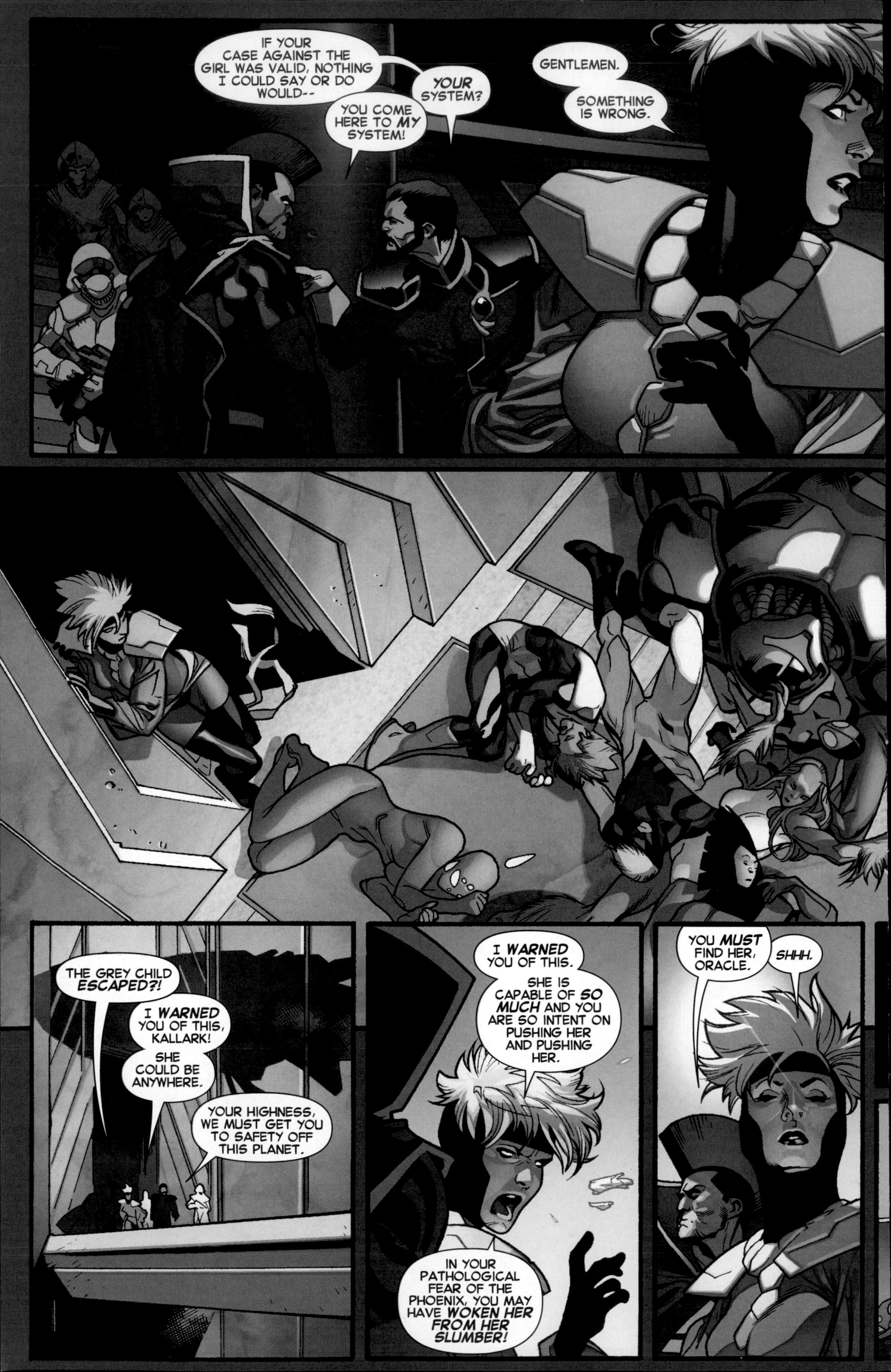

IF YOUR CASE AGAINST THE GIRL WAS VALID, NOTHING I COULD SAY OR DO WOULD--
YOU COME HERE TO *MY* SYSTEM!
YOUR SYSTEM?
GENTLEMEN.
SOMETHING IS WRONG.
THE GREY CHILD *ESCAPED?!*
I *WARNED* YOU OF THIS, KALLARK!
SHE COULD BE ANYWHERE.
YOUR HIGHNESS, WE MUST GET YOU TO SAFETY OFF THIS PLANET.
I *WARNED* YOU OF THIS.
SHE IS CAPABLE OF *SO MUCH* AND YOU ARE SO INTENT ON PUSHING HER AND PUSHING HER.
IN YOUR PATHOLOGICAL FEAR OF THE PHOENIX, YOU MAY HAVE *WOKEN HER FROM HER SLUMBER!*
YOU *MUST* FIND HER, ORACLE.
SHHH.

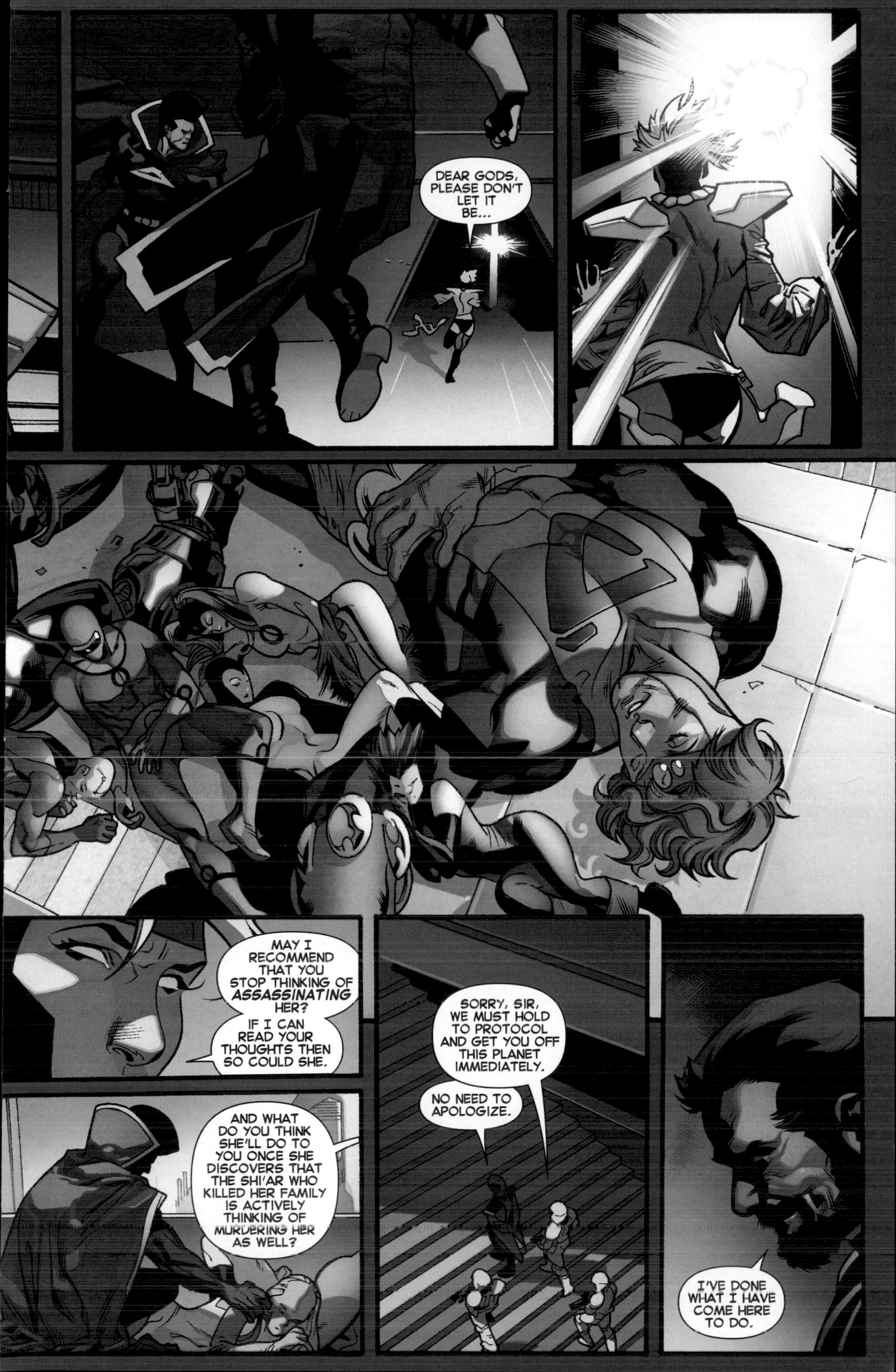
DEAR GODS, PLEASE DON'T LET IT BE...
MAY I RECOMMEND THAT YOU STOP THINKING OF *ASSASSINATING* HER?
IF I CAN READ YOUR THOUGHTS THEN SO COULD SHE.
AND WHAT DO YOU THINK SHE'LL DO TO YOU ONCE SHE DISCOVERS THAT THE SHI'AR WHO KILLED HER FAMILY IS ACTIVELY THINKING OF MURDERING HER AS WELL?
SORRY, SIR, WE MUST HOLD TO PROTOCOL AND GET YOU OFF THIS PLANET IMMEDIATELY.
NO NEED TO APOLOGIZE.
I'VE DONE WHAT I HAVE COME HERE TO DO.

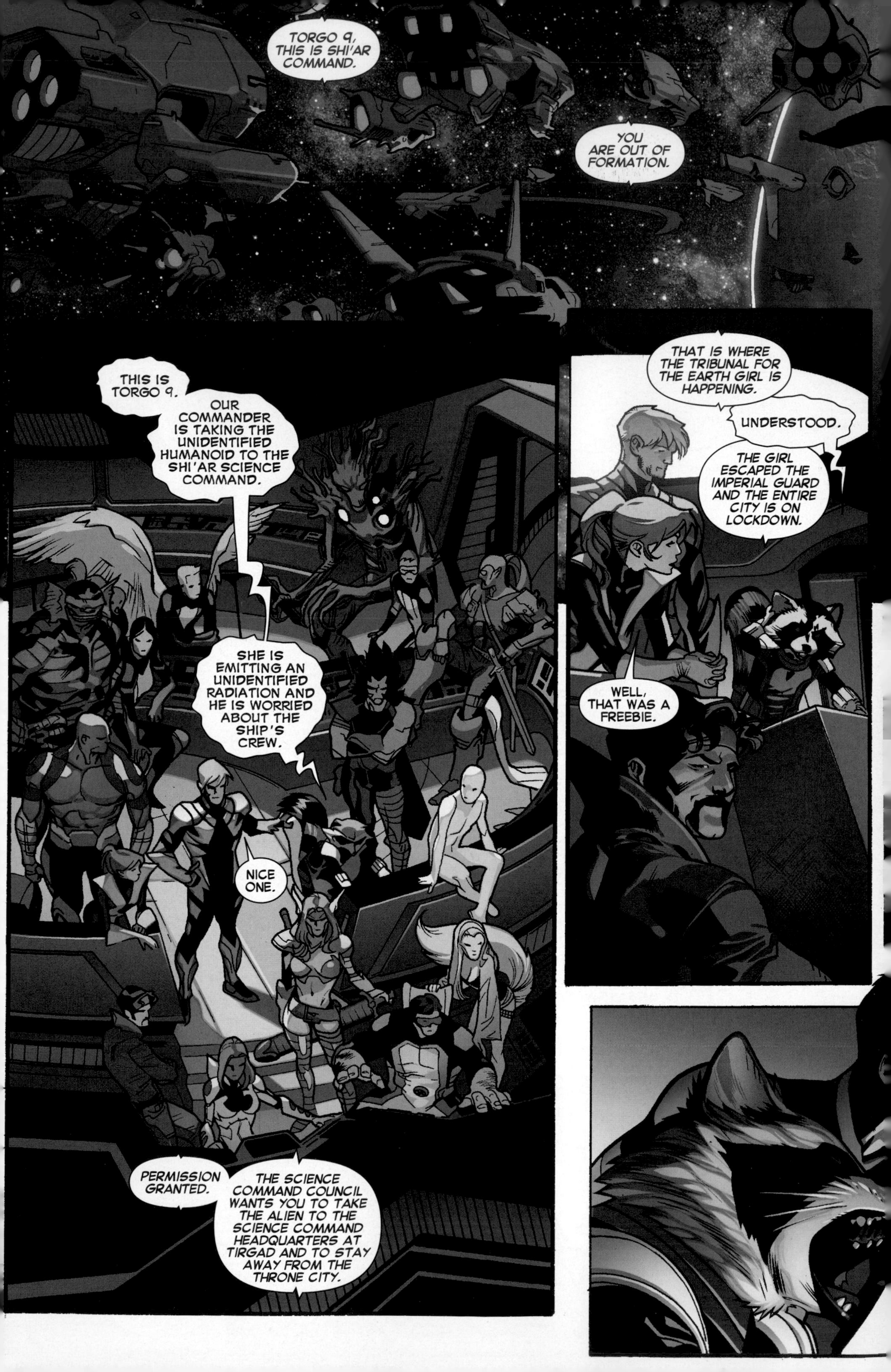
TORGO 9, THIS IS SHI'AR COMMAND.
YOU ARE OUT OF FORMATION.
THIS IS TORGO 9.
OUR COMMANDER IS TAKING THE UNIDENTIFIED HUMANOID TO THE SHI'AR SCIENCE COMMAND.
SHE IS EMITTING AN UNIDENTIFIED RADIATION AND HE IS WORRIED ABOUT THE SHIP'S CREW.
NICE ONE.
PERMISSION GRANTED.
THE SCIENCE COMMAND COUNCIL WANTS YOU TO TAKE THE ALIEN TO THE SCIENCE COMMAND HEADQUARTERS AT TIRGAD AND TO STAY AWAY FROM THE THRONE CITY.
THAT IS WHERE THE TRIBUNAL FOR THE EARTH GIRL IS HAPPENING.
UNDERSTOOD.
THE GIRL ESCAPED THE IMPERIAL GUARD AND THE ENTIRE CITY IS ON LOCKDOWN.
WELL, THAT WAS A FREEBIE.

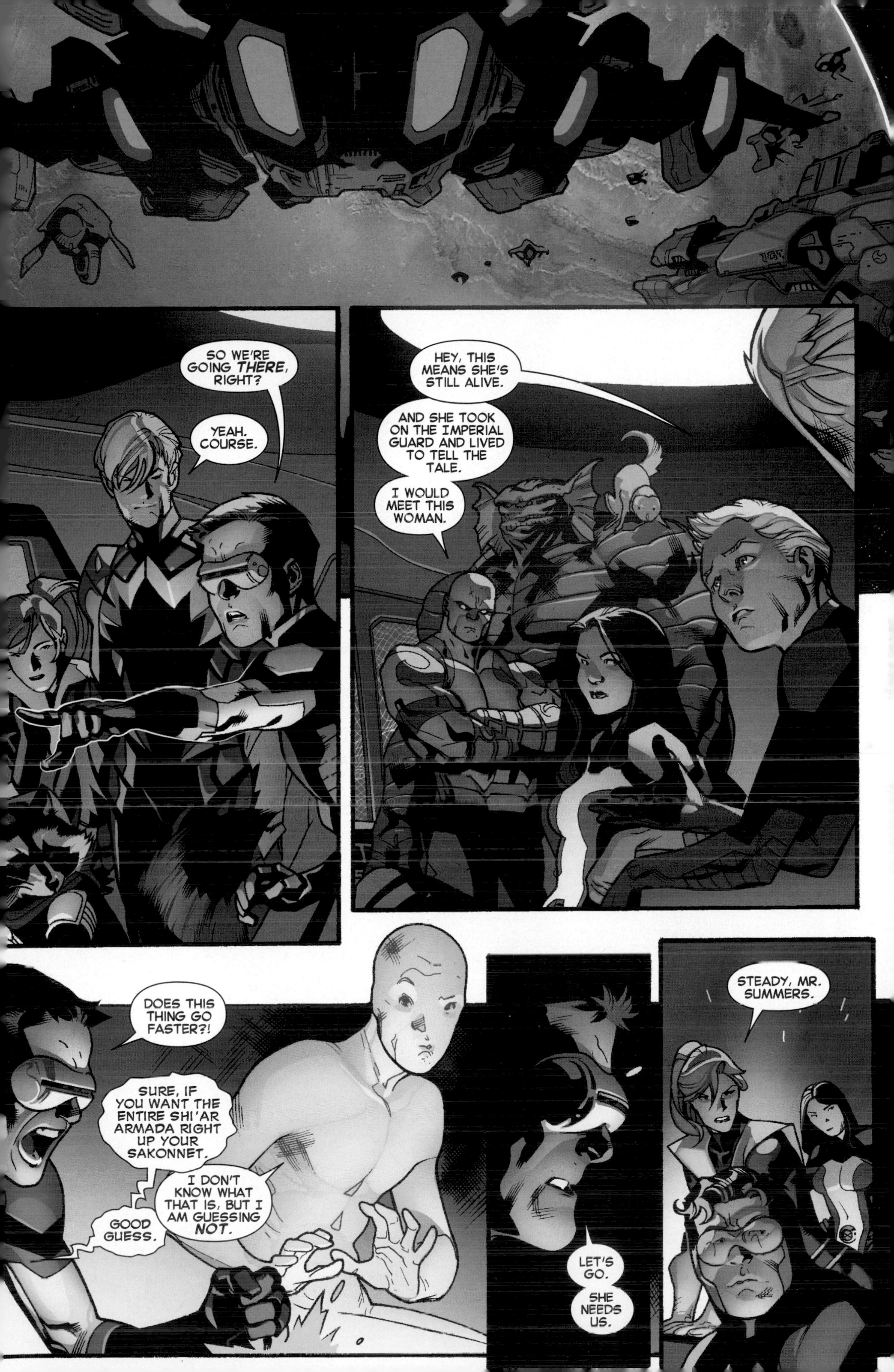
SO WE'RE GOING *THERE*, RIGHT?
YEAH. COURSE.
HEY, THIS MEANS SHE'S STILL ALIVE.
AND SHE TOOK ON THE IMPERIAL GUARD AND LIVED TO TELL THE TALE.
I WOULD MEET THIS WOMAN.
DOES THIS THING GO FASTER?!
SURE, IF YOU WANT THE ENTIRE SHI'AR ARMADA RIGHT UP YOUR SAKONNET.
I DON'T KNOW WHAT THAT IS, BUT I AM GUESSING *NOT*.
GOOD GUESS.
LET'S GO.
SHE NEEDS US.
STEADY, MR. SUMMERS.

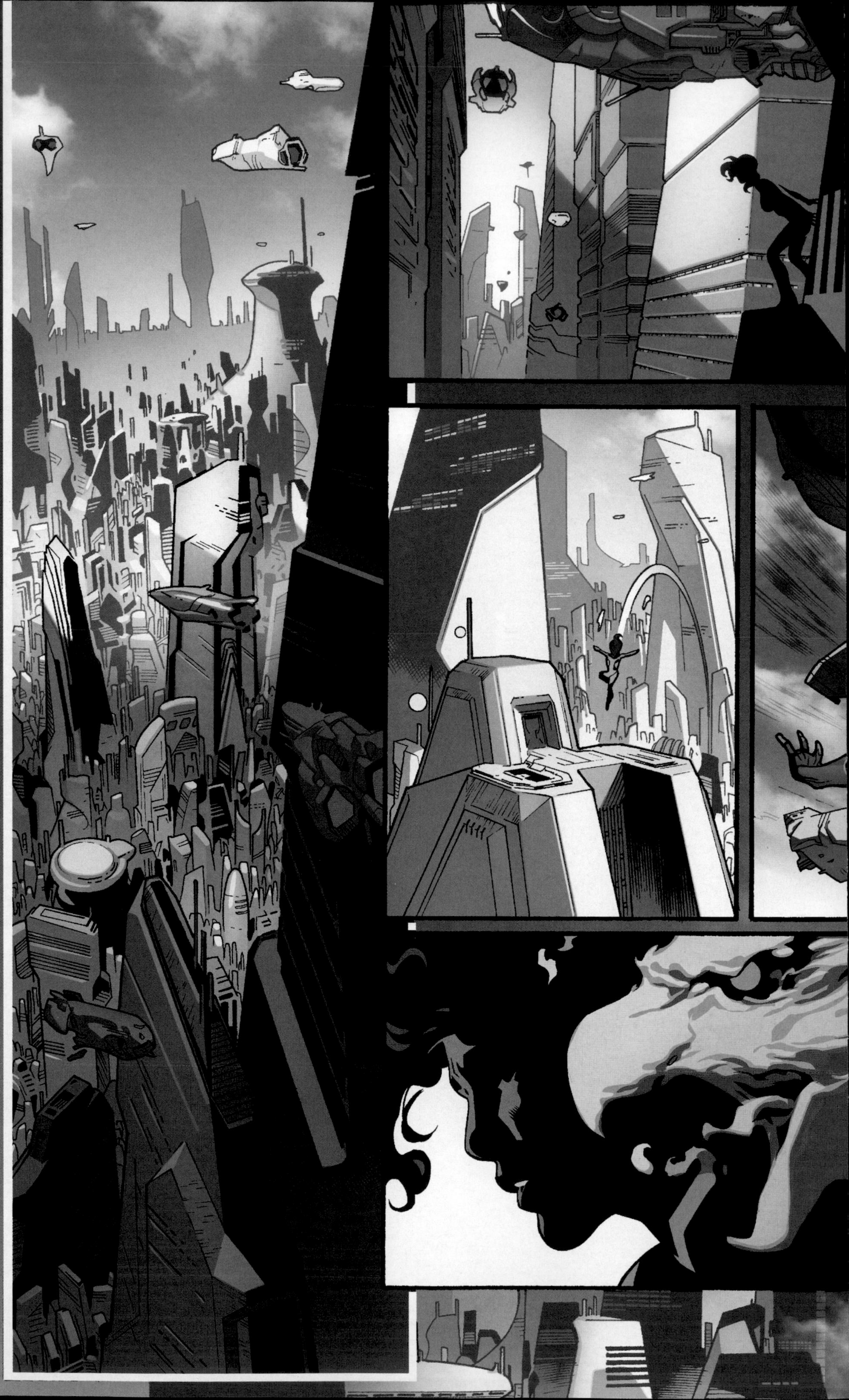

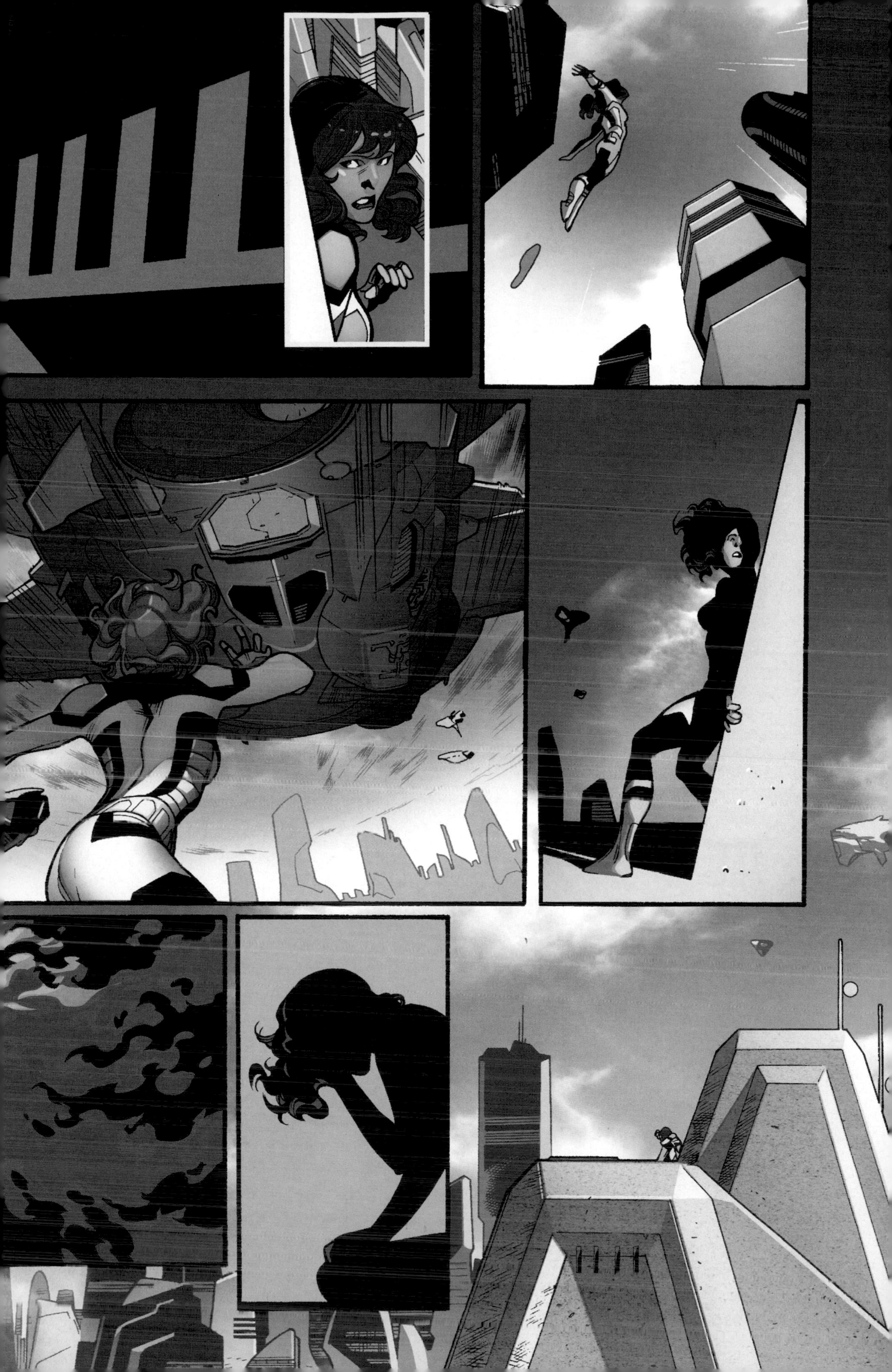

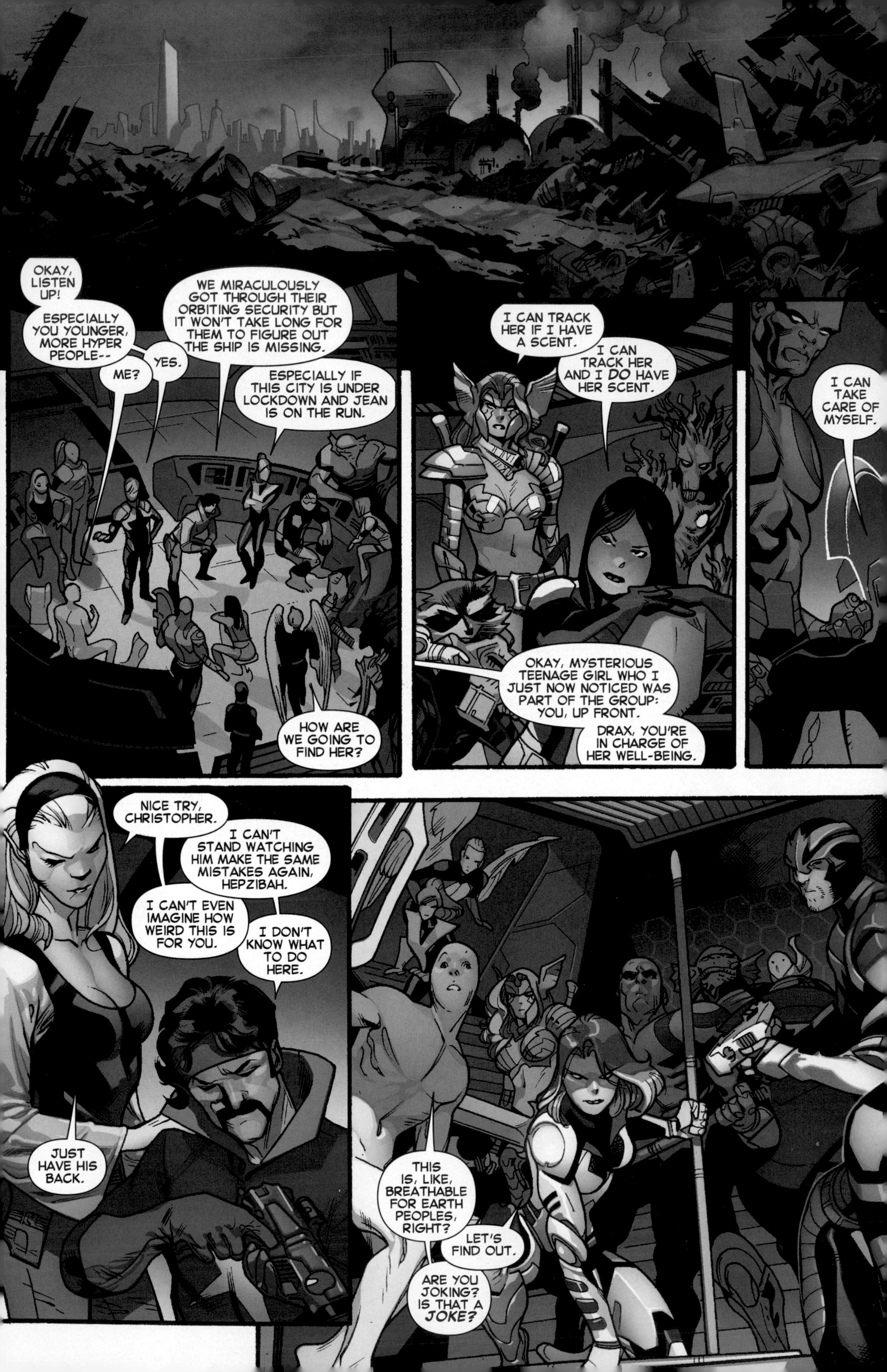
OKAY, LISTEN UP!
ESPECIALLY YOU YOUNGER, MORE HYPER PEOPLE--
ME?
YES.
WE MIRACULOUSLY GOT THROUGH THEIR ORBITING SECURITY BUT IT WON'T TAKE LONG FOR THEM TO FIGURE OUT THE SHIP IS MISSING.
ESPECIALLY IF THIS CITY IS UNDER LOCKDOWN AND JEAN IS ON THE RUN.
HOW ARE WE GOING TO FIND HER?
I CAN TRACK HER IF I HAVE A SCENT.
I CAN TRACK HER AND I DO HAVE HER SCENT.
OKAY, MYSTERIOUS TEENAGE GIRL WHO I JUST NOW NOTICED WAS PART OF THE GROUP: YOU, UP FRONT.
DRAX, YOU'RE IN CHARGE OF HER WELL-BEING.
I CAN TAKE CARE OF MYSELF.
NICE TRY, CHRISTOPHER.
I CAN'T STAND WATCHING HIM MAKE THE SAME MISTAKES AGAIN, HEPZIBAH.
I CAN'T EVEN IMAGINE HOW WEIRD THIS IS FOR YOU.
I DON'T KNOW WHAT TO DO HERE.
JUST HAVE HIS BACK.
THIS IS, LIKE, BREATHABLE FOR EARTH PEOPLES, RIGHT?
LET'S FIND OUT.
ARE YOU JOKING? IS THAT A JOKE?

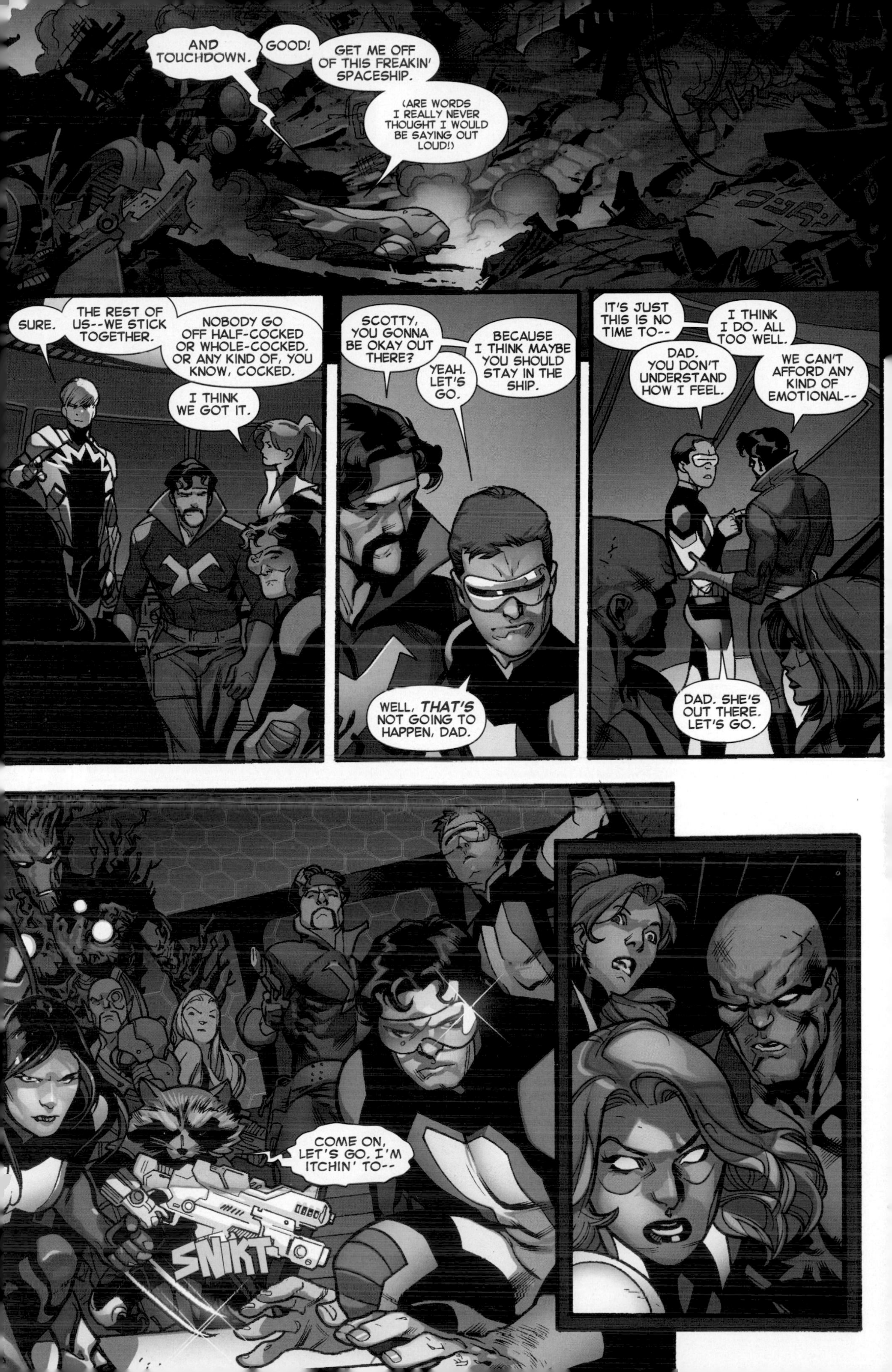
AND TOUCHDOWN.
GOOD!
GET ME OFF OF THIS FREAKIN' SPACESHIP.
(ARE WORDS I REALLY NEVER THOUGHT I WOULD BE SAYING OUT LOUD!)
SURE.
THE REST OF US--WE STICK TOGETHER.
NOBODY GO OFF HALF-COCKED OR WHOLE-COCKED. OR ANY KIND OF, YOU KNOW, COCKED.
I THINK WE GOT IT.
SCOTTY, YOU GONNA BE OKAY OUT THERE?
YEAH. LET'S GO.
BECAUSE I THINK MAYBE YOU SHOULD STAY IN THE SHIP.
WELL, *THAT'S* NOT GOING TO HAPPEN, DAD.
IT'S JUST THIS IS NO TIME TO--
I THINK I DO. ALL TOO WELL.
DAD. YOU DON'T UNDERSTAND HOW I FEEL.
WE CAN'T AFFORD ANY KIND OF EMOTIONAL--
DAD. SHE'S OUT THERE. LET'S GO.
COME ON, LET'S GO. I'M ITCHIN' TO--
SNIKT

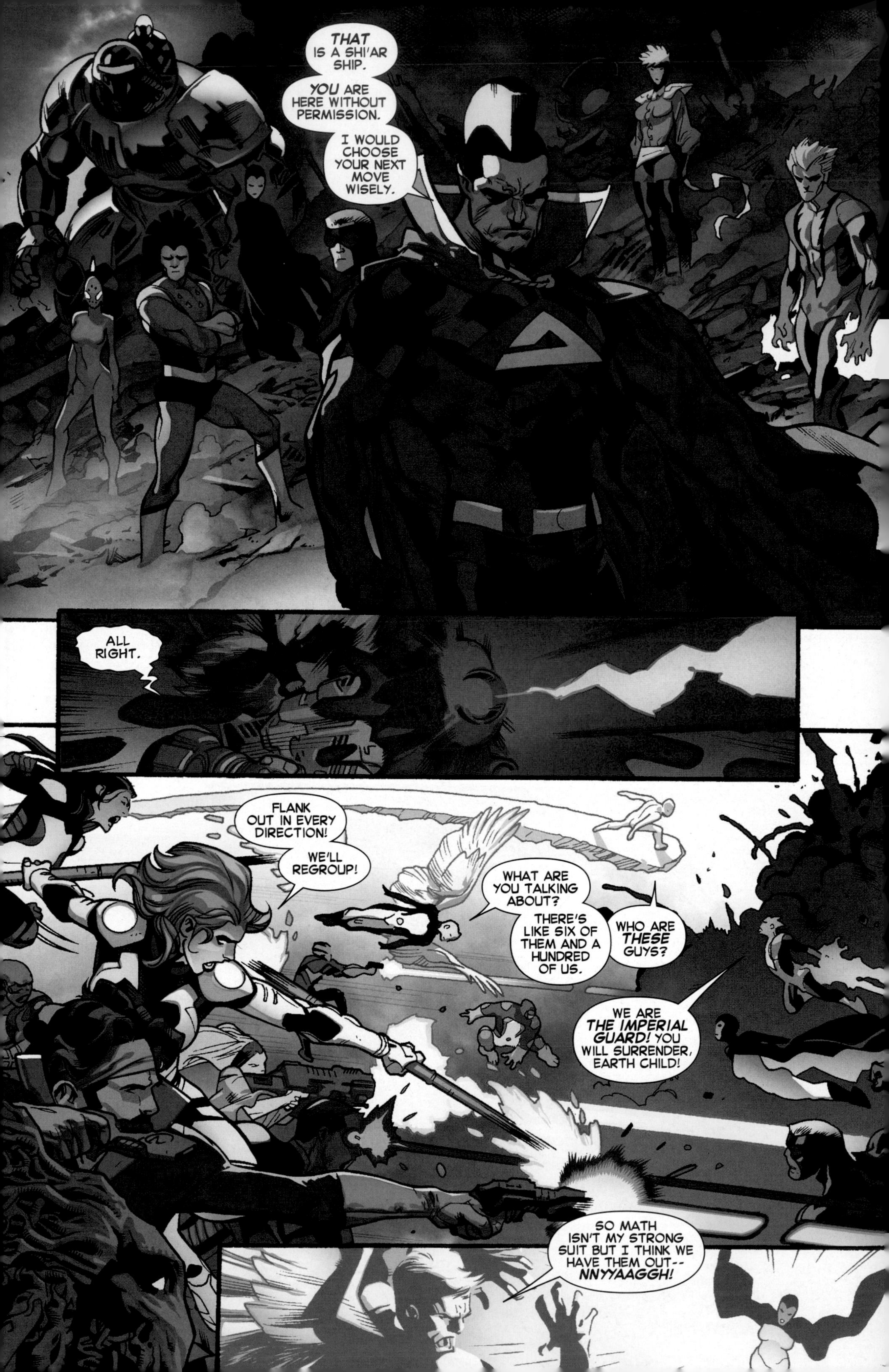
THAT IS A SHI'AR SHIP.
YOU ARE HERE WITHOUT PERMISSION.
I WOULD CHOOSE YOUR NEXT MOVE WISELY.
ALL RIGHT.
FLANK OUT IN EVERY DIRECTION!
WE'LL REGROUP!
WHAT ARE YOU TALKING ABOUT?
THERE'S LIKE SIX OF THEM AND A HUNDRED OF US.
WHO ARE THESE GUYS?
WE ARE THE IMPERIAL GUARD! YOU WILL SURRENDER, EARTH CHILD!
SO MATH ISN'T MY STRONG SUIT BUT I THINK WE HAVE THEM OUT-- NNYYAAGGH!

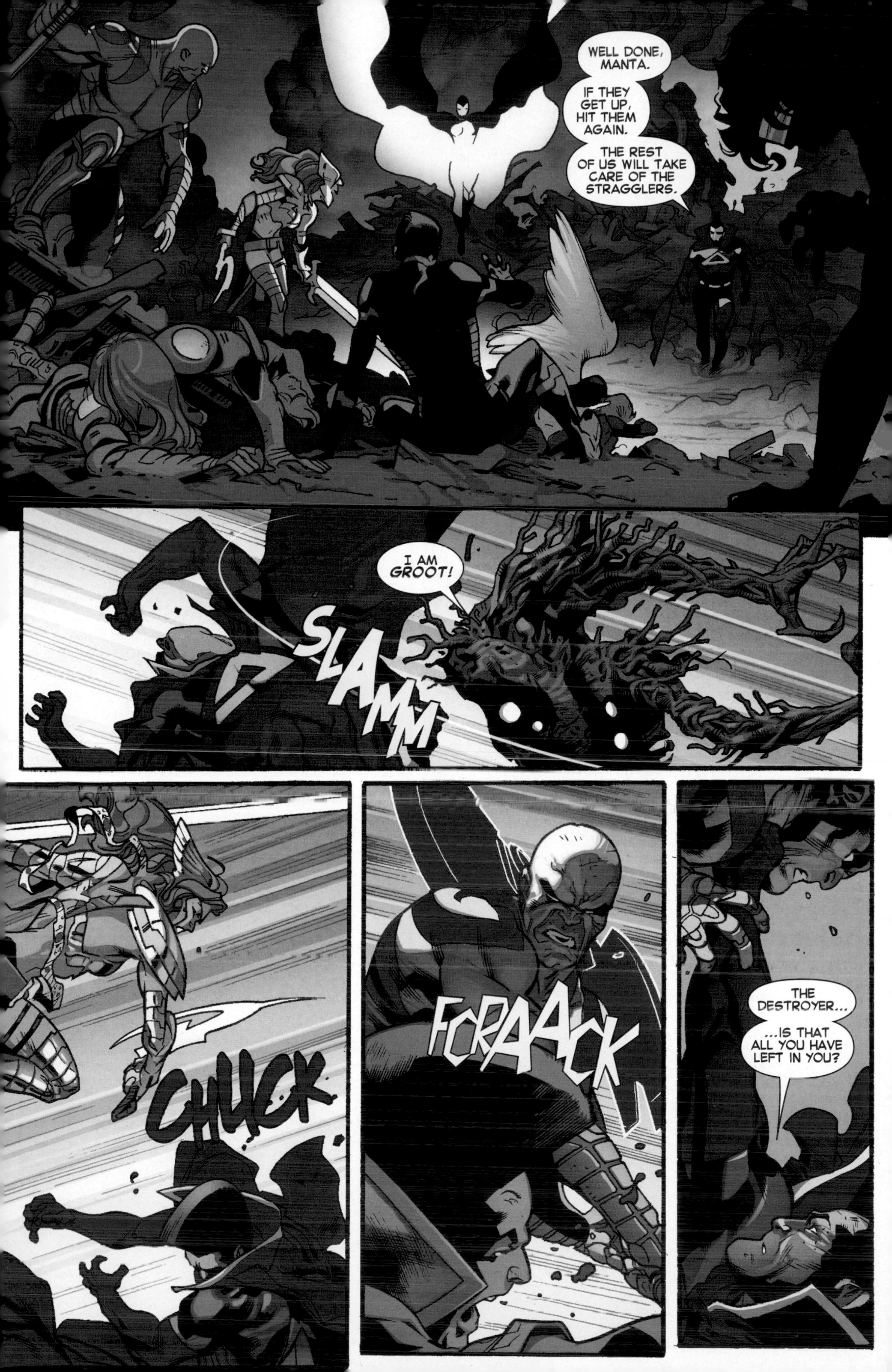
WELL DONE, MANTA.
IF THEY GET UP, HIT THEM AGAIN.
THE REST OF US WILL TAKE CARE OF THE STRAGGLERS.
I AM GROOT!
SLAMM
CHUCK
FCRAAACK
THE DESTROYER...
...IS THAT ALL YOU HAVE LEFT IN YOU?

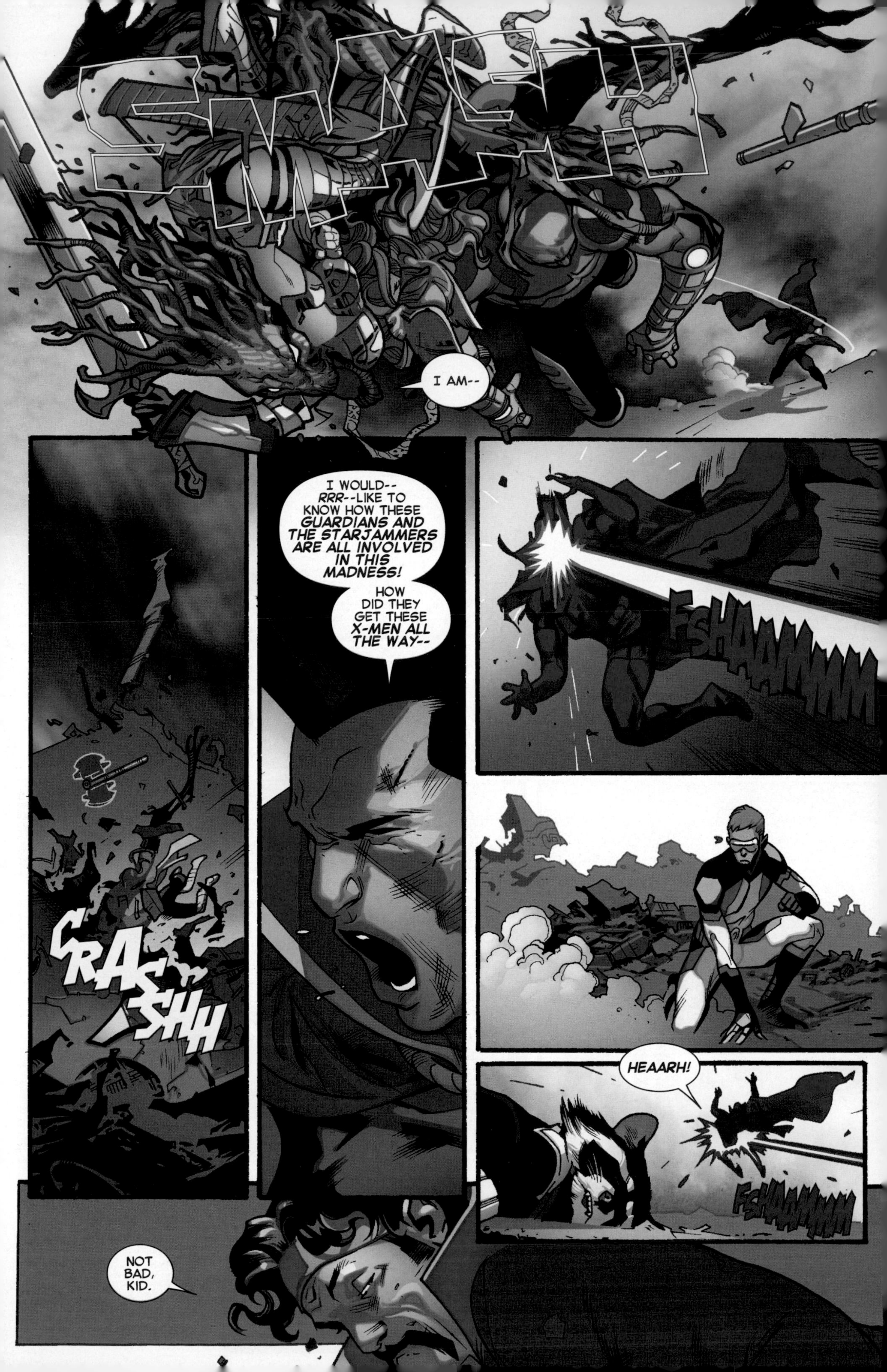
I AM--
I WOULD-- RRR--LIKE TO KNOW HOW THESE GUARDIANS AND THE STARJAMMERS ARE ALL INVOLVED IN THIS MADNESS!
HOW DID THEY GET THESE X-MEN ALL THE WAY--
CRASHH
HEAARH!
NOT BAD, KID.

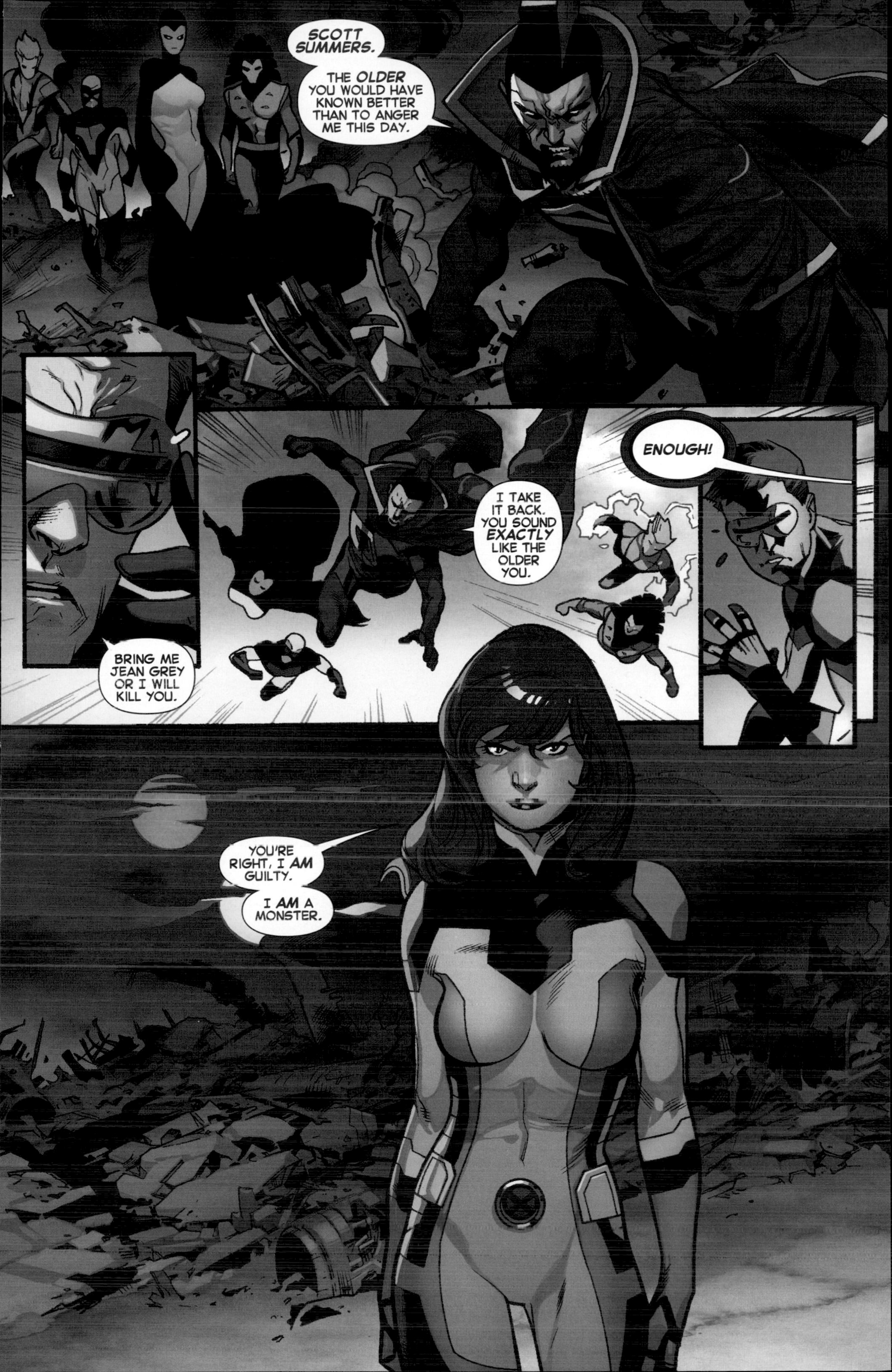
SCOTT SUMMERS.
THE OLDER YOU WOULD HAVE KNOWN BETTER THAN TO ANGER ME THIS DAY.
BRING ME JEAN GREY OR I WILL KILL YOU.
I TAKE IT BACK. YOU SOUND EXACTLY LIKE THE OLDER YOU.
ENOUGH!
YOU'RE RIGHT, I AM GUILTY.
I AM A MONSTER.

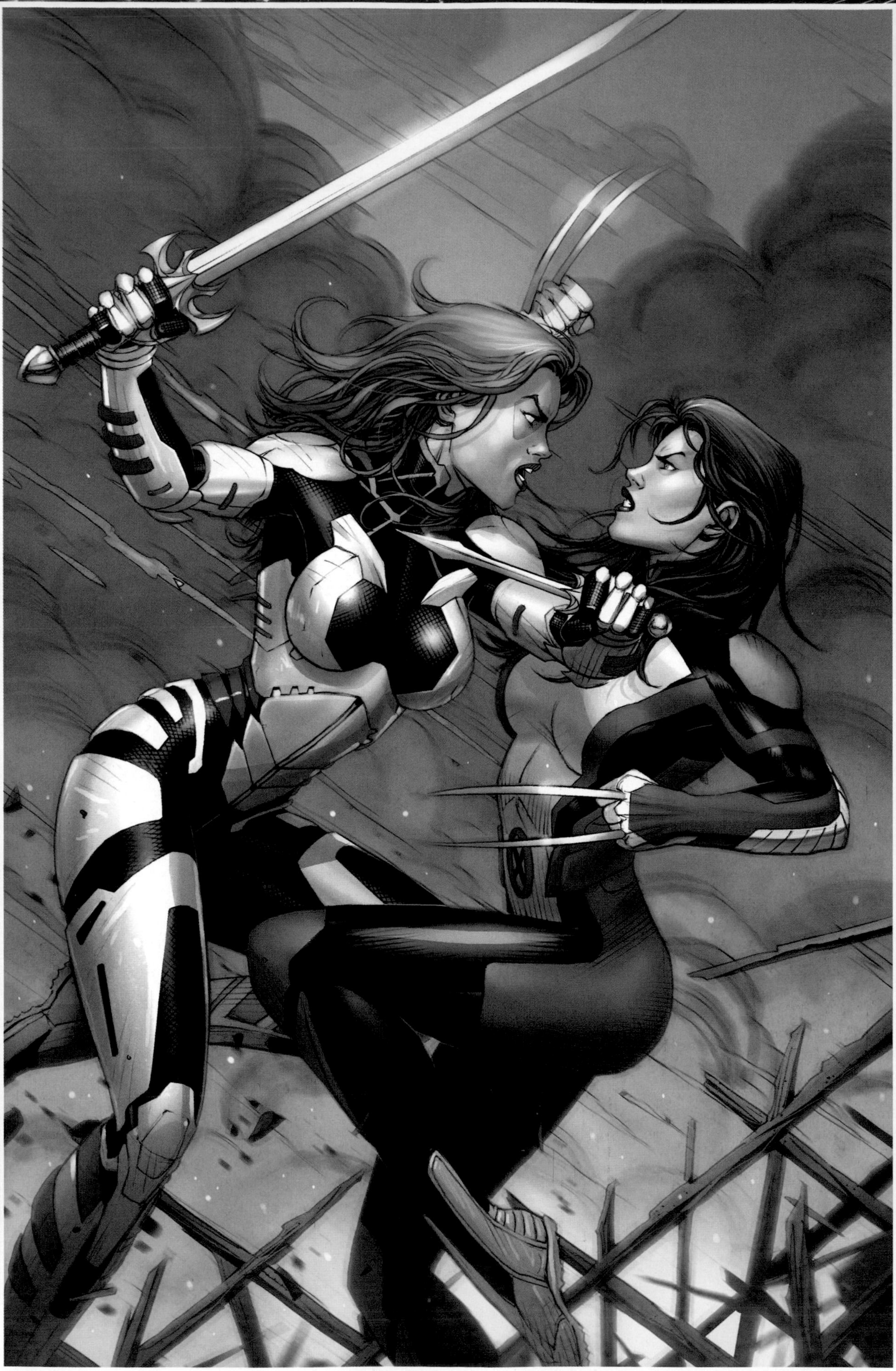

***GUARDIANS OF THE GALAXY #13* VARIANT**
BY DALE KEOWN & JASON KEITH

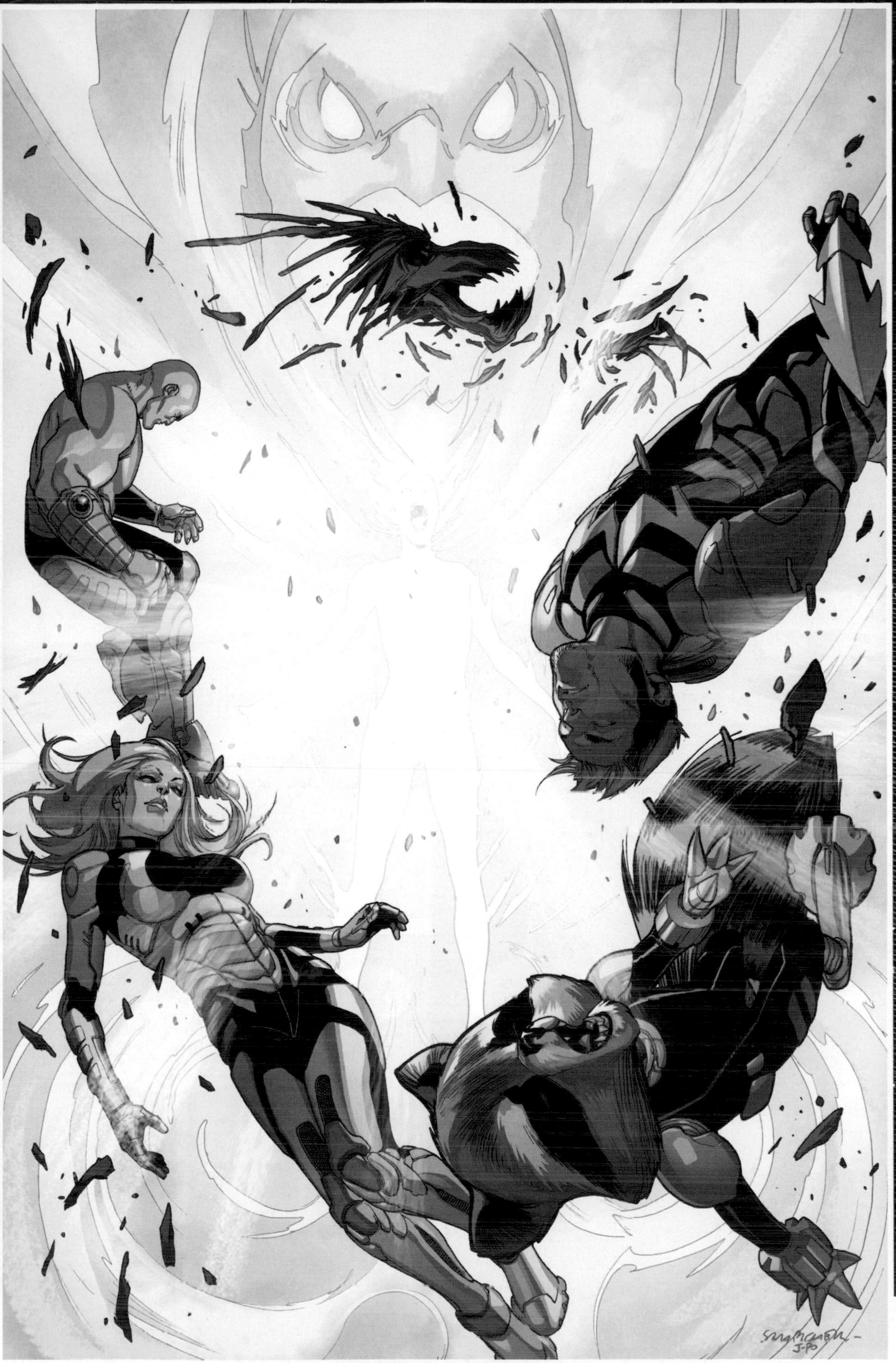

GUARDIANS OF THE GALAXY 13

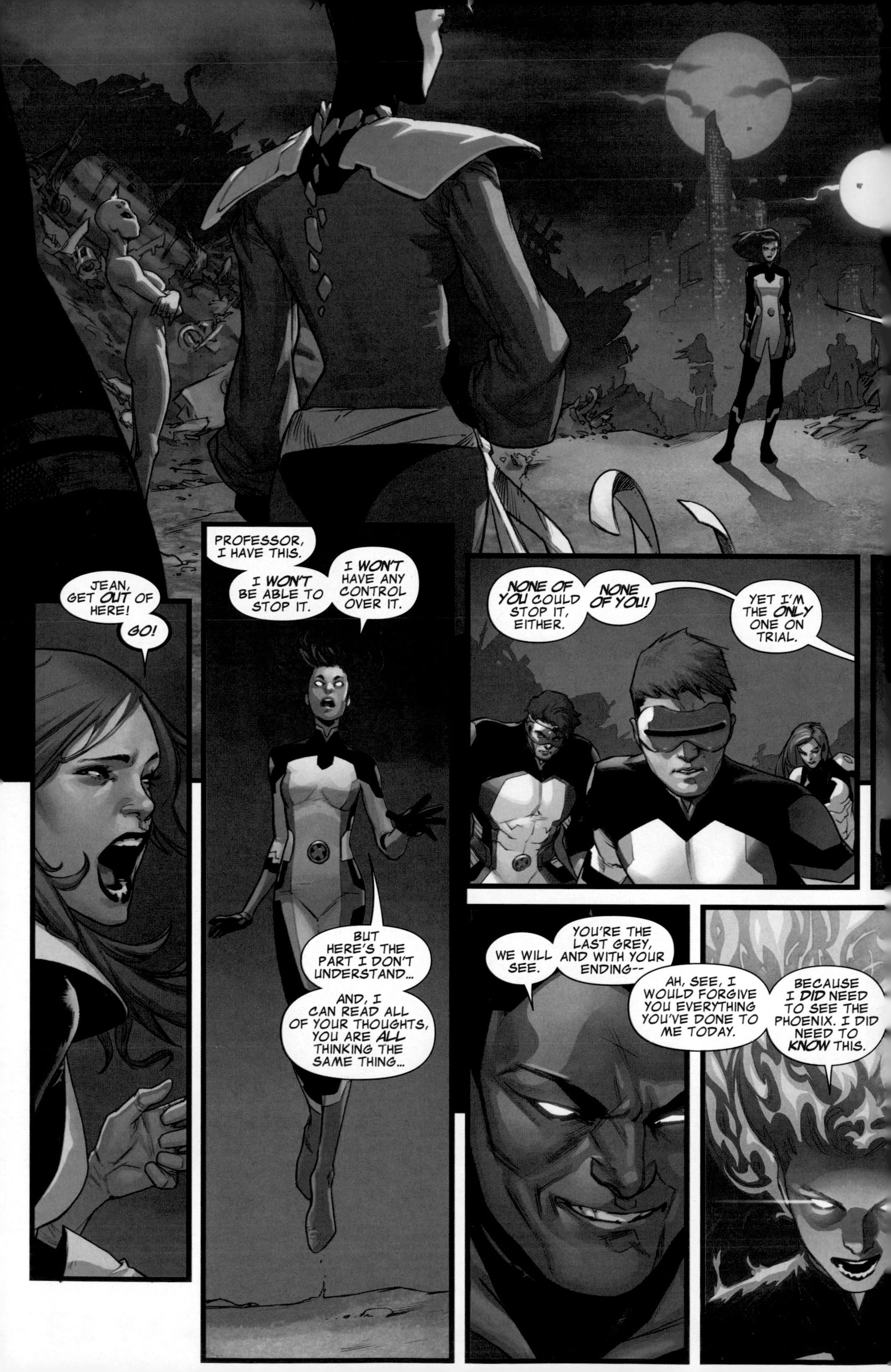
JEAN, GET OUT OF HERE! GO!
PROFESSOR, I HAVE THIS.
I WON'T BE ABLE TO STOP IT.
I WON'T HAVE ANY CONTROL OVER IT.
BUT HERE'S THE PART I DON'T UNDERSTAND...
AND, I CAN READ ALL OF YOUR THOUGHTS, YOU ARE ALL THINKING THE SAME THING...
NONE OF YOU COULD STOP IT, EITHER.
NONE OF YOU!
YET I'M THE ONLY ONE ON TRIAL.
WE WILL SEE.
YOU'RE THE LAST GREY, AND WITH YOUR ENDING--
AH, SEE, I WOULD FORGIVE YOU EVERYTHING YOU'VE DONE TO ME TODAY.
BECAUSE I DID NEED TO SEE THE PHOENIX. I DID NEED TO KNOW THIS.

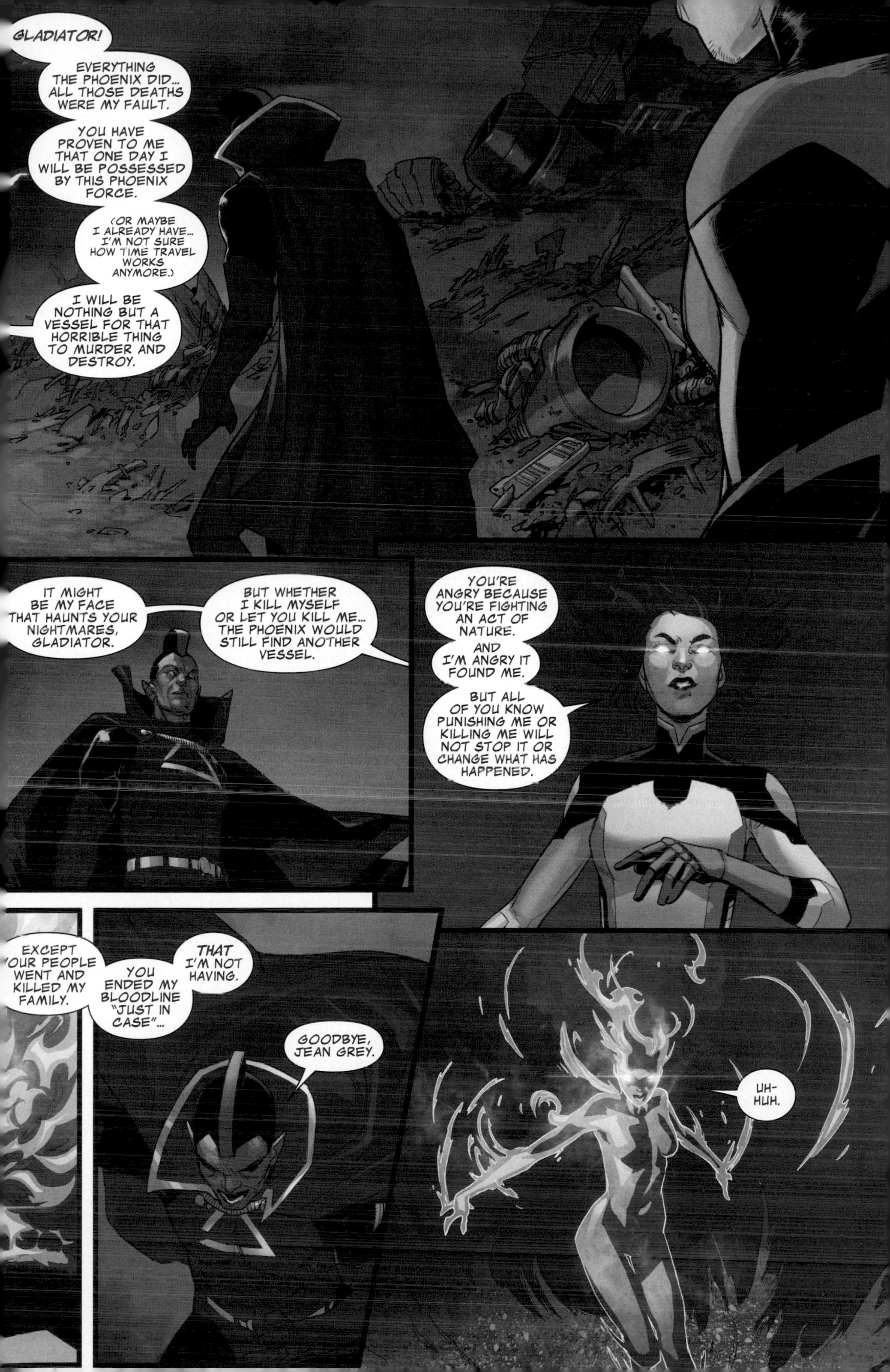
GLADIATOR!
EVERYTHING THE PHOENIX DID... ALL THOSE DEATHS WERE MY FAULT.
YOU HAVE PROVEN TO ME THAT ONE DAY I WILL BE POSSESSED BY THIS PHOENIX FORCE.
(OR MAYBE I ALREADY HAVE... I'M NOT SURE HOW TIME TRAVEL WORKS ANYMORE.)
I WILL BE NOTHING BUT A VESSEL FOR THAT HORRIBLE THING TO MURDER AND DESTROY.
IT MIGHT BE MY FACE THAT HAUNTS YOUR NIGHTMARES, GLADIATOR.
BUT WHETHER I KILL MYSELF OR LET YOU KILL ME... THE PHOENIX WOULD STILL FIND ANOTHER VESSEL.
YOU'RE ANGRY BECAUSE YOU'RE FIGHTING AN ACT OF NATURE.
AND I'M ANGRY IT FOUND ME.
BUT ALL OF YOU KNOW PUNISHING ME OR KILLING ME WILL NOT STOP IT OR CHANGE WHAT HAS HAPPENED.
EXCEPT YOUR PEOPLE WENT AND KILLED MY FAMILY.
YOU ENDED MY BLOODLINE "JUST IN CASE"...
THAT I'M NOT HAVING.
GOODBYE, JEAN GREY.
UH-HUH.

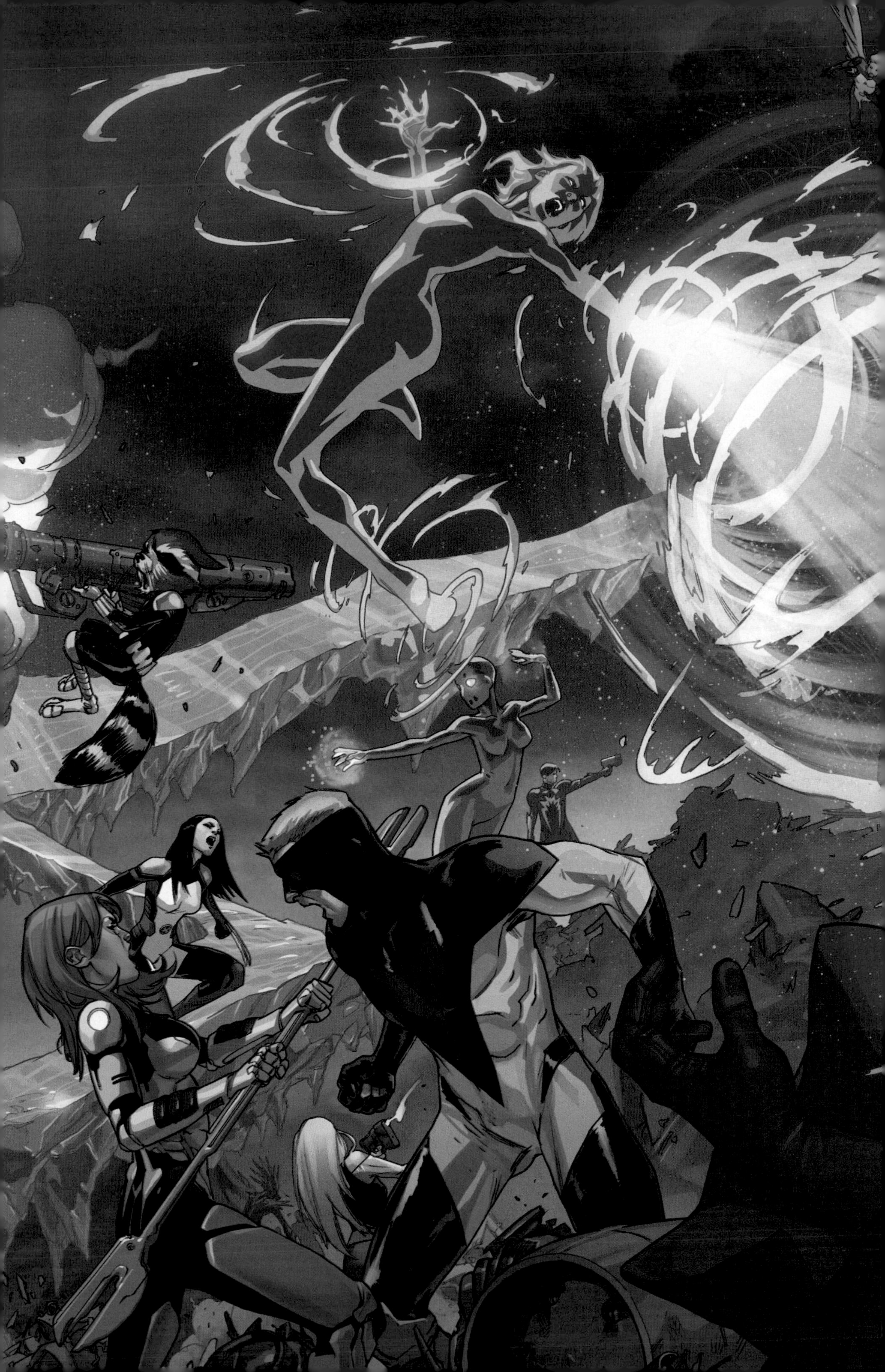

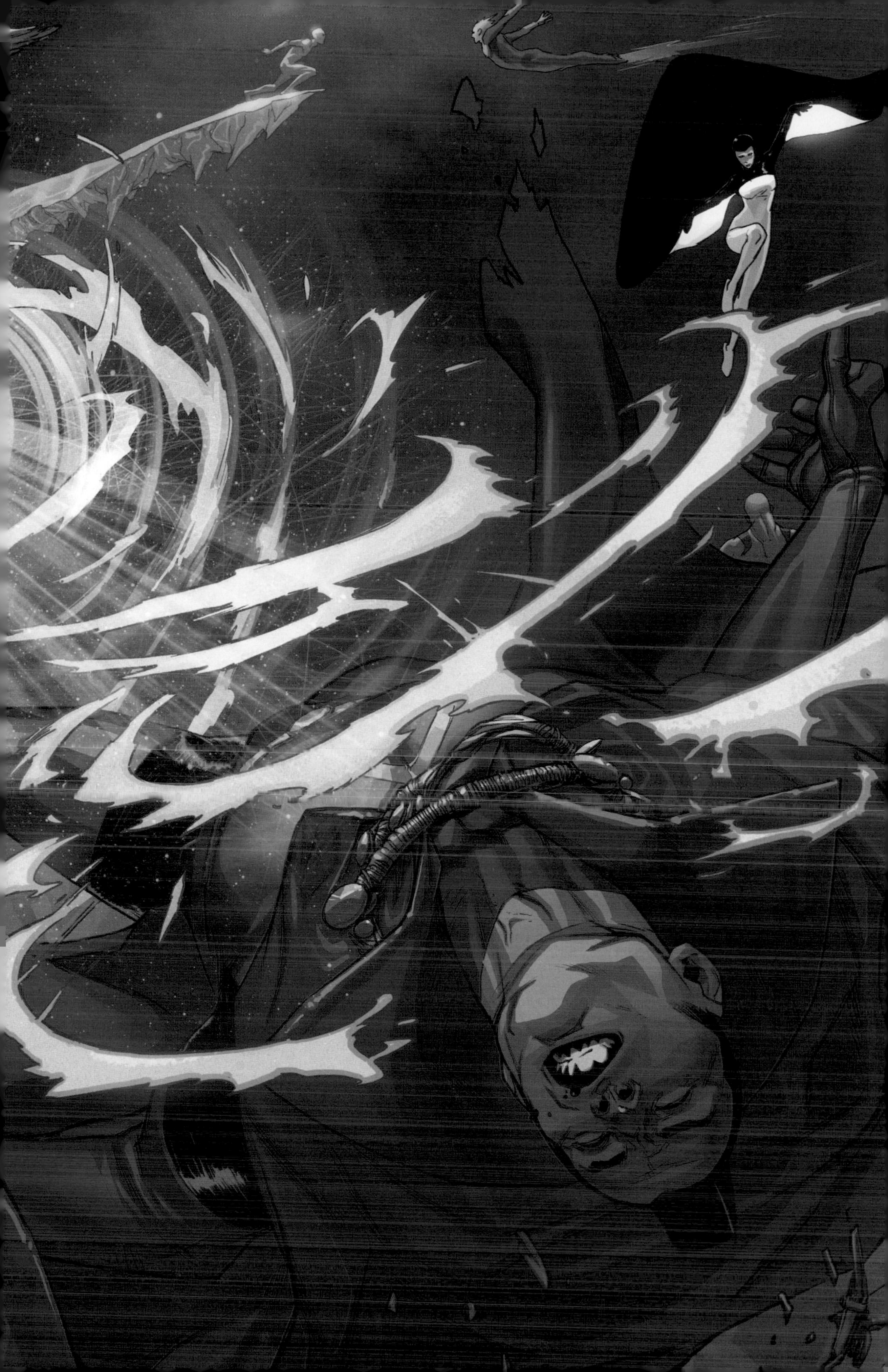

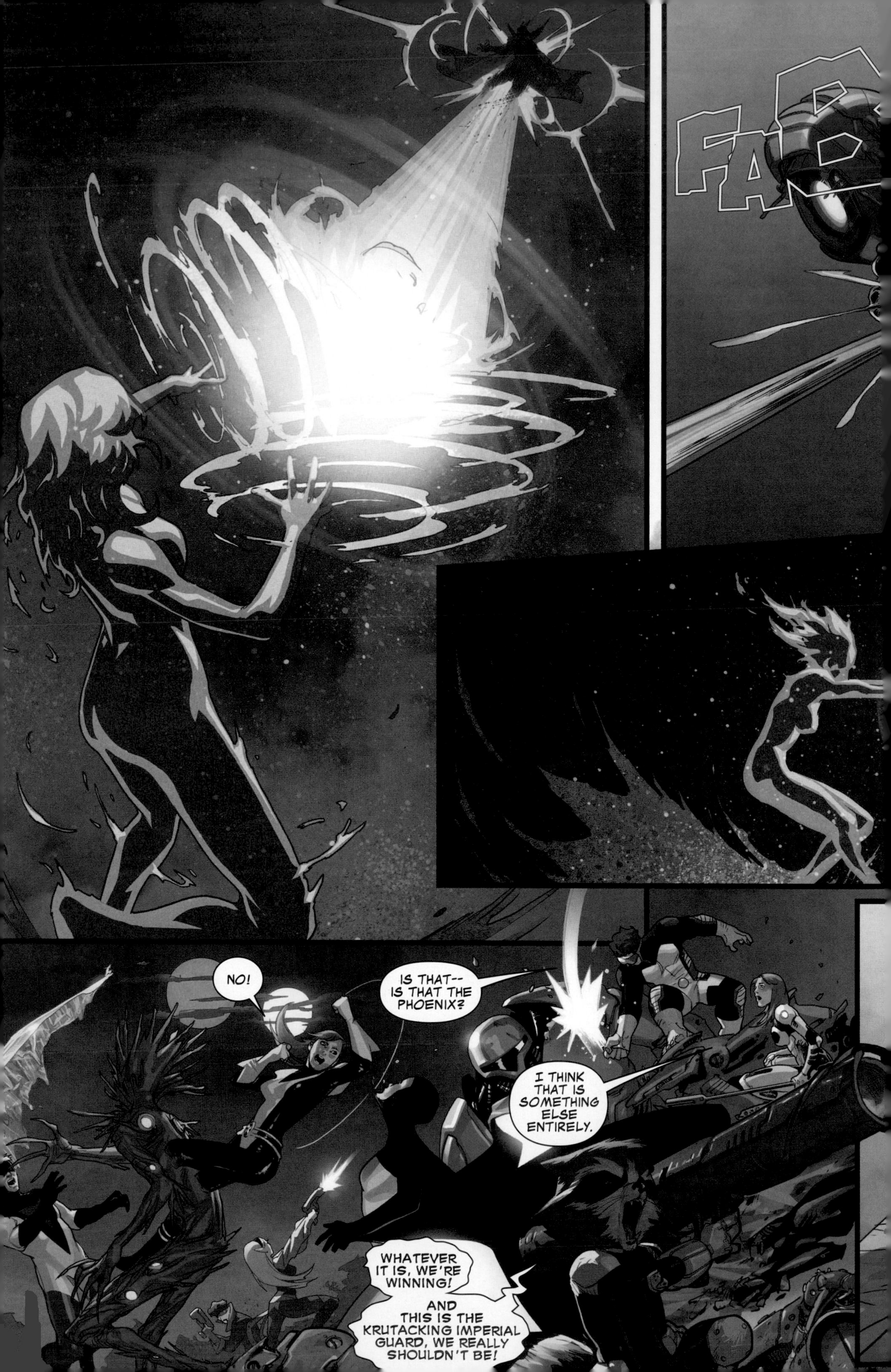
FA-
NO!
IS THAT-- IS THAT THE PHOENIX?
I THINK THAT IS SOMETHING ELSE ENTIRELY.
WHATEVER IT IS, WE'RE WINNING!
AND THIS IS THE KRUTACKING IMPERIAL GUARD, WE REALLY SHOULDN'T BE!

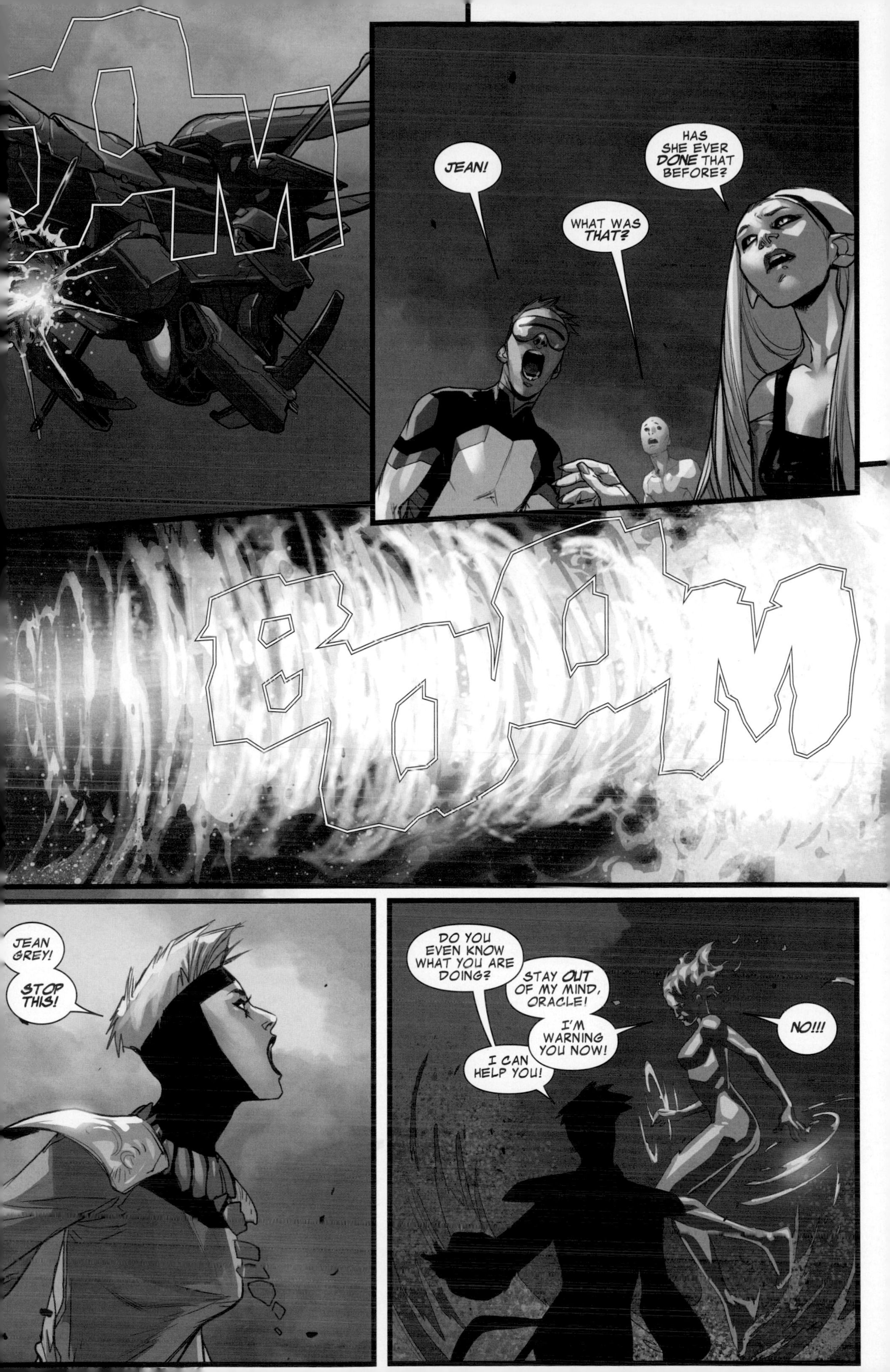

OOM
JEAN!
HAS SHE EVER DONE THAT BEFORE?
WHAT WAS THAT?
BOOM
JEAN GREY!
STOP THIS!
DO YOU EVEN KNOW WHAT YOU ARE DOING?
STAY OUT OF MY MIND, ORACLE!
I'M WARNING YOU NOW!
I CAN HELP YOU!
NO!!!

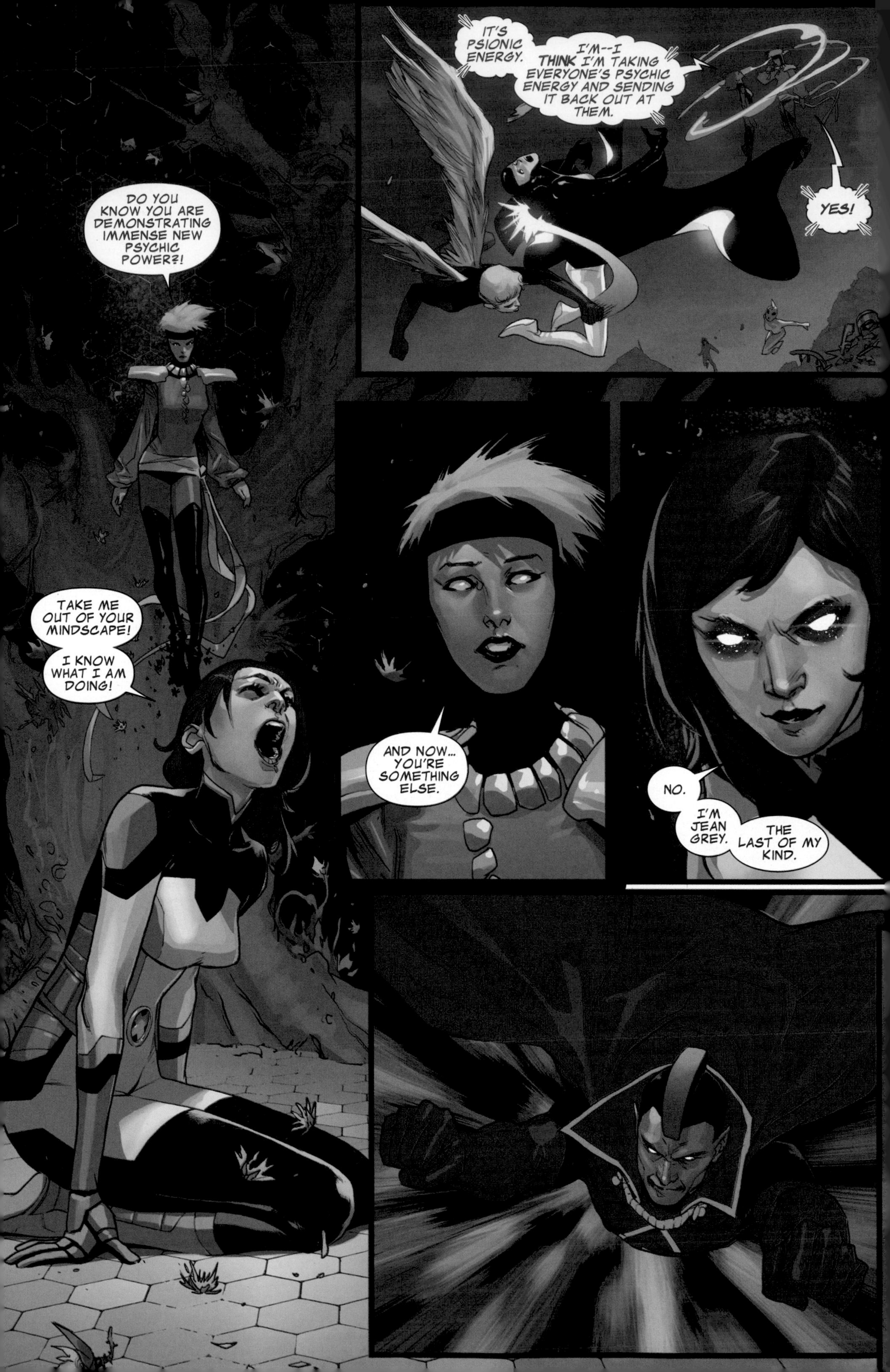
DO YOU KNOW YOU ARE DEMONSTRATING IMMENSE NEW PSYCHIC POWER?!
IT'S PSIONIC ENERGY.
I'M--I THINK I'M TAKING EVERYONE'S PSYCHIC ENERGY AND SENDING IT BACK OUT AT THEM.
YES!
TAKE ME OUT OF YOUR MINDSCAPE!
I KNOW WHAT I AM DOING!
AND NOW... YOU'RE SOMETHING ELSE.
NO.
I'M JEAN GREY.
THE LAST OF MY KIND.

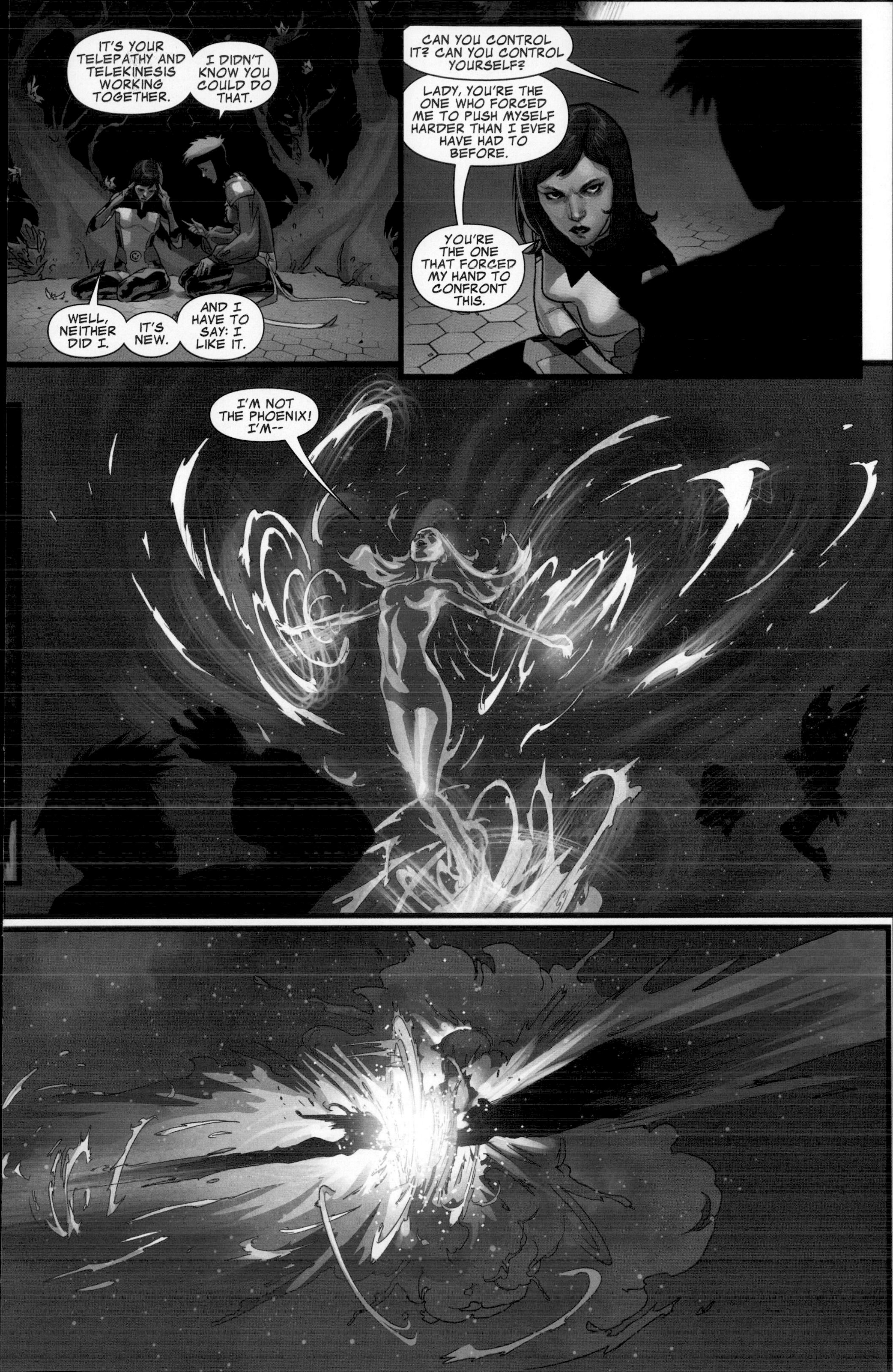
IT'S YOUR TELEPATHY AND TELEKINESIS WORKING TOGETHER.
I DIDN'T KNOW YOU COULD DO THAT.
WELL, NEITHER DID I.
IT'S NEW.
AND I HAVE TO SAY: I LIKE IT.
CAN YOU CONTROL IT? CAN YOU CONTROL YOURSELF?
LADY, YOU'RE THE ONE WHO FORCED ME TO PUSH MYSELF HARDER THAN I EVER HAVE HAD TO BEFORE.
YOU'RE THE ONE THAT FORCED MY HAND TO CONFRONT THIS.
I'M NOT THE PHOENIX! I'M--

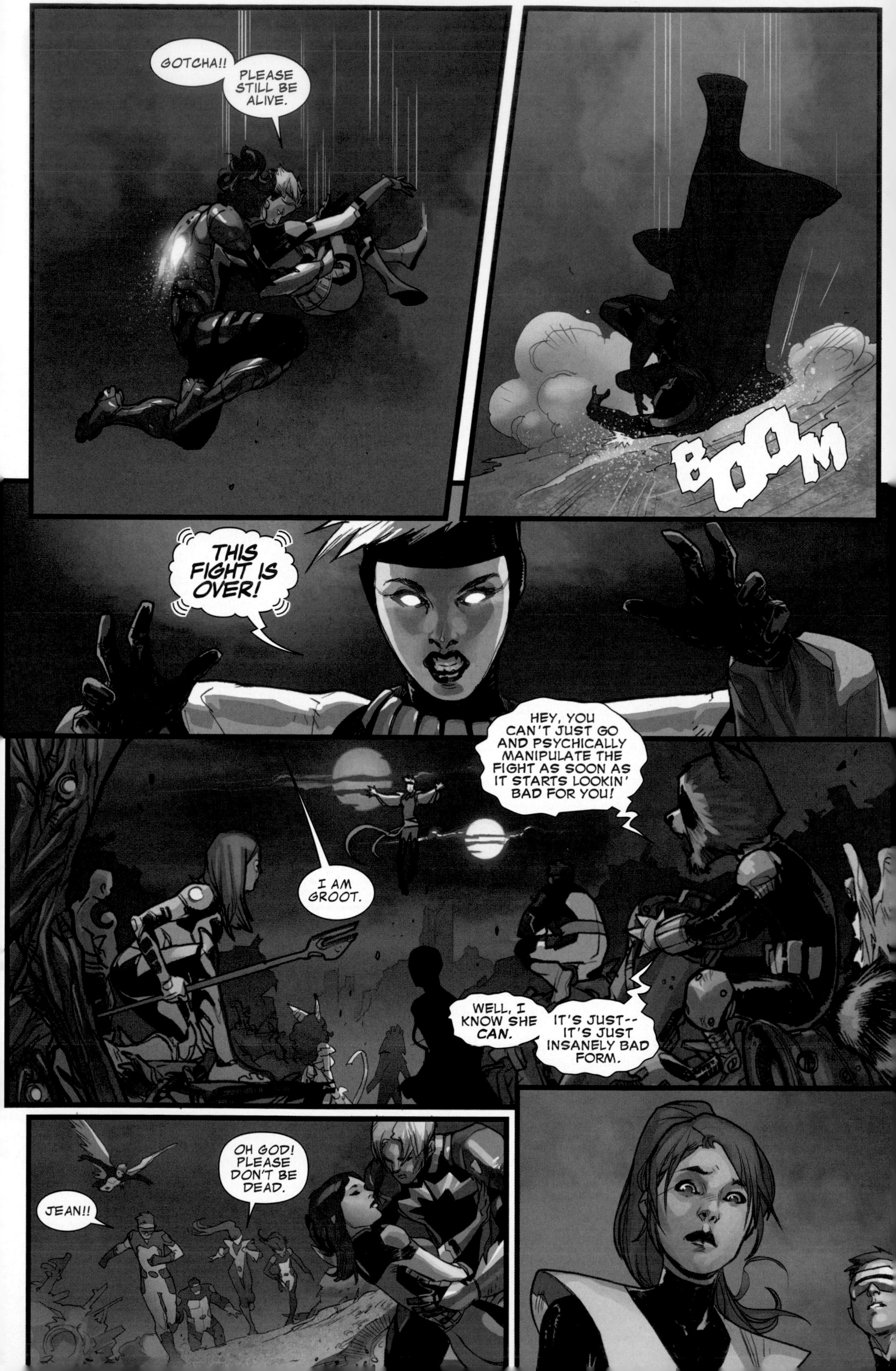
GOTCHA!!
PLEASE STILL BE ALIVE.
BOOM
THIS FIGHT IS OVER!
HEY, YOU CAN'T JUST GO AND PSYCHICALLY MANIPULATE THE FIGHT AS SOON AS IT STARTS LOOKIN' BAD FOR YOU!
I AM GROOT.
WELL, I KNOW SHE CAN.
IT'S JUST-- IT'S JUST INSANELY BAD FORM.
JEAN!!
OH GOD! PLEASE DON'T BE DEAD.

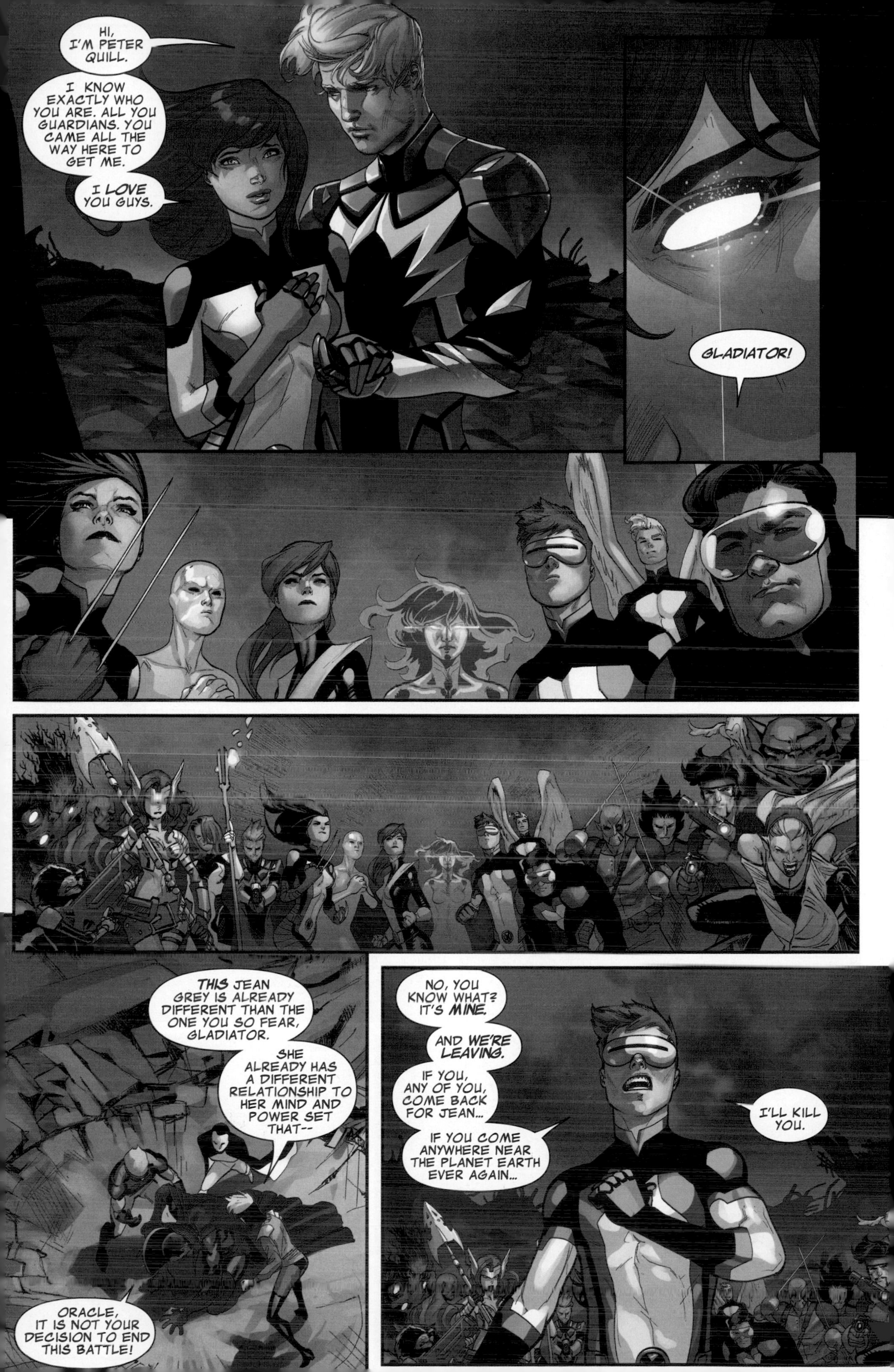
HI, I'M PETER QUILL.
I KNOW EXACTLY WHO YOU ARE. ALL YOU GUARDIANS. YOU CAME ALL THE WAY HERE TO GET ME.
I LOVE YOU GUYS.
GLADIATOR!
THIS JEAN GREY IS ALREADY DIFFERENT THAN THE ONE YOU SO FEAR, GLADIATOR.
SHE ALREADY HAS A DIFFERENT RELATIONSHIP TO HER MIND AND POWER SET THAT--
ORACLE, IT IS NOT YOUR DECISION TO END THIS BATTLE!
NO, YOU KNOW WHAT? IT'S MINE.
AND WE'RE LEAVING.
IF YOU, ANY OF YOU, COME BACK FOR JEAN...
IF YOU COME ANYWHERE NEAR THE PLANET EARTH EVER AGAIN...
I'LL KILL YOU.

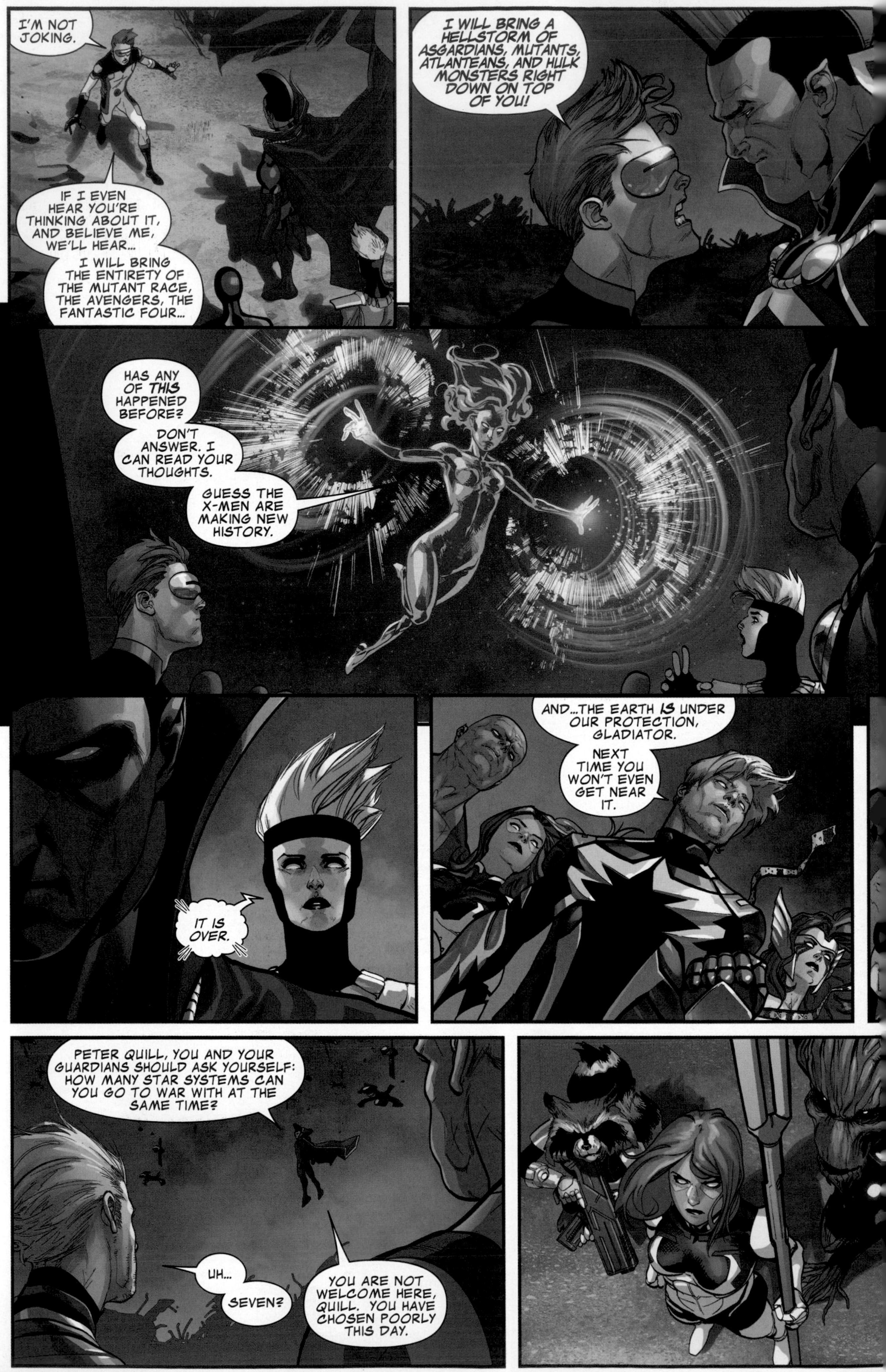
I'M NOT JOKING.
IF I EVEN HEAR YOU'RE THINKING ABOUT IT, AND BELIEVE ME, WE'LL HEAR...
I WILL BRING THE ENTIRETY OF THE MUTANT RACE, THE AVENGERS, THE FANTASTIC FOUR...
I WILL BRING A HELLSTORM OF ASGARDIANS, MUTANTS, ATLANTEANS, AND HULK MONSTERS RIGHT DOWN ON TOP OF YOU!
HAS ANY OF THIS HAPPENED BEFORE?
DON'T ANSWER. I CAN READ YOUR THOUGHTS.
GUESS THE X-MEN ARE MAKING NEW HISTORY.
IT IS OVER.
AND...THE EARTH IS UNDER OUR PROTECTION, GLADIATOR.
NEXT TIME YOU WON'T EVEN GET NEAR IT.
PETER QUILL, YOU AND YOUR GUARDIANS SHOULD ASK YOURSELF: HOW MANY STAR SYSTEMS CAN YOU GO TO WAR WITH AT THE SAME TIME?
UH...
SEVEN?
YOU ARE NOT WELCOME HERE, QUILL. YOU HAVE CHOSEN POORLY THIS DAY.

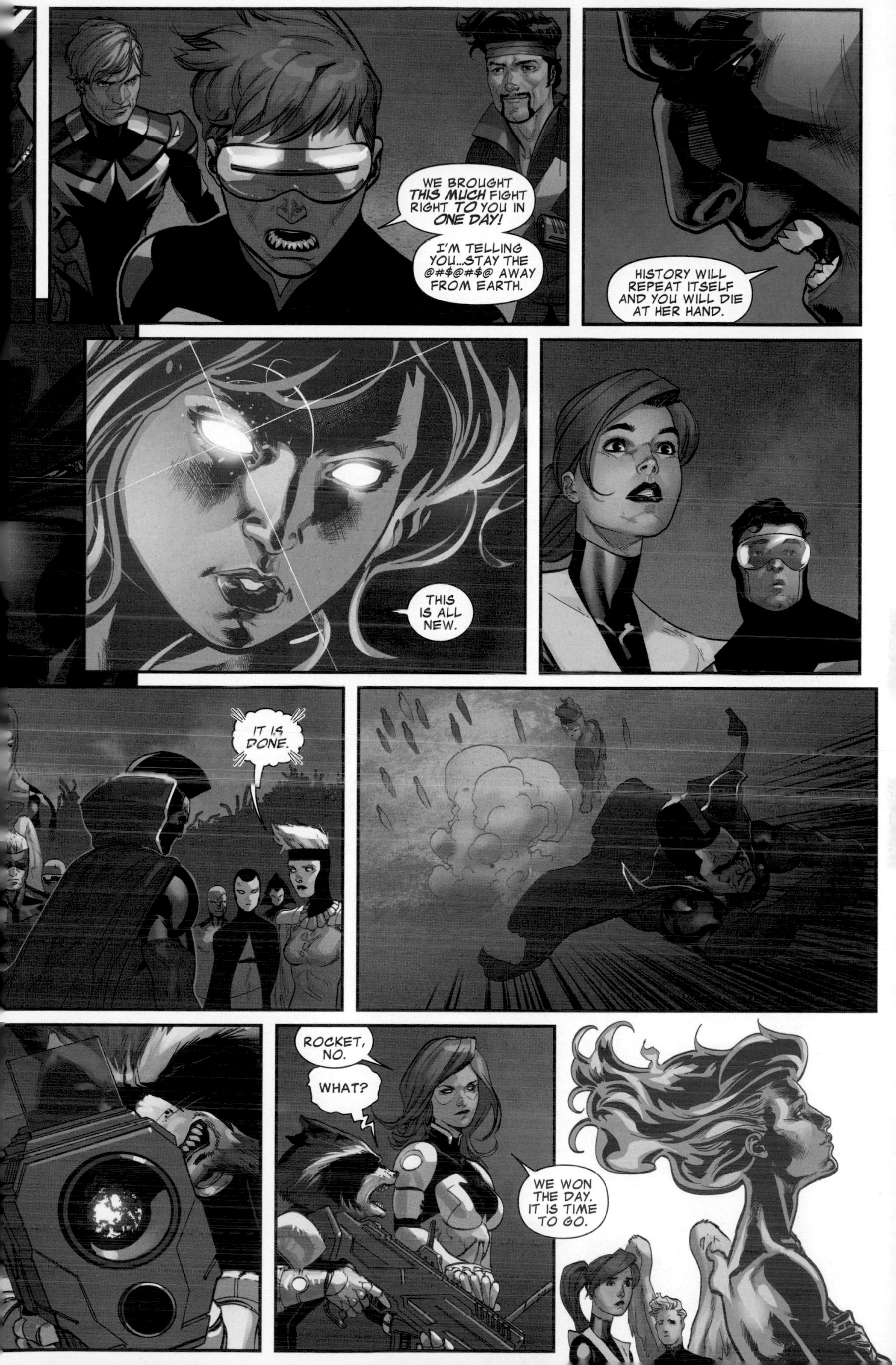
WE BROUGHT THIS MUCH FIGHT RIGHT TO YOU IN ONE DAY!
I'M TELLING YOU...STAY THE @#$@#$@ AWAY FROM EARTH.
HISTORY WILL REPEAT ITSELF AND YOU WILL DIE AT HER HAND.
THIS IS ALL NEW.
IT IS DONE.
ROCKET, NO.
WHAT?
WE WON THE DAY. IT IS TIME TO GO.

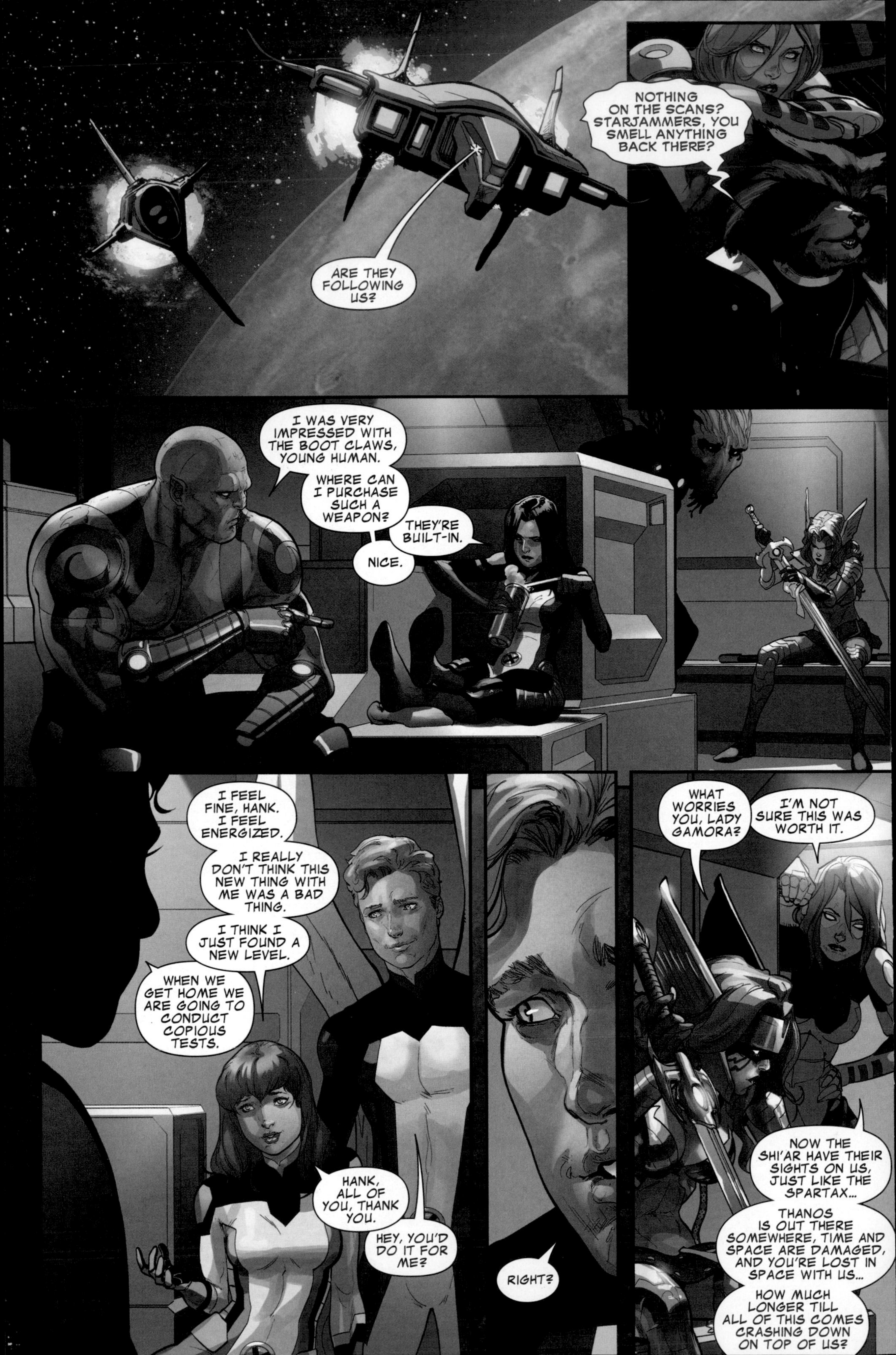
NOTHING ON THE SCANS? STARJAMMERS, YOU SMELL ANYTHING BACK THERE?
ARE THEY FOLLOWING US?
I WAS VERY IMPRESSED WITH THE BOOT CLAWS, YOUNG HUMAN.
WHERE CAN I PURCHASE SUCH A WEAPON?
THEY'RE BUILT-IN.
NICE.
I FEEL FINE, HANK. I FEEL ENERGIZED.
I REALLY DON'T THINK THIS NEW THING WITH ME WAS A BAD THING.
I THINK I JUST FOUND A NEW LEVEL.
WHEN WE GET HOME WE ARE GOING TO CONDUCT COPIOUS TESTS.
HANK, ALL OF YOU, THANK YOU.
HEY, YOU'D DO IT FOR ME?
RIGHT?
WHAT WORRIES YOU, LADY GAMORA?
I'M NOT SURE THIS WAS WORTH IT.
NOW THE SHI'AR HAVE THEIR SIGHTS ON US, JUST LIKE THE SPARTAX...
THANOS IS OUT THERE SOMEWHERE, TIME AND SPACE ARE DAMAGED, AND YOU'RE LOST IN SPACE WITH US...
HOW MUCH LONGER TILL ALL OF THIS COMES CRASHING DOWN ON TOP OF US?

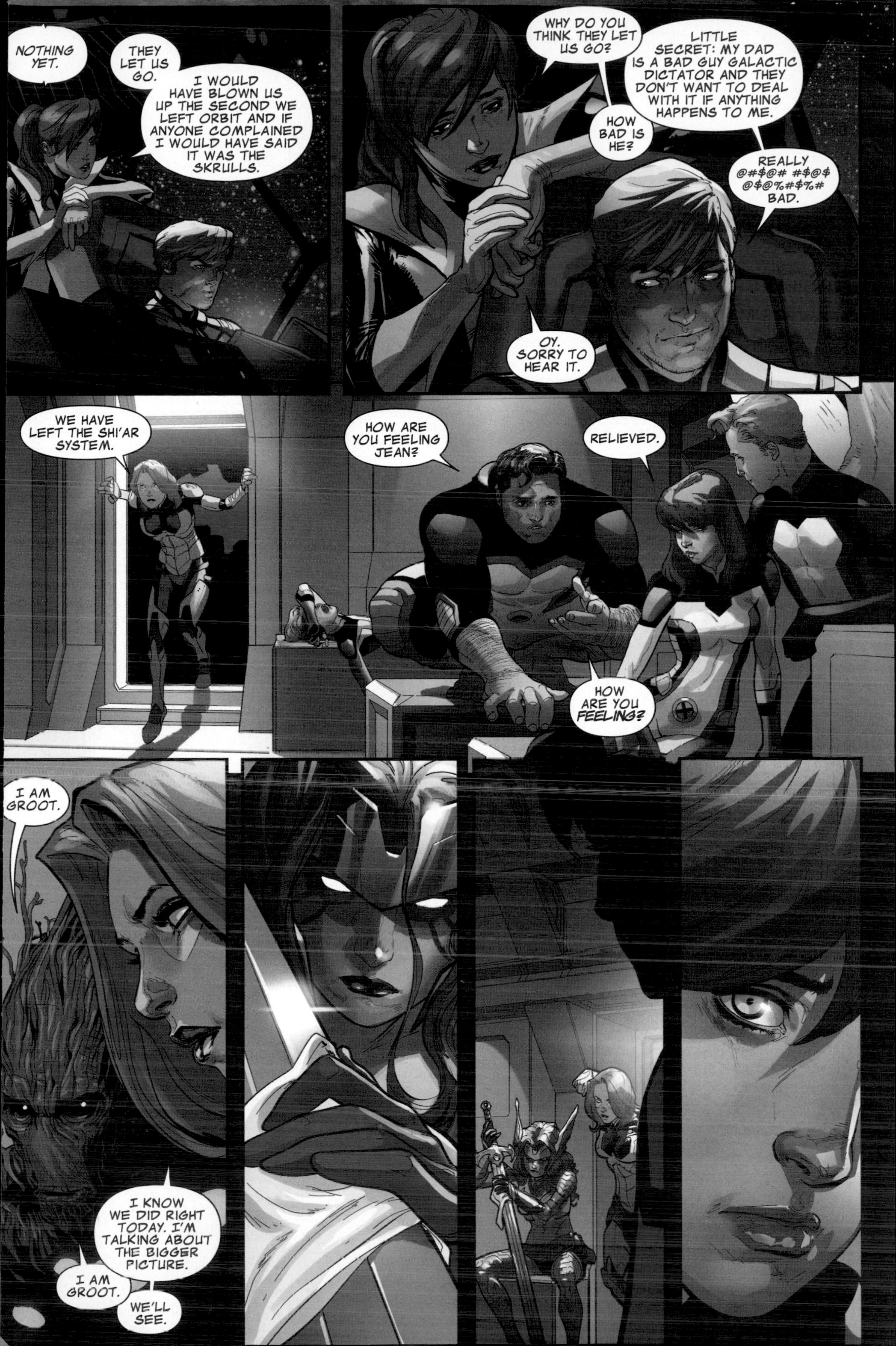
NOTHING YET.
THEY LET US GO.
I WOULD HAVE BLOWN US UP THE SECOND WE LEFT ORBIT AND IF ANYONE COMPLAINED I WOULD HAVE SAID IT WAS THE SKRULLS.
WHY DO YOU THINK THEY LET US GO?
LITTLE SECRET: MY DAD IS A BAD GUY GALACTIC DICTATOR AND THEY DON'T WANT TO DEAL WITH IT IF ANYTHING HAPPENS TO ME.
HOW BAD IS HE?
REALLY @#$@# #$@$ @$@%#$%# BAD.
OY. SORRY TO HEAR IT.
WE HAVE LEFT THE SHI'AR SYSTEM.
HOW ARE YOU FEELING JEAN?
RELIEVED.
HOW ARE YOU FEELING?
I AM GROOT.
I KNOW WE DID RIGHT TODAY. I'M TALKING ABOUT THE BIGGER PICTURE.
I AM GROOT.
WE'LL SEE.

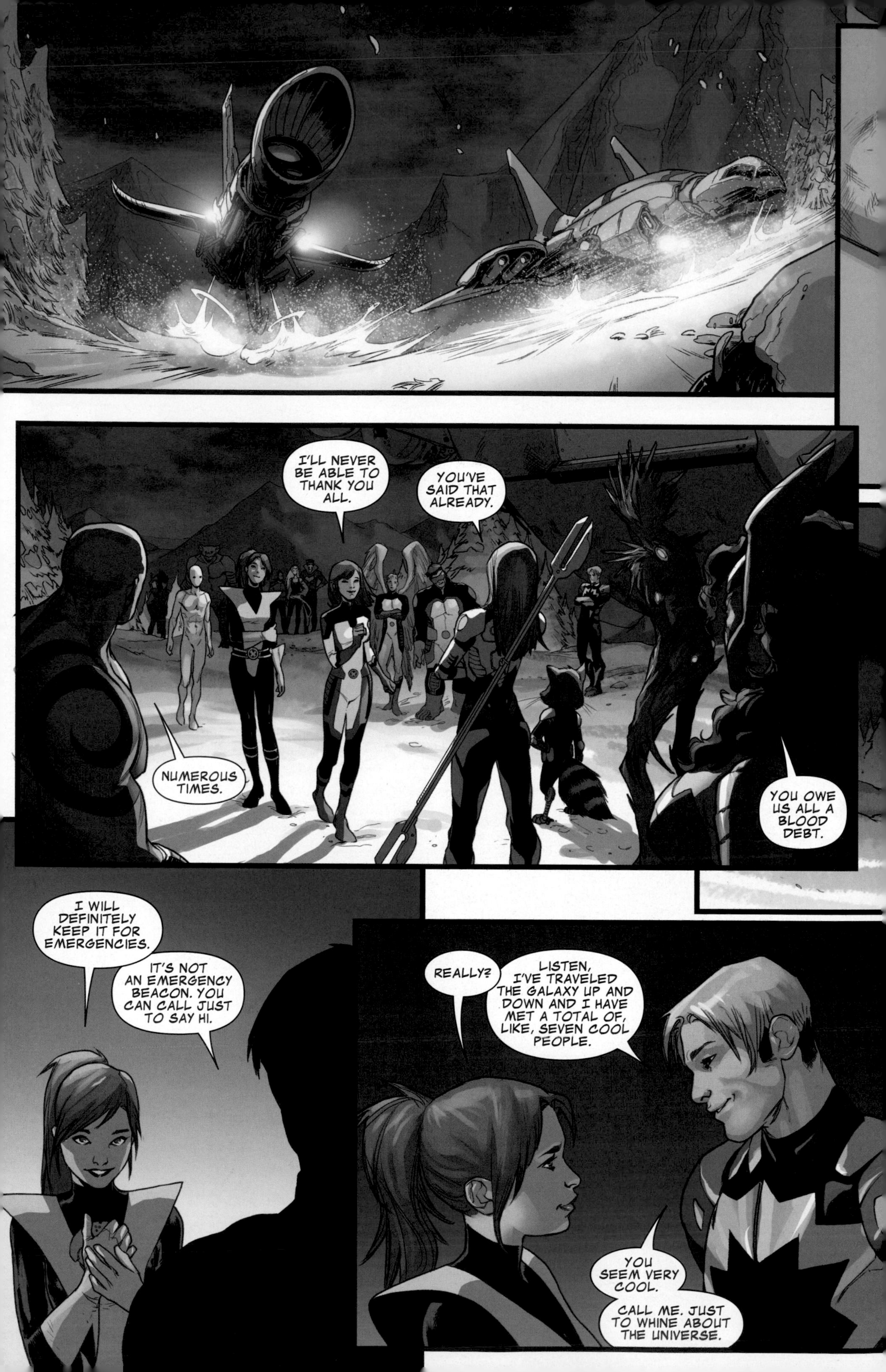

I'LL NEVER BE ABLE TO THANK YOU ALL.
YOU'VE SAID THAT ALREADY.
NUMEROUS TIMES.
YOU OWE US ALL A BLOOD DEBT.
I WILL DEFINITELY KEEP IT FOR EMERGENCIES.
IT'S NOT AN EMERGENCY BEACON. YOU CAN CALL JUST TO SAY HI.
REALLY?
LISTEN, I'VE TRAVELED THE GALAXY UP AND DOWN AND I HAVE MET A TOTAL OF, LIKE, SEVEN COOL PEOPLE.
YOU SEEM VERY COOL.
CALL ME. JUST TO WHINE ABOUT THE UNIVERSE.

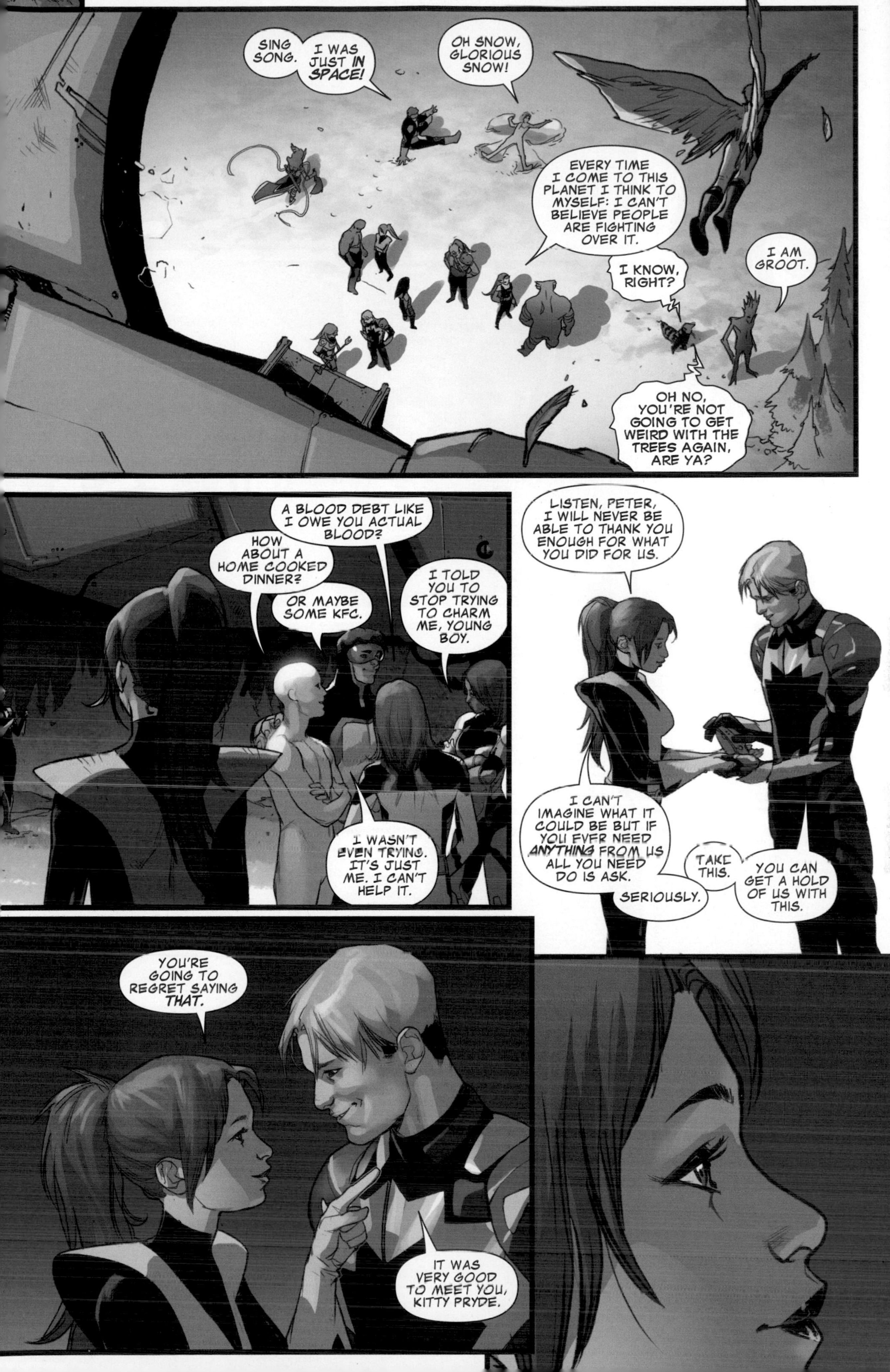
SING SONG.
I WAS JUST IN SPACE!
OH SNOW, GLORIOUS SNOW!
EVERY TIME I COME TO THIS PLANET I THINK TO MYSELF: I CAN'T BELIEVE PEOPLE ARE FIGHTING OVER IT.
I KNOW, RIGHT?
I AM GROOT.
OH NO, YOU'RE NOT GOING TO GET WEIRD WITH THE TREES AGAIN, ARE YA?
A BLOOD DEBT LIKE I OWE YOU ACTUAL BLOOD?
HOW ABOUT A HOME COOKED DINNER?
OR MAYBE SOME KFC.
I TOLD YOU TO STOP TRYING TO CHARM ME, YOUNG BOY.
I WASN'T EVEN TRYING. IT'S JUST ME. I CAN'T HELP IT.
LISTEN, PETER, I WILL NEVER BE ABLE TO THANK YOU ENOUGH FOR WHAT YOU DID FOR US.
I CAN'T IMAGINE WHAT IT COULD BE BUT IF YOU EVER NEED ANYTHING FROM US ALL YOU NEED DO IS ASK.
SERIOUSLY.
TAKE THIS.
YOU CAN GET A HOLD OF US WITH THIS.
YOU'RE GOING TO REGRET SAYING THAT.
IT WAS VERY GOOD TO MEET YOU, KITTY PRYDE.

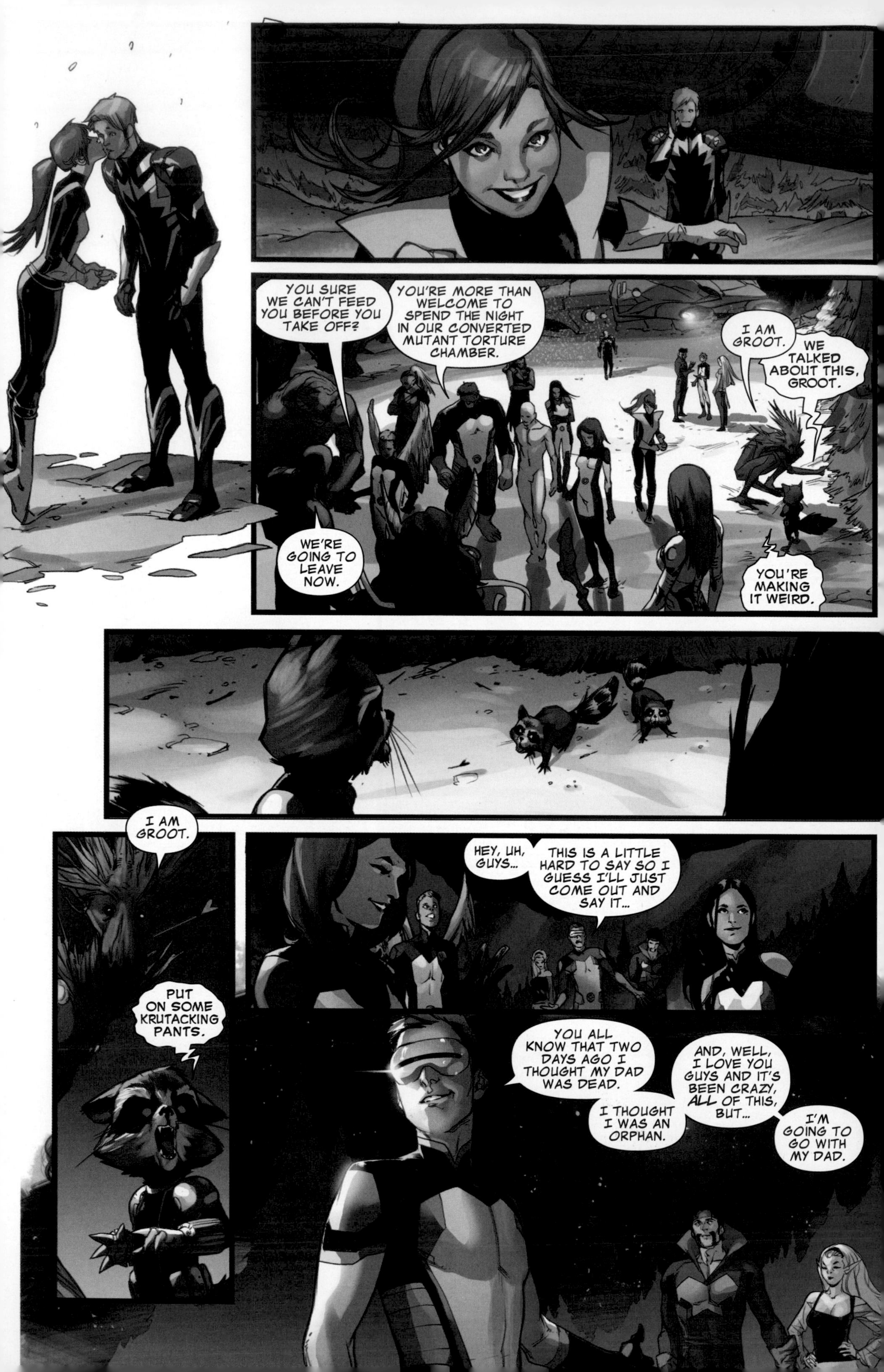
YOU SURE WE CAN'T FEED YOU BEFORE YOU TAKE OFF?
YOU'RE MORE THAN WELCOME TO SPEND THE NIGHT IN OUR CONVERTED MUTANT TORTURE CHAMBER.
WE'RE GOING TO LEAVE NOW.
I AM GROOT.
WE TALKED ABOUT THIS, GROOT.
YOU'RE MAKING IT WEIRD.
I AM GROOT.
PUT ON SOME KRUTACKING PANTS.
HEY, UH, GUYS...
THIS IS A LITTLE HARD TO SAY SO I GUESS I'LL JUST COME OUT AND SAY IT...
YOU ALL KNOW THAT TWO DAYS AGO I THOUGHT MY DAD WAS DEAD.
I THOUGHT I WAS AN ORPHAN.
AND, WELL, I LOVE YOU GUYS AND IT'S BEEN CRAZY, ALL OF THIS, BUT...
I'M GOING TO GO WITH MY DAD.

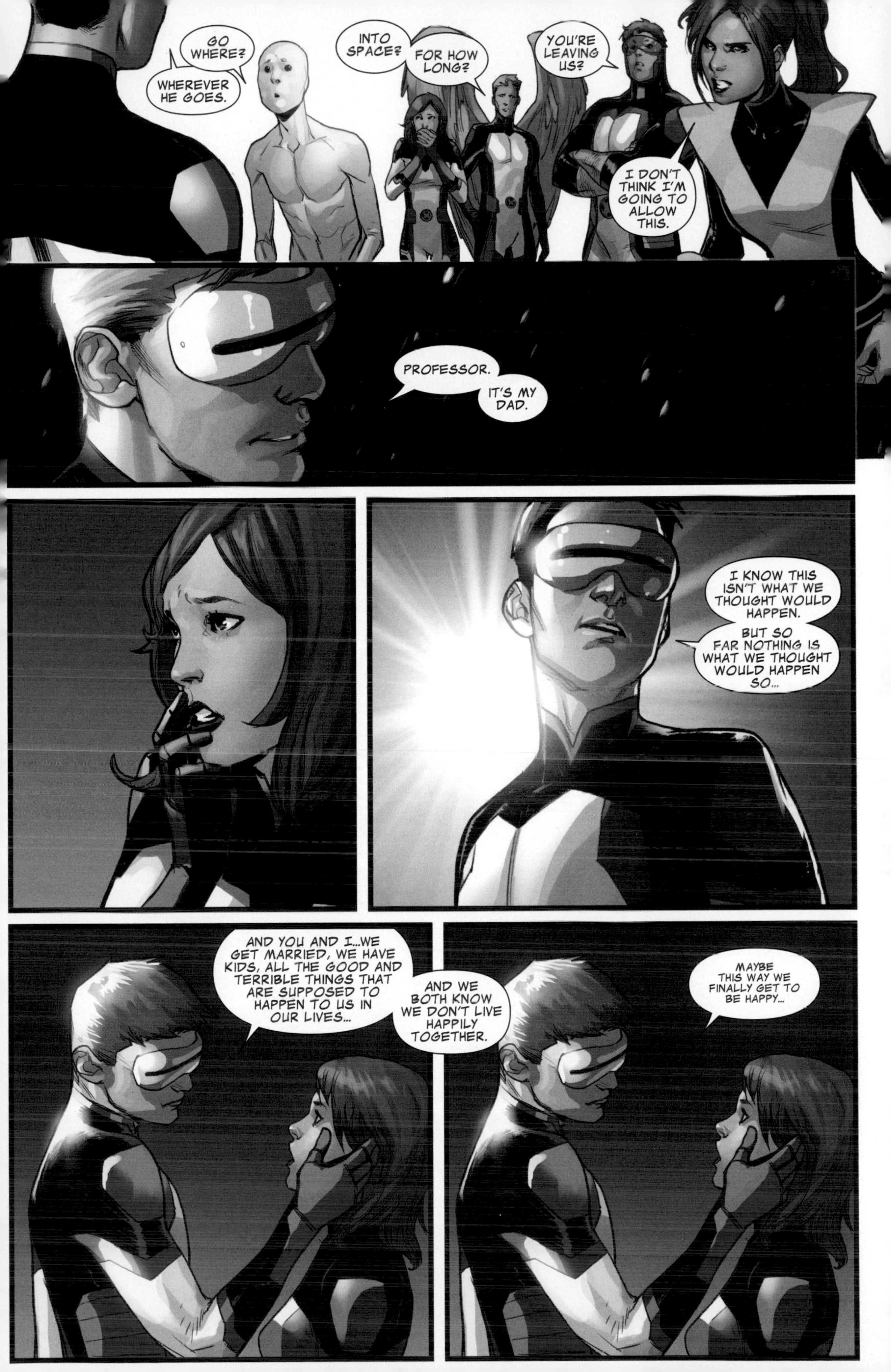
GO WHERE?
WHEREVER HE GOES.
INTO SPACE?
FOR HOW LONG?
YOU'RE LEAVING US?
I DON'T THINK I'M GOING TO ALLOW THIS.
PROFESSOR.
IT'S MY DAD.
I KNOW THIS ISN'T WHAT WE THOUGHT WOULD HAPPEN.
BUT SO FAR NOTHING IS WHAT WE THOUGHT WOULD HAPPEN SO...
AND YOU AND I...WE GET MARRIED, WE HAVE KIDS, ALL THE GOOD AND TERRIBLE THINGS THAT ARE SUPPOSED TO HAPPEN TO US IN OUR LIVES...
AND WE BOTH KNOW WE DON'T LIVE HAPPILY TOGETHER.
MAYBE THIS WAY WE FINALLY GET TO BE HAPPY...

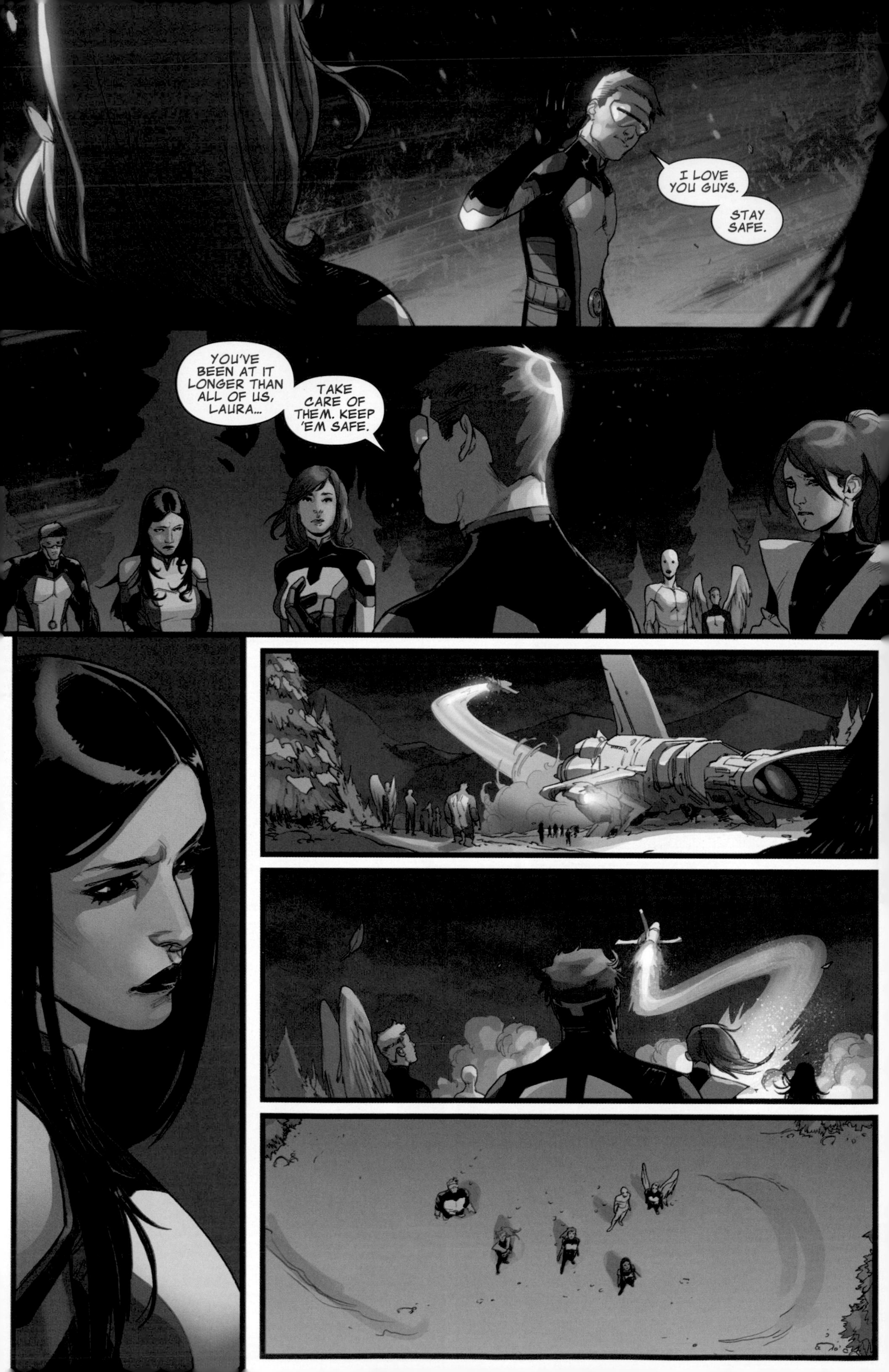

I LOVE YOU GUYS.
STAY SAFE.
YOU'VE BEEN AT IT LONGER THAN ALL OF US, LAURA...
TAKE CARE OF THEM. KEEP 'EM SAFE.

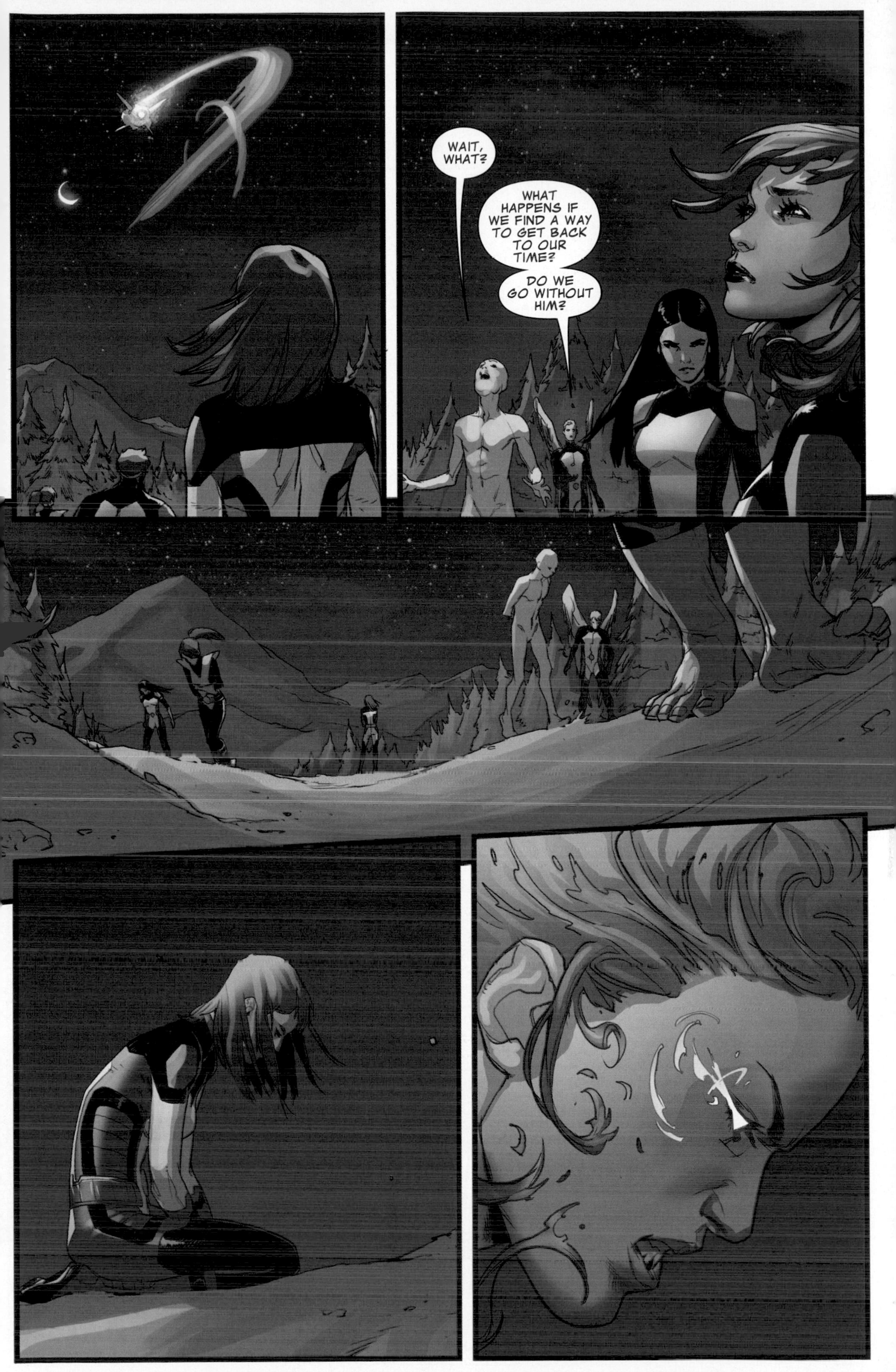
WAIT, WHAT?
WHAT HAPPENS IF WE FIND A WAY TO GET BACK TO OUR TIME?
DO WE GO WITHOUT HIM?

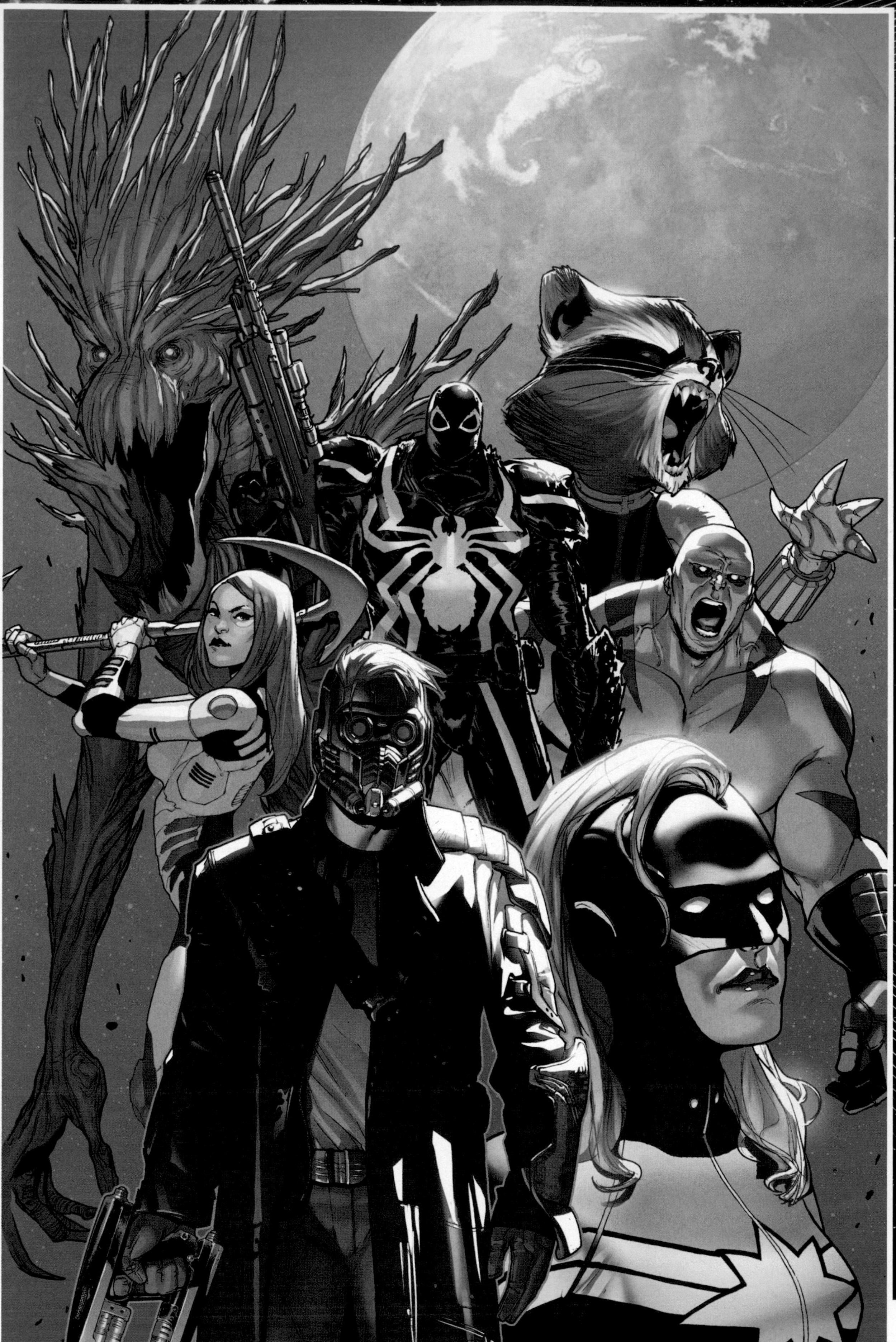

FREE COMIC BOOK DAY 2014 (GUARDIANS OF THE GALAXY) 1

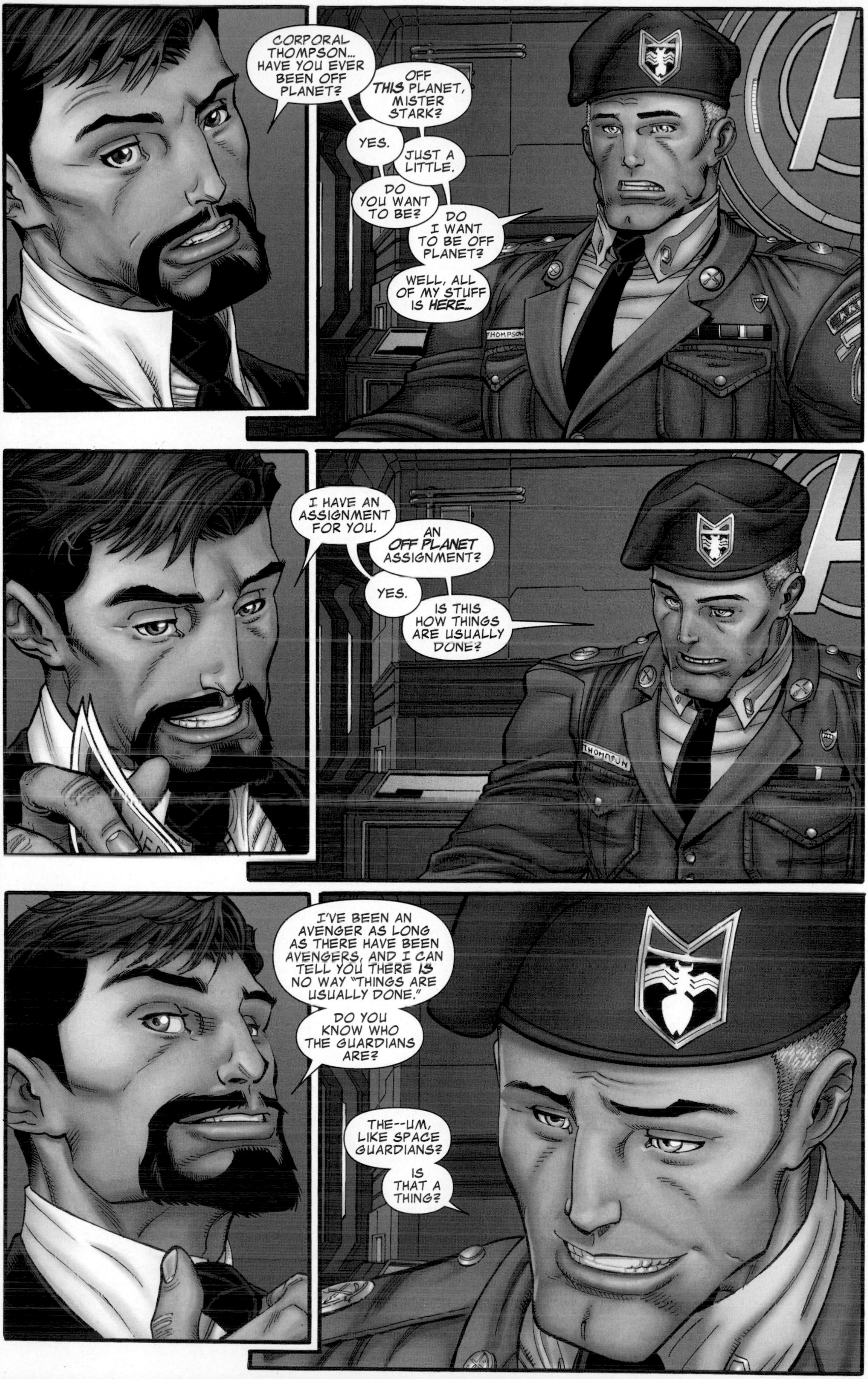
CORPORAL THOMPSON... HAVE YOU EVER BEEN OFF PLANET?
OFF THIS PLANET, MISTER STARK?
YES.
JUST A LITTLE.
DO YOU WANT TO BE?
DO I WANT TO BE OFF PLANET?
WELL, ALL OF MY STUFF IS HERE...
THOMPSON
I HAVE AN ASSIGNMENT FOR YOU.
AN OFF PLANET ASSIGNMENT?
YES.
IS THIS HOW THINGS ARE USUALLY DONE?
I'VE BEEN AN AVENGER AS LONG AS THERE HAVE BEEN AVENGERS, AND I CAN TELL YOU THERE IS NO WAY "THINGS ARE USUALLY DONE."
DO YOU KNOW WHO THE GUARDIANS ARE?
THE--UM, LIKE SPACE GUARDIANS?
IS THAT A THING?

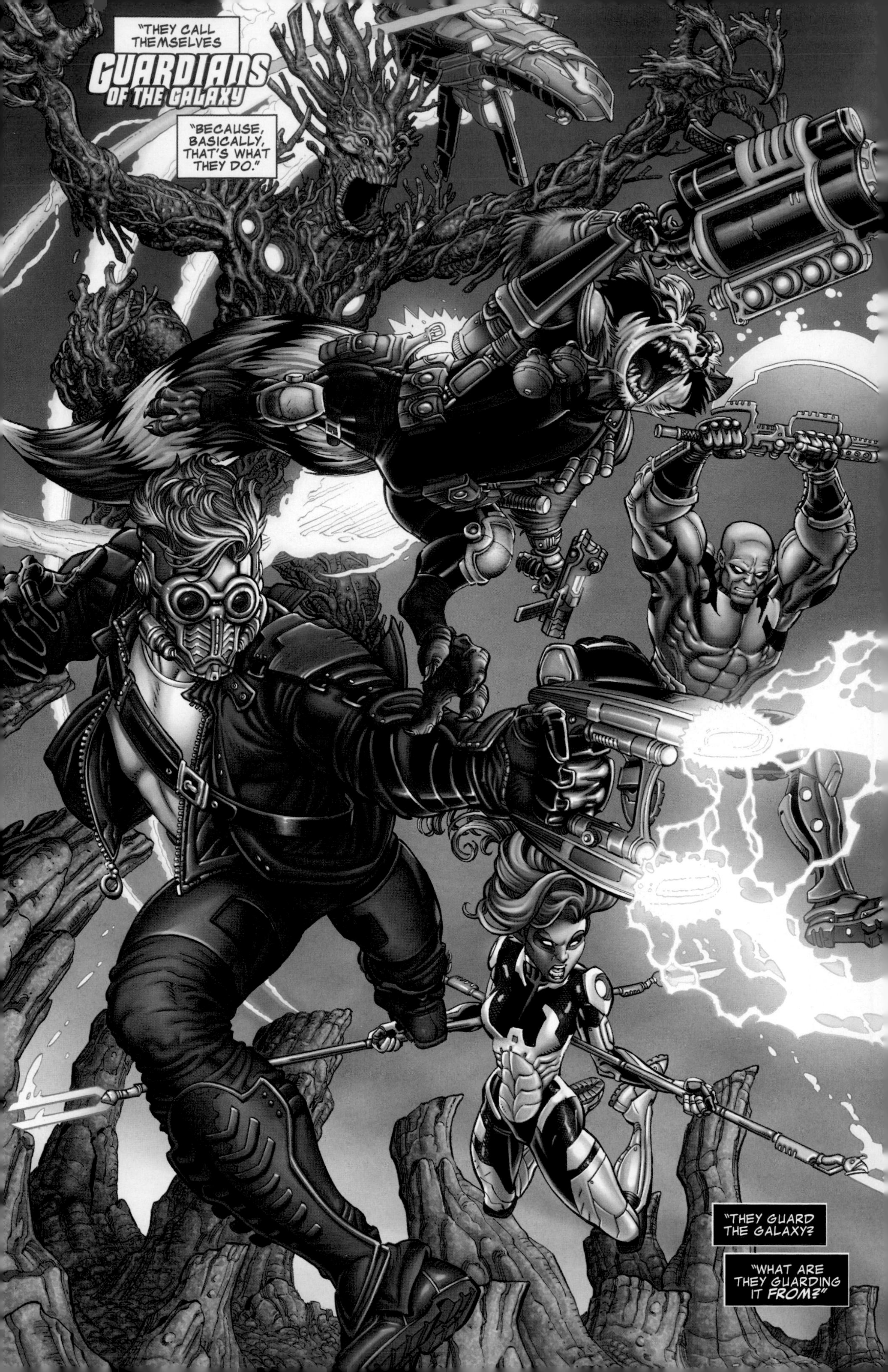
"THEY CALL THEMSELVES
GUARDIANS OF THE GALAXY
"BECAUSE, BASICALLY, THAT'S WHAT THEY DO."
"THEY GUARD THE GALAXY?
"WHAT ARE THEY GUARDING IT FROM?"

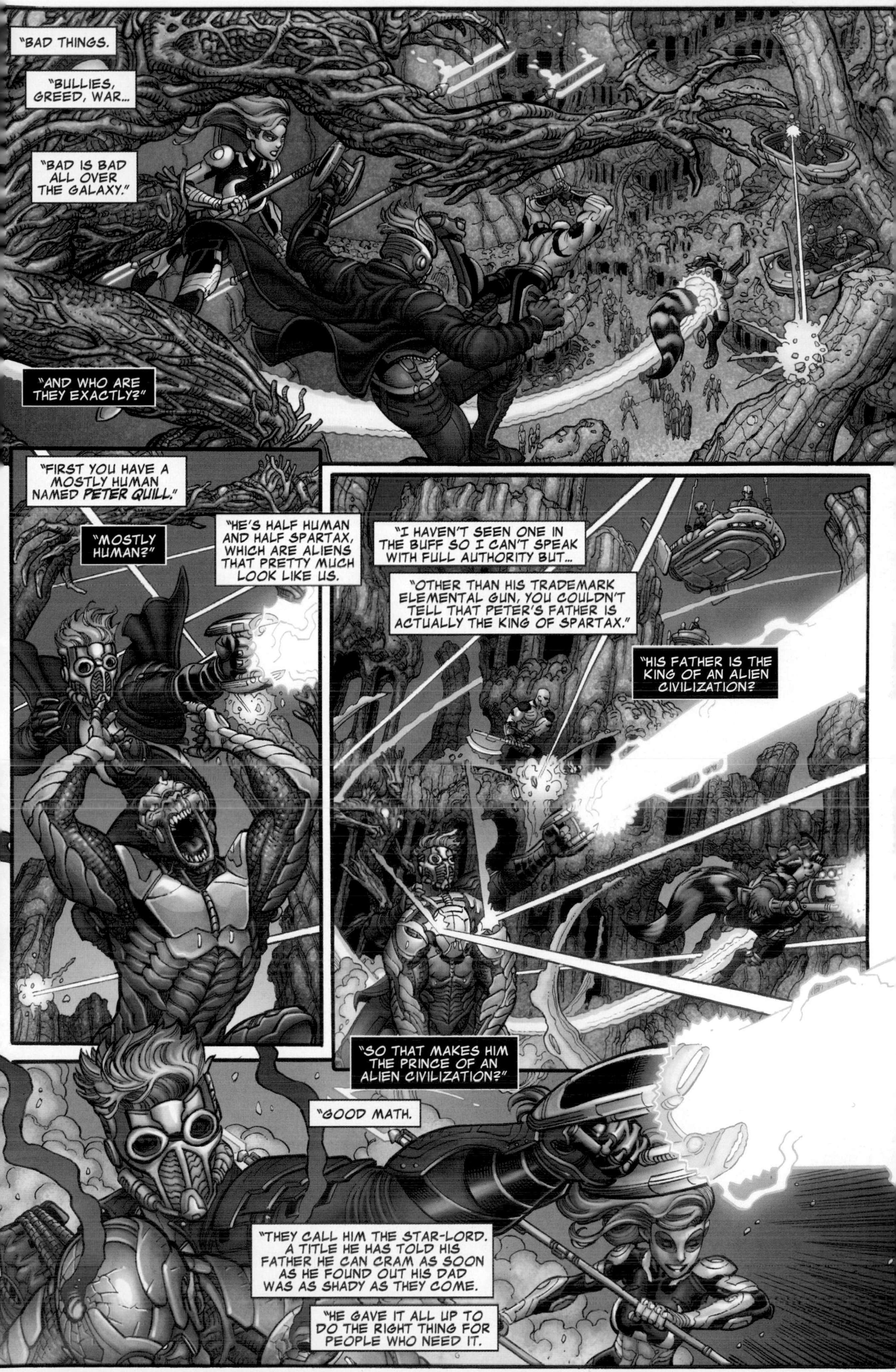

"BAD THINGS.
"BULLIES, GREED, WAR...
"BAD IS BAD ALL OVER THE GALAXY."
"AND WHO ARE THEY EXACTLY?"
"FIRST YOU HAVE A MOSTLY HUMAN NAMED PETER QUILL."
"MOSTLY HUMAN?"
"HE'S HALF HUMAN AND HALF SPARTAX, WHICH ARE ALIENS THAT PRETTY MUCH LOOK LIKE US.
"I HAVEN'T SEEN ONE IN THE BUFF SO I CAN'T SPEAK WITH FULL AUTHORITY BUT...
"OTHER THAN HIS TRADEMARK ELEMENTAL GUN, YOU COULDN'T TELL THAT PETER'S FATHER IS ACTUALLY THE KING OF SPARTAX."
"HIS FATHER IS THE KING OF AN ALIEN CIVILIZATION?
"SO THAT MAKES HIM THE PRINCE OF AN ALIEN CIVILIZATION?"
"GOOD MATH.
"THEY CALL HIM THE STAR-LORD. A TITLE HE HAS TOLD HIS FATHER HE CAN CRAM AS SOON AS HE FOUND OUT HIS DAD WAS AS SHADY AS THEY COME.
"HE GAVE IT ALL UP TO DO THE RIGHT THING FOR PEOPLE WHO NEED IT.

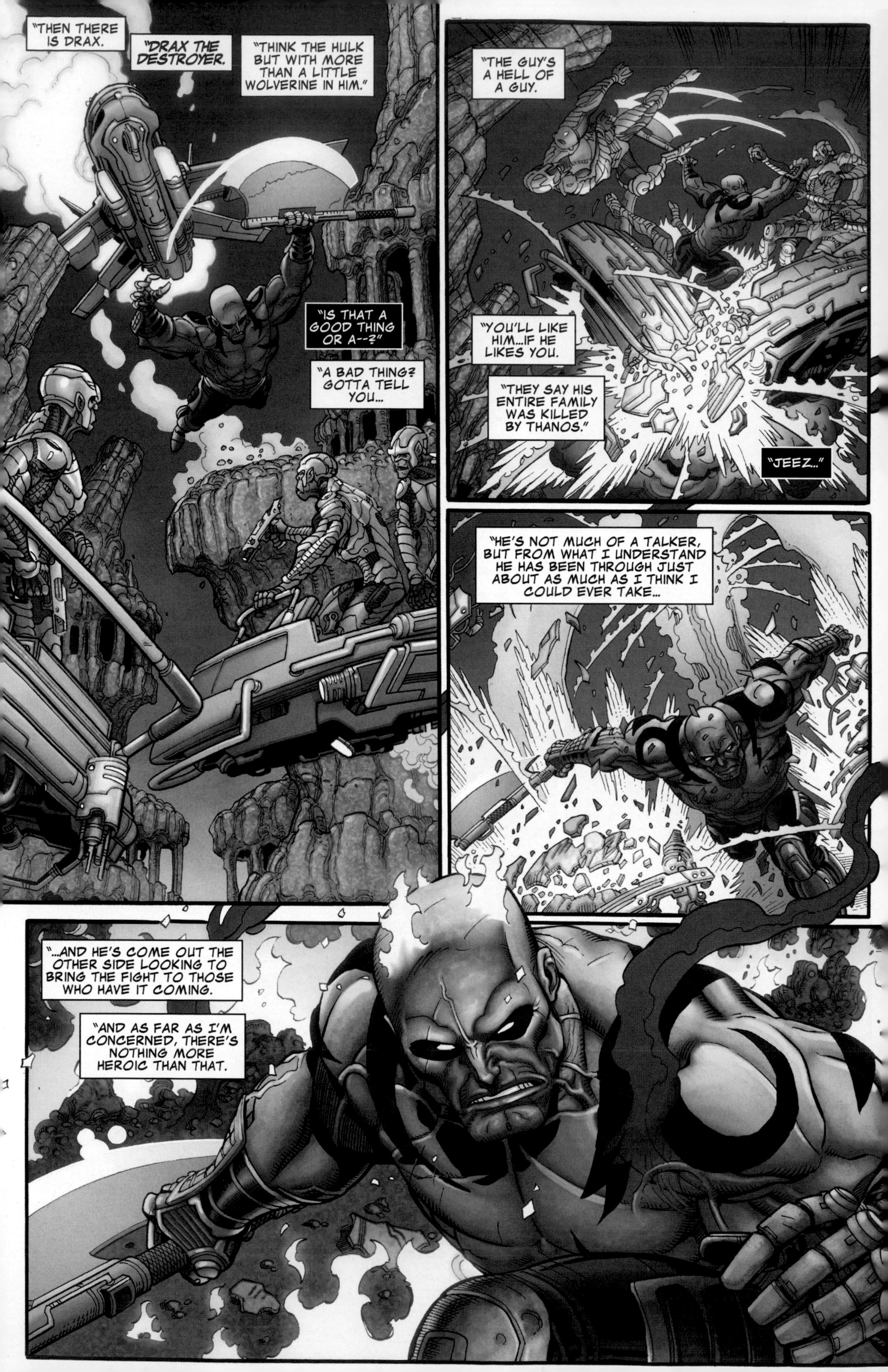
"THEN THERE IS DRAX.
"DRAX THE DESTROYER.
"THINK THE HULK BUT WITH MORE THAN A LITTLE WOLVERINE IN HIM."
"IS THAT A GOOD THING OR A--?"
"A BAD THING? GOTTA TELL YOU...
"THE GUY'S A HELL OF A GUY.
"YOU'LL LIKE HIM...IF HE LIKES YOU.
"THEY SAY HIS ENTIRE FAMILY WAS KILLED BY THANOS."
"JEEZ..."
"HE'S NOT MUCH OF A TALKER, BUT FROM WHAT I UNDERSTAND HE HAS BEEN THROUGH JUST ABOUT AS MUCH AS I THINK I COULD EVER TAKE...
"...AND HE'S COME OUT THE OTHER SIDE LOOKING TO BRING THE FIGHT TO THOSE WHO HAVE IT COMING.
"AND AS FAR AS I'M CONCERNED, THERE'S NOTHING MORE HEROIC THAN THAT.

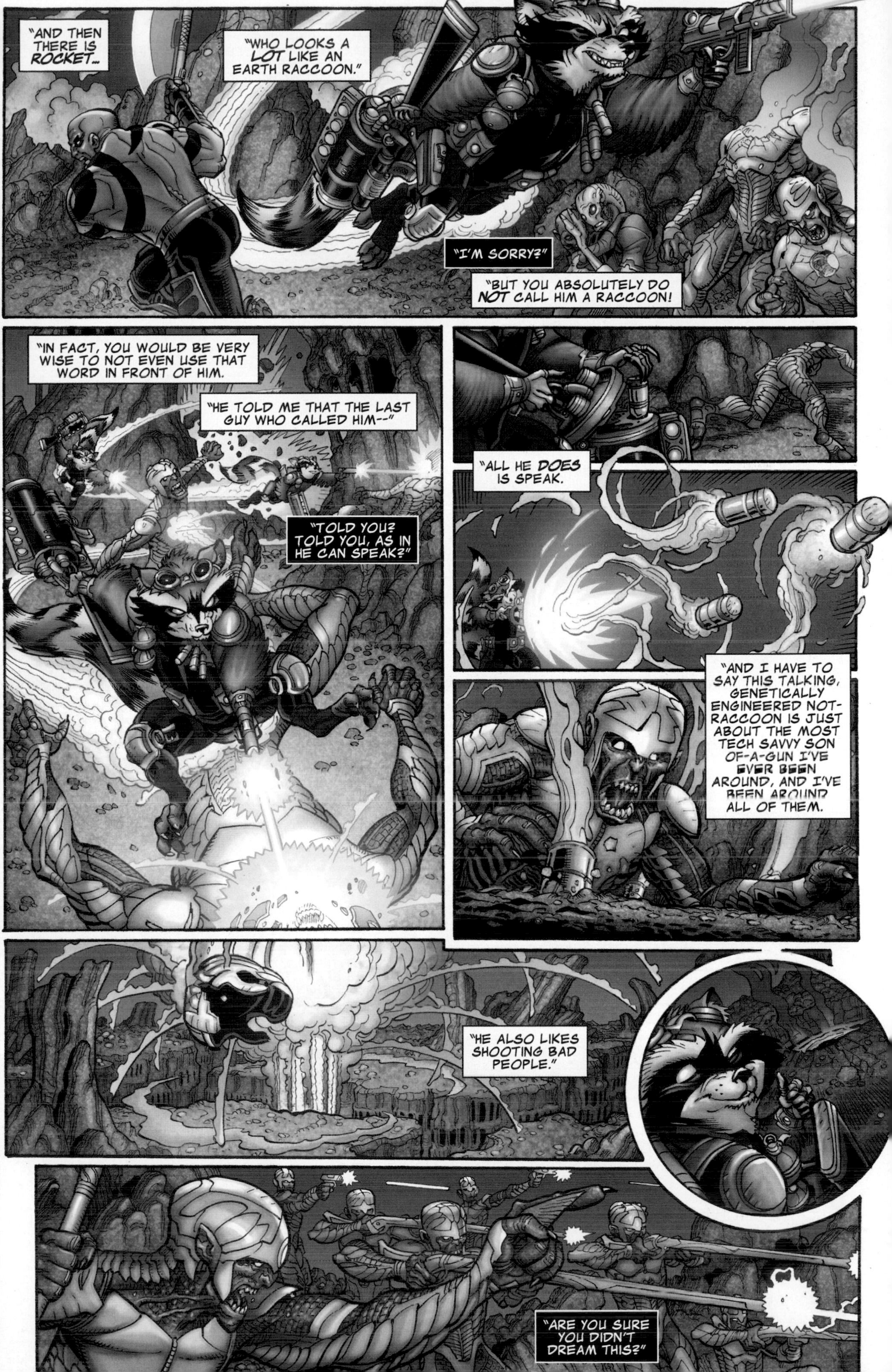
"AND THEN THERE IS ROCKET...
"WHO LOOKS A LOT LIKE AN EARTH RACCOON."
"I'M SORRY?"
"BUT YOU ABSOLUTELY DO NOT CALL HIM A RACCOON!
"IN FACT, YOU WOULD BE VERY WISE TO NOT EVEN USE THAT WORD IN FRONT OF HIM.
"HE TOLD ME THAT THE LAST GUY WHO CALLED HIM--"
"TOLD YOU? TOLD YOU, AS IN HE CAN SPEAK?"
"ALL HE DOES IS SPEAK.
"AND I HAVE TO SAY THIS TALKING, GENETICALLY ENGINEERED NOT-RACCOON IS JUST ABOUT THE MOST TECH SAVVY SON OF-A-GUN I'VE EVER BEEN AROUND, AND I'VE BEEN AROUND ALL OF THEM.
"HE ALSO LIKES SHOOTING BAD PEOPLE."
"ARE YOU SURE YOU DIDN'T DREAM THIS?"

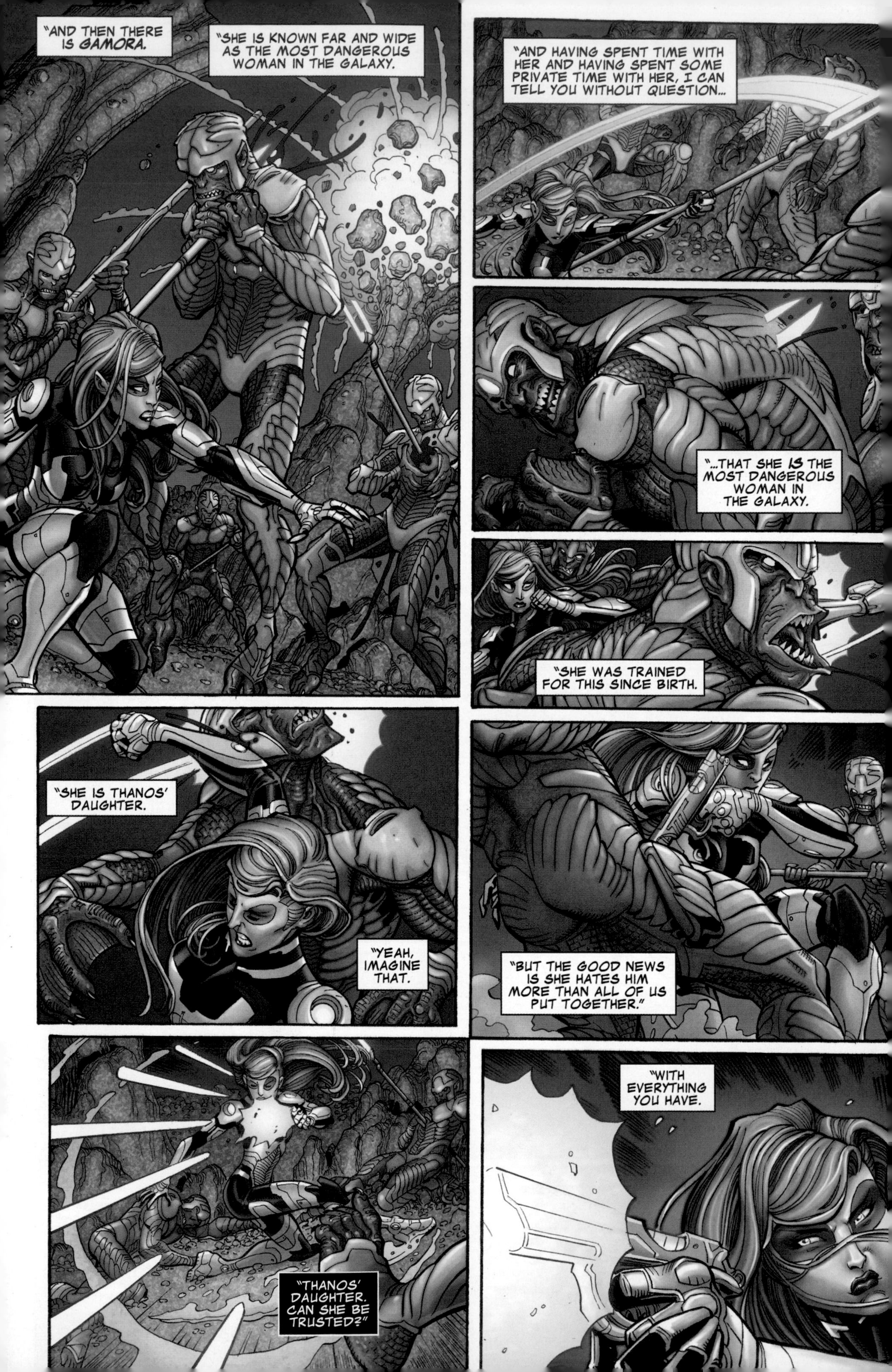
"AND THEN THERE IS GAMORA.
"SHE IS KNOWN FAR AND WIDE AS THE MOST DANGEROUS WOMAN IN THE GALAXY.
"AND HAVING SPENT TIME WITH HER AND HAVING SPENT SOME PRIVATE TIME WITH HER, I CAN TELL YOU WITHOUT QUESTION...
"...THAT SHE IS THE MOST DANGEROUS WOMAN IN THE GALAXY.
"SHE WAS TRAINED FOR THIS SINCE BIRTH.
"SHE IS THANOS' DAUGHTER.
"YEAH, IMAGINE THAT.
"BUT THE GOOD NEWS IS SHE HATES HIM MORE THAN ALL OF US PUT TOGETHER."
"THANOS' DAUGHTER. CAN SHE BE TRUSTED?"
"WITH EVERYTHING YOU HAVE.

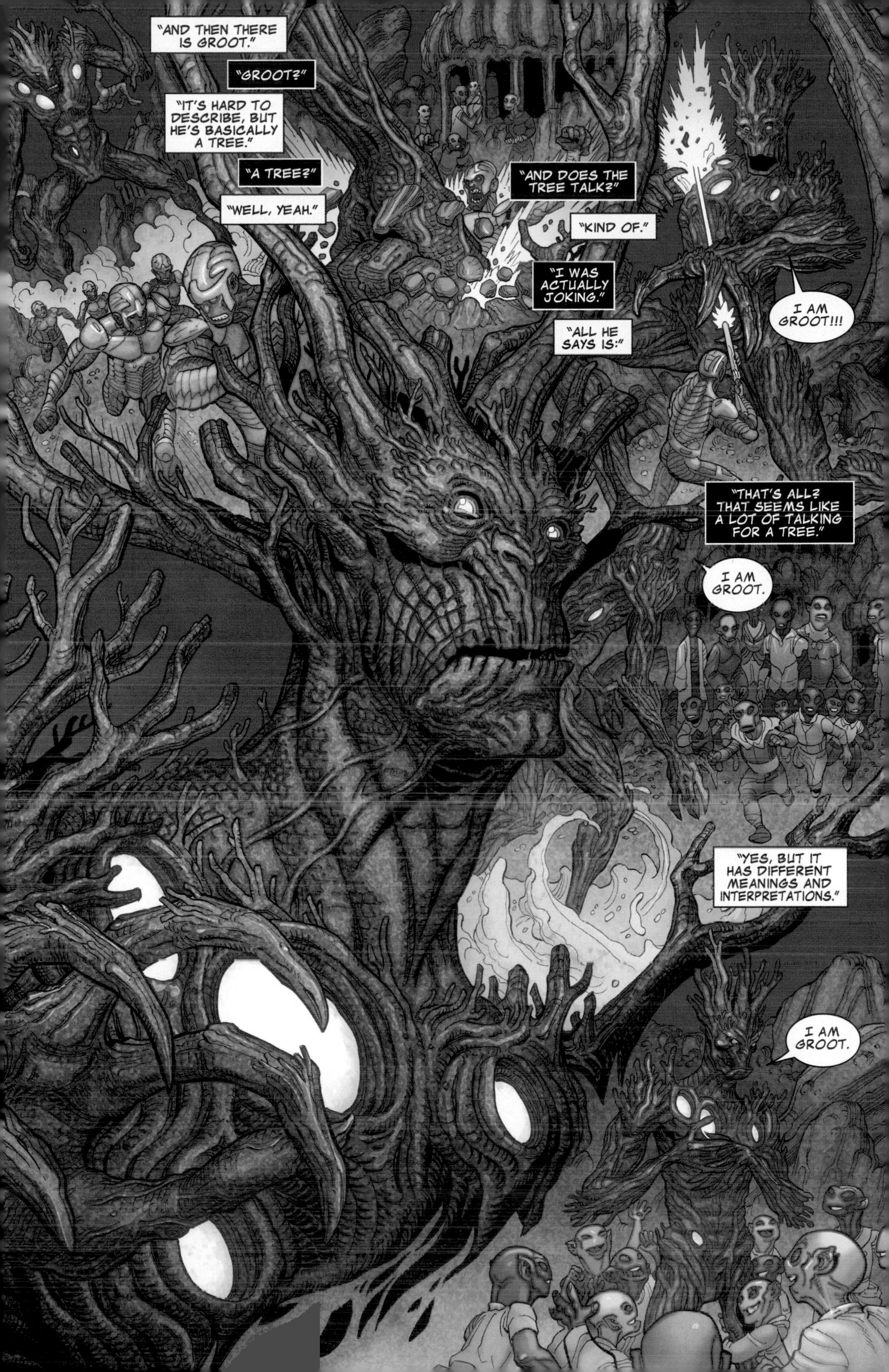
"AND THEN THERE IS GROOT."
"GROOT?"
"IT'S HARD TO DESCRIBE, BUT HE'S BASICALLY A TREE."
"A TREE?"
"WELL, YEAH."
"AND DOES THE TREE TALK?"
"KIND OF."
"I WAS ACTUALLY JOKING."
"ALL HE SAYS IS:"
I AM GROOT!!!
"THAT'S ALL? THAT SEEMS LIKE A LOT OF TALKING FOR A TREE."
I AM GROOT.
"YES, BUT IT HAS DIFFERENT MEANINGS AND INTERPRETATIONS."
I AM GROOT.

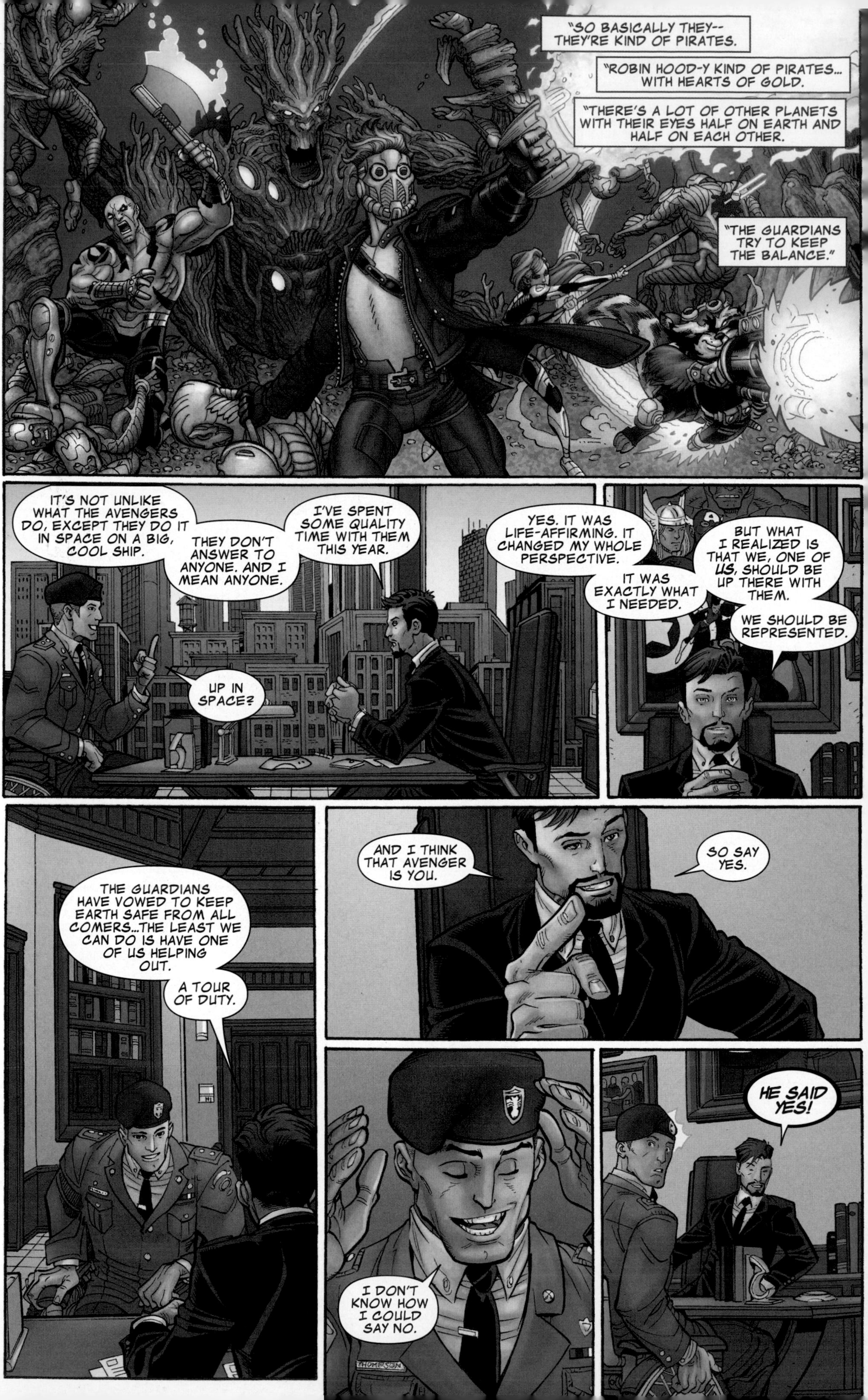

"SO BASICALLY THEY-- THEY'RE KIND OF PIRATES.
"ROBIN HOOD-Y KIND OF PIRATES... WITH HEARTS OF GOLD.
"THERE'S A LOT OF OTHER PLANETS WITH THEIR EYES HALF ON EARTH AND HALF ON EACH OTHER.
"THE GUARDIANS TRY TO KEEP THE BALANCE."
IT'S NOT UNLIKE WHAT THE AVENGERS DO, EXCEPT THEY DO IT IN SPACE ON A BIG, COOL SHIP.
THEY DON'T ANSWER TO ANYONE. AND I MEAN ANYONE.
I'VE SPENT SOME QUALITY TIME WITH THEM THIS YEAR.
UP IN SPACE?
YES. IT WAS LIFE-AFFIRMING. IT CHANGED MY WHOLE PERSPECTIVE.
IT WAS EXACTLY WHAT I NEEDED.
BUT WHAT I REALIZED IS THAT WE, ONE OF US, SHOULD BE UP THERE WITH THEM.
WE SHOULD BE REPRESENTED.
THE GUARDIANS HAVE VOWED TO KEEP EARTH SAFE FROM ALL COMERS...THE LEAST WE CAN DO IS HAVE ONE OF US HELPING OUT.
A TOUR OF DUTY.
AND I THINK THAT AVENGER IS YOU.
SO SAY YES.
I DON'T KNOW HOW I COULD SAY NO.
HE SAID YES!

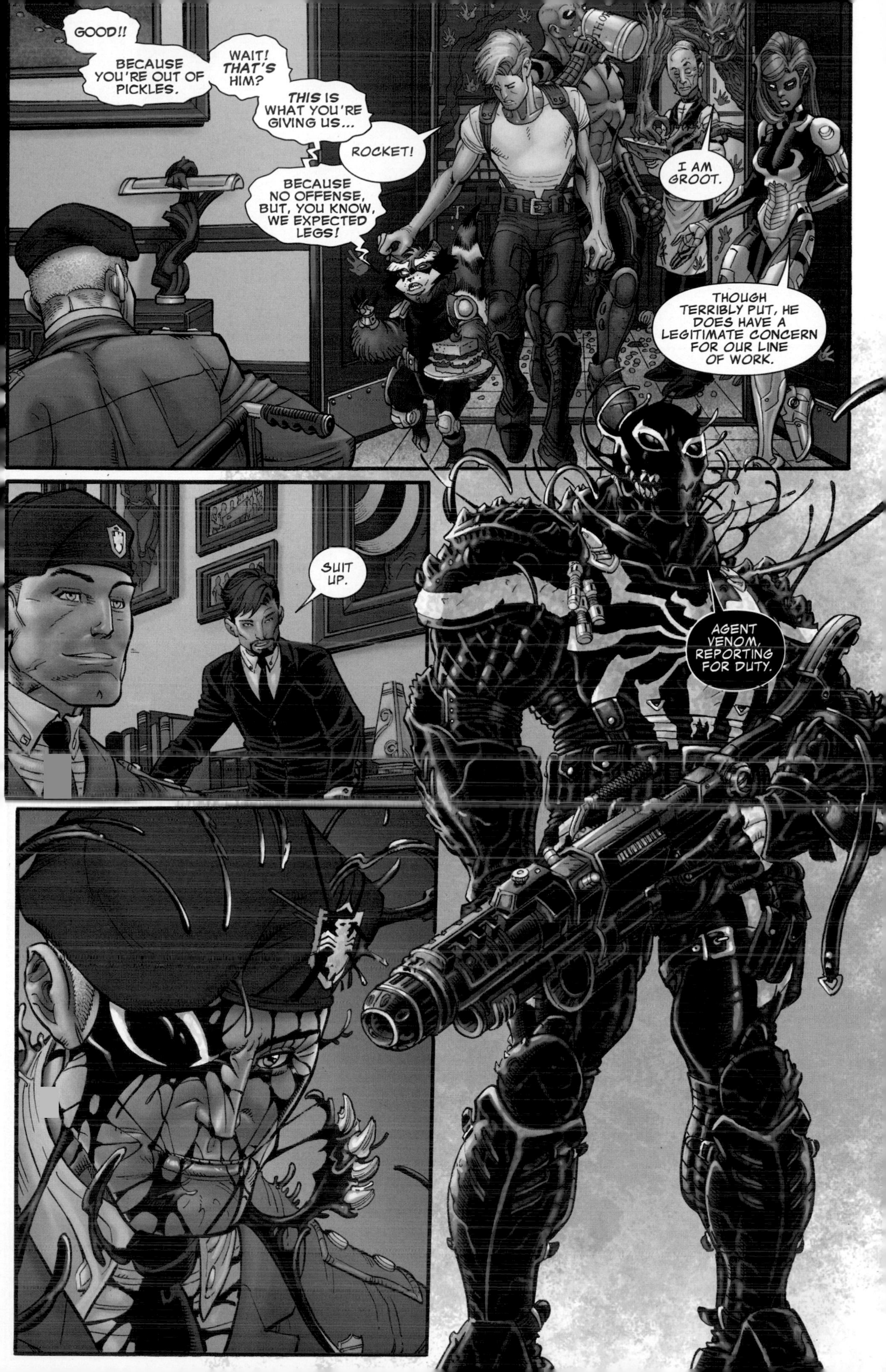
GOOD!!
BECAUSE YOU'RE OUT OF PICKLES.
WAIT! THAT'S HIM?
THIS IS WHAT YOU'RE GIVING US...
ROCKET!
BECAUSE NO OFFENSE, BUT, YOU KNOW, WE EXPECTED LEGS!
I AM GROOT.
THOUGH TERRIBLY PUT, HE DOES HAVE A LEGITIMATE CONCERN FOR OUR LINE OF WORK.
SUIT UP.
AGENT VENOM, REPORTING FOR DUTY.

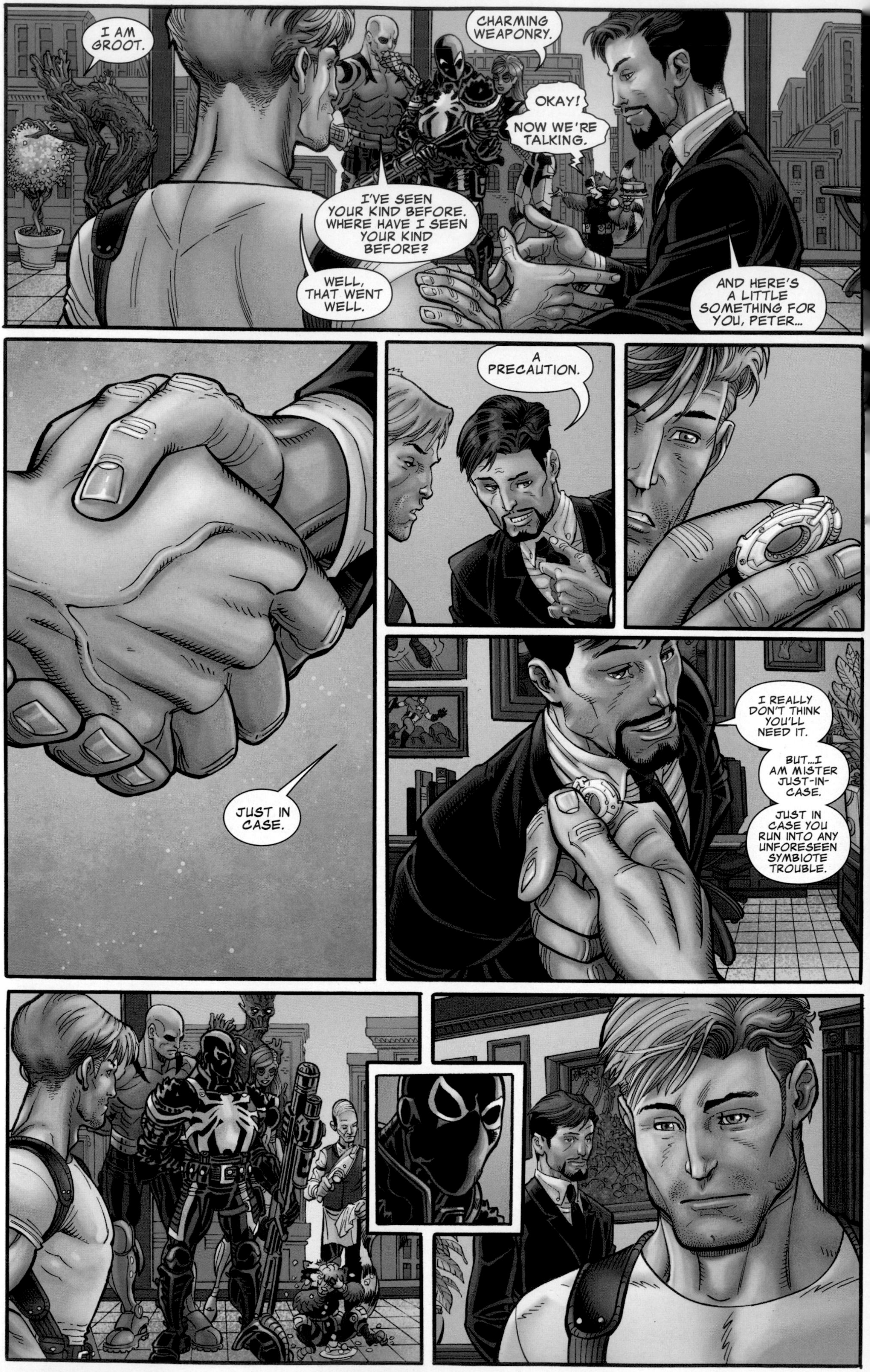
I AM GROOT.
CHARMING WEAPONRY.
OKAY!
NOW WE'RE TALKING.
I'VE SEEN YOUR KIND BEFORE. WHERE HAVE I SEEN YOUR KIND BEFORE?
WELL, THAT WENT WELL.
AND HERE'S A LITTLE SOMETHING FOR YOU, PETER...
A PRECAUTION.
JUST IN CASE.
I REALLY DON'T THINK YOU'LL NEED IT.
BUT...I AM MISTER JUST-IN-CASE.
JUST IN CASE YOU RUN INTO ANY UNFORESEEN SYMBIOTE TROUBLE.

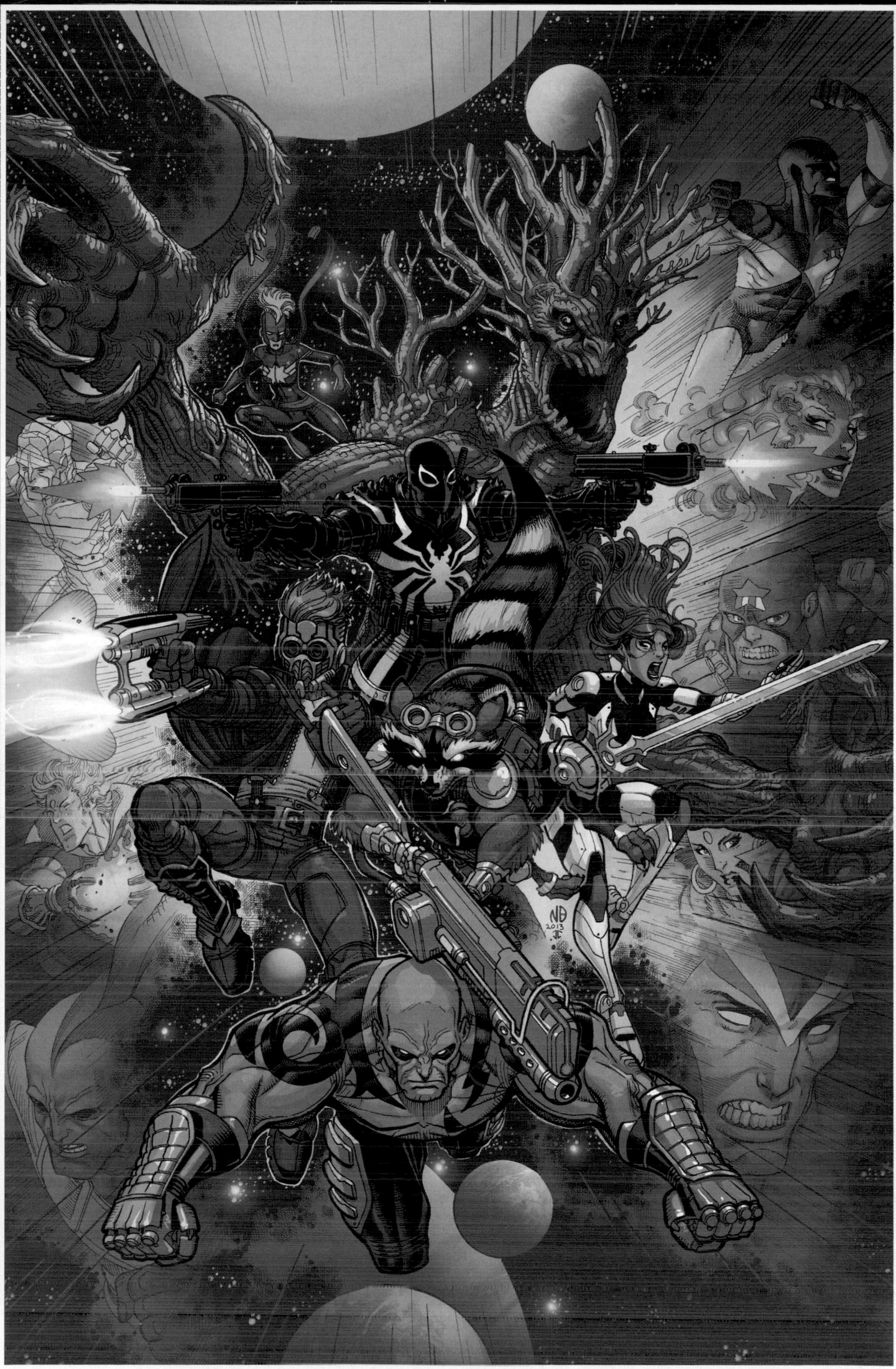

GUARDIANS OF THE GALAXY 14

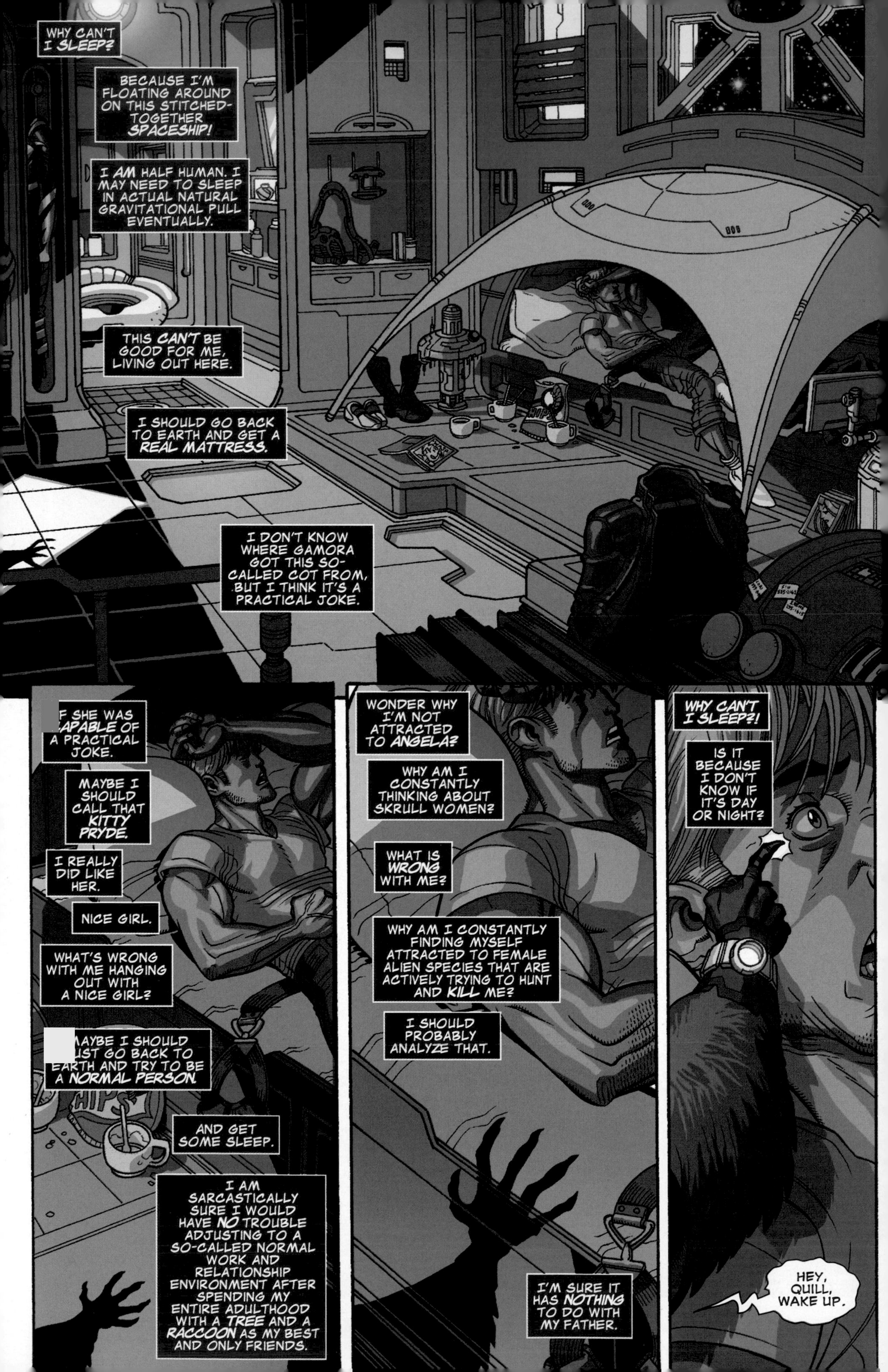
WHY CAN'T I SLEEP?
BECAUSE I'M FLOATING AROUND ON THIS STITCHED-TOGETHER SPACESHIP!
I AM HALF HUMAN. I MAY NEED TO SLEEP IN ACTUAL NATURAL GRAVITATIONAL PULL EVENTUALLY.
THIS CAN'T BE GOOD FOR ME, LIVING OUT HERE.
I SHOULD GO BACK TO EARTH AND GET A REAL MATTRESS.
I DON'T KNOW WHERE GAMORA GOT THIS SO-CALLED COT FROM, BUT I THINK IT'S A PRACTICAL JOKE.
F SHE WAS APABLE OF A PRACTICAL JOKE.
MAYBE I SHOULD CALL THAT KITTY PRYDE.
I REALLY DID LIKE HER.
NICE GIRL.
WHAT'S WRONG WITH ME HANGING OUT WITH A NICE GIRL?
AYBE I SHOULD UST GO BACK TO EARTH AND TRY TO BE A NORMAL PERSON.
AND GET SOME SLEEP.
I AM SARCASTICALLY SURE I WOULD HAVE NO TROUBLE ADJUSTING TO A SO-CALLED NORMAL WORK AND RELATIONSHIP ENVIRONMENT AFTER SPENDING MY ENTIRE ADULTHOOD WITH A TREE AND A RACCOON AS MY BEST AND ONLY FRIENDS.
WONDER WHY I'M NOT ATTRACTED TO ANGELA?
WHY AM I CONSTANTLY THINKING ABOUT SKRULL WOMEN?
WHAT IS WRONG WITH ME?
WHY AM I CONSTANTLY FINDING MYSELF ATTRACTED TO FEMALE ALIEN SPECIES THAT ARE ACTIVELY TRYING TO HUNT AND KILL ME?
I SHOULD PROBABLY ANALYZE THAT.
I'M SURE IT HAS NOTHING TO DO WITH MY FATHER.
WHY CAN'T I SLEEP?!
IS IT BECAUSE I DON'T KNOW IF IT'S DAY OR NIGHT?
HEY, QUILL, WAKE UP.

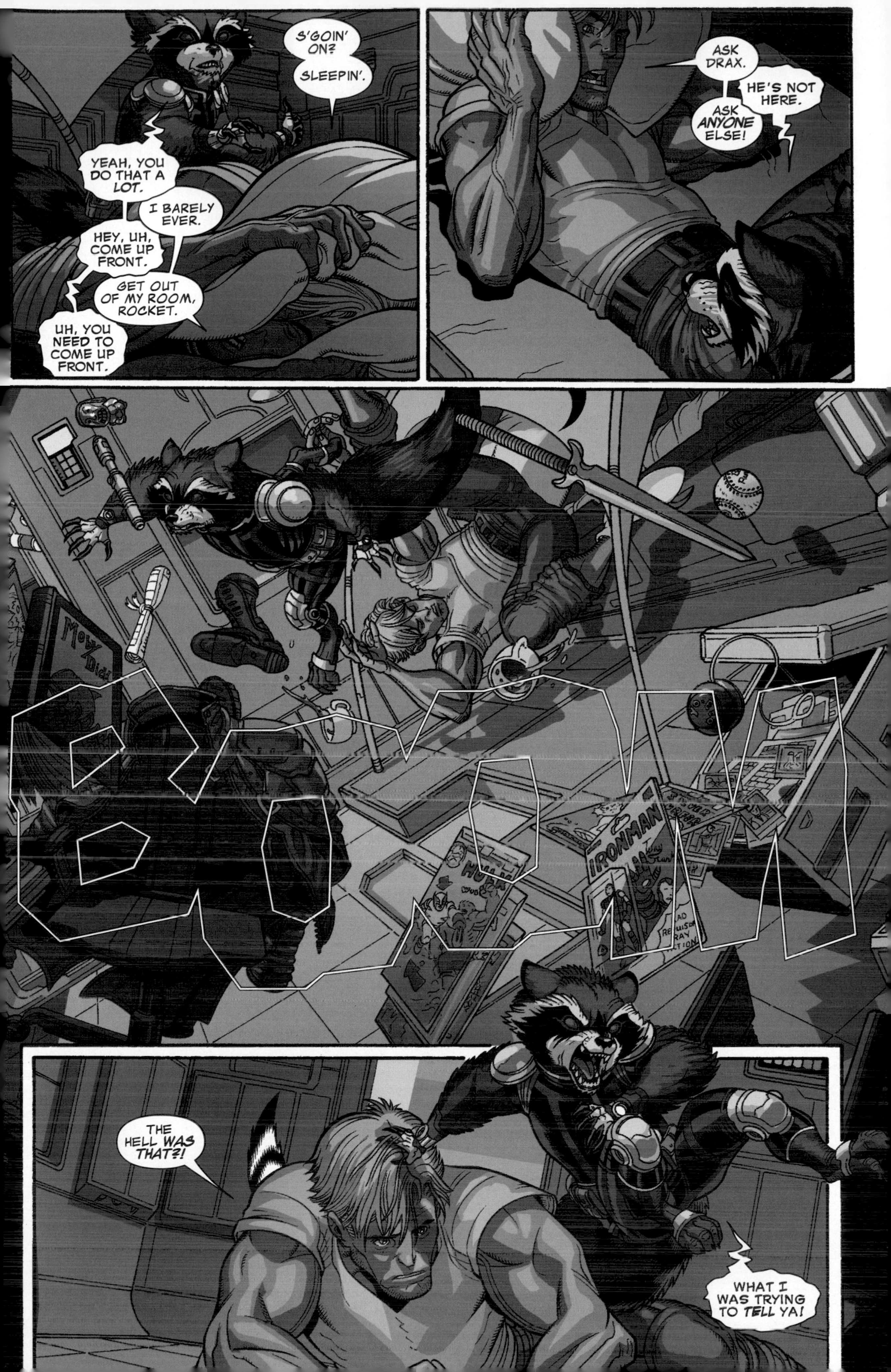
S'GOIN' ON?
SLEEPIN'.
YEAH, YOU DO THAT A LOT.
I BARELY EVER.
HEY, UH, COME UP FRONT.
GET OUT OF MY ROOM, ROCKET.
UH, YOU NEED TO COME UP FRONT.
ASK DRAX.
HE'S NOT HERE.
ASK ANYONE ELSE!
THE HELL WAS THAT?!
WHAT I WAS TRYING TO TELL YA!

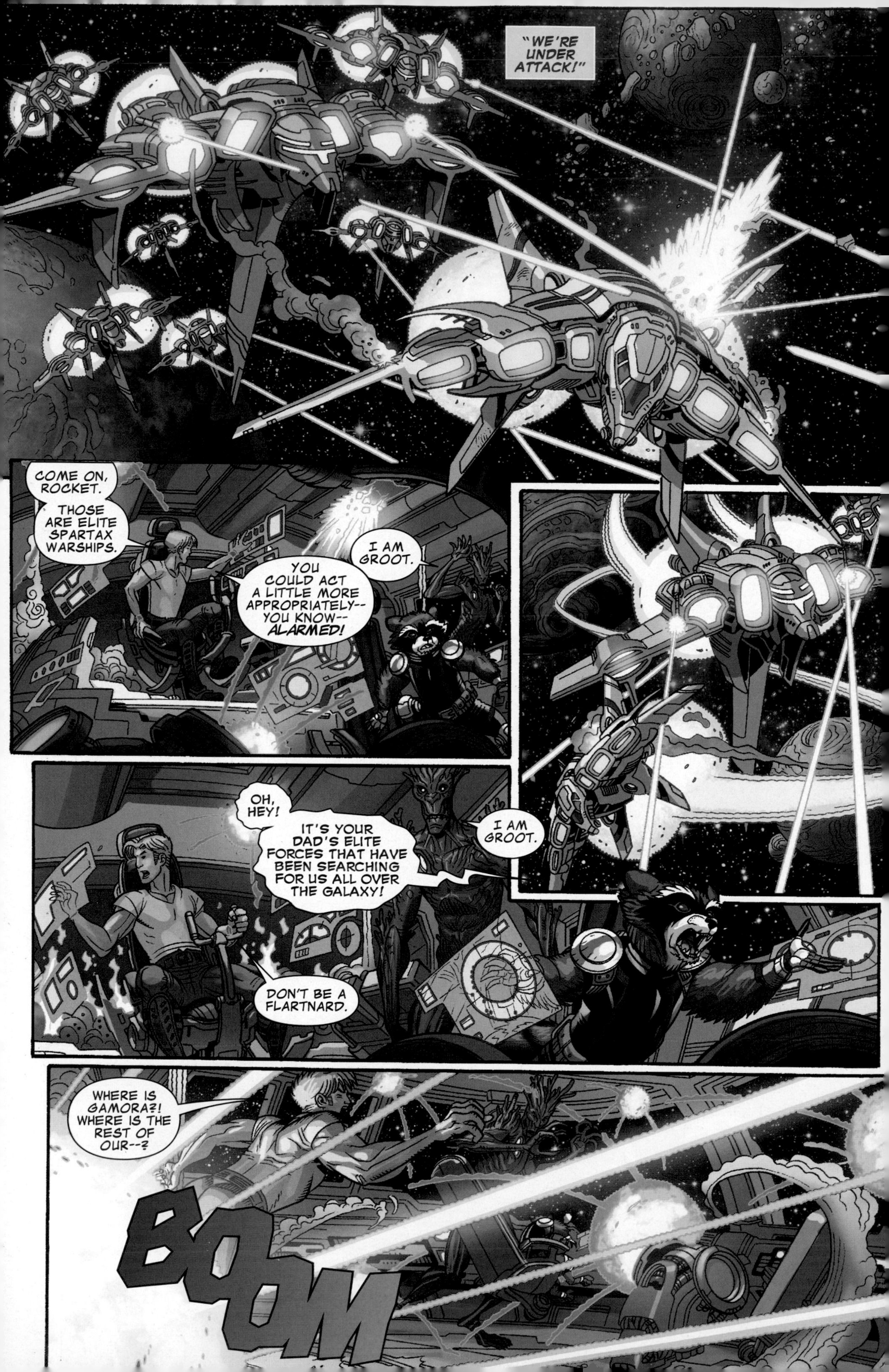
"WE'RE UNDER ATTACK!"
COME ON, ROCKET.
THOSE ARE ELITE SPARTAX WARSHIPS.
YOU COULD ACT A LITTLE MORE APPROPRIATELY-- YOU KNOW-- ALARMED!
I AM GROOT.
OH, HEY!
IT'S YOUR DAD'S ELITE FORCES THAT HAVE BEEN SEARCHING FOR US ALL OVER THE GALAXY!
I AM GROOT.
DON'T BE A FLARTNARD.
WHERE IS GAMORA?! WHERE IS THE REST OF OUR--?
BOOOM

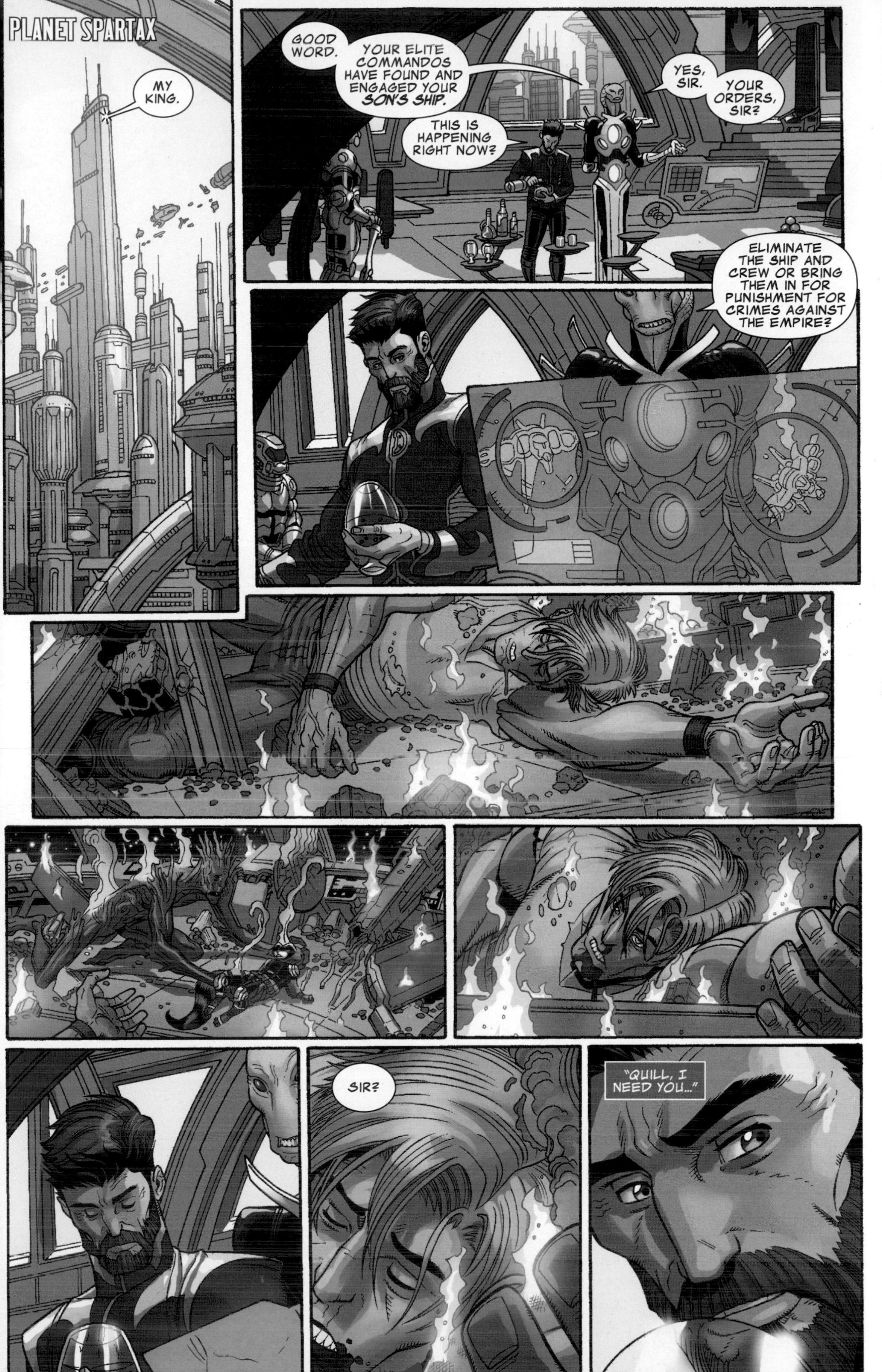
PLANET SPARTAX
MY KING.
GOOD WORD.
YOUR ELITE COMMANDOS HAVE FOUND AND ENGAGED YOUR SON'S SHIP.
THIS IS HAPPENING RIGHT NOW?
YES, SIR.
YOUR ORDERS, SIR?
ELIMINATE THE SHIP AND CREW OR BRING THEM IN FOR PUNISHMENT FOR CRIMES AGAINST THE EMPIRE?
SIR?
"QUILL, I NEED YOU..."

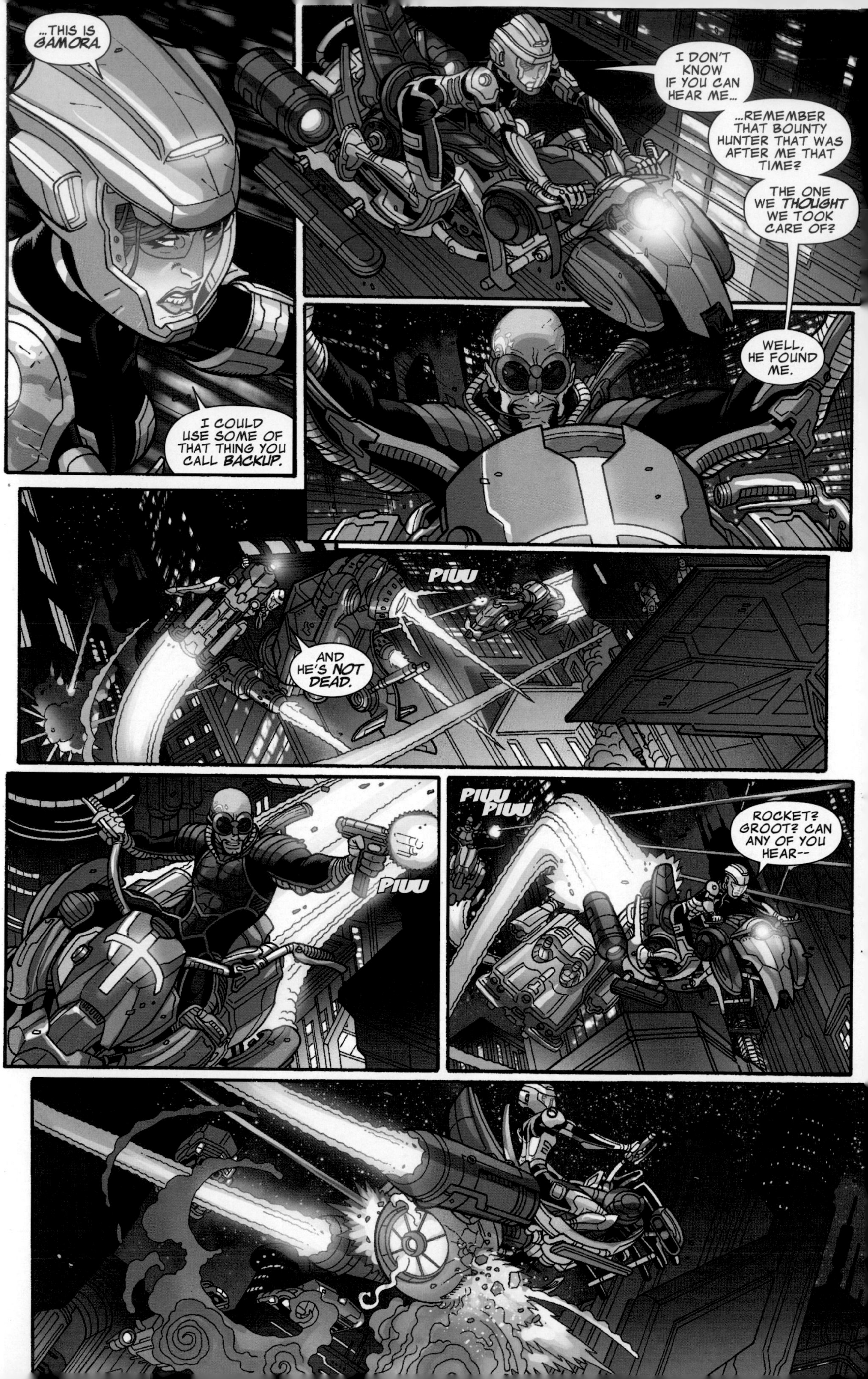
...THIS IS GAMORA.
I COULD USE SOME OF THAT THING YOU CALL BACKUP.
I DON'T KNOW IF YOU CAN HEAR ME...
...REMEMBER THAT BOUNTY HUNTER THAT WAS AFTER ME THAT TIME?
THE ONE WE THOUGHT WE TOOK CARE OF?
WELL, HE FOUND ME.
PIUU
AND HE'S NOT DEAD.
PIUU
PIUU PIUU
ROCKET? GROOT? CAN ANY OF YOU HEAR--

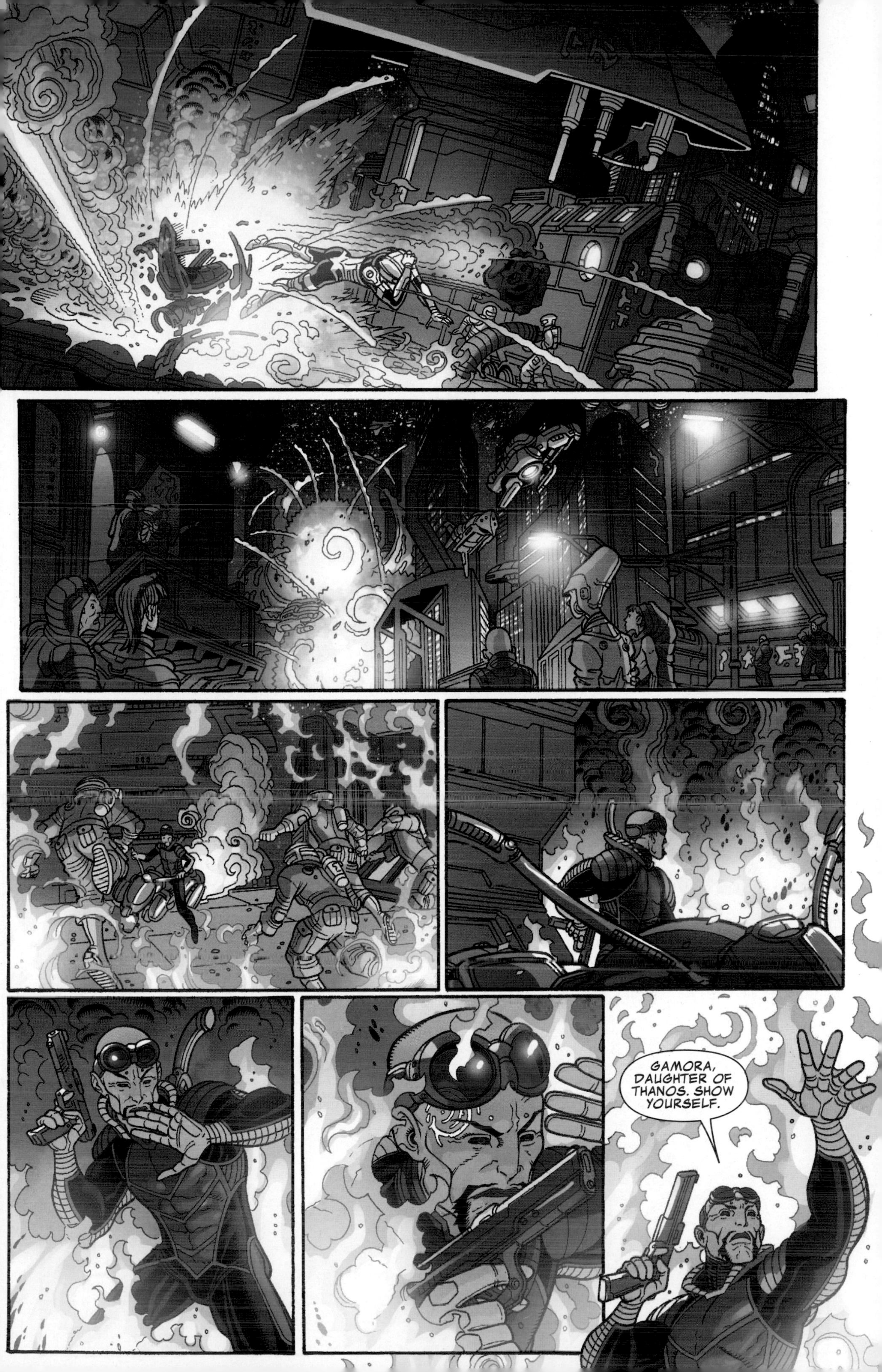
GAMORA, DAUGHTER OF THANOS. SHOW YOURSELF.

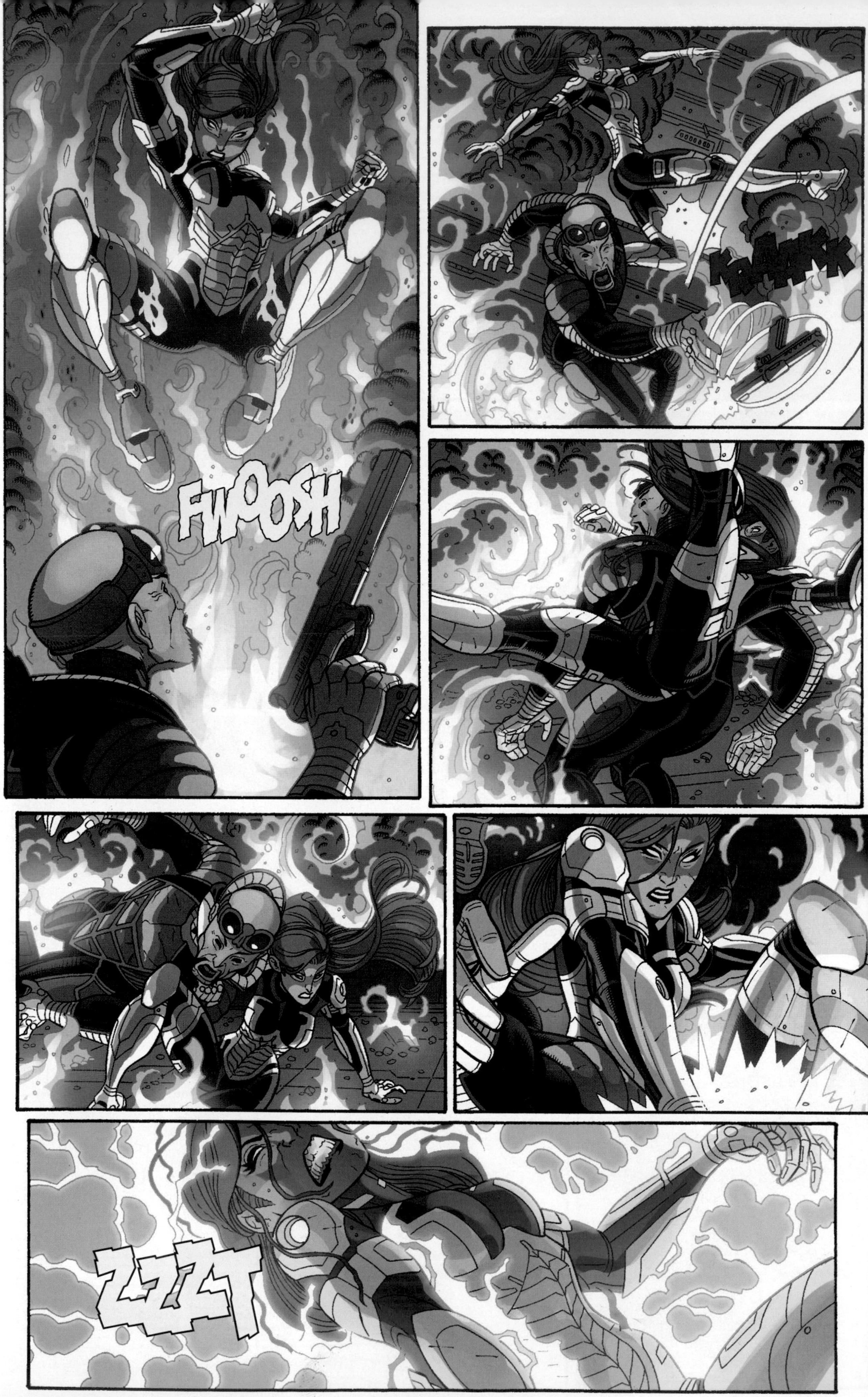
FWOOSH
ZZZT

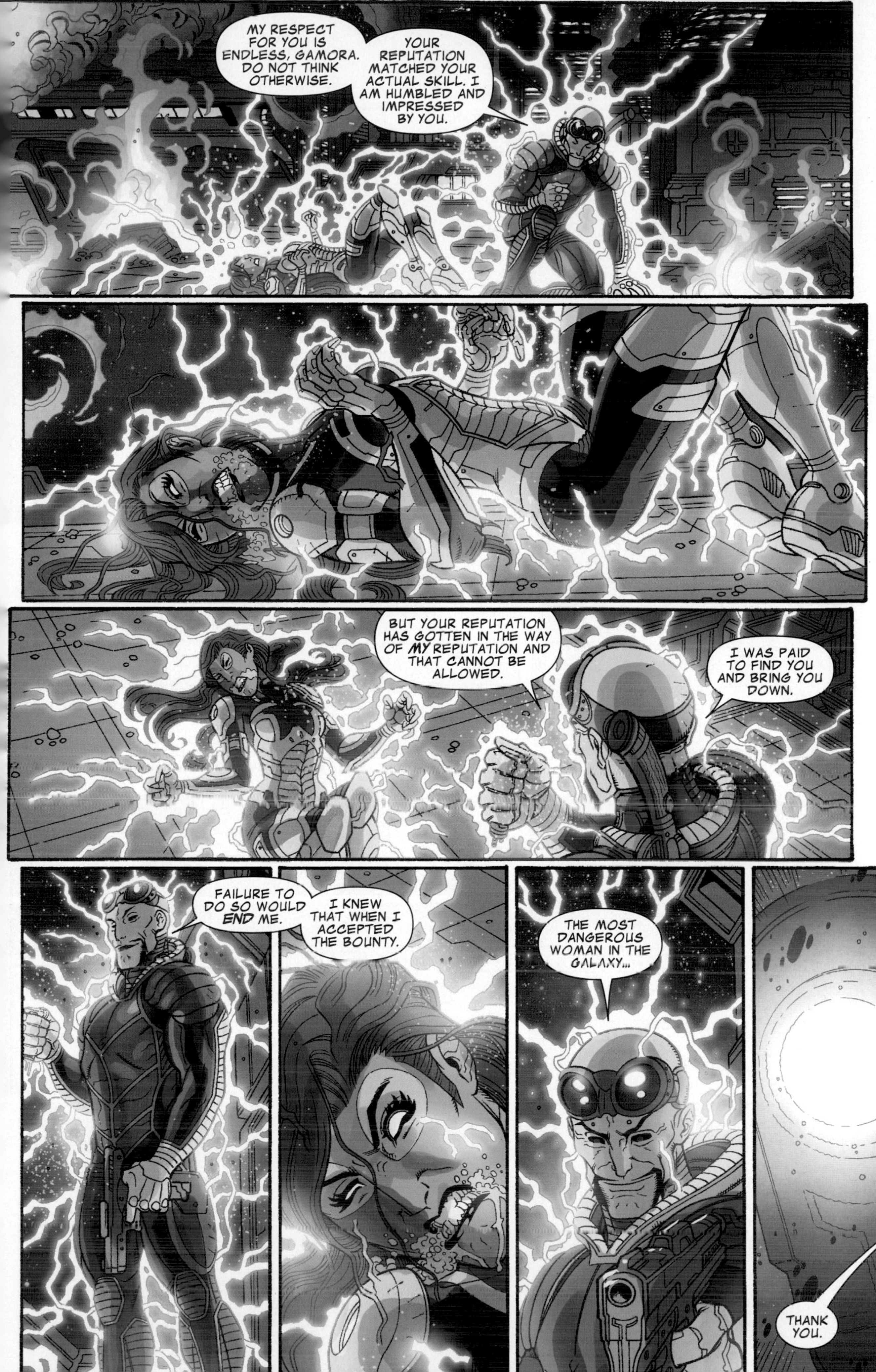
MY RESPECT FOR YOU IS ENDLESS, GAMORA. DO NOT THINK OTHERWISE.
YOUR REPUTATION MATCHED YOUR ACTUAL SKILL. I AM HUMBLED AND IMPRESSED BY YOU.
BUT YOUR REPUTATION HAS GOTTEN IN THE WAY OF MY REPUTATION AND THAT CANNOT BE ALLOWED.
I WAS PAID TO FIND YOU AND BRING YOU DOWN.
FAILURE TO DO SO WOULD END ME.
I KNEW THAT WHEN I ACCEPTED THE BOUNTY.
THE MOST DANGEROUS WOMAN IN THE GALAXY...
THANK YOU.

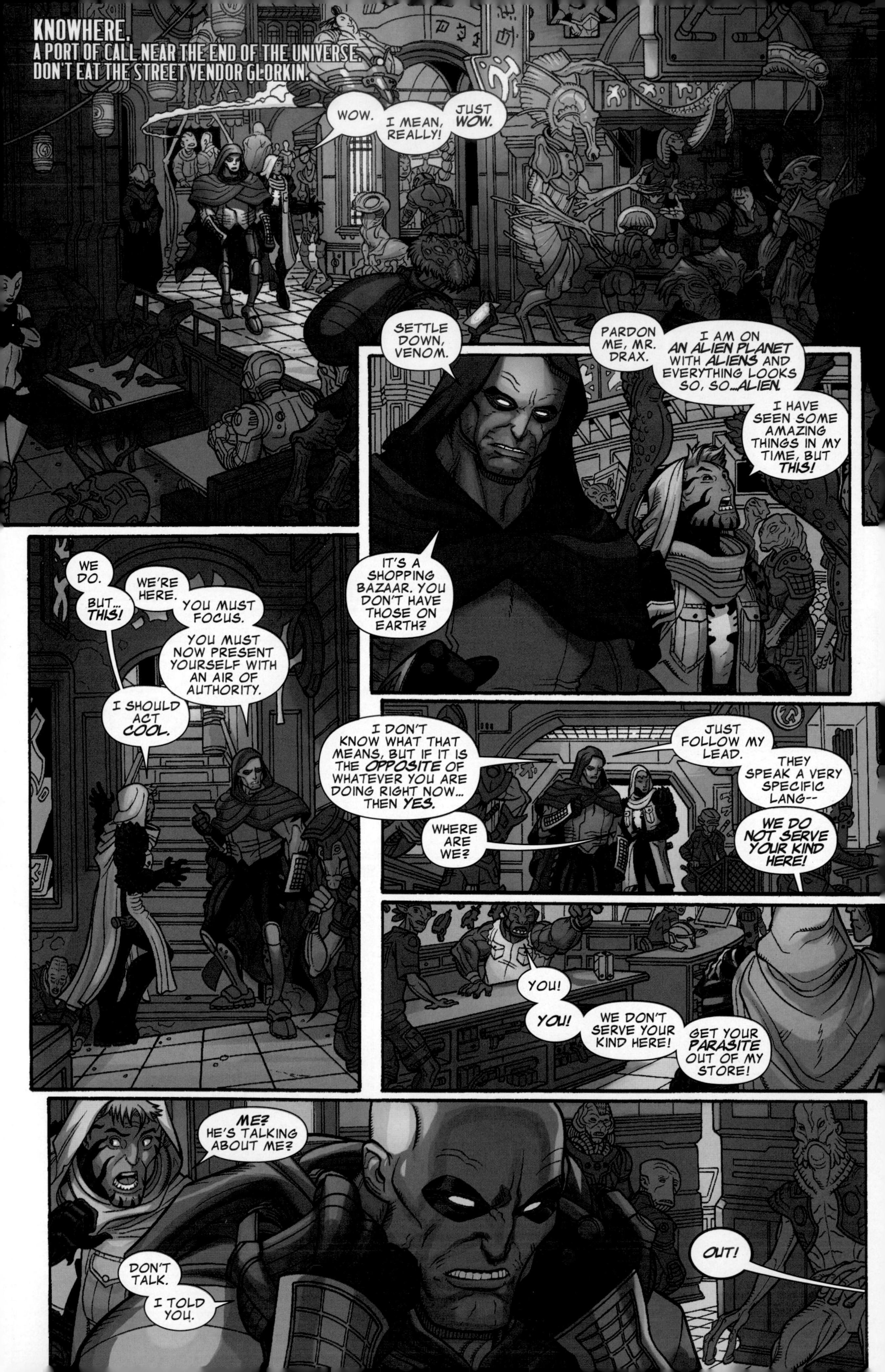
KNOWHERE.
A PORT OF CALL NEAR THE END OF THE UNIVERSE.
DON'T EAT THE STREET VENDOR GLORKIN.
WOW.
I MEAN, REALLY!
JUST WOW.
SETTLE DOWN, VENOM.
PARDON ME, MR. DRAX.
I AM ON AN ALIEN PLANET WITH ALIENS AND EVERYTHING LOOKS SO, SO...ALIEN.
I HAVE SEEN SOME AMAZING THINGS IN MY TIME, BUT THIS!
IT'S A SHOPPING BAZAAR. YOU DON'T HAVE THOSE ON EARTH?
WE DO.
BUT... THIS!
WE'RE HERE.
YOU MUST FOCUS.
YOU MUST NOW PRESENT YOURSELF WITH AN AIR OF AUTHORITY.
I SHOULD ACT COOL.
I DON'T KNOW WHAT THAT MEANS, BUT IF IT IS THE OPPOSITE OF WHATEVER YOU ARE DOING RIGHT NOW... THEN YES.
JUST FOLLOW MY LEAD.
THEY SPEAK A VERY SPECIFIC LANG--
WHERE ARE WE?
WE DO NOT SERVE YOUR KIND HERE!
YOU!
YOU!
WE DON'T SERVE YOUR KIND HERE!
GET YOUR PARASITE OUT OF MY STORE!
ME? HE'S TALKING ABOUT ME?
DON'T TALK.
I TOLD YOU.
OUT!

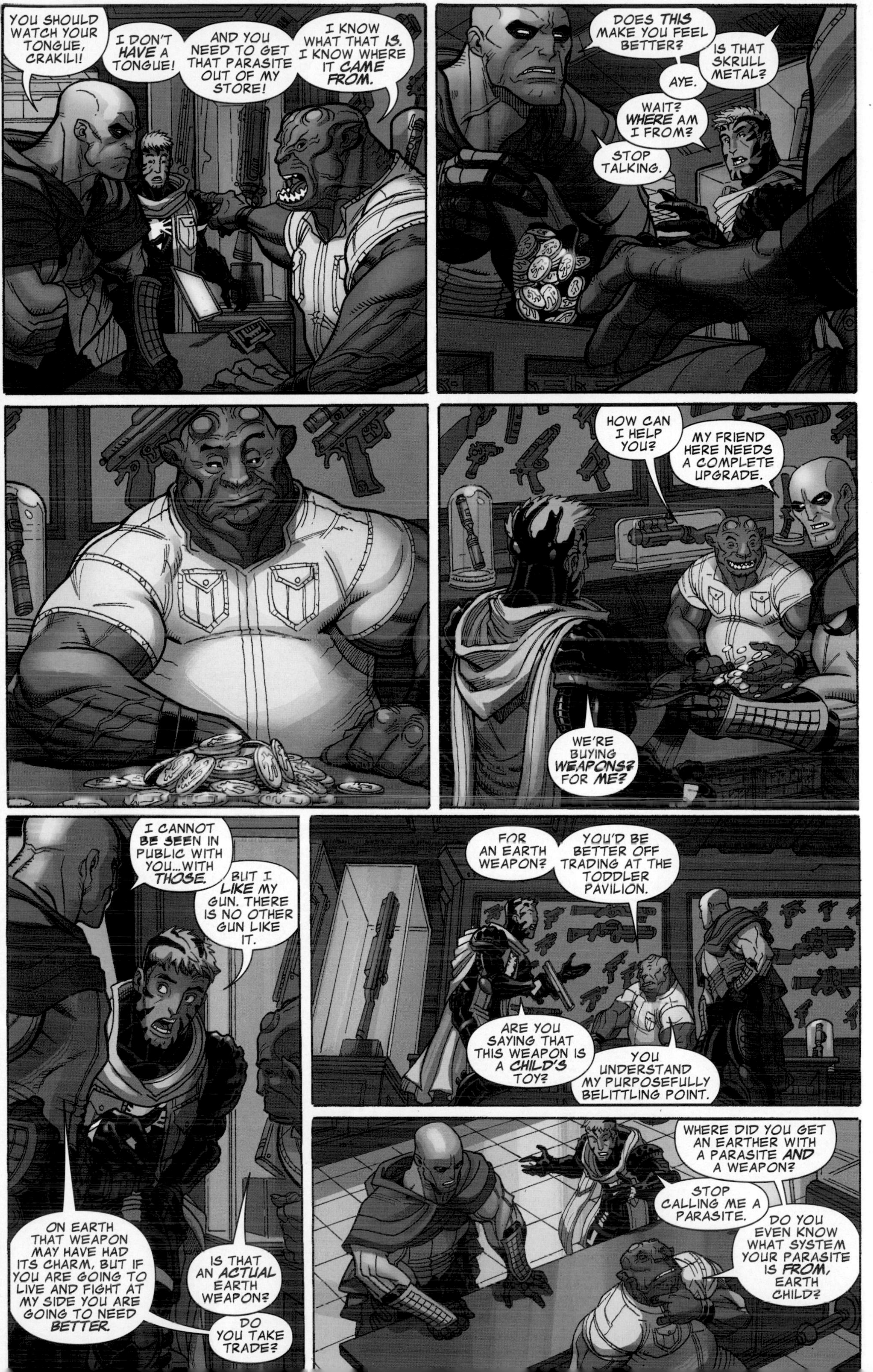

YOU SHOULD WATCH YOUR TONGUE, CRAKILI!
I DON'T HAVE A TONGUE!
AND YOU NEED TO GET THAT PARASITE OUT OF MY STORE!
I KNOW WHAT THAT IS. I KNOW WHERE IT CAME FROM.
DOES THIS MAKE YOU FEEL BETTER?
IS THAT SKRULL METAL?
AYE.
WAIT? WHERE AM I FROM?
STOP TALKING.
HOW CAN I HELP YOU?
MY FRIEND HERE NEEDS A COMPLETE UPGRADE.
WE'RE BUYING WEAPONS? FOR ME?
I CANNOT BE SEEN IN PUBLIC WITH YOU...WITH THOSE.
BUT I LIKE MY GUN. THERE IS NO OTHER GUN LIKE IT.
ON EARTH THAT WEAPON MAY HAVE HAD ITS CHARM, BUT IF YOU ARE GOING TO LIVE AND FIGHT AT MY SIDE YOU ARE GOING TO NEED BETTER.
IS THAT AN ACTUAL EARTH WEAPON?
DO YOU TAKE TRADE?
FOR AN EARTH WEAPON?
YOU'D BE BETTER OFF TRADING AT THE TODDLER PAVILION.
ARE YOU SAYING THAT THIS WEAPON IS A CHILD'S TOY?
YOU UNDERSTAND MY PURPOSEFULLY BELITTLING POINT.
WHERE DID YOU GET AN EARTHER WITH A PARASITE AND A WEAPON?
STOP CALLING ME A PARASITE.
DO YOU EVEN KNOW WHAT SYSTEM YOUR PARASITE IS FROM, EARTH CHILD?

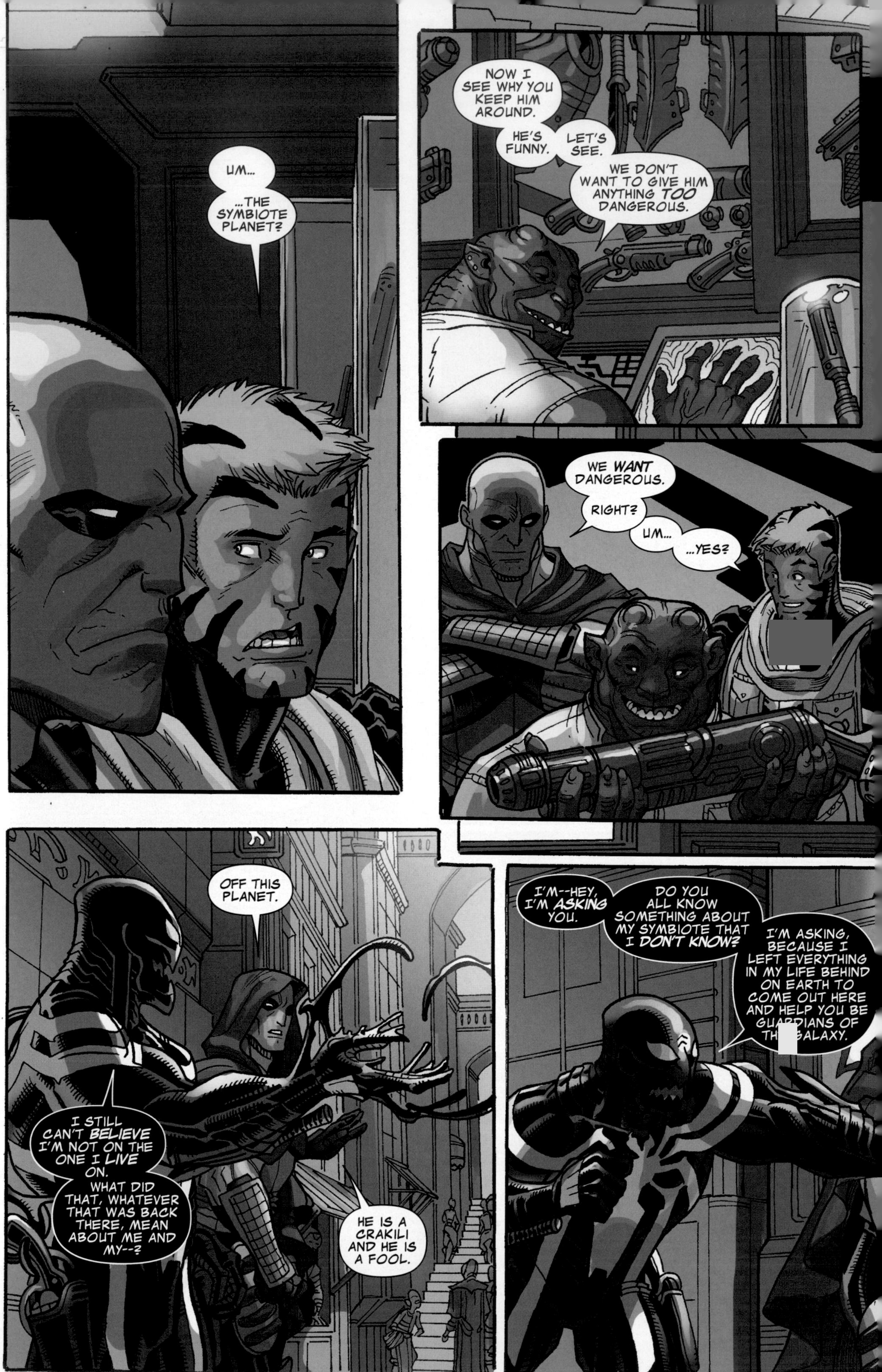
UM...
...THE SYMBIOTE PLANET?
NOW I SEE WHY YOU KEEP HIM AROUND.
HE'S FUNNY.
LET'S SEE.
WE DON'T WANT TO GIVE HIM ANYTHING *TOO* DANGEROUS.
WE *WANT* DANGEROUS.
RIGHT?
UM...
...YES?
OFF THIS PLANET.
I STILL CAN'T *BELIEVE* I'M NOT ON THE ONE I *LIVE* ON.
WHAT DID THAT, WHATEVER THAT WAS BACK THERE, MEAN ABOUT ME AND MY--?
HE IS A CRAKILI AND HE IS A FOOL.
I'M--HEY, I'M *ASKING* YOU.
DO YOU ALL KNOW SOMETHING ABOUT MY SYMBIOTE THAT I *DON'T KNOW?*
I'M ASKING, BECAUSE I LEFT EVERYTHING IN MY LIFE BEHIND ON EARTH TO COME OUT HERE AND HELP YOU BE GUARDIANS OF TH GALAXY.

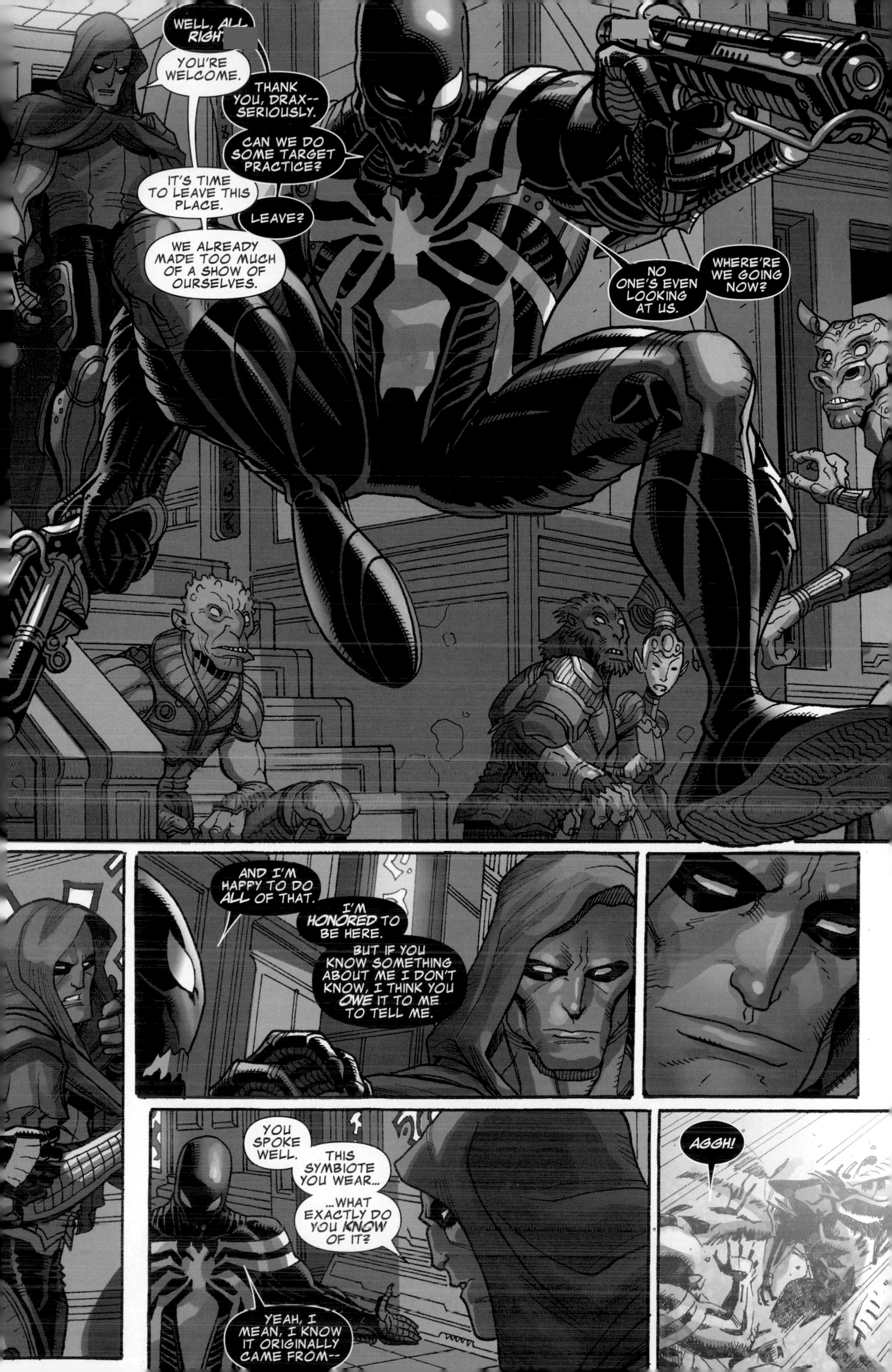
WELL, ALL RIGH
YOU'RE WELCOME.
THANK YOU, DRAX-- SERIOUSLY.
CAN WE DO SOME TARGET PRACTICE?
IT'S TIME TO LEAVE THIS PLACE.
LEAVE?
WE ALREADY MADE TOO MUCH OF A SHOW OF OURSELVES.
NO ONE'S EVEN LOOKING AT US.
WHERE'RE WE GOING NOW?
AND I'M HAPPY TO DO ALL OF THAT.
I'M HONORED TO BE HERE.
BUT IF YOU KNOW SOMETHING ABOUT ME I DON'T KNOW, I THINK YOU OWE IT TO ME TO TELL ME.
YOU SPOKE WELL.
THIS SYMBIOTE YOU WEAR...
...WHAT EXACTLY DO YOU KNOW OF IT?
YEAH, I MEAN, I KNOW IT ORIGINALLY CAME FROM--
AGGH!

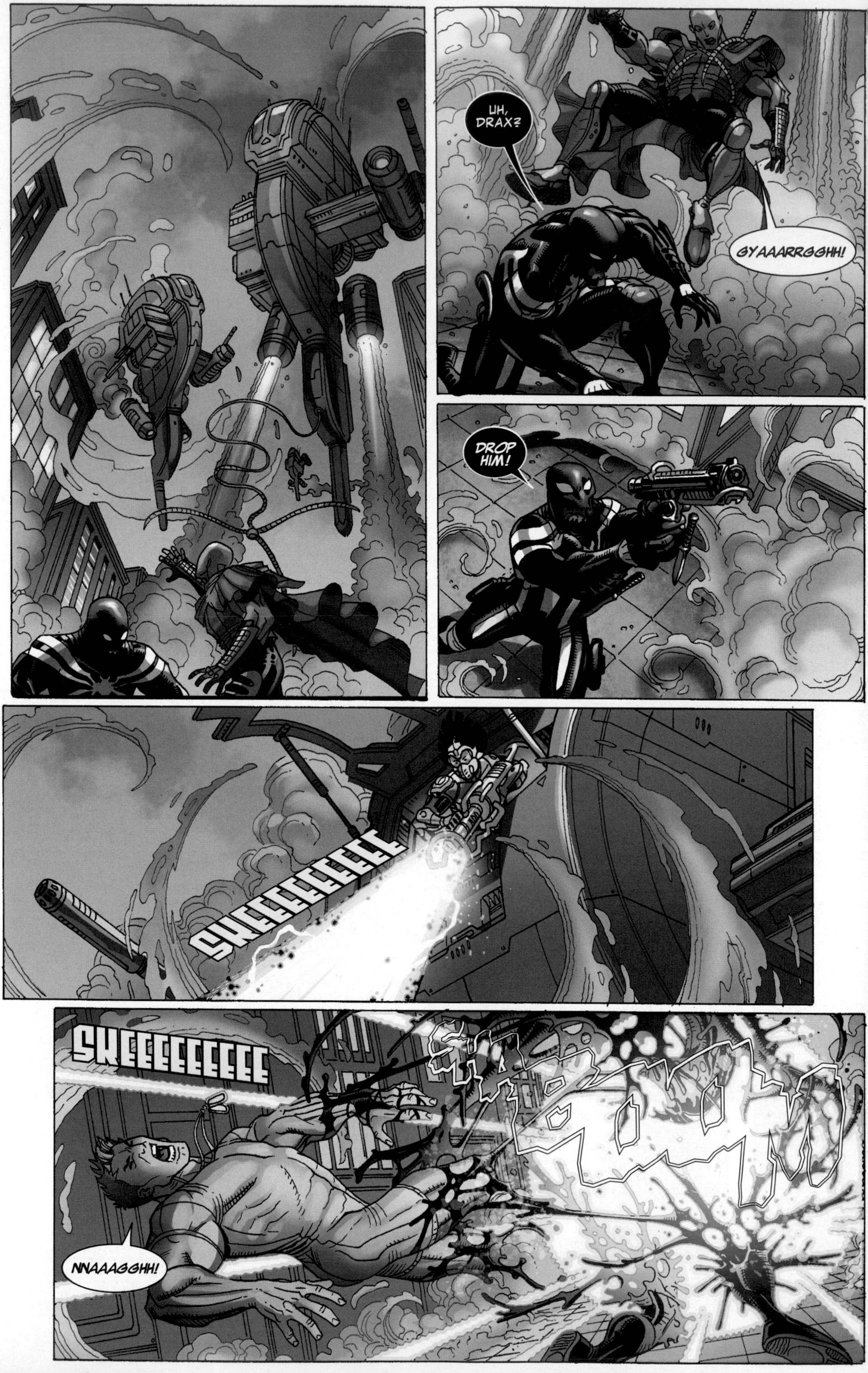
UH, DRAX?
GYAAARRGGHH!
DROP HIM!
SKEEEEEEEEE
SKEEEEEEEEE
NNAAAGGHH!

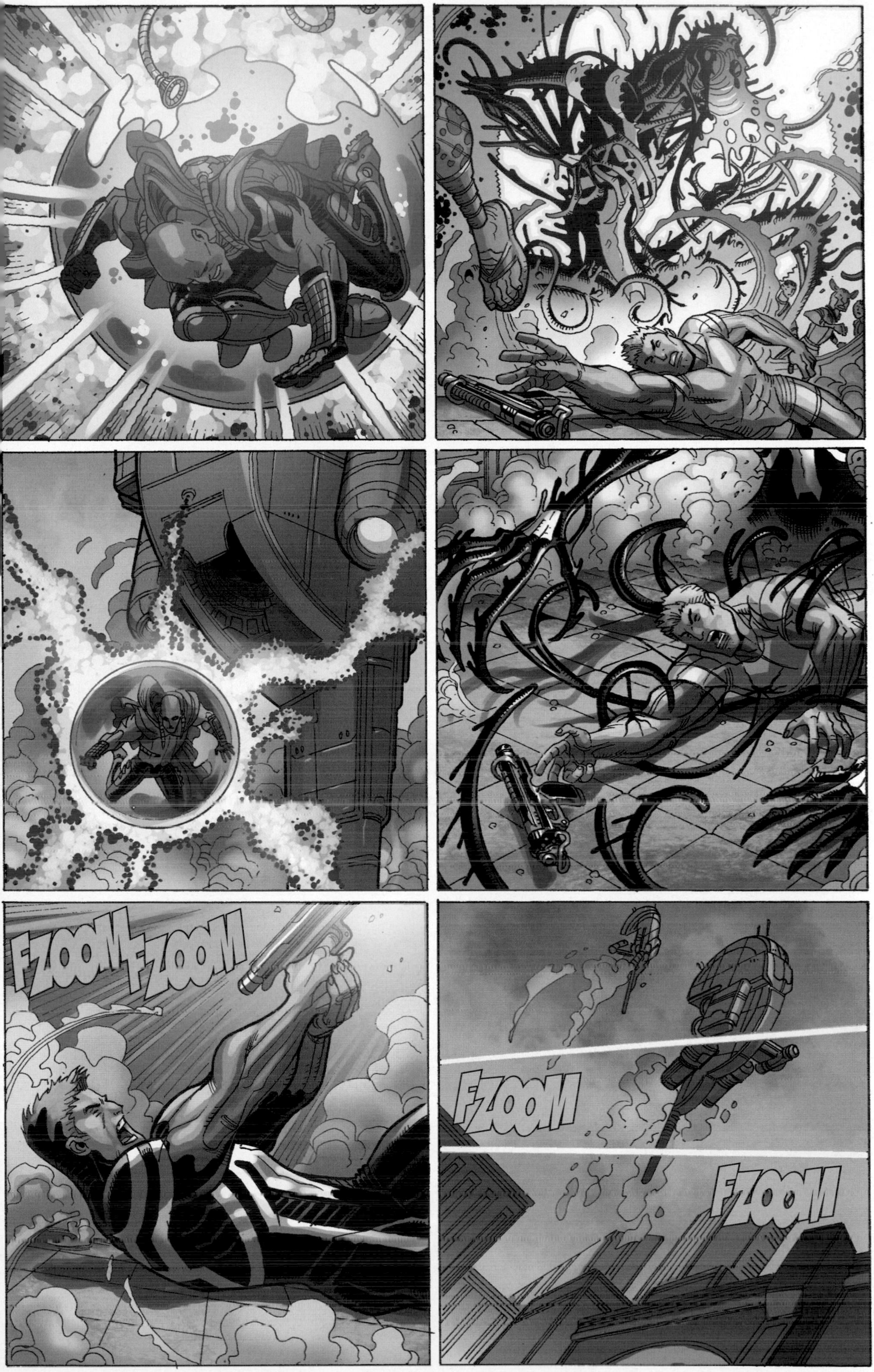
FZOOM FZOOM
FZOOM
FZOOM

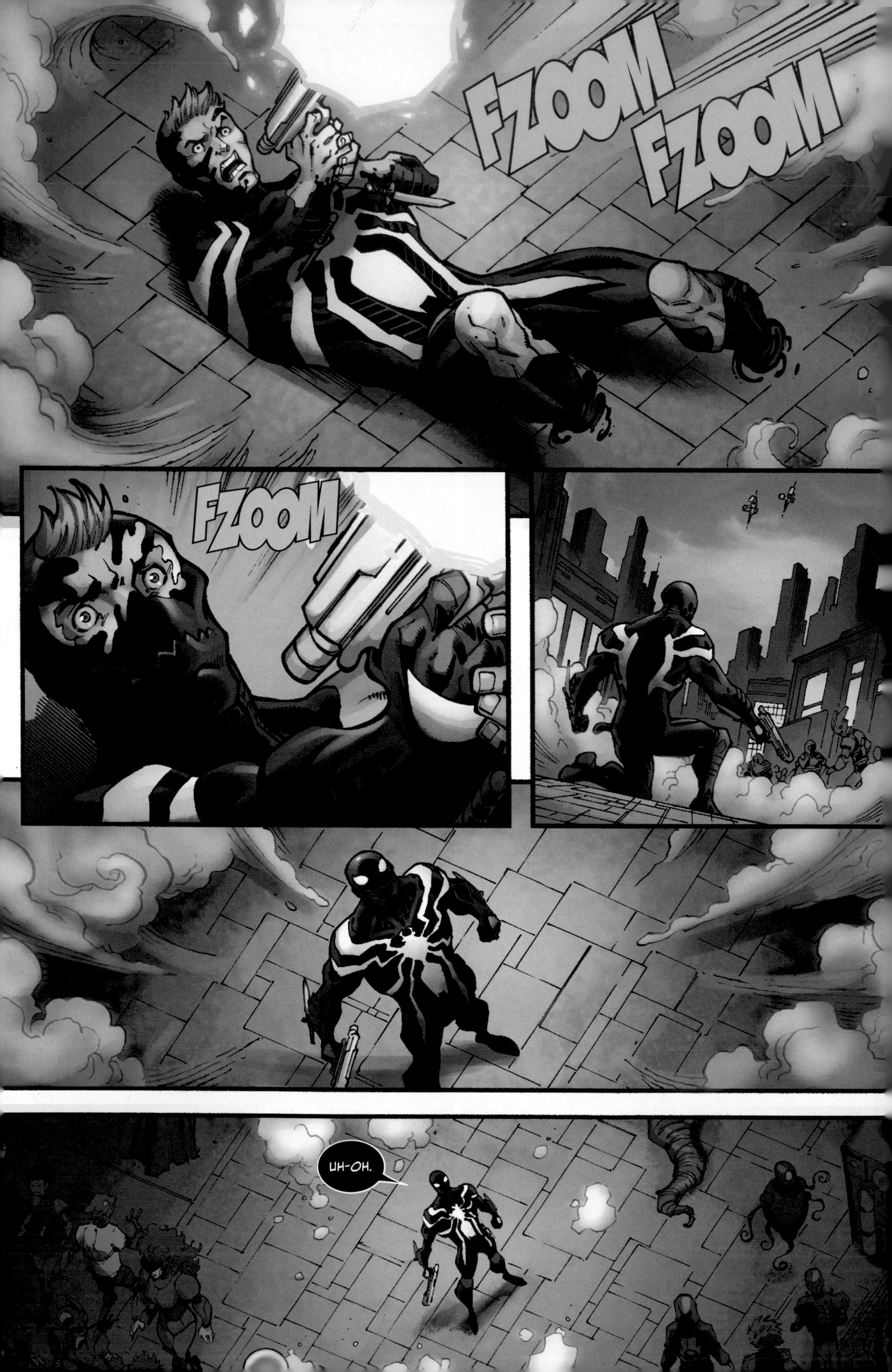
FZOOM
FZOOM
FZOOM
UH-OH.

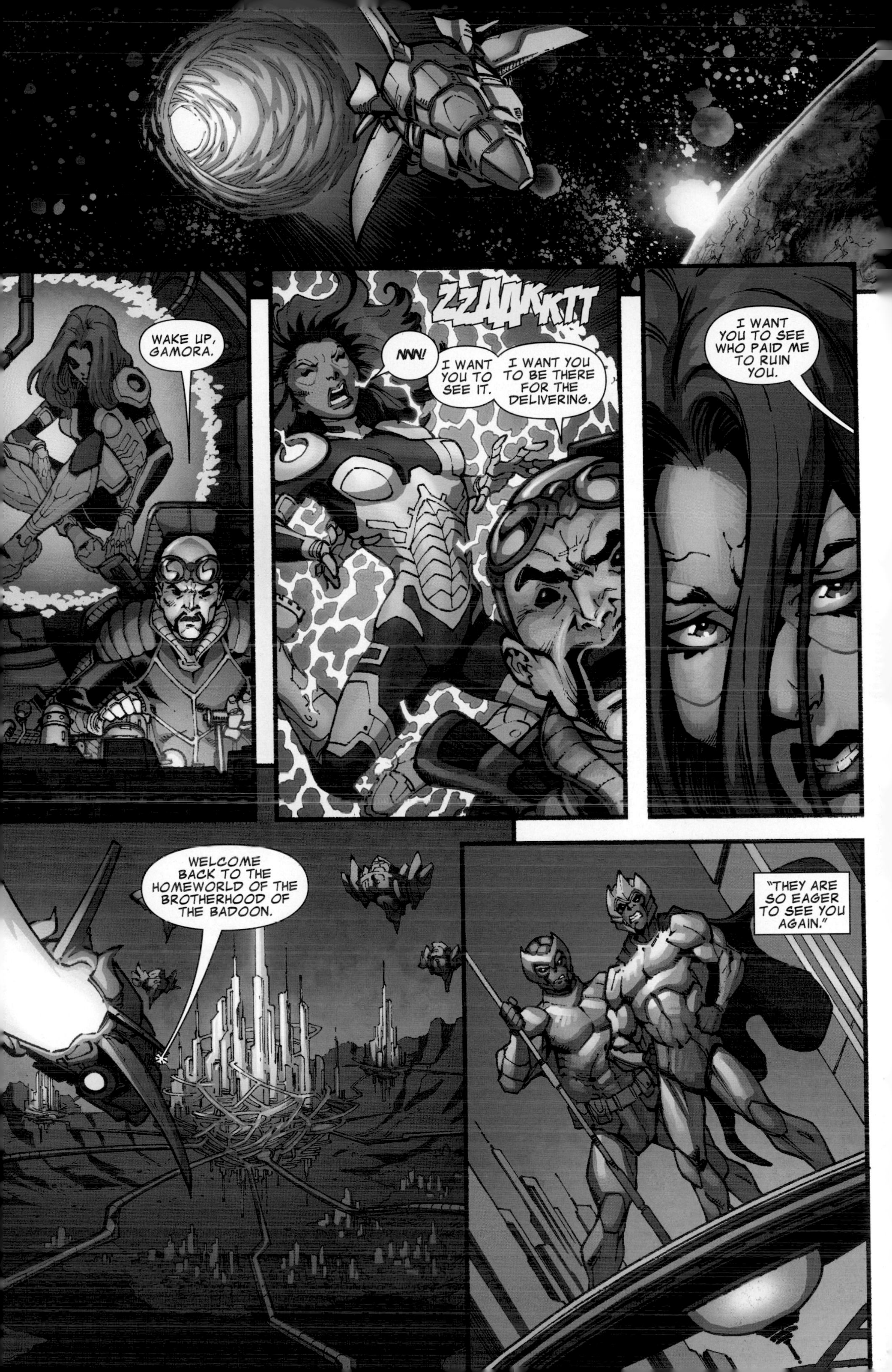

WAKE UP, GAMORA.
ZZAAKKTT
NNN!
I WANT YOU TO SEE IT.
I WANT YOU TO BE THERE FOR THE DELIVERING.
I WANT YOU TO SEE WHO PAID ME TO RUIN YOU.
WELCOME BACK TO THE HOMEWORLD OF THE BROTHERHOOD OF THE BADOON.
"THEY ARE SO EAGER TO SEE YOU AGAIN."

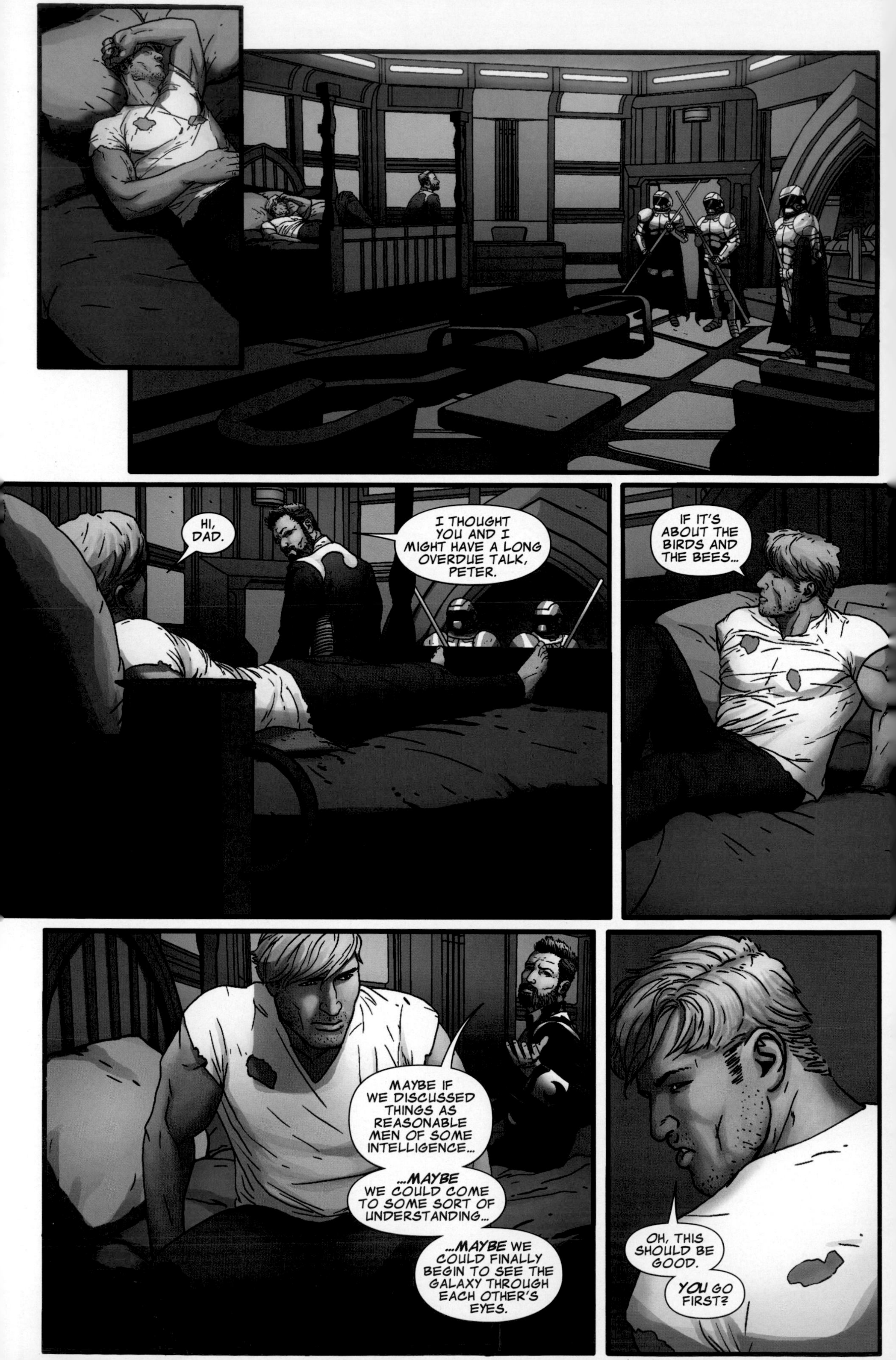
HI, DAD.
I THOUGHT YOU AND I MIGHT HAVE A LONG OVERDUE TALK, PETER.
IF IT'S ABOUT THE BIRDS AND THE BEES...
MAYBE IF WE DISCUSSED THINGS AS REASONABLE MEN OF SOME INTELLIGENCE...
...MAYBE WE COULD COME TO SOME SORT OF UNDERSTANDING...
...MAYBE WE COULD FINALLY BEGIN TO SEE THE GALAXY THROUGH EACH OTHER'S EYES.
OH, THIS SHOULD BE GOOD.
YOU GO FIRST?

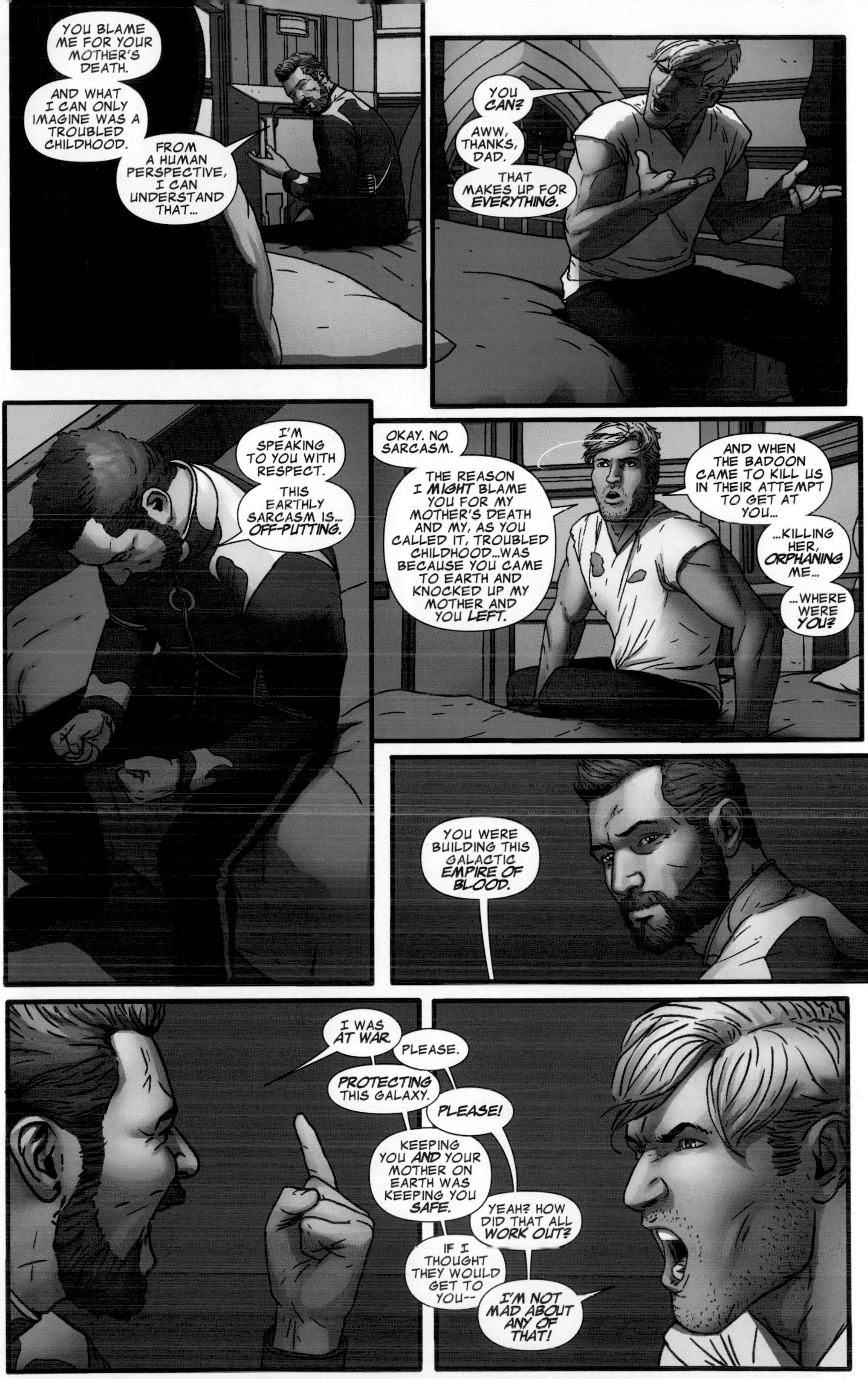
YOU BLAME ME FOR YOUR MOTHER'S DEATH.
AND WHAT I CAN ONLY IMAGINE WAS A TROUBLED CHILDHOOD.
FROM A HUMAN PERSPECTIVE, I CAN UNDERSTAND THAT...
YOU CAN?
AWW, THANKS, DAD.
THAT MAKES UP FOR EVERYTHING.
I'M SPEAKING TO YOU WITH RESPECT.
THIS EARTHLY SARCASM IS... OFF-PUTTING.
OKAY. NO SARCASM.
THE REASON I MIGHT BLAME YOU FOR MY MOTHER'S DEATH AND MY, AS YOU CALLED IT, TROUBLED CHILDHOOD...WAS BECAUSE YOU CAME TO EARTH AND KNOCKED UP MY MOTHER AND YOU LEFT.
AND WHEN THE BADOON CAME TO KILL US IN THEIR ATTEMPT TO GET AT YOU...
...KILLING HER, ORPHANING ME...
...WHERE WERE YOU?
YOU WERE BUILDING THIS GALACTIC EMPIRE OF BLOOD.
I WAS AT WAR.
PLEASE.
PROTECTING THIS GALAXY.
PLEASE!
KEEPING YOU AND YOUR MOTHER ON EARTH WAS KEEPING YOU SAFE.
YEAH? HOW DID THAT ALL WORK OUT?
IF I THOUGHT THEY WOULD GET TO YOU--
I'M NOT MAD ABOUT ANY OF THAT!

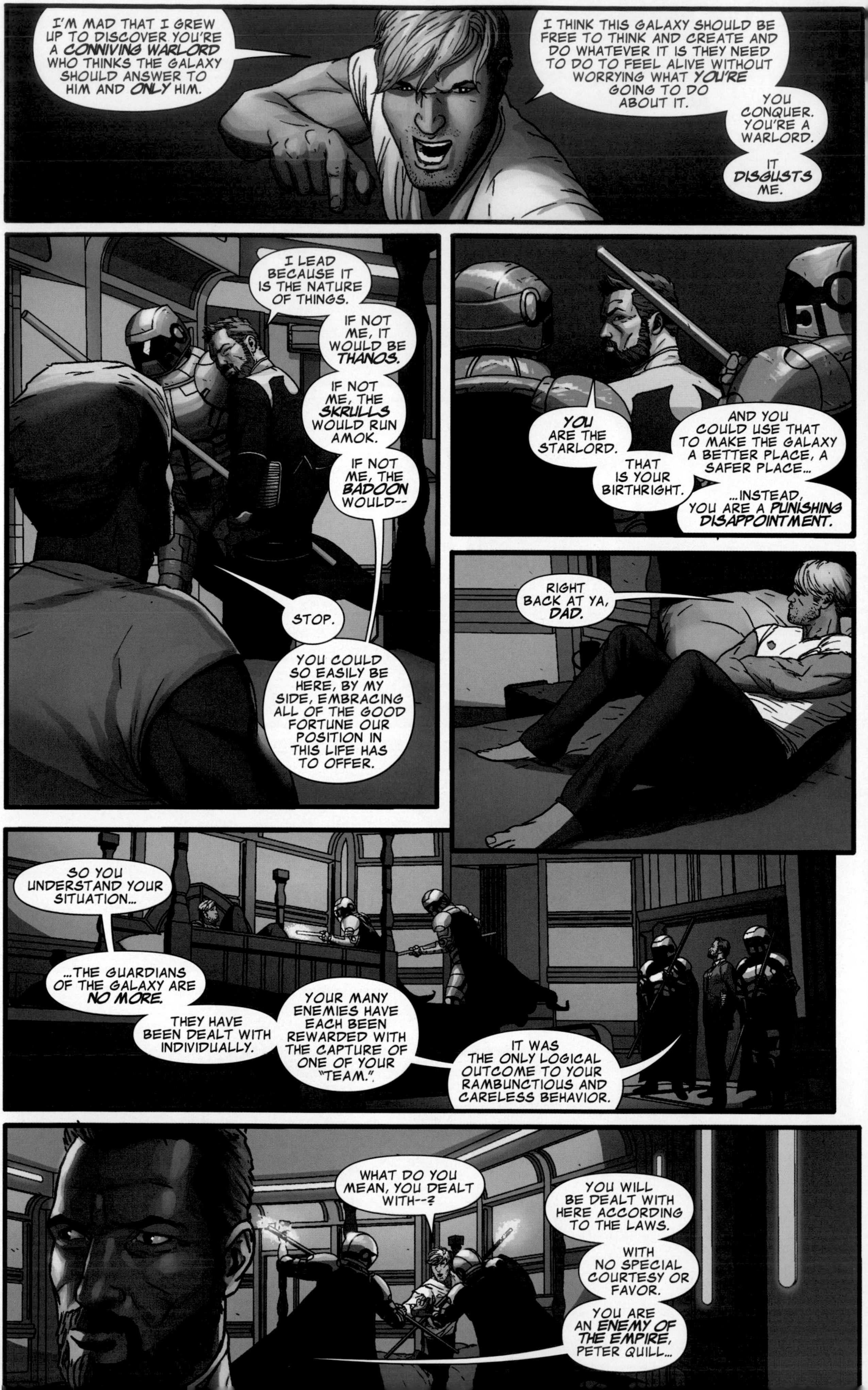

I'M MAD THAT I GREW UP TO DISCOVER YOU'RE A CONNIVING WARLORD WHO THINKS THE GALAXY SHOULD ANSWER TO HIM AND ONLY HIM.
I THINK THIS GALAXY SHOULD BE FREE TO THINK AND CREATE AND DO WHATEVER IT IS THEY NEED TO DO TO FEEL ALIVE WITHOUT WORRYING WHAT YOU'RE GOING TO DO ABOUT IT.
YOU CONQUER. YOU'RE A WARLORD.
IT DISGUSTS ME.
I LEAD BECAUSE IT IS THE NATURE OF THINGS.
IF NOT ME, IT WOULD BE THANOS.
IF NOT ME, THE SKRULLS WOULD RUN AMOK.
IF NOT ME, THE BADOON WOULD--
STOP.
YOU COULD SO EASILY BE HERE, BY MY SIDE, EMBRACING ALL OF THE GOOD FORTUNE OUR POSITION IN THIS LIFE HAS TO OFFER.
YOU ARE THE STARLORD.
THAT IS YOUR BIRTHRIGHT.
AND YOU COULD USE THAT TO MAKE THE GALAXY A BETTER PLACE, A SAFER PLACE...
...INSTEAD, YOU ARE A PUNISHING DISAPPOINTMENT.
RIGHT BACK AT YA, DAD.
SO YOU UNDERSTAND YOUR SITUATION...
...THE GUARDIANS OF THE GALAXY ARE NO MORE.
THEY HAVE BEEN DEALT WITH INDIVIDUALLY.
YOUR MANY ENEMIES HAVE EACH BEEN REWARDED WITH THE CAPTURE OF ONE OF YOUR "TEAM."
IT WAS THE ONLY LOGICAL OUTCOME TO YOUR RAMBUNCTIOUS AND CARELESS BEHAVIOR.
WHAT DO YOU MEAN, YOU DEALT WITH--?
YOU WILL BE DEALT WITH HERE ACCORDING TO THE LAWS.
WITH NO SPECIAL COURTESY OR FAVOR.
YOU ARE AN ENEMY OF THE EMPIRE, PETER QUILL...

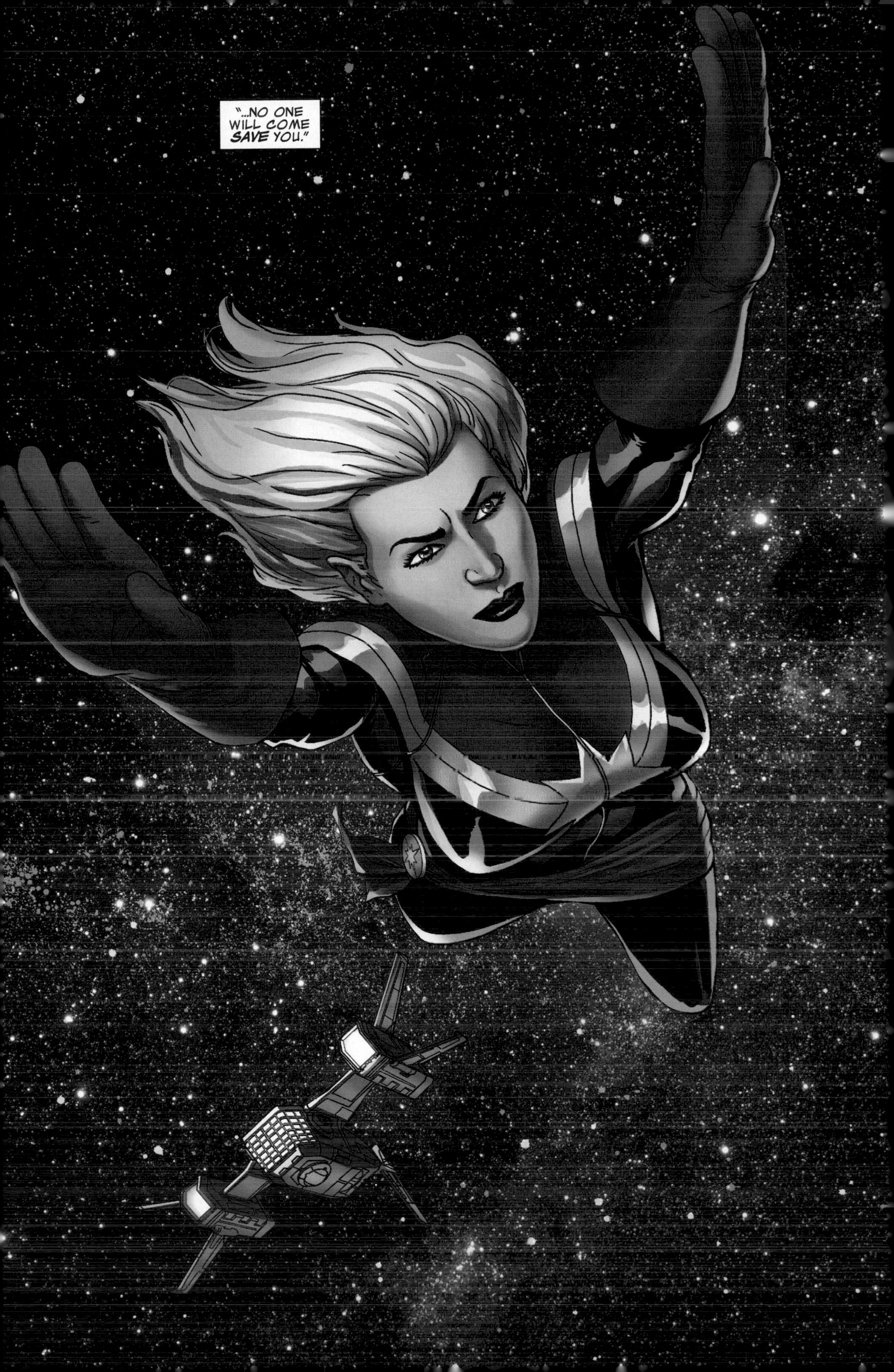
"...NO ONE WILL COME SAVE YOU."

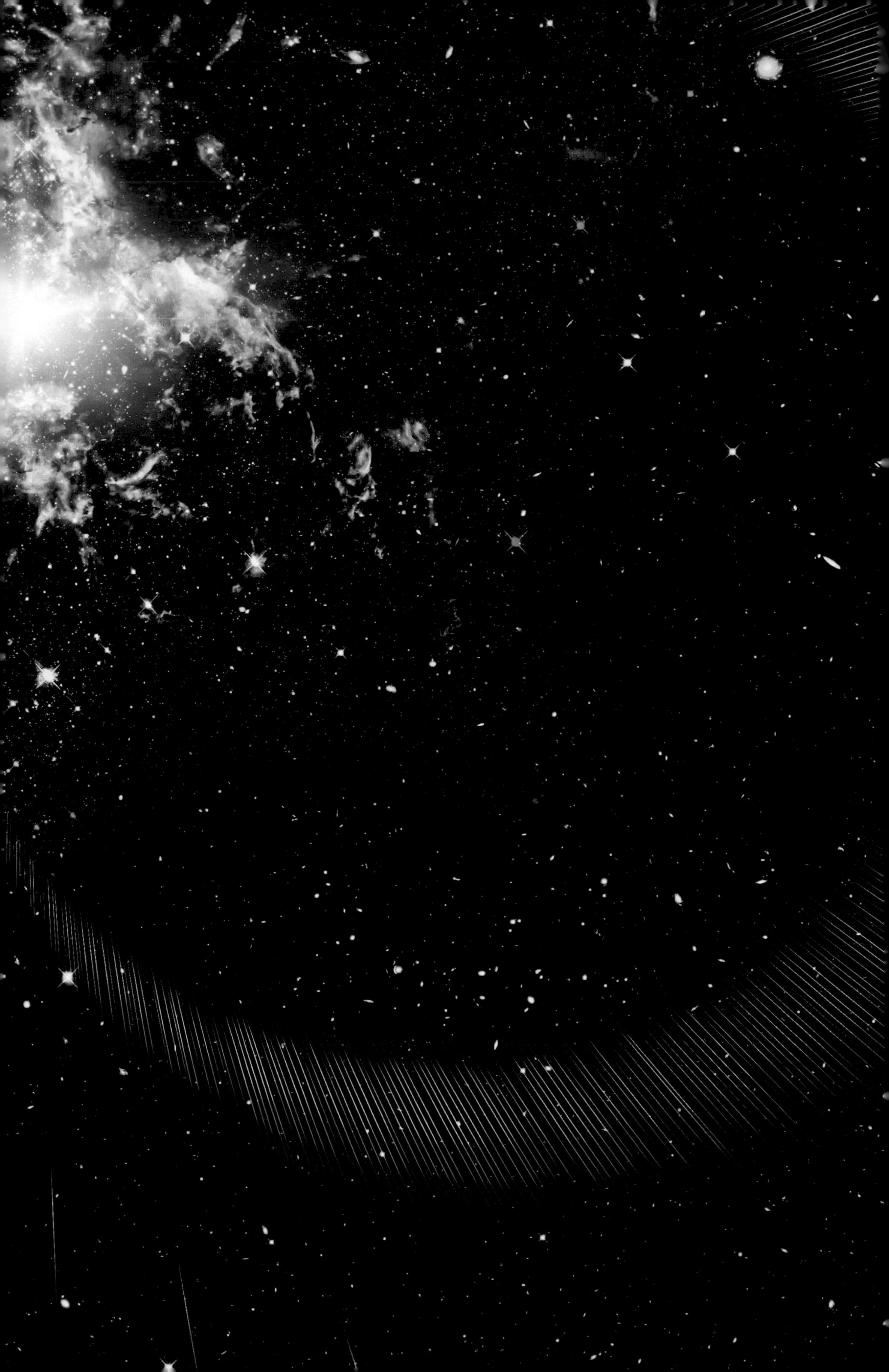

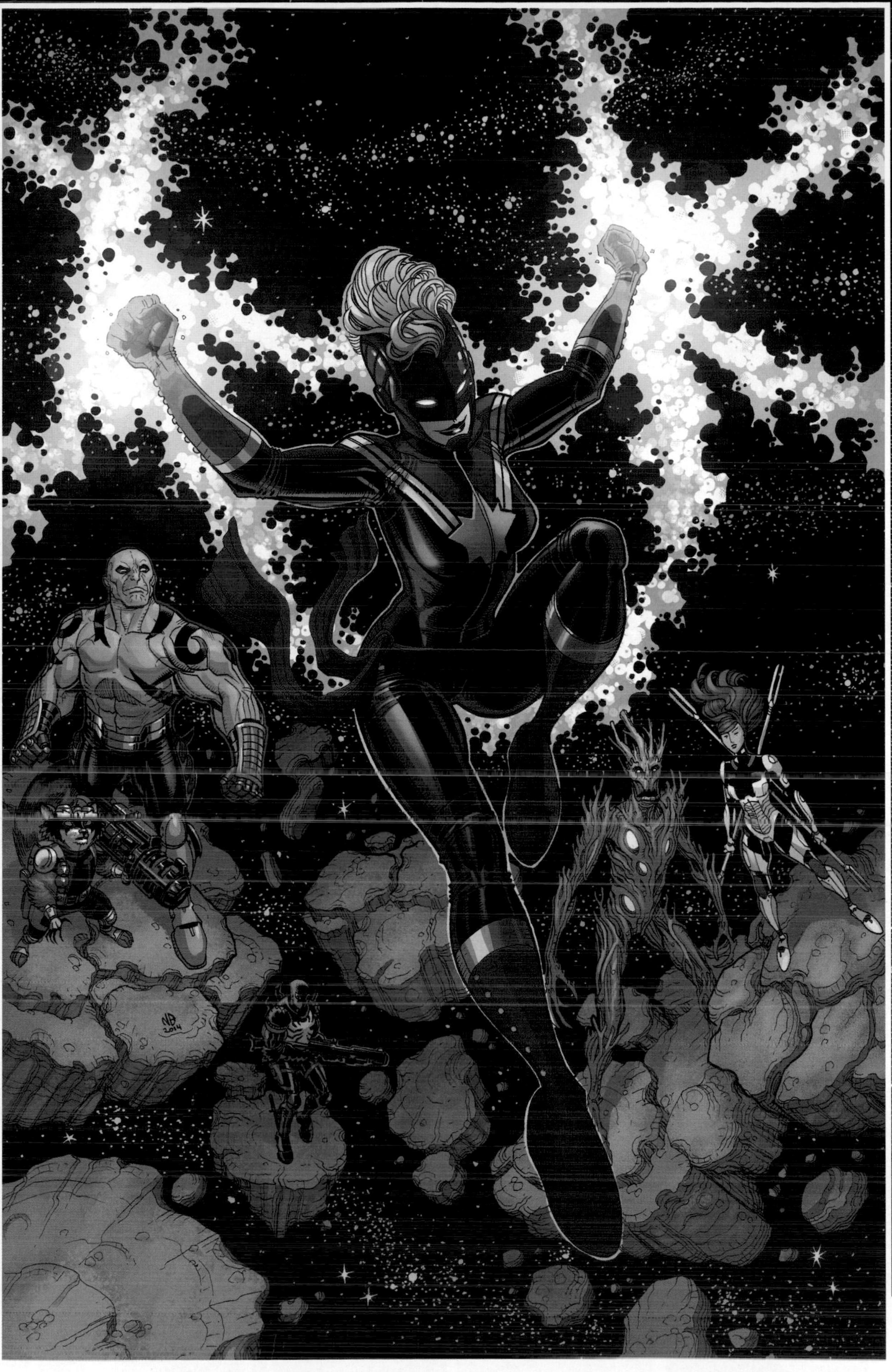

NA
2014

GUARDIANS OF THE GALAXY 15

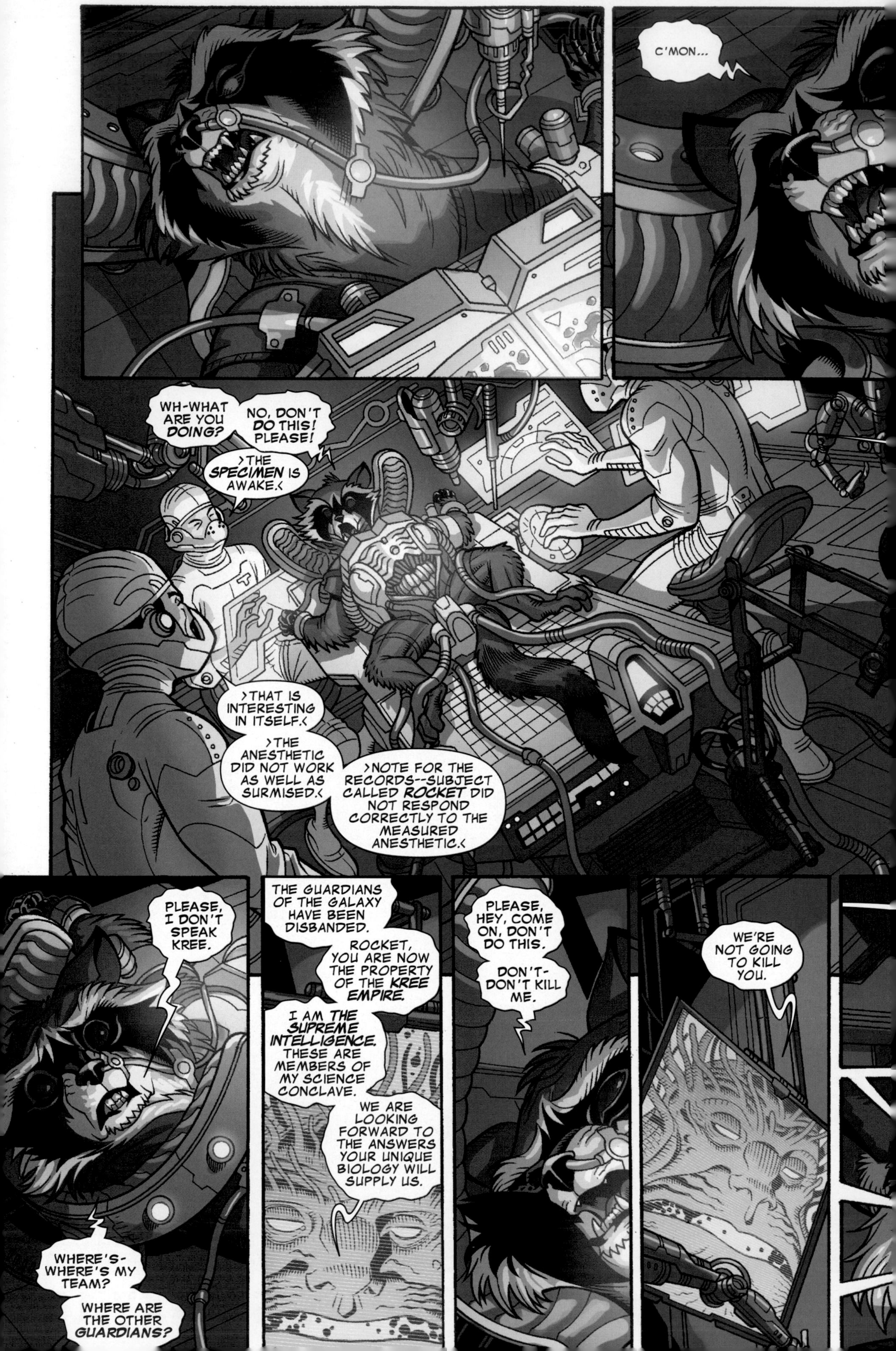
C'MON...
WH-WHAT ARE YOU DOING?
NO, DON'T DO THIS! PLEASE!
>THE SPECIMEN IS AWAKE.<
>THAT IS INTERESTING IN ITSELF.<
>THE ANESTHETIC DID NOT WORK AS WELL AS SURMISED.<
>NOTE FOR THE RECORDS--SUBJECT CALLED ROCKET DID NOT RESPOND CORRECTLY TO THE MEASURED ANESTHETIC.<
PLEASE, I DON'T SPEAK KREE.
WHERE'S- WHERE'S MY TEAM?
WHERE ARE THE OTHER GUARDIANS?
THE GUARDIANS OF THE GALAXY HAVE BEEN DISBANDED.
ROCKET, YOU ARE NOW THE PROPERTY OF THE KREE EMPIRE.
I AM THE SUPREME INTELLIGENCE. THESE ARE MEMBERS OF MY SCIENCE CONCLAVE.
WE ARE LOOKING FORWARD TO THE ANSWERS YOUR UNIQUE BIOLOGY WILL SUPPLY US.
PLEASE, HEY, COME ON, DON'T DO THIS.
DON'T- DON'T KILL ME.
WE'RE NOT GOING TO KILL YOU.

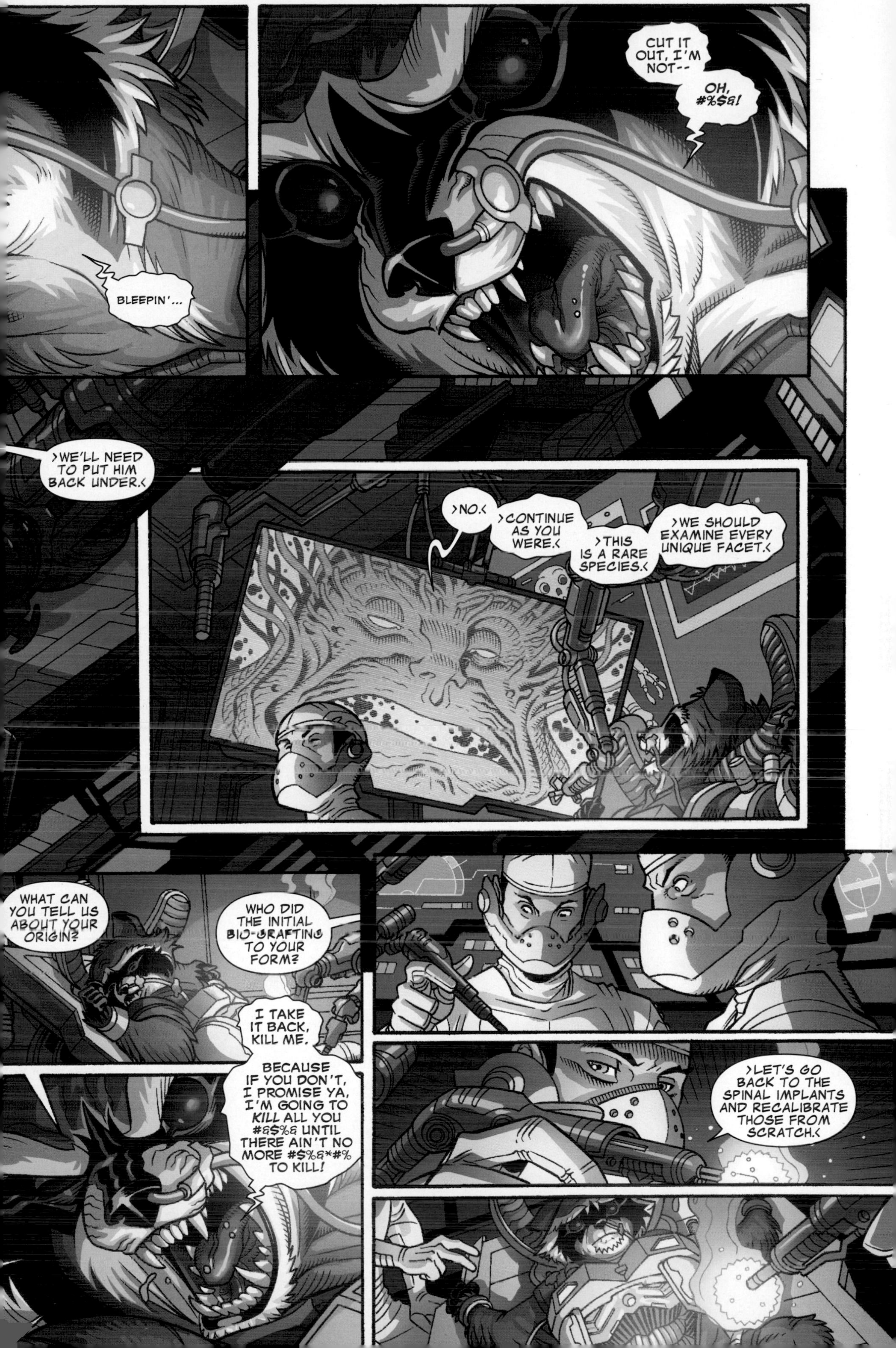
BLEEPIN'...
CUT IT OUT, I'M NOT--
OH, #%$&!
>WE'LL NEED TO PUT HIM BACK UNDER.<
>NO.<
>CONTINUE AS YOU WERE.<
>THIS IS A RARE SPECIES.<
>WE SHOULD EXAMINE EVERY UNIQUE FACET.<
WHAT CAN YOU TELL US ABOUT YOUR ORIGIN?
WHO DID THE INITIAL BIO-GRAFTING TO YOUR FORM?
I TAKE IT BACK, KILL ME.
BECAUSE IF YOU DON'T, I PROMISE YA, I'M GOING TO KILL ALL YOU #&$%& UNTIL THERE AIN'T NO MORE #$%&*#% TO KILL!
>LET'S GO BACK TO THE SPINAL IMPLANTS AND RECALIBRATE THOSE FROM SCRATCH.<

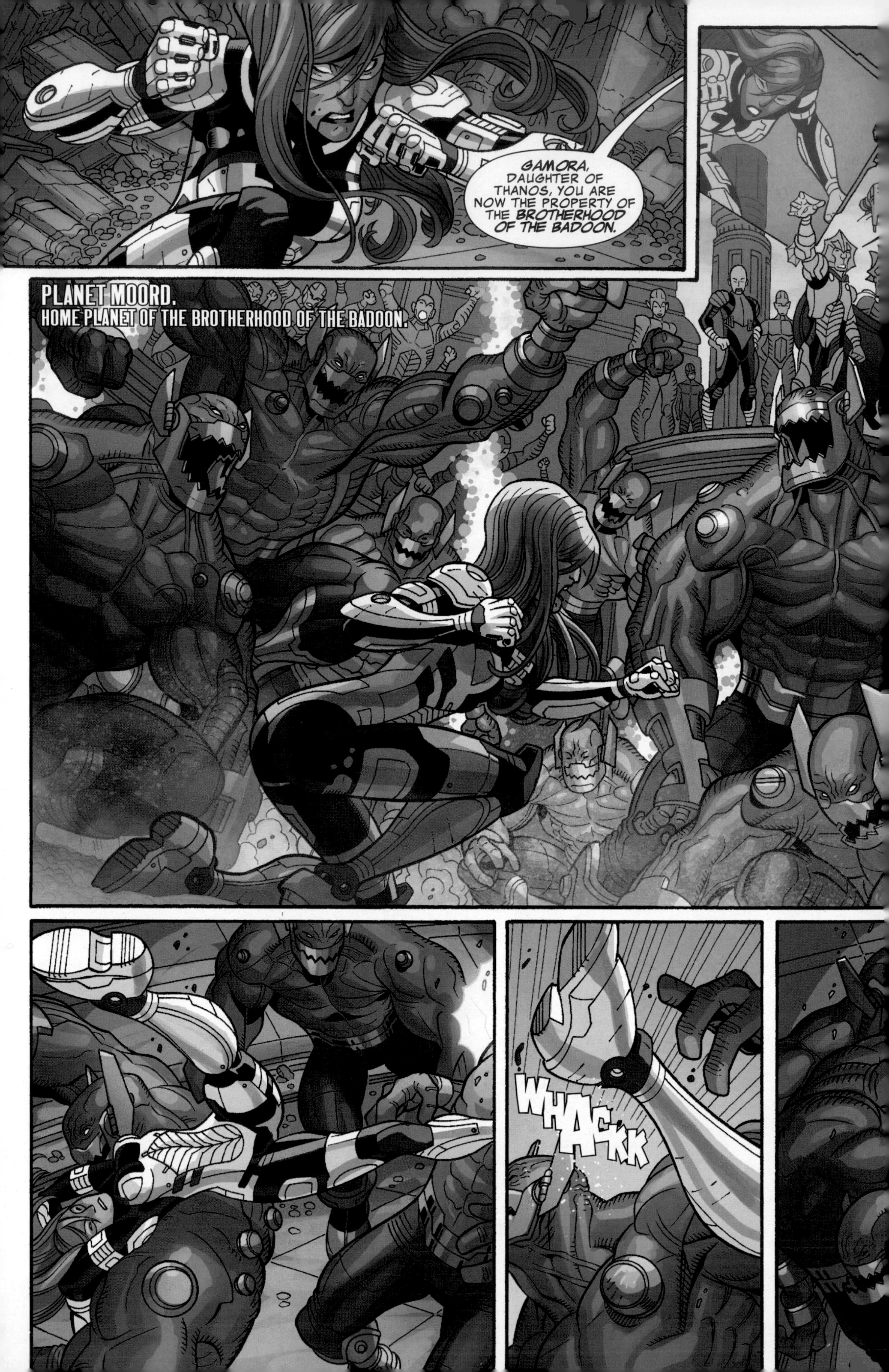
GAMORA, DAUGHTER OF THANOS, YOU ARE NOW THE PROPERTY OF THE BROTHERHOOD OF THE BADOON.
PLANET MOORD.
HOME PLANET OF THE BROTHERHOOD OF THE BADOON.
WHACKK

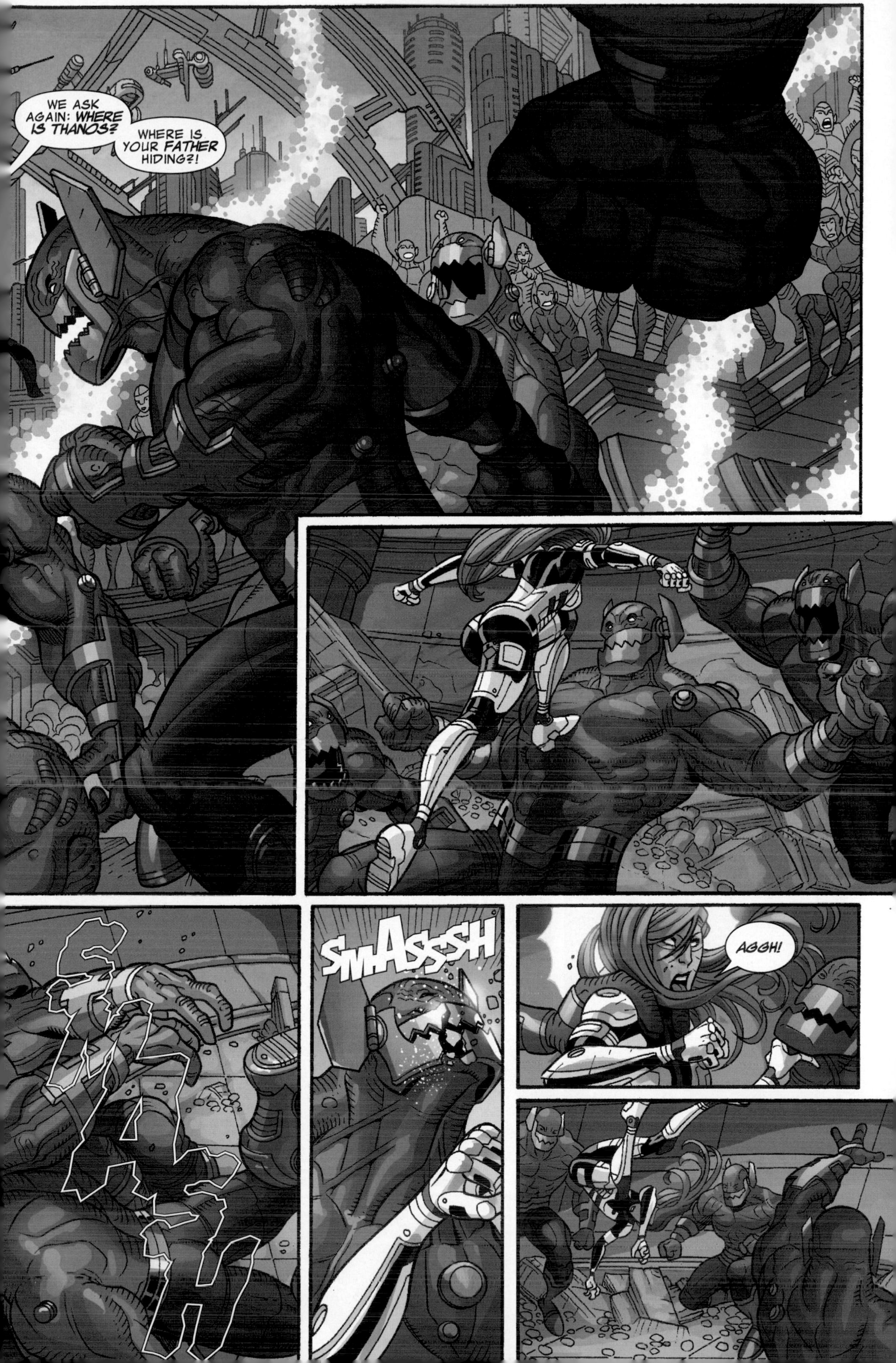
WE ASK AGAIN: WHERE IS THANOS?
WHERE IS YOUR FATHER HIDING?!
SMASSSH
AGGH!

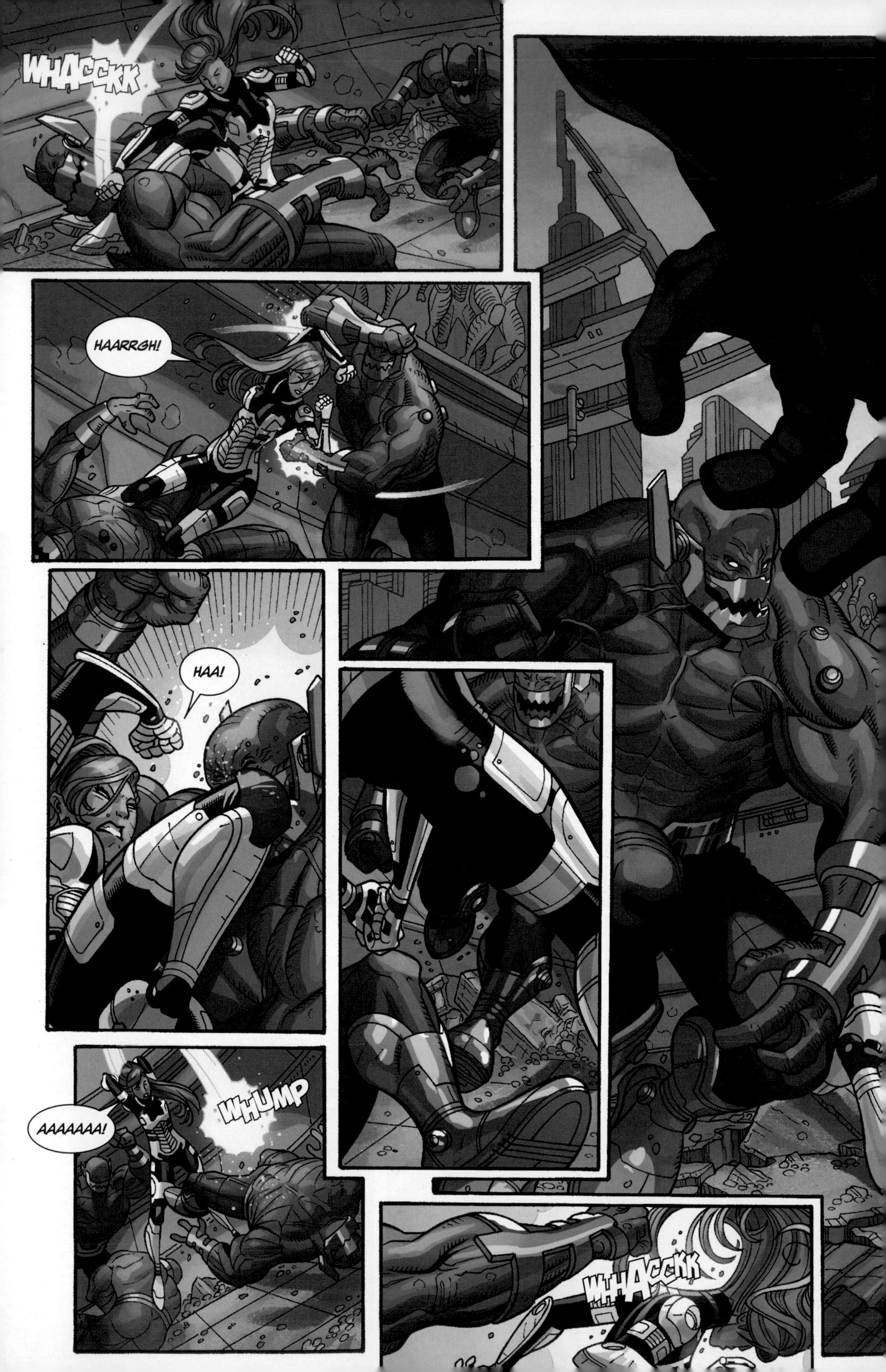
WHACCKK
HAARRGH!
HAA!
AAAAAAA!
WHUMP
WHACCKK

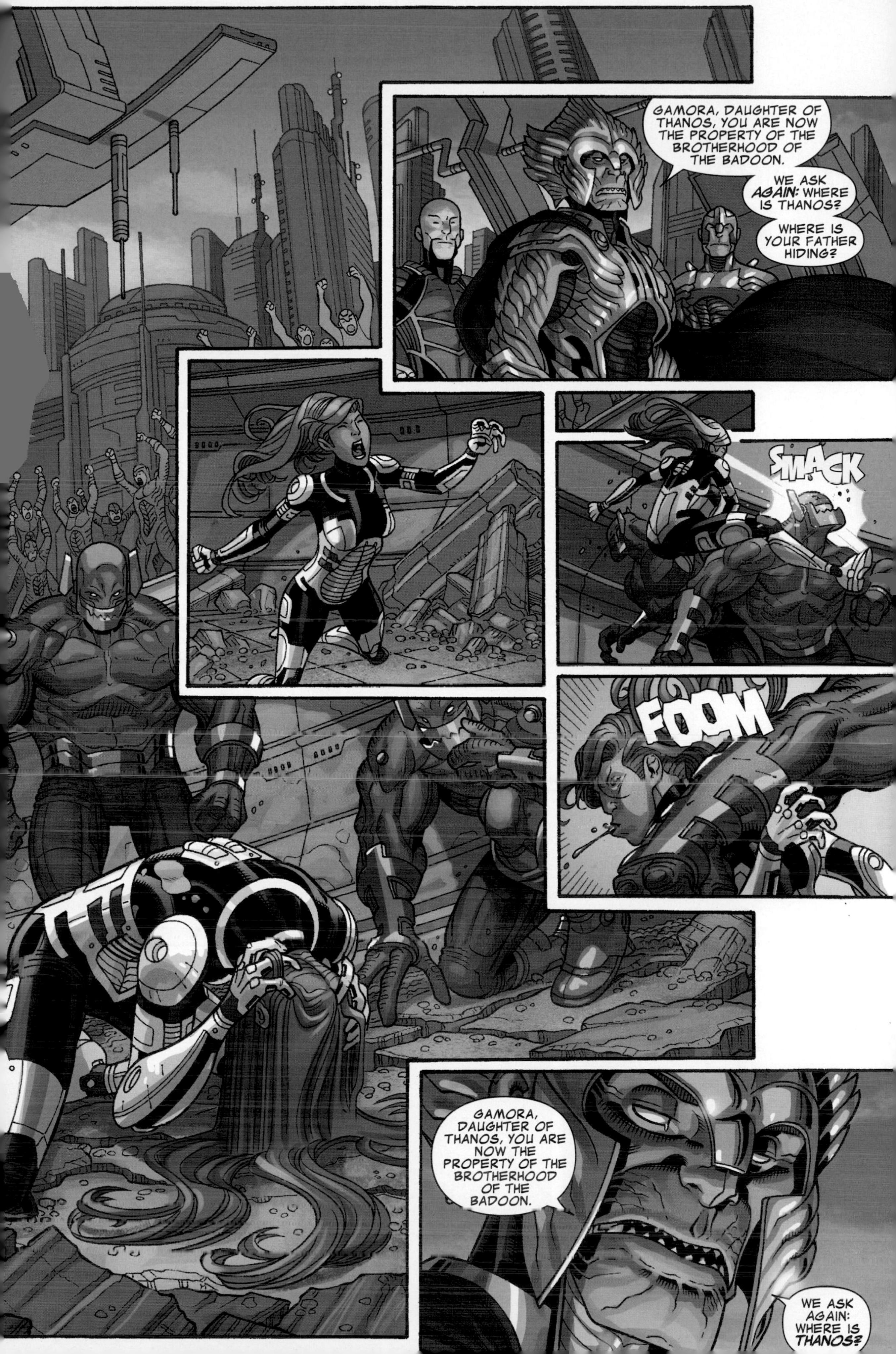
GAMORA, DAUGHTER OF THANOS, YOU ARE NOW THE PROPERTY OF THE BROTHERHOOD OF THE BADOON.
WE ASK AGAIN: WHERE IS THANOS?
WHERE IS YOUR FATHER HIDING?
SMACK
FOOM
GAMORA, DAUGHTER OF THANOS, YOU ARE NOW THE PROPERTY OF THE BROTHERHOOD OF THE BADOON.
WE ASK AGAIN: WHERE IS THANOS?

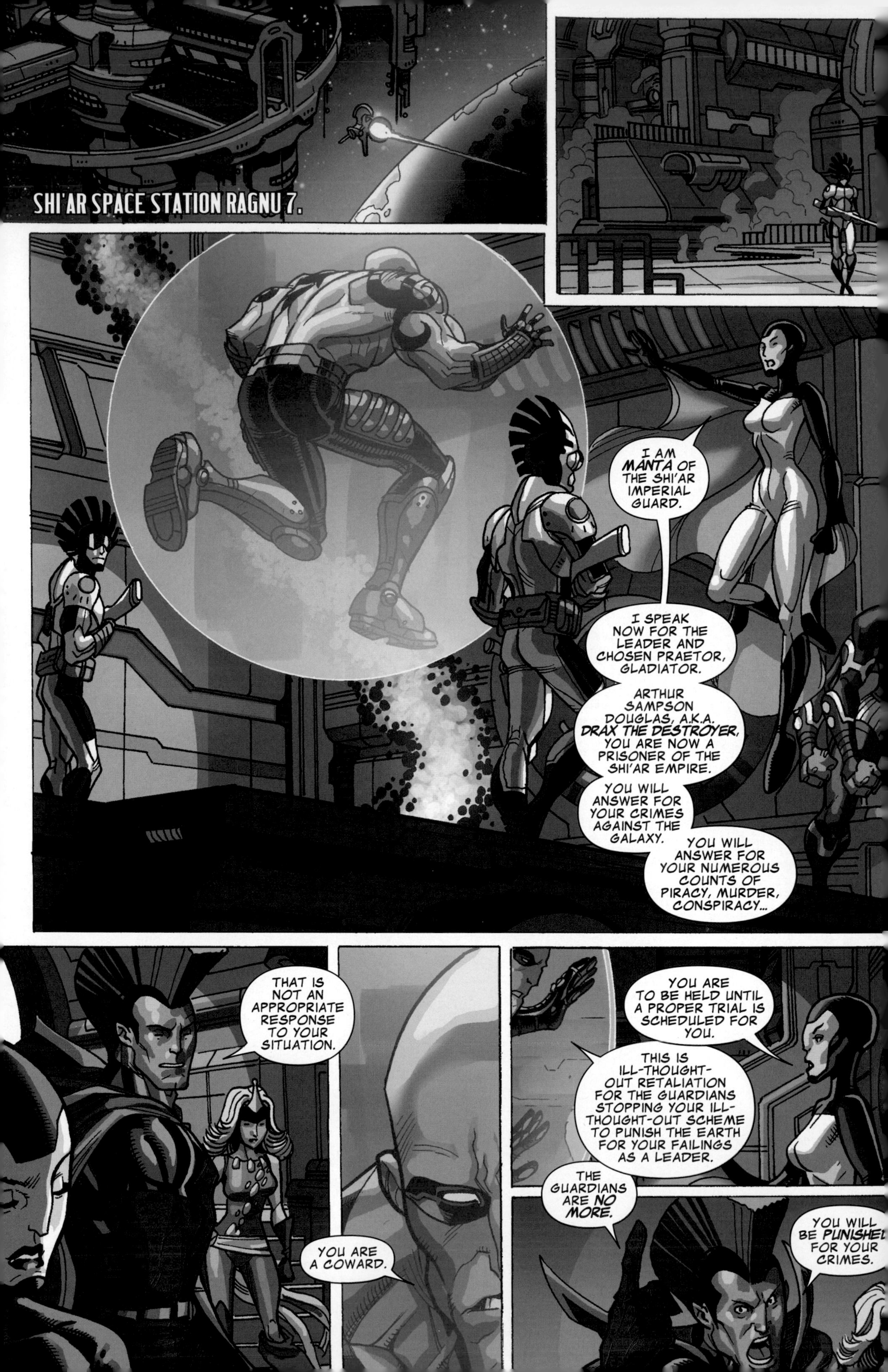
SHI'AR SPACE STATION RAGNU 7.
I AM MANTA OF THE SHI'AR IMPERIAL GUARD.
I SPEAK NOW FOR THE LEADER AND CHOSEN PRAETOR, GLADIATOR.
ARTHUR SAMPSON DOUGLAS, A.K.A. DRAX THE DESTROYER, YOU ARE NOW A PRISONER OF THE SHI'AR EMPIRE.
YOU WILL ANSWER FOR YOUR CRIMES AGAINST THE GALAXY.
YOU WILL ANSWER FOR YOUR NUMEROUS COUNTS OF PIRACY, MURDER, CONSPIRACY...
THAT IS NOT AN APPROPRIATE RESPONSE TO YOUR SITUATION.
YOU ARE A COWARD.
YOU ARE TO BE HELD UNTIL A PROPER TRIAL IS SCHEDULED FOR YOU.
THIS IS ILL-THOUGHT-OUT RETALIATION FOR THE GUARDIANS STOPPING YOUR ILL-THOUGHT-OUT SCHEME TO PUNISH THE EARTH FOR YOUR FAILINGS AS A LEADER.
THE GUARDIANS ARE NO MORE.
YOU WILL BE PUNISHED FOR YOUR CRIMES.

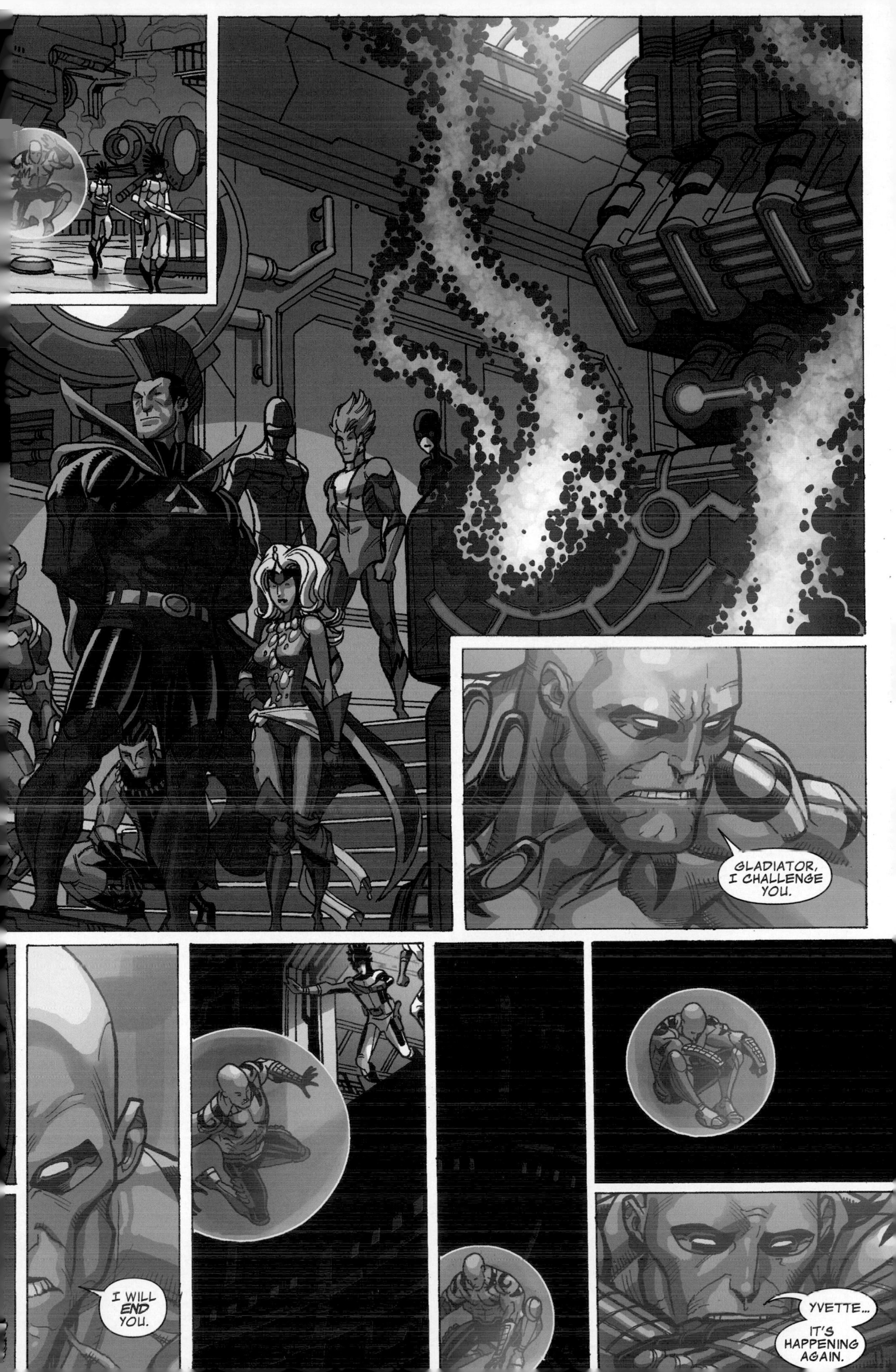
GLADIATOR, I CHALLENGE YOU.
I WILL END YOU.
YVETTE...
IT'S HAPPENING AGAIN.

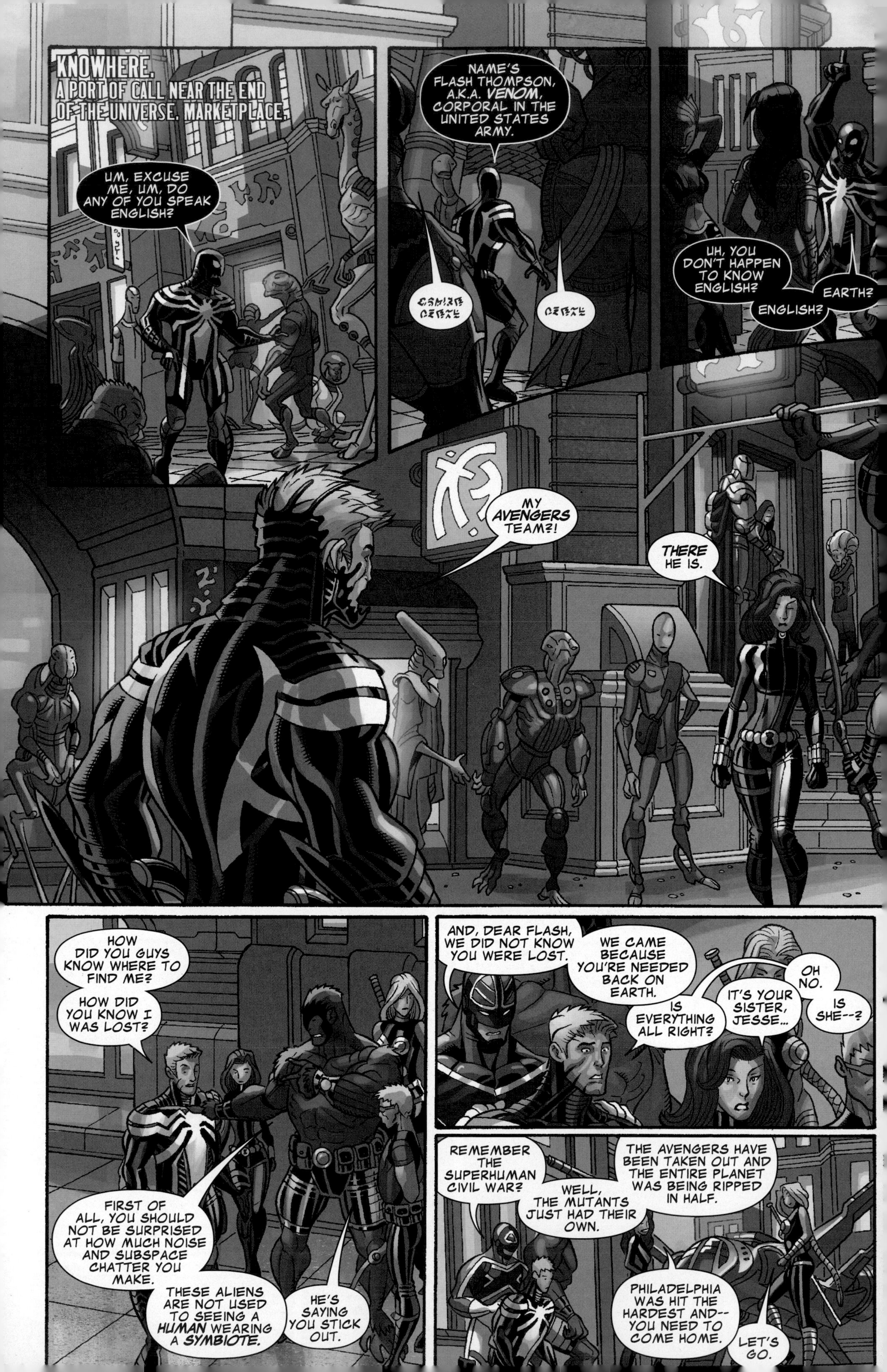
KNOWHERE.
A PORT OF CALL NEAR THE END OF THE UNIVERSE. MARKETPLACE.
UM, EXCUSE ME, UM, DO ANY OF YOU SPEAK ENGLISH?
NAME'S FLASH THOMPSON, A.K.A. VENOM, CORPORAL IN THE UNITED STATES ARMY.
UH, YOU DON'T HAPPEN TO KNOW ENGLISH?
EARTH?
ENGLISH?
MY AVENGERS TEAM?!
THERE HE IS.
HOW DID YOU GUYS KNOW WHERE TO FIND ME?
HOW DID YOU KNOW I WAS LOST?
FIRST OF ALL, YOU SHOULD NOT BE SURPRISED AT HOW MUCH NOISE AND SUBSPACE CHATTER YOU MAKE.
THESE ALIENS ARE NOT USED TO SEEING A HUMAN WEARING A SYMBIOTE.
HE'S SAYING YOU STICK OUT.
AND, DEAR FLASH, WE DID NOT KNOW YOU WERE LOST.
WE CAME BECAUSE YOU'RE NEEDED BACK ON EARTH.
IS EVERYTHING ALL RIGHT?
IT'S YOUR SISTER, JESSE...
OH NO.
IS SHE--?
REMEMBER THE SUPERHUMAN CIVIL WAR?
WELL, THE MUTANTS JUST HAD THEIR OWN.
THE AVENGERS HAVE BEEN TAKEN OUT AND THE ENTIRE PLANET WAS BEING RIPPED IN HALF.
PHILADELPHIA WAS HIT THE HARDEST AND-- YOU NEED TO COME HOME.
LET'S GO.

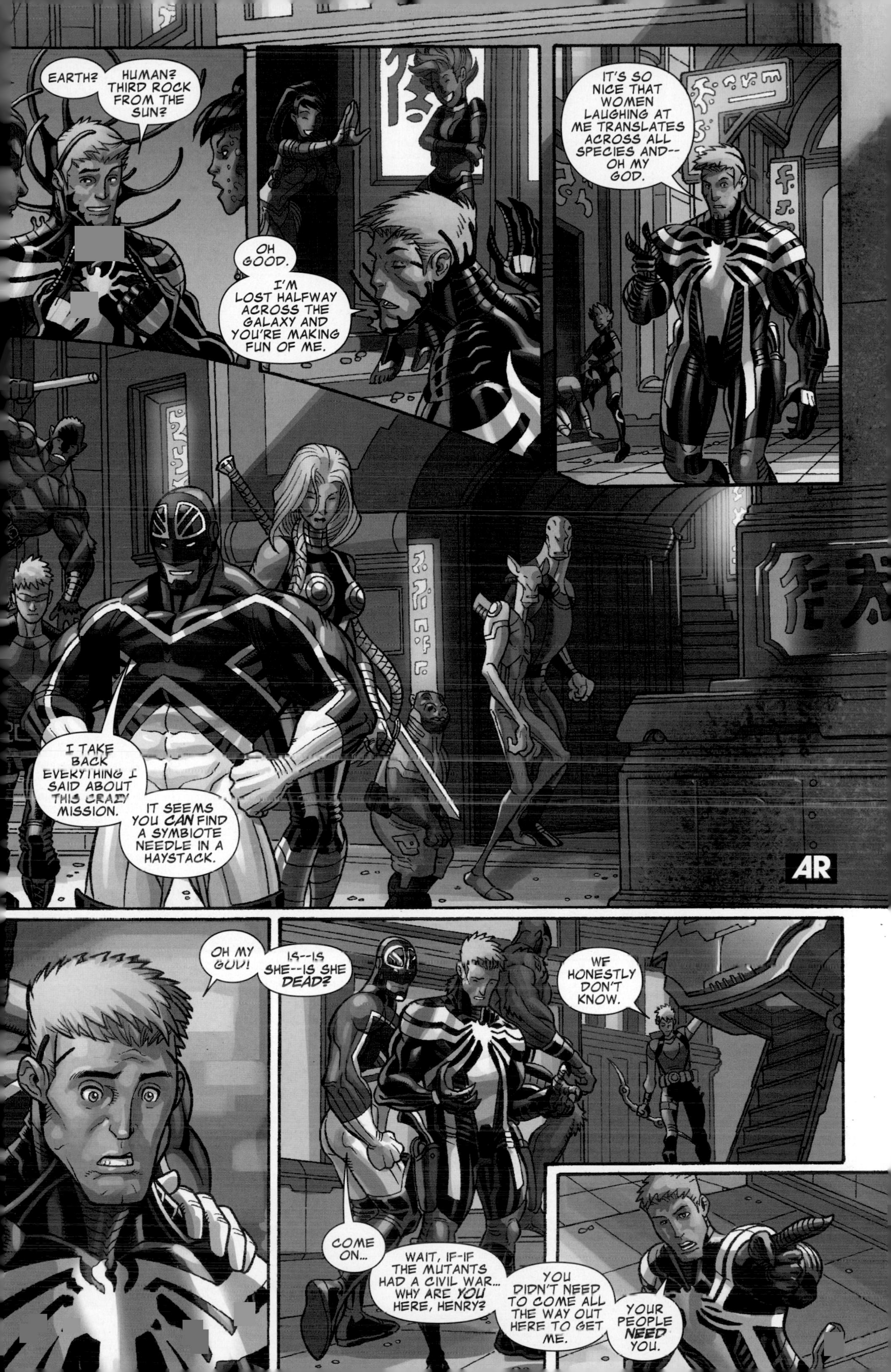
EARTH?
HUMAN? THIRD ROCK FROM THE SUN?
OH GOOD.
I'M LOST HALFWAY ACROSS THE GALAXY AND YOU'RE MAKING FUN OF ME.
IT'S SO NICE THAT WOMEN LAUGHING AT ME TRANSLATES ACROSS ALL SPECIES AND-- OH MY GOD.
I TAKE BACK EVERYTHING I SAID ABOUT THIS CRAZY MISSION.
IT SEEMS YOU CAN FIND A SYMBIOTE NEEDLE IN A HAYSTACK.
AR
OH MY GOD!
IS--IS SHE--IS SHE DEAD?
WE HONESTLY DON'T KNOW.
COME ON...
WAIT, IF-IF THE MUTANTS HAD A CIVIL WAR... WHY ARE YOU HERE, HENRY?
YOU DIDN'T NEED TO COME ALL THE WAY OUT HERE TO GET ME.
YOUR PEOPLE NEED YOU.

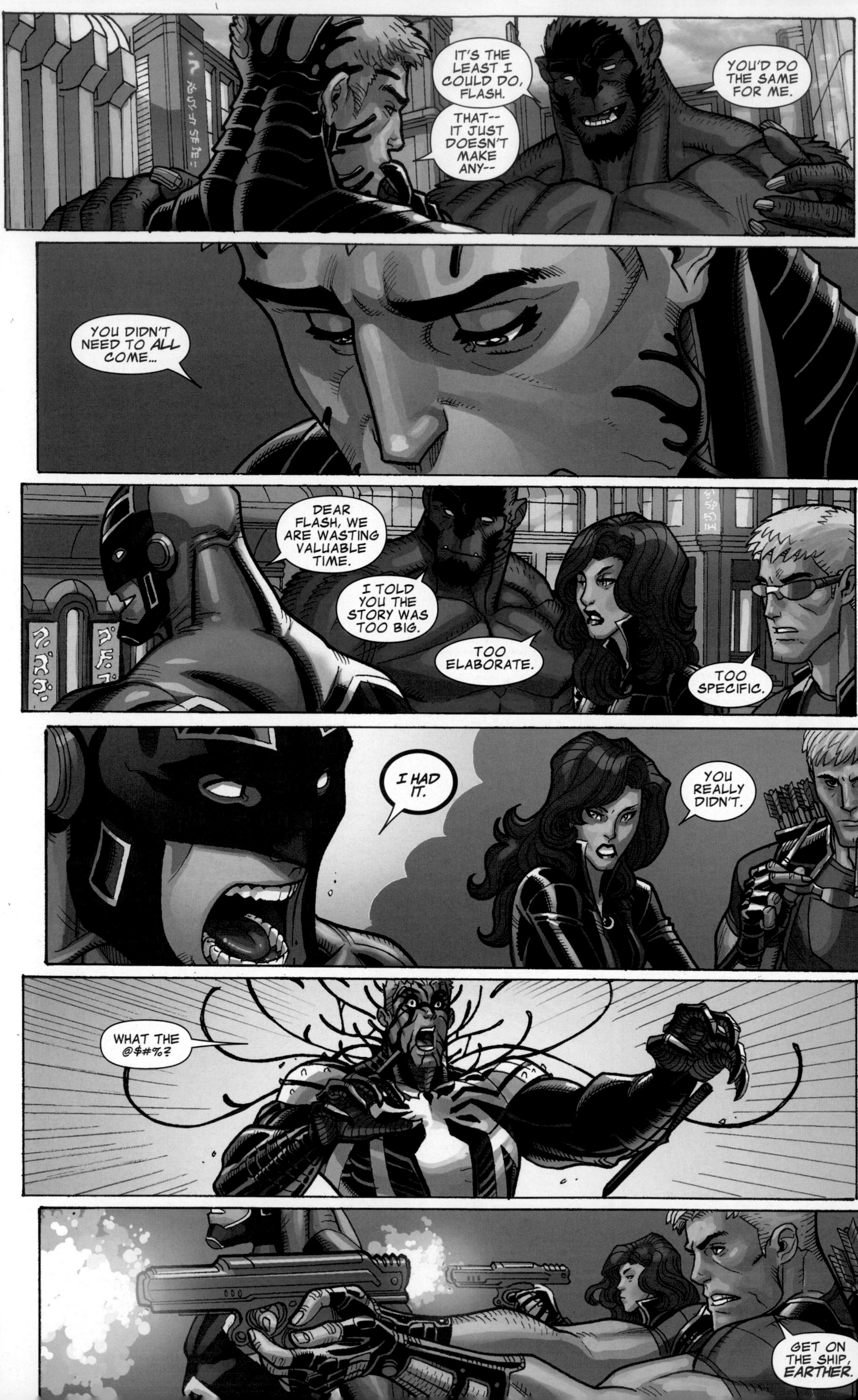
IT'S THE LEAST I COULD DO, FLASH.
YOU'D DO THE SAME FOR ME.
THAT-- IT JUST DOESN'T MAKE ANY--
YOU DIDN'T NEED TO ALL COME...
DEAR FLASH, WE ARE WASTING VALUABLE TIME.
I TOLD YOU THE STORY WAS TOO BIG.
TOO ELABORATE.
TOO SPECIFIC.
I HAD IT.
YOU REALLY DIDN'T.
WHAT THE @$#%?
GET ON THE SHIP, EARTHER.

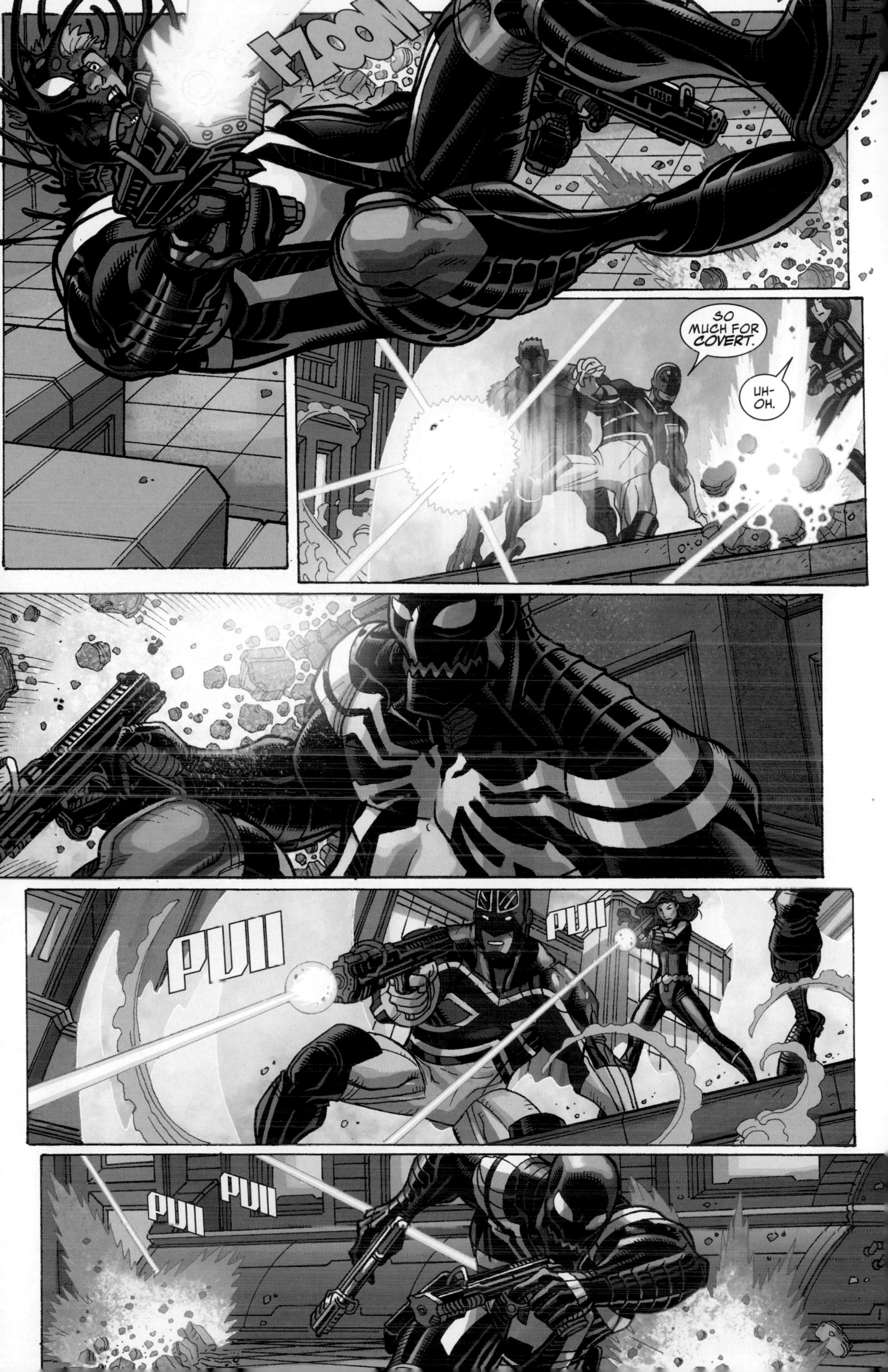
FZOOM
SO MUCH FOR COVERT.
UH-OH.
PUII
PUII
PUII
PUII

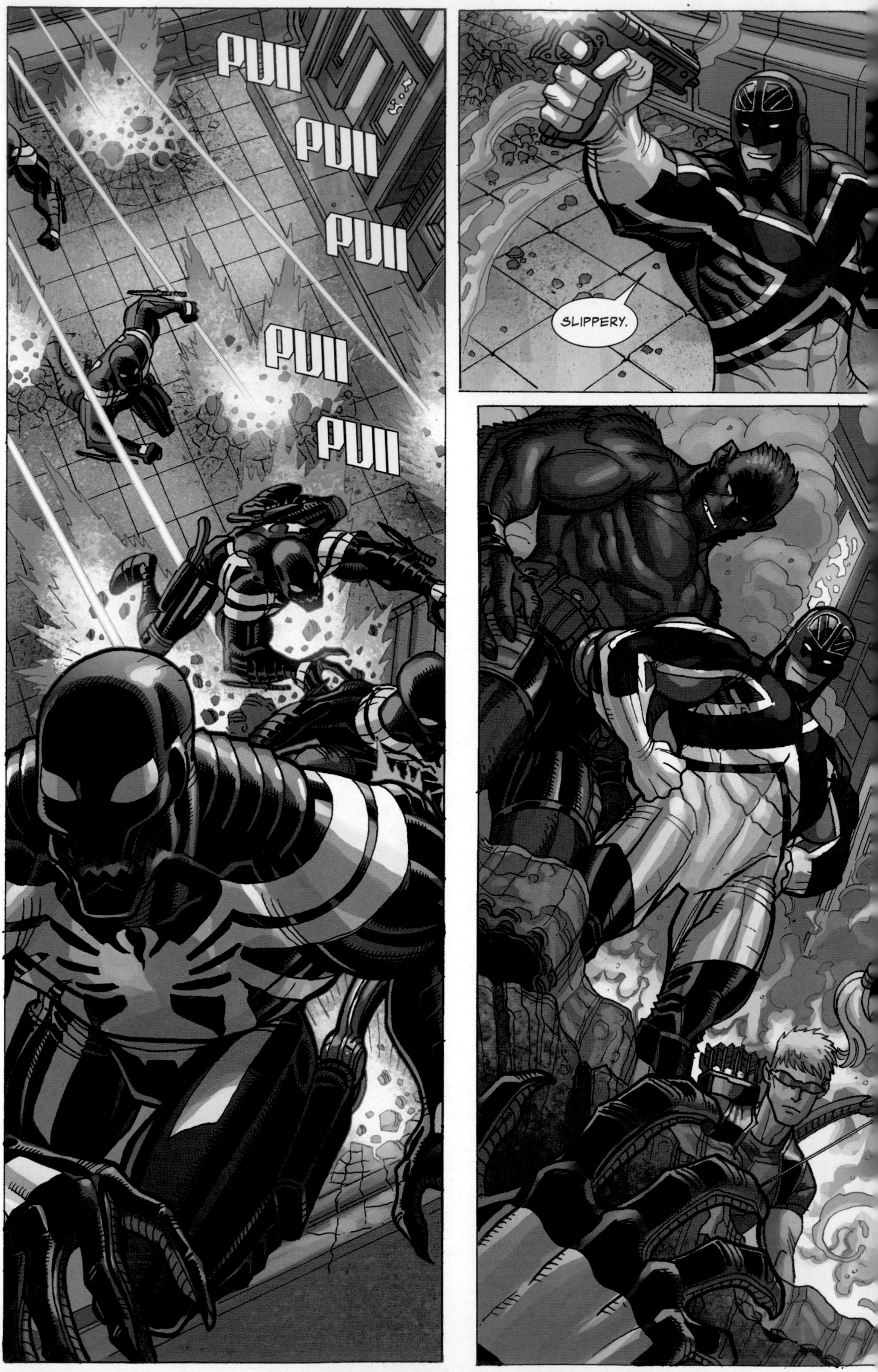
PVII
PVII
PVII
PVII
PVII
SLIPPERY.

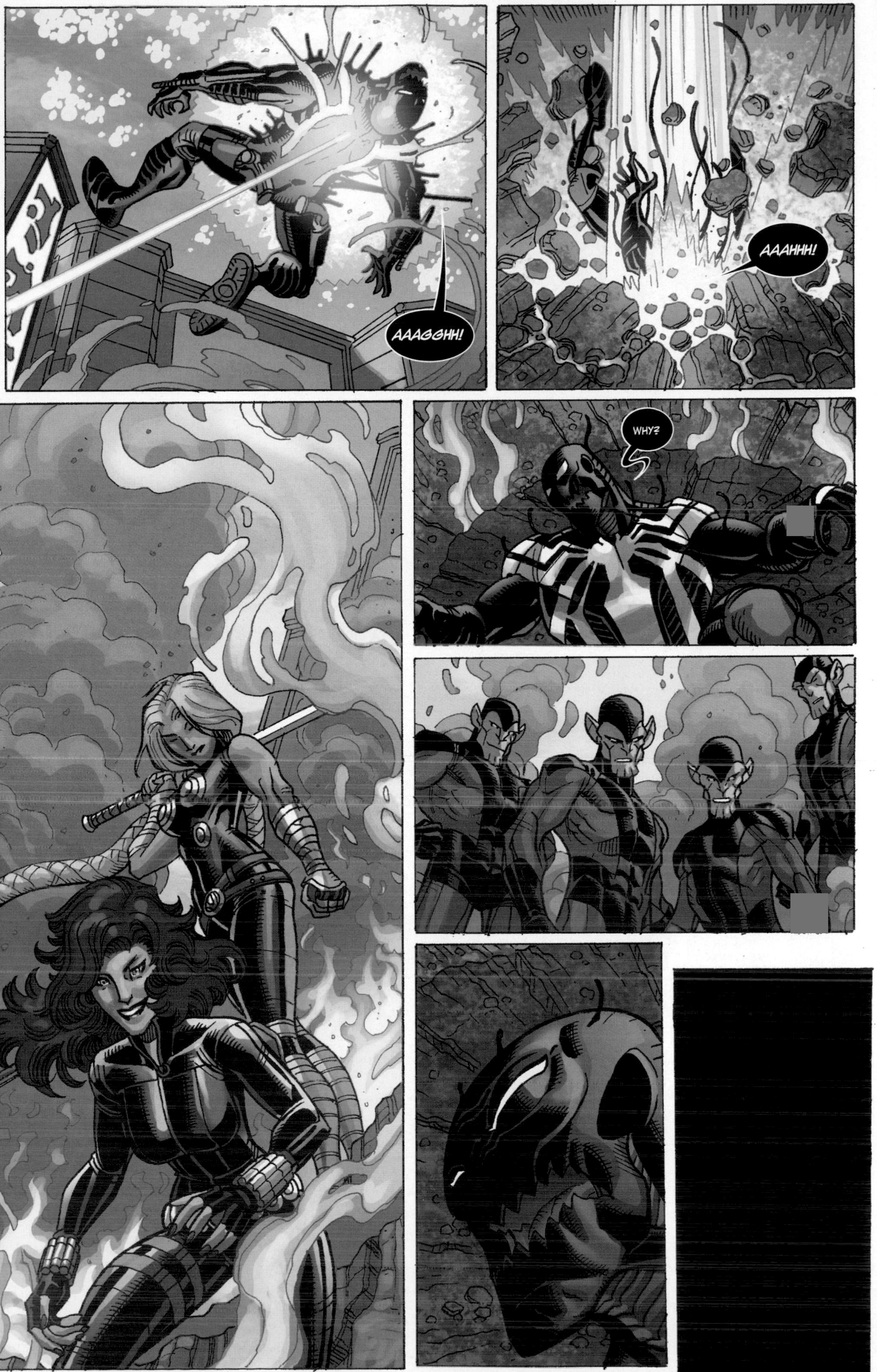
AAAGGHH!
AAAHHH!
WHY?

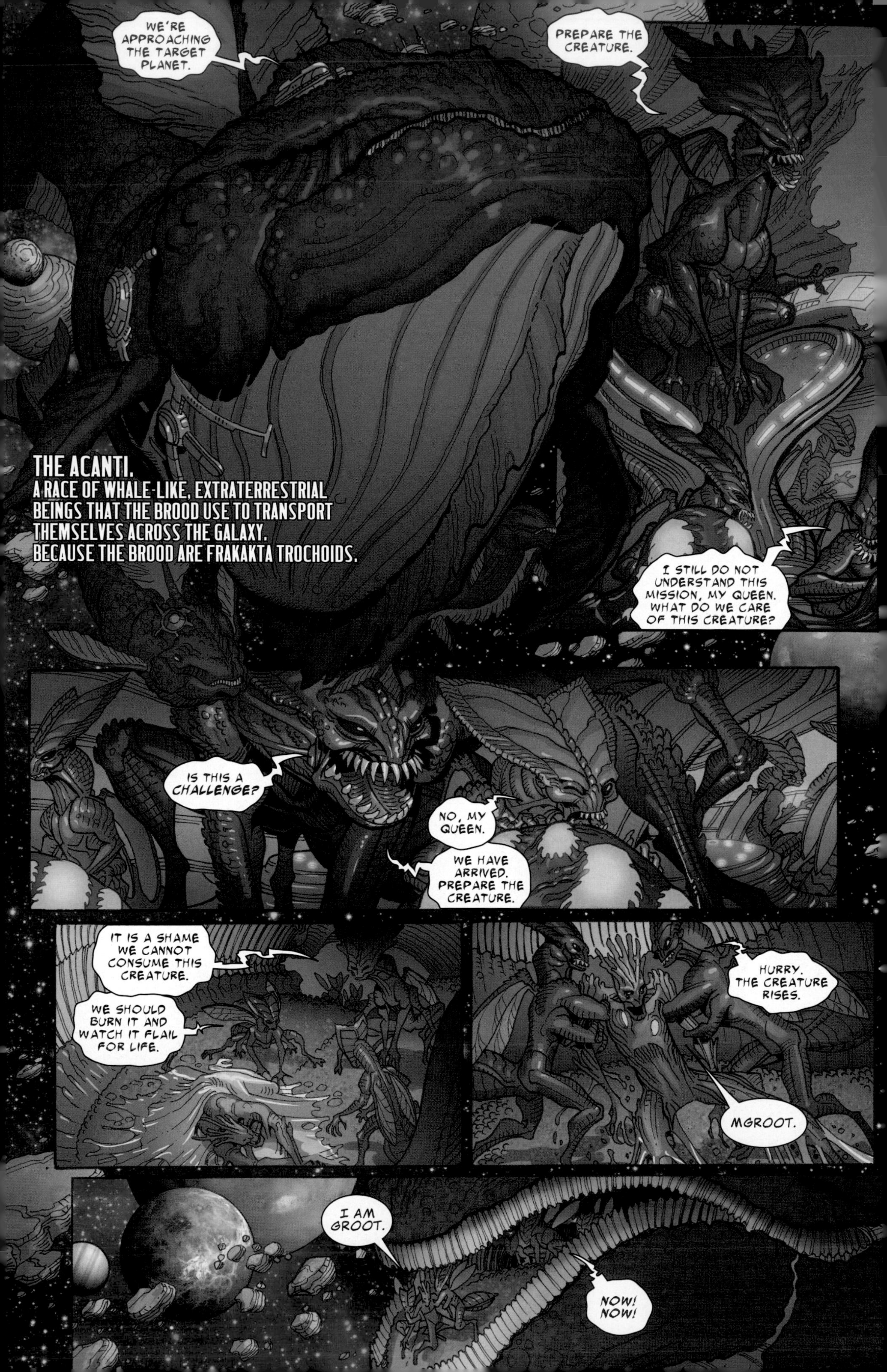
WE'RE APPROACHING THE TARGET PLANET.
PREPARE THE CREATURE.
THE ACANTI.
A RACE OF WHALE-LIKE, EXTRATERRESTRIAL BEINGS THAT THE BROOD USE TO TRANSPORT THEMSELVES ACROSS THE GALAXY.
BECAUSE THE BROOD ARE FRAKAKTA TROCHOIDS.
I STILL DO NOT UNDERSTAND THIS MISSION, MY QUEEN. WHAT DO WE CARE OF THIS CREATURE?
IS THIS A CHALLENGE?
NO, MY QUEEN.
WE HAVE ARRIVED. PREPARE THE CREATURE.
IT IS A SHAME WE CANNOT CONSUME THIS CREATURE.
WE SHOULD BURN IT AND WATCH IT FLAIL FOR LIFE.
HURRY. THE CREATURE RISES.
MGROOT.
I AM GROOT.
NOW! NOW!

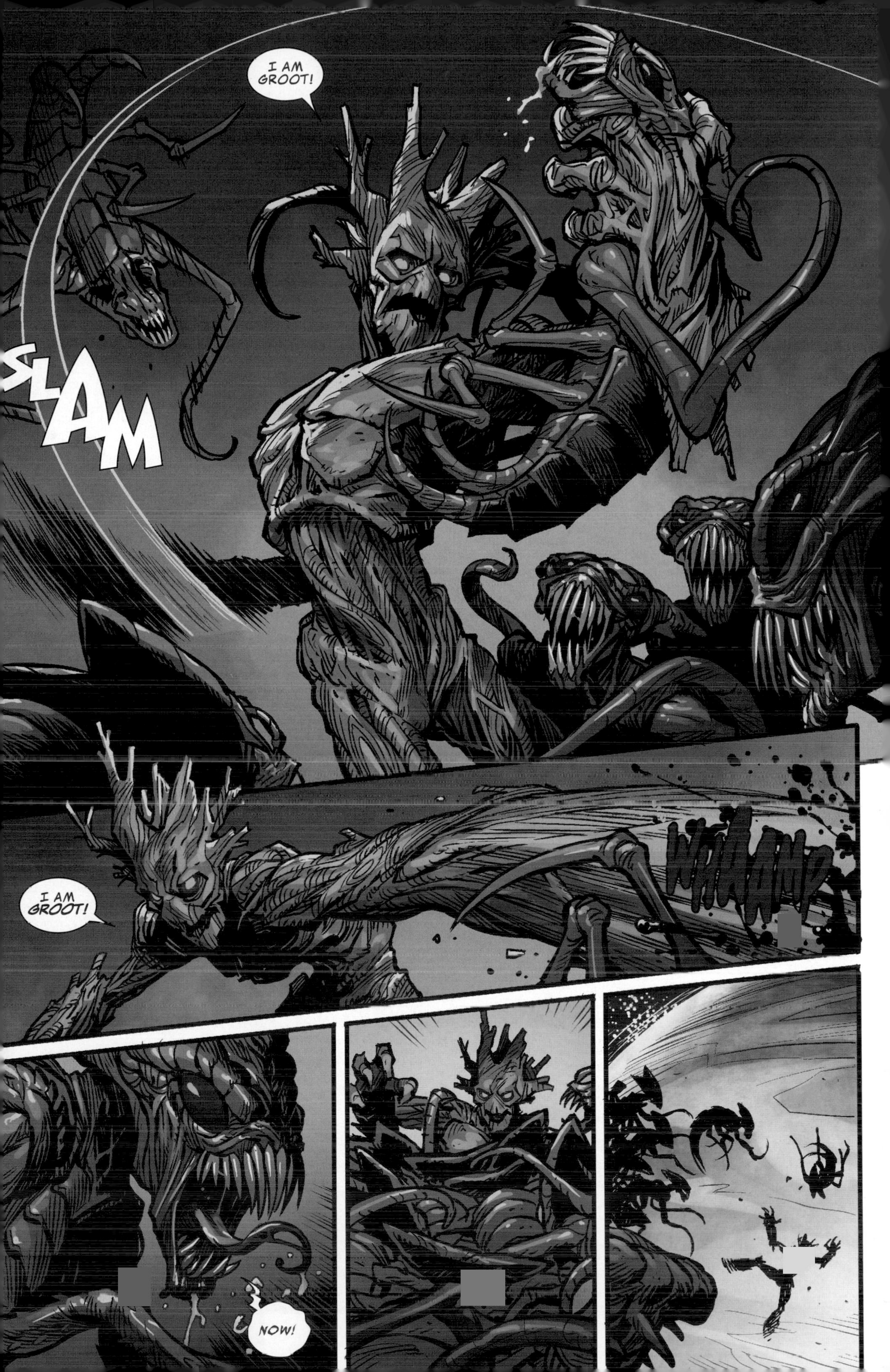
I AM GROOT!
SLAM
I AM GROOT!
WHAAMP
NOW!

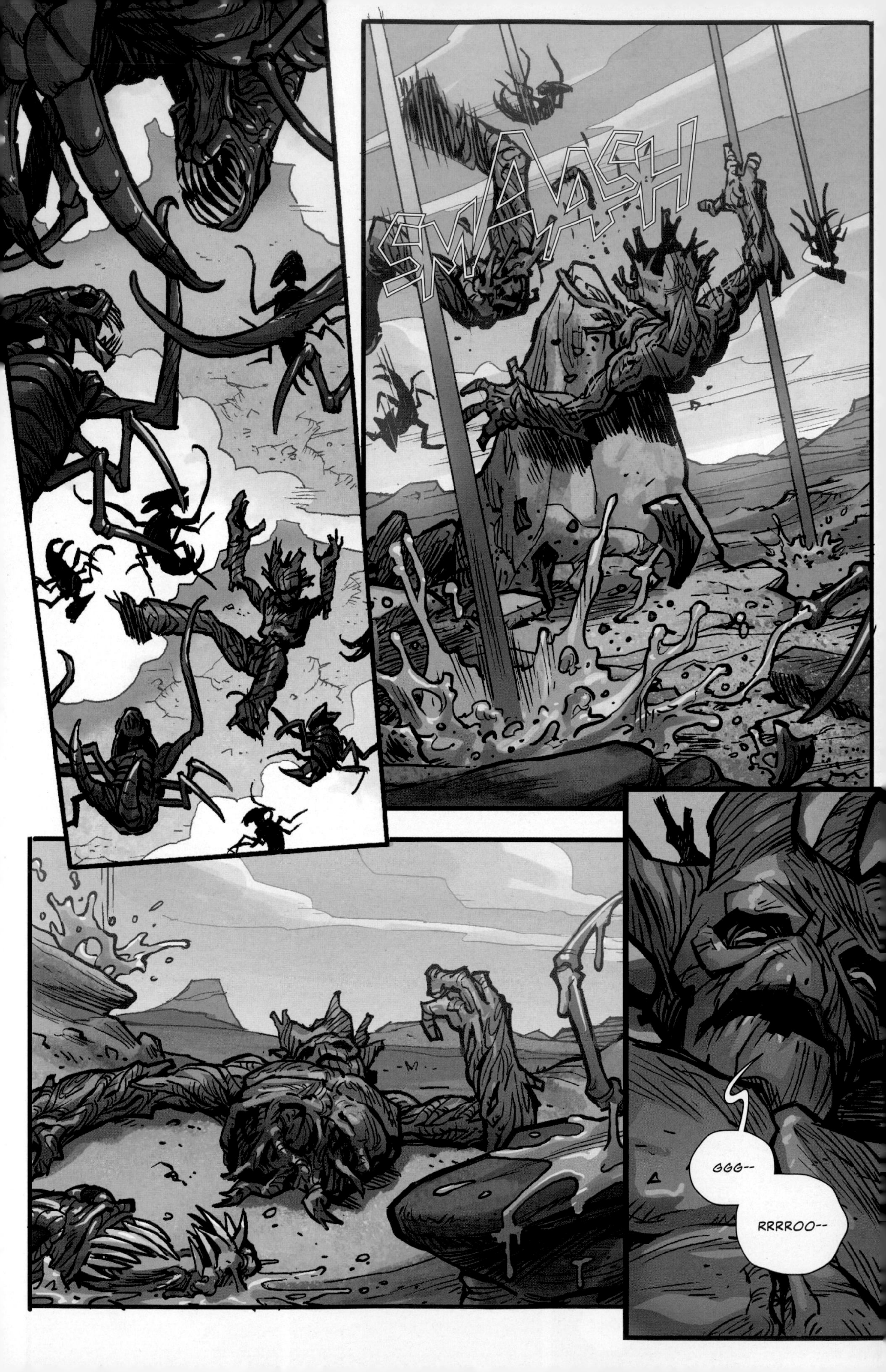
SWAAASH
GGG--
RRRROO--

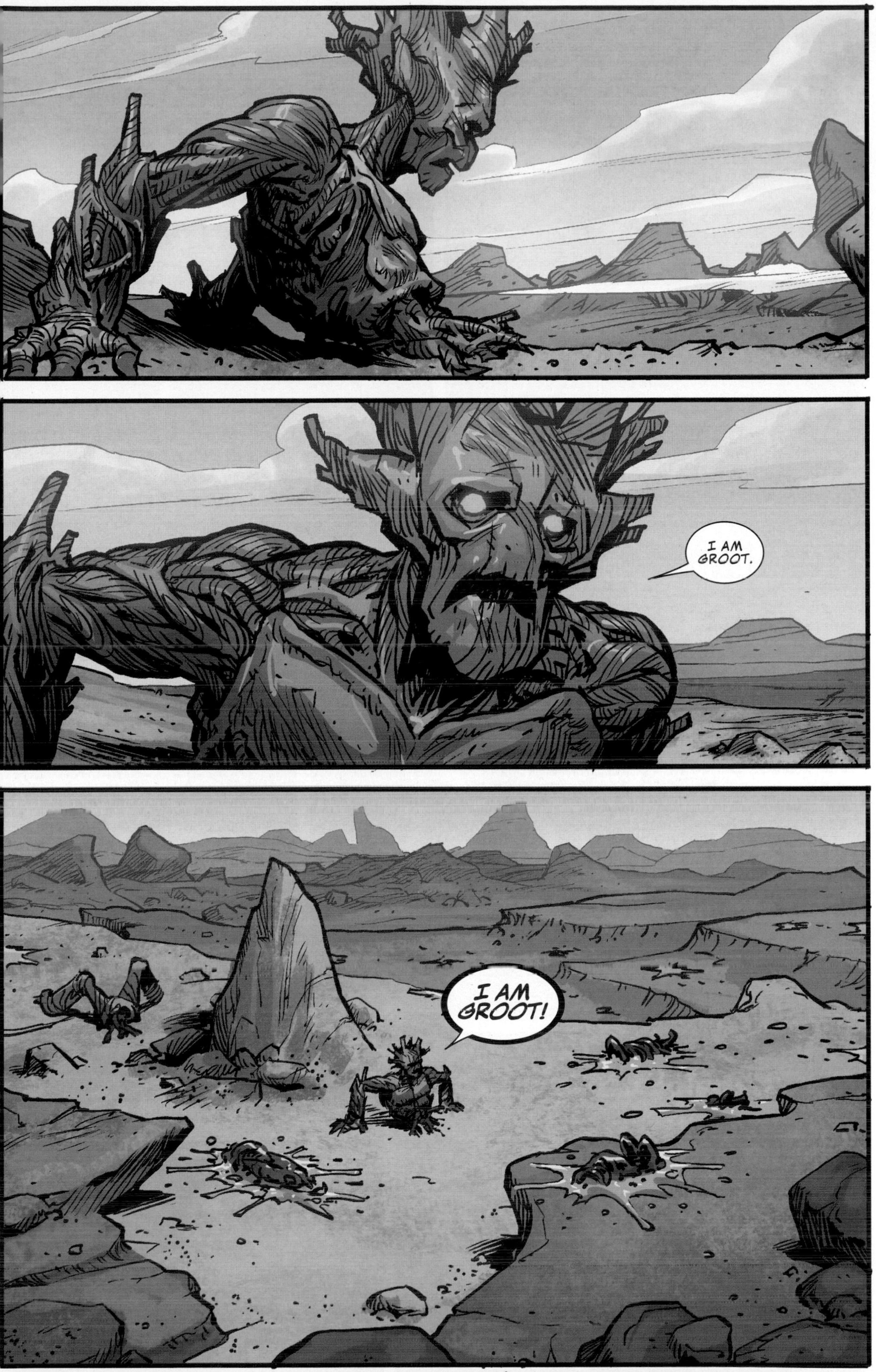
I AM GROOT.
I AM GROOT!

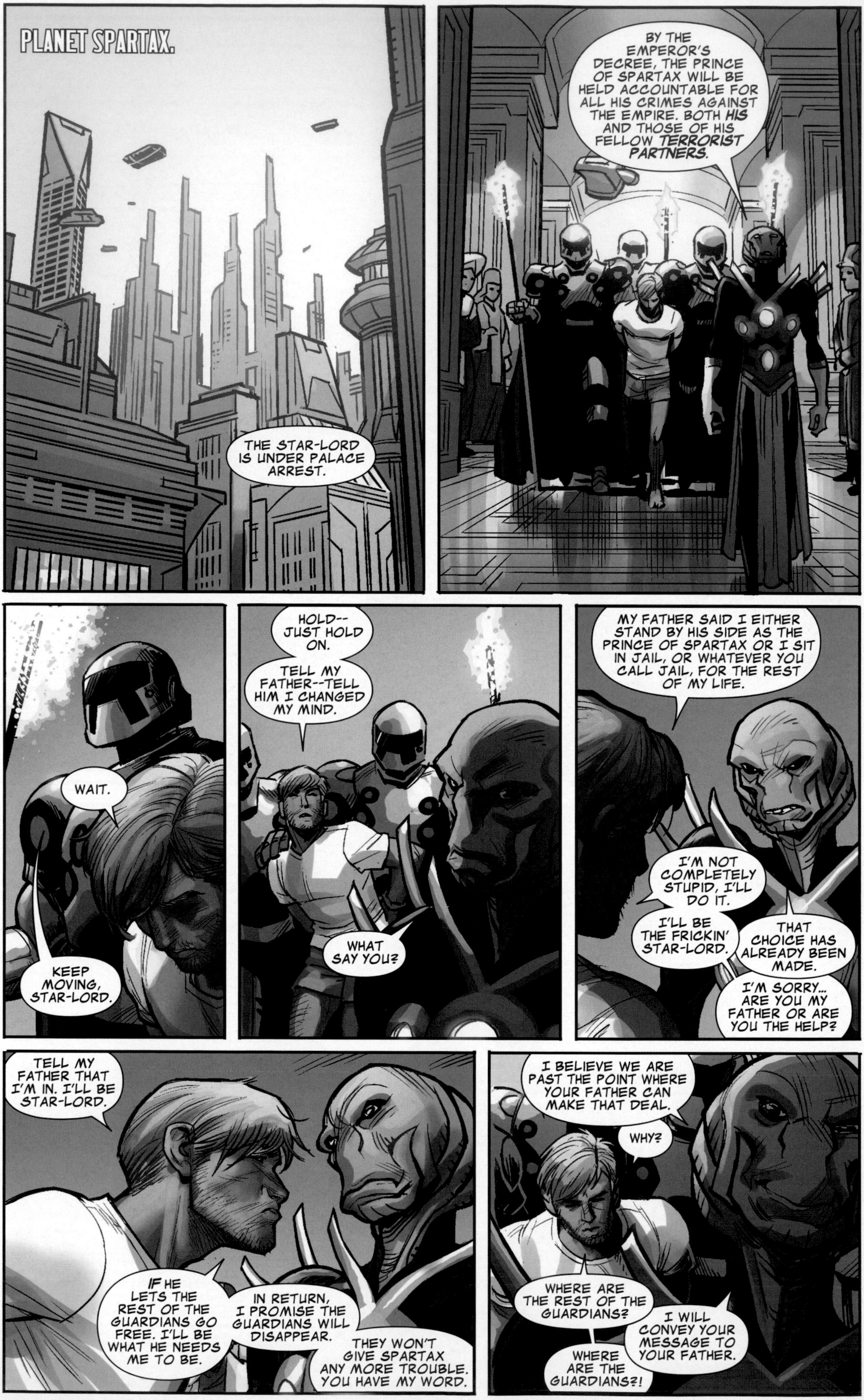
PLANET SPARTAX.
THE STAR-LORD IS UNDER PALACE ARREST.
BY THE EMPEROR'S DECREE, THE PRINCE OF SPARTAX WILL BE HELD ACCOUNTABLE FOR ALL HIS CRIMES AGAINST THE EMPIRE. BOTH HIS AND THOSE OF HIS FELLOW TERRORIST PARTNERS.
WAIT.
KEEP MOVING, STAR-LORD.
HOLD-- JUST HOLD ON.
TELL MY FATHER--TELL HIM I CHANGED MY MIND.
WHAT SAY YOU?
MY FATHER SAID I EITHER STAND BY HIS SIDE AS THE PRINCE OF SPARTAX OR I SIT IN JAIL, OR WHATEVER YOU CALL JAIL, FOR THE REST OF MY LIFE.
I'M NOT COMPLETELY STUPID, I'LL DO IT.
I'LL BE THE FRICKIN' STAR-LORD.
THAT CHOICE HAS ALREADY BEEN MADE.
I'M SORRY... ARE YOU MY FATHER OR ARE YOU THE HELP?
TELL MY FATHER THAT I'M IN. I'LL BE STAR-LORD.
IF HE LETS THE REST OF THE GUARDIANS GO FREE. I'LL BE WHAT HE NEEDS ME TO BE.
IN RETURN, I PROMISE THE GUARDIANS WILL DISAPPEAR.
THEY WON'T GIVE SPARTAX ANY MORE TROUBLE. YOU HAVE MY WORD.
I BELIEVE WE ARE PAST THE POINT WHERE YOUR FATHER CAN MAKE THAT DEAL.
WHY?
WHERE ARE THE REST OF THE GUARDIANS?
WHERE ARE THE GUARDIANS?!
I WILL CONVEY YOUR MESSAGE TO YOUR FATHER.

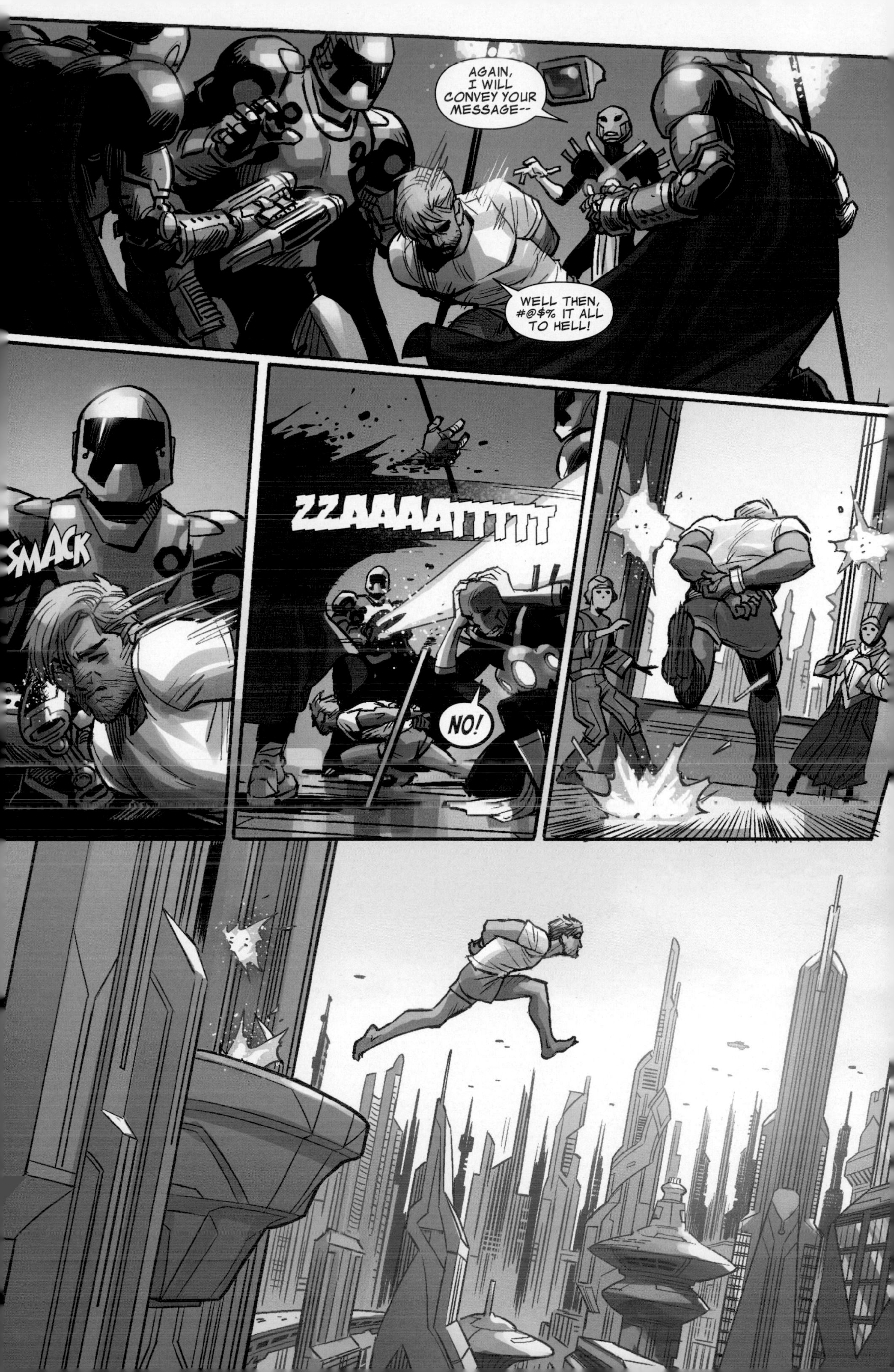
AGAIN, I WILL CONVEY YOUR MESSAGE--
WELL THEN, #@$% IT ALL TO HELL!
SMACK
ZZAAAAATTTTT
NO!

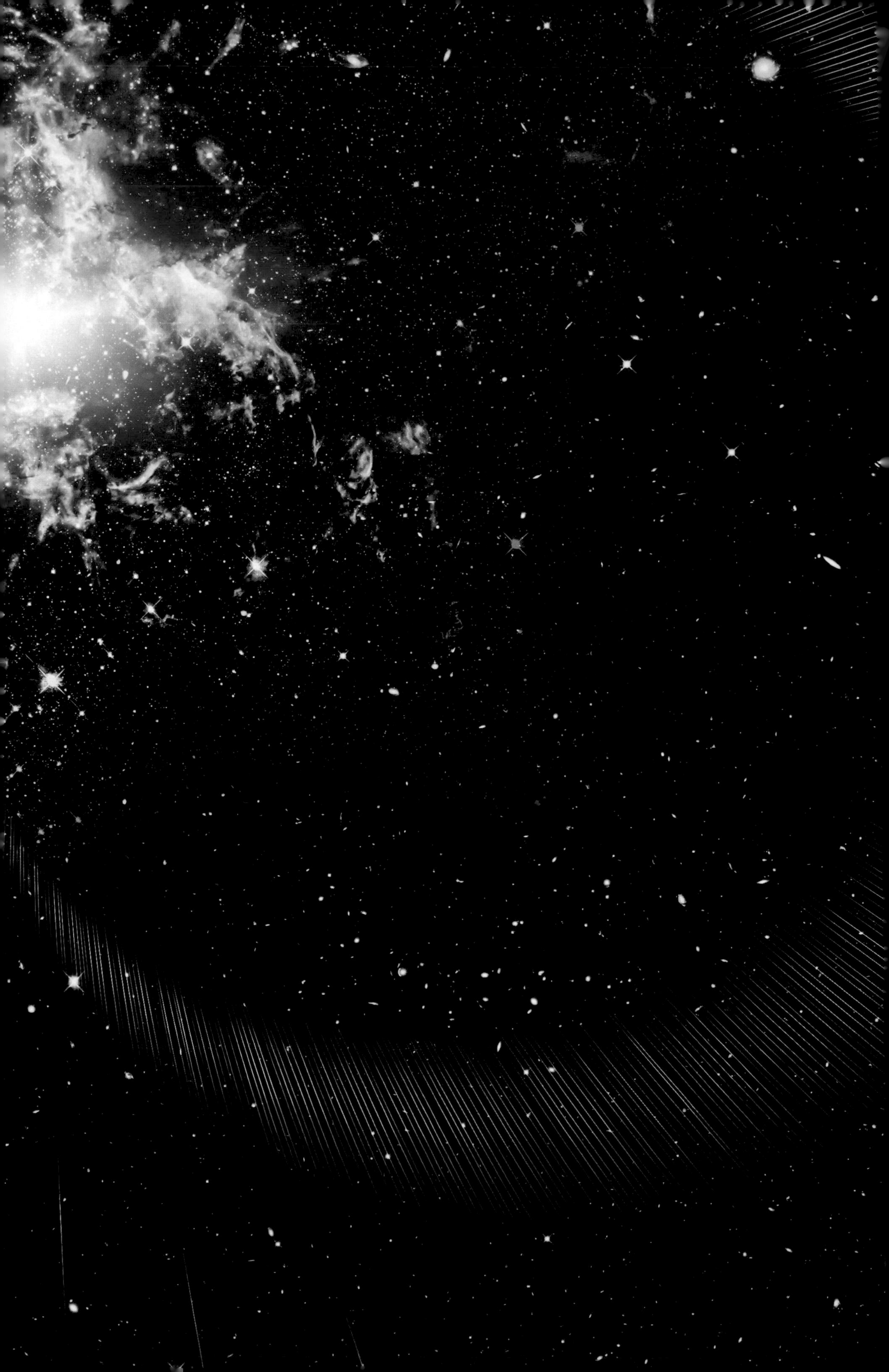

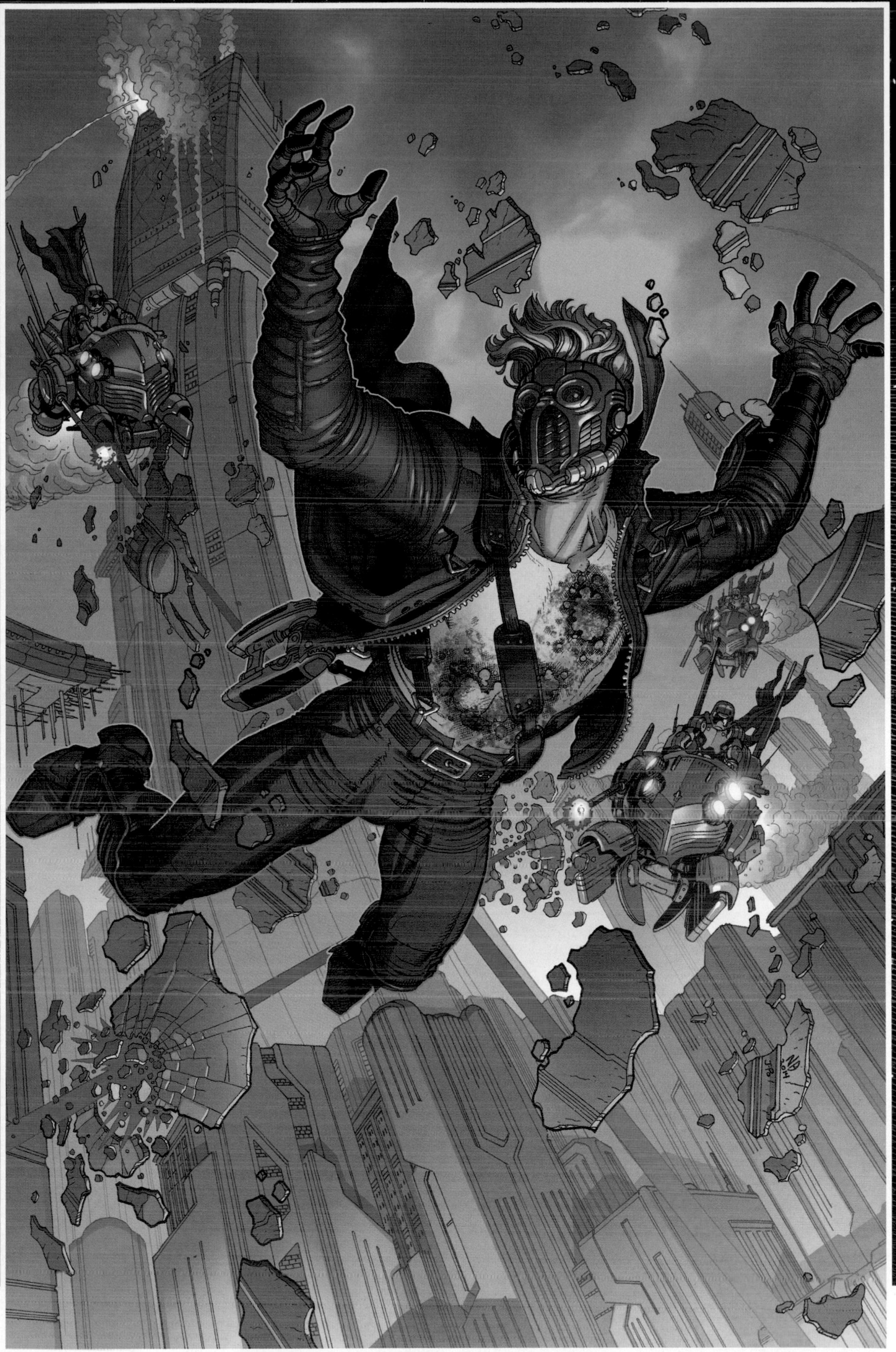

GUARDIANS OF THE GALAXY 16

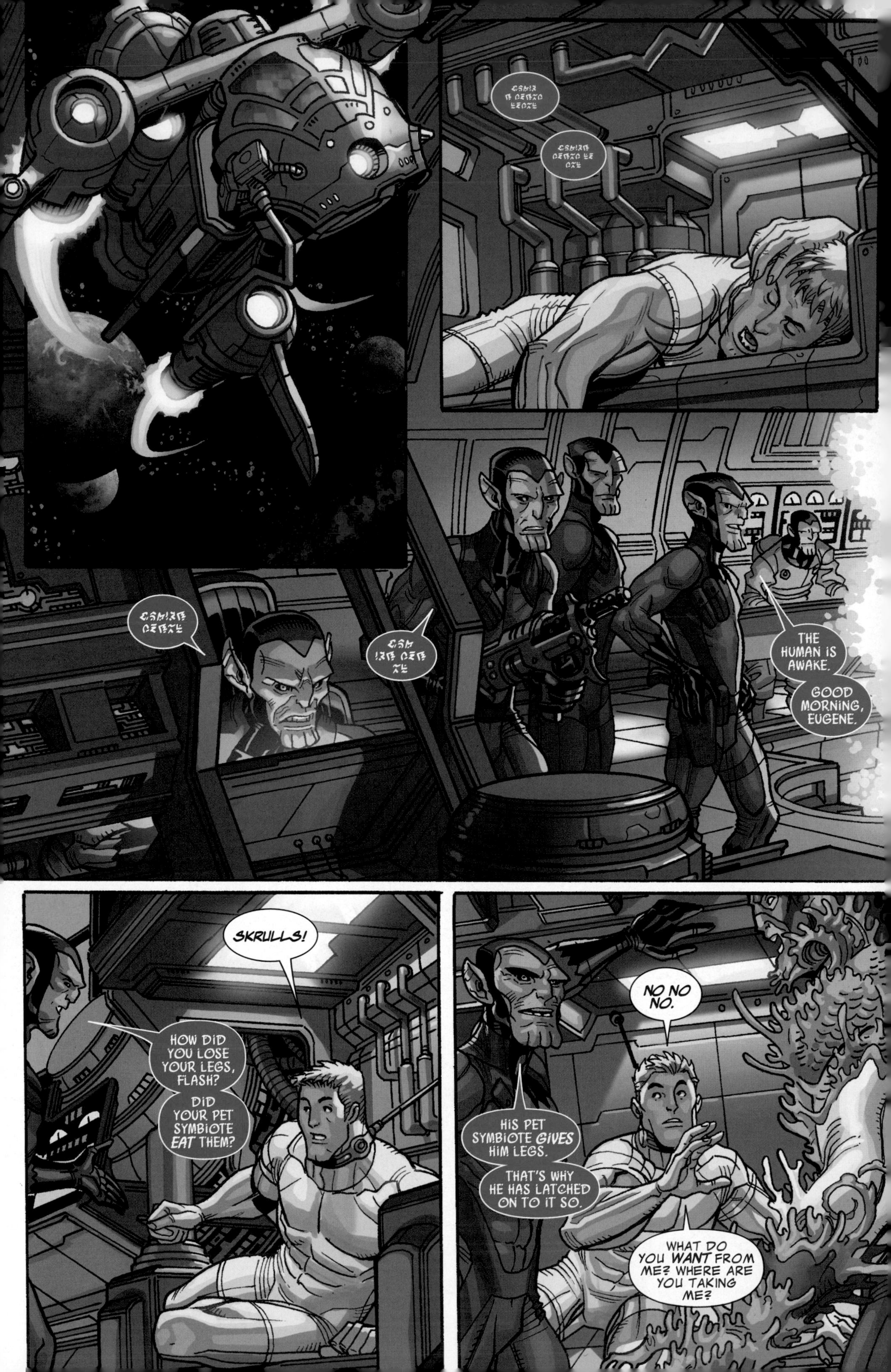
THE HUMAN IS AWAKE.
GOOD MORNING, EUGENE.
SKRULLS!
HOW DID YOU LOSE YOUR LEGS, FLASH?
DID YOUR PET SYMBIOTE EAT THEM?
NO NO NO.
HIS PET SYMBIOTE GIVES HIM LEGS.
THAT'S WHY HE HAS LATCHED ON TO IT SO.
WHAT DO YOU WANT FROM ME? WHERE ARE YOU TAKING ME?

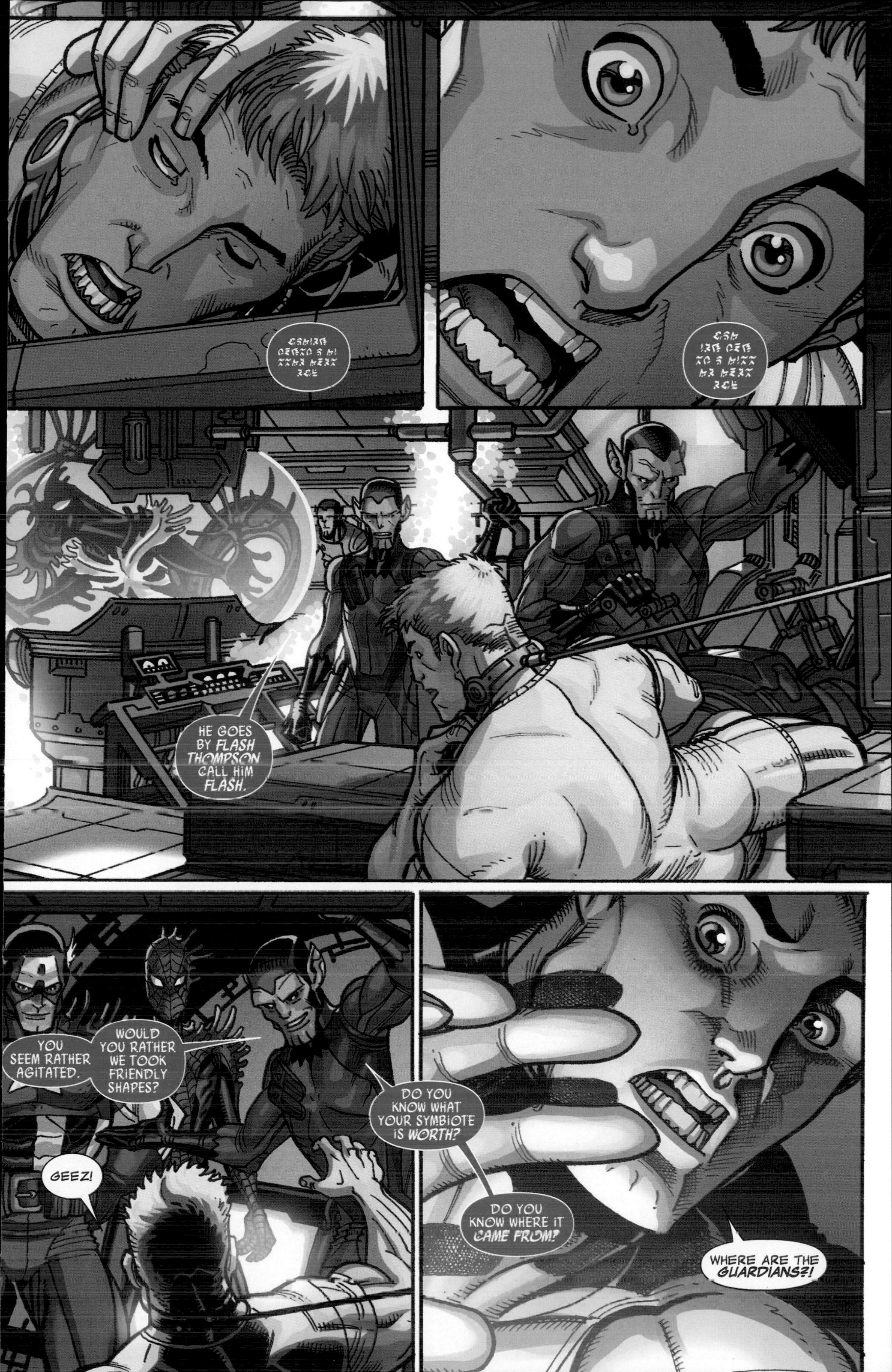
HE GOES BY FLASH THOMPSON. CALL HIM FLASH.
YOU SEEM RATHER AGITATED.
WOULD YOU RATHER WE TOOK FRIENDLY SHAPES?
DO YOU KNOW WHAT YOUR SYMBIOTE IS WORTH?
GEEZ!
DO YOU KNOW WHERE IT CAME FROM?
WHERE ARE THE GUARDIANS?!

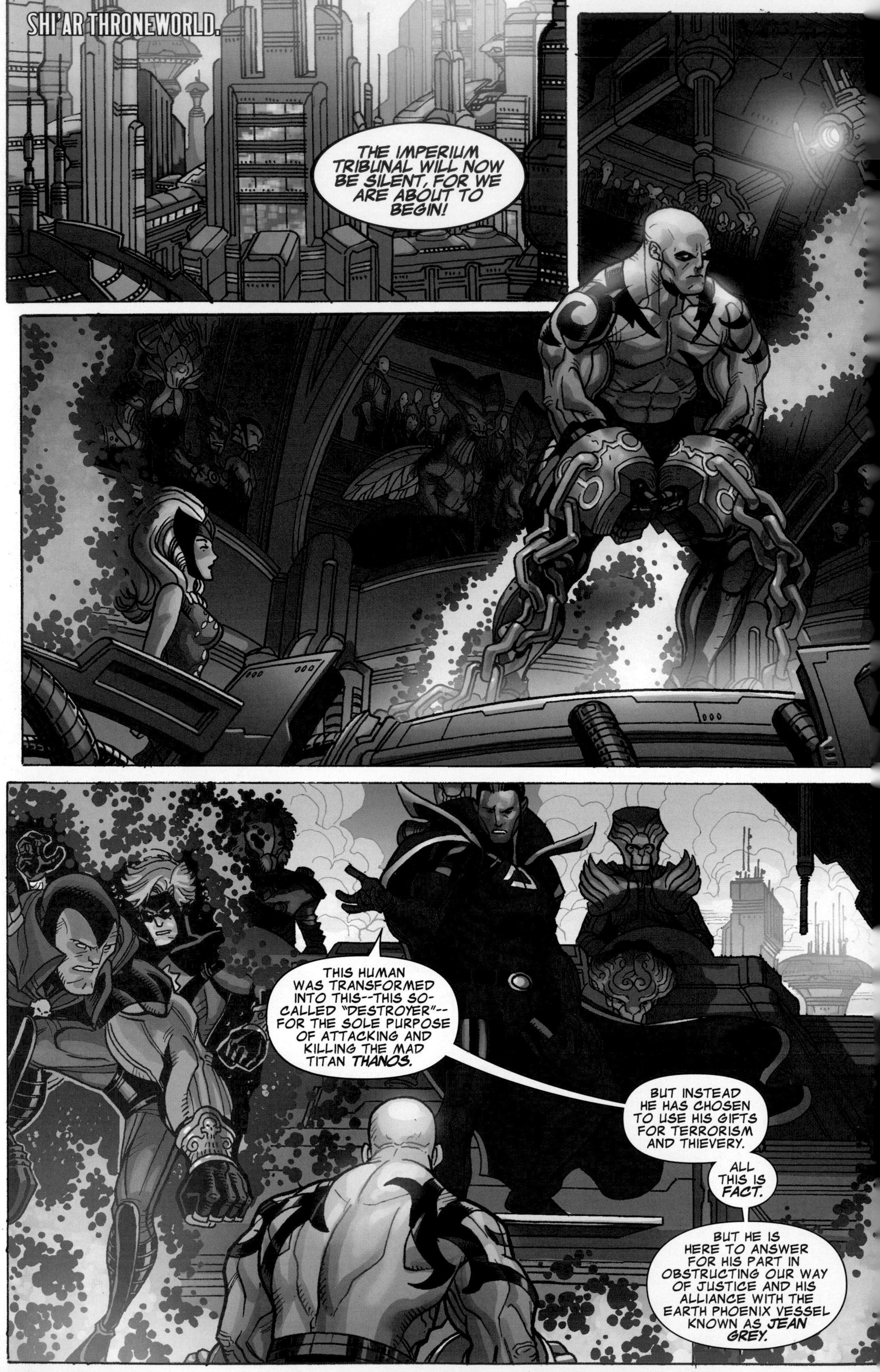
SHI'AR THRONEWORLD.
THE IMPERIUM TRIBUNAL WILL NOW BE SILENT, FOR WE ARE ABOUT TO BEGIN!
THIS HUMAN WAS TRANSFORMED INTO THIS--THIS SO-CALLED "DESTROYER"--FOR THE SOLE PURPOSE OF ATTACKING AND KILLING THE MAD TITAN THANOS.
BUT INSTEAD HE HAS CHOSEN TO USE HIS GIFTS FOR TERRORISM AND THIEVERY.
ALL THIS IS FACT.
BUT HE IS HERE TO ANSWER FOR HIS PART IN OBSTRUCTING OUR WAY OF JUSTICE AND HIS ALLIANCE WITH THE EARTH PHOENIX VESSEL KNOWN AS JEAN GREY.

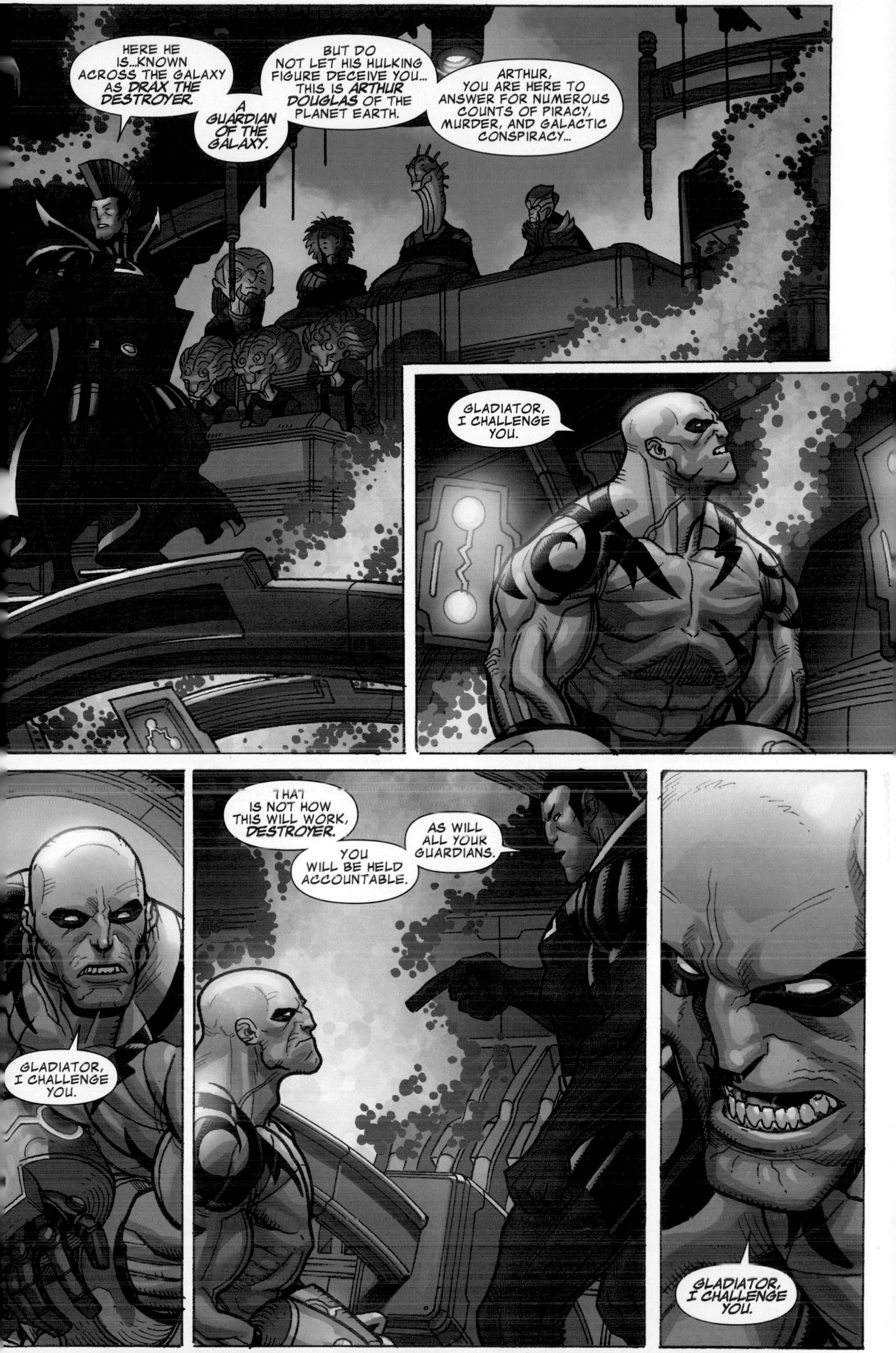
HERE HE IS...KNOWN ACROSS THE GALAXY AS DRAX THE DESTROYER.
A GUARDIAN OF THE GALAXY.
BUT DO NOT LET HIS HULKING FIGURE DECEIVE YOU... THIS IS ARTHUR DOUGLAS OF THE PLANET EARTH.
ARTHUR, YOU ARE HERE TO ANSWER FOR NUMEROUS COUNTS OF PIRACY, MURDER, AND GALACTIC CONSPIRACY...
GLADIATOR, I CHALLENGE YOU.
GLADIATOR, I CHALLENGE YOU.
THAT IS NOT HOW THIS WILL WORK, DESTROYER.
YOU WILL BE HELD ACCOUNTABLE.
AS WILL ALL YOUR GUARDIANS.
GLADIATOR, I CHALLENGE YOU.

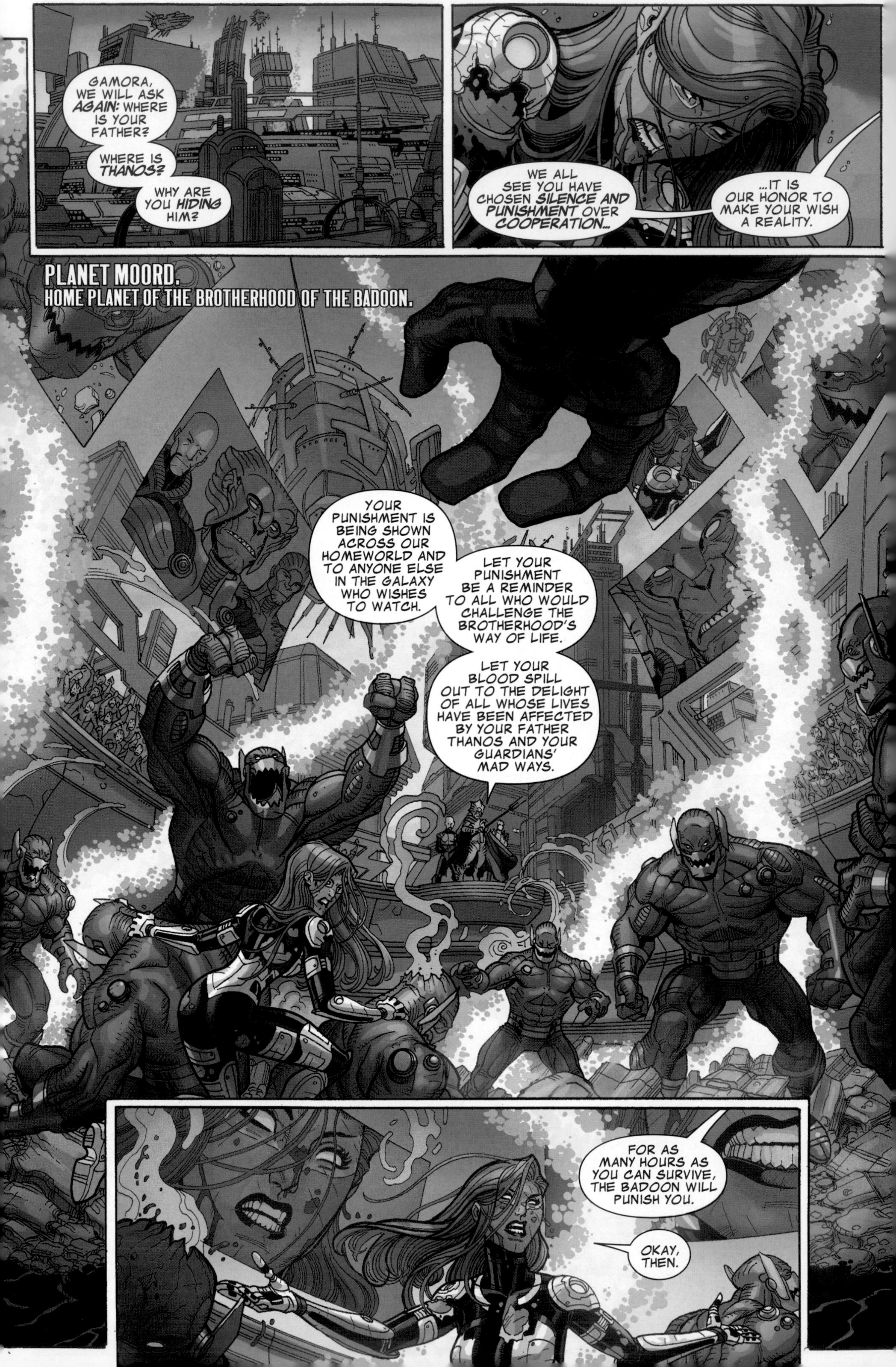
GAMORA, WE WILL ASK AGAIN: WHERE IS YOUR FATHER?
WHERE IS THANOS?
WHY ARE YOU HIDING HIM?
WE ALL SEE YOU HAVE CHOSEN SILENCE AND PUNISHMENT OVER COOPERATION...
...IT IS OUR HONOR TO MAKE YOUR WISH A REALITY.
PLANET MOORD.
HOME PLANET OF THE BROTHERHOOD OF THE BADOON.
YOUR PUNISHMENT IS BEING SHOWN ACROSS OUR HOMEWORLD AND TO ANYONE ELSE IN THE GALAXY WHO WISHES TO WATCH.
LET YOUR PUNISHMENT BE A REMINDER TO ALL WHO WOULD CHALLENGE THE BROTHERHOOD'S WAY OF LIFE.
LET YOUR BLOOD SPILL OUT TO THE DELIGHT OF ALL WHOSE LIVES HAVE BEEN AFFECTED BY YOUR FATHER THANOS AND YOUR GUARDIANS' MAD WAYS.
FOR AS MANY HOURS AS YOU CAN SURVIVE, THE BADOON WILL PUNISH YOU.
OKAY, THEN.

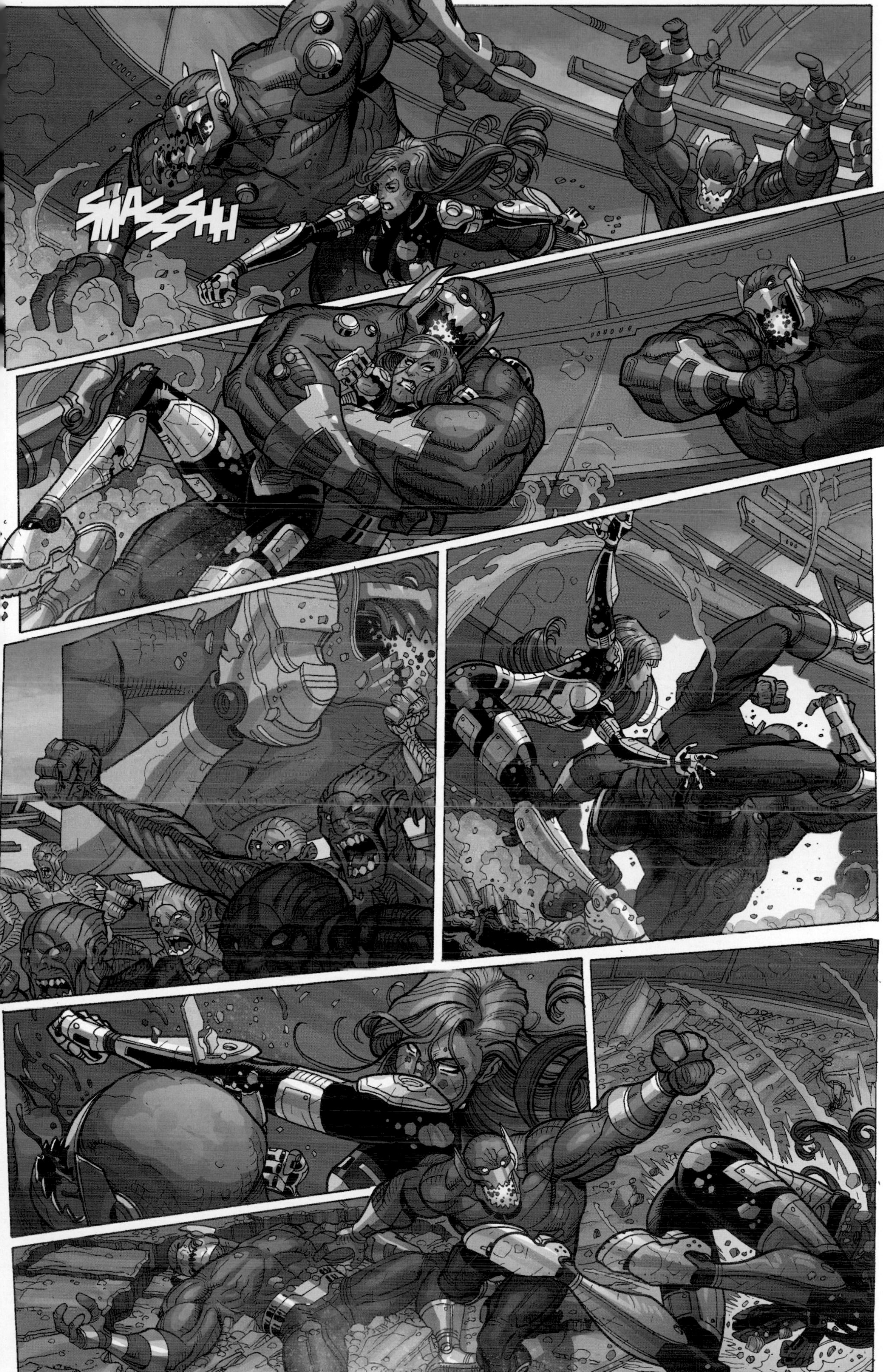
SMASSHH

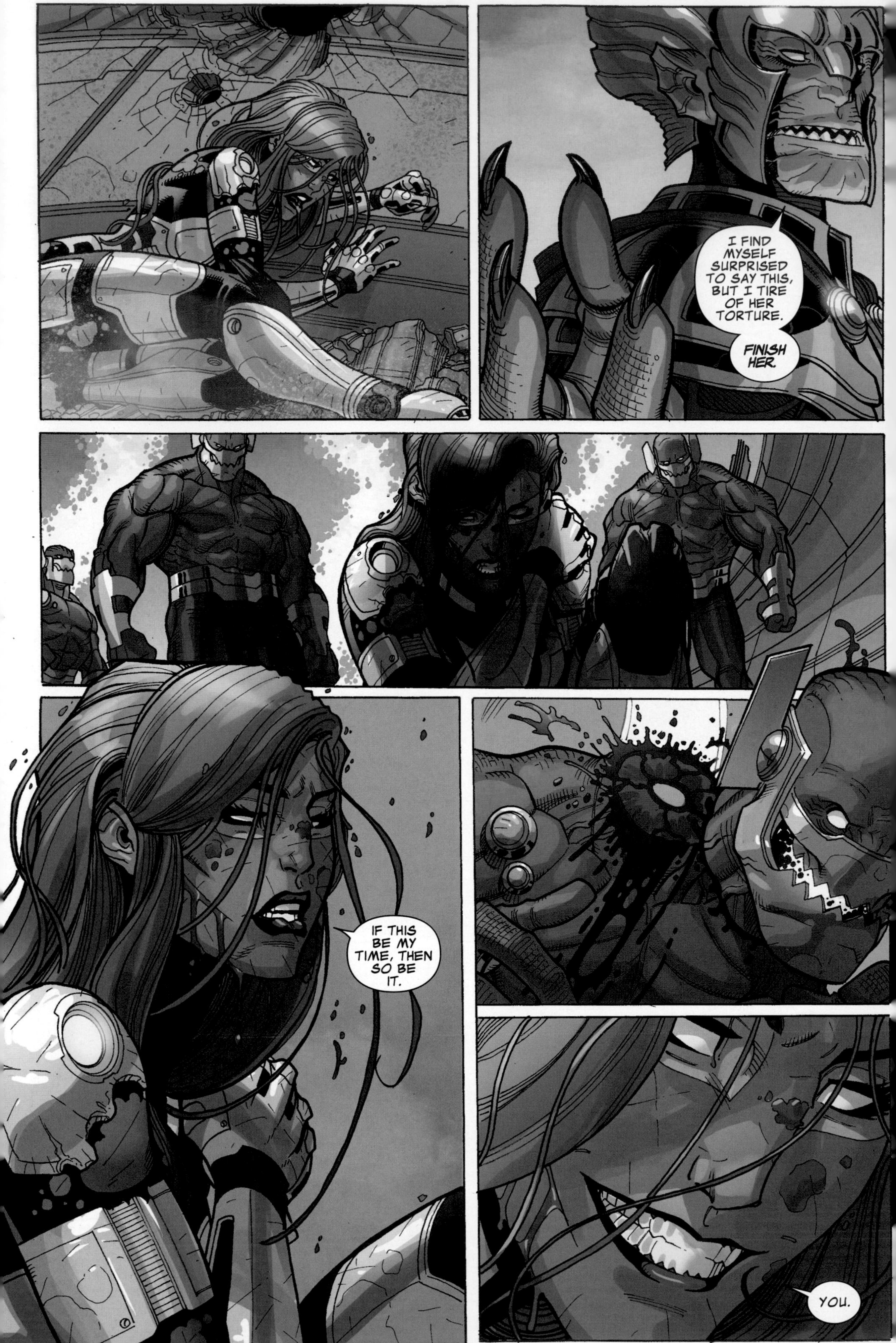
I FIND MYSELF SURPRISED TO SAY THIS, BUT I TIRE OF HER TORTURE.
FINISH HER.
IF THIS BE MY TIME, THEN SO BE IT.
YOU.

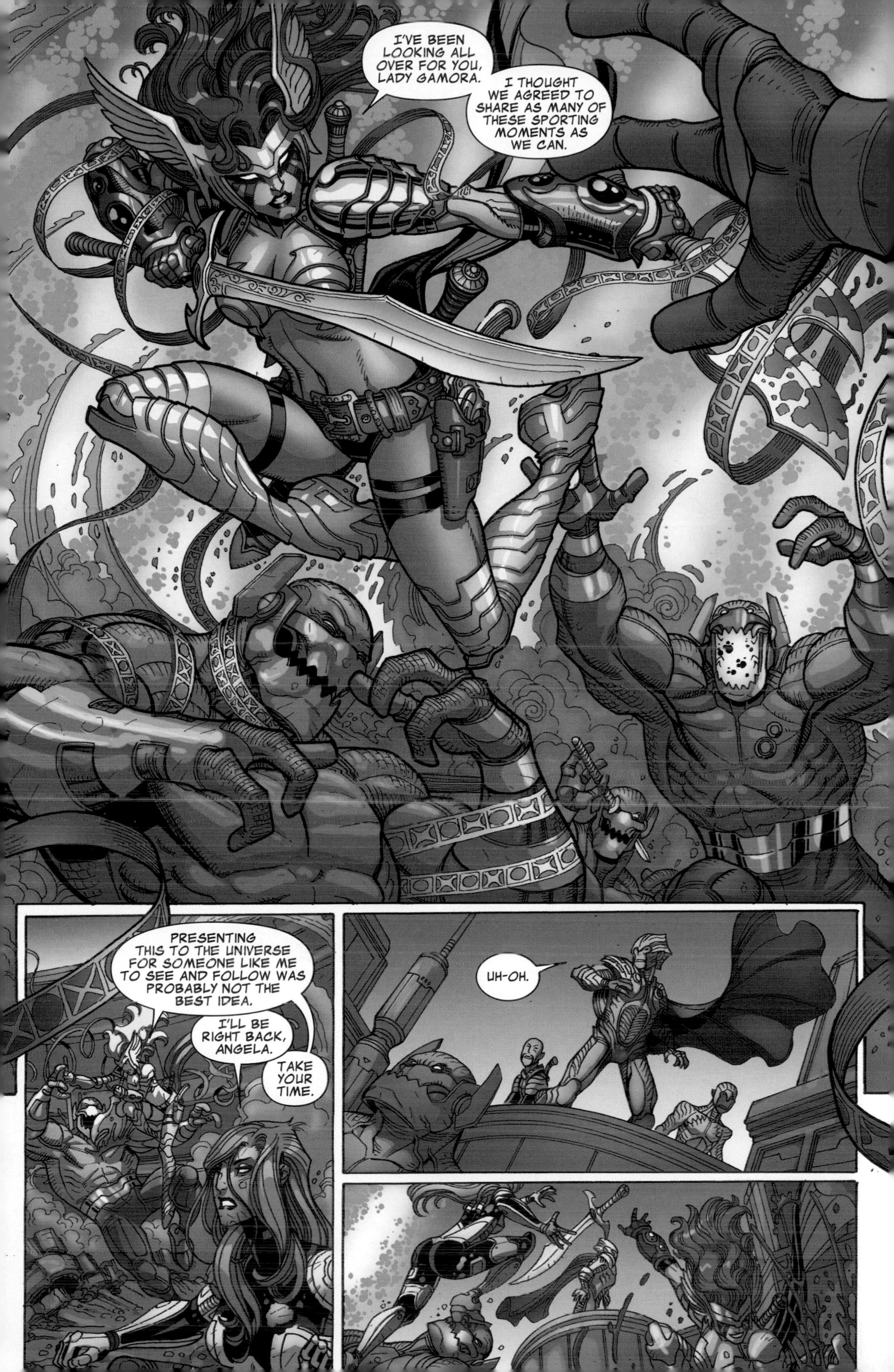
I'VE BEEN LOOKING ALL OVER FOR YOU, LADY GAMORA.
I THOUGHT WE AGREED TO SHARE AS MANY OF THESE SPORTING MOMENTS AS WE CAN.
PRESENTING THIS TO THE UNIVERSE FOR SOMEONE LIKE ME TO SEE AND FOLLOW WAS PROBABLY NOT THE BEST IDEA.
I'LL BE RIGHT BACK, ANGELA.
TAKE YOUR TIME.
UH-OH.

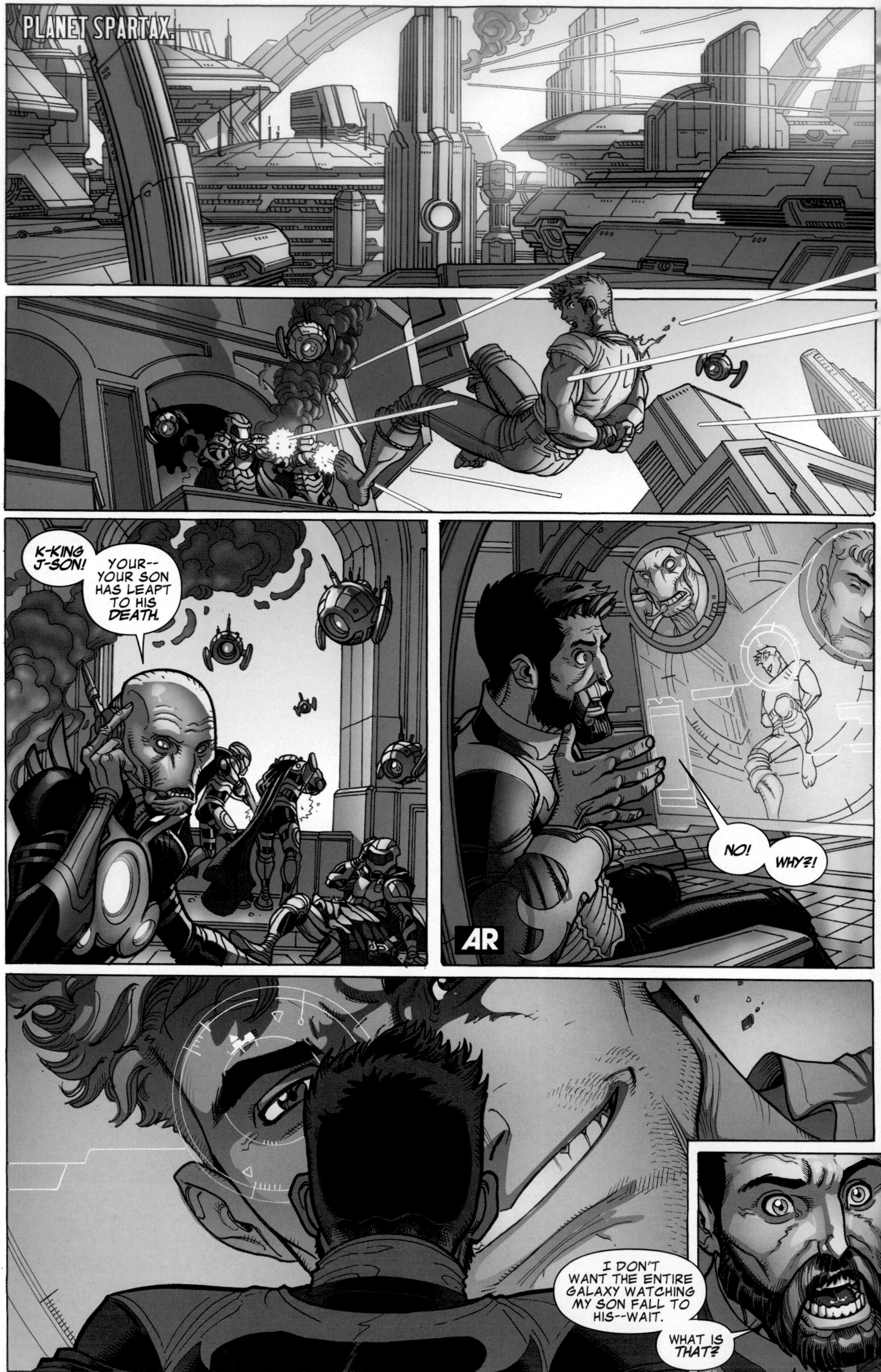
PLANET SPARTAX.
K-KING J-SON!
YOUR-- YOUR SON HAS LEAPT TO HIS DEATH.
NO!
WHY?!
AR
I DON'T WANT THE ENTIRE GALAXY WATCHING MY SON FALL TO HIS--WAIT.
WHAT IS THAT?

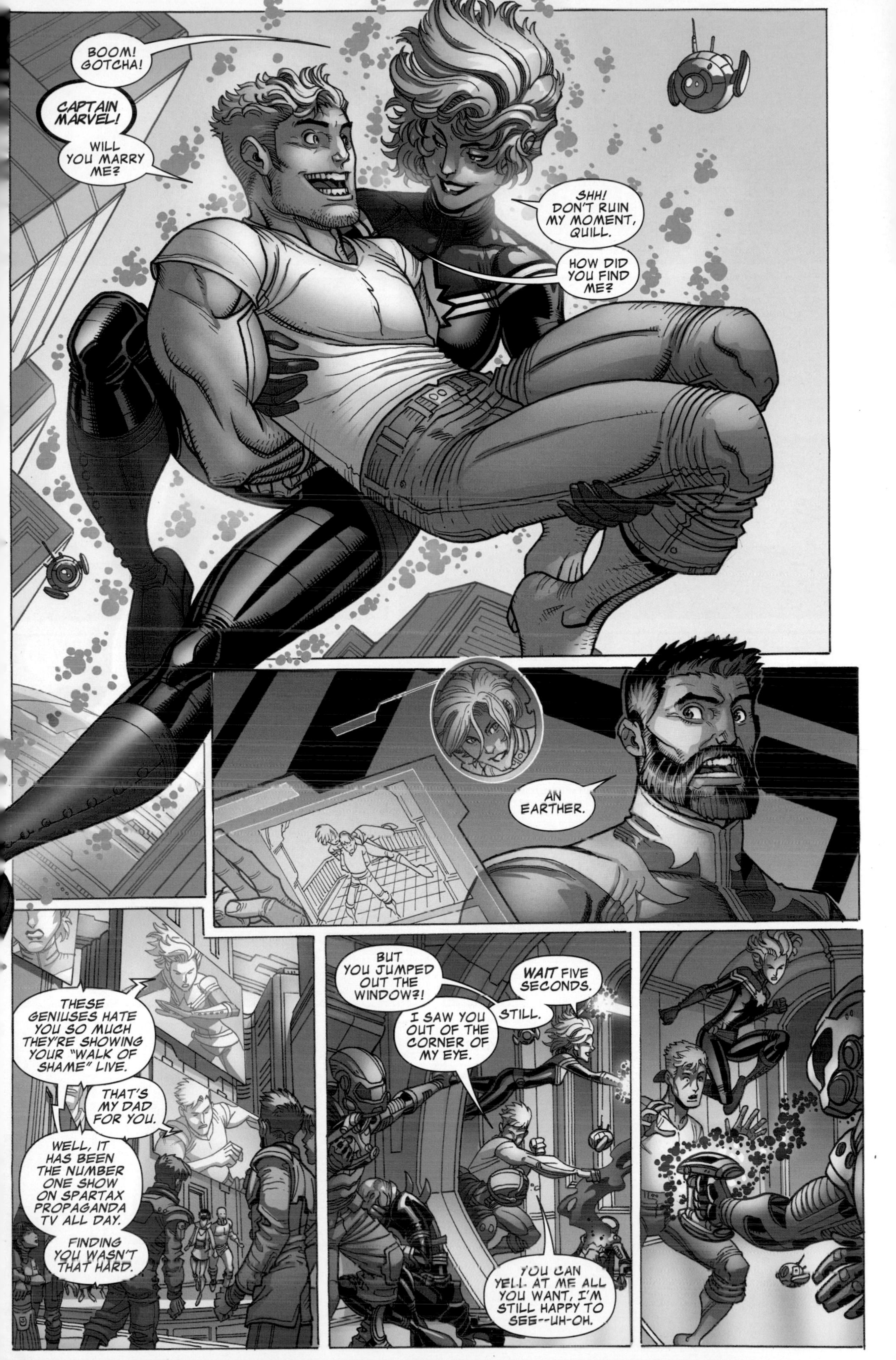
BOOM! GOTCHA!
CAPTAIN MARVEL!
WILL YOU MARRY ME?
SHH! DON'T RUIN MY MOMENT, QUILL.
HOW DID YOU FIND ME?
AN EARTHER.
THESE GENIUSES HATE YOU SO MUCH THEY'RE SHOWING YOUR "WALK OF SHAME" LIVE.
THAT'S MY DAD FOR YOU.
WELL, IT HAS BEEN THE NUMBER ONE SHOW ON SPARTAX PROPAGANDA TV ALL DAY.
FINDING YOU WASN'T THAT HARD.
BUT YOU JUMPED OUT THE WINDOW?!
WAIT FIVE SECONDS.
STILL.
I SAW YOU OUT OF THE CORNER OF MY EYE.
YOU CAN YELL AT ME ALL YOU WANT, I'M STILL HAPPY TO SEE--UH-OH.

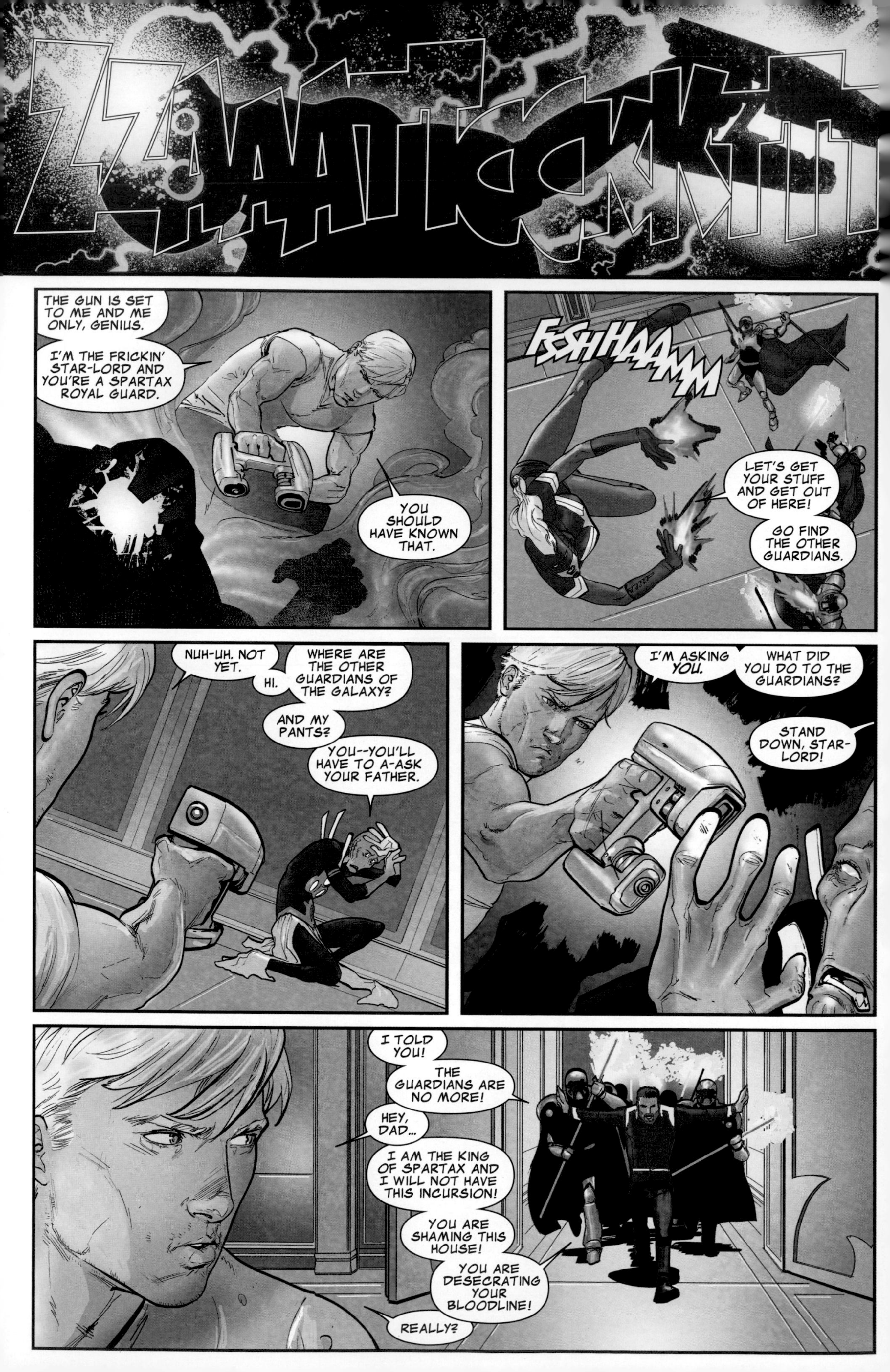
ZZWAAAKKKOOOMMKKTTT
THE GUN IS SET TO ME AND ME ONLY, GENIUS.
I'M THE FRICKIN' STAR-LORD AND YOU'RE A SPARTAX ROYAL GUARD.
YOU SHOULD HAVE KNOWN THAT.
FSSHHAAMMM
LET'S GET YOUR STUFF AND GET OUT OF HERE!
GO FIND THE OTHER GUARDIANS.
NUH-UH. NOT YET.
HI.
WHERE ARE THE OTHER GUARDIANS OF THE GALAXY?
AND MY PANTS?
YOU--YOU'LL HAVE TO A-ASK YOUR FATHER.
I'M ASKING YOU.
WHAT DID YOU DO TO THE GUARDIANS?
STAND DOWN, STAR-LORD!
I TOLD YOU!
THE GUARDIANS ARE NO MORE!
HEY, DAD...
I AM THE KING OF SPARTAX AND I WILL NOT HAVE THIS INCURSION!
YOU ARE SHAMING THIS HOUSE!
YOU ARE DESECRATING YOUR BLOODLINE!
REALLY?

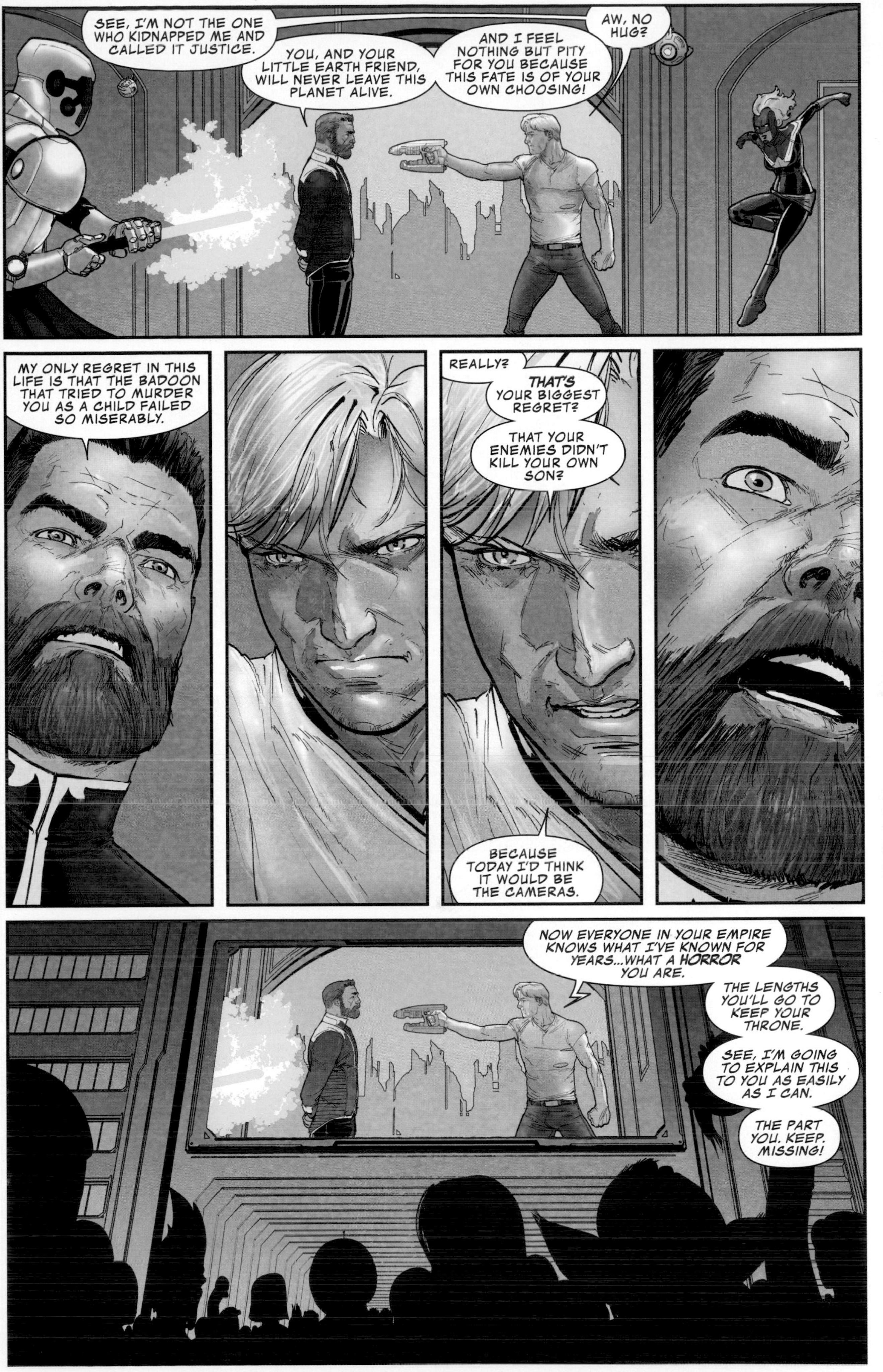
SEE, I'M NOT THE ONE WHO KIDNAPPED ME AND CALLED IT JUSTICE.
YOU, AND YOUR LITTLE EARTH FRIEND, WILL NEVER LEAVE THIS PLANET ALIVE.
AND I FEEL NOTHING BUT PITY FOR YOU BECAUSE THIS FATE IS OF YOUR OWN CHOOSING!
AW, NO HUG?
MY ONLY REGRET IN THIS LIFE IS THAT THE BADOON THAT TRIED TO MURDER YOU AS A CHILD FAILED SO MISERABLY.
REALLY?
THAT'S YOUR BIGGEST REGRET?
THAT YOUR ENEMIES DIDN'T KILL YOUR OWN SON?
BECAUSE TODAY I'D THINK IT WOULD BE THE CAMERAS.
NOW EVERYONE IN YOUR EMPIRE KNOWS WHAT I'VE KNOWN FOR YEARS...WHAT A *HORROR* YOU ARE.
THE LENGTHS YOU'LL GO TO KEEP YOUR THRONE.
SEE, I'M GOING TO EXPLAIN THIS TO YOU AS EASILY AS I CAN.
THE PART YOU. KEEP. MISSING!

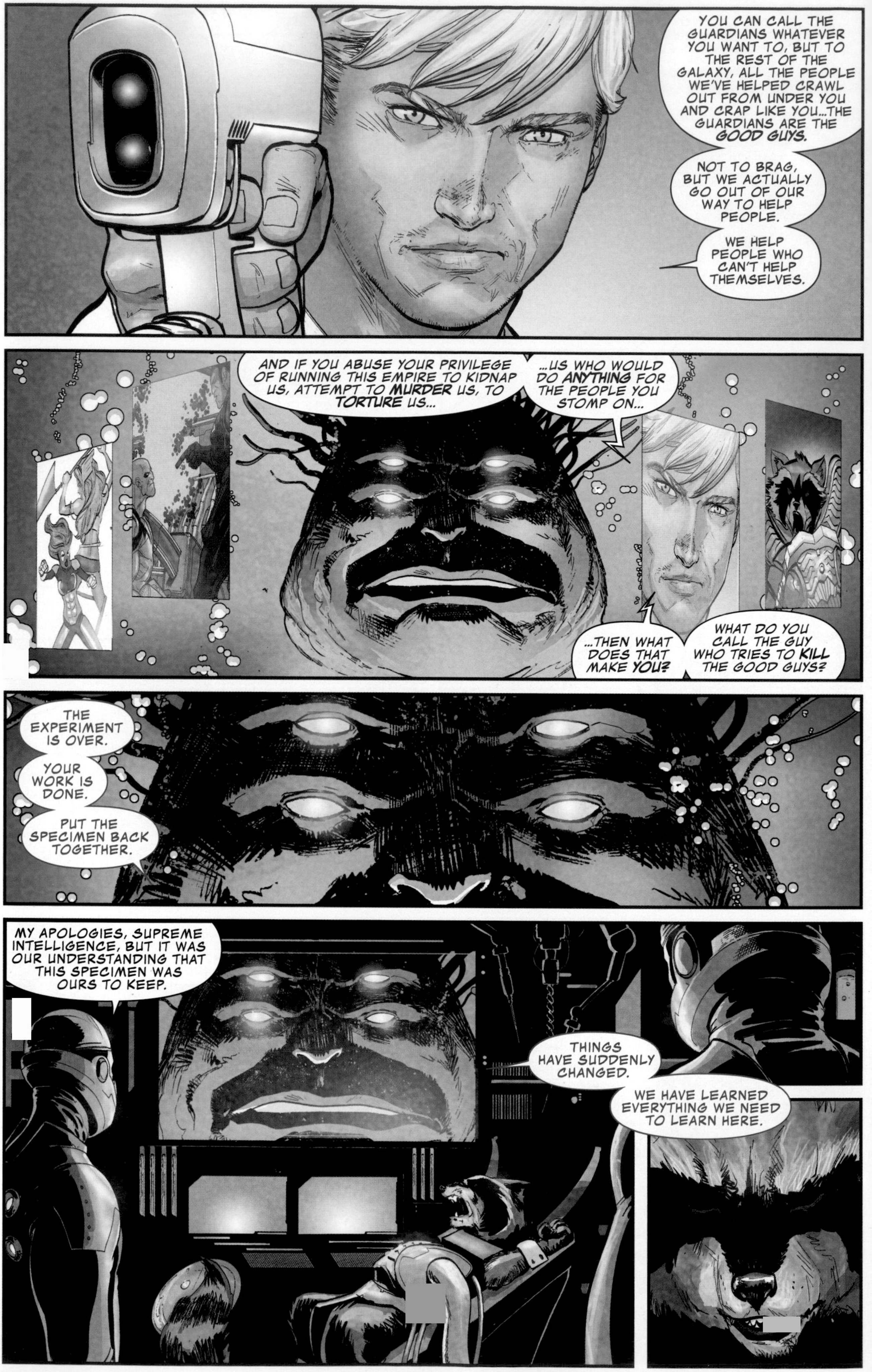
YOU CAN CALL THE GUARDIANS WHATEVER YOU WANT TO, BUT TO THE REST OF THE GALAXY, ALL THE PEOPLE WE'VE HELPED CRAWL OUT FROM UNDER YOU AND CRAP LIKE YOU...THE GUARDIANS ARE THE GOOD GUYS.
NOT TO BRAG, BUT WE ACTUALLY GO OUT OF OUR WAY TO HELP PEOPLE.
WE HELP PEOPLE WHO CAN'T HELP THEMSELVES.
AND IF YOU ABUSE YOUR PRIVILEGE OF RUNNING THIS EMPIRE TO KIDNAP US, ATTEMPT TO MURDER US, TO TORTURE US...
...US WHO WOULD DO ANYTHING FOR THE PEOPLE YOU STOMP ON...
...THEN WHAT DOES THAT MAKE YOU?
WHAT DO YOU CALL THE GUY WHO TRIES TO KILL THE GOOD GUYS?
THE EXPERIMENT IS OVER.
YOUR WORK IS DONE.
PUT THE SPECIMEN BACK TOGETHER.
MY APOLOGIES, SUPREME INTELLIGENCE, BUT IT WAS OUR UNDERSTANDING THAT THIS SPECIMEN WAS OURS TO KEEP.
THINGS HAVE SUDDENLY CHANGED.
WE HAVE LEARNED EVERYTHING WE NEED TO LEARN HERE.

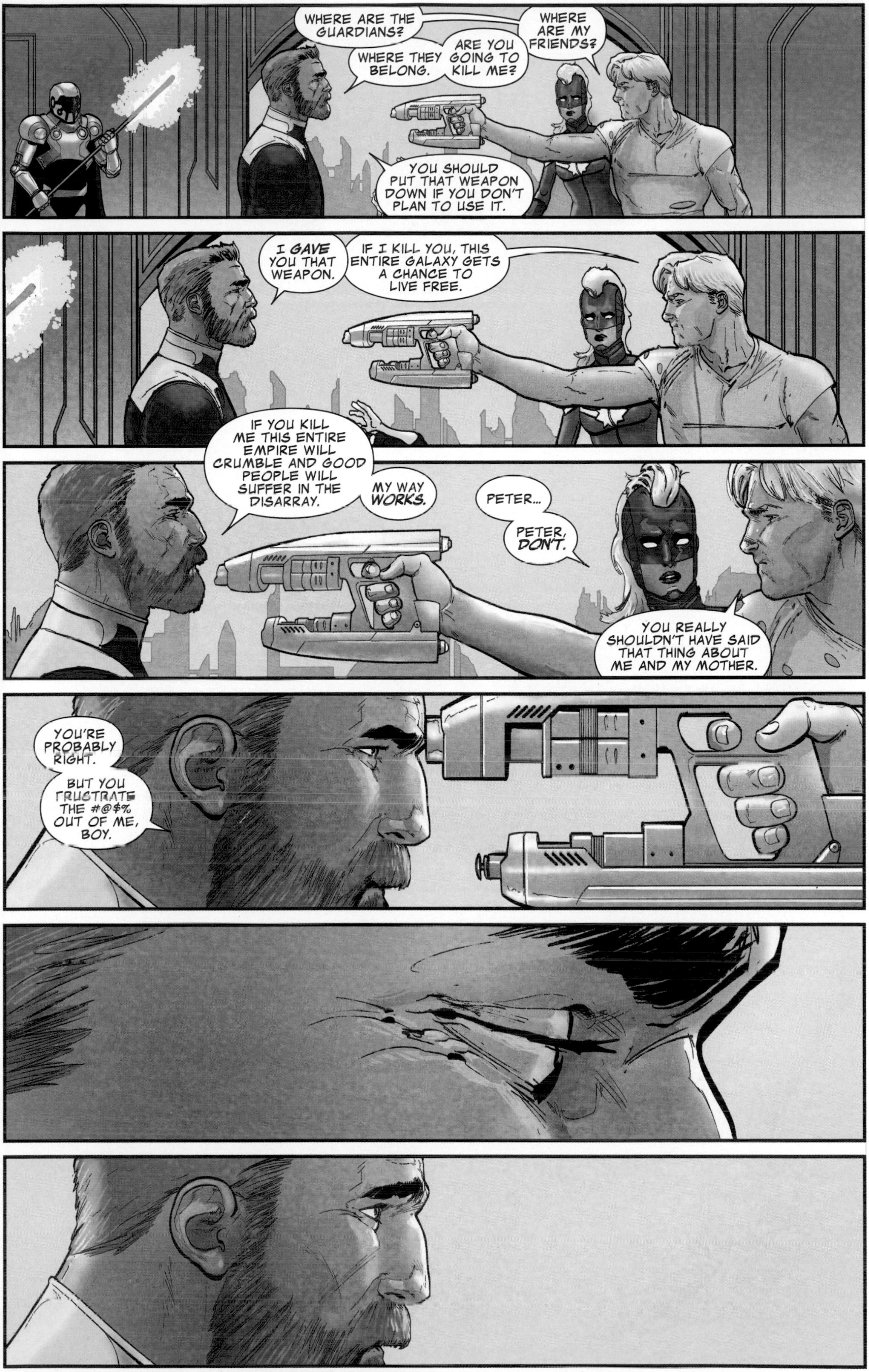
WHERE ARE THE GUARDIANS?
WHERE THEY BELONG.
WHERE ARE MY FRIENDS?
ARE YOU GOING TO KILL ME?
YOU SHOULD PUT THAT WEAPON DOWN IF YOU DON'T PLAN TO USE IT.
I *GAVE* YOU THAT WEAPON.
IF I KILL YOU, THIS ENTIRE GALAXY GETS A CHANCE TO LIVE FREE.
IF YOU KILL ME THIS ENTIRE EMPIRE WILL CRUMBLE AND GOOD PEOPLE WILL SUFFER IN THE DISARRAY.
MY WAY *WORKS.*
PETER...
PETER, *DON'T.*
YOU REALLY SHOULDN'T HAVE SAID THAT THING ABOUT ME AND MY MOTHER.
YOU'RE PROBABLY RIGHT.
BUT YOU FRUSTRATE THE #@$% OUT OF ME, BOY.

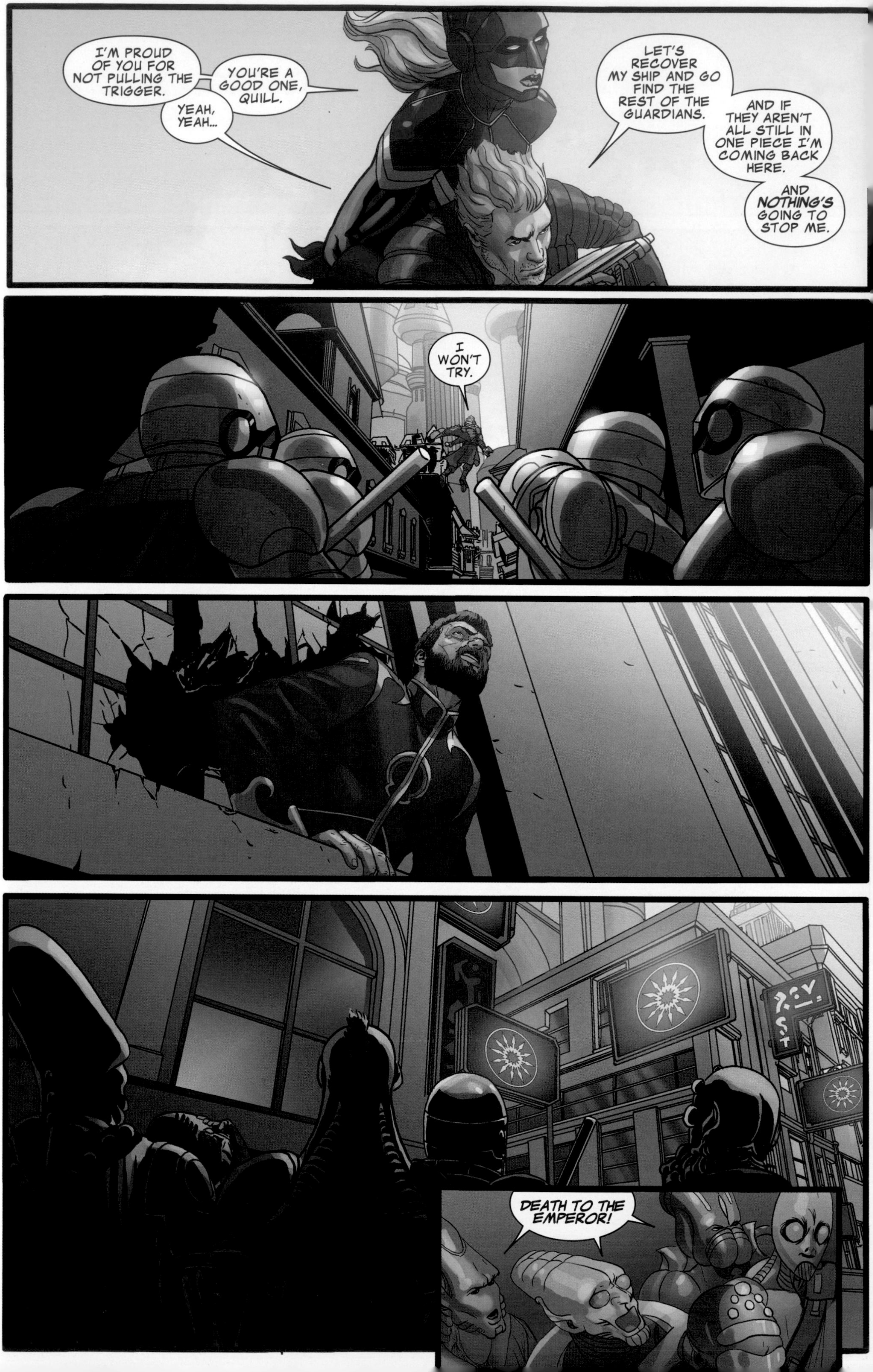
I'M PROUD OF YOU FOR NOT PULLING THE TRIGGER.
YOU'RE A GOOD ONE, QUILL.
YEAH, YEAH...
LET'S RECOVER MY SHIP AND GO FIND THE REST OF THE GUARDIANS.
AND IF THEY AREN'T ALL STILL IN ONE PIECE I'M COMING BACK HERE.
AND NOTHING'S GOING TO STOP ME.
I WON'T TRY.
DEATH TO THE EMPEROR!

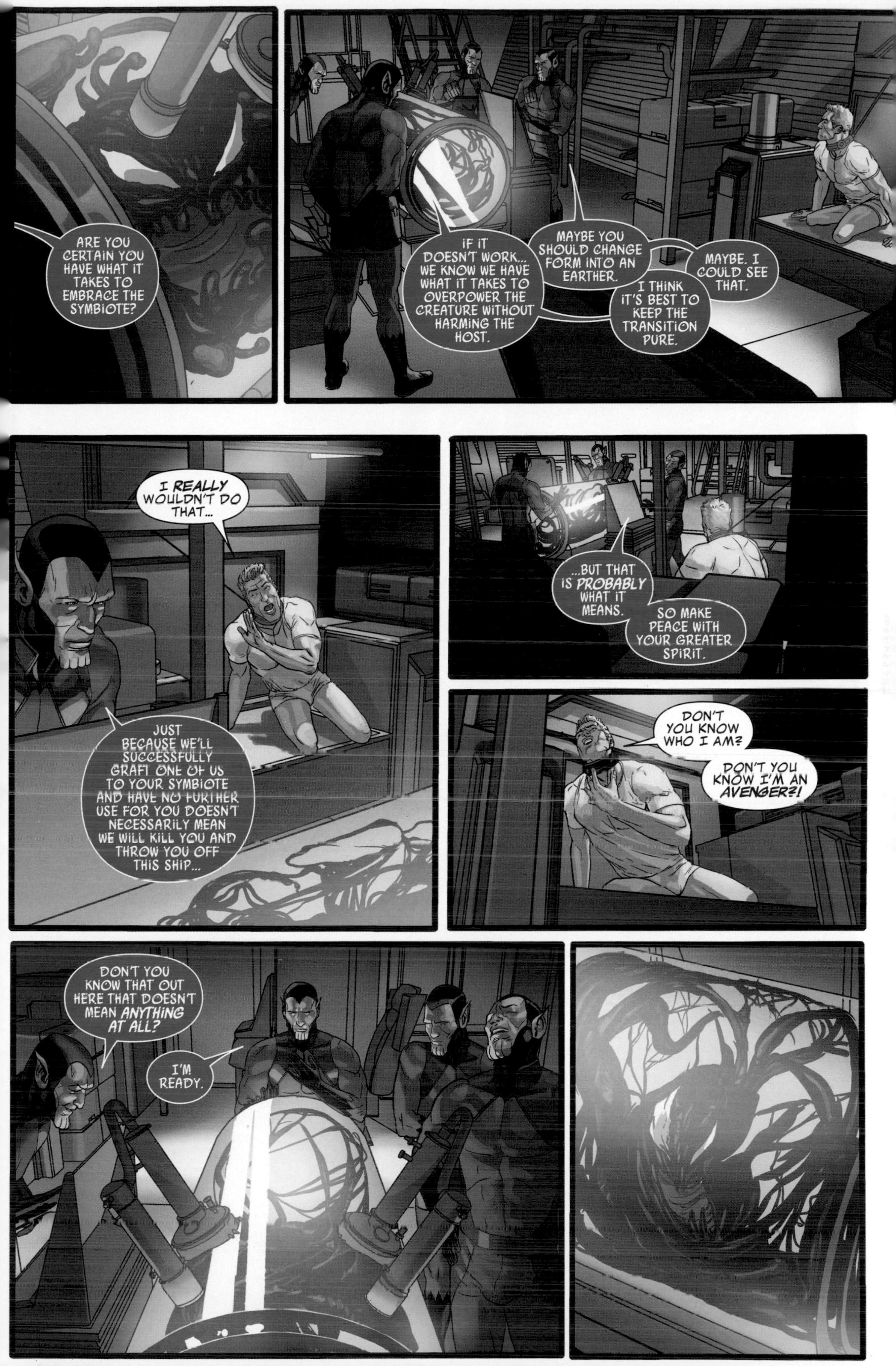
ARE YOU CERTAIN YOU HAVE WHAT IT TAKES TO EMBRACE THE SYMBIOTE?
IF IT DOESN'T WORK... WE KNOW WE HAVE WHAT IT TAKES TO OVERPOWER THE CREATURE WITHOUT HARMING THE HOST.
MAYBE YOU SHOULD CHANGE FORM INTO AN EARTHER.
MAYBE. I COULD SEE THAT.
I THINK IT'S BEST TO KEEP THE TRANSITION PURE.
I REALLY WOULDN'T DO THAT...
JUST BECAUSE WE'LL SUCCESSFULLY GRAFT ONE OF US TO YOUR SYMBIOTE AND HAVE NO FURTHER USE FOR YOU DOESN'T NECESSARILY MEAN WE WILL KILL YOU AND THROW YOU OFF THIS SHIP...
...BUT THAT IS PROBABLY WHAT IT MEANS.
SO MAKE PEACE WITH YOUR GREATER SPIRIT.
DON'T YOU KNOW WHO I AM?
DON'T YOU KNOW I'M AN AVENGER?!
DON'T YOU KNOW THAT OUT HERE THAT DOESN'T MEAN ANYTHING AT ALL?
I'M READY.

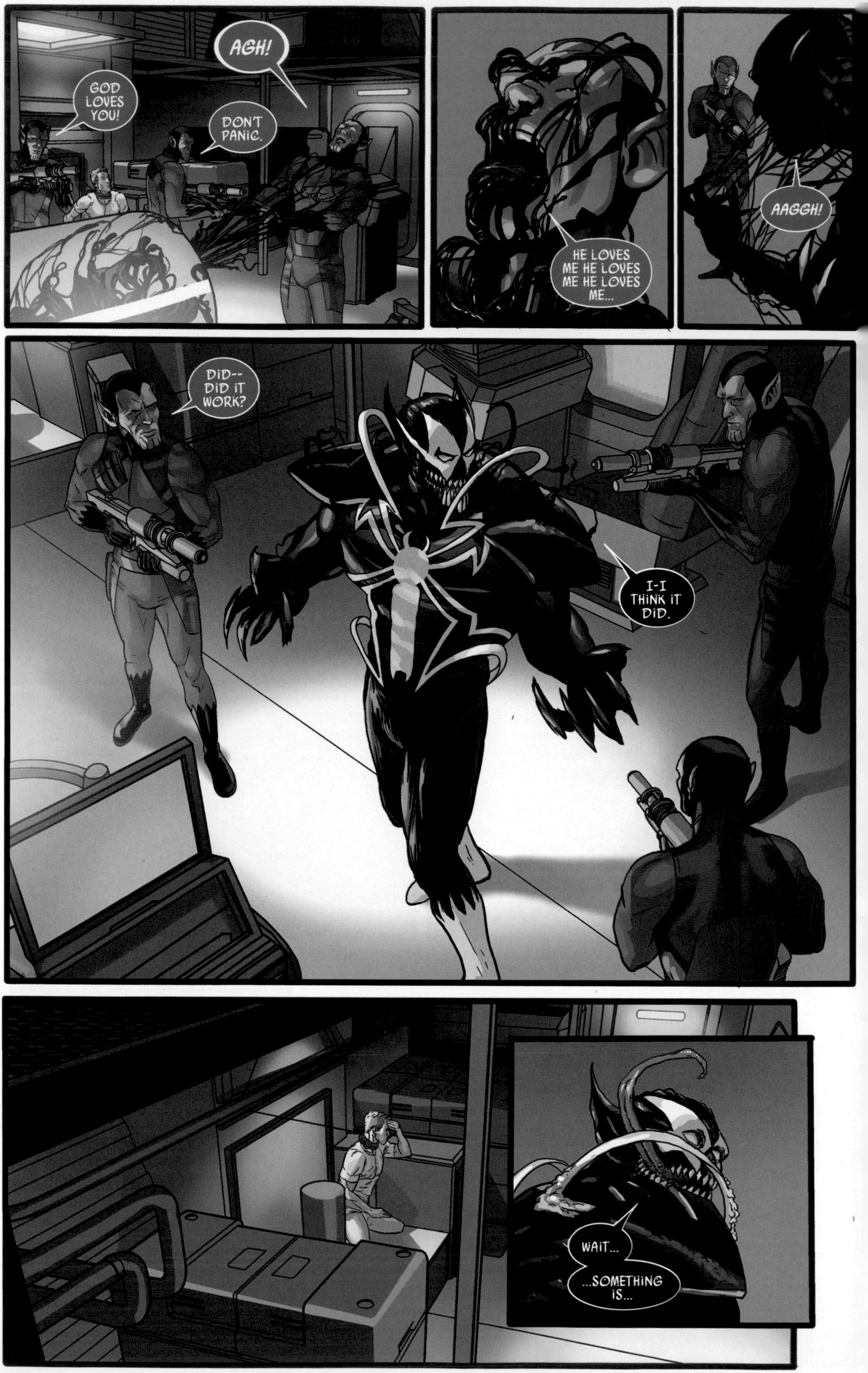
AGH!
GOD LOVES YOU!
DON'T PANIC.
HE LOVES ME HE LOVES ME HE LOVES ME...
AAGGH!
DID-- DID IT WORK?
I-I THINK IT DID.
WAIT...
...SOMETHING IS...

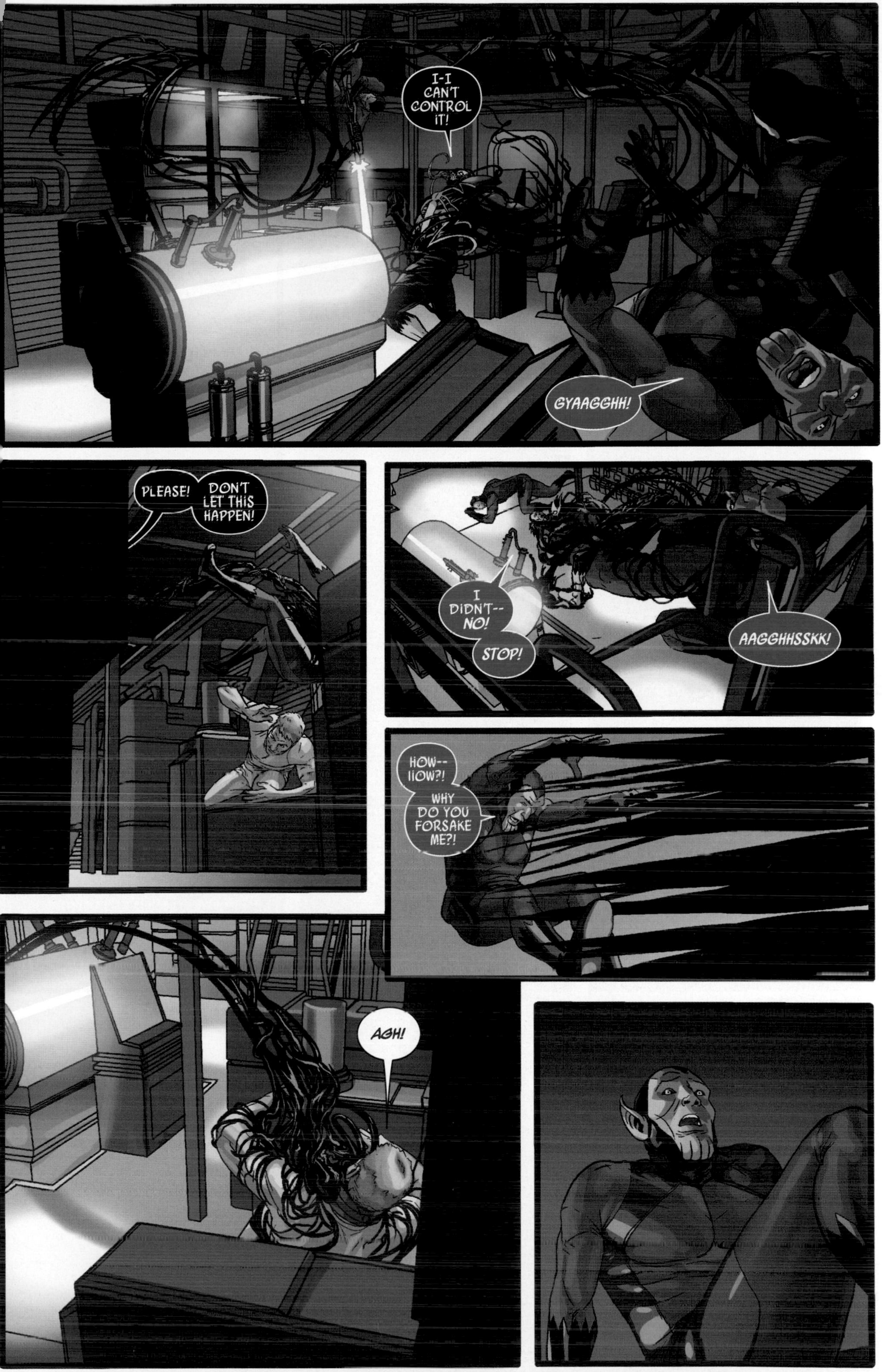
I-I CAN'T CONTROL IT!
GYAAGGHH!
PLEASE!
DON'T LET THIS HAPPEN!
I DIDN'T-- NO!
STOP!
AAGGHHSSKK!
HOW-- HOW?!
WHY DO YOU FORSAKE ME?!
AGH!

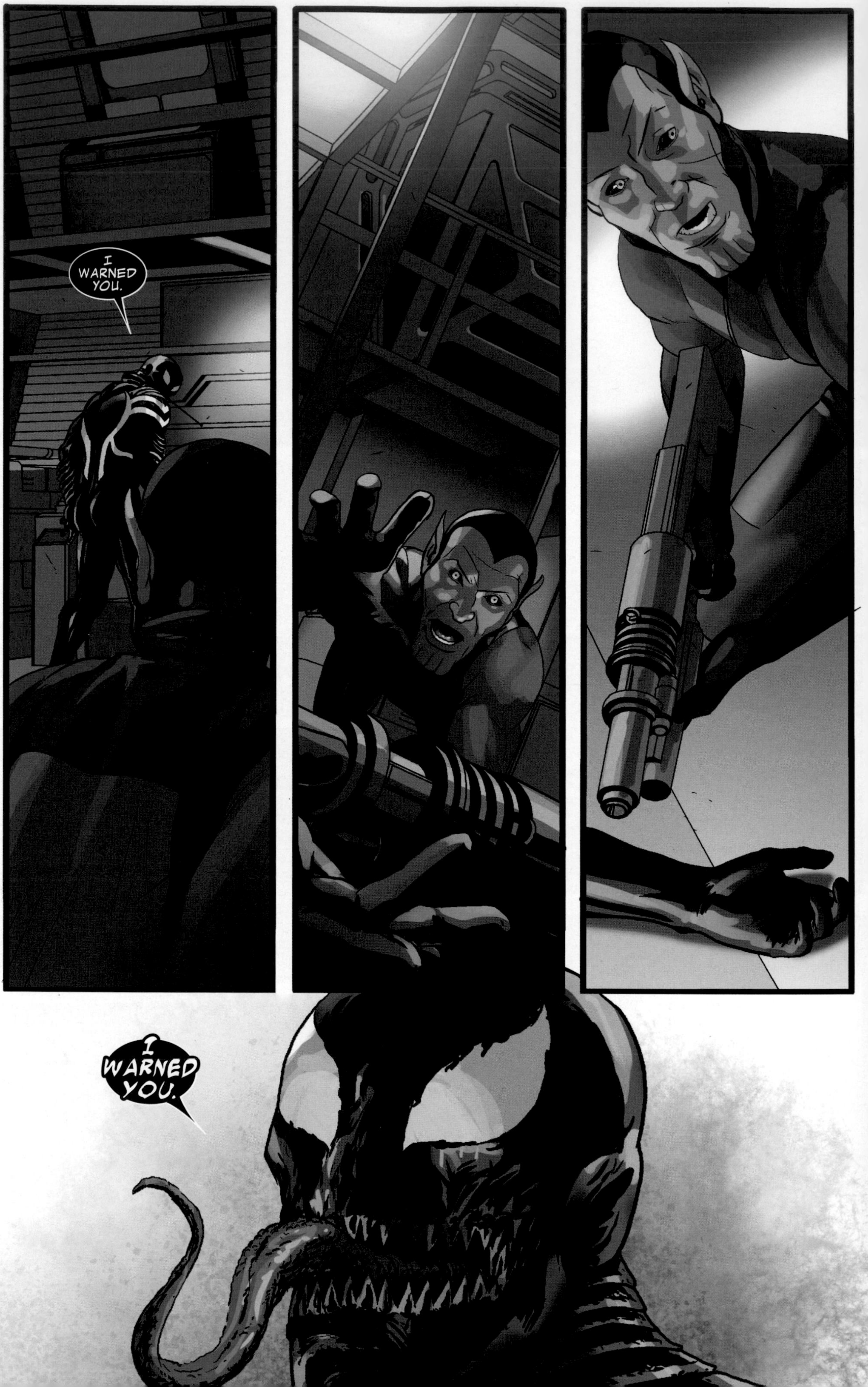
I WARNED YOU.
I WARNED YOU.

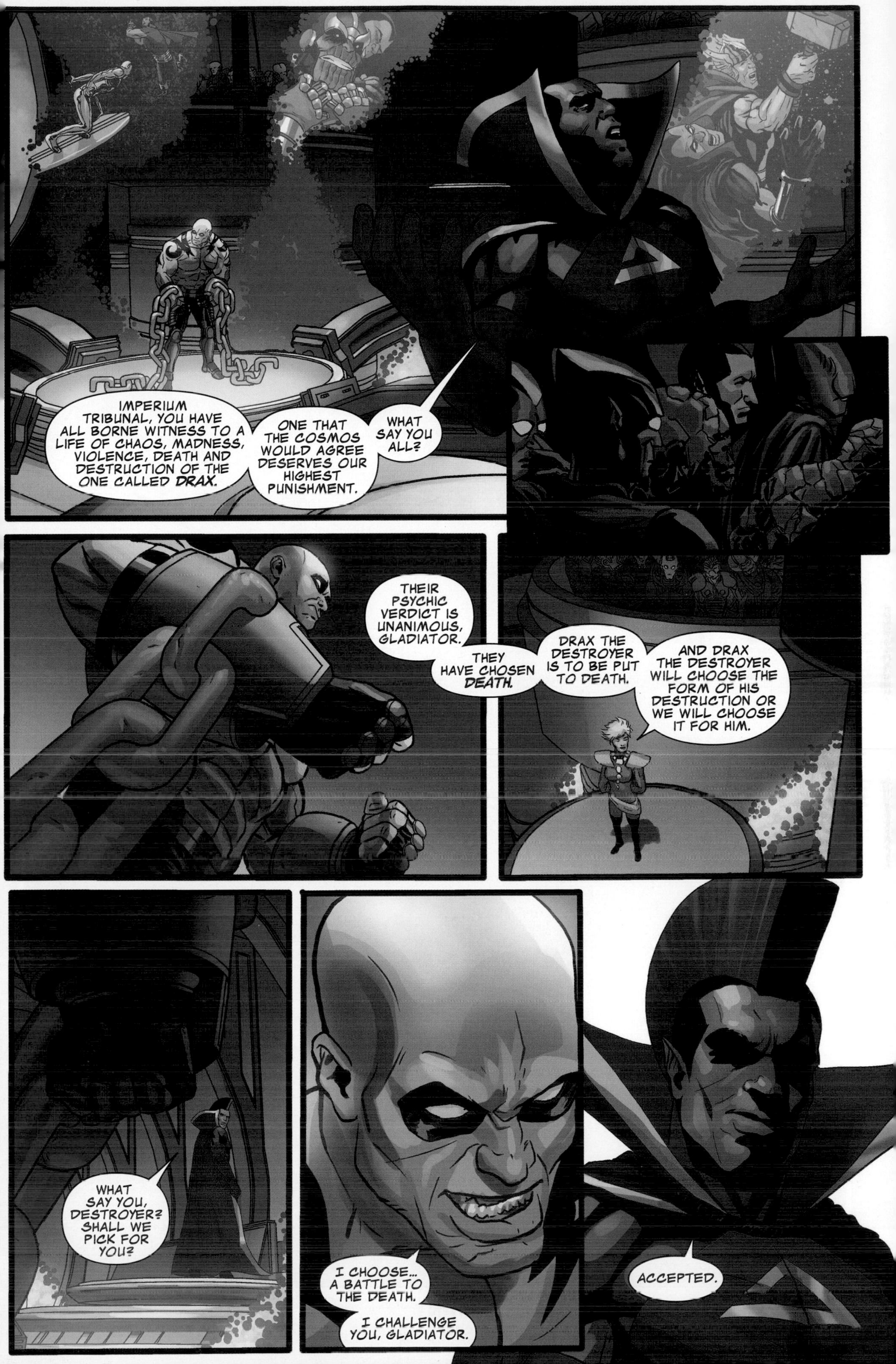

IMPERIUM TRIBUNAL, YOU HAVE ALL BORNE WITNESS TO A LIFE OF CHAOS, MADNESS, VIOLENCE, DEATH AND DESTRUCTION OF THE ONE CALLED DRAX.
ONE THAT THE COSMOS WOULD AGREE DESERVES OUR HIGHEST PUNISHMENT.
WHAT SAY YOU ALL?
THEIR PSYCHIC VERDICT IS UNANIMOUS, GLADIATOR.
THEY HAVE CHOSEN DEATH.
DRAX THE DESTROYER IS TO BE PUT TO DEATH.
AND DRAX THE DESTROYER WILL CHOOSE THE FORM OF HIS DESTRUCTION OR WE WILL CHOOSE IT FOR HIM.
WHAT SAY YOU, DESTROYER? SHALL WE PICK FOR YOU?
I CHOOSE... A BATTLE TO THE DEATH.
I CHALLENGE YOU, GLADIATOR.
ACCEPTED.

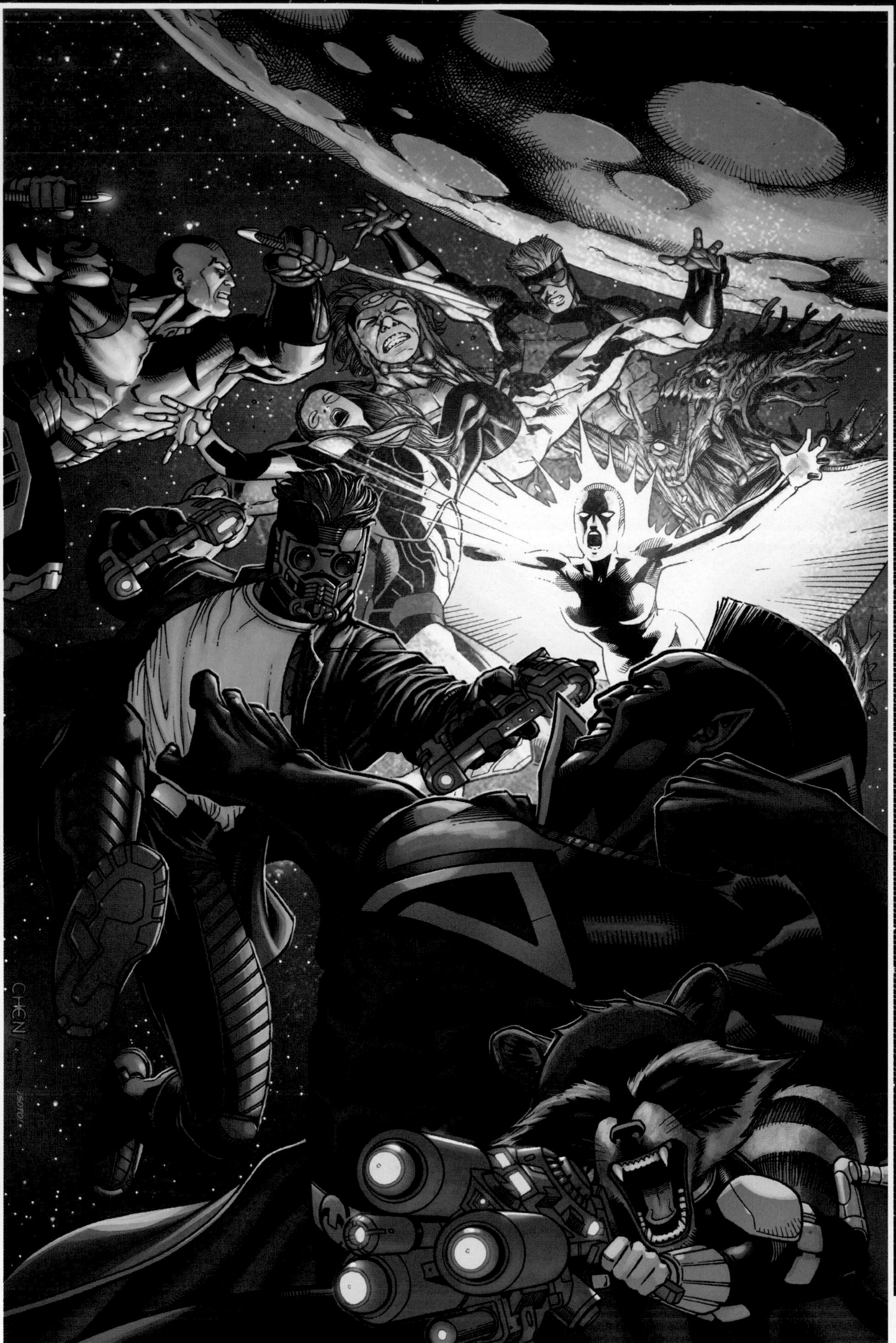
CHEN

***GUARDIANS OF THE GALAXY #17* VARIANT**
BY SEAN CHEN, MARK MORALES & CHRIS SOTOMAYOR

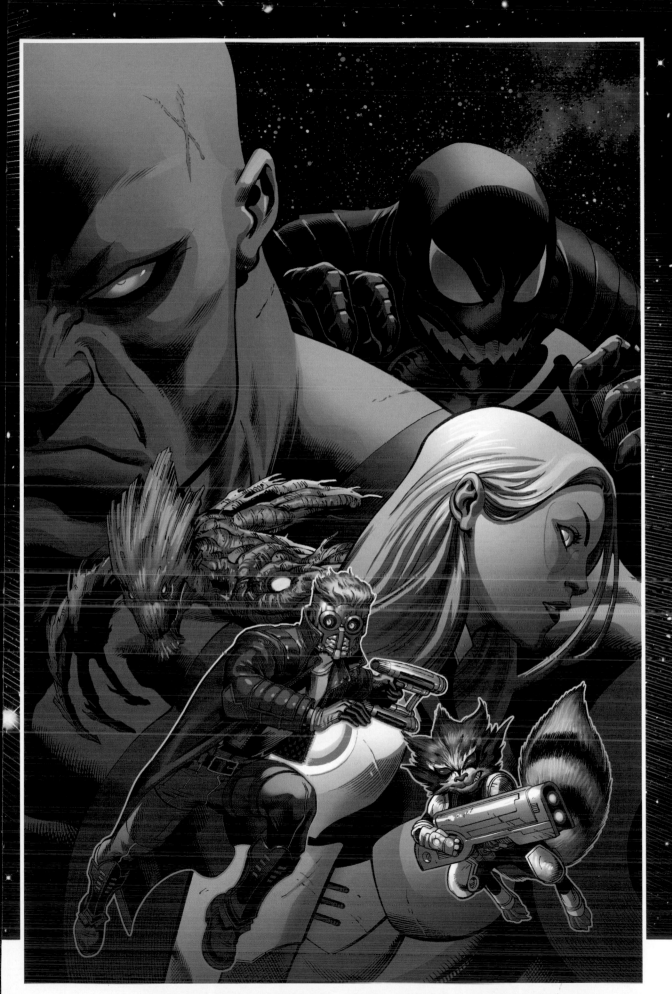

GUARDIANS OF THE GALAXY 17

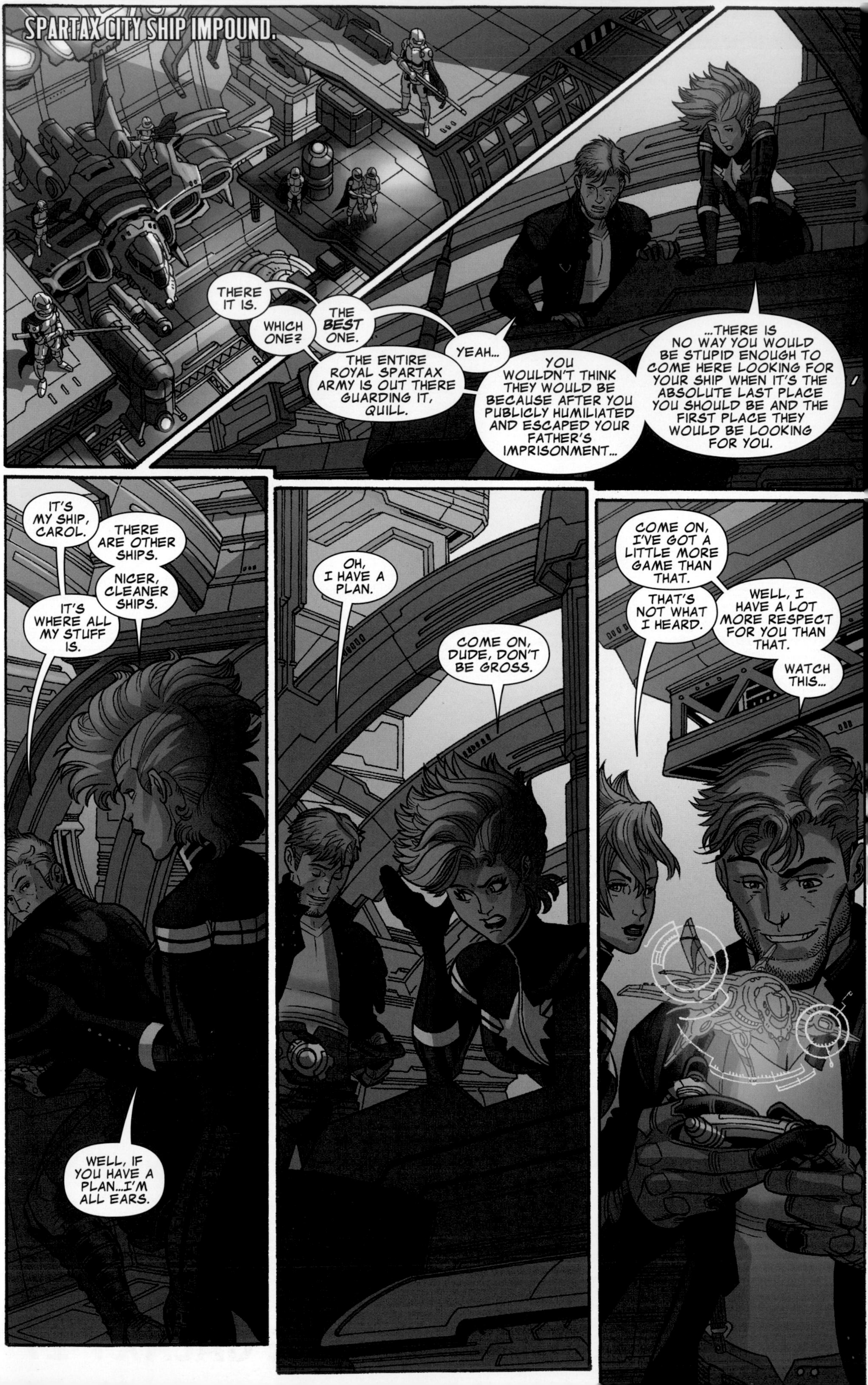
SPARTAX CITY SHIP IMPOUND.
THERE IT IS.
WHICH ONE?
THE BEST ONE.
YEAH...
THE ENTIRE ROYAL SPARTAX ARMY IS OUT THERE GUARDING IT, QUILL.
YOU WOULDN'T THINK THEY WOULD BE BECAUSE AFTER YOU PUBLICLY HUMILIATED AND ESCAPED YOUR FATHER'S IMPRISONMENT...
...THERE IS NO WAY YOU WOULD BE STUPID ENOUGH TO COME HERE LOOKING FOR YOUR SHIP WHEN IT'S THE ABSOLUTE LAST PLACE YOU SHOULD BE AND THE FIRST PLACE THEY WOULD BE LOOKING FOR YOU.
IT'S MY SHIP, CAROL.
THERE ARE OTHER SHIPS.
NICER, CLEANER SHIPS.
IT'S WHERE ALL MY STUFF IS.
WELL, IF YOU HAVE A PLAN...I'M ALL EARS.
OH, I HAVE A PLAN.
COME ON, DUDE, DON'T BE GROSS.
COME ON, I'VE GOT A LITTLE MORE GAME THAN THAT.
THAT'S NOT WHAT I HEARD.
WELL, I HAVE A LOT MORE RESPECT FOR YOU THAN THAT.
WATCH THIS...

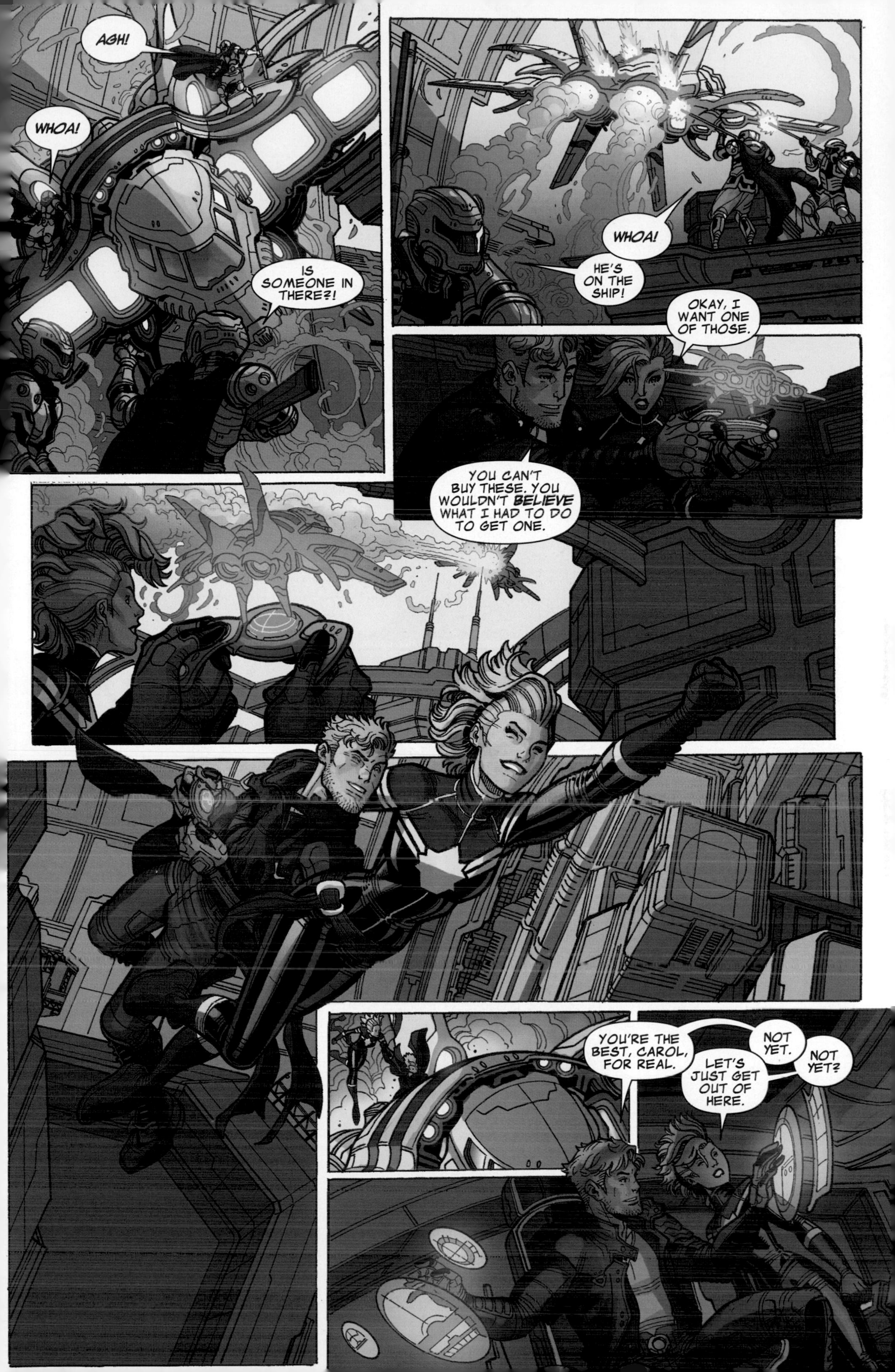
AGH!
WHOA!
IS SOMEONE IN THERE?!
WHOA!
HE'S ON THE SHIP!
OKAY, I WANT ONE OF THOSE.
YOU CAN'T BUY THESE. YOU WOULDN'T BELIEVE WHAT I HAD TO DO TO GET ONE.
YOU'RE THE BEST, CAROL, FOR REAL.
NOT YET.
NOT YET?
LET'S JUST GET OUT OF HERE.

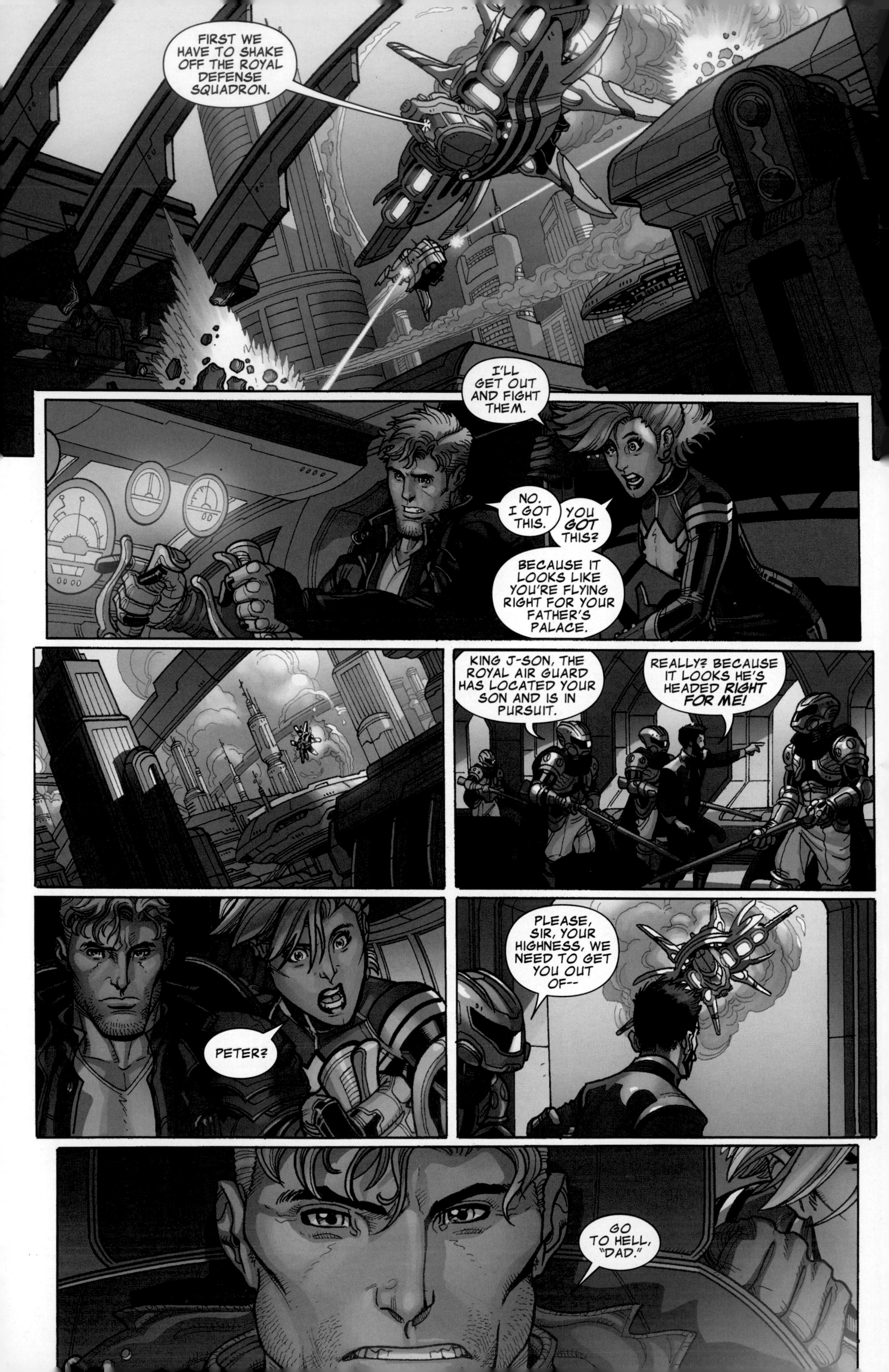

FIRST WE HAVE TO SHAKE OFF THE ROYAL DEFENSE SQUADRON.
I'LL GET OUT AND FIGHT THEM.
NO. I GOT THIS.
YOU GOT THIS?
BECAUSE IT LOOKS LIKE YOU'RE FLYING RIGHT FOR YOUR FATHER'S PALACE.
KING J-SON, THE ROYAL AIR GUARD HAS LOCATED YOUR SON AND IS IN PURSUIT.
REALLY? BECAUSE IT LOOKS HE'S HEADED RIGHT FOR ME!
PETER?
PLEASE, SIR, YOUR HIGHNESS, WE NEED TO GET YOU OUT OF--
GO TO HELL, "DAD."

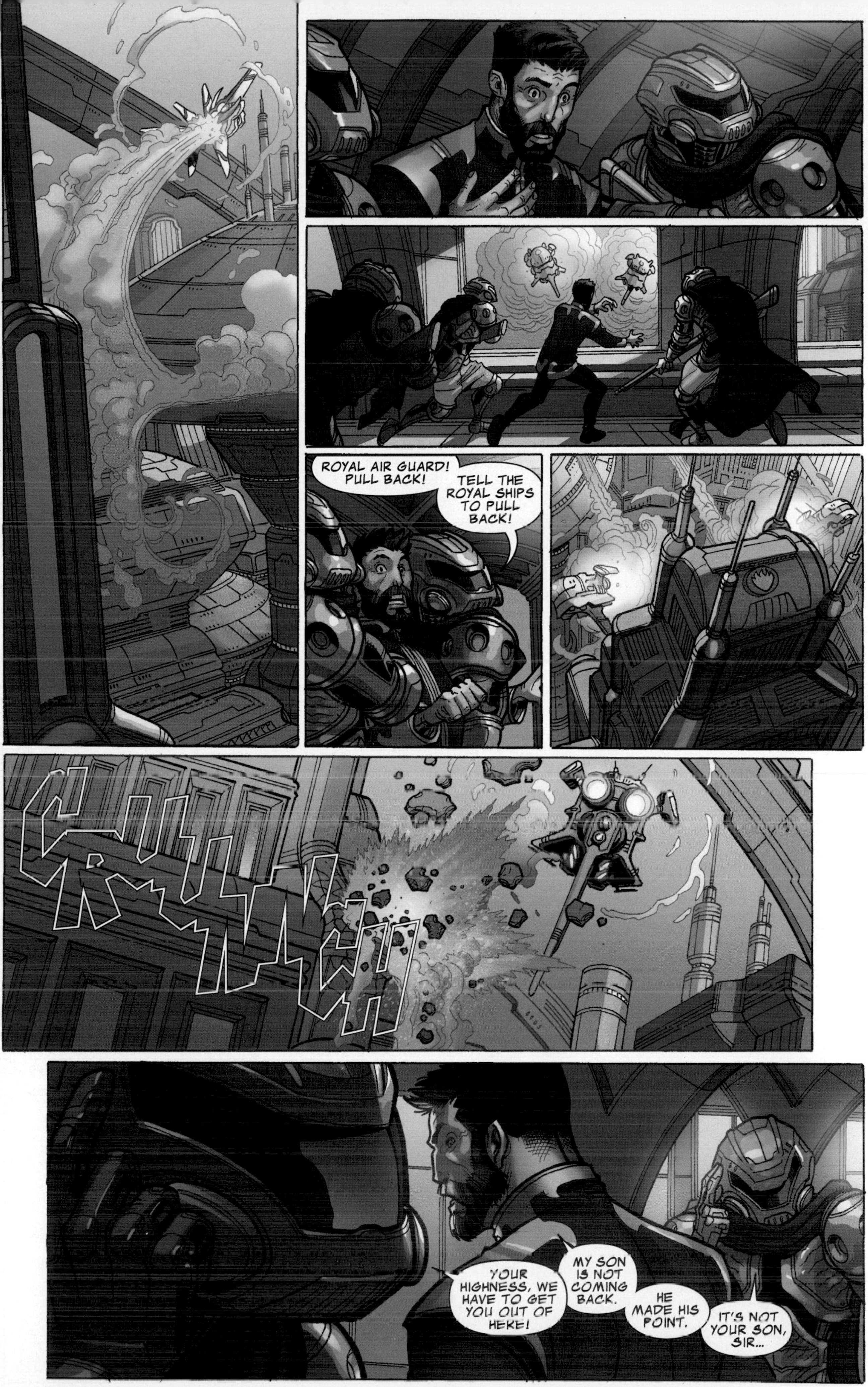
ROYAL AIR GUARD! PULL BACK!
TELL THE ROYAL SHIPS TO PULL BACK!
CRUNCH
YOUR HIGHNESS, WE HAVE TO GET YOU OUT OF HERE!
MY SON IS NOT COMING BACK.
HE MADE HIS POINT.
IT'S NOT YOUR SON, SIR...

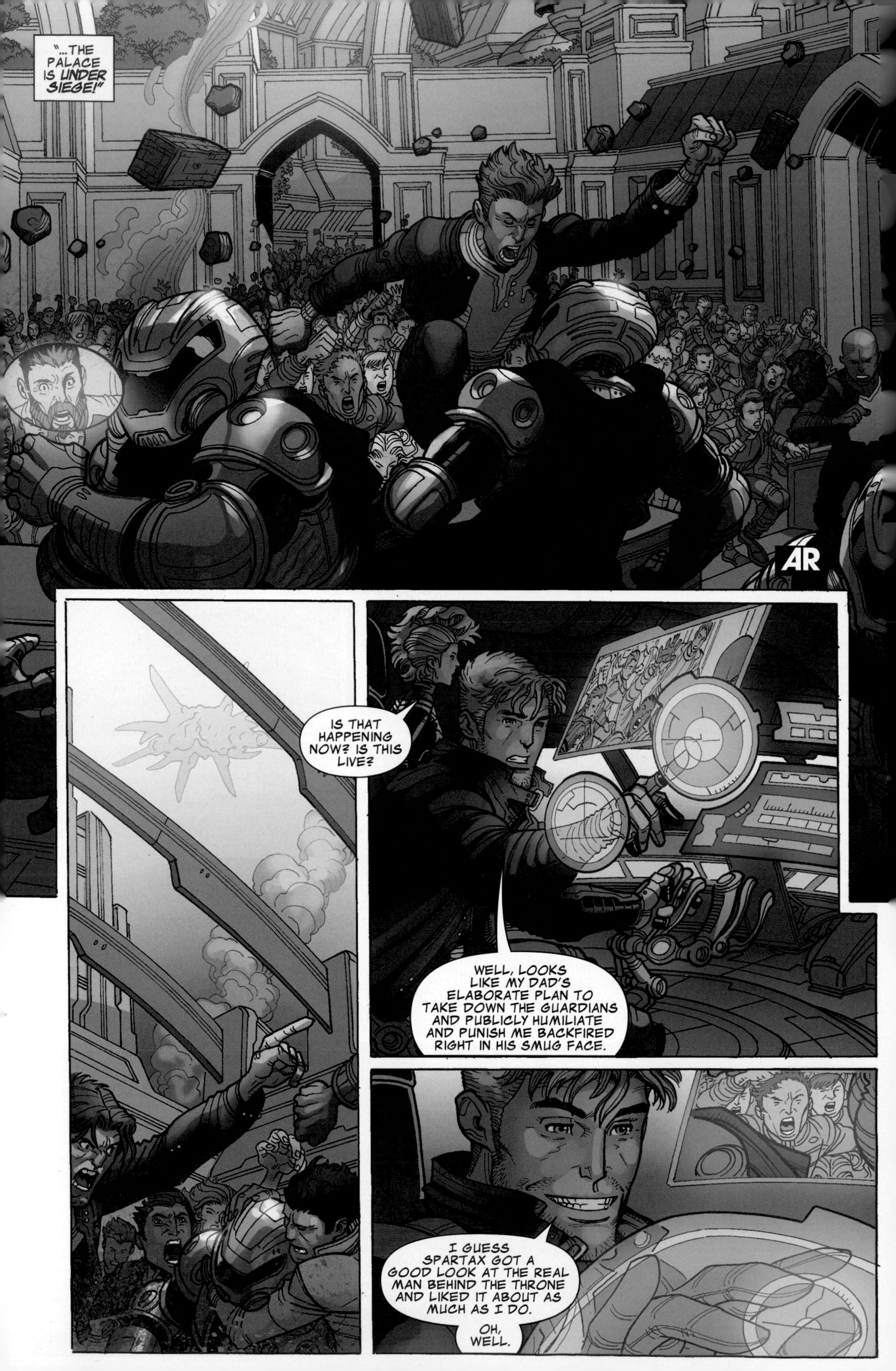
"...THE PALACE IS UNDER SIEGE!"
AR
IS THAT HAPPENING NOW? IS THIS LIVE?
WELL, LOOKS LIKE MY DAD'S ELABORATE PLAN TO TAKE DOWN THE GUARDIANS AND PUBLICLY HUMILIATE AND PUNISH ME BACKFIRED RIGHT IN HIS SMUG FACE.
I GUESS SPARTAX GOT A GOOD LOOK AT THE REAL MAN BEHIND THE THRONE AND LIKED IT ABOUT AS MUCH AS I DO.
OH, WELL.

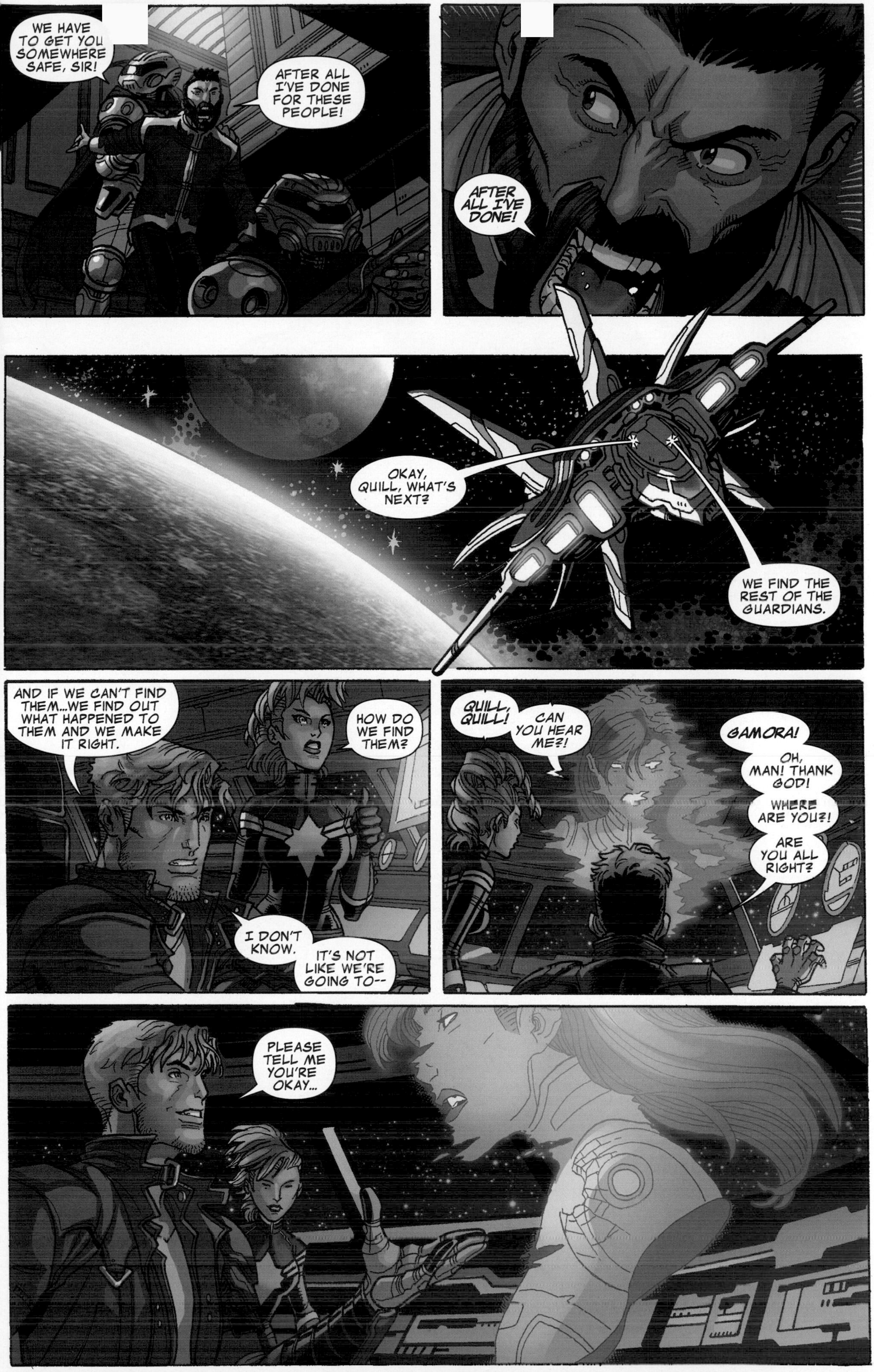
WE HAVE TO GET YOU SOMEWHERE SAFE, SIR!
AFTER ALL I'VE DONE FOR THESE PEOPLE!
AFTER ALL I'VE DONE!
OKAY, QUILL, WHAT'S NEXT?
WE FIND THE REST OF THE GUARDIANS.
AND IF WE CAN'T FIND THEM...WE FIND OUT WHAT HAPPENED TO THEM AND WE MAKE IT RIGHT.
HOW DO WE FIND THEM?
I DON'T KNOW.
IT'S NOT LIKE WE'RE GOING TO--
QUILL, QUILL!
CAN YOU HEAR ME?!
GAMORA!
OH, MAN! THANK GOD!
WHERE ARE YOU?!
ARE YOU ALL RIGHT?
PLEASE TELL ME YOU'RE OKAY...

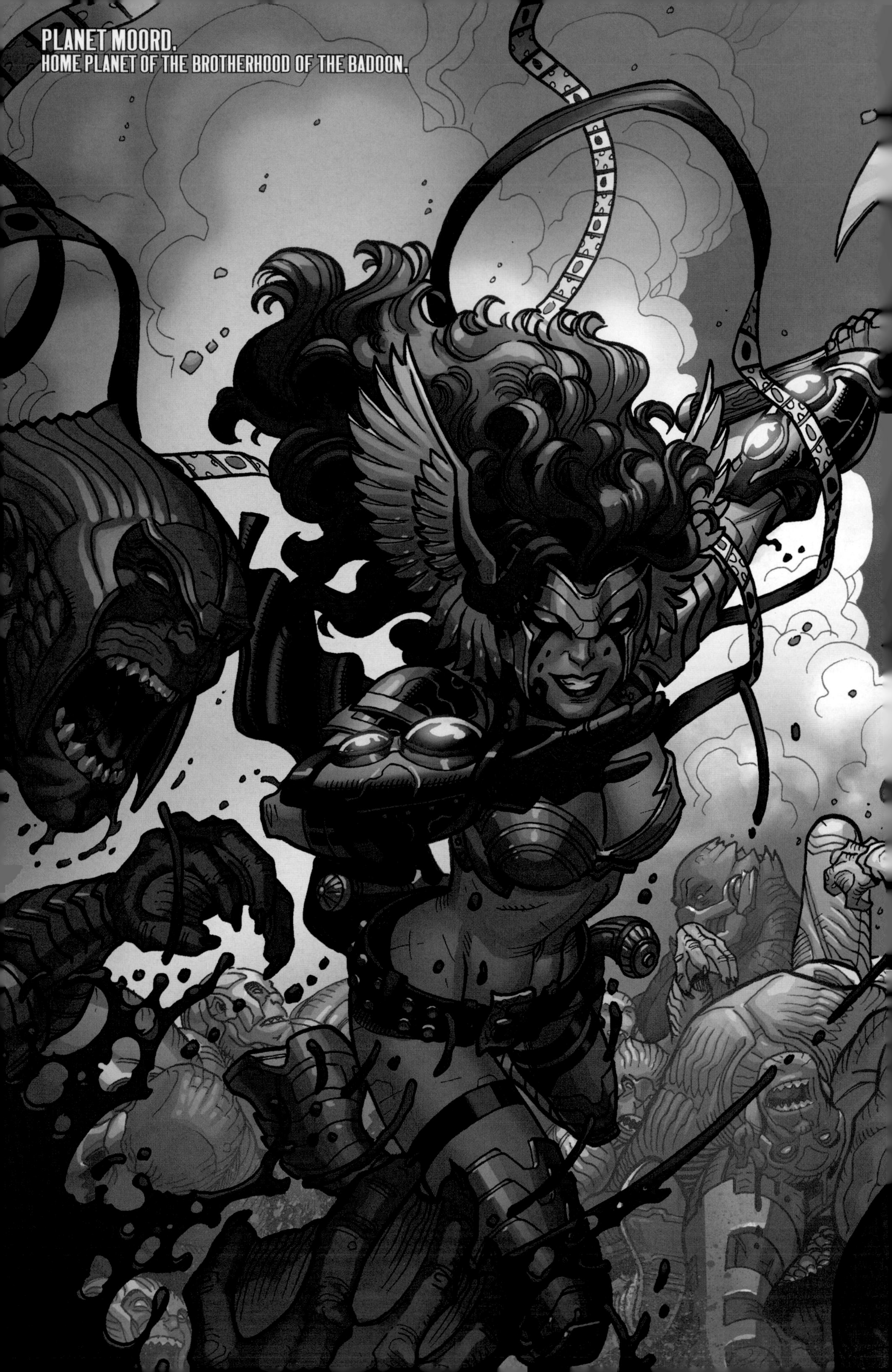
PLANET MOORD.
HOME PLANET OF THE BROTHERHOOD OF THE BADOON.

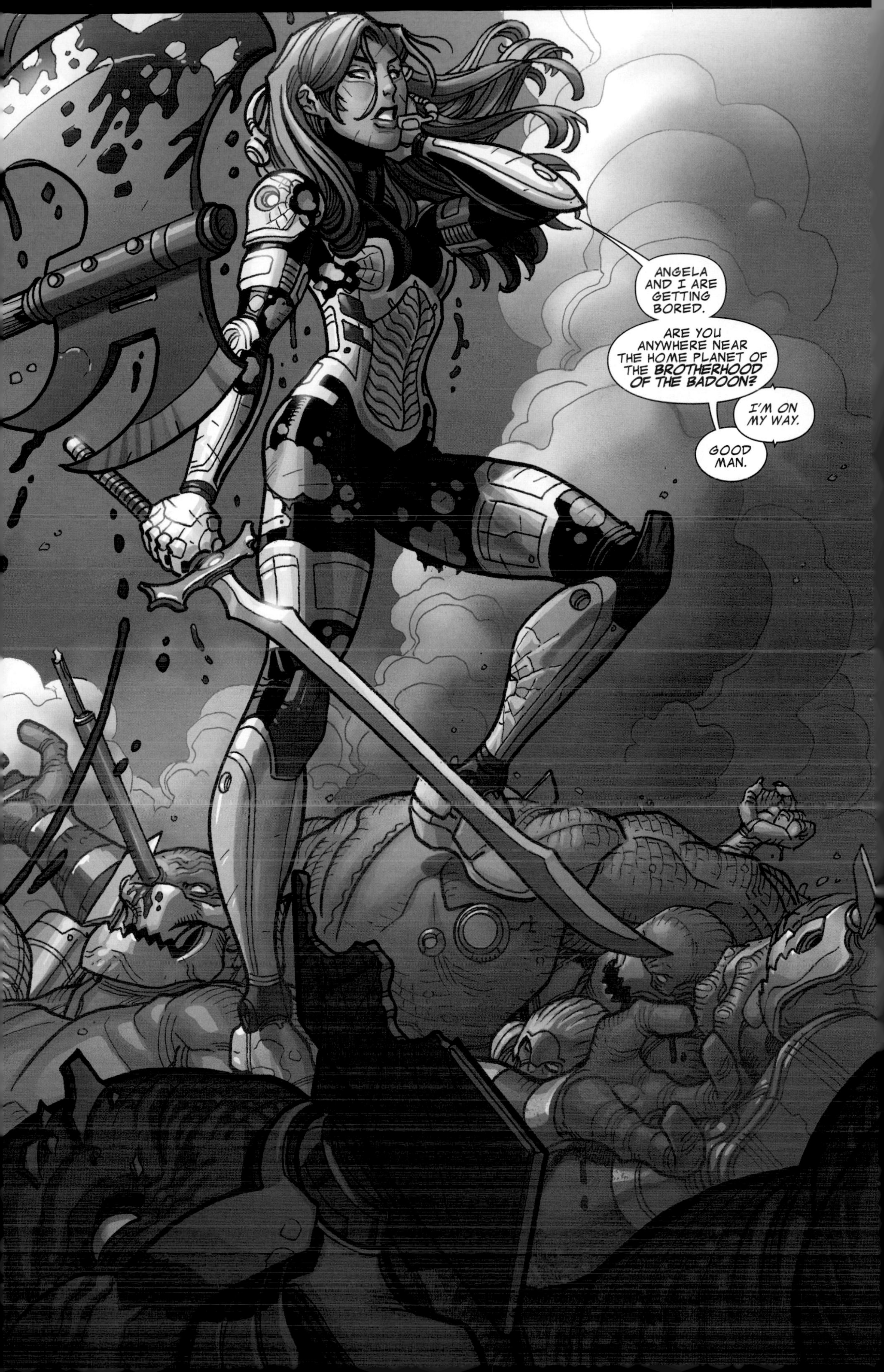
ANGELA AND I ARE GETTING BORED.
ARE YOU ANYWHERE NEAR THE HOME PLANET OF THE **BROTHERHOOD OF THE BADOON?**
I'M ON MY WAY.
GOOD MAN.

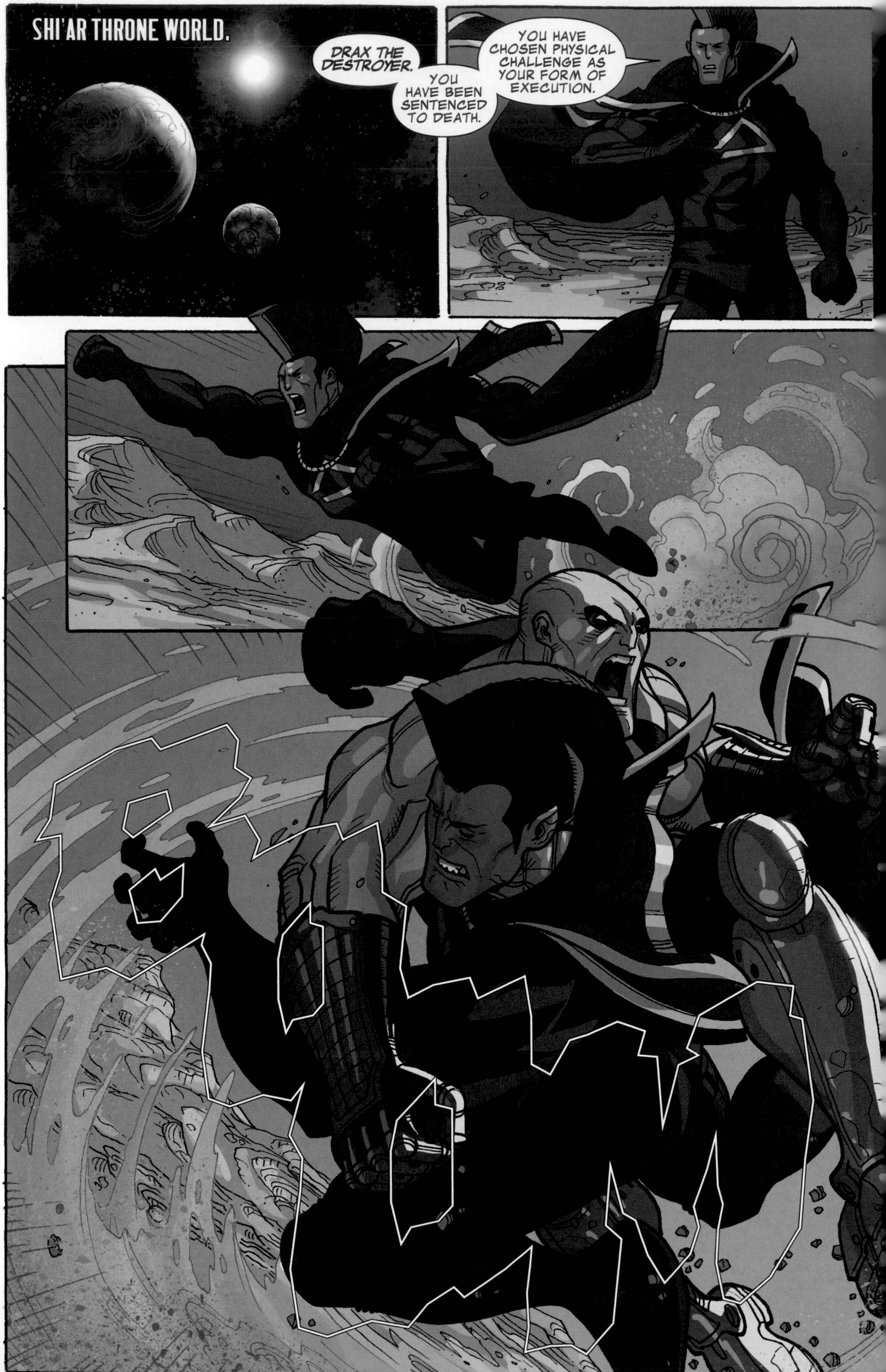
SHI'AR THRONE WORLD.
DRAX THE DESTROYER.
YOU HAVE BEEN SENTENCED TO DEATH.
YOU HAVE CHOSEN PHYSICAL CHALLENGE AS YOUR FORM OF EXECUTION.

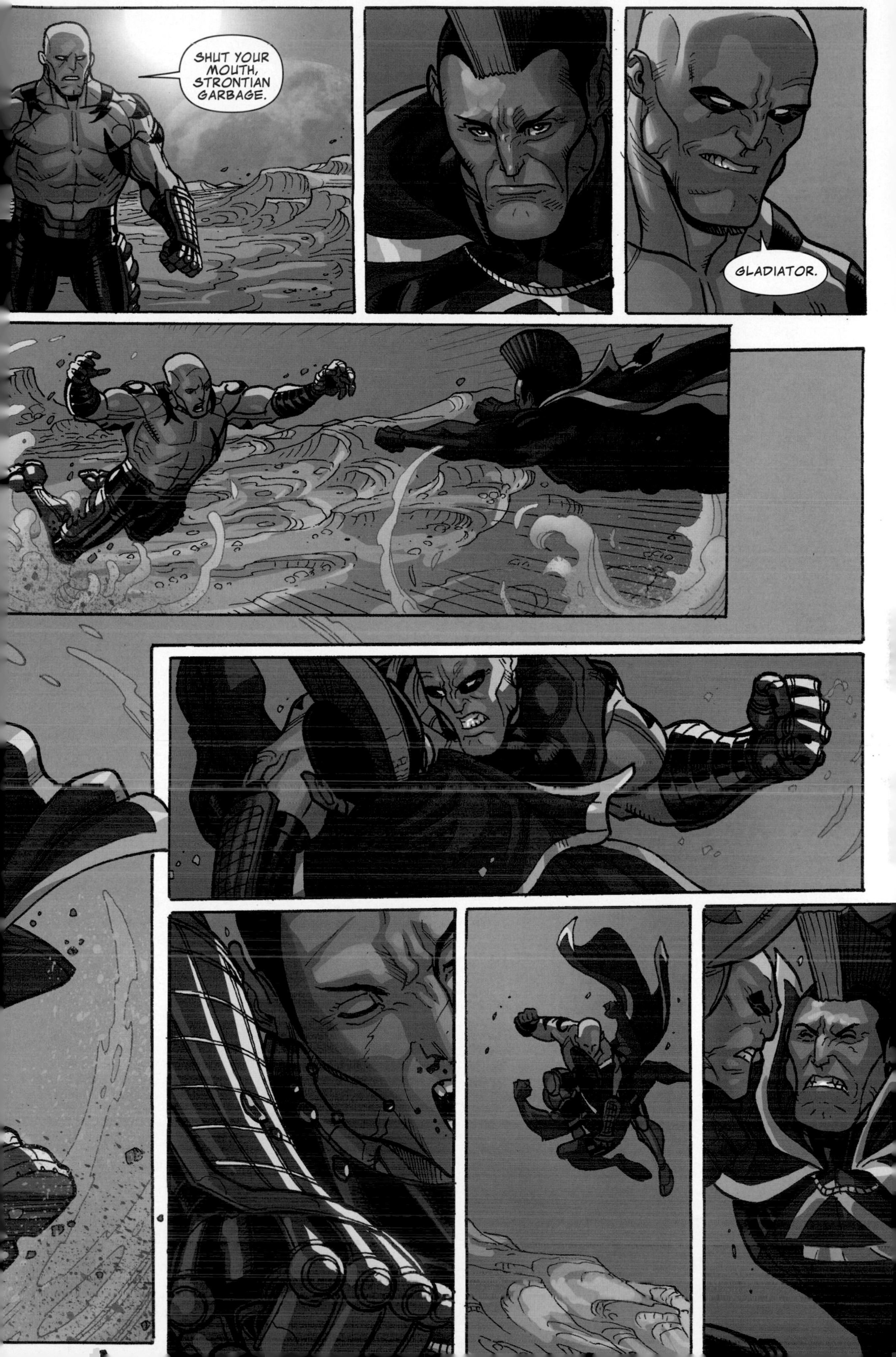
SHUT YOUR MOUTH, STRONTIAN GARBAGE.
GLADIATOR.

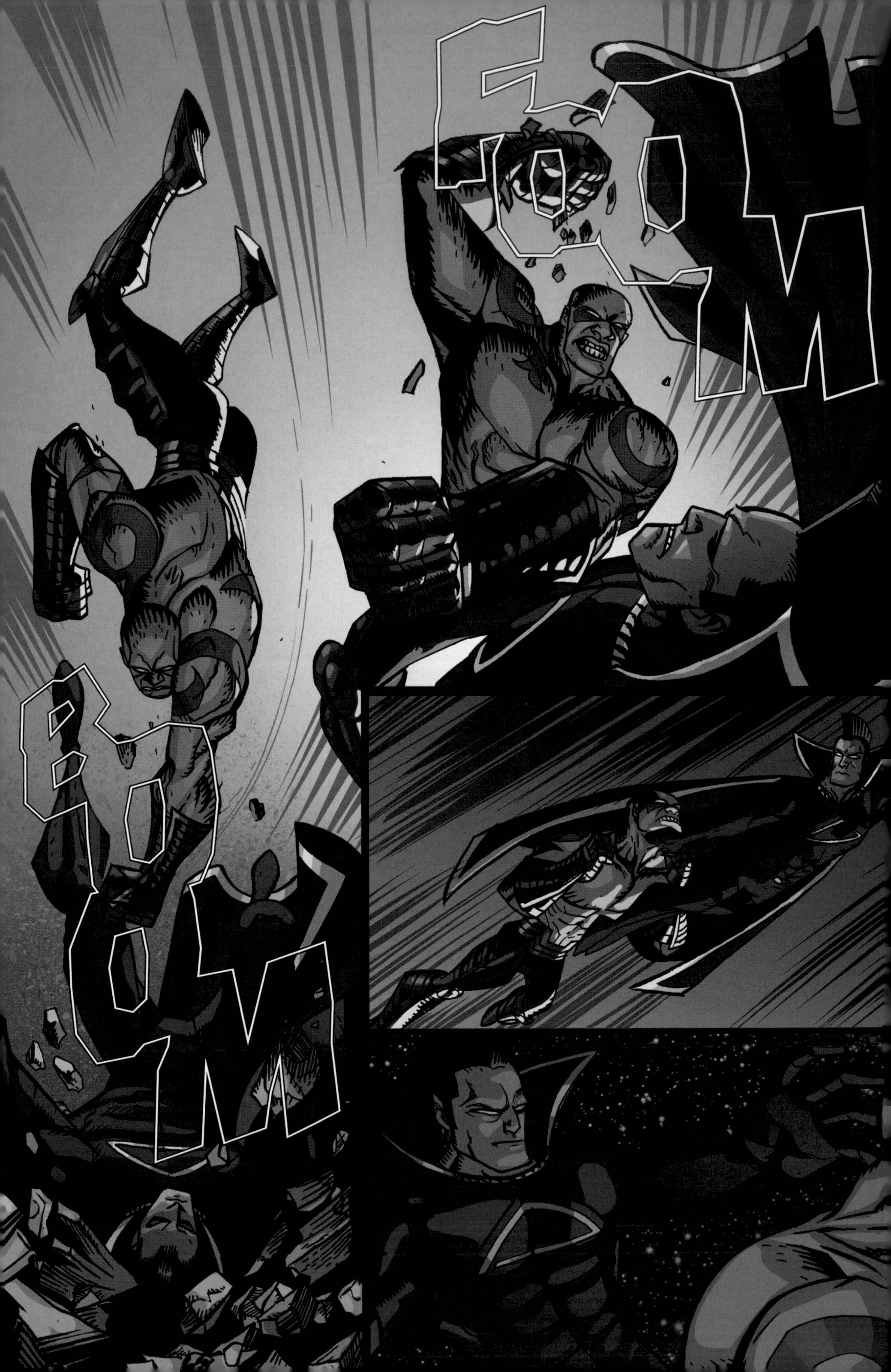
FOOM
BOOM

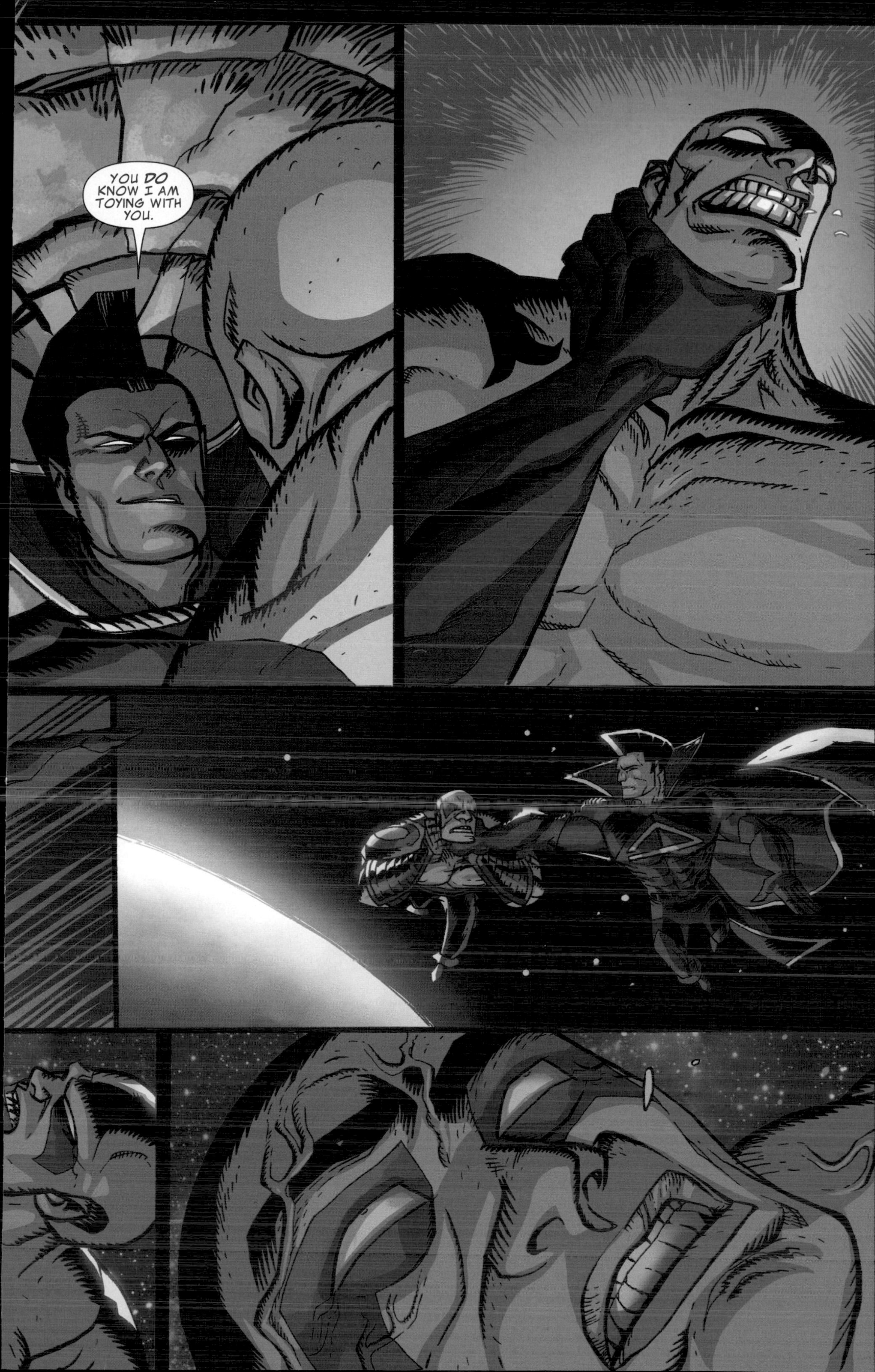
YOU DO KNOW I AM TOYING WITH YOU.

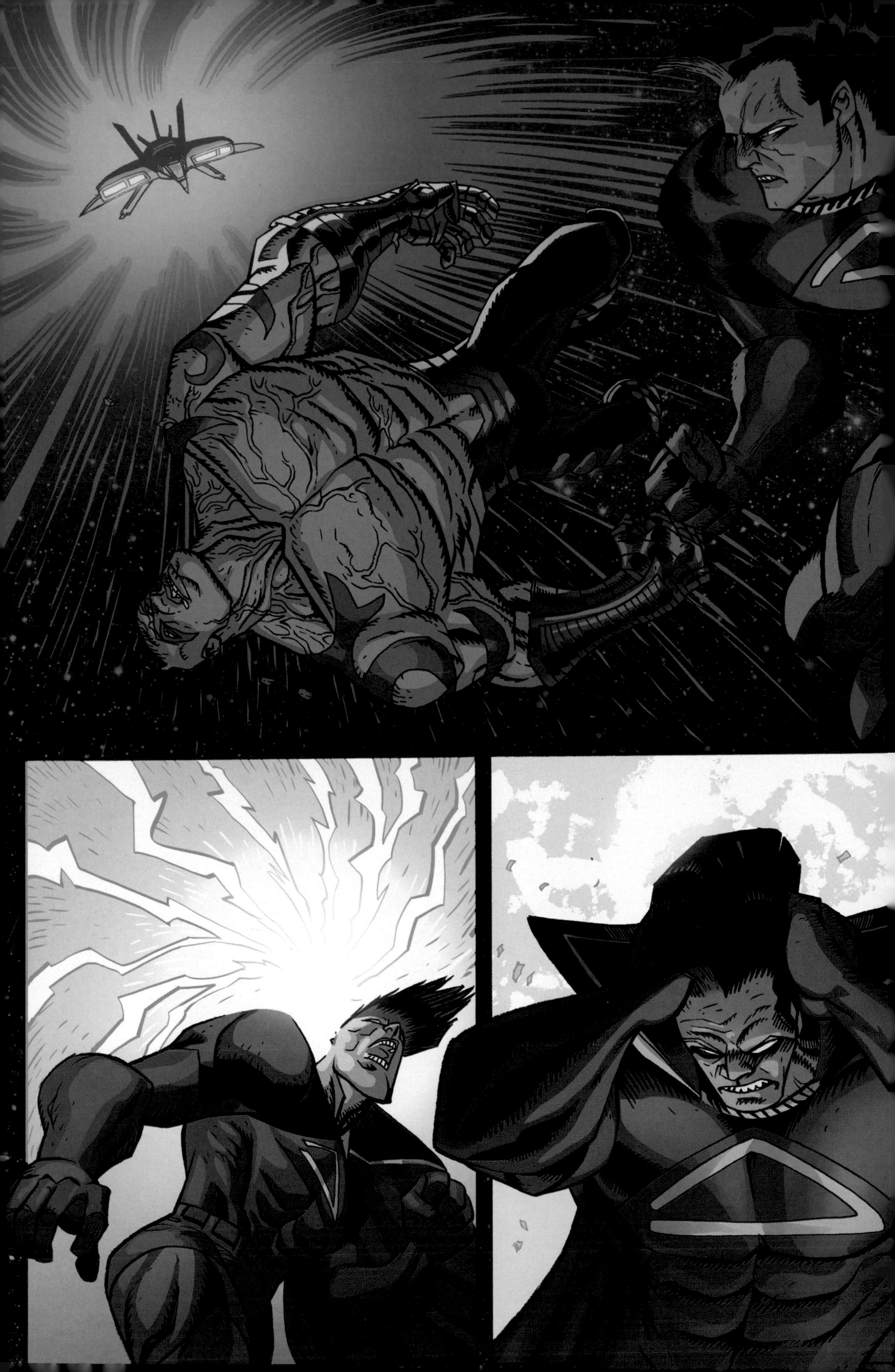

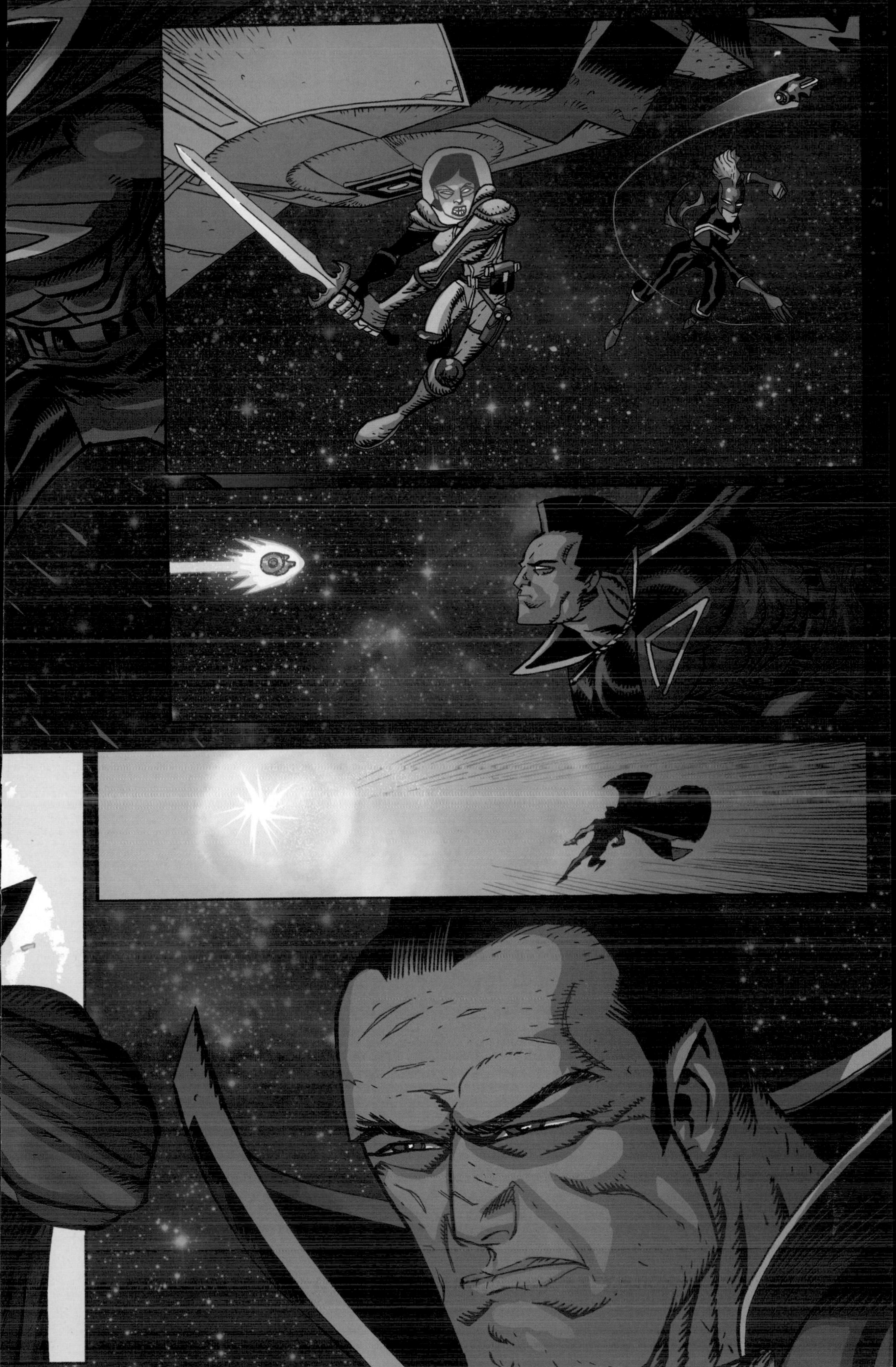

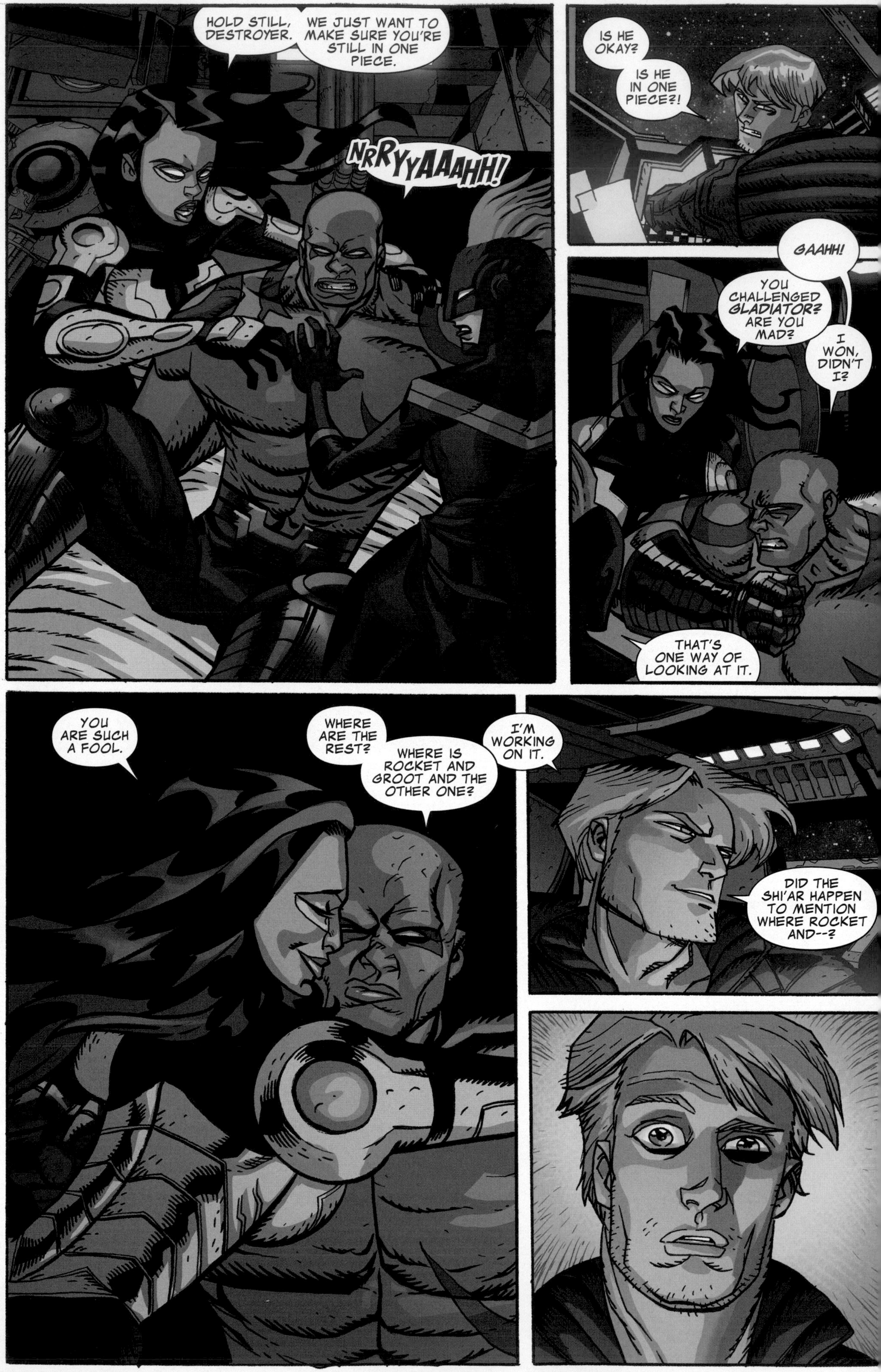
HOLD STILL, DESTROYER.
WE JUST WANT TO MAKE SURE YOU'RE STILL IN ONE PIECE.
NRRYYAAAHH!
IS HE OKAY?
IS HE IN ONE PIECE?!
GAAHH!
YOU CHALLENGED GLADIATOR? ARE YOU MAD?
I WON, DIDN'T I?
THAT'S ONE WAY OF LOOKING AT IT.
YOU ARE SUCH A FOOL.
WHERE ARE THE REST?
WHERE IS ROCKET AND GROOT AND THE OTHER ONE?
I'M WORKING ON IT.
DID THE SHI'AR HAPPEN TO MENTION WHERE ROCKET AND--?

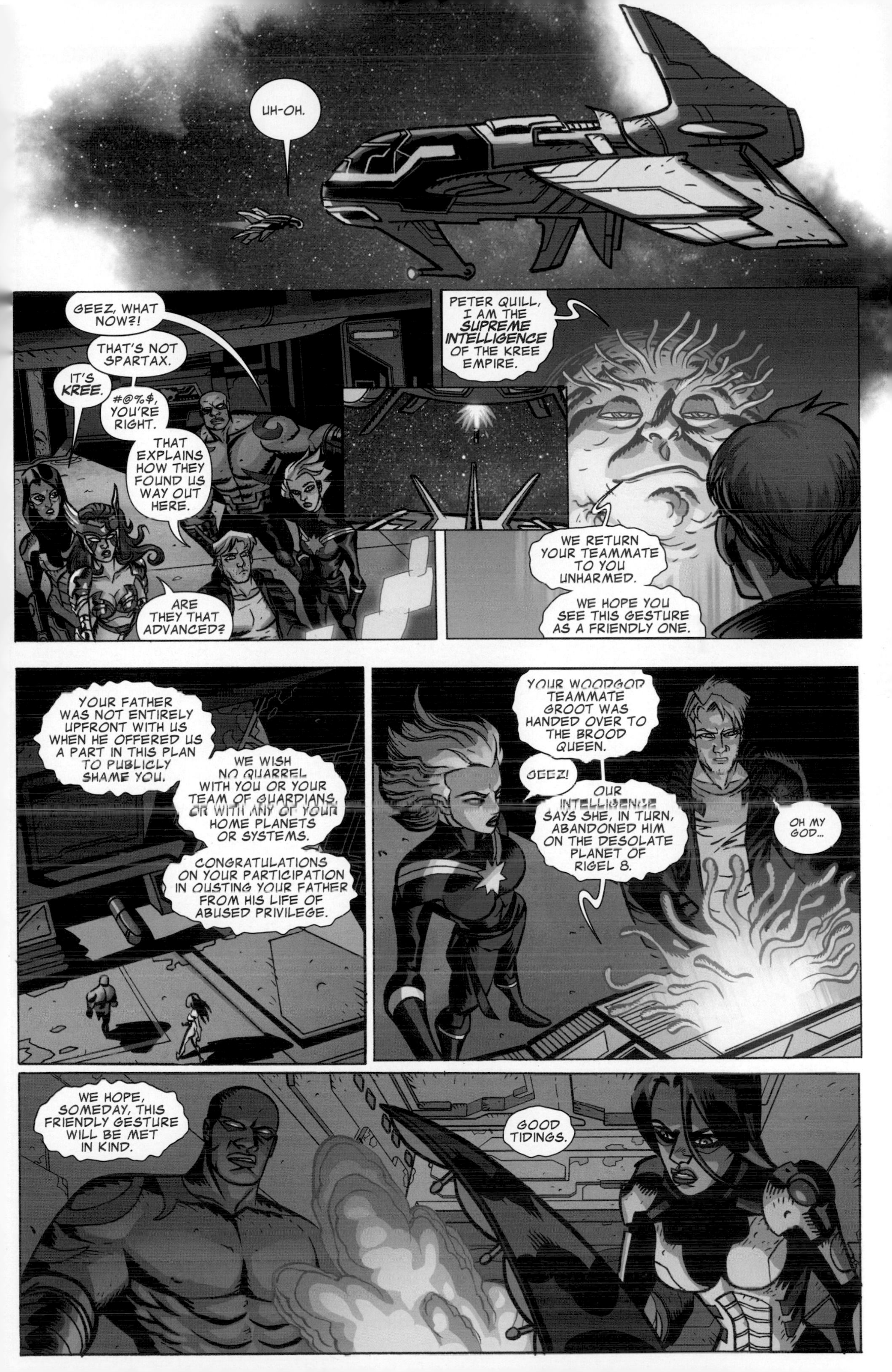
UH-OH.
GEEZ, WHAT NOW?!
THAT'S NOT SPARTAX.
IT'S KREE.
#@%$, YOU'RE RIGHT.
THAT EXPLAINS HOW THEY FOUND US WAY OUT HERE.
ARE THEY THAT ADVANCED?
PETER QUILL, I AM THE SUPREME INTELLIGENCE OF THE KREE EMPIRE.
WE RETURN YOUR TEAMMATE TO YOU UNHARMED.
WE HOPE YOU SEE THIS GESTURE AS A FRIENDLY ONE.
YOUR FATHER WAS NOT ENTIRELY UPFRONT WITH US WHEN HE OFFERED US A PART IN THIS PLAN TO PUBLICLY SHAME YOU.
WE WISH NO QUARREL WITH YOU OR YOUR TEAM OF GUARDIANS, OR WITH ANY OF YOUR HOME PLANETS OR SYSTEMS.
CONGRATULATIONS ON YOUR PARTICIPATION IN OUSTING YOUR FATHER FROM HIS LIFE OF ABUSED PRIVILEGE.
YOUR WOODGOD TEAMMATE GROOT WAS HANDED OVER TO THE BROOD QUEEN.
GEEZ!
OUR INTELLIGENCE SAYS SHE, IN TURN, ABANDONED HIM ON THE DESOLATE PLANET OF RIGEL 8.
OH MY GOD...
WE HOPE, SOMEDAY, THIS FRIENDLY GESTURE WILL BE MET IN KIND.
GOOD TIDINGS.

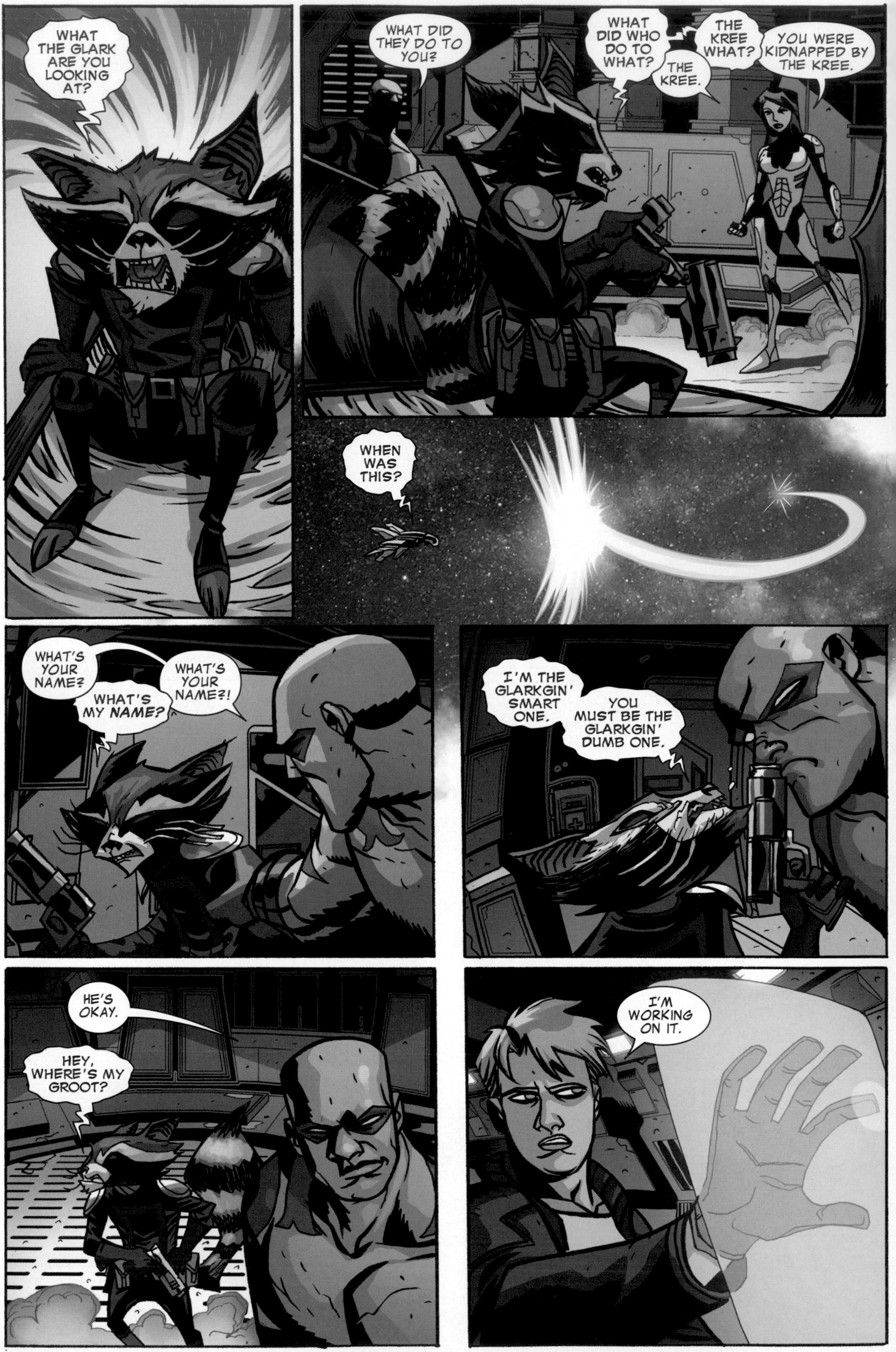

WHAT THE GLARK ARE YOU LOOKING AT?
WHAT DID THEY DO TO YOU?
WHAT DID WHO DO TO WHAT?
THE KREE.
THE KREE WHAT?
YOU WERE KIDNAPPED BY THE KREE.
WHEN WAS THIS?
WHAT'S YOUR NAME?
WHAT'S MY NAME?
WHAT'S YOUR NAME?!
I'M THE GLARKGIN' SMART ONE.
YOU MUST BE THE GLARKGIN' DUMB ONE.
HEY, WHERE'S MY GROOT?
HE'S OKAY.
I'M WORKING ON IT.

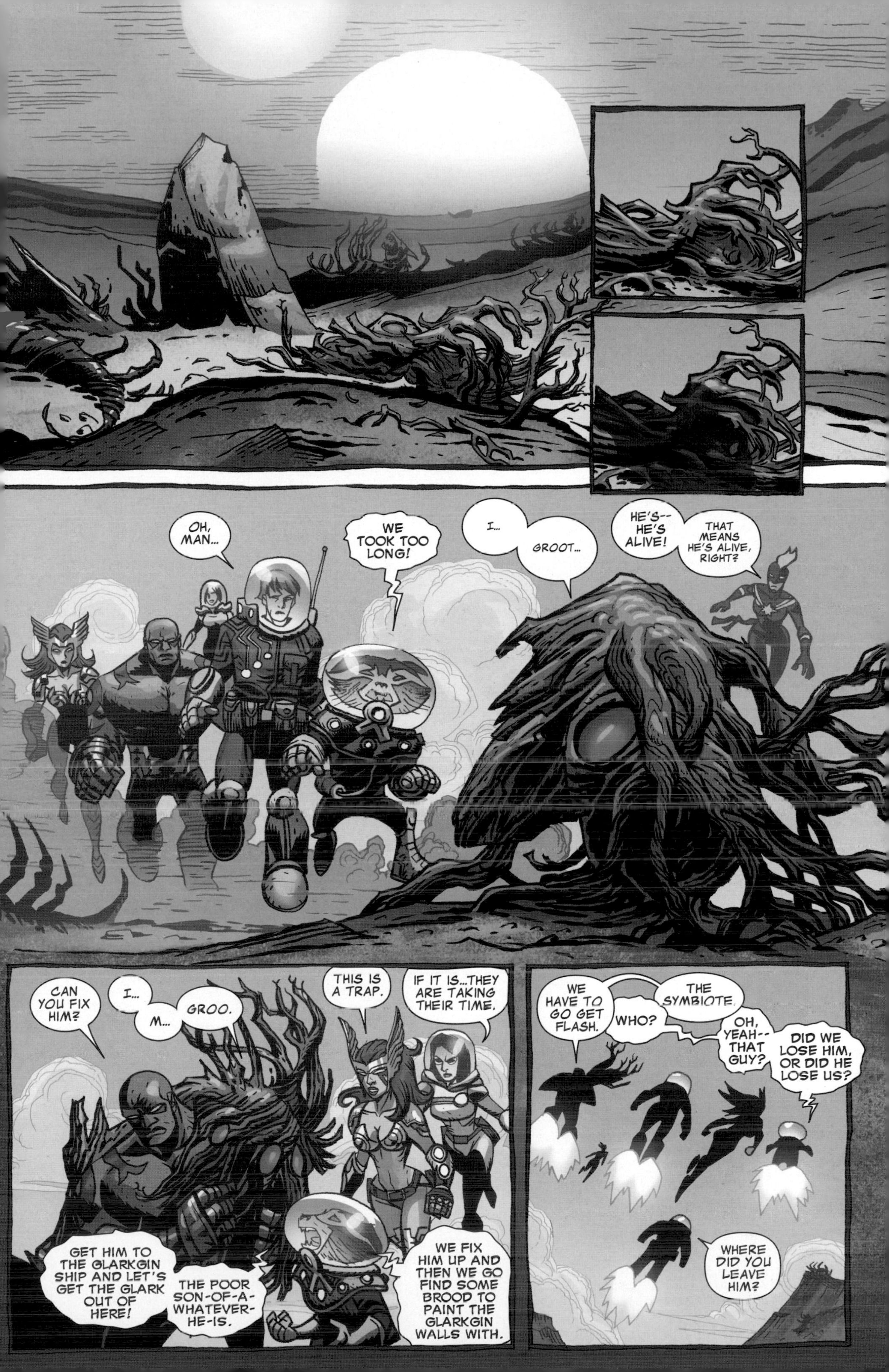

OH, MAN...
WE TOOK TOO LONG!
I...
GROOT...
HE'S-- HE'S ALIVE!
THAT MEANS HE'S ALIVE, RIGHT?
CAN YOU FIX HIM?
I...
M...
GROO.
THIS IS A TRAP.
IF IT IS...THEY ARE TAKING THEIR TIME.
GET HIM TO THE GLARKGIN SHIP AND LET'S GET THE GLARK OUT OF HERE!
THE POOR SON-OF-A-WHATEVER-HE-IS.
WE FIX HIM UP AND THEN WE GO FIND SOME BROOD TO PAINT THE GLARKGIN WALLS WITH.
WE HAVE TO GO GET FLASH.
WHO?
THE SYMBIOTE.
OH, YEAH-- THAT GUY?
DID WE LOSE HIM, OR DID HE LOSE US?
WHERE DID YOU LEAVE HIM?

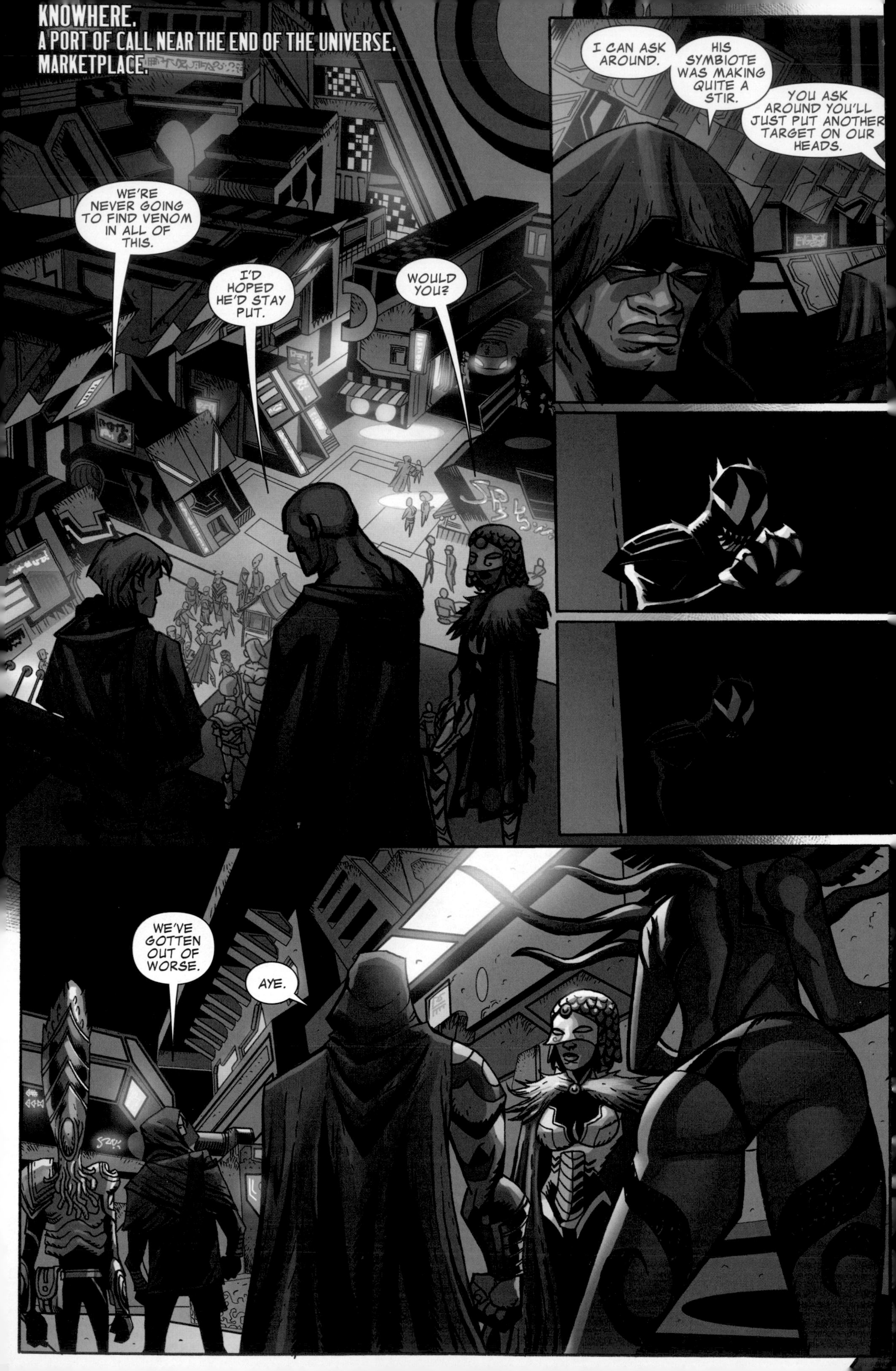
KNOWHERE.
A PORT OF CALL NEAR THE END OF THE UNIVERSE.
MARKETPLACE.
WE'RE NEVER GOING TO FIND VENOM IN ALL OF THIS.
I'D HOPED HE'D STAY PUT.
WOULD YOU?
I CAN ASK AROUND.
HIS SYMBIOTE WAS MAKING QUITE A STIR.
YOU ASK AROUND YOU'LL JUST PUT ANOTHER TARGET ON OUR HEADS.
WE'VE GOTTEN OUT OF WORSE.
AYE.

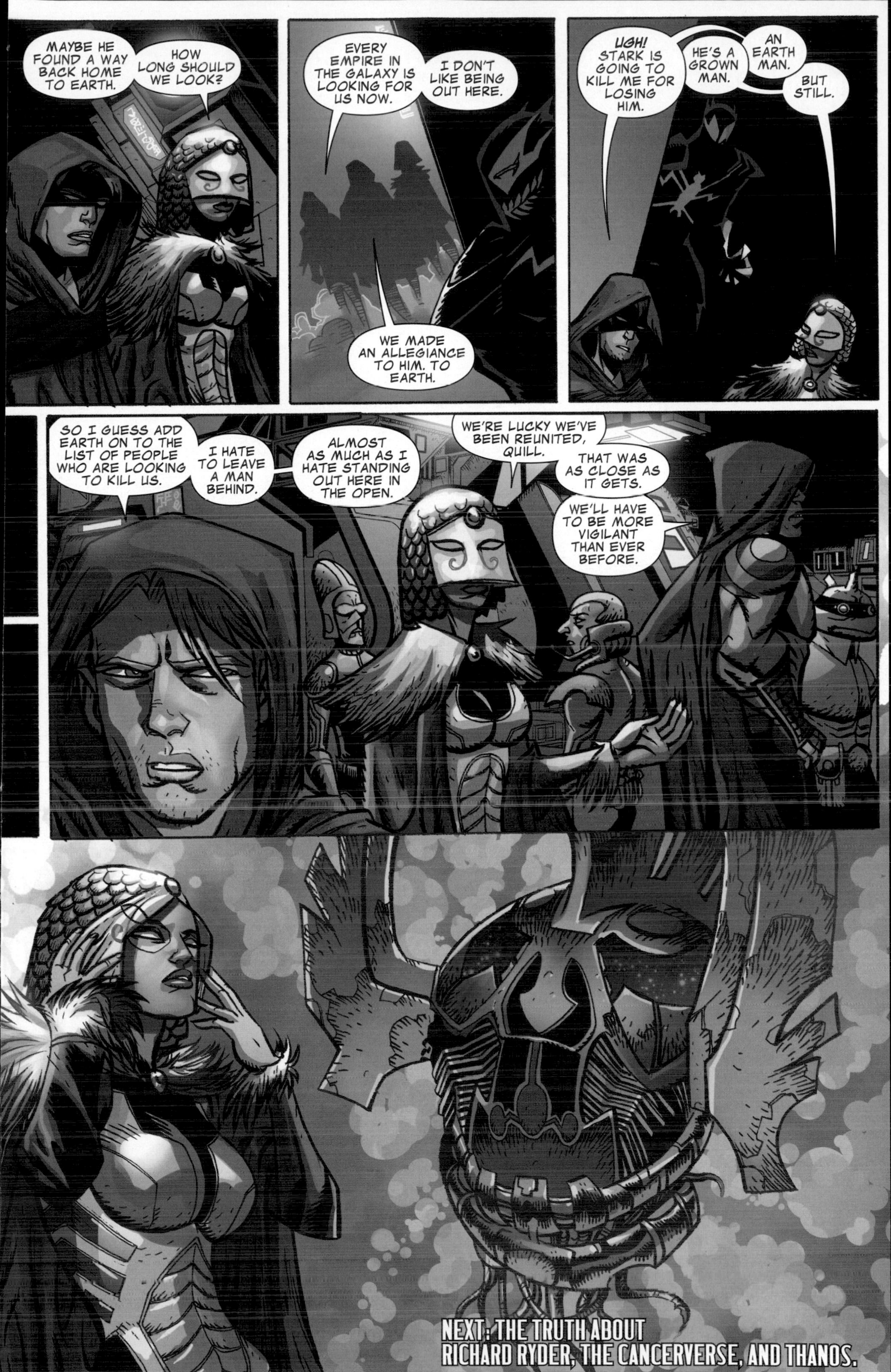
MAYBE HE FOUND A WAY BACK HOME TO EARTH.
HOW LONG SHOULD WE LOOK?
EVERY EMPIRE IN THE GALAXY IS LOOKING FOR US NOW.
I DON'T LIKE BEING OUT HERE.
WE MADE AN ALLEGIANCE TO HIM. TO EARTH.
UGH! STARK IS GOING TO KILL ME FOR LOSING HIM.
HE'S A GROWN MAN.
AN EARTH MAN.
BUT STILL.
SO I GUESS ADD EARTH ON TO THE LIST OF PEOPLE WHO ARE LOOKING TO KILL US.
I HATE TO LEAVE A MAN BEHIND.
ALMOST AS MUCH AS I HATE STANDING OUT HERE IN THE OPEN.
WE'RE LUCKY WE'VE BEEN REUNITED, QUILL.
THAT WAS AS CLOSE AS IT GETS.
WE'LL HAVE TO BE MORE VIGILANT THAN EVER BEFORE.
NEXT: THE TRUTH ABOUT
RICHARD RYDER, THE CANCERVERSE, AND THANOS.

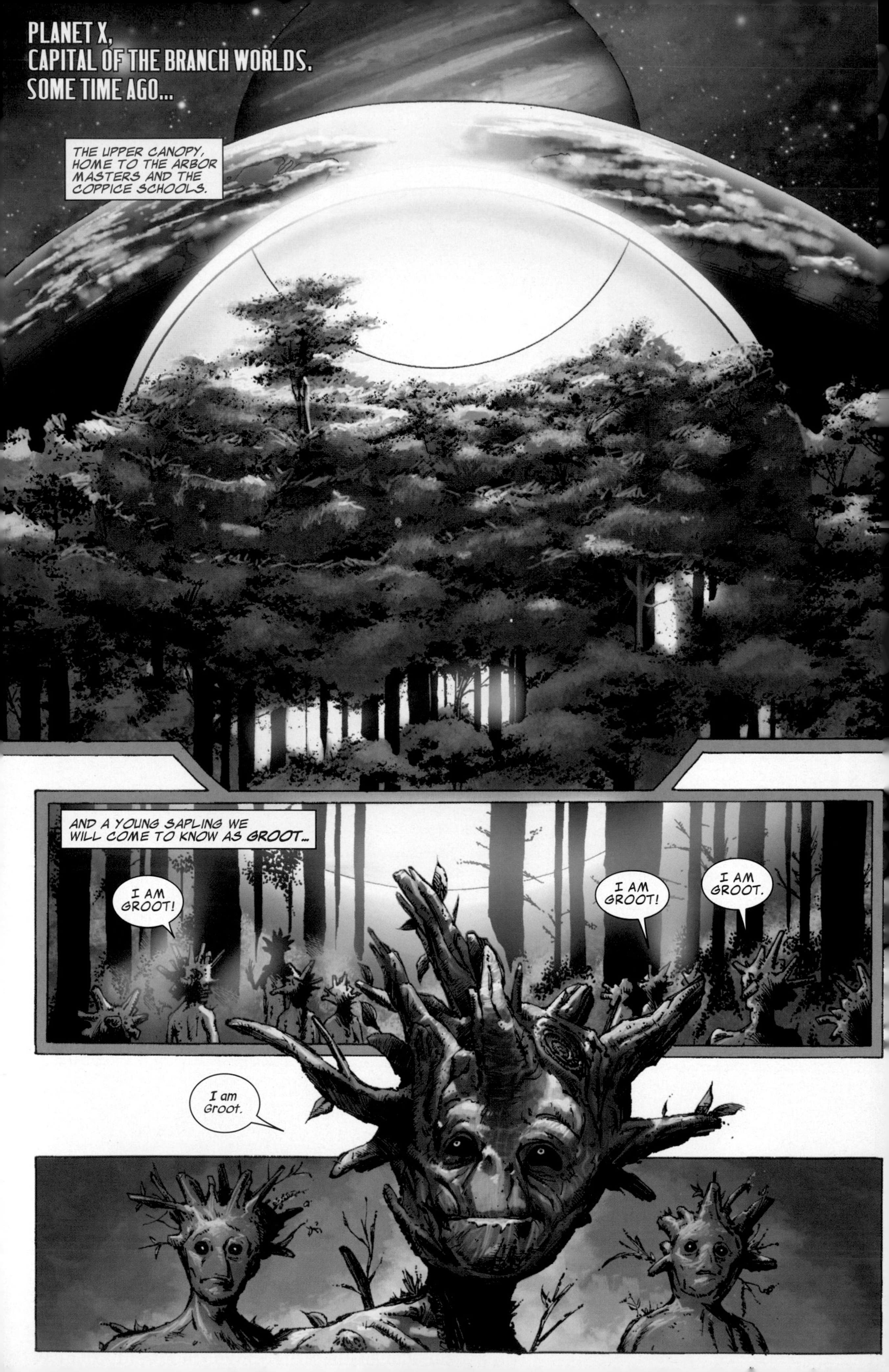
PLANET X,
CAPITAL OF THE BRANCH WORLDS.
SOME TIME AGO...
THE UPPER CANOPY, HOME TO THE ARBOR MASTERS AND THE COPPICE SCHOOLS.
AND A YOUNG SAPLING WE WILL COME TO KNOW AS GROOT...
I AM GROOT!
I AM GROOT!
I AM GROOT.
I am Groot.

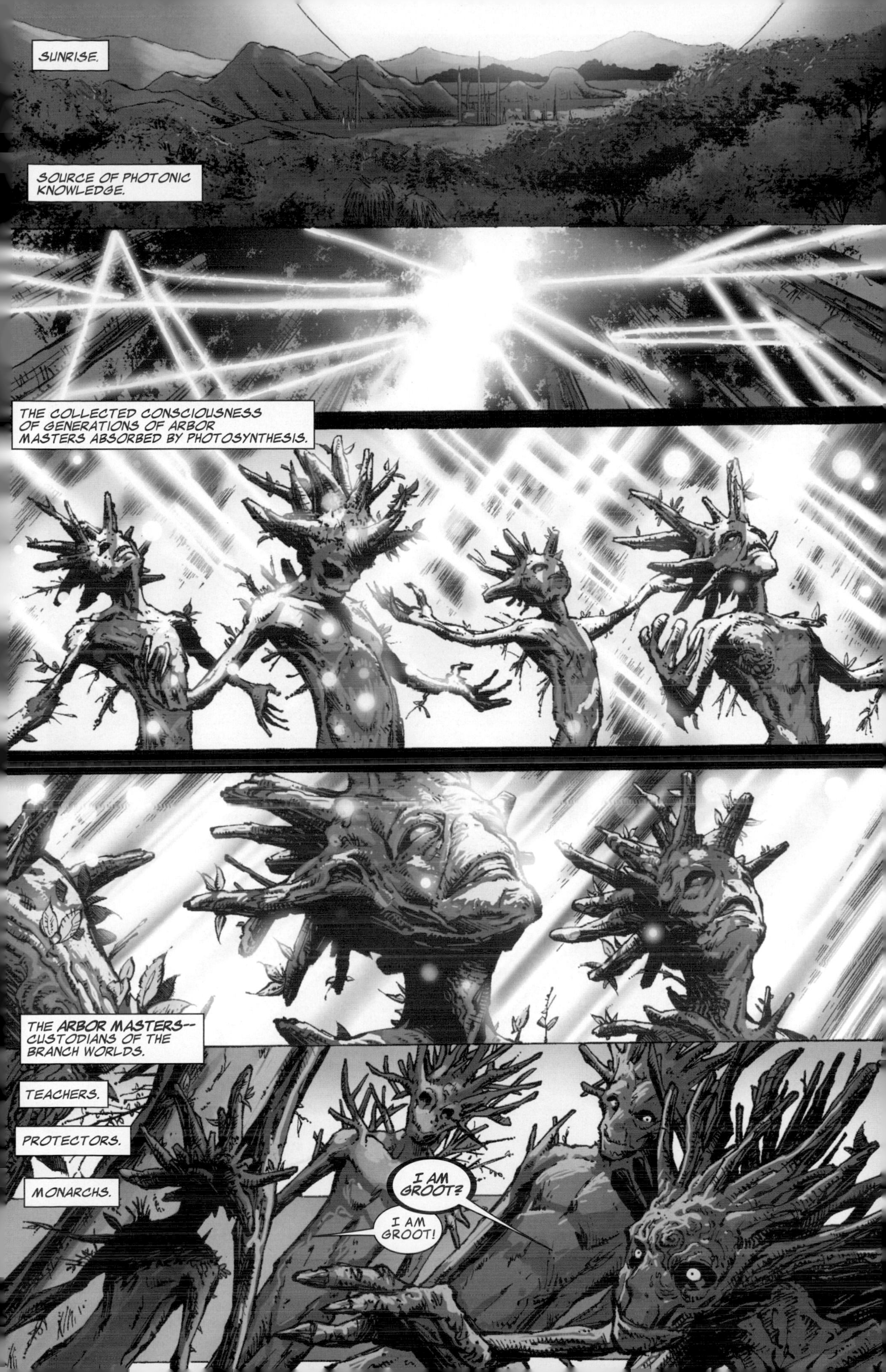
SUNRISE.
SOURCE OF PHOTONIC KNOWLEDGE.
THE COLLECTED CONSCIOUSNESS OF GENERATIONS OF ARBOR MASTERS ABSORBED BY PHOTOSYNTHESIS.
THE ARBOR MASTERS-- CUSTODIANS OF THE BRANCH WORLDS.
TEACHERS.
PROTECTORS.
MONARCHS.
I AM GROOT?
I AM GROOT!

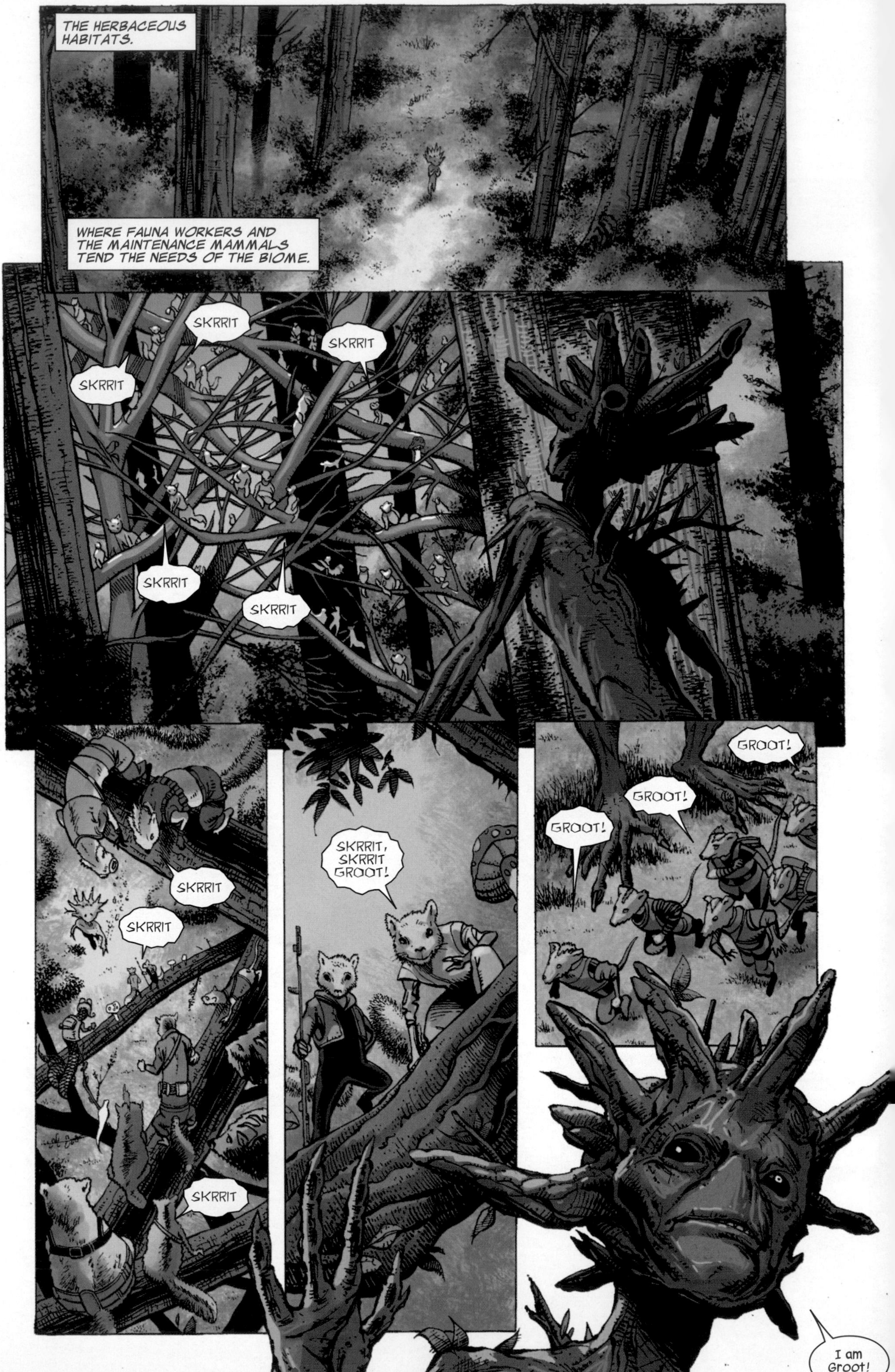
THE HERBACEOUS HABITATS.
WHERE FAUNA WORKERS AND THE MAINTENANCE MAMMALS TEND THE NEEDS OF THE BIOME.
SKRRIT
SKRRIT
SKRRIT
SKRRIT
SKRRIT
SKRRIT
SKRRIT
SKRRIT
SKRRIT
SKRRIT, SKRRIT GROOT!
GROOT!
GROOT!
GROOT!
I am Groot!

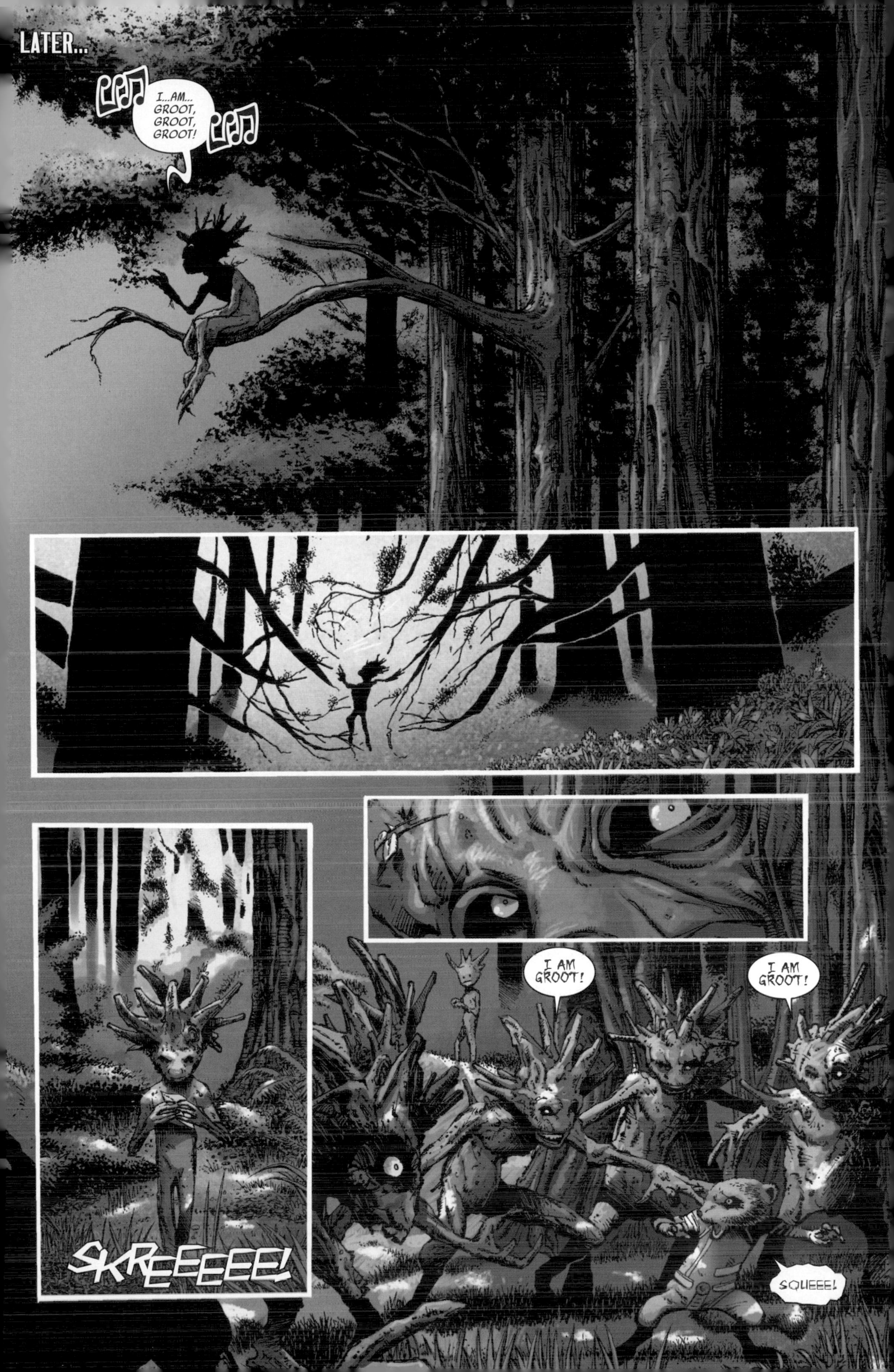
LATER...
I...AM... GROOT, GROOT, GROOT!
I AM GROOT!
I AM GROOT!
SKREEEEEE!
SQUEEE!

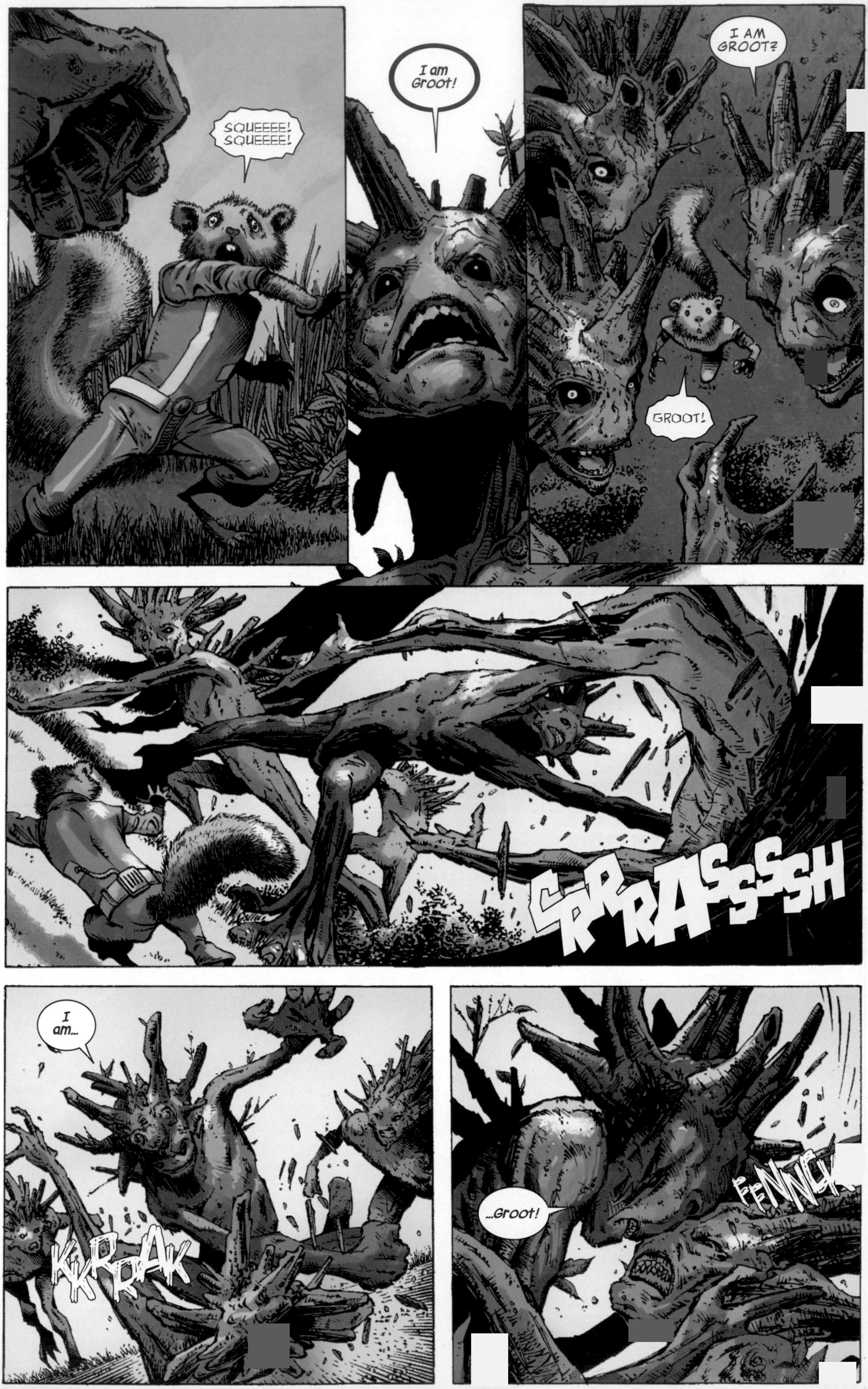
SQUEEEE! SQUEEEE!
I am Groot!
I AM GROOT?
GROOT!
CRRRASSSSH
I am...
KRRAK
...Groot!
FFNNG

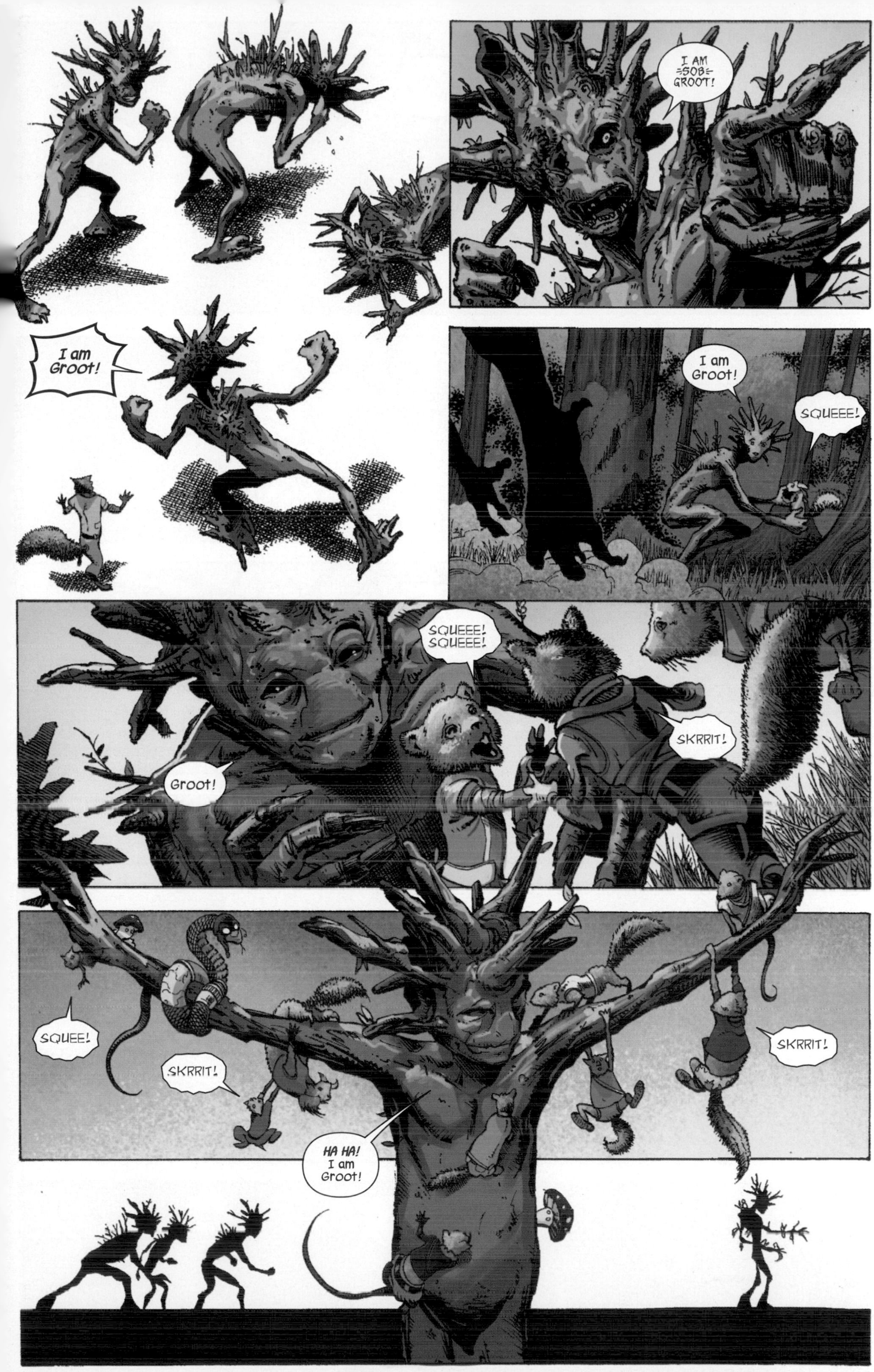
I AM SOB GROOT!
I am Groot!
I am Groot!
SQUEEE!
SQUEEE! SQUEEE!
SKRRIT!
Groot!
SQUEE!
SKRRIT!
SKRRIT!
HA HA! I am Groot!

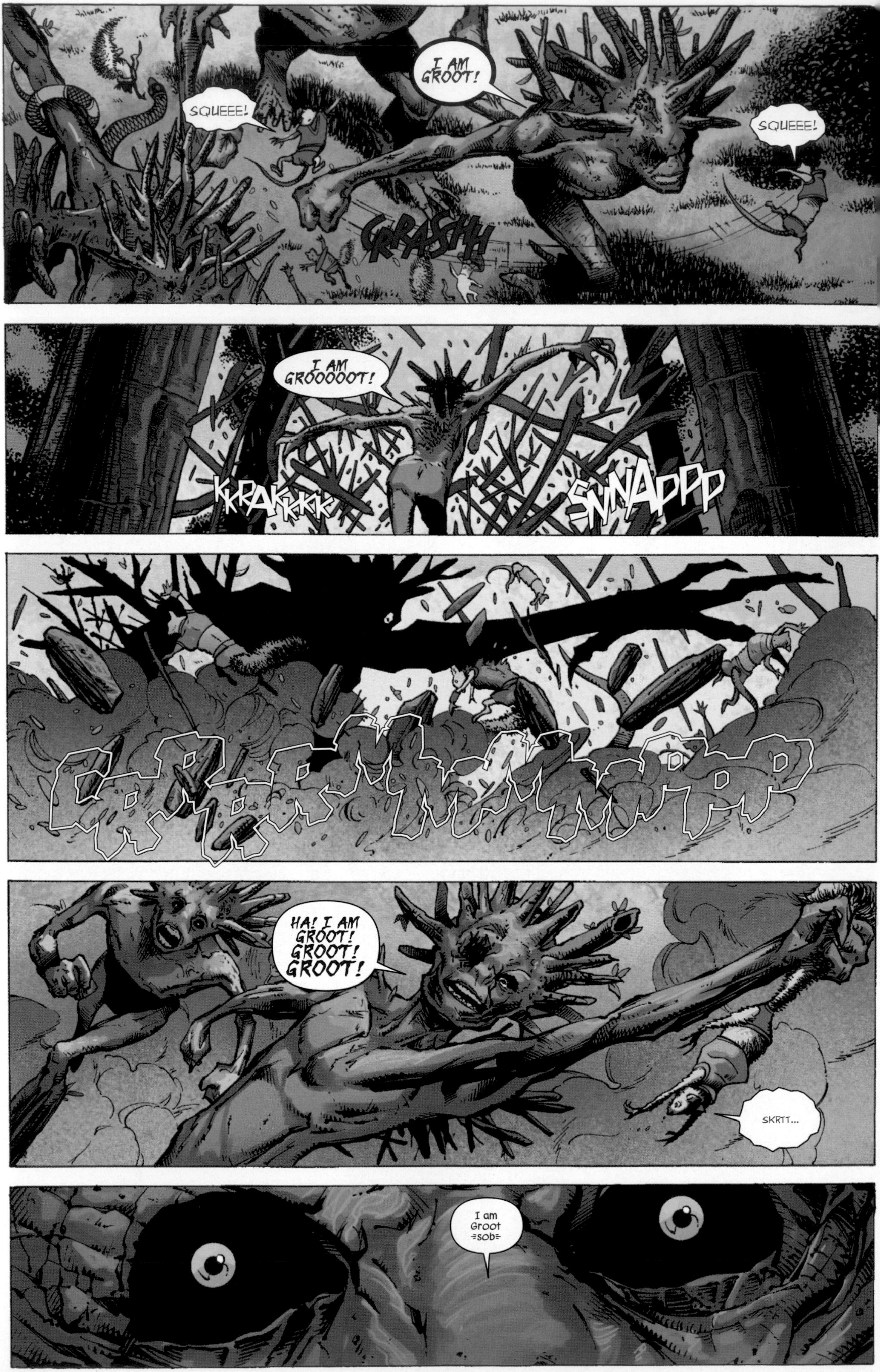
SQUEEE!
I AM GROOT!
SQUEEE!
CRASHH
I AM GROOOOOT!
KKRAKKKKK
SNNAPPP
HA! I AM GROOT! GROOT! GROOT!
SKRTT...
I am Groot
=sob=

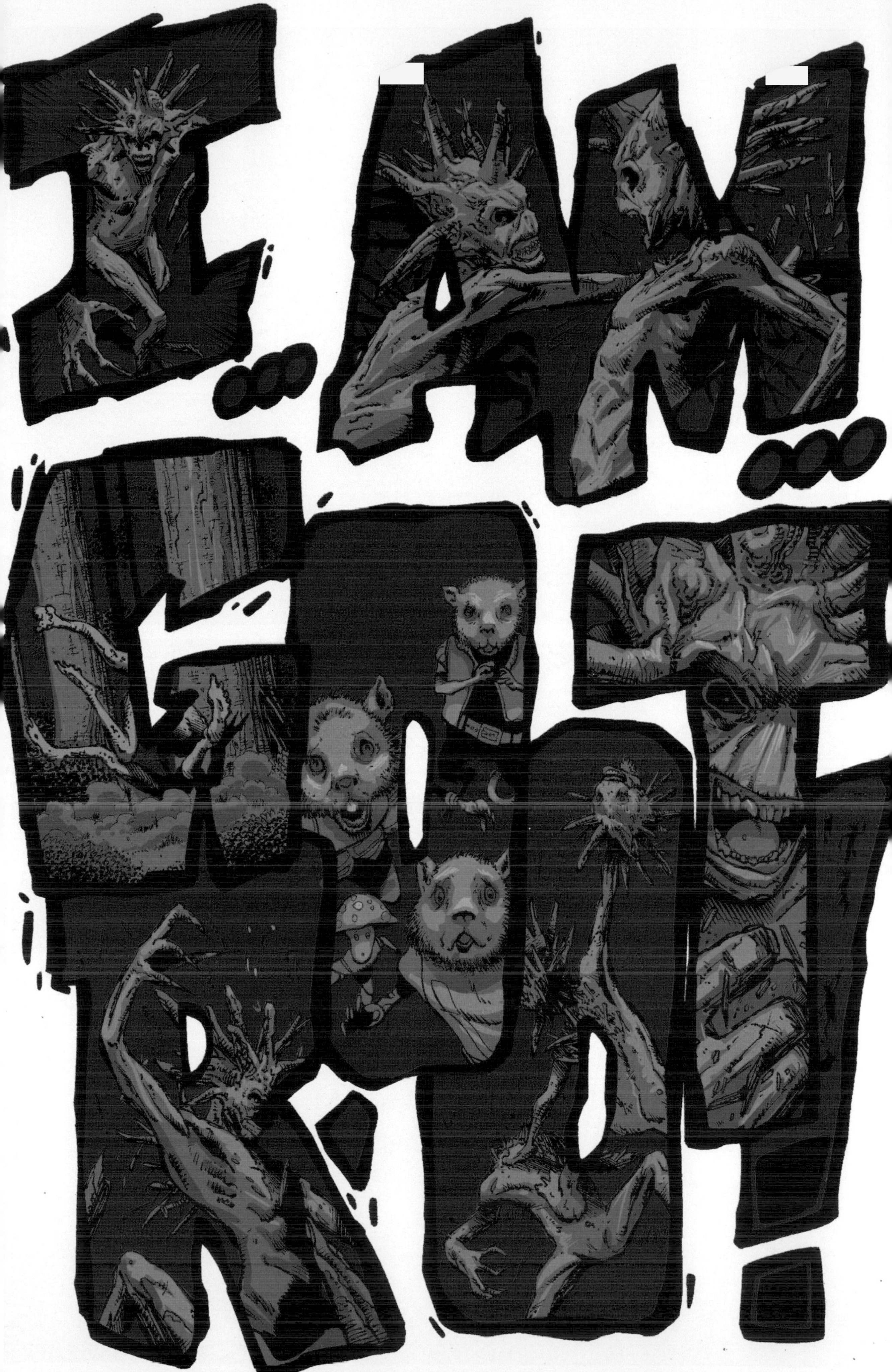
I... AM... GROOT!

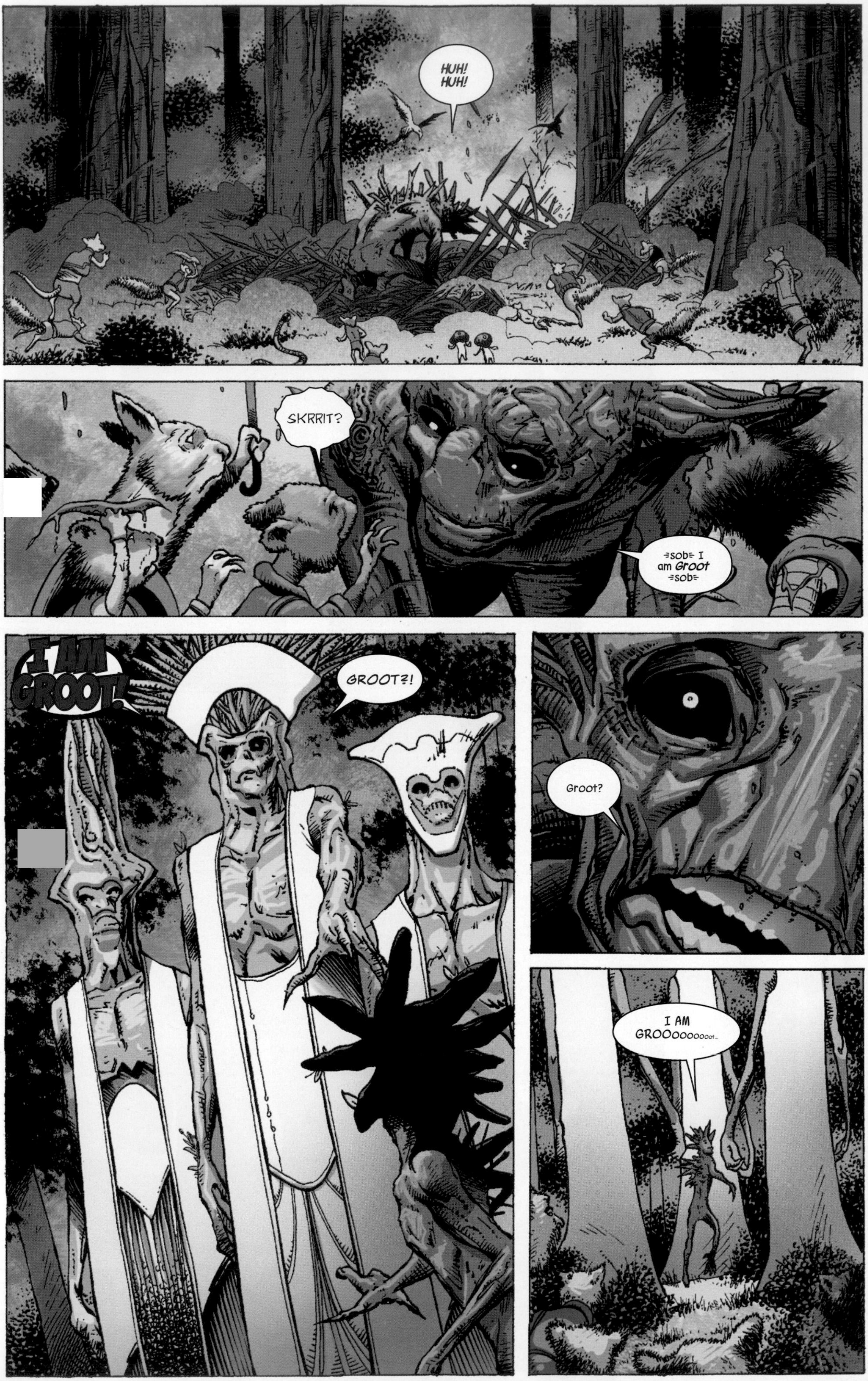
HUH! HUH!
SKRRIT?
=sob= I am Groot =sob=
I AM GROOT!
GROOT?!
Groot?
I AM GROOoooooooot...

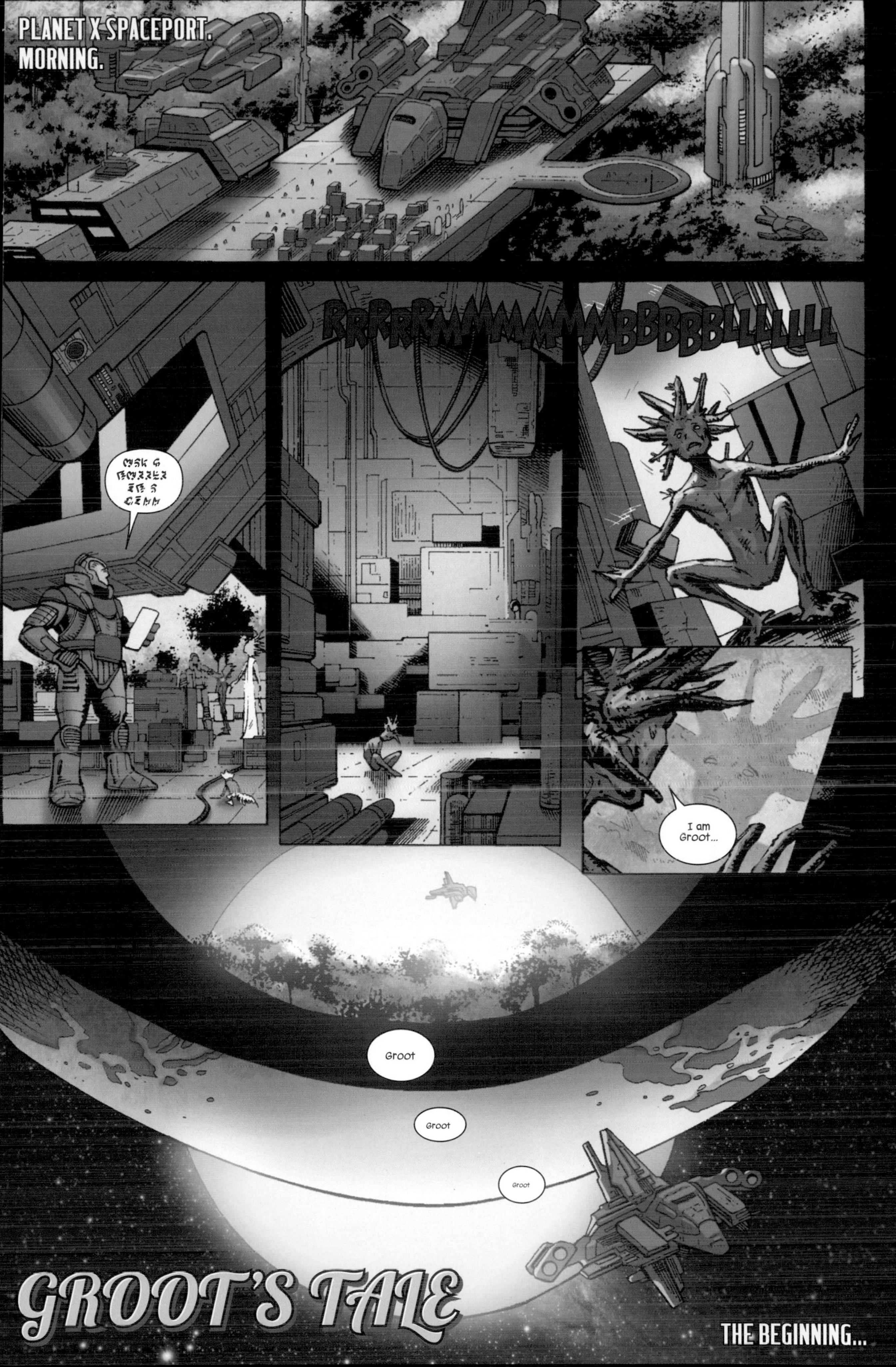
PLANET X SPACEPORT. MORNING.
RRRRRMMMMMMMMMBBBBBLLLLLL
I am Groot...
Groot
Groot
Groot
GROOT'S TALE
THE BEGINNING...

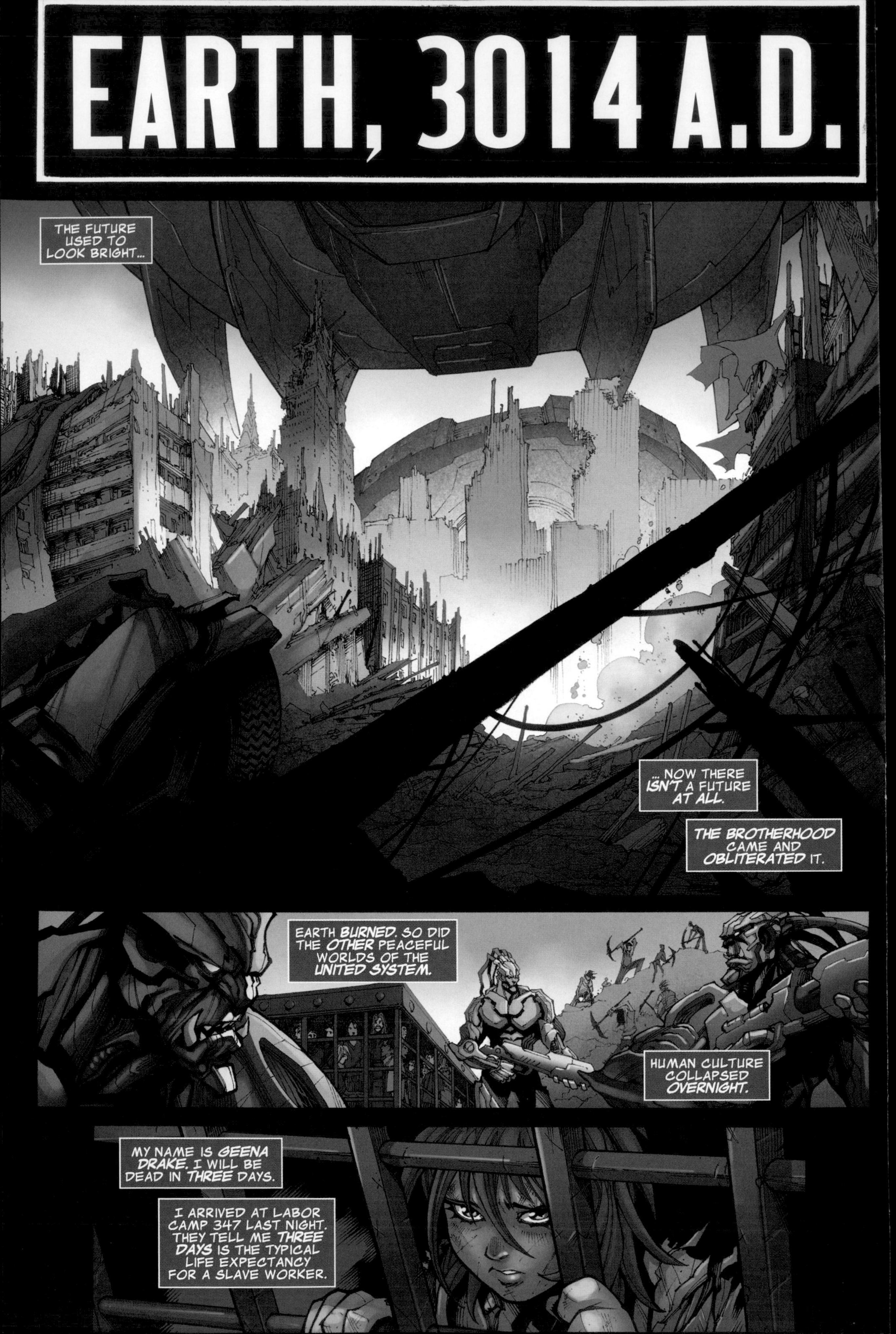

EARTH, 3014 A.D.
THE FUTURE USED TO LOOK BRIGHT...
...NOW THERE ISN'T A FUTURE AT ALL.
THE BROTHERHOOD CAME AND OBLITERATED IT.
EARTH BURNED. SO DID THE OTHER PEACEFUL WORLDS OF THE UNITED SYSTEM.
HUMAN CULTURE COLLAPSED OVERNIGHT.
MY NAME IS GEENA DRAKE. I WILL BE DEAD IN THREE DAYS.
I ARRIVED AT LABOR CAMP 347 LAST NIGHT. THEY TELL ME THREE DAYS IS THE TYPICAL LIFE EXPECTANCY FOR A SLAVE WORKER.

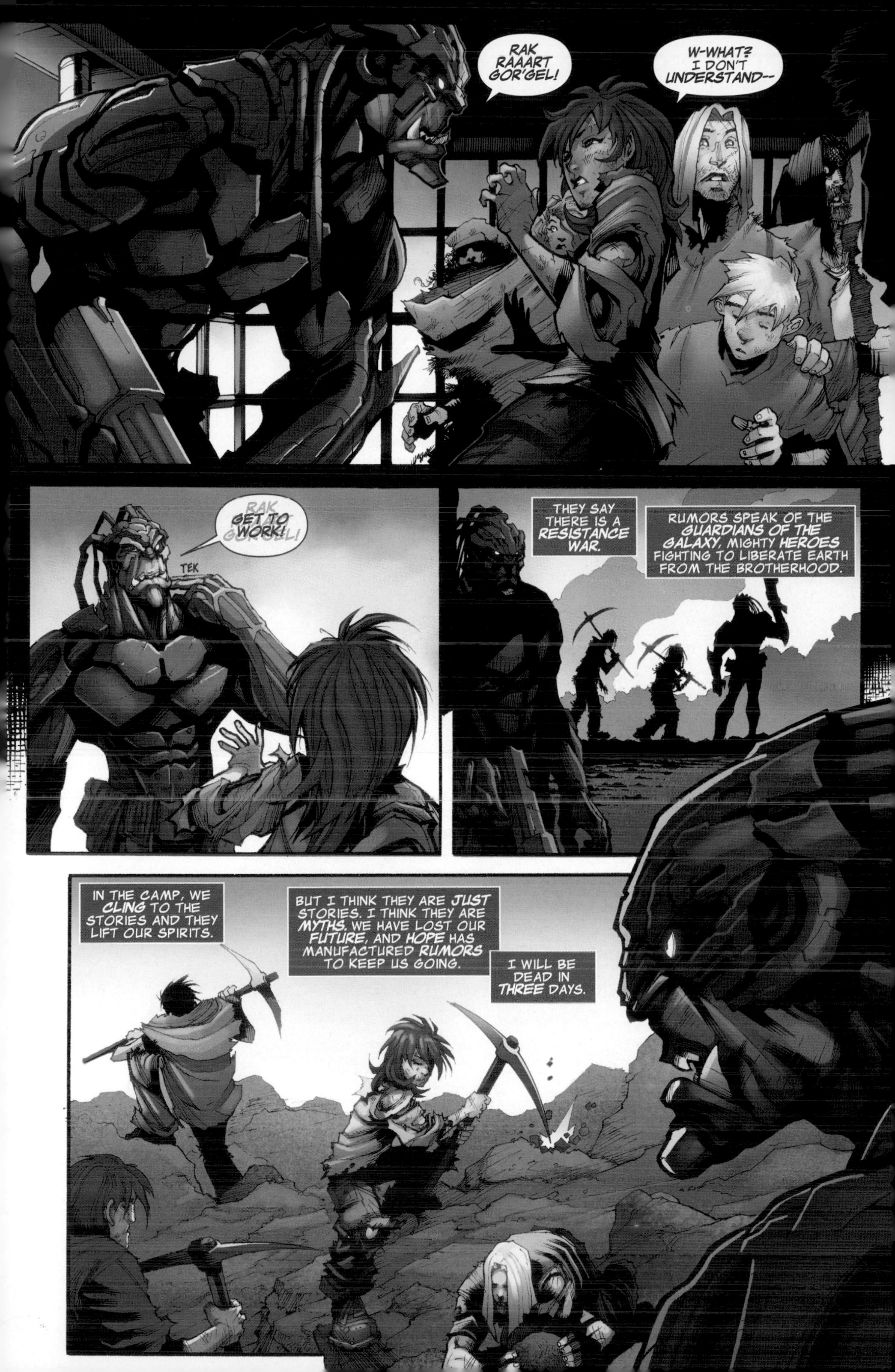
RAK RAAART GOR'GEL!
W-WHAT? I DON'T UNDERSTAND--
GET TO WORK!
TEK
THEY SAY THERE IS A RESISTANCE WAR.
RUMORS SPEAK OF THE GUARDIANS OF THE GALAXY, MIGHTY HEROES FIGHTING TO LIBERATE EARTH FROM THE BROTHERHOOD.
IN THE CAMP, WE CLING TO THE STORIES AND THEY LIFT OUR SPIRITS.
BUT I THINK THEY ARE JUST STORIES. I THINK THEY ARE MYTHS. WE HAVE LOST OUR FUTURE, AND HOPE HAS MANUFACTURED RUMORS TO KEEP US GOING.
I WILL BE DEAD IN THREE DAYS.

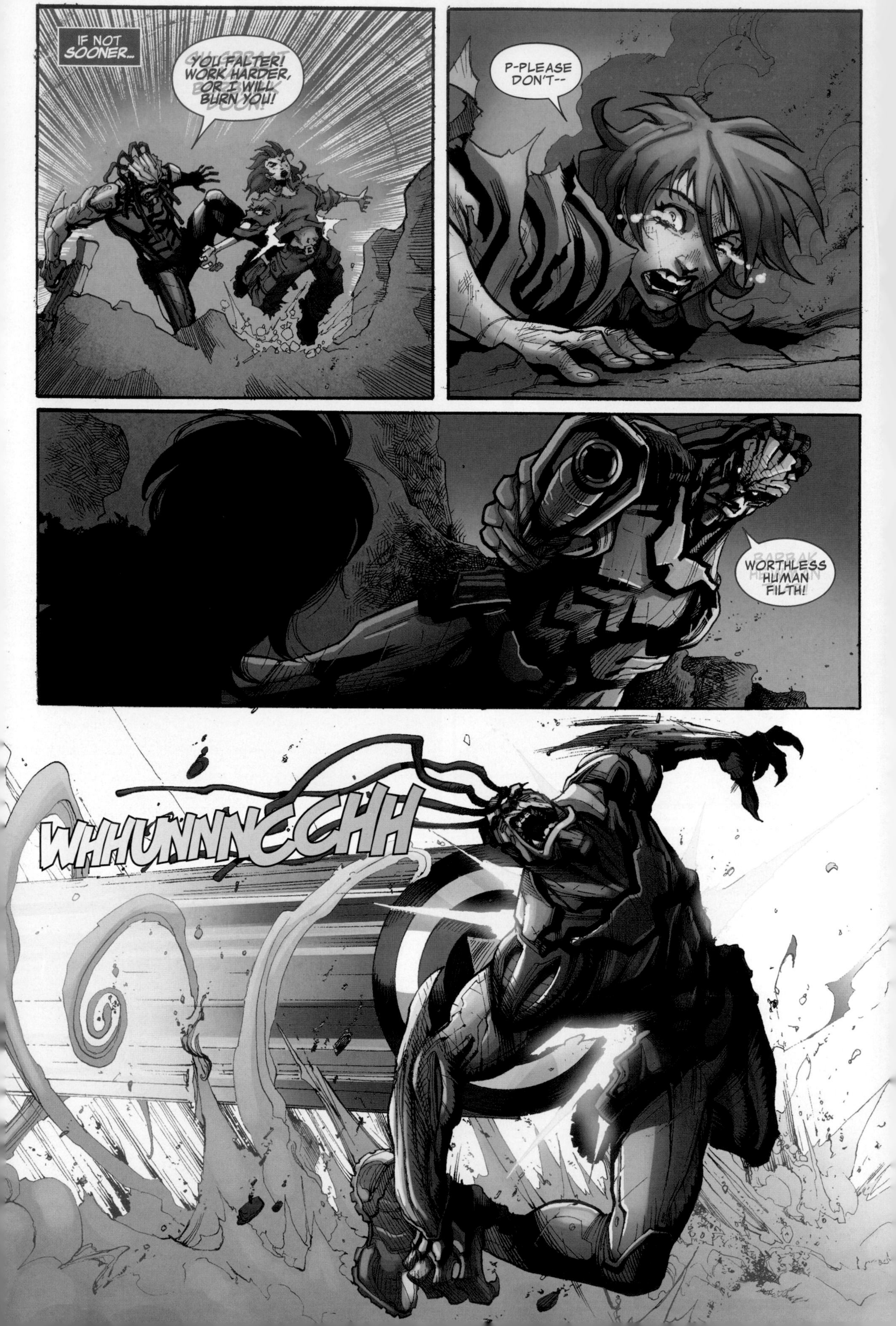
IF NOT SOONER...
YOU FALTER! WORK HARDER, OR I WILL BURN YOU!
P-PLEASE DON'T--
WORTHLESS HUMAN FILTH!
WHHUNNNCCHH

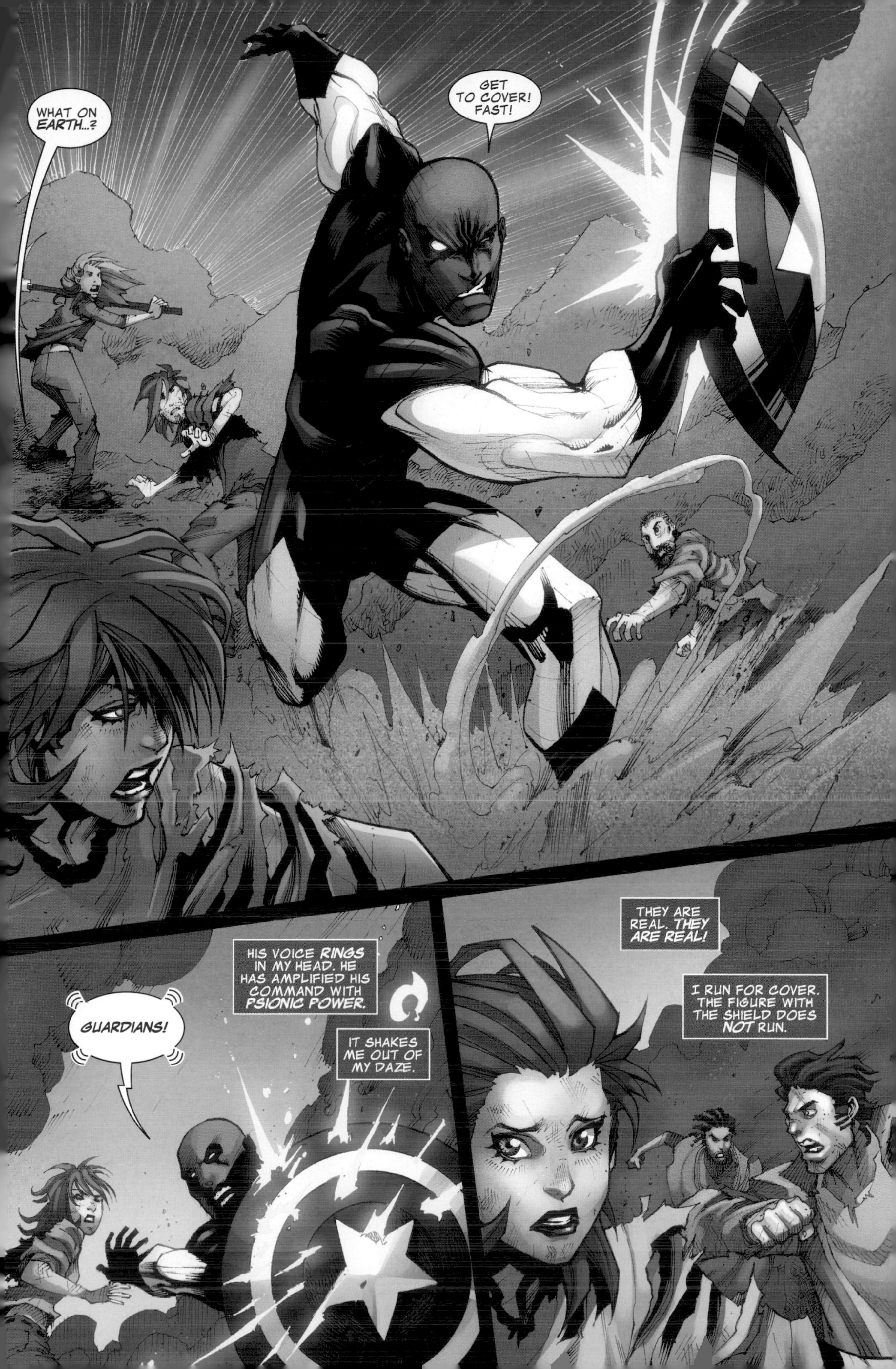
WHAT ON EARTH...?
GET TO COVER! FAST!
GUARDIANS!
HIS VOICE RINGS IN MY HEAD. HE HAS AMPLIFIED HIS COMMAND WITH PSIONIC POWER.
IT SHAKES ME OUT OF MY DAZE.
THEY ARE REAL. THEY ARE REAL!
I RUN FOR COVER. THE FIGURE WITH THE SHIELD DOES NOT RUN.

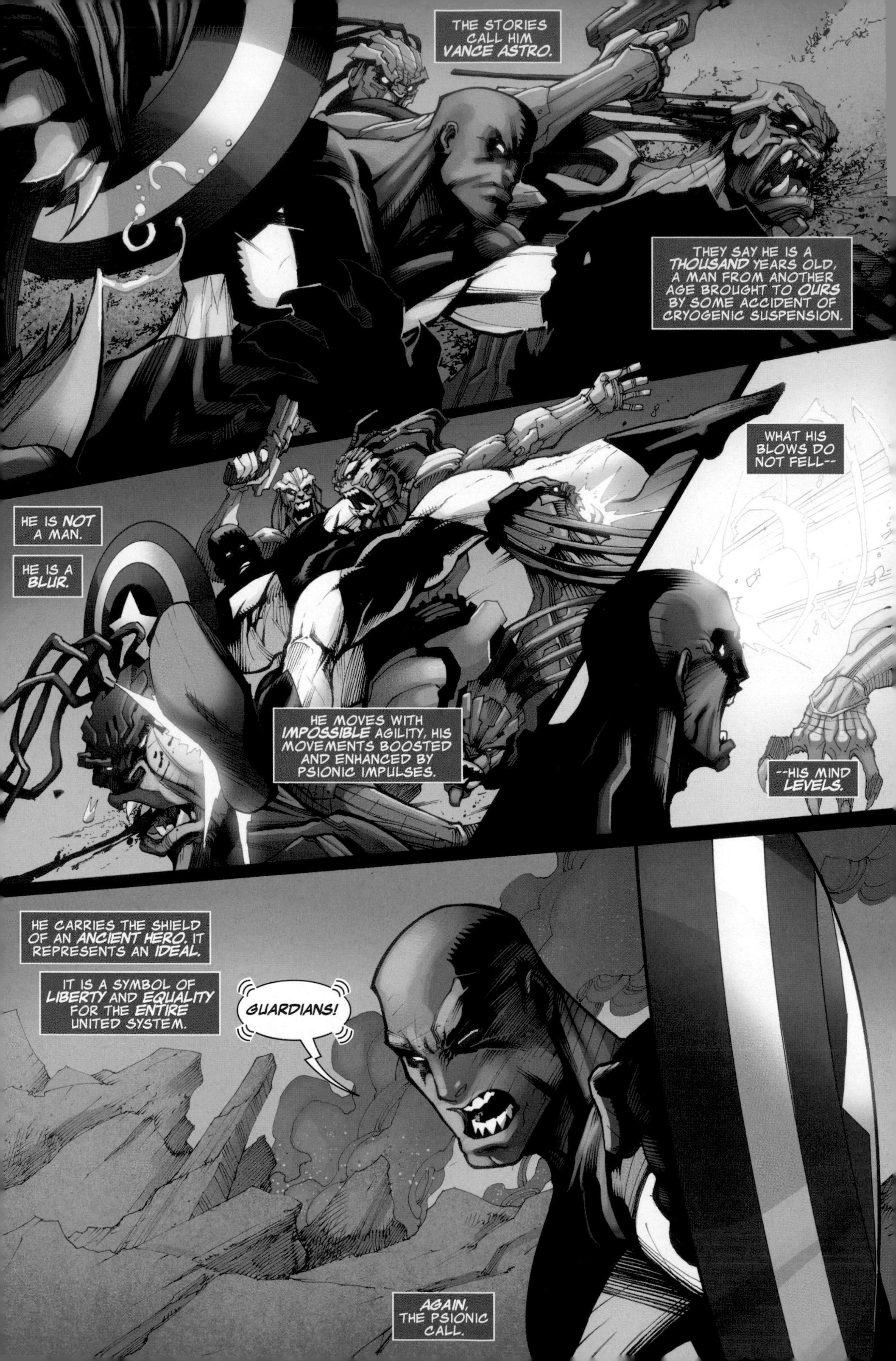
THE STORIES CALL HIM VANCE ASTRO.
THEY SAY HE IS A THOUSAND YEARS OLD, A MAN FROM ANOTHER AGE BROUGHT TO OURS BY SOME ACCIDENT OF CRYOGENIC SUSPENSION.
HE IS NOT A MAN.
HE IS A BLUR.
HE MOVES WITH IMPOSSIBLE AGILITY, HIS MOVEMENTS BOOSTED AND ENHANCED BY PSIONIC IMPULSES.
WHAT HIS BLOWS DO NOT FELL--
--HIS MIND LEVELS.
HE CARRIES THE SHIELD OF AN ANCIENT HERO. IT REPRESENTS AN IDEAL.
IT IS A SYMBOL OF LIBERTY AND EQUALITY FOR THE ENTIRE UNITED SYSTEM.
GUARDIANS!
AGAIN, THE PSIONIC CALL.

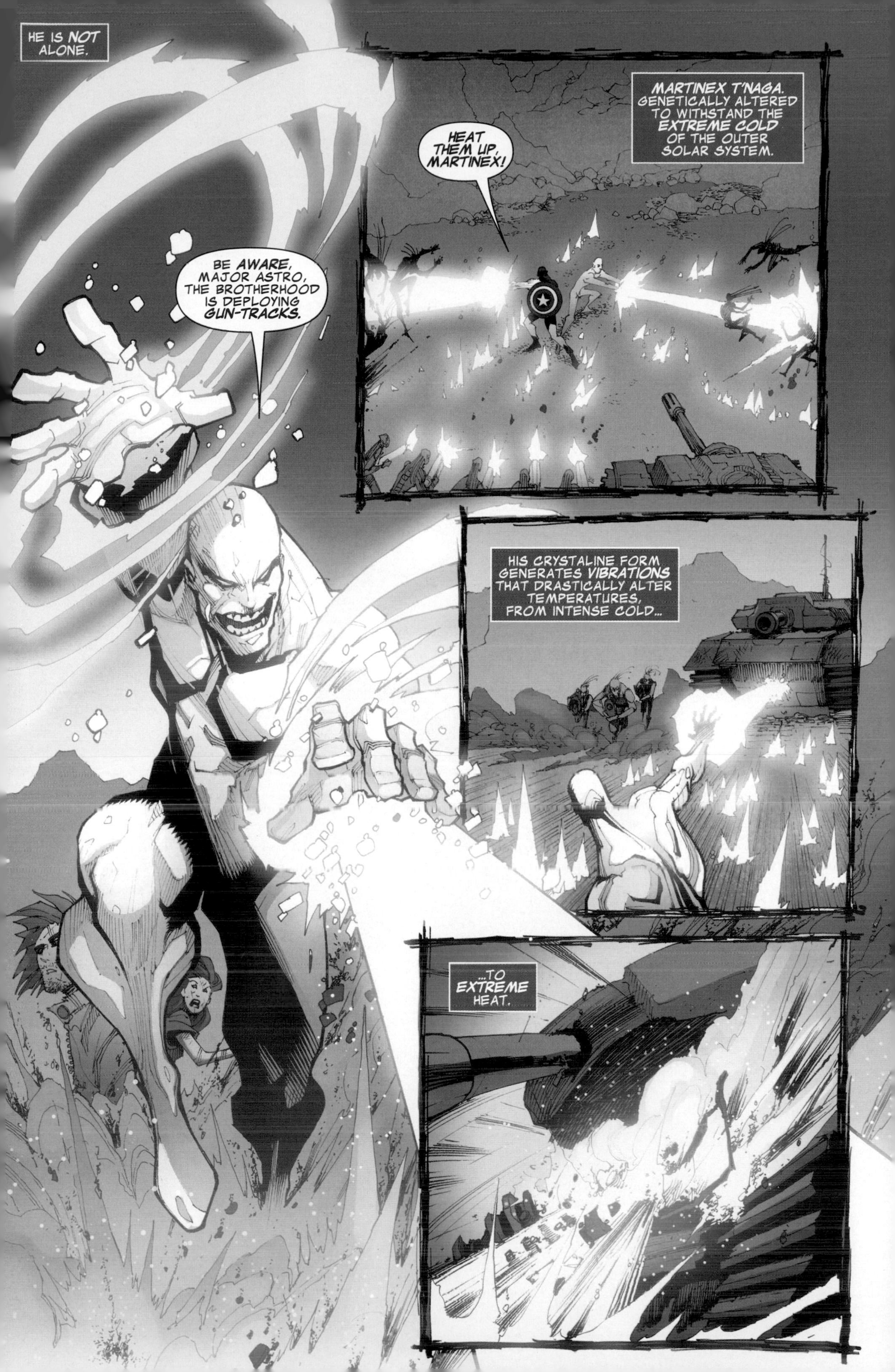
HE IS NOT ALONE.
MARTINEX T'NAGA. GENETICALLY ALTERED TO WITHSTAND THE EXTREME COLD OF THE OUTER SOLAR SYSTEM.
HEAT THEM UP, MARTINEX!
BE AWARE, MAJOR ASTRO, THE BROTHERHOOD IS DEPLOYING GUN-TRACKS.
HIS CRYSTALINE FORM GENERATES VIBRATIONS THAT DRASTICALLY ALTER TEMPERATURES, FROM INTENSE COLD...
...TO EXTREME HEAT.

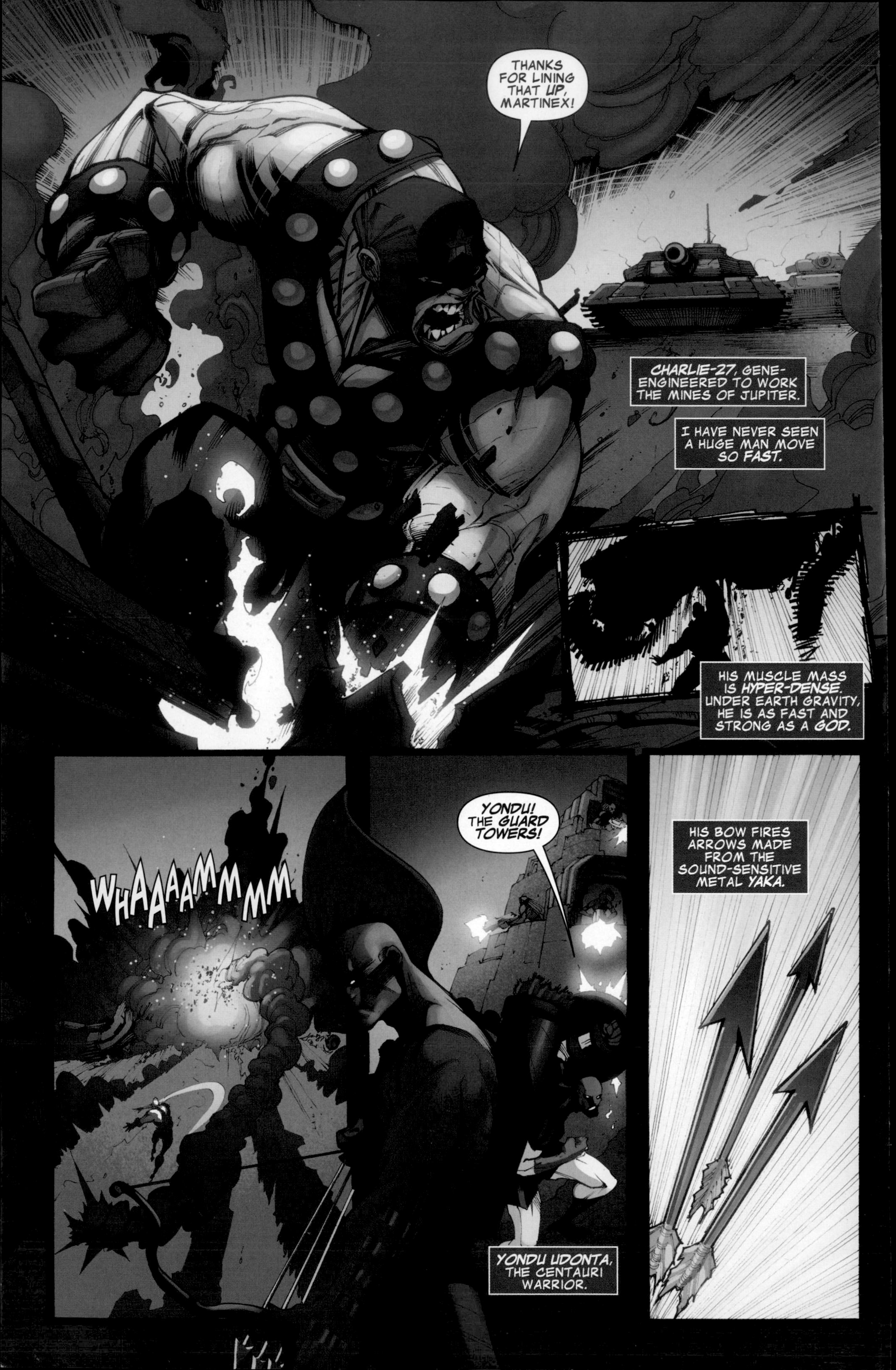
THANKS FOR LINING THAT UP, MARTINEX!
CHARLIE-27, GENE-ENGINEERED TO WORK THE MINES OF JUPITER.
I HAVE NEVER SEEN A HUGE MAN MOVE SO FAST.
HIS MUSCLE MASS IS HYPER-DENSE. UNDER EARTH GRAVITY, HE IS AS FAST AND STRONG AS A GOD.
WHAAAAMMMMM
YONDU! THE GUARD TOWERS!
YONDU UDONTA, THE CENTAURI WARRIOR.
HIS BOW FIRES ARROWS MADE FROM THE SOUND-SENSITIVE METAL YAKA.

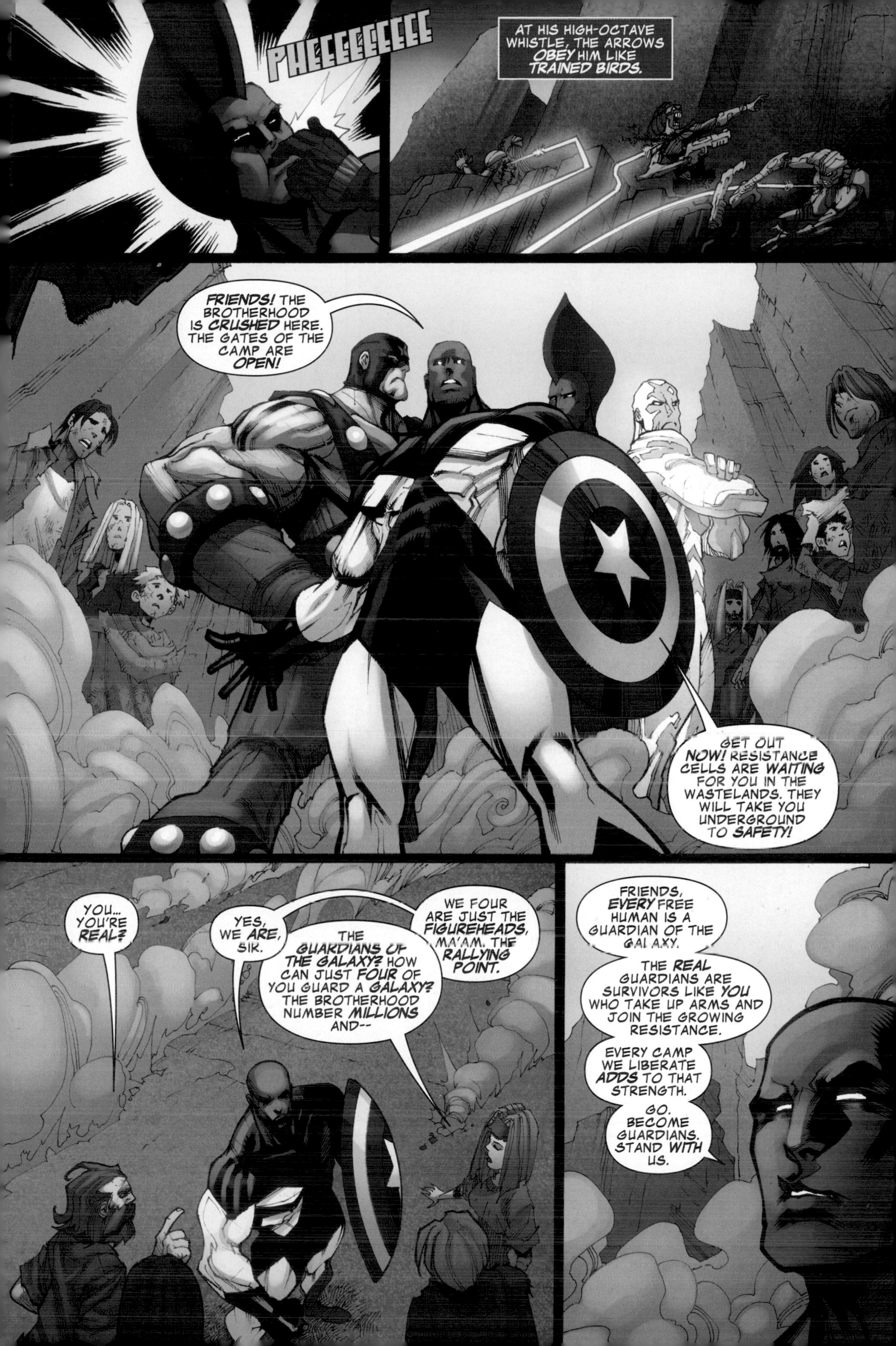
PHEEEEEEEEEE
AT HIS HIGH-OCTAVE WHISTLE, THE ARROWS OBEY HIM LIKE TRAINED BIRDS.
FRIENDS! THE BROTHERHOOD IS CRUSHED HERE. THE GATES OF THE CAMP ARE OPEN!
GET OUT NOW! RESISTANCE CELLS ARE WAITING FOR YOU IN THE WASTELANDS. THEY WILL TAKE YOU UNDERGROUND TO SAFETY!
YOU... YOU'RE REAL?
YES, WE ARE, SIR.
THE GUARDIANS OF THE GALAXY? HOW CAN JUST FOUR OF YOU GUARD A GALAXY? THE BROTHERHOOD NUMBER MILLIONS AND--
WE FOUR ARE JUST THE FIGUREHEADS, MA'AM. THE RALLYING POINT.
FRIENDS, EVERY FREE HUMAN IS A GUARDIAN OF THE GALAXY.
THE REAL GUARDIANS ARE SURVIVORS LIKE YOU WHO TAKE UP ARMS AND JOIN THE GROWING RESISTANCE.
EVERY CAMP WE LIBERATE ADDS TO THAT STRENGTH.
GO. BECOME GUARDIANS. STAND WITH US.

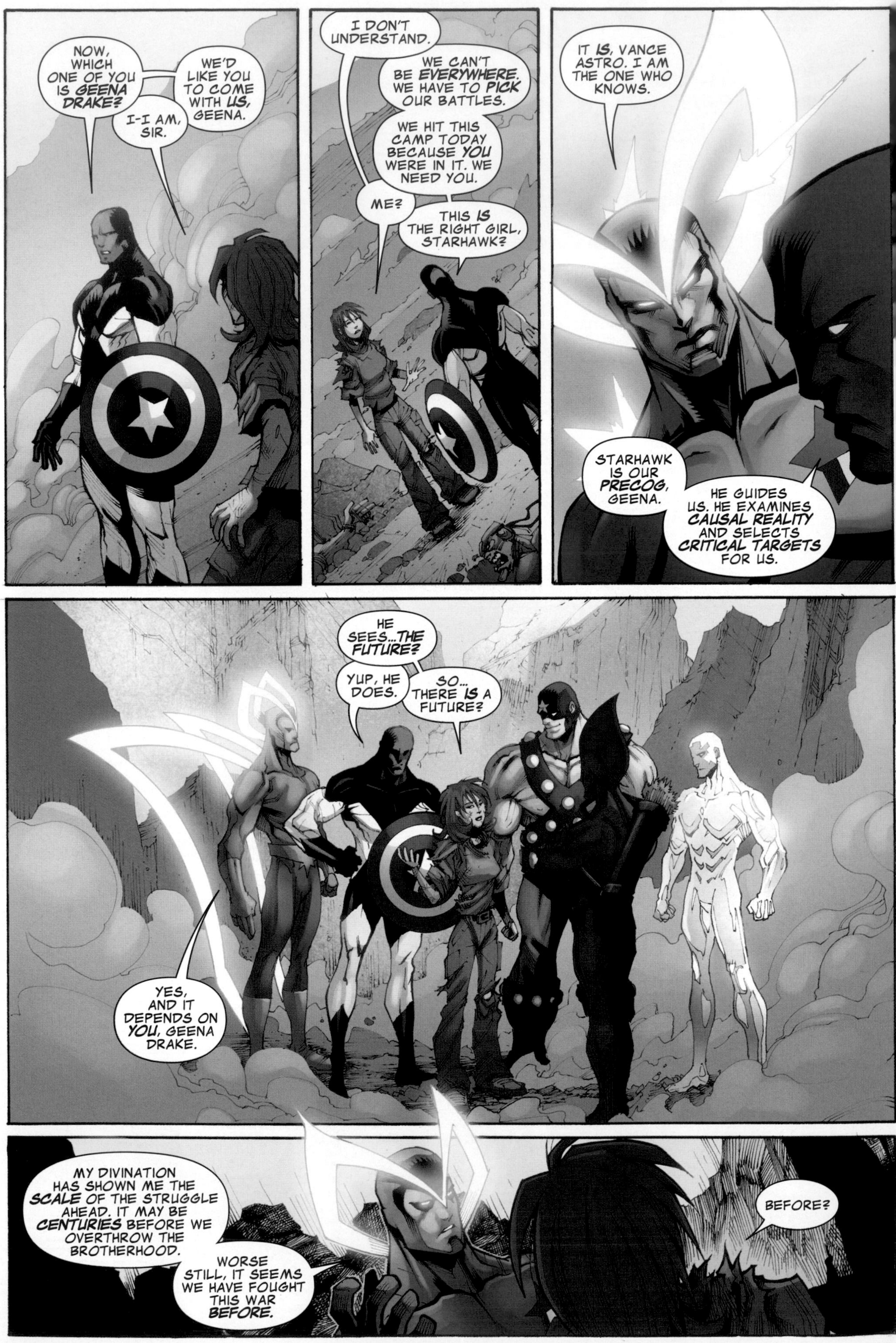
NOW, WHICH ONE OF YOU IS GEENA DRAKE?
WE'D LIKE YOU TO COME WITH US, GEENA.
I-I AM, SIR.
I DON'T UNDERSTAND.
WE CAN'T BE EVERYWHERE. WE HAVE TO PICK OUR BATTLES.
WE HIT THIS CAMP TODAY BECAUSE YOU WERE IN IT. WE NEED YOU.
ME?
THIS IS THE RIGHT GIRL, STARHAWK?
IT IS, VANCE ASTRO. I AM THE ONE WHO KNOWS.
STARHAWK IS OUR PRECOG, GEENA.
HE GUIDES US. HE EXAMINES CAUSAL REALITY AND SELECTS CRITICAL TARGETS FOR US.
HE SEES...THE FUTURE?
YUP, HE DOES.
SO... THERE IS A FUTURE?
YES, AND IT DEPENDS ON YOU, GEENA DRAKE.
MY DIVINATION HAS SHOWN ME THE SCALE OF THE STRUGGLE AHEAD. IT MAY BE CENTURIES BEFORE WE OVERTHROW THE BROTHERHOOD.
WORSE STILL, IT SEEMS WE HAVE FOUGHT THIS WAR BEFORE.
BEFORE?

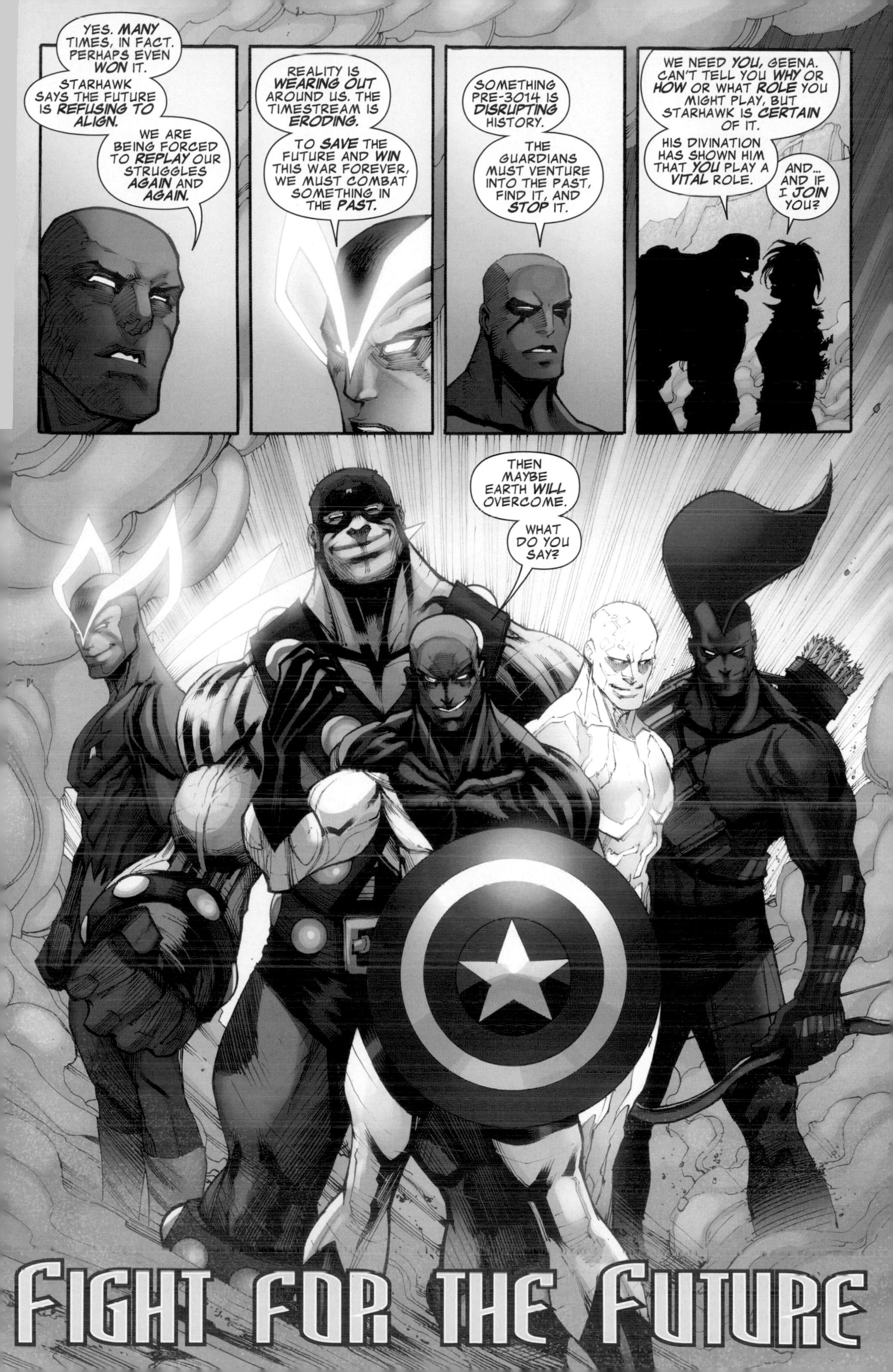
YES. MANY TIMES, IN FACT. PERHAPS EVEN WON IT.
STARHAWK SAYS THE FUTURE IS REFUSING TO ALIGN.
WE ARE BEING FORCED TO REPLAY OUR STRUGGLES AGAIN AND AGAIN.
REALITY IS WEARING OUT AROUND US. THE TIMESTREAM IS ERODING.
TO SAVE THE FUTURE AND WIN THIS WAR FOREVER, WE MUST COMBAT SOMETHING IN THE PAST.
SOMETHING PRE-3014 IS DISRUPTING HISTORY.
THE GUARDIANS MUST VENTURE INTO THE PAST, FIND IT, AND STOP IT.
WE NEED YOU, GEENA. CAN'T TELL YOU WHY OR HOW OR WHAT ROLE YOU MIGHT PLAY, BUT STARHAWK IS CERTAIN OF IT.
HIS DIVINATION HAS SHOWN HIM THAT YOU PLAY A VITAL ROLE.
AND... AND IF I JOIN YOU?
THEN MAYBE EARTH WILL OVERCOME.
WHAT DO YOU SAY?
FIGHT FOR THE FUTURE

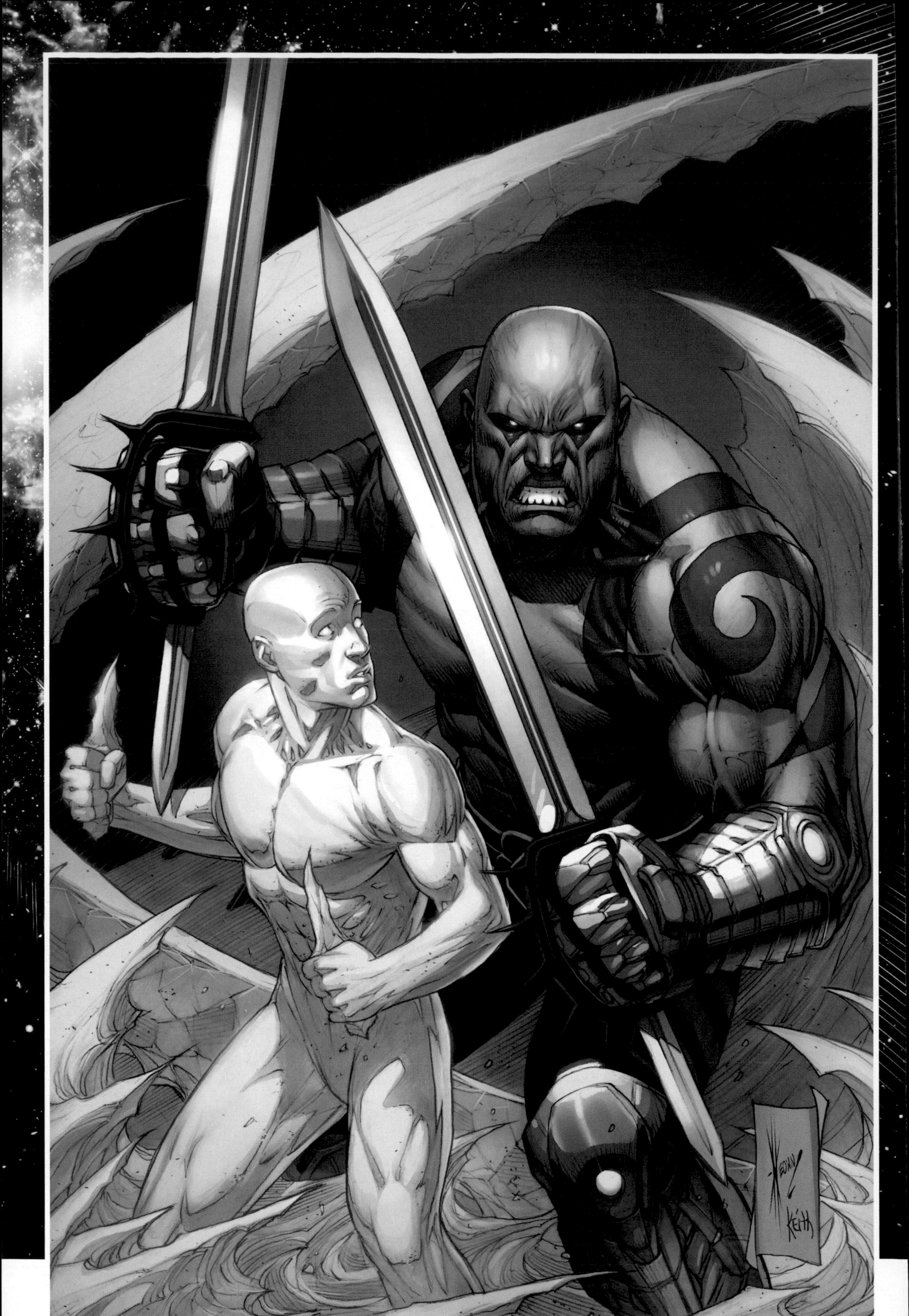
KEOWN
KEITH

***ALL-NEW X-MEN* #22 VARIANT**
BY DALE KEOWN & JASON KEITH

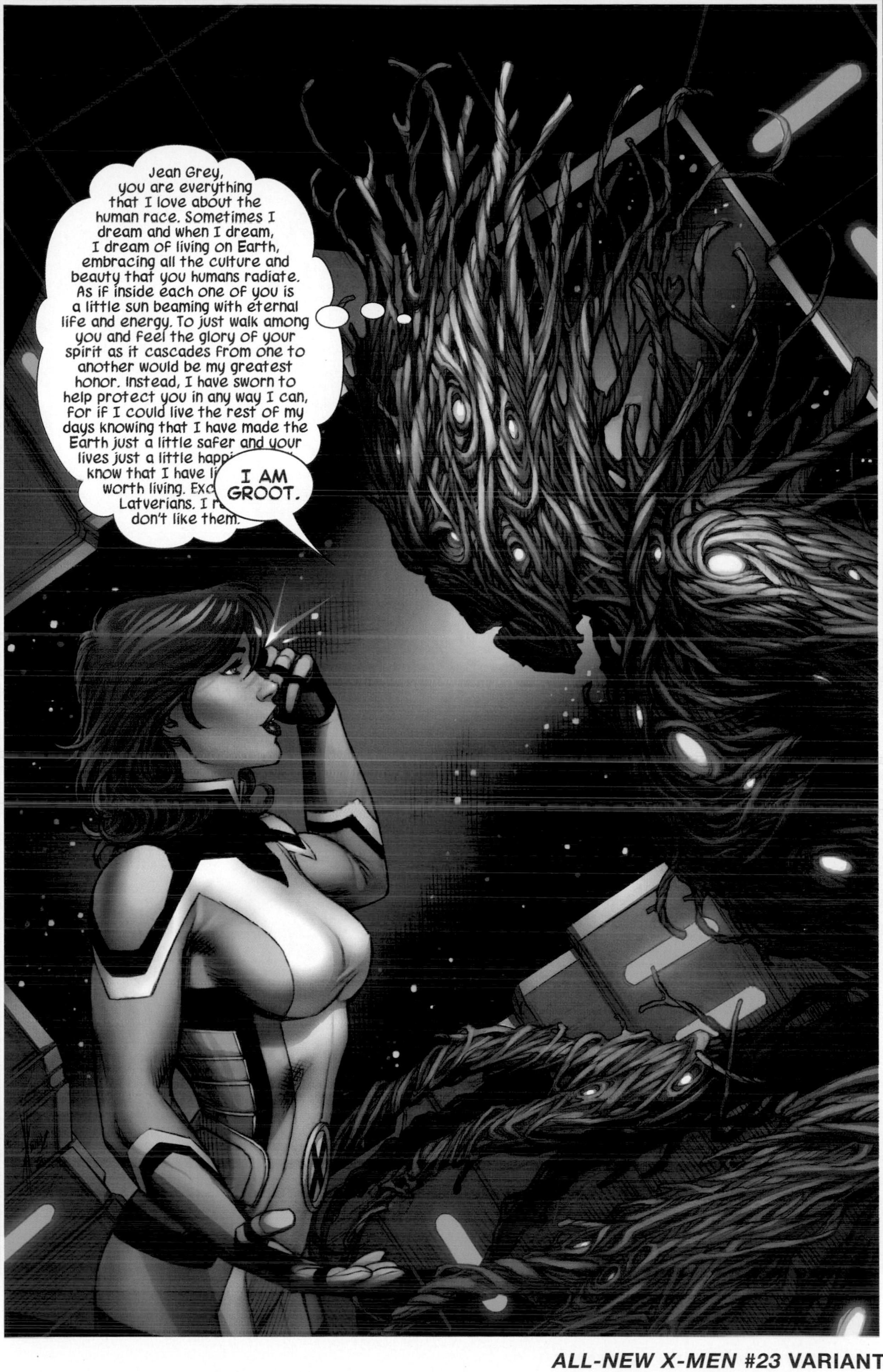

***ALL-NEW X-MEN* #23 VARIANT**
BY DALE KEOWN & JASON KEITH

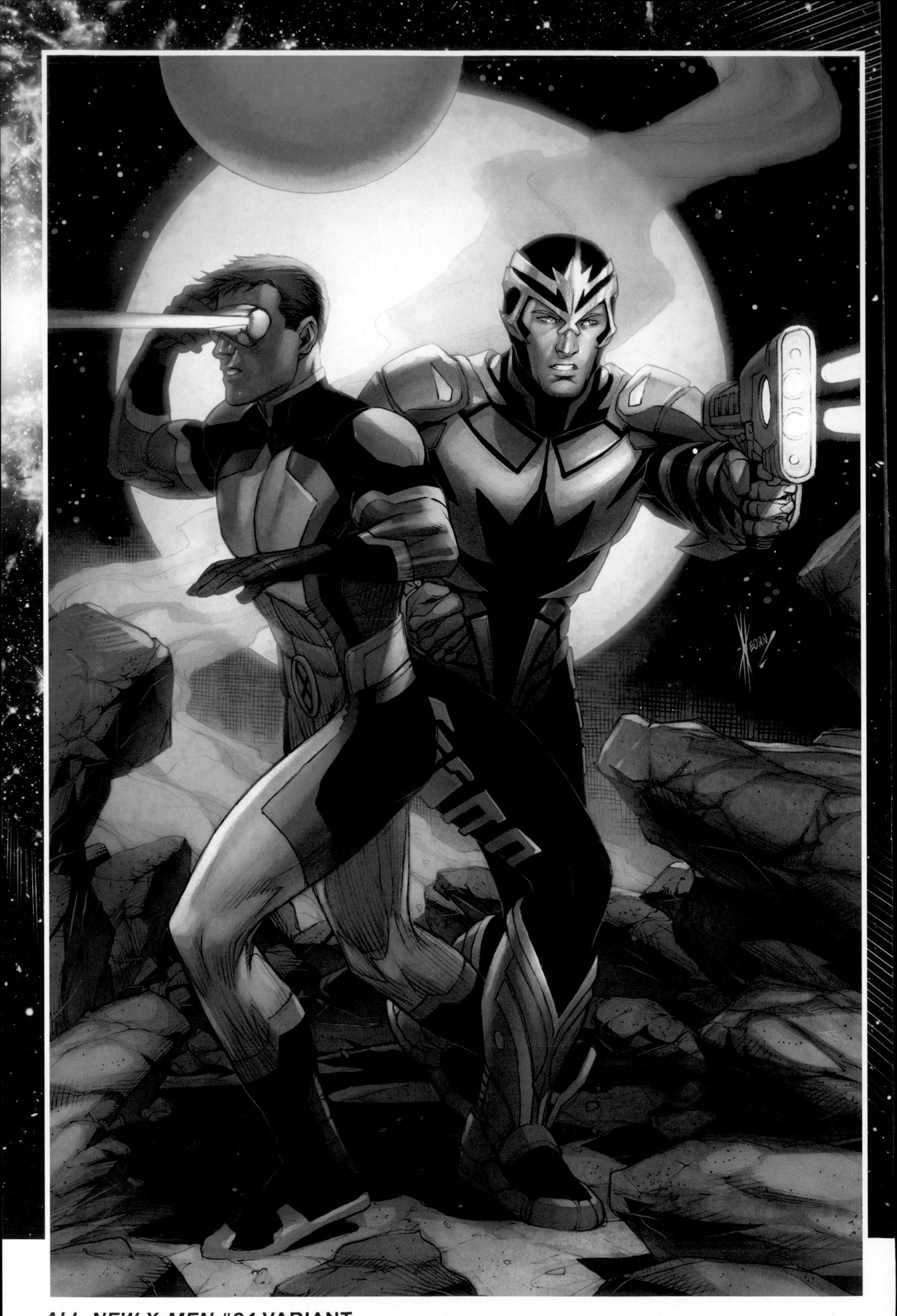

***ALL-NEW X-MEN* #24 VARIANT**
BY DALE KEOWN & JASON KEITH

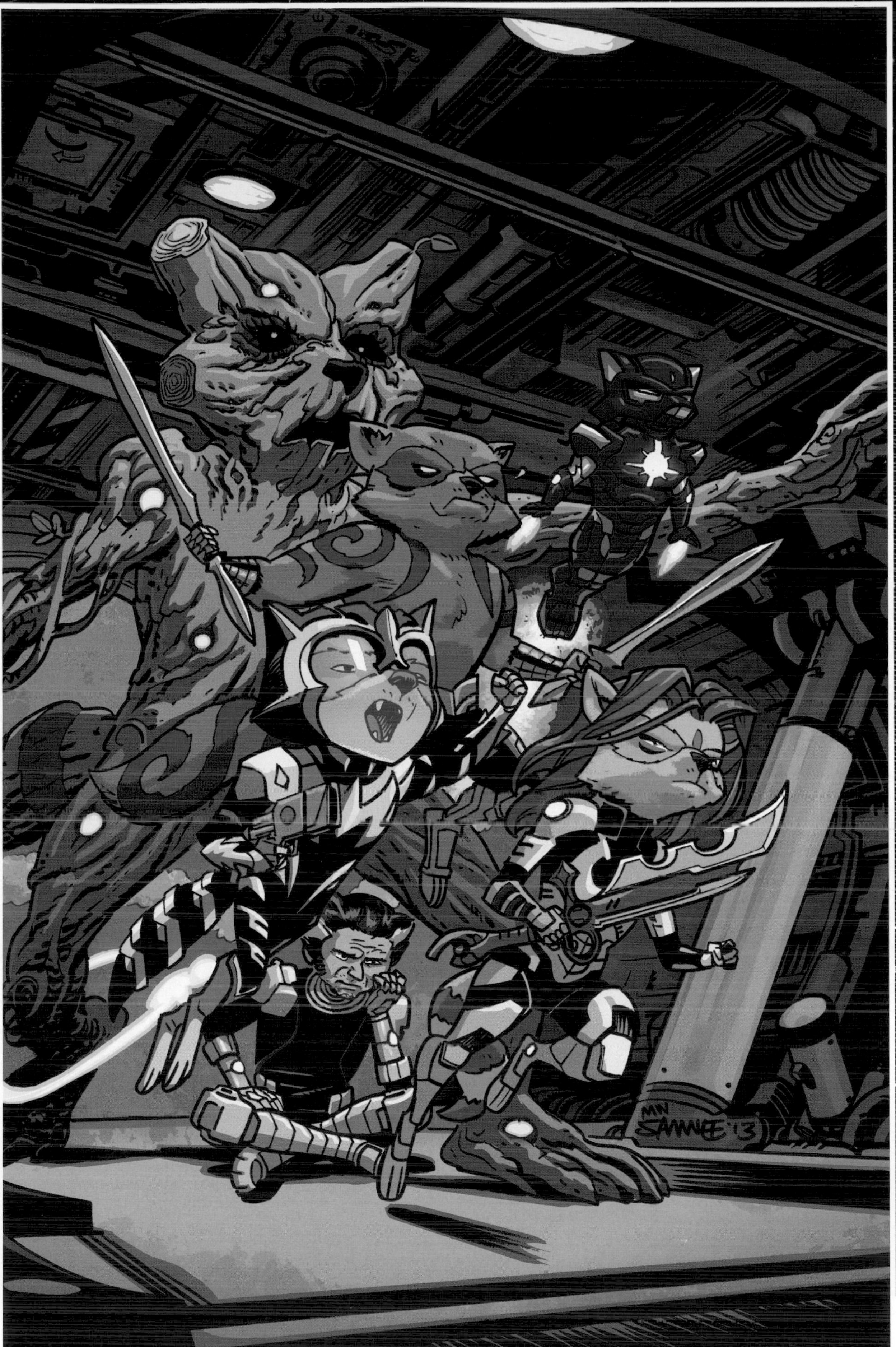

GUARDIANS OF THE GALAXY #11 **ANIMAL VARIANT**
BY CHRIS SAMNEE & MATTHEW WILSON

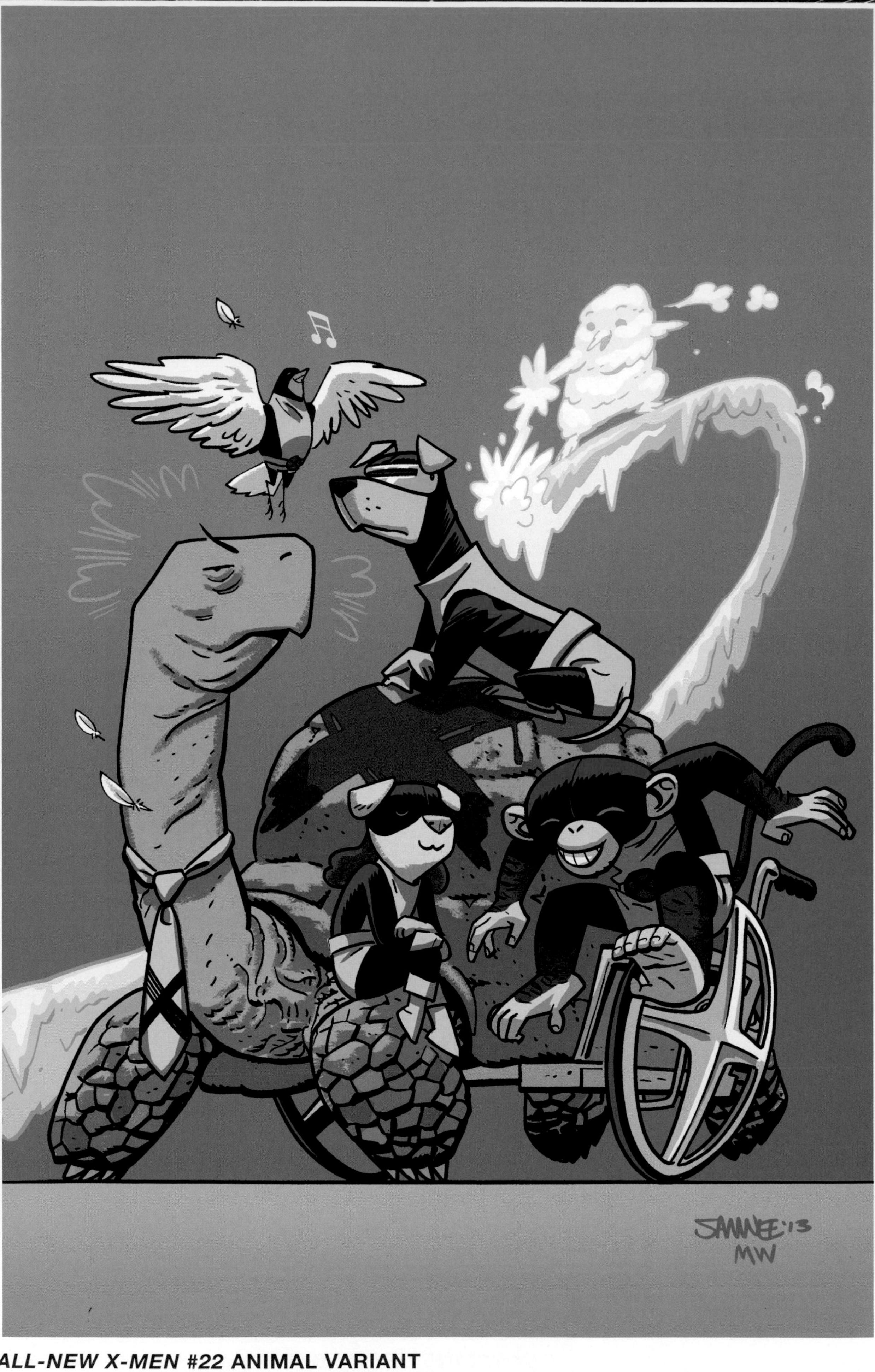
SAMNEE '13
MW

***ALL-NEW X-MEN* #22 ANIMAL VARIANT**
BY CHRIS SAMNEE & MATTHEW WILSON

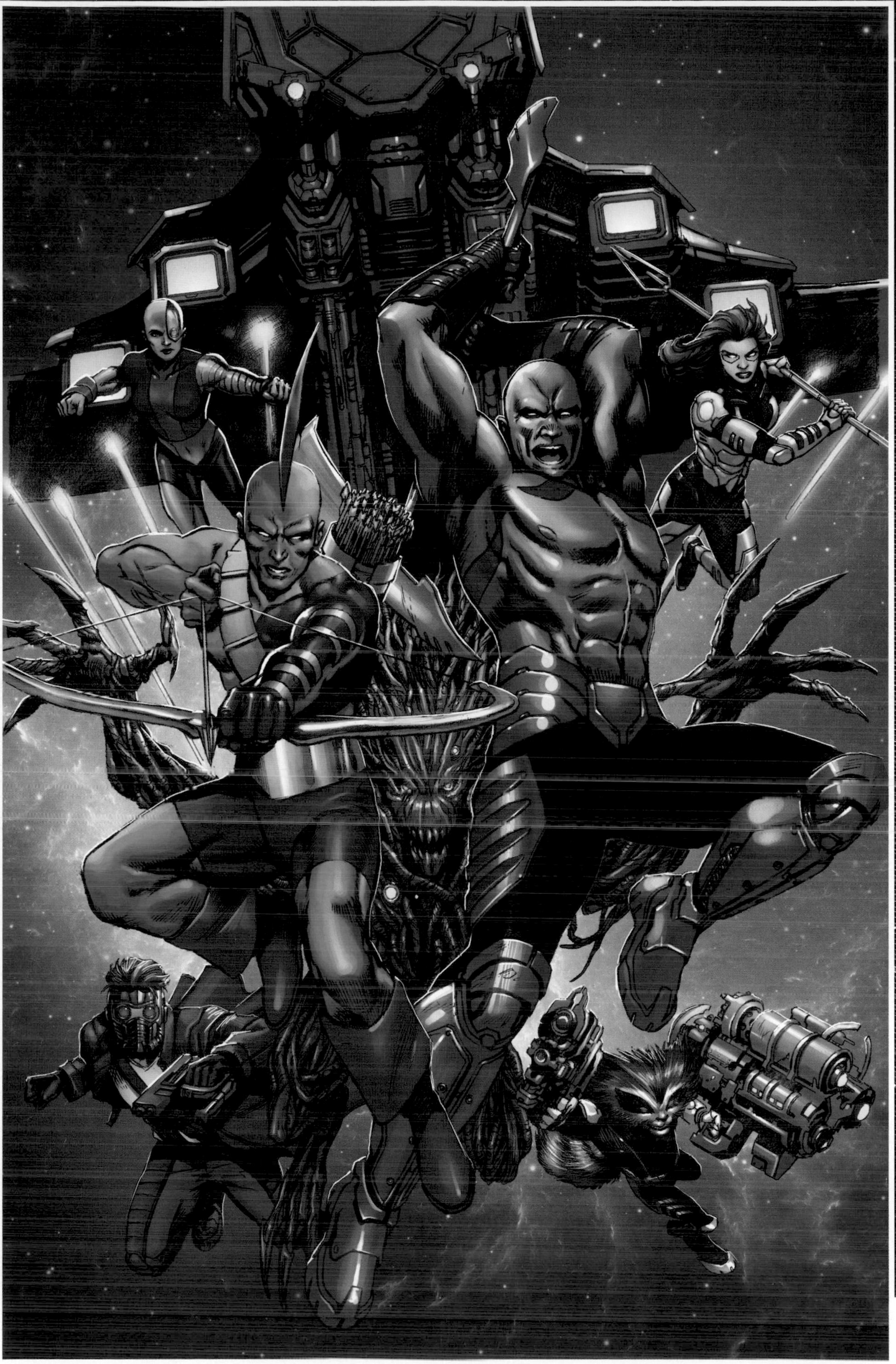

***GUARDIANS OF THE GALAXY #17* WIZARD WORLD VARIANT**
BY ALVARO MARTINEZ & CHRIS SOTOMAYOR

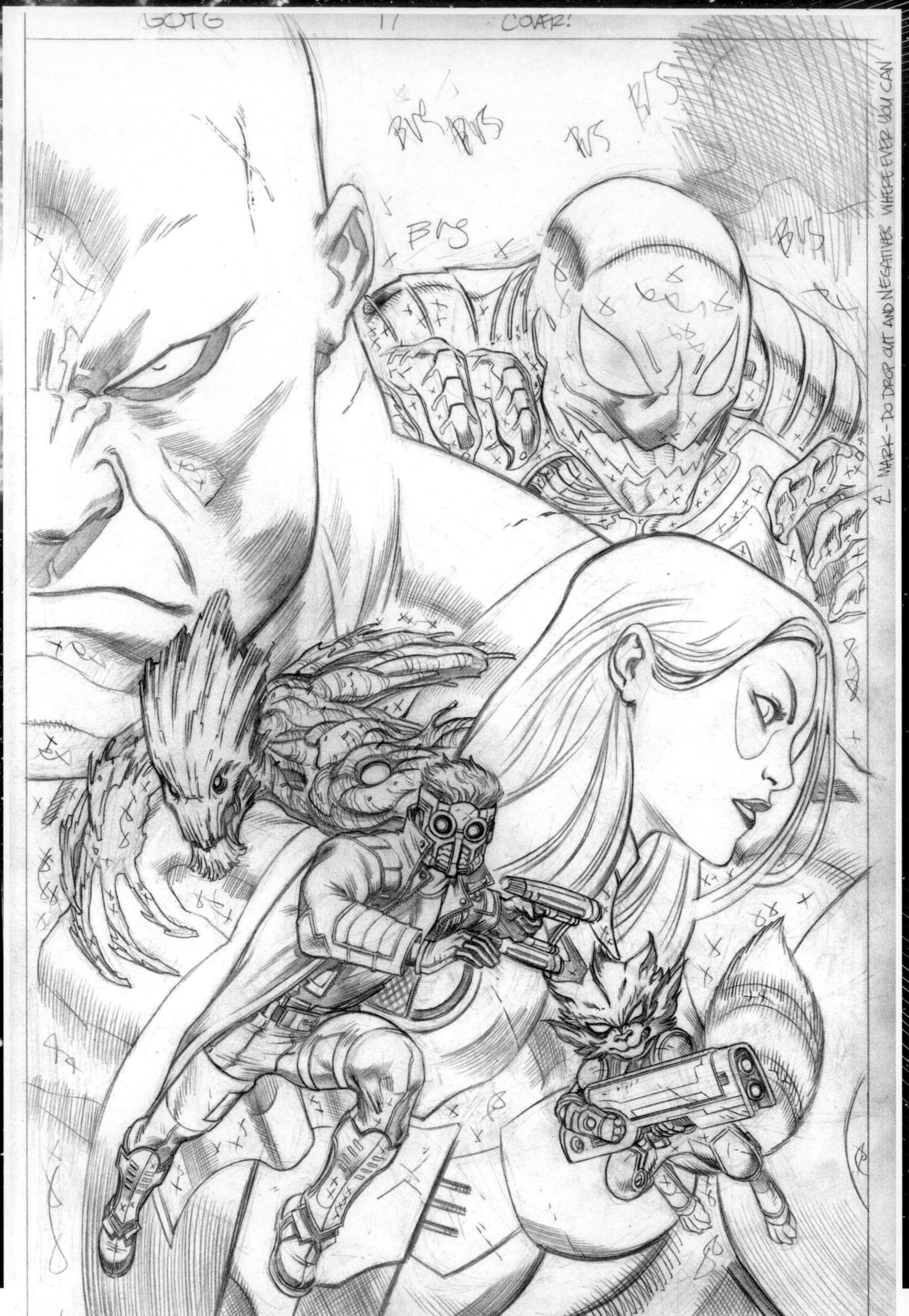
GOTG 17 COVER!
MARK - DO DROP OUT AND NEGATIVES WHEREVER YOU CAN

***GUARDIANS OF THE GALAXY* #17**
COVER PENCILS BY ED MCGUINNESS

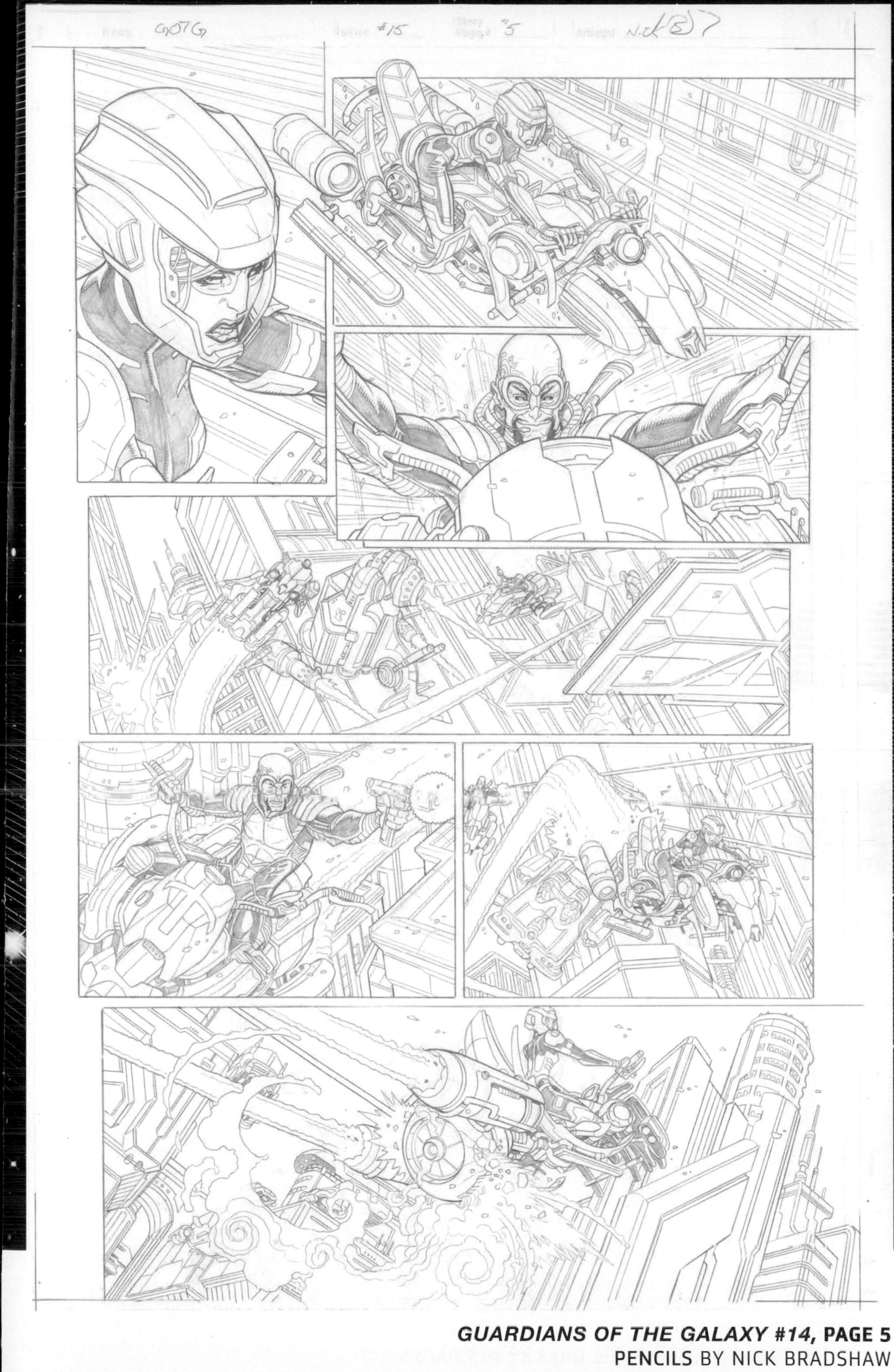
GOTG
#15
5

***GUARDIANS OF THE GALAXY #14*, PAGE 5**
PENCILS BY NICK BRADSHAW

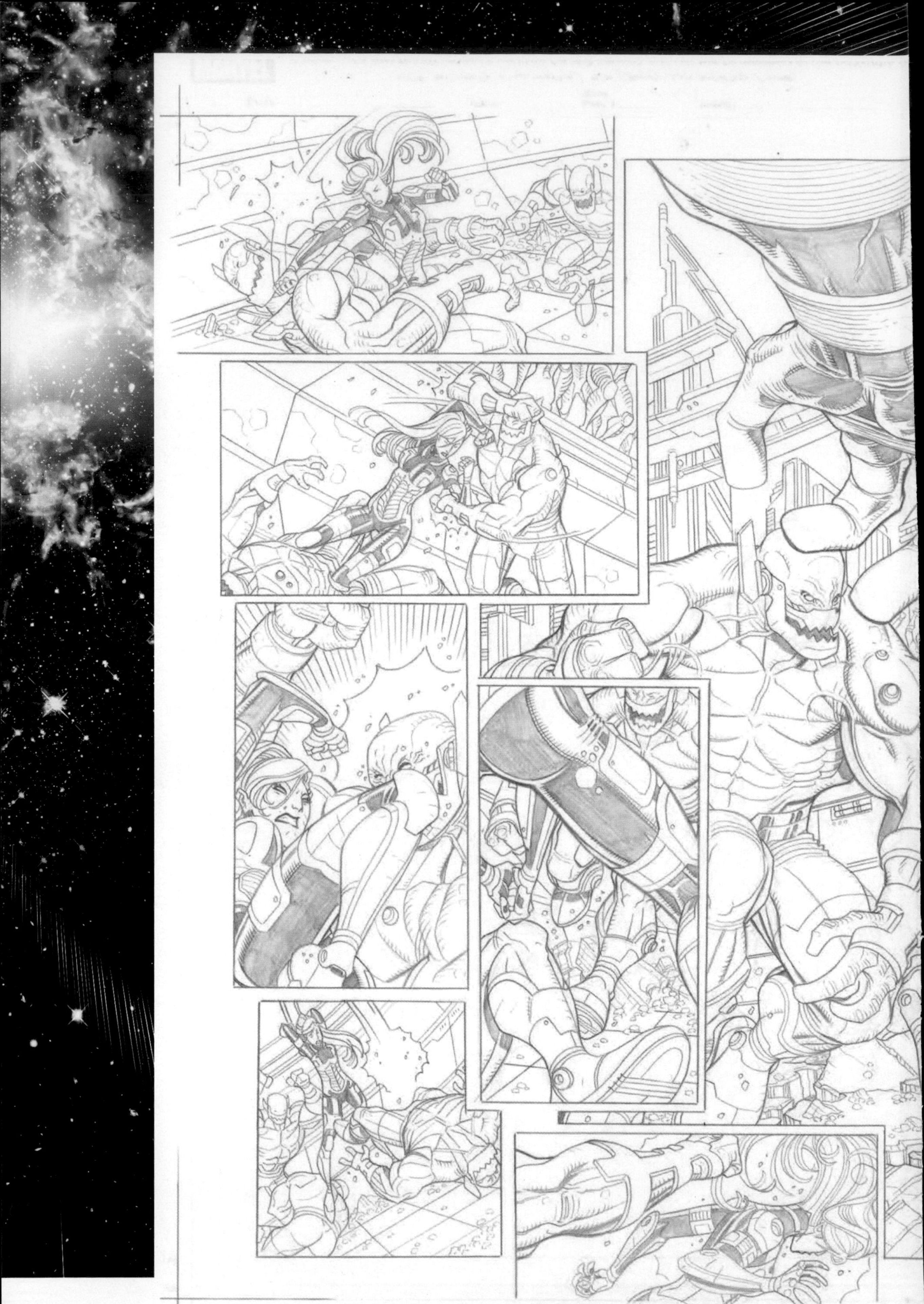

GUARDIANS OF THE GALAXY #15,PAGES 6-7

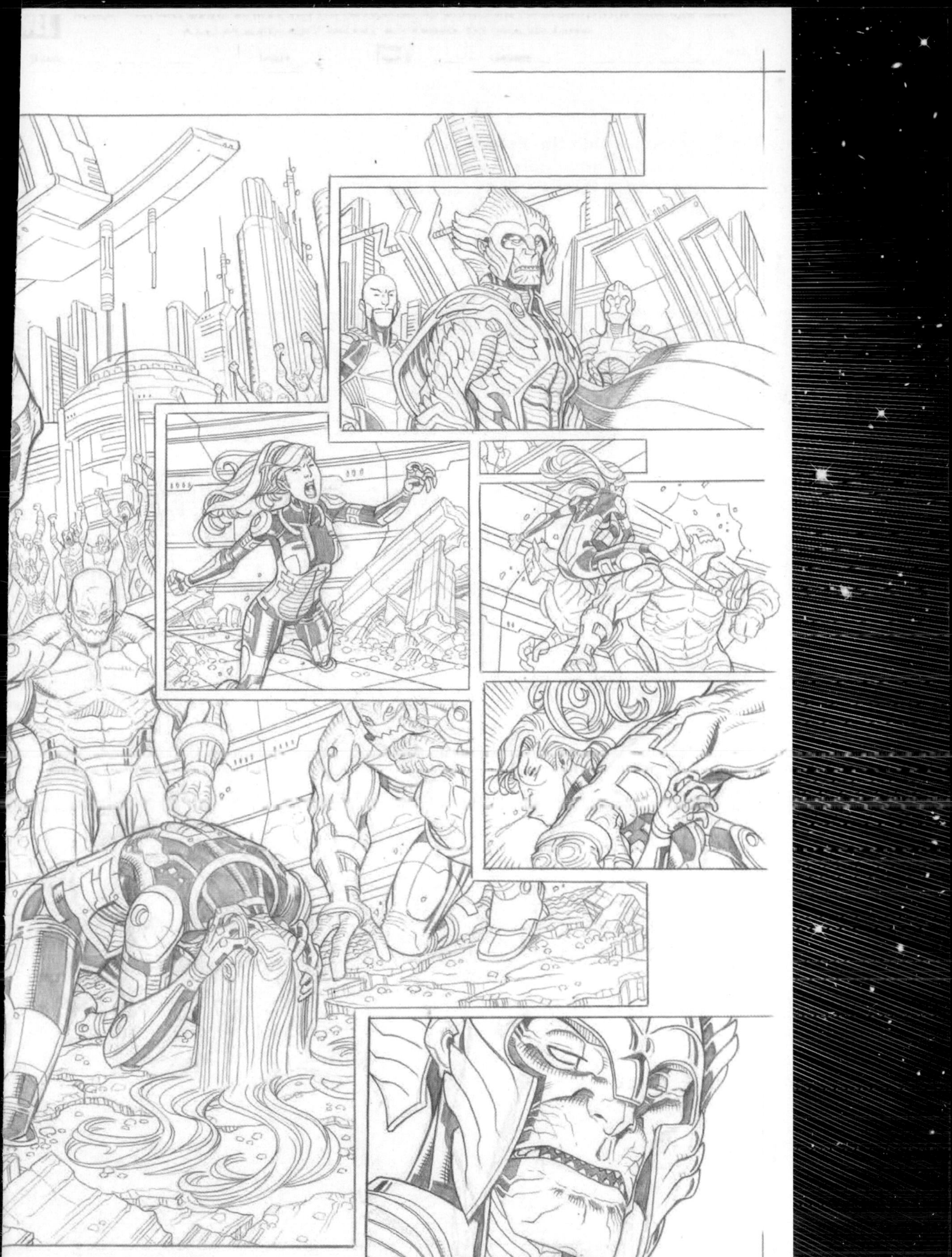

PENCILS BY NICK BRADSHAW

MARVEL AR AUGMENTED REALITY

MARVEL AUGMENTED REALITY (AR) ENHANCES AND CHANGES THE WAY YOU EXPERIENCE COMICS!

TO ACCESS THE FREE MARVEL AR CONTENT IN THIS BOOK*:

1. Locate the AR logo within the comic.
2. Go to Marvel.com/AR in your web browser.
3. Search by series title to find the corresponding AR.
4. Enjoy Marvel AR!

*All AR content that appears in this book has been archived and will be available only at Marvel.com/AR – no longer in the Marvel AR App. Content subject to change and availability.

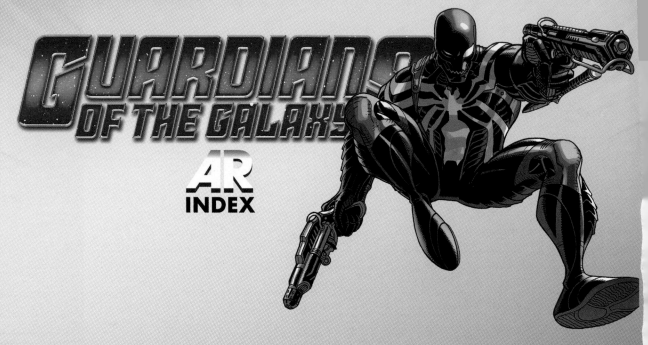

GUARDIANS OF THE GALAXY

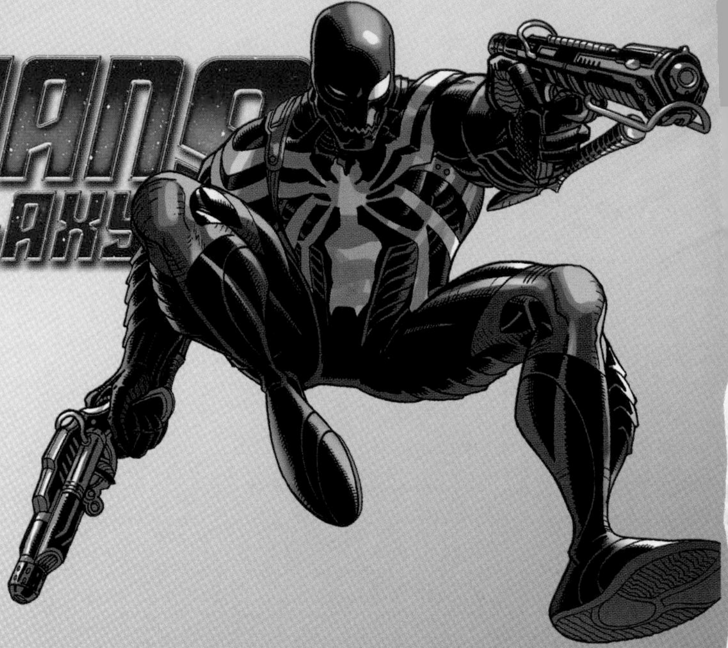

AR INDEX